Data Network Design,
Third Edition

Data Network Design, Third Edition

DARREN **SPOHN**,
TINA **BROWN**,
AND SCOTT **GRAU**

McGraw-Hill/Osborne

New York Chicago San Francisco
Lisbon London Madrid Mexico City Milan
New Delhi San Juan Seoul Singapore Sydney Toronto

McGraw-Hill/Osborne
2600 Tenth Street
Berkeley, California 94710
U.S.A.

To arrange bulk purchase discounts for sales promotions, premiums, or fund-raisers, please contact **McGraw-Hill**/Osborne at the above address. For information on translations or book distributors outside the U.S.A., please see the International Contact Information page immediately following the index of this book.

Data Network Design, Third Edition

1234567890 FGR FGR 0198765432

ISBN 0-07-219312-3

Publisher	**Copy Editor**
Brandon A. Nordin	Laura Ryan
Vice President & Associate Publisher	**Proofreader**
Scott Rogers	Susie Elkind
Acquisitions Editor	**Indexer**
Franny Kelly	Claire Splan
Project Editor	**Composition**
Jennifer Malnick	Apollo Publishing Services,
Acquisitions Coordinator	Lucie Ericksen
Emma Acker	**Illustrators**
Technical Editor	Michael Mueller, Lyssa Wald
Chuck Larrieu	**Series Design**
	Peter F. Hancik

This book was composed with Corel VENTURA™ Publisher.

CONTENTS

Part II

Physical Layer Technologies

Part III

Protocols and Interfaces: Layer 2

Part IV

Protocols and Interfaces: Layer 3

Part V

Requirements, Planning, and Choosing Technology

Part VI

Choosing the Service Provider

Part VII

Network Design and Management

PREFACE

Reader, commonly called courteous or gentle Reader. I am a Data Network Designer—extraordinary, being of my own creation—not vain enough to fancy myself an Expert, nor visionary enough to hope I shall one day become an official Industry Pundit. The doors of the College open to me as a harmless enthusiast, not as a worshipful member. I have no tabard to my back, crown to my brows, no authority, no office; I am guiltless of grants, and unacquainted with fees (well, that's not entirely true…); but I am devoted to the study of Data Network Design, and may truly call myself a "Network Designer", as I have long and diligently pursued the subject by a path, largely untrodden I believe by others before the first edition, though several had crossed the track. Are you inclined to keep me company and see where it will lead us? For the end, I tell you fairly, is yet to seek. If so, have with you. I will guide you as well as I can, and as far as I know. No great distance, perchance; but I will rather declare my ignorance than willfully misdirect your steps, for I look upon our journey as one in quest of Truth; and he would ill deserve to find her, who should lie by the way.[*]

---

[*] Modified from the preface to the 3rd Edition of J.R. Planché's *The Pursuivant of Arms; Or, Heraldry Founded Upon Facts*, 1874.)

I "borrowed" and slightly rewrote J. R. Planché's introduction to his third edition because it fit so well with what we are trying to do with this Third Edition of *Data Network Design*—bring to the reader the best efforts known to designing data networks. I am joined in this edition by two of my most trusted and experienced friends and colleagues, Tina Brown and Scott Grau. Together we have over 45 years experience in designing, implementing, and managing data networks. It is with this theoretical and practical experience that we write this third edition.

PURPOSE OF THIS BOOK

The primary purpose of this book is to teach the science and art of designing a data network. We have attempted to provide the reader an all encompassing text on how to plan, design, build, implement, manage, and secure both simple and complex data networks for both enterprises (end users) and service providers. The chapter flow is chronological, making the book a true implementation guide that can also be used as a reference guide or textbook.

Science is defined by *Webster's* as "knowledge covering general truth, or operation of general laws especially as attained and tested through scientific method." Art is defined as "skill acquired by experience or study" and relates more to a talent, knack, or ability to perform. Therefore, data network design is an art that demands the study and mastery of many sciences (technologies), and much practice!

The science aspects of data network design include learning the major transmission, multiplexing, bridging, switching, and routing technologies prevalent at the turn of the 21st century. Thus, one goal is to provide detailed educational and operational descriptions of all the dominant access (including LAN) and backbone (WAN) technologies and services. We next educate and give the reader insight into future dominant technologies. Our disciplines include

▼　Private Line—Electrical (DSx) and Optical (SONET, WDM, DWDM)

■　Frame Relay

■　ATM

■　IP suite, including TCP and PPP

■　Dial, DSL, and Cable Modem Access

■　LAN: Ethernet, Token Ring, FDDI

■　SAN: HIPPI, ESCON, FICON, FCS

■　MPLS, Packet over SONET, and Wireless

■　Voice over Packet

■　X.25 Packet Switching and SMDS

■　Security Technologies, including packet filtering and application proxies

▲　Network Management Technologies, including SMNP and OSI

The *art* of network design is how to select and implement the required technologies and services into your network design. First, of course, you will need to learn how to gather the business and technical requirements, and then how to design the network using these technologies and services

As stated above, the book takes the reader through the entire network design process, from compiling the requirements through design and into optimization and management techniques—the true art of data network design. Tried and true methods are presented, augmented by new developments in the industry that teach the art of network design. Our goal is to provide a tome complete with referenced technical details and real-world experience. The core chapters present a *broad scope* of data and computer communications standards, architectures, hardware, software, protocols, technologies, and services as they relate to designing data networks. Voice network design is given some coverage, specifically as it relates to integration and convergence with the data network.

For the core technology and services chapters, emphasis is placed on the predominant technologies as of the turn of the century and emerging technologies of the next decade, including packet, frame, and cell-switched services like IP, Frame Relay, ATM, and MPLS; predominant LAN standards like Ethernet; and predominant WAN transmission standards like SONET, Packet over SONET, WDM, and DWDM. All these acronyms will be explained in great detail with this book. This book is designed to walk the reader chronologically through the process of a data network design using these LAN and WAN technologies and services, paying attention to both the technical and business decisions required. Small attention will be given to application and desktop design, as this topic would comprise several texts itself. It is the author's intent to provide a broad overview of these topics with insight into practical design aspects of each, allowing the reader to perform an end-to-end network design. Standards and reference pointers are provided to the reader for further detailed study.

The logical and physical design of hardware and software is not the only process in a network design. Network designs encompass many aspects including making the business case, compiling the requirements, choosing the technology, planning for capacity, selecting the vendor, and weighing all the issues before the actual design begins. After these efforts have produced a workable design plan, there are additional issues that must be addressed, including operations, maintenance, security, and management support structures. While resolution of many of these additional tasks often falls to the project manager, many other people must be involved in the many processes affecting the integrity of the design and must assess the impact of each decision as it relates to the overall network design. A further goal is to teach the network designer how to accomplish all these efforts.

A more detailed design book, resplendent with addressing schemes, detailed protocol structures, discrete circuit operations, and additional protocol specifics would take volumes. A separate book could be published on each protocol, technology, and service—and in fact there are hundreds of books available for each technology presented within this book. The primary purpose of this text, however, is to provide a *comprehensive overview* of the prevalent LAN and WAN technologies and services, how to identify the need for these services and then select the appropriate technology/service and their providers, and complete the entire data network design process.

INTENDED AUDIENCE

This text is designed for data communications novices through advanced design engineers, including all levels of communications management. Some business and data communications basics are provided in the beginning chapters. The text presents design material at a high level, assuming the reader has access to resources or colleagues with a background in basic data communications and a working knowledge of transmission basics. Although this skill level is assumed, some discussion on hardware and protocol basics is provided. The book serves as professional reading as well as a desktop reference guide for the engineer and manager, and has been used in many college classrooms around the world. This text has also been translated into multiple languages, and the study and use of data network design is global in nature. Many highly successful engineers and managers have used prior editions of this book as their beginning guide to data communications, to secure their first job in the field, or as their first curriculum in the science—we hope this latest edition lives up to their expectations.

It is important to note that almost this entire text has been rewritten from the second edition. The authors offer their thanks to everyone for their submissions, corrections, and comments.

OVERVIEW OF THIS BOOK

Data Network Design, *Third Edition*, is divided into eight parts.

▼ **Part I, "Data Communications: Business Drivers and Networking Directions,"** provides a broad overview of the business drivers, technical drivers, standards, and networking directions that have shaped modern day data communications. Also provides an introduction to the key principles of transmission, hardware types, circuit types, common protocols and architectures, and multiplexing and switching technologies.

■ **Chapter 1, "Data Communication: Past to Future,"** defines data network design from the evolution and history of communications; through modern day network infrastructures and their business and technical requirements, applications, and enablers; to a view of the next generation network.

■ **Chapter 2, "Understanding the Standards and Their Makers,"** presents the major national and global industry standards organizations, forums, and the processes of standardization.

▲ **Chapter 3, "Introduction to Transmission Technologies,"** presents the common network topologies, circuits, connections, hardware, and transmission types, along with the fundamentals of bridging, switching, and routing.

Each technology chapter in Parts II through IV explain protocol structure, format, interfaces, and theory. They also contain software, hardware, and design recommendations.

▼ **Part II, "Physical Layer Technologies,"** introduces the reader to the basics of the OSIRM Layer 1 protocols, interfaces, hardware, software, and services.

- **Chapter 4, "Multiplexing and Switching Technologies: An Overview,"** provides an overview of multiplexer and switching technologies, including circuit and packet switching.

- **Chapter 5, "Optical Networking,"** covers SONET/SDH and DWDM. The discussion covers history of optical network, network topologies, and types of optical equipment.

- **Chapter 6, "Physical Layer Protocols and Access Technologies,"** provides the reader with a study of physical layer protocols and media, working models, and detailed protocol descriptions of the most common forms of consumer and corporate access, including Dial, ISDN, DSL, Cable, wireless, and satellite.

- **Part III, "Protocols and Interfaces: Layer 2,"** introduces the reader to the basics of the OSIRM Layer 2 protocols, interfaces, hardware, software, and services.

- **Chapter 7, "Common Protocols and Interfaces in the LAN Environment,"** starts with a discussion of the LLC and MAC sublayers, moves to detailed coverage of Ethernet, Token Ring, and FDDI, and concludes with coverage of bridging protocols and a study of switching in the LAN environment.

- **Chapter 8, "Frame Relay,"** covers the FR standards, interfaces, protocol structure, transmission theory, hardware, service, performance engineering, and design topics such as port/PVC sizing, open and closed loop architecture comparison, and VoFR.

- **Chapter 9, "Common WAN Protocols: ATM,"** covers the ATM standards, interfaces, protocol structure, transmission theory, hardware, service, performance engineering, and design topics.

- **Part IV, "Protocols and Interfaces: Layer 3,"** introduces the reader to the basics of the OSIRM Layer 3 and higher protocols, interfaces, hardware, software, and services.

- **Chapter 10, "Common Protocols and Interfaces in the Upper Layers (TCP/IP),"** presents the definition, standards, protocols, transmission theory, operation, and service provided by IP. Includes common routing protocols (OSPF, RIP, BGP, E-IGRP) and lower and higher layer protocols associated with IP (ICMP, IGMP, ARP, TCP, and UDP). Comes with a detailed IP addressing example.

- **Chapter 11, Mature Packet Switched Protocols,"** covers X.25 and SMDS legacy protocols and services.

- **Part V, "Requirements, Planning, and Choosing Technology,"** steps the reader through defining data network design requirements, performing the traffic analysis and capacity-planning process, and comparing circuit- , packet- , frame- , and cell-switched technologies.

- **Chapter 12, "Requirements Definition,"** provides an understanding of different business and technical challenges and requirements. Discusses the process of understanding current or planned protocols and traffic requirements.

- **Chapter 13, "Traffic Engineering and Capacity Planning,"** provides a summary of common traffic analysis, engineering, and capacity planning techniques for circuit and packet switched services with specific design recommendations. Also covers evaluation and selection of design tools.

- **Chapter 14, "Technology Comparisons,"** provides numerous business, technology, and service comparisons of LAN and WAN technologies and services. Analyzes pros and cons of private versus public networking.

- **Part VI, "Choosing the Service Provider,"** assists the reader in analyzing and selecting a service provider.

- **Chapter 15, "Choosing Service Providers,"** provides guidelines for the RFI/RFP process and criteria for choosing a service provider and future relationship with them. Extends coverage to international network and service providers.

- **Part VII, "Network Design and Management,"** deals with the design and management of networks—from access through backbone, and including security, documentation, and network management.

- **Chapter 16, "Access Network Design"** starts with the access design—the point where the user accesses the network or public network service.

- **Chapter 17, "Backbone Network Design,"** continues with the backbone design. The backbone is often a switched-network service. This chapter also contains some valuable practical insights on network tuning.

- **Chapter 18, "Securing Your Network,"** covers the issues that must be addressed to secure your network design, including how to identify security requirements, understanding threats and safeguards, writing and implementing the security policy, designing the firewall and VPN, and identifying intrusion detection systems.

- **Chapter 19, "Documentation and Network Management,"** identifies and details key documentation that accompanies the network design and the predominant network management protocols, architectures, and disciplines.

- **Part VIII, "Emerging Technologies,"** introduces the reader to new technologies on the horizon at the time of publication.

- **Chapter 20, "What's New on the Horizon,"** covers MPLS, VDSL, Wireless, PoS, optical switching and routing, metro Ethernet, and Voice over Packet.

- ▲ **Part IX, "Appendixes,"** contains **Appendix A**, which lists the major acronyms and abbreviations used in the book. **Appendix B** provides a reference of national and international standards sources. **Appendix C** gives a reference table for creating IP network address masks. **Appendix D** provides a summary of all IP network addressing. **Appendix E** provides a glossary of defined common terms associated with the technologies, architectures, services, and protocols encountered throughout the book.

ACKNOWLEDGMENTS

Many people have helped us prepare this book. They have provided comments on various drafts, information on products and services, and other value-added services. For the third edition, we would like to thank Franny Kelly, Tracy Dunkelberger, Chuck Larrieu, and Jenny Malnick, all at McGraw-Hill/Osborne.

Many people assisted Darren Spohn on the second edition, and we would again like to recognize Mr. Jerry Davis of NetSolve; Mr. Joel Adams of Adams Capital Management; Mr. Ron Appleton and Mr. Brian Noel of AT&T; Mr. Bill Backus of Bell Laboratories; Mr. Jim Gayton and Mr. Chuck Sullivan of Cascade Communications; Mr. Doug Hantula and Mr. David O'Leary, and Mr. Dave Travis of Cisco Systems; Mr. Scott Grau of E-net; Mr. Bill Flannigan of Fastcom; Mr. Gary Kessler of MAN Technology Corporation; Mr. Curtis Brownmiller, Mr. Mike Conn, Mr. Herb Frizzell Sr., Dr. David McDysan, Mr. Paul Metzger, and Mr. Scott Thompson of MCI; Mr. Jorge Chong, Mr. Steve Davies, Mr. Mark Hofer, Mr. Penn Rabb, Mr. Michael Turner, and Mr. Craig Tysdal of NetSolve; and Mr. Dave Runnels of Sprint, along with other colleagues who over the last 14 years have shared their knowledge and expertise. Special thanks also went to Mr. Herb Frizzell, Sr., for both the English style and syntax review as well as select submissions, and for enduring the many edits for the second edition; Senior Editing Supervisor Stephen Smith, Senior Editor Steven Elliot, Assistant Editor Donna Namarato, and all the rest of the staff at McGraw-Hill/Osborne who assisted me on the project. They have helped me develop a greater understanding and appreciation for data network design.

And finally, for helping on the first edition, thanks go to Mr. Gene Wahlberg of Bay Networks; Mr. Arthur Henley of E-net; Mr. Ed Braunston of General DataCom; Mr. Charan Khurana and Ms. Margot Peterson of IBM; Ms. Beverly Dygart of MAKE Systems; Mr. Gary Kessler of MAN Technology Corporation; Mr. Lance Boxer, Mr. Carl Geib, Dr. David McDysan, and Mr. Paul Metzger of MCI; and Dr. James F. Mollenauer of Technical Strategy Associates. Without their help second and third editions would not have been possible.

This book does not reflect any policy, position, or posture of Spohn & Associates. A caveat should be added that this work was not funded or supported financially by Spohn & Associates or by its corporate resources. Ideas and concepts expressed are strictly those of the authors. Information pertaining to specific vendor or service provider products is based upon open literature freely provided and adapted as required. Our friends and associates at Spohn & Associates did support the project, especially as it defocused our time and energies away from the success of our business, and for their support are hereby thanked. This includes Robert Arroyo, Chas Baker, Denise Batek, Paulette Becker, Phil Cowell, Susan Crim, Steve Davies, Ron Davis, Scott Harrington, Ed Higgins, Mike Mallow, Eric Martineau, Bob Mitchell, Jim Nichols, Michelle Perry, Steve Roos, Wendy Savage, Kathy Thomas, Christi Vacca, Stacy Webber, and Javan Wiener.

Special thanks go to Bob Mitchell for updating all the appendices and helping to gather data, and Mark Ollom for some of the graphics creation.

And to my wife, Becky, and sons Alexander and Cameron—their never-ending support and love throughout has helped me accomplish this project.

The combined support and assistance of these people has made this book possible.
—*Darren L. Spohn*

The first edition of this book was dedicated to my parents, Karl and Regina, and best friend (and wife), Becky. I added a dedication to our first son, Alexander, in the second edition. In this third edition I add a dedication to our youngest son, Cameron. And I continue to believe, more so every day, that there is nothing better in this world than family.
—*DLS*

I would like to thank my husband, Eric, for his love and support; my son, Jason, for his ability to make me smile even when I am juggling too much in my career; my spirited leader, Darren, for this opportunity as well as the many others; and Annamarie, Al, and Richard for their guidance and for teaching me that all is possible with the love of family.
—*TB*

I would like to thank my wife, Cindy, and my sons, Christopher and Aaron, and my parents, Edward and Rose, for their extra patience and support. Thanks to Scott Brigham for his guidance when I was starting out, Arthur Henley for his over 10 years of mentoring and friendship, and Marcus McEwen for his friendship and support. Thanks to Brown for listening to my complaining and to Darren for the opportunity and friendship.
—*SAG*

INTRODUCTION

Voice, data, and video—which of these three methods of information communications do you use every day? The answer is probably all three. Every day we talk on a fixed or cellular phone, interface with a computing device that stores, sends, and/or receives data at work and at home (this could include browsing the Internet or even retrieving cash from an ATM machine!), and watch television/DVDs/tapes at home or at work. But how is this information "networked" among those human interface devices—phones, computers, and video display or recorders. What are the various network elements that comprise the communications infrastructure? These interface devices often rely on complex data communications networks to aggregate, store, interpret, transmit, and receive this "data" across the neighborhood or across the world. It is with these data communications networks, or more specifically their design, that we deal with in this book.

Data communications users are constantly demanding more bandwidth and network resources. Consumers now demand broadband access to the home—from 64,000 bps dial to DSL and cable modem speeds that exceed 1.5 Mbps. Bandwidth requirements have gone mobile through wireless, although still fall far short of true "broadband." Portable cellular phones now support a variety of capabilities such as e-mail, Internet access and browsing, contact manager capabilities similar to a PDA, voice recognition, two-way paging, and fax—all require more bandwidth, faster processors, and more juice.

In the corporate environment, bandwidth- and processor-hungry client-server applications have reached most corporate desktops. Enterprise resource planning (ERP) tools used to improve automation and productivity, voice-data-video integration at the desktop, increased file sizes for databases and medical imaging files, huge cross-country and international file transfers, and desktop video conferencing are just a few corporate applications driving the need for more bandwidth. Of course, faster machines with more memory are required to run these applications and store the massive amounts of information, and thus servers partnered with gigabit-per-second processor-driven workstations have been deployed. The combination of these applications and computing platforms have ushered in a new age of distributed computing. So we see that as data-transfer and storage bandwidth requirements for text, video, voice, and imaging traffic increase exponentially, the network transport requirements required to transport that traffic increase proportionately, and sometimes nonproportionately.

The number of bandwidth units required for each application increases as the price of bandwidth per unit decreases. So users turn to technology and service alternatives that offer less expensive and more flexible bandwidth. A host of services stand ready to provide flexible, on-demand bandwidth, including IP, FR, ATM, DSL, and cable are available. The trick is choosing which one or combination thereof is best for your network.

Now let's carry this requirement past the enterprise or intranet level, and into the global extranet community. We are now living in a distributed, extranet-oriented data world. Everyone needs access to everyone else's data. The best example of this trend is the public Internet. For the cost of a low-speed dial connection, anyone can communicate with anyone else in the world who has access to this public Internet. E-mail, file transfers, stock quotes, research, news, radio, web site hosting, on-line gaming—the only real limitations are your connect speed and ability to pay for or find what you want. The Internet created the world's first electronic global community. Let's now take this one step further into the corporate world. Enterprises can use the public Internet to build virtual private networks (VPNs) between their sites. These are often called Edge-VPNs or Customer premises equipment (CPE)–based VPNs. And there are many private, or virtually private (VPNs), non-Internet alternatives we will soon discuss. But beware the criminal element—use of the public Internet as a communications medium requires strict management and security measures. So now the public Internet carries consumer and corporate traffic, and everyone has the ability to communication with each other over this extranet.

The focus of this book is on designing corporate enterprise and service providers networks. Let's first discuss the networking requirements of the enterprise. Building networks with many meshed dedicated circuits have become the exception as switched public and private data networks and services now span the globe. It is a given that everything from workstations and servers to mainframe computers need to talk to one another the same way people in the voice world pick up the phone and dial a global phone number recognized anyone in the world. IP addressing has brought us this same capability in the data world. The rise of telecommuting and the proliferation of the mobile worker has brought a host of wireless access and transport alternatives into the mainstream. The aggregation of these wireless and wireline requirements has caused the market for high-speed data transport to continue to accelerate. We have entered the Gigabit Age, where the predominant LAN protocol is quickly becoming Gigabit Ethernet (GbE). Average WAN and Internet access is still not into the gigabit-per-second speed (remaining firmly entrenched in the multimegabit range), but metro Ethernet speeds are pushing the envelope in that direction. This book will explore all predominant broadband LAN and WAN technologies and services that will support these networks.

Routing/switching is in the process of merging within the LAN and WAN. Within the LAN, routing/switching in many cases has merged. This merging of routing and switching is also happening in the WAN through the implementation of MPLS networks. MPLS carrier–provided services offer the enterprise user the ability to achieve all the capabilities of an IP VPN with all the benefits of a connection-oriented service like FR and ATM. Frame relay and ATM continue to grow, representing a multibillion dollar market. The IP connectivity market has grown primarily in three areas: remote VPN access through dial, DSL, and cable using the public Internet (replacing old modem pools), corporate site-to-site IP VPNs over private IP networks or the public Internet, and dedicated corporate Internet access (through IP, FR, or ATM service ports).

This discussion now brings us to the design and optimization of service provider networks. This text devotes at least two chapters to the design of industrial strength, carrier-class access and backbone networks that can offer the broadband services mentioned above. Service providers worldwide have fallen on tough times in the early part of the 21st century. The last decade yielded a huge growth spurt of service providers and services—designed and deployed to stay ahead of the bandwidth requirement explosion. Massive investments were made in SONET, WDM, and DWDM deployments and fiber overbuilds in the anticipation that this user-spending growth would continue exponentially. The debate still rages on whether the world has too much or too little fiber, but the reality is that service providers need to be more judicial on how they support and grow their networks. Rapid expansion has yielded to network optimization. Therefore, the service provider network designer must understand not only design using these new optical and "legacy" electrical technologies and services, but more importantly how to optimize the traffic management and engineering of these networks.

New technologies continue to emerge and compete with legacy services for market share. Packet over SONET offers a cost-effective alternative to point-to-point gigabit transport. Toll-quality voice can now be transported and switched over almost very packet-based service—for example VoIP, VoFR, and VoATM—but there is a price to be paid in opportunity bandwidth and user complexity. The falling PSTN switched voice rates have made VoPacket less economically feasible for most corporations than it was just a few years earlier. The various derivatives of DSL (e.g. VDSL) continue to offer cost-effective broadband access alternatives for consumer and corporate Internet and FR access, and cable modem continues to lead DSL deployment as local access providers struggle to upgrade legacy infrastructure.

Into this chaos steps the data network design engineer. All of these trends in legacy and emerging technology and services have an impact on the overall design. Designing a data network to handle a diverse user application and technology base is a complex task, let alone the LAN and WAN technology and service selection and support challenges. Capacity requirements begin to boggle the mind as LAN users project peak traffic periods of up to 50:1. With X.25 packet switching, the network provided many services that made the user rely on the network for error correction of data and end-to-end link-level data integrity. Packet, frame, and cell networks push this requirement to the end-user CPE and the devices running the applications, and require the end user to apply much more intelligence with higher-layer protocols when transporting data or risk loss and retransmission. Now, designers who once had to worry only about how long it would take to move or access data are now faced with data-transport protocols that promise to deliver a majority of the data, while leaving the discovery of lost data and subsequent retransmission to the transport through application layers. WAN design is more so today intricately tied to LAN design. Design spans from the application through the LAN and into and across the WAN, and each element in the network can affect every other part of it. Over this all ride the requirements of application delay, loss, jitter, and throughput. Decisions must be made on whether Class of Service will suffice or if Quality of Service is required. Couple this with multiple protocol and architecture environments and you have quite a challenge in designing a single homogeneous network.

The data network designer must now bridge the gap between data-transport services and user applications and services, physical- and data-link layer protocols and higher-layer protocols. This means building a network that involves both local area and wide area communications. The new developments discussed will bridge the gap between these historically separate LAN and WAN domains and provide the end user with the information required to perform a design that spans both environments. Large-scale, wide-area public networks and services are available that provide connectivity that is flexible and easy to install, with a small amount of delay and high throughput, while offering flexible bandwidth and pricing. The network designer must also know how to design the network from the perspectives of both the user and the service provider. The user typically sees the network as a utility, a network cloud that should provide ubiquitous connectivity with excellent performance and availability at low or no cost. The network or service provider's perspective is much different. The network is comprised of many pieces and parts—hardware, software, circuits—that have various technology and service options and constant price-performance trade-offs. The goal of the network designer is to bring together those two perspectives and build a network that as best as possible meets all requirements at as low a cost as possible. Understanding and quantifying these trade-offs are part of the art of network design.

And finally, after learning the technologies and services available, many users ask the classic question, "Which technology or service should I use?" This book will show that the answer to this question is based on many factors and may have several answers. There is rarely a single solution, and the decision of which technology and service to use generally comes down to what is best for the applications and what is affordable—price versus performance and functionality—as well as what causes the least change for users and what positions them the best for future expansion.

HOW TO USE THIS BOOK FOR COURSES

Many state universities use *Data Network Design* in their engineering and management curriculums. The book is designed similar to a textbook in that it teaches the science of data network design in a chronological and logical order, with technology examples augmented by numerous graphics.

Chapters to be taught in a basic architectures, protocols, technologies, and services course (PT1) are Chapters 1 through 7, and 14. Chapters to be taught in an advanced protocols and technologies course (PT2) are Chapters 8 through 14, and 18 through 20. The student should have a minimum working knowledge of the material contained in Chapters 1 through 4.

Chapters to be included in a pure design course (ND1) are the entire book, with focus on Chapters 12 through 19. The student should have a minimum working knowledge of Chapters 1 through 4, and some knowledge of the material covered in Chapters 5 through 10.

The material in this book can be taught and covered in two or three semesters. Three semesters' worth of study, along with the suggested course outlines and guidelines for selecting the course material, are outlined earlier. There is some overlap, and the recommended progression is from the basic course PT1 to the advanced course PT2, and finally to the pure design course ND1, with both design tool and test scenario hand calculated network design labs for engineering curriculums. PT2 and ND1 should begin with the overview chapters shown to reaffirm a working knowledge of basic protocols and their operation, since the advanced protocols are modifications or perturbations of simpler or more complex protocol operations. Labs should contain design problems based on the cumulative knowledge gained from the class reading and outside reading assignments (recent technology updates). The exercises should involve multiple design problems. Special or final exams (all or a portion) should include at least one multiprotocol or multitechnology network design problem. Students should be encouraged to use the text as a "working document," noting any changes as the standards are revised and updated. The authors will continue to publish updated editions of this book as appropriate technology changes may warrant, and welcome suggested changes or corrections from readers in writing (current address may be obtained from McGraw-Hill/Osborne) or via e-mail (bookinfo@spohncentral.com).

HOW TO OBTAIN TRAINING BASED ON THIS BOOK

Spohn Training, Inc., has an entire curriculum of courses built around *Data Network Design* and the technology and services defined in this book. Please see our web site at www.spohntraining.com for a complete list of courses.

AUTHOR'S DISCLAIMER

Accurate and timely information is provided up to the date of publication. While all of the standards presented in the second edition are now final, some of the standards used in this third edition are recommendations or draft standards at the time of writing and are assumed will become final soon after publication. At times, the author will present material that is practical in a large-scale design, but is simply not possible in the normal small-business communications environment. Also, in many cases, examples are presented on a larger scale. The presented material must be scaled down on a case-by-case basis. Many data communications networks operate and will continue to run quite well on dedicated private lines, but eventually the economics of switched or routed technologies and services, even on the smallest scale, are worth investigating. Please excuse the blatant assumption that the user is ready to implement these advanced technologies—in many cases it will take some time before they can be implemented. Also, please excuse any personal biases that may have crept into the text.

PART I

Data Communications: Business Drivers and Networking Directions

CHAPTER 1

Data Communication: Past to Future

This chapter focuses first on defining data network design and identifying the need for a data communications network. We first turn our attention to a discussion of the historical directions of computing and networking. After describing modern day legacy communications, we explore the computing and networking directions that will carry us through the first few decades of the twenty-first century.

A short review of recent late twentieth century history shows a major shift of resources (people, systems, infrastructure, and funding) away from voice and towards data communications, as data traffic volumes far outpace those of legacy voice. This acceleration is precipitated by the information revolution and an increased dependence, from consumers to the largest corporations, upon data communications. In this process, we explore the world from the perspective of the information technology executive, network manager, and engineer, focusing on legacy, mature, and future technologies with a view toward emerging technologies of the early twenty-first century.

WHAT IS NETWORK DESIGN?

Network design, specifically data network design, is a broad field of study. It encompasses and interacts with almost every aspect of the business and relies heavily on its integration with technology. Data is defined as information from which conclusions are drawn. *Data* is often used in the plural to refer to multiple collections of information. Data can reside in microcomputers, minicomputers, mainframes, routers, switches, storage devices, personal digital assistants (PDAs), cell phones, and even the human brain.

Data units are generally grouped into bits and bytes (8 bits to a byte), and these units, in multiples, form data streams. Sending data streams over a medium from one point to another is called *data transport*. The medium that delivers data from point A to point B or point C is called a *network*. Devices attached to and within this network can perform functions on the data such as bridging, routing, switching, and multiplexing, to name a few. Figure 1-1 depicts a sample data communications network of three sites, where point A serves as the headquarters and points B and C as remote access sites. This example is oversimplified to demonstrate that the network extends from the output port on a user device to the input port on a remote destination user B or C device. Transport is across a Wide Area Network (WAN), and two of the most popular and well-known networks in the world are the Public Switched Telephone Network (PSTN) and the Internet.

Data network design does not just focus on the transport of data. It is a broad field of study encompassing the creation of a communications infrastructure that comprehends all of the following:

▼ User applications

■ Network architectures, infrastructures, and topologies

▲ Public standards, services, protocols, data transport techniques

The field of study also includes network analysis, planning, and implementation. It goes beyond simply understanding the technical details of protocols connecting one element of hardware or software to another to facilitate data transfer and the knowledge of standards

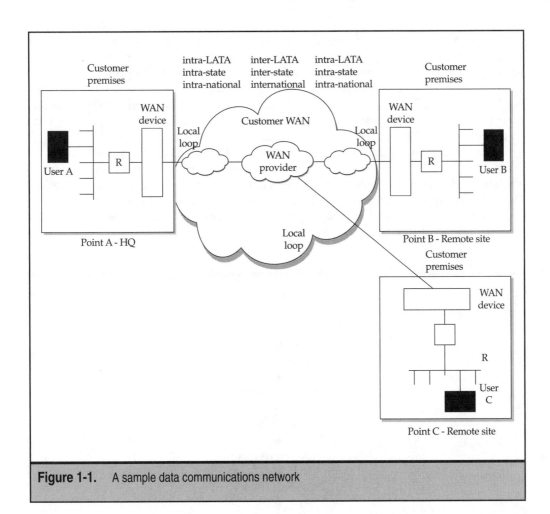

Figure 1-1.   A sample data communications network

and basic telecommunications. Data communications networks are designed with the primary purpose of enabling consumers or businesses to communicate in some form or fashion. In other words, a data network is designed and exists to enable the business. At the highest level, it is one tool to accomplish the mission and vision of a business; at the lowest level, it is a composite of hardware and software designed to pass bits of data from one point to another.

The role of the people who build and manage these networks has changed over time. Specialization by network engineers and managers in a single networking discipline, operating system, or application is no longer enough. Focus cannot be split between voice and data traffic, or the local area network (LAN) and wide area network (WAN), or the server and router worlds, but instead must be directed at all components as a single system. The lines of demarcation from the desktop to the WAN transport have greatly blurred, while overriding issues such as security and disaster recovery integrate and span all these worlds.

The internetworking portion of design deals with the interconnectivity of multiple applications, protocols, and devices into a single or multiple network infrastructures and service. One of the key features of a good design is that it is built to support both present and future requirements. A network is defined as a snare or catching device that, once built, attracts and catches many applications not originally destined to be supported. Over time, businesses almost always become more dependent and interdependent with their networks. The snare concept will become more evident in subsequent chapters.

Network design can be viewed as a series of chronological events that start with determining the business requirements to managing and securing the network after it is implemented. Figure 1-2 shows the steps taken in this text to perform a network design. The order in which these steps are presented can be organized to the network designer's preference. This text has been designed to walk the reader through this chronological process of network design.

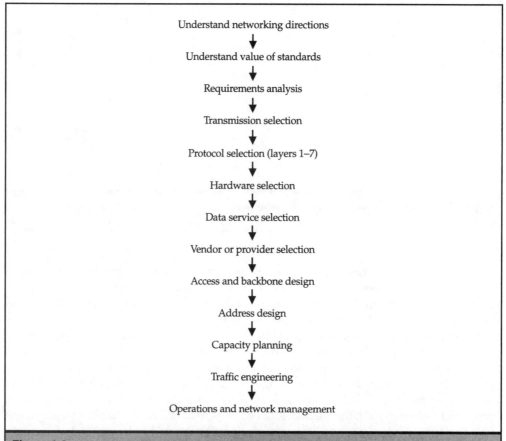

Understand networking directions

↓

Understand value of standards

↓

Requirements analysis

↓

Transmission selection

↓

Protocol selection (layers 1–7)

↓

Hardware selection

↓

Data service selection

↓

Vendor or provider selection

↓

Access and backbone design

↓

Address design

↓

Capacity planning

↓

Traffic engineering

↓

Operations and network management

Figure 1-2.   Network design steps

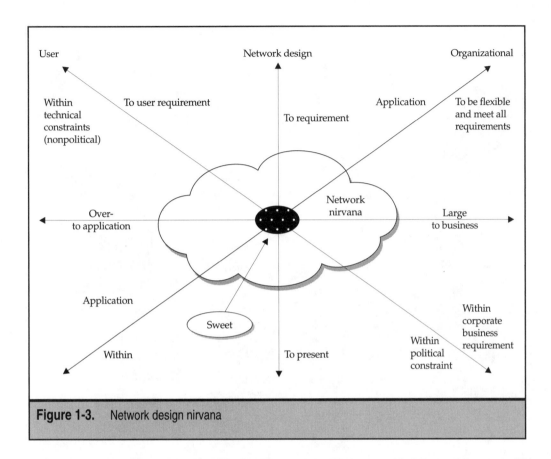

Figure 1-3.   Network design nirvana

The network designer constantly strives to achieve *network nirvana*, or the point where the network design comes as close as possible to meeting the requirements of both the end users (think desktop application performance and availability) and the business (think budget, return on investment (ROI), and politics). These needs are often in conflict. Reaching this balance point between each end of the spectrum is the art of network design. Figure 1-3 illustrates the many factors—business and technical, economic and political—that influence the network design. The art of network design is achieving the most cost-effective and robust design that falls in the "sweet spot."

A data communications network, when designed efficiently, can and does become the lifeblood of a business organization. The new network can create and enable many opportunities not available under the old style of communications, such as deployment of new applications (desktop video-conferencing, e-mail, file sharing, Internet access, telecommuting, and mobile access) to increase productivity, achieve IT cost savings, and many other benefits discussed in this book. It can also be extremely detrimental to the business and your career if designed incorrectly.

Figure 1-4 depicts the user's view of a data communications network, showing a few of the many types of user-to-network devices prevalent in today's networks.

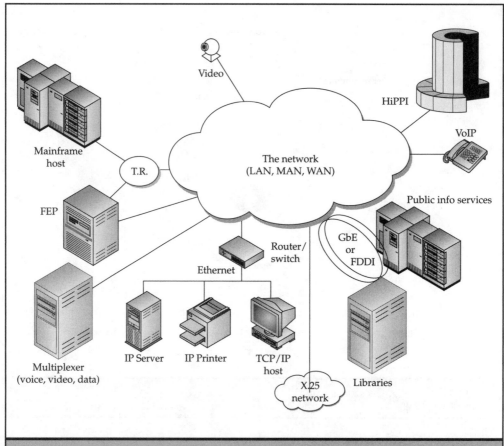

Figure 1-4.   Data communications network with user-to-network interfaces

First-generation network design consisted of engineering primarily for the transport of voice or low-speed data traffic over dedicated private line facilities. The entire communications infrastructure before 1960 was based primarily on analog technology. In this era, data communications adapted to the analog world. The 1980s saw massive deployments of synchronous digital transmission facilities. Voice communications were digitized and multiplexed into high-capacity digital transmission facilities. This was the beginning of the categorization of voice as low-speed data. Computer data traffic at this time was also low-speed, consisting primarily of terminal to mainframe communications. Computing devices (the personal computer and network devices like routers, bridges, and switches as we know them today) were in their infancy.

A myriad of developments in analog, digital, and optical transport technologies has brought us into the current information era, founded primarily on high-speed—

characterized in the millions (mega), billions (giga), and now trillions (tera) of bits per second—digital and now optical transport, switching, and routing technologies. One of the most significant factors in the evolution and acceleration of the information era has been the digitization of transport networks. Digital technology increased network, switch, and computer performance, and optical technology optimized the transport of that traffic across the metro and wide area network. The same digital and optical technologies have enabled the construction of global transport networks capable of providing subscriber service for all forms of voice, video, and data traffic—even assuring specific and controllable quality-of-service parameters.

Digital technologies have rapidly yielded ground to optical technologies. Optical technology innovations that have taken place since the early 1990s have dramatically increased the amount of bandwidth available on a single strand of fiber, and this bandwidth is much needed for applications that become more graphical and bandwidth intensive on almost a daily basis.

Network design, which once started with just the transparent transport of voice and data over dedicated facilities, now has to comprise all protocol interactions from user applications through network protocols and encompass local (LAN), metropolitan (MAN), and wide (WAN) area networks physical and logical connectivity.

Thus, our charter is to understand all aspects of network design in order to make comprehensive decisions when designing a network. A working understanding of solid design principles enables the design engineer or manager to successfully plan, design, build, implement, manage, optimize, and secure a data communications network from conception through continued operation. The engineer or manager must clearly comprehend the fundamental concepts of network design as presented in this book. The engineer or manager must also understand that change is the way networks operate. Network traffic and networking options continue to accelerate. Data transport and application formats change, speed and throughput requirements increase at exponential rates, vendors strive to produce products to meet standards under development or create new standards, and more efficient technologies emerge at a rate that makes hardware and software seem obsolete almost before it is deployed into the network.

This book deals primarily with network design relating to computer and data communications networks. A data communications network design is defined as a complete communications system-level design encompassing user premises and access (ingress and egress), the transportation medium and data transport elements, as well as all internal and external factors that affect, manage, or interact with the communications medium. A data communications network domain includes the hardware, software, security, management, and any other subsets of the communications network. Many people would say it is constrained to the WAN, MAN, and LAN, but in reality it extends into the desktop and up to the user applications. This list is far from comprehensive, but includes the basic elements.

We will focus on the network at both a micro and macro level, from detailed architecture and protocol design to high-level systems design. We will also study network design from the user perspective *into* the network, and from the network perspective *outward* toward the end user.

BACKGROUND: DEFINING DATA COMMUNICATIONS NEEDS

The first step in the process of data network design is to define the business need for data communications, which should then be prioritized with respect to other needs in the organization. A data network design or optimization should go through the same business analysis process—return on investment (ROI) business case study—as any other corporate expense. We start this process by focusing on the needs of the users and their applications, evaluating the effectiveness of the current communications technology, looking at the priorities of future requirements, and reviewing corporate needs driving the necessity for communications.

Business staffing changes as organizations bulk up on resources in good times, and reduce staffing in crunch times, but one thing is constant: The organization—primarily its personnel's and applications' communications patterns—will continue to drive the need for each individual to have access to more data and to communicate with more users and shared resources. The primary patterns are

▼ A drive for longer or "follow-the-sun" work hours

■ Data that is graphically and bandwidth intensive

▲ A desire for any-to-any extranet communications patterns

The Internet is the best example of this trend, where even the casual consumer browses more frequently, downloads progressively more graphically bandwidth-intensive content, check stock quotes, and wants to chat with his or her closest friends simultaneously.

The business user community is facing these same issues. In the 1980s, this change was borne out by the move from hierarchical System Network Architecture (SNA) host-based networks to LANs at the local level. In the 1990s, computing took the shape of more peer-to-peer internetworking over the Internet or intranet across the corporate wide area network, distributing more and more processing down to the desktop and handing over the brains of the network to client-server–based applications. The first decade of the twenty-first century finds users building their own virtual private intranets, internets, and extranets over private and public data service platforms. But the pattern is the same—more time computing, more bandwidth per compute, and more connectivity between the computers. So we find that as computers and computing power proliferates, so does the need for more data communications. Users will always find use for more bandwidth, and will always need more bandwidth, but our study centers on business. Businesses, due to their accelerating reliance on communications networks, are constantly being driven to increase their reliance on less expensive, user-controllable, multiple-platform communications access in a multivendor environment. As the business becomes increasingly reliant on data communications, the network becomes a force that must be reckoned with.

Demand for corporate and government communications increases each year—slower in some, much faster in others, but inexorably more—while the per unit cost of bandwidth for data services decreases daily. Many scenarios fuel this growth including the following:

▼ Increased LAN and application interconnectivity between departments, customers, and suppliers

■ The continued movement of mainframe applications to a distributed client-server architecture

■ The movement of applications into the network (application service provider's [ASP] and e-commerce models)

▲ The emergence of a new class of image and graphics-intensive interactive applications

A large number of possible scenarios exist, each leading to the same conclusion: businesses continue to experience an explosion of data traffic (defined as voice, video, and true data) that requires communication throughout the business to meet ever-increasing demands for high-performance computing to and between every desktop.

How can these increased data requirements, phenomenal growth of user applications, processing power, and demand for connectivity and bandwidth be defined and understood? How can this parallel shift from hierarchical to flat, decentralized, and distributed applications and networks and organizations be quantified? This chapter provides answers to these questions and more of an in-depth look at perspectives on past, current, and future communications architectures, changes in applications, and the technologies that provide the enabler to change.

FROM VOICE NETWORKS TO DATA NETWORKS

A dramatic shift from voice communications networks to data communications networks has occurred over the past 20 years. Data communications now affects many aspects of our lives: stock market transactions, medical research networks, electronic mail, Internet access, corporate file and calendar sharing, online gaming, and even the Automatic Teller Machines (the other ATM!) that provide us with money on practically every street corner. What chain of events made data communications become so integral to our daily life in the last generation? How did the move occur so quickly from voice networks using analog transmission facilities; to voice networks using digital transmission facilities; to all digital transmission facilities integrating voice, data, and video traffic; to a hybrid digital and optical network that is converging legacy voice and data along with blurring the line between access and backbone networks? With these questions in mind, this chapter now begins with a review of the evolution of communications. For those readers preparing to skip this section, a word of warning: Those who do not study history are doomed to repeat it! Only by studying history can one come close to predicting the future, as history always repeats itself. As background, the history of voice communications is presented as the precursor to data communications.

Brief History of Communications

Figure 1-5 depicts a view of the history of communication along the dimensions of analog versus digital encoding and synchronous versus asynchronous timing, or scheduling. The beginnings of spoken human communication are estimated to be over 50,000 years old. The issue with using complex languages for communications is that both the sender and receiver must speak (or be able to translate) the same language! This concept is the same for all voice and data protocols.

Graphic images have been found in caves over 20,000 years old. Graphics eliminated the need to translate languages, but were limited in the data that could be communicated (unless you believe in the axiom "a picture is worth a thousand words"). Written records over 5000 years old have been found. Finally, man had the ability to record data and send it over great distances. But this took time.

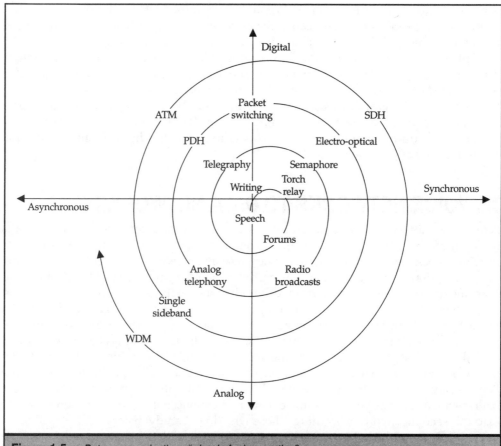

Figure 1-5. Data communications "wheel of reincarnation"

Armies did not have satellites to track troop movements 2000 years ago. So, as many inventions are borne out of necessity, the Greeks traded analog communications for optical. Digital long-distance optical communications began before the birth of Christ when the ancient Greeks used digital and optical communications to relay information using placement of torches on towers at relay stations. The Greeks and Romans helped us prepare for later forms of data communication by popularizing *scheduled* public announcements and speeches that served as early examples of broadcast communications, as well as individual, *unscheduled* communication in forums and debates. Our ancestors taught us well—whereas it took the Greeks 2000 years to go from analog to optical communications, our twentieth-century Geeks did the same in 20 years.

In the seventeenth and eighteenth centuries, optical telegraphy was used extensively in Europe. Later, Samuel F. B. Morse invented electrical telegraphy in 1846, marking the beginning of modern digital electromagnetic communications. Radiotelegraphy was invented shortly afterwards by G. Marconi. Broadcast analog radio communications of audio signals followed in the late nineteenth and early twentieth centuries. This technology was also applied to analog voice communication in the same time frame.

Television signal broadcasting became commercially viable in the late 1940s. Then, in the 1950s, the conversion of analog voice to digital signals in the Plesiochronous Digital Hierarchy (PDH) began in large metropolitan areas to make better use of installed cabling. This was followed by the invention of packet switching in the 1960s as an offshoot of research into secure military communication networks. Fiber-optic transmission and the concept of synchronous digital transmission were introduced in the early 1980s. Analog transmission of voice had a brief renaissance using Single Side Band (SSB) in the 1980s. Asynchronous Transfer Mode (ATM) then moved the wheel of technology around the circle back into the domain of digital asynchronous communication.

The next major leap in emerging technology is Wavelength Division Multiplexing (WDM), and Dense Wavelength Division Multiplexing (DWDM), which is analog and asynchronous and uses colors of light to extend the available bandwidth of a single fiber-optic fiber well into the terabits per second. The speed (transfer) of communication has increased geometrically over time through each of these evolving phases of technology.

This is not a perfect analogy—sometimes the wheel spins faster than at other times. For example, in the current day we move from Asynchronous Transfer Mode (ATM), an asynchronous digital technology, all the way around to Wavelength Division Multiplexing (WDM), an asynchronous, analog technology.

The military has been a key user of data communications networks throughout history, and most inventions were discovered and developed to solve militaristic needs. The telegraph was significant to the Union forces in the Civil War, where near instant communications of army locations and sizes across the entire theatre gave a distinct advantage to the North. Many data processing and early computer systems were developed during World War II, when systems integration was driven by the necessity to reduce complexity. After World War II, the command and control centers, weapons and sensor systems, voice networks, and the computers that ran these systems needed to be centrally controlled within one interconnected communications network. This was the beginning of the U.S. Department of Defense (DoD) telecommunications architecture.

The next major advance by the DoD was the establishment of the Advanced Research Projects Agency NETwork (ARPANET). ARPANET was established in 1971 as the first packet-switched network. This data network connected military and civilian locations, as well as universities. In 1983, a majority of ARPANET users, including European and Pacific Rim contingents, were split off to form the Defense Data Network (DDN)—also referred to as MILNET. Some locations in the U.S. and Europe remained with ARPANET, and are now merged with the DARPA Internet, which provides connectivity to many universities and national telecommunications networks. The original ARPANET was decommissioned in 1990. Many of the advances in computer communications, including routing and networking protocols, have been developed through experience on the Internet and related projects.

The explosive growth of the Internet has occurred in tandem to the explosive growth in consumer and corporate broadband requirements. It is curious to note these two requirements—corporate and consumer—tend to leapfrog each other. Up until recently, consumer 56-Kbps dial-up connections could not compete with corporate DS1 speeds. Now consumer xDSL and cable modem services are more ubiquitous than equal speed corporate connectivity, and, in fact, many corporations are evaluating these two technologies as alternatives to private line and frame relay access. But we will see later that consumer access is much different than corporate transport.

Packet switching had its hand in this evolution. Host-based networks accessed by local and remote terminals evolved through the use of private networks and later packet-switched services. The primary example is the IBM Systems Network Architecture (SNA). This architecture provides the platform for many dumb terminals and workstations to communicate with an intelligent host or mainframe in a hierarchical, or star, fashion. This hierarchy was developed for two reasons:

▼ Collecting expensive intelligence at the host and allowing the terminals to have little resident intelligence was the most cost-effective trade-off.

▲ Transmission facilities that could be shared at the access point, as with multipoint circuits, were much more cost-effective than dedicated point-to-point circuits to every site.

Later, packet-switched access enabled even greater efficiencies, until the point where client-server distributed computing created traffic patterns that destroyed hierarchical topology design and required distributed, meshed architectures. The primary driver for distributed computing and these changes was the Local Area Network (LAN).

LANs were the next major development in the computer communications networking environment, with the advent of Ethernet produced by Xerox, DEC, and Intel in 1974. Token Ring ruled the IBM environment, and Ethernet ruled most of the rest. Today, Ethernet is clearly the predominant LAN standard. Client-server architectures and distributed processing across the LAN, MAN, and WAN signaled the beginning of modern data communications.

This ends the short course on the "History of Data 101." Now we move on to more recent data history starting in the 1990s.

A Recent History of Data Communications

One of the primary challenges faced by many corporations today is how to cope with the move from a controlled application and protocol environment with structured and centralized applications to one of individual choice across multiple protocols and architectures. Tie this to the switching and routing required across a flattening of interconnected LAN networks to support the astounding rate of personal computer proliferation (read exponentially increasing network traffic requirements) and you have a *paradigm shift* (and the most common buzz word of the decade!). This network flattening and shift to client-server computing began the (r)evolution , sometimes called the "Information Revolution," of the corporate data network. What started as a personal computer designed for home use has now become a corporate necessity on every desktop (and laptop).

In the 1990s, it was a natural evolutionary choice for the visionary network design engineer to address the users in these two very different islands of information—the distributed LAN interconnecting desktops supporting client-server applications based primarily on Ethernet and IP, and the centralized mainframe Management Information Systems (MIS) arena supporting legacy systems and SNA protocols used for billing and accounting—by creating a common environment using routers and switches to achieve interworking and interconnectivity. As these two worlds merged, it created a tremendous opportunity for network device providers (switches, routers, hubs, and so forth) and service providers (offering various types of Virtual Private Network [VPN] services).

The falling costs, complexity, and increased ubiquity phenomenon of LAN and WAN routers and switches enabled enhanced LAN and routed protocol connectivity. This is very similar to what happened when the minicomputers invaded mainframe turf and the cost of minis fell to departmental budget approval levels, bypassing corporate MIS budget approval. Routers enabled the segmentation of the corporate LAN effectively into user groups, which further enabled interdepartmental connectivity of diverse LAN technologies and protocols in a cost-effective manner. Many "home-grown" router and switch networks placed cost and control more in the hands of the end user than they have ever been before.

In the late 1980s and early 1990s, many users asked themselves the question, "Why conform to corporate MIS dictates when you can build your own departmental LAN and handle 90 percent of your data processing needs?" But with this independence came complexity and hidden costs, as corporations learned that having legacy and new age networking platforms and applications required more than twice the support! Hence, when there was a need to interconnect these LANs with each other or with the legacy systems, the legacy MIS manager and "entrepreneurial" LAN managers had to work together in order to integrate access from the LANs to the VAX and IBM mainframes. For many years, and for many corporations even today, these two worlds remained as separate cost centers with duplicate support staff.

In addition, WAN interconnectivity often went beyond the scope of a single LAN manager and had costs that had to be shared across multiple LANs. The router also found its place here as the gateway to the WAN and continued the user-control wave into the 1990s. Today, the line from the desktop through the LAN and into the WAN has blurred, exacerbated by the placement of the applications *within* the network with the move to E-commerce and by Application Service Providers (ASPs). For a while it looked as though this integration role would eventually be conceded to ATM switches and services around the turn of the century, but that has not been the case. But the popularity of the Internet, and easy, cheap networking using Ethernet, changed all of that.

IP, FR, and ATM arrived in this era of expanding, even euphoric, expectations from users caught up in this new wave of freedom. The high-performance workstations and servers deploying 100 MbE and GbE, and who required multimedia services (voice, data, or video) lead the next data communications revolution. Many of the legacy systems were tied to new-age routed networks through gateways or conversion to Token Ring LAN interfaces with routing, while others were just rewritten in client-server applications and replaced over time. The MIS manager still needed to focus attention on the design and maintenance of the host and front-end processor systems because many mission-critical applications still resided there, at least until they could be ported to client-server Enterprise Resource Planning (ERP) applications like Oracle Financials, PeopleSoft, BAAN, and JD Edwards.

The LAN and WAN manager positions merged with the MIS or IT manager role, and this single individual now needs to focus on the needs of the high-performance workstation user and server, while continuing to enhance the support provided to the users employing legacy technology. Bringing the requirements of these two divergent realms into a single ubiquitous and seamless network is essential. You should not become caught up in the glamour of a single integration technology such as ATM or IP until a clear path is defined for migrating mission-critical applications from an older technology to a newer one. Again, the snare concept tells us that a well-designed network that was once intended for a single application and protocol will easily snare many more applications and protocols throughout its life; so make sure your single network infrastructure is the right one!

THE TELEPHONE NETWORK: CURRENT NETWORK INFRASTRUCTURE

History continually repeats itself, and voice and data communications history is no exception to the rule. Voice communications has a long history of competition, starting with the telegraph and box phone, through the extension of long lines business across the country, and into modern-day divestiture and open competition. This evolution, a by-product of national policy, has been cyclic—competition, regulation, natural monopoly, deregulation, and again competition.

Now for a short trip through the history of the U.S. telephone network—the worlds largest VPN! It took many competitive efforts to achieve what we have today in the United States. AT&T, plagued by independent telephone competition at the beginning of the century, succeeded in building a government-sanctioned natural monopoly only to lose it again during divestiture. Now, as traditional IntereXchange Carriers (IXCs) move into the local access business and Local Exchange Carriers (LECs) move into long-haul (inter-LATA) service, the lines again blur. The dot-com bust at the turn of the century had its own special consequences on regulation, eventually for the betterment of all.

The United States

The telephone was patented on March 7, 1876, by Alexander Graham Bell. The first box telephone was patented the next year, on January 30, 1877. That same year, over 600 telephones were connected to each other via point-to-point private lines. Mr. Bell also carried his invention to Europe in 1877 and demonstrated its operation to Queen Victoria and other world dignitaries. Thus, the information era of telecommunications was born. On January 28, 1878, the first telephone exchange was opened in New Haven, Connecticut, and an operator switched users manually at "central." The number of exchanges spread rapidly until the New England Telephone Company was formed on February 12, 1878.

Throughout the next three years many companies changed hands. Companies like Western Union, the National Bell Telephone Company, and the American Speaking Telephone Company competed over telephone rights. In November 1879, an agreement was reached that Western Union would remain solely in the telegraph business and the National Bell Telephone Company, which became the American Bell Telephone Company, would remain solely in the telephone business.

The next major development was the formation of the American Telephone and Telegraph Company (AT&T) in 1885. This company was formed as a subsidiary of the American Bell Telephone Company to handle the nation's long lines business, but AT&T grew and in 1900 absorbed the Bell Company. Later, in 1911, AT&T organized territorial divisions called Bell Associated Companies, which in turn paid licensing fees to AT&T for patents. Throughout the early part of the century, AT&T fought a hard battle against independent telephone competition, buying out those they could and refusing to connect to others. The Kingsbury commitment was made by AT&T in 1913 under government regulatory pressure, allowing independents to interconnect with AT&T. In 1921, the Graham Act was passed by Congress, legitimizing AT&T as a "natural monopoly." From this point until divestiture, AT&T enjoyed the status of a monopoly.

The AT&T monopoly comprised AT&T Headquarters, 23 Bell Associated Companies, Western Electric Company, and Bell Telephone Laboratories. This monopoly was broken up in 1982 during what is called "divestiture." The Modified Final Judgment (MFJ) was issued by Judge Harold Greene of the U.S. District Court in Washington, D.C., for AT&T to divest itself of all of the Bell Operating Companies (BOCs). Figure 1-6 shows each of the post-divestiture Regional Bell Operating Companies (RBOCs) and their areas of coverage. These seven RBOCs were

▼ Pacific Telesis

■ U.S. West

■ SBC Communications

- ■ Ameritech
- ■ Bell South
- ■ Bell Atlantic
- ▲ NYNEX

Another major decision at divestiture was to not allow RBOCs to manufacture Customer Premises Equipment (CPE). One hundred sixty Local Area Transport Areas (LATAs) were designated for local access. Independent telephone companies could elect to come under the LATA plan or not; most larger ones did. The RBOCs could provide service within designated LATA areas only, leaving the long-distance companies—AT&T, MCI, and Sprint—to provide the inter-LATA connectivity. AT&T was split into AT&T Communications and AT&T Technologies and forbidden to use the Bell system logo. The most recent form of legislation having an all-encompassing effect on the industry was the Telecommunications Bill of 1996. This legislature allows for competition in long-distance, local, cellular, and cable industries. Thus, AT&T and the other legacy interexchange carriers

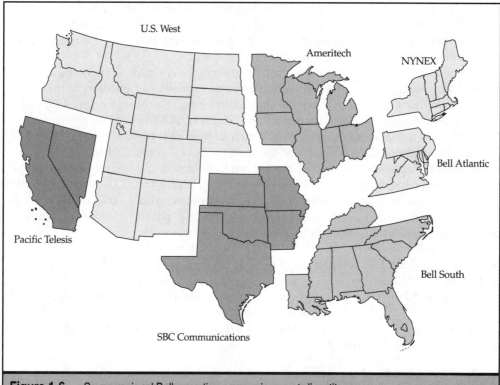

Figure 1-6.   Seven regional Bell operating companies: post-divestiture

(IXCs) have an opportunity to compete in the local markets, and vice versa with the legacy RBOCs (at least the ones that have not been purchased by an IXC or another RBOC!).

Data communications networks evolved in much the same way as voice networks, as we will see in subsequent chapters.

International Network Infrastructures

The European and Pacific Rim telephone industry has evolved in a similar manner as the U.S. industry. The historical model was for the predominant telecommunications carrier to be owned by government entities through what are called postal telegraph and telephone (PTT) agencies. Many of the more industrialized countries have moved from the PTT environment and sold off government-owned entities to public markets and owners, or allowed national and foreign competition into some or all of their telecommunications markets.

In the United States, communications entities are privately owned but loosely regulated by governmental agencies. In Europe, South and Central America, and the Pacific Rim, many countries have opened telecommunications and services to local or foreign competition. Those PTTs that remain are typically both operated *and* regulated by the government. Many of the remaining PTT monopolies are being realigned into two organizations—traditional services such as local dial tone, and competitive services such as virtual private and switched network services. Multinational (transnational) companies helped force this change as their requirements for cost-effective telecommunications often drive the decision on what county to do business in. In fact, many multinational communications companies like AT&T Cable & Wireless are challenging local PTTs or the dominant carrier for access and transport services. The competitive environment that prevails in the U.S. since the AT&T breakup has followed internationally.

Voice as Low-Speed Data

A standard voice-grade channel can be accurately represented by a 64-Kbps (or 56-Kbps) data stream. Nyquist's sampling theorem states that the number of samples taken from an analog signal must be taken at a rate more than *twice* the bandwidth of its signal for it to be accurately reproduced. Therefore, the minimum sampling rate for a 4000-Hz bandwidth voice channel is 8000 samples per second. Employing 8 (or 7) bits per sample yields a 64-Kbps (or 56-Kbps) data stream. The coding of each voice sample is performed using one of two different nonlinear companding (COMpression/exPANDING) schemes, called μ-Law in North America and A-Law elsewhere. In fact, while voice is typically transmitted at 64 Kbps, many digital encoding and compression techniques now enable a voice channel to be transmitted at speeds as low as 8 kbps.

The 64-Kbps representation of voice was first used for engineering and economic reasons to multiplex more voice conversations onto bundles of twisted pairs in crowded conduits, mainly in urban areas of the United States in the mid-1950s. Twenty-four voice channels were multiplexed onto a single twisted pair in what was known as a T1 repeater system, using a DS1 signal format. The scarce resource of twisted pairs was now utilized at 2400 percent of its previous capacity, a tremendous enhancement! The fact that these multiplexing methods could be used for the purpose of data communications came later.

Voice is very sensitive to delay and variations in delay (jitter), somewhat loss-sensitive, and requires a fixed amount of bandwidth (typically 64 Kbps) per voice call. Users do not tolerate appreciable delay during a full-duplex or half-duplex conversation, because it can inhibit interaction or result in annoying echo, nor will they accept sentence-flow garbling by the loss of entire syllables. Variations in delay can cause the speaker's voice to become unrecognizable, or render the speech unintelligible. The loss of small portions of syllables or words in voice communications is usually acceptable, however. Satellite transmission delay, which most people have experienced, is a good example of the effects of large delay (in terms of echo) and the impact on interactive conversation. Certain packet technologies such as ATM can handle delay-sensitive voice traffic almost as well as a dedicated private line, while other technologies such as frame relay and IP require strict traffic engineering to provide the consistent high quality of service required to carry this type of traffic.

Voice and Data over the Current Network Infrastructure

The public telephone network naturally evolved from a narrow-band to a broadband hierarchy based upon circuit economic considerations such as the aggregation of circuits into a common medium (24 DS0 circuits onto a single DS1, 28 DS1s onto a single DS3, and so forth). Figure 1-7 depicts the classical five-level public telephone network hierarchy developed to minimize cost and achieve traffic engineering economies of scale, which resulted in a corresponding increase in bandwidth at higher levels in the hierarchy. Customer locations are connected to the telephone network by a *local loop* (also called a trunk) that is provided by narrow-band twisted pair access lines to the lowest level of the hierarchy, the Class 5 central office telephone switch. A *twisted pair* is composed of multiple wires that are twisted to minimize impairments in analog transmission such as crosstalk and interference. These twisted pairs are bundled into cables and then aggregated at the central office. Generally, if the distance traversed is greater than a few miles, the local loops are aggregated into larger bandwidths for transmission over microwave, copper, or optical fiber. Indeed, the DS1 and DS3 multiplex levels were created for this very reason, their use for data occurring by later invention and innovation rather than initial design.

Historically, Class 5 switches were directly connected, or else connected to larger Class 4 tandem switches, which were then connected to even larger tandem switches such as the Class 3 and 2. The final route choice was via Class 1 switches connected at the highest bandwidth aggregate level. In general, switches are larger at higher levels in the hierarchy, even though a Class 5 switch in a large metropolitan area can be quite large.

Recent voice networks are connected in a flatter, more distributed network of fully interconnected Class 4 or 5 switches. The number of levels has not yet ubiquitously been reduced to one, but in many cases there are only two or three levels in a hierarchical phone network. Again, this parallels the move of most major businesses from a hierarchical organization to a flatter, distributed organization.

Voice channels are time division multiplexed and transmitted over digital and optical transmission systems. When compared to data, the main difference is that voice calls are circuit switched, whereas data can be message, packet, cell, or circuit switched as

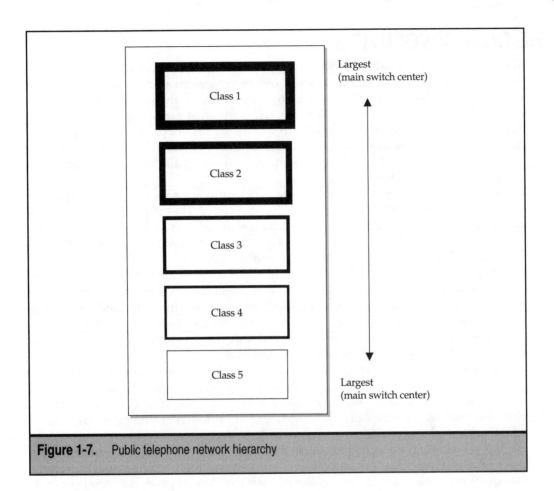

Figure 1-7. Public telephone network hierarchy

described in Chapter 4. Both voice and data applications require large amounts of bandwidth, but for different reasons. Data applications require large bandwidth to support the peak rate of applications, while voice requires large amounts of aggregate bandwidth to multiplex large numbers of individual voice circuits.

One interesting point is that historically, personal computer users who access the Internet at home have used their analog phone "voice" lines for a much longer duration than for actual voice calls. Consider casual Internet browsing for hours at a time versus a three-minute average voice call duration. The voice network perceives this traffic as a voice call until it can hand it off to a modem on the data network, when in effect these are actually data calls. As telecommuting and access to the Internet from home increase, it begs the question, how much "voice" traffic is really "data" traffic in unstructured form? Consumer broadband access alternatives like xDSL and cable modems have greatly relieved the PSTN of these long duration calls by placing the home user directly onto the data network at much higher speeds than standard 56-Kbps modem dial speeds.

THE DATA REVOLUTION

The 1990s yielded a broadband data revolution with a rallying cry of "bandwidth-on-demand!" The expectation of bandwidth-on-demand was created by the LAN where a user shared a high-speed medium with many other users, having access to the full shared medium bandwidth on demand. This worked well when every user required only a small portion of the shared medium, but became a significant problem as the power of desktop technology increased while Ethernet capability remained at 10 Mbps for many years. Eventually, in the late 1990s, Ethernet deployments of 100 Mbps proliferated, and again the LAN was no longer the bottleneck.

As we move to a graphic-intensive world with high-powered servers directly attached to LANs, the need for 1000 Mbps Ethernet (GbE) is growing. The key point here is that LAN bandwidth is cheap, whereas WAN bandwidth is extremely expensive. As a case in point, consider the cost of a five-station 100-Mbps LAN: Five 100-Mbps Ethernet Network Interface Cards (NICs) and an eight-port hub can cost less than $300, thus providing each user with potentially up to a 100-Mbps transmission. But move to the WAN and we find the *monthly* charge for 100 Mbps (two 45-Mbps DS3s) could cost ten times the *one-time* cost of the LAN. We can see that the concept of cost-effective bandwidth-on-demand is most critical in the WAN. Bandwidth-on-demand expectations for the WAN are driven by users requiring near-LAN connect speeds across the WAN, but at cost-effective rates. This is one of the primary drivers for packet-switched and routed services.

There is another interpretation of bandwidth-on-demand advocated by those using circuit switched technologies. With circuit switching, a user requests bandwidth and is either granted the full request or is denied access completely (that is, blocked). This is similar to making a phone call—the call either goes through or you get a busy signal. ISDN and V.90 dial access services are two prime examples.

This section shows how the growth in data communications has taken the lead over that of voice communications in total volume, revenue for service providers, and the introduction of new managed and value-add services. The discussion then moves on to cover how various services best meet application needs in terms of bandwidth (capacity and throughput), delay, and burstiness (defined as the ratio of the peak traffic rate to the average traffic rate). The section concludes with the observation that the data revolution continues to be global, social, and economic in scope.

Data Communications Takes the Lead

Data traffic continues to grow at double-digit growth annually, far outpacing the average growth of voice, which averages only 6 to 8 percent per year. The consequence of this differential in growth is plotted in Figure 1-8, which projects the U.S. common carrier voice and data services revenues for the growth rates cited previously. These growth rates have remained constant, and now, based on many figures (as projected in the last edition of this text), data network revenue exceeds voice network revenue for a majority of service providers. Of course, many factors cause these growth rates to change, such as the dot-com bust at the turn of the century, so these numbers will vary. However, it makes the point that

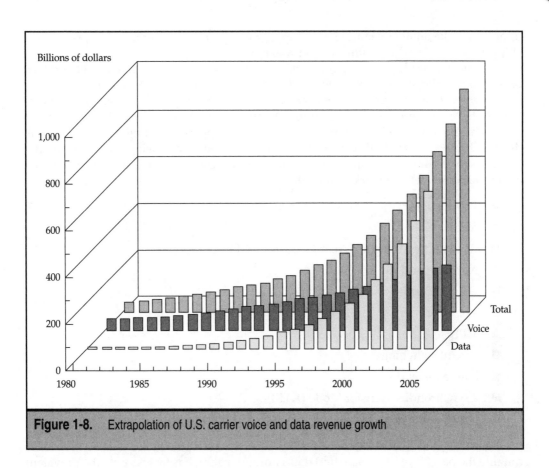

Figure 1-8.   Extrapolation of U.S. carrier voice and data revenue growth

we are in the era of data communications dominance over voice. Collaborative computing, electronic mail with attachments, file transfers, local area network interconnection, interactive, graphics-intensive applications, and emerging computer communications applications like voice recognition and desktop video-conferencing represent just a few examples of how data communications traffic is far exceeding that of voice communications.

For companies that rely on their communications and information flow as the lifeblood of their business, effective and highly available data communications cannot only give them a competitive edge, it can put them on a leading edge. Corporations seek return on investment (ROI) and improved time to market results from their communications spending. The network must truly enable the business. But this leading edge can create both benefits and risks. Once a business experiences effective data communications, it becomes "hooked" on its own network. The data and computer communications network quickly becomes the lifeblood of the company, and downtime is no longer an inconvenience, but can cause loss of revenue, legal implications, regulatory embarrassment, or a host of other damaging influences. Take, for example, the financial services company whose data communications network transmits information for millions of dollars in funds transfered per hour, where a one-hour outage can cost the company millions of dollars. Take another example of a shipping company that operates on a just-in-time shipping schedule, where information transfer is critical.

A company needs voice network communications, but a private voice network can only become so large since it is limited by the company's size. Voice communications traffic can be forecast and has predictable characteristics. On the other hand, data communications traffic characteristics can be a different ball game with new rules. Once a company uses a data network, traffic patterns now resemble shoppers spending patterns in a mall during Christmas—with little to no predictability or pattern while being extremely bursty.

Key services and switching technologies that represent existing and emerging data communications service markets include

▼ Private lines

■ X.25

■ IP, including transport, remote access, and Internet access

■ Narrow-band ISDN

■ DSL and cable

■ Vo packet

■ MPLS

■ Circuit switching

■ Frame Relay (FR)

■ Asynchronous Transfer Mode (ATM)

▲ SONET and Dense Wavelength Division Multiplexing (DWDM)

Figure 1-9 shows the time frame for the introduction of the major data services over roughly the past 30 years. Broadband data communication has fast become the prevalent market since the 1990s within the United States and most of Europe and at the forefront are private lines, DSL, cable, frame relay, IP, ATM, SONET, and D/WDM. The 1990s can be called the era of interworking, simply because of the widespread use of these broadband technologies and services and the internetworking of LANs, where frame relay, IP, and ATM have lead the charge. Not shown in this figure are the many forms of wireless communications services now emerging, as most mobile and fixed wireless services do not approach broadband speeds today.

Business Relies on Data Communications

A major portion of most corporate budgets is devoted to the care and feeding of data communications networks, yet the level of dependence of a corporation on its data communications network is not always readily apparent. An optimized network that has 100 percent availability, reliability, and has consistently high performance can be taken for granted, despite demonstrating the exact return on investment being sought. Unfortunately, it takes the chaos that occurs when the network goes down to show the corporation how fundamental the data communications network is to the successful operation of any business. Computers, terminals, modems, facsimile machines, security systems, and

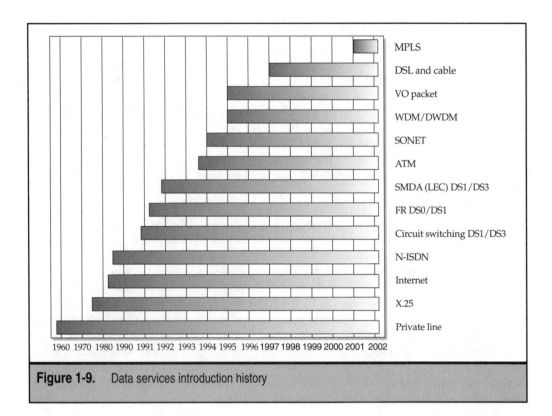

Figure 1-9.   Data services introduction history

the telephone systems all send the traffic across the data communications network, and rely on its optimization. A well-designed network can enable a business, while a poorly designed one can disable the business. Thus, design of a data communications network can have a direct impact on the success or failure of a business.

Cost also plays a major role in determining network needs, and often is driven more by the cost of services provided by the carrier, or actually running the network, than by the actual equipment costs. Often, services supplied by service providers or vendors are expensed, whereas the purchase of equipment is a depreciated capital expenditure. Equipment expenses often turn out to be a small part of the total expenses of operating a network, eclipsed by the cost of people, tools, and the process of network operations.

A New World Order for Data?

Corporate global enterprise networks are proliferating at an astonishing rate as international circuit costs decline, foreign governments open up telecommunications infrastructures to competition, and service ubiquity increases. We have believed for over a decade that these changes have pointed to a new world order for data communications, and we must become familiar with and participate in this new world order to survive.

The data communications market is truly a global community, supported by international standards for equipment interconnection and digital and optical transmission infrastructures. International data service (PL, FR, ATM, IP, SONET, and DWDM) connectivity continues to grow faster than transoceanic cables and fiber can be installed, as evidenced by the bandwidth on these cables being sold months and sometimes years in advance of their completed installation.

International switched and packet services are booming, with current product offerings providing a broad range of switched service speeds and technologies from low-speed dial-up Internet access available in almost every country to high-speed gigabit-per-second connectivity in large metropolitan cities. Most of the civilized world has now been connected by fiber optic transmission systems. In fact, a single fiber-optic cable can carry more than 1 terahertz, or 1000 gigahertz, of capacity with a bit error rate (BER) of one bit per million.

Political, technological, economic, and regulatory changes worldwide have spurred international data network interoperability. Legislature such as the North American Free Trade Agreement (NAFTA) has spurred U.S. interests in Mexico and Canada. Significant growth and connectivity has occurred in the United States, Europe, the Pacific Rim, and Southeast Asia. Markets in South America, New Zealand, Australia, Russia, and countries once part of the Eastern Bloc and the now-defunct Soviet Union have been slower to emerge, but are gaining momentum through the development of infrastructures based on state-of-the-art technology. Many of these countries are skipping older (intermediate) technologies and building infrastructure with newer technologies, in effect leap-frogging over intermediate technologies (but still often not building networks with leading-edge, state-of-the-art technologies—China is a great example). Wireless has been a key technology deployed in these countries. Postal, Telegraphy, and Telephony (PTT) monopolies are realigning with open market competition, making worldwide advanced data communications a reality.

The 1990s saw a surge in mergers and strategic partnerships, and the term *coopetition* (a blend of cooperation and competition) was coined in the communications industry. Every day the sun would rise on a new international merger or partnership among carriers, hardware vendors, PTTs, governmental agencies, and small companies who fill niche markets, and many among old rivals. Many joint ventures sprang up both nationally and internationally, ranging from computer manufacturers trying to capture market share to large interexchange and international carriers vying for entrance into foreign markets.

The turn of the century saw many of these mergers and acquisitions fail, as exorbitant prices paid for companies months earlier seemed ridiculous when those same companies were worth pennies on the dollar. Many of these companies were struggling through a recession and trying to consolidate and survive, and only the strong and cash-rich were succeeding. But the cycle goes on, and soon we predict the same cycle of megamergers and acquisitions will return, albeit probably at less ridiculous levels.

APPLICATIONS AND KEY ENABLERS

Consumer and commercial applications are changing and evolving, creating a need for more bandwidth-on-demand and more any-to-any communications. Requirements for LAN and WAN bandwidth accelerate faster than power to the desktop, as evidenced by application connectivity patterns or one-to-many and many-to-many. Take for example e-mail. A decade ago users would send a small text file. Later, they would attach a spreadsheet or word processor document. More recently, they tend to attach large graphics files, or database files, and send the e-mails to more people within their LAN and across the WAN. Combined exponential growths in computing power and the nonlinear growth in inter-communications have created an overall demand for data communications that is greater than exponential. These factors, together referred to as the *accelerating bandwidth principle*, is further accelerated itself by the increased power of the desktop computer. Multimedia is one example of a high-speed bandwidth application requiring a high-speed communications network. We will explain this principle later in this section.

Consumer and Commercial Applications

Consumer service applications requiring high bandwidth are enabling technologies such as xDSL and cable modems running IP and ATM protocols. These applications require high flexibility and performance, and include

▼ Entertainment imaging

■ Home-shopping services employing multimedia voice, data, image, and video using online databases and catalogs

■ Video-on-demand for popular movies

■ E-mail and multimedia messaging systems

▲ Interactive multimedia applications and online gaming

Some applications require not only broadband service but also the capability of a broadcast public service. These include

▼ Distance learning

■ Online video libraries for home study

■ Video desktop training courses

▲ Video- and music-on-demand

Many commercial public service applications are pushing the envelope for high and flexible bandwidths such as

▼ LAN/MAN/WAN seamless interconnectivity and internetworking

■ Telecommuting and SOHO applications (VPNs)

■ Distributed and remote database access

■ Large file transfer and real-time access to files

■ Electronic and desktop publishing

■ Graphic-intensive industrial engineering applications (such as, CAD, CAM, CAE, and CIM) online

- ■ Collaborative computing such as groupware
- ■ Cooperative computing such as concurrent CAD/CAM concurrent engineering
- ■ Integrated voice, video, data multiplexing, and switching
- ■ Terminal-to-mainframe communications
- ■ Video conferencing
- ■ CD-ROM servers
- ■ Inventory control systems
- ■ Multimedia applications to the desktop (such as, e-mail)
- ■ Electronic fund transfer (EFT)
- ■ Medical imaging
- ■ Financial modeling
- ■ Electronic commerce
- ■ Collapsed backbone campus networks
- ■ Seamless interworking with legacy systems using ATM
- ▲ Enterprise Reserve Planning (ERP) tools

Many of these applications have reached wide-scale deployment, driving the need for greater amounts and more flexible bandwidth.

Application Demand for Bandwidth

Deployment of the bandwidth-intensive applications detailed in the preceding section can increase revenues or provide cost consolidation efficiencies. These applications can also improve business metrics like faster accounts receivable or billing and potentially save lives—for example, real-time medical imaging. In general, they can change the dynamics of the business or the life of the user. People are becoming increasingly more reliant on visual or image information rather than audio or text information, as predicted by the old but accurate adage that a picture is worth a thousand words. The increase in telecommuting and conducting business from the home illustrates the trend to rely on visual or image information. Internet browsing of text-only pages has yielded to flash graphics and browser-based e-commerce. I even receive multimedia Christmas cards through an e-mail that links to a multimedia web site!

The partnering and buyout of cable firms in the late 1990s by information transport and telecommunications providers portended a major change in the infrastructure for providing interactive multimedia networking to the home, signaling the wide-scale deployment of cable modem service and effectively upgrading users from 56 Kbps to 10 Mbps. xDSL deployments by second-tier providers attempted the same thing, only to disappear and sell off their assets to legacy Tier 1 providers after the dot-com burst. It is interesting to note that the three top xDSL providers together achieved market capitalization in the billions of dollars but many of their assets were eventually sold for a fraction of that amount.

As new technologies emerge, their proponents often look for a single "killer application" for success. Often, the case is that a technology or service will enable many applications to work together successfully in the desktop or the local, campus, metropolitan, and wide area network. And more often, it is the technology that is the easiest and most cost-effective to implement and support that wins, rather than the best technology.

How do we characterize applications and their use of the network? Application information transport requirements can be broken down into two generic types: an object of fixed size that must be transferred from point A to point B, and a stream of information to be transferred that can be characterized by a certain data rate, bandwidth, or throughput requirement. Multimedia involves combinations of these basic information transfers. The tradeoffs in response time, throughput, and the number of simultaneous applications must be supported by the technologies that transport them, as we will illustrate later through several simple examples.

Figure 1-10 shows the time to transfer an object of a certain size at a specific and constant transfer rate. Along the horizontal axis, a number of common information objects are listed as an illustration of the object size in units of millions of bytes (megabytes or MB).

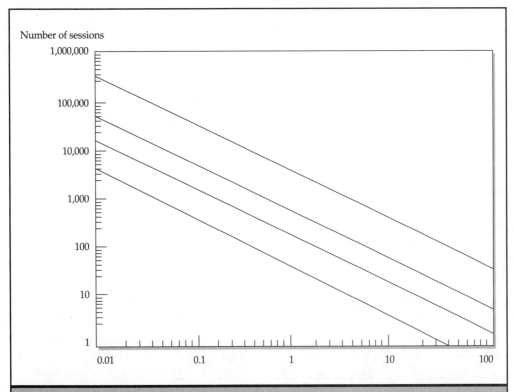

Figure 1-10.   Object transfer time as a function of bandwidth

The general rule is that the time required to transfer the information decreases as the transfer rate is increased. A real-time application like live voice or video would require immediate transfer in the tens-of-milliseconds range to maintain "life-like" quality. The utility of the service in an interactive, near-real-time mode is usually perceived as requiring a transfer time of no more than a few seconds. A non-real-time or batch application such as a file transfer or hard drive backup may require many seconds up to minutes, or even hours, for transfer of an object (such as a large file or multiple files).

Now let's look at applications such as audio and video that require a constant and fixed amount of bandwidth. This bandwidth may be a fixed, continuous amount or an average amount, each with its own impact upon the application.

Figure 1-11 plots the number of these applications requiring a certain fixed bandwidth that can be supported by allocated bandwidths of 50 Mbps (megabits per second)

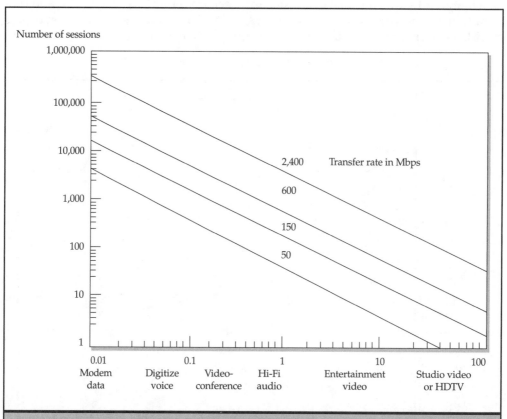

Figure 1-11.   Number of fixed rate application sessions supported

and higher. In general, as the bandwidth required by each application increases, the number of simultaneous applications supported decreases. For example, if two file transfers are sent simultaneously over a 64-Kbps circuit, they each could receive 32 Kbps of bandwidth. But if two more file transfers were added (for a total of four simultaneous file transfers), each file transfer could receive 16 Kbps of the total 64 Kbps available, assuming no protocol overhead. Of course, allocating more overall bandwidth increases the number of fixed-rate applications that can be supported. All packet switching technologies allow the support of many applications of different rates in the same network; however, each uses different quality- and class-of-service (QoS/CoS) techniques to attempt or guarantee bandwidth to each application, and are not illustrated in this figure.

New Multimedia Applications

Today's application trends all demonstrate a move toward visual reality—a dynamic, interactive visual representation of information rather than just textual or simple, static graphical representation. *Multimedia* is a term often used to represent the combination and presentation of multiple forms of data to the user, often including voice, video, and data interactive transfer.

Multimedia has taken the user community by storm. Stereo-quality sound cards and speakers and business quality video cards are now commonplace in most home computers, and many users sport microphones and small cameras. Multimedia has found its mainstream in the commercial market with many of the applications mentioned previously. Technologies such as ATM are being deployed to offer the capability to support time-sensitive traffic, typically voice or video, and offer enhanced delivery options such as point-to-multipoint and eventually broadcast. High-speed multicast applications may include a broadcast of a video-conferencing application that includes text and video. Applications that can take advantage of the attributes of broadband data technologies such as ATM and IP VPNs are now appearing to support true voice, data, and video traffic integration with guaranteed Quality of Service (QoS) or attempted Class of Service (CoS) for each traffic type. These technologies allow bandwidth and connectivity to be flexibly and dynamically allocated.

Figure 1-12 shows a multimedia desktop workstation in Chicago. The person is holding a videoconference with four other individuals in New York, London, Paris, and Washington, D.C. In this example, an automatic translation server could be connected for language conversion between the parties speaking different languages (not shown in the figure). Using ATM technology, an ATM interface card in the Chicago workstation could combine the video of the built-in monitor camera, the telephone, and text data into a single 155-Mbps ATM transmission stream to a local ATM switch. The ATM switch then broadcasts the voice, data, and video to switches at all four locations through intervening ATM WANs in the global ATM network. Of course, each of the sites could do the same in return. In order for this application to be effective, all attendees would need to have four

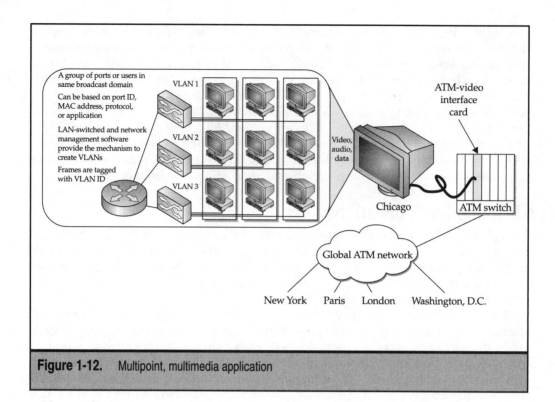

Figure 1-12. Multipoint, multimedia application

individual pop-up screens on their workstations so that they could see the other participants. Multicast video-conferencing connections can be controlled by a conference option, where the originator dynamically controls the choice of recipients. A "meet me"
type conference is also available. This capability can also be performed with e-learning
platforms running IP as shown in Figure 1-12, although the quality of service could be
highly variable.

The Accelerating Bandwidth Principle

The processing speed of a CPU sitting on the average desktop is measured in millions of instructions per second (MIPS). This machine would have filled a medium-sized office building 25 years ago. In fact, desktop workstations can offer more than a billion instructions per
second (BIPS) of computing power, sporting processors in the GHz. Not only are the centralized MIPS of yesteryear distributed in the computing power on the desktop today, but
also the need to interconnect these distributed computing devices continues to grow. This
growth in internetwork communications is required of new distributed processing applications like groupware and collaborative computing, shared databases, desktop video

conferencing, shared workspaces, multimedia, and electronic mail. Combining these two trends of an increase in computing power and application bandwidth requirements along with the need for any-to-any communications results in the *accelerating bandwidth principle*.

This need for accelerating bandwidth constantly outdates legacy LAN and WAN network bandwidths. Witness Ethernet, where initially 10 Mbps, even if utilized at only 40 percent efficiency, initially offered a tremendous amount of bandwidth in the local area. As workstation power and application demands increased, however, Ethernet LANs "ran out of gas" and had to be segmented to increase bandwidth and resegmented until in some cases there was only one workstation per Ethernet segment. Ethernet switches were designed to increase capacity within the LAN and break the bottleneck of the common bus that Ethernet 10 Mbps used to provide. Then 100-Mbps Ethernet came on the scene, supercharging legacy 10-Mbps Ethernet until in the last decade all Ethernet cards appeared in 10/100-Mbps auto-sensing mode at a fraction of the cost of 10-Mbps Ethernet NICs only a few years ago. FDDI, which had a short run of popularity, and Ethernet 100 Mbps were invented to provide ten times more bandwidth (100 Mbps) than Ethernet 10 Mbps, but on leading-edge server networking, even FDDI and 100-Mbps Ethernet became a bandwidth constraint, and we turned to 1000-Mbps Ethernet, or Gigabit Ethernet (GigE). But as the speed of Ethernet increases, distance decreases.

As a further illustration of the explosive growth that can be caused by open interconnection, observe the tremendous growth rate of traffic on the public Internet—still estimated at 20 to 25 percent per month! Furthermore, with the advent of audio and video multicast, the demand outstrips Internet capacity on occasion. Reference the Victoria Secret Internet broadcast that annually creates new records for Internet congestion!

Required connectivity is driven by the method in which business is performed, flow of information, and the nature of the organizational structure. In a flatter, distributed, empowered organization each individual may send, or provide access to, information in a peer-to-peer manner that would only have been sent upwards in the preceding, hierarchical organization. The following shows how the combined exponential growths in computing power and the nonlinear growth in intercommunications create an overall demand for data communications that is greater than exponential. These phenomena are collectively referred to as the *accelerating bandwidth principle*. Before exploring this concept, let's first review Amdahl's law.

Amdahl's law states that the average application requires processing cycles, storage, and data communication speeds in roughly equal proportion, namely 1 MIPS, 1 MB, and 1 Mbps. In the accelerating bandwidth principle, the claim is that this rule no longer holds true.

Figure 1-13 illustrates the accelerating bandwidth principle. The curve labeled MIPS/ desk represents the exponential growth in computing power at the desktop at a rate of approximately 175 percent growth every two years. The curve labeled Mbps/MIPS represents the nonlinear growth of the required data communication of approximately 3 percent

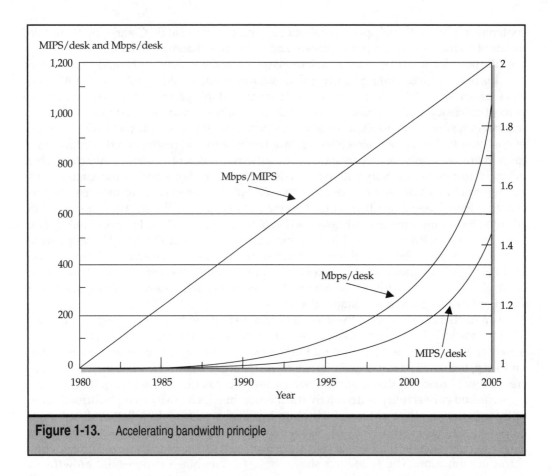

Figure 1-13. Accelerating bandwidth principle

per year, resulting in a doubling of Amdahl's law of the proportion of bandwidth to processing power over 25 years. The curve labeled Mbps/desk, which is the product of MIPS/desk and Mbps/MIPS, represents the data communications bandwidth predicted by the accelerating bandwidth principle.

When I first published the accelerating bandwidth theory in the early 1990s, it pointed to the inadequacy of Ethernet and FDDI and illustrated the need for true Gigabit-per-second (Gbps) networking. We now see that projection coming true in the deployment of GbE deployments in both the LAN and the MAN, and that far more bandwidth is required across the LAN and MAN than at the desktop.

Another way to offset the increasing need for communications bandwidth is the use of improved compression that reduces the amount of data requiring transmission. However, compression only yields improvement up to the information theoretic limits.

Applications and business needs expand to fill the opportunities that technology can provide cost-effectively. One example is Microsoft Windows, whose code continues to expand to fill the ever-growing hard drive space available to the personal computer. Another example is the amount of audio and graphical Internet content that has been enabled by wide-scale deployment of xDSL and cable modems. (The Internet would not be as prevalent in our daily lives if we only had 56-Kbps dial access!) The usage of computing and communications by applications is largely driven by the cost of the computing devices and software, along with the bandwidth that connects them. And while basic computing and communications costs have been declining dramatically for the last 20 years, applications have become more communications bandwidth intensive and use up more computing power and processing. All these trends beg the question, when will bandwidth be less expensive than computing resources? In other words, when will we do our computing inside the network instead of at the premises?

Figure 1-14 plots over time the costs of desktop processing, desktop hard drive storage, desktop RAM, LAN bandwidth, and WAN bandwidth. Desktop processing is measured as $ per MHz of CPU (multi-GHz in 2003). Desktop hard-drive storage was

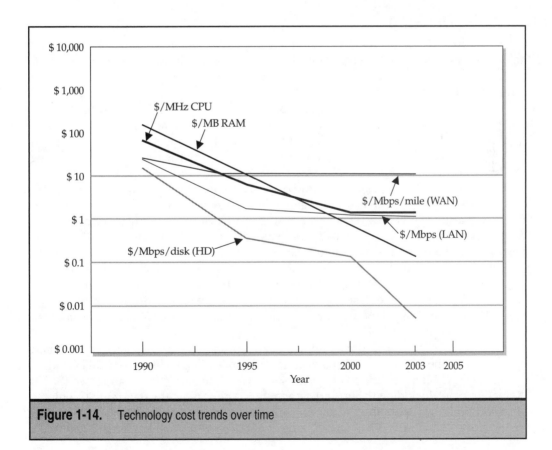

Figure 1-14.   Technology cost trends over time

measured in $ per MB (hard drives are now measured in GBs). Desktop RAM was measured in $ per MB. LAN bandwidth was measured in $ per Mbps, understanding that it is mostly capital cost and wiring. WAN bandwidth was measured in $ per Mbps per mile, and was the hardest to quantify since private line pricing is all across the board (we took averages). All of these costs decrease over time, but it can be seen that the cost of local storage is decreasing more rapidly than the cost of WAN bandwidth. The exponential increase in computing speed and accessible memory is a well-established trend, driven by integrated circuit technology that will continue to extend well into the 21st century. Recent trends in processor and memory technology may even exceed exponential growth! Note that the cost of transmission is decreasing much slower than all other trends, and in some markets is increasing. The rapid drop in the cost of local storage has tracked to LAN bandwidth, but not WAN bandwidth, showing that the WAN is still the bottleneck. The vision of network computers running applications within the network and requesting applications on demand never materialized in force because the cost of local processing and storage dropped much faster than WAN bandwidth, and this trend is despite services like FR, ATM, IP VPNs, and even the public Internet.

Power to the Desktop

Obviously, one of the biggest trends influencing the explosion of bandwidth requirements and the subsequent success of transport technologies like FR, ATM, and IP is the proliferation of computing power to the desktop and its subsequent use in distributed computing. Personal computer and workstation processing power (MIPS, displayed to the user as MHz), memory size (once MB, now GB, and soon TB), and display size (Megapixels and now Gigapixels) are increasing at an exponential rate. This increase, coupled with an ever-increasing need to interconnect these desktops and laptops, is occurring at a rate faster than the computing performance metrics due to the accelerating bandwidth principle.

Personal computers (PCs) such as the Apple computer were born in "garage shops" and were initially looked at as toys for games and other amusements. That has changed as the PC matured and had an even more powerful offspring referred to as a workstation. Workstations, also called clients or hosts, have now taken the premier position in the computing industry as a requirement for every home user through corporate executive.

From the PC's humble beginnings, as software applications were developed and speeds and memory increased while costs dropped, the larger computer manufacturers began to notice PCs on the desks of users who previously had a "dumb" terminal connected to the host. The personal computer was legitimized by the IBM announcement of its personal computer in 1983.

In an ironic twist of fate, IBM attempted to set a proprietary *de facto* industry standard by introducing the micro-channel architecture, not making it open like the initial PC Industry Standard Architecture (ISA). Soon after, several other manufacturers surpassed IBM in PC market share, including the upstart garage shop Apple! Now the standard PC with the Microsoft Windows operating system is clearly the worldwide standard of choice.

The PC has provided the user with the device for desktop access to the world of information. Mass storage of information has shrunk to a fraction of its original size and cost. Now the critical element is no longer hardware, but software. Indeed, the cost of software over the life of a modern PC can easily exceed that of the hardware investment.

Since 1983, the PC has been the industry standard for corporate and government micro-computing. Figure 1-15 shows the growth in the number of professionals using PCs. This trend has continued to the point where virtually every desktop has a personal computer, where mobile and wireless personal computing devices have gone beyond the laptop to the palmtop, and to Personal Digital Assistants (PDAs).

COMMUNICATIONS TECHNOLOGIES AS ENABLERS

The applications driving the need for high-performance data communications networks—in particular, a high-bandwidth LAN and WAN—have already been reviewed. This section now explores technology that enables the business. Technology enablers take on many forms, from the need for higher speeds, increased flexibility, improved efficiency, and support for multiple traffic types to support required for entirely new applications. To understand where a technology is going and its short- and long-term benefit to the user, you must first understand the S-curves of technological evolution and the phases by which it is accepted (or rejected) by users.

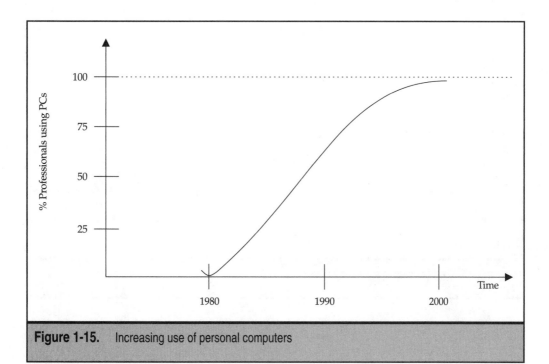

Figure 1-15. Increasing use of personal computers

S-Curves of Technological Evolution

The evolution of a technology can be viewed as an S-curve on an X-Y axis, where the horizontal axis is time and the vertical axis is the maturity or market penetration of the technology. Notice Figure 1-16 where FR, ATM, IP-VPN, and MPLS are portrayed. Notice that FR began deployment in 1990, picked up steam with phenomenal growth rate of greater than 200 percent per year in 1993–95, and in 1996 became a commodity market—but still with a high growth rate. FR led the charge in flexible bandwidth-on-demand services in the latter part of the 1990s along with ATM offering higher access speeds. Simultaneously, users began turning to IP access and transport services using private and public (including the Internet) in the 1990s, and IP services have seen even greater growth at the turn of the century. Note that FR and ATM are predominantly WAN technologies, whereas IP is found in both LAN and WAN. We also see technologies like private lines maturing over time and being replaced by these new packet switched technologies. Sometimes a technology will never reach the drastic growth cycle and die out, as did ISDN and SMDS, as well as ATM in the LAN.

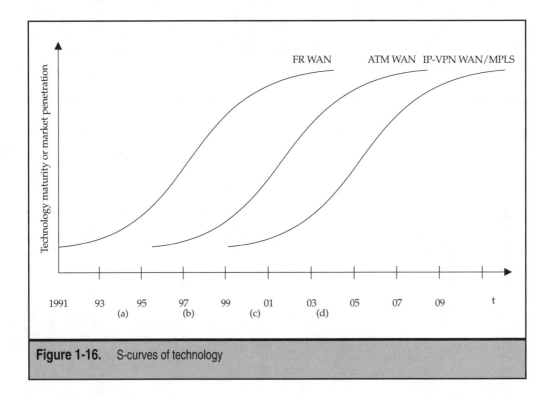

Figure 1-16.   S-curves of technology

Technology Acceptance Phases

Another way to measure a technology's success might be in how well it is able to catch the wave of technological innovation. Technology innovations are like waves crashing on a beach—many waves continually come in, but every twelfth wave or so is larger than the others.

Technology innovations and subsequent market penetrations follow a similar pattern. The bell curve of classic market or product life cycles is presented in Figure 1-17. Timing is the key, along with ease of use and deployment and cost-effectiveness. The life cycles of the technologies presented in this book are illustrated in Figure 1-18. As time evolves and technologies age and are replaced by new ones, their market penetration wanes. One example of a current technology wave eclipsing frame relay and ATM is IP VPNs, another is optical and/or wavelength switching replacing SONET. Dense Wavelength Division Multiplexing (DWDM) is quickly becoming the next generation transport technology of choice, slowly replacing legacy SONET systems (while integrating and interoperating with them simultaneously). The relative values and timing of each technology in this figure are not intended to be precise, but merely to illustrate a possible future scenario. No technology will last forever, and legacy technologies generally take a long time to disappear from the scene.

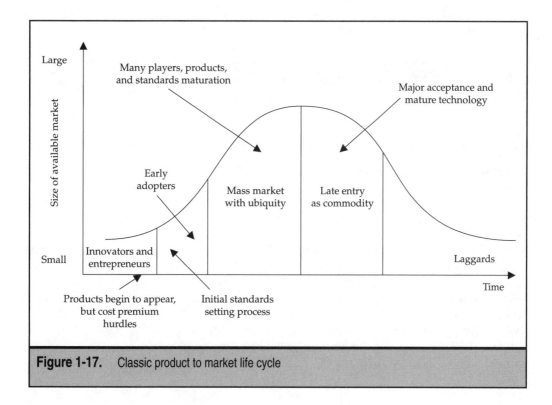

Figure 1-17.   Classic product to market life cycle

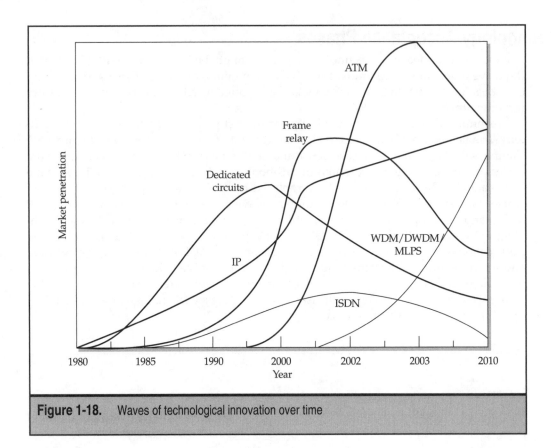

Figure 1-18.   Waves of technological innovation over time

High-Performance Digital Transmission

Older network protocols implemented complex procedures just to ensure that a packet could be reliably sent from node to node, sometimes requiring multiple retransmissions over noisy analog links. Error correction and retransmission was performed at each switch within the network. The simplification of network switching protocols is primarily a result of essentially error-free physical layer communications over digital and optical facilities versus the older error-prone analog facilities. The infrequent occurrence of errors and associated retransmission is then achieved cost-effectively in end systems, allowing for higher throughput and lower delay. Simpler network transport protocols, such as frame relay and ATM, and internetworking protocols like IP, rely on the performance of digital fiber-optic transmission that provides low error rates, typically on the order of 10^{-12}. The cost-effective availability of plesiochronous digital transmission rates such as DS1, DS3, and SONET rates of STS-Nc is a key enabler for high-speed broadband services.

FR, ATM, and IP Technology Enablers

FR, ATM, and IP deserve a spotlight in this section, as they are the leading communications technology enablers . Chapters 9 and 10 will discuss these technologies in much greater detail. ATM is a multiplexing and switching technology that is designed for flexibility at the expense of efficiency, offering multiple levels of quality of service for multimedia traffic. For any *single* application it is usually possible to find a better data communications technique, but ATM excels where it is desirable for applications with different performance, quality of service, and business requirements to be performed on the same computer, multiplexer, router, switch, and/or network. For these applications, the flexibility of ATM can result in a solution that is more cost-effective than several separate, individually optimized technologies.

Let's compare the multiplexer technology revolution of the 1980s to the proliferation of FR and ATM technology in the late 1990s. The widespread use of T1 multiplexers in the 1980s was predicted to be a precursor to a wave of T3 (which is the common name for DS3, as explained in Chapter 4) multiplexer deployment, which was never fully deployed. Understanding the reasons for the T1 multiplexer success and the lack of the adoption of T3 multiplexers is central to placing the potential benefits of FR and ATM in perspective. T1 multiplexers allowed high-performance, relatively low-cost DS1 (colloquially called T1) facilities to be shared between a variety of applications on a quasistatic basis using Time Division Multiplexing (TDM). TDM bandwidth allocation is not well suited to high-performance, bursty data communications. The growth in demand for data communications has increased dramatically, but the demand for TDM-based service has not kept pace with the overall demand for bandwidth. DS3 speeds are over 28 times that of the DS1, but cost only five to ten times more. The economics and restrictions of TDM of the T3 multiplexer were simply never justified for most users because better choices for public services were available within the planning horizon, such as FR, SMDS, and ATM.

FR and ATM offer the capability to extend the LAN or MAN across the WAN at speeds comparable to the LAN or MAN but at a much lower cost, because the bandwidth and switches are economically shared across many users, as shown in Figure 1-19. Instead of having to funnel the bandwidth of interconnected LANs down to the lower bandwidth provided by the static allocation of TDM connecting sites via DS1s in the DS3 access line, as shown in Figure 1-19A, FR and ATM provide LANs the capability to burst up to the full port speed across the WAN, as shown in Figure 1-19B. This figure shows how TDM LAN interconnection takes much longer to transfer data, as shown by the time slots of actual usage on the access lines.

Since all users do not burst simultaneously, and indeed are controlled so that they cannot, access to peak bandwidth on demand can be accommodated almost all of the time. Extreme economies of scale can be obtained by integrating multiple applications on the same physical network. This is why FR and ATM are ideal technologies for LAN interconnect traffic. A mention must be made for IP transport, as it too provides the same statistical multiplexing capabilities as FR and ATM, but without the guaranteed quality of service (QoS) capabilities. Rather, IP used attempted Class of Service (CoS) for bandwidth and application prioritization.

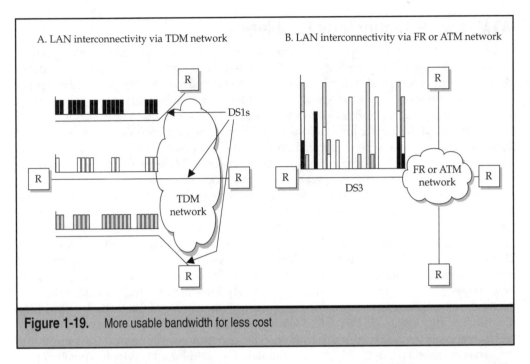

Figure 1-19. More usable bandwidth for less cost

The need for public network packet services like FR, ATM, and IP has grown rapidly as users have found the capital cost of building a private packet-switched WAN is huge, compared with using a shared, partitioned, public network service. Hence the term Virtual Private Network (VPN) is applied to FR, ATM, and IP services that are provisioned with *virtual* connections across a public packet service yet appear *private* to the end users. A financial interest can also play a part here, too, since expense dollars are paid for public services in lieu of capital dollars spent for private equipment. Within many corporations the expense-oriented approach can be more readily justified and is more appealing than the capital-intensive approach.

Technology that Future-Proofs Your Investment

Always look for a technology or service that can future-proof or protect your investment. This concept is the essence of achieving ROI on your network investment. While FR, ATM, and IP seem to be the technology leaders for the first decade, standards continue to evolve and generations of equipment can be separated by only a few years or even months. Many public service providers in the 1990s made ATM a core part of their backbone and service offerings, thus achieving the benefit of flexibility and scalability.

Today, they are turning to Multi-Protocol Label Switching (MPLS) to achieve that flexibility and scalability as their switched and routed platforms merge. Flexibility and scalability take on many forms. Being able to increase the number and size of switches, users, and circuits in a scalable manner is a key benefit. Support for a distributed architecture for high reliability is another benefit. The capability to upgrade network elements to faster processors, as well as upgrade routers, switches, hubs, and workstations to the same standards-based architecture, is also a potential benefit. No technology will remain efficient and cost-effective forever, but the flexibility and scalability of carefully selected hardware and software can potentially provide a longer life cycle for the LAN and WAN, which "future-proofs" your network investment.

CORPORATE INFRASTRUCTURE CHANGES

Transmission infrastructures continue to evolve and change with the proliferation of high-performance fiber-optic facilities based on SONET, WDM, and DWDM technologies—changes all required for end-to-end broadband networking. Networks have evolved from centralized to distributed processing, fueled by the move toward distributed computing, client-server, and IP internetworking.

This shift has caused traditional SNA legacy protocols to merge with internetworking protocols like TCP/IP. LAN, MAN, and WAN technologies have merged in the process, as LANs demand native transfer speeds across the MAN and WAN. Shared media has been replaced by wire speed LAN switches as multi-user LANs ran out of speed (bandwidth) and users began to segment LANs populated by fewer users, combining single user LAN segments with LAN switches. Distributed routing and switching technology moved to the periphery of the network, where it was more cost-effective, and a whole new family of optical switches emerged. The cost of bandwidth in the LAN and WAN continues to decrease rapidly, and advances in fiber-optic transmission technology, such as DWDM, has drastically lowered the cost of WAN transport bandwidth.

We will now review this evolution in corporate LAN and WAN transmission infrastructures.

WAN Transmission Infrastructure Evolution

International and national WAN transmission infrastructures in modern countries have found digital facilities largely replaced by fiber-optics facilities even more rapidly than analog facilities were previously displaced by digital transmission systems. Satellite communication continues to provide a high-quality digital transmission medium for connectivity to remote areas or as backup to terrestrial facilities, and there are even satellites designed specifically to handle ATM traffic. Fiber-optic transmission using DWDM has replaced legacy microwave and digital transmission facilities along all major traffic routes and most thinner "spur" routes. Just about every major metropolitan area is now wired with one or multiple fiber rings, with access speeds now reaching into the terabits. Significant deployment of fiber to the curb and to the home is now beginning, fast on the heels of copper broadband services like xDSL and cable.

Modern digital and fiber-optic transmissions are ushering in a new baseline for the performance of data communications, just as digital transmission made long-distance-calling sound quality as good as local calls just 15 years ago. The impact and benefits of high-performance digital transmission over fiber optics is a recurring theme throughout this book. These changes in the remodernization of the fiber infrastructure have accelerated the move toward broadband networking.

From Centralized to Distributed Networks

Computer communications networks have evolved from centralized mainframe computing, through the minicomputer era, and into the era in the last 30 years of the distributed personal computer workstation and server. The first data computer communications networks resembled a hierarchical, or star, topology. Access from remote sites homed back to a central location where the mainframe computer resided (usually a legacy IBM S/390 host or DEC VAX). Figure 1-20 shows this centralized, hierarchical computer network topology.

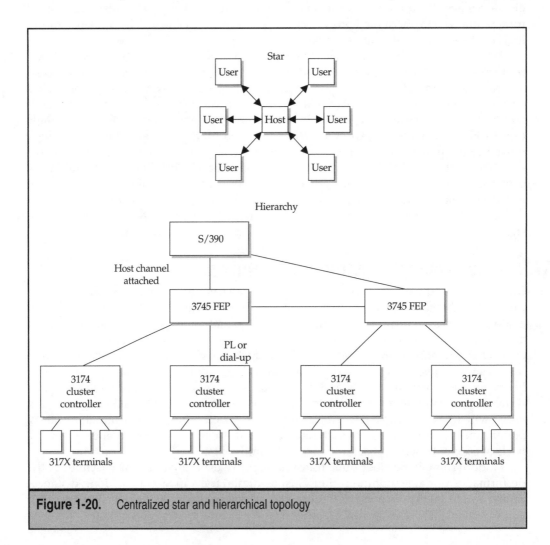

Figure 1-20.   Centralized star and hierarchical topology

Note that the star and hierarchy are actually different ways of drawing the same centralized network topology. Loss of the main hub site meant an entire network outage.

Organizations and networks have evolved in parallel, making the transition from hierarchical to distributed structures, both requiring greater interconnection and more productivity from each element or individual. This move from a hierarchical structure to a distributed structure is called *flattening*. In networks, flattening means there are fewer network elements but greater logical interconnection. In organizations, flattening is often referred to as the elimination of middle management, which requires greater horizontal communication and interaction within the organization. This trend continues as the corporation and later the network infrastructure is continually re-engineered to support ever-changing computing and communication requirements of increased connectivity and communications.

Figure 1-21 illustrates this parallel between organizational and network flattening; in this case, from a five-tier hierarchical design to a more distributed three-tier network that provides for fewer hierarchical interactions, as shown by the horizontal arrows. Each box represents an employee/manager or a router/switch/hub. Note the peer-to-peer communications flows.

Distributed Computing and Client-Server Networking

Today, almost all shared computing is accomplished through distributed processing and client-server relationships. *Distributed processing* is defined as the distribution of network intelligence and processing to many network sites and computing devices, where each site or device communicates on a peer-to-peer level, rather than through a centralized hierarchy. *Client-server* architectures have emerged from this trend toward distributed computing, enabling client workstations to communicate with distributed servers for their core information. These servers provide the means for multiple clients to share applications on a single or multiple servers, with a license fee required only for the actively used applications. Client workstations then operate only a shell of the original application retrieved from the server, but still often have enough computing power to run their own applications should the server be unavailable. Servers are also used to share expensive resources such as printers, CD-ROM jukeboxes, mass storage, and software.

Most sites now have the intelligence and capability to communicate with many other sites directly on a peer-to-peer level, rather than through a centralized computer or site. Client-server computing distributes the actual storage and processing of information among many sites as opposed to storing and processing all information at a single, centralized location. This model reflects the increasingly flatter organizational structure and the need for increased connectivity and communications shown previously. One counter move to this distribution is the use of Storage Area Networks (SANs) to centralize storage farms. Figure 1-22 illustrates a computer communications network supporting the distributed client-server architecture. Note that a server may be locally attached to a router or remotely accessed across the WAN.

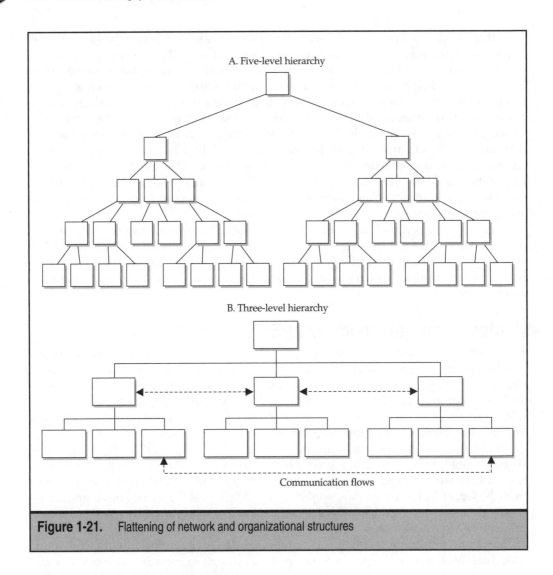

A. Five-level hierarchy

B. Three-level hierarchy

Communication flows

Figure 1-21. Flattening of network and organizational structures

IBM SNA and Internetwork Protocol Convergence

The architectural differences between IBM's hierarchical SNA protocol structure and newer Internet protocol (IP)-based routed networks are significant, but Token Ring and IP routing interfaces are available for most of these legacy systems enabling network convergence between the two worlds. Many devices explored in the following chapters allow for SNA traffic to be combined with true routable traffic in a routed or switched architectural environment. Successful implementations using these technologies has allowed thousands of companies to successfully migrate from traditional SNA to FR, ATM, and IP architectures.

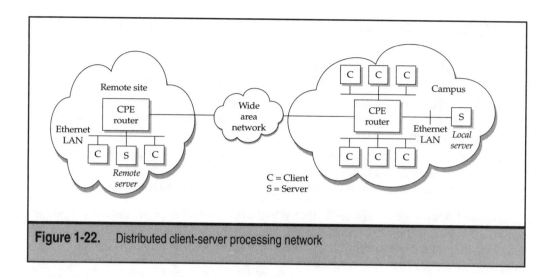

Figure 1-22.   Distributed client-server processing network

The Need for LAN/MAN/WAN Connectivity

Almost every major corporate location has one or multiple LANs. LAN traffic, which once was constricted across WAN speeds that were significantly lower than LAN speeds, are now using broadband access services capable of providing true LAN connect speeds across the WAN. These include xDSL, broadband cable, and Gigabit Ethernet, to name a few.

Two general scenarios found in most corporations drive the need for greater LAN connectivity across the wide area. The first is the increased need for interconnection between distributed computing devices on disparate LANs. The second is the logical extension of the LAN across wider geographic areas. The geographically dispersed LANs now have a range of connectivity choices—from dedicated circuits to switched wide area and metropolitan area networks and broadband data services. The choice of technology and services is based upon many factors, not just cost. The paramount goal is to define the business need to connect these disparate networks, determine which technology or service can cost-effectively provide the required connectivity, and implement that solution. Networking geographies have been defined in many ways. The following six definitions are used throughout the book:

▼ **Local Area Network (LAN)**   Distance on the order of 0.1 km (350 ft), providing local connectivity, typically within a building, floor, or room. A LAN segment can be shared among many users, or as few as a single dedicated host.

■ **Campus Area Network (CAN)**   Distance on the order of 1 km (1.6 mi.), providing connectivity between buildings in the same general campus area.

■ **Metropolitan Area Network (MAN)**   Distance on the order of 10 km (30 mi.), providing regional connectivity, typically between campuses over the geographic area associated with a major population center.

■ **Wide Area Network (WAN)**   Distance on the order of 100 to 10,000 km (60 to 6000 mi.), providing national connectivity.

■ **Global Area Network (GAN)**   Distance on the order of 1000 to 20,000 km (600 to 12,000 mi.) or more, providing connectivity between nations.

■ **Virtual Local Area Network (VLAN)**   Distance varies from a few feet to thousands of kilometers, providing virtual LAN connectivity to geographically diverse users, appearing as if they share the same physical LAN.

▲ **Storage Area Network (SAN)**   High-speed network used to interconnect servers with data storage devices used predominately in large networks or for user communities requiring a large amount of data to be maintained.

Typical LAN speeds, which were limited in the early 1990s to tens of millions of bits per second (that is, 10-Mbps Ethernet), are now typically hundreds of millions of bits per second (100-Mbps Ethernet), and billions of bits per second (Gbps Ethernet or GigE). LAN interconnect speeds have followed the trend.

Once the LAN is established and operational, many factors drive the LAN to expand in physical and logical size. The amount of data traffic continues to grow, along with the bridges, routers, hubs, switches, and gateways required to transport, switch, and route the traffic. Worldwide LAN interconnection is a reality of life for many international corporations—witness the Internet and recent proliferation of public and private IP VPN service offerings. The business drivers for expanding local area networking usually fall into one or more of the following categories:

▼ Increased inter-LAN (intranet) and extranet traffic

■ Remote and mobile access to LAN-based resources

■ Higher available transmission rates at equal or similar cost

■ Increased host and application function and performance

■ Cross-domain routing or cross-mainframe access requirements

■ Geographical extension of LAN resources required

■ Software/hardware upgrade requirements

▲ Expansion of the business through growth or acquisition

The technology drivers of internetworking LANs led to the hybrid use of private data networks in conjunction with public WAN services. This has occurred with a strong emphasis toward delivering bandwidth-on-demand through packet-switched services. One interpretation of bandwidth-on-demand arose in the LAN environment, where many users shared a single high-bandwidth medium. At any instant, only one user was likely to be active and hence had the entire shared medium bandwidth available for his or her use. Hence, bandwidth was not dedicated and was available to users on demand. The realization of this concept within networks other than those on a shared medium can be seen in the packet-switched architectures of FR, ATM, and IP.

Another interpretation is analogous to the switched telephone network, where a call (demand) is placed for bandwidth. The call attempt usually succeeds, failing only with a small blocking probability, and hence is also interpreted as bandwidth-on-demand (albeit in a fixed bandwidth nature).

Users spend much more money on service and support than hardware and software. This statistic shows the decreasing cost of the equipment in relation to the cost to support that equipment, and as opposed to the increasing cost of support systems required to run the LAN. Anyone trying to build his or her own VPN will find this out quickly. As further evidence of this trend, the use of high-bandwidth circuits and services to support these growing LANs just about doubles each year for the average Fortune 500 company.

One attempt to contain the bandwidth explosion is to actually decrease the need for bandwidth through the use of efficient coding and compression techniques. One example is the decrease in the coding rates of video conferencing, North American Television Standard Coding (NTSC), and High Definition TeleVision (HDTV) over time. Acceptable video conferencing for business can be achieved at DS0 (64 Kbps) rates today, but business video conferencing still remains at a minimum of 384 Kbps. NTSC coding was achieved at DS3 (45 Mbps) rates in the late 1980s, and is now at the DS1 (1.5 Mbps) rate for noninteractive programming. The need for 150 Mbps for HDTV transmission has also evaporated due to similar increases in coding efficiencies. Of course, the improvements in coding efficiencies are limited by the actual information content of the signal. In general, these schemes for efficient coding and compression arise when bandwidth is inordinately expensive, or a competitive niche occurs that justifies the expense of such coding or compression.

The Proliferation of LAN Switching

Normal LAN and MAN technologies—Ethernet (IEEE 802.3), Token Ring (IEEE 802.5), and FDDI (ANSI X3.139 or ISO 9314)—all connect to network devices through a shared medium, as shown in Figure 1-23A. Bandwidth is shared between all users on the shared medium with each user potentially having access to the entire bandwidth. A problem occurs when more than a few users are active on a 10- or 100-Mbps Ethernet, resulting in a usable throughput of less than 4 or 30 Mbps, respectively. Capacity begins to become the limiting factor. Token Ring and FDDI achieve better utilization than 10-Mbps Ethernet through a more sophisticated bandwidth-sharing protocol, but when the users' desktop rate begins to approach the shared medium's speed, there is no choice but to move to the next higher-speed shared medium LAN solution (100-Mbps, 1-Gbps, or even 10-Gbps Ethernet) or to segment the LANs with fewer users. The consequence is that the number of users per LAN segment has continually decreased, creating the market for switching hubs, also called LAN or Layer 2 switches, as shown in Figure 1-23B. Mostly, this segmentation would be performed with expensive routers. As workstations and more likely server processors and bus I/O speeds increase, the LAN environment connecting these devices reduces to a single host per LAN segment connected to a LAN switch, as shown on the right-hand side of Figure 1-23C. ATM can also offer a scalable LAN alternative to shared-medium solutions.

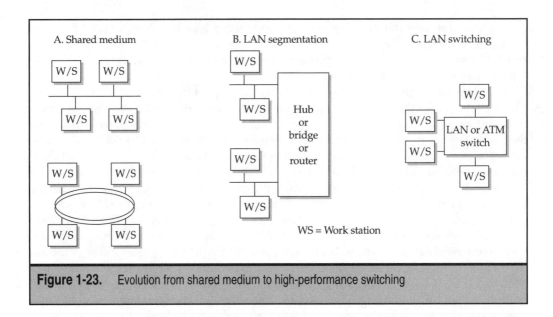

Figure 1-23. Evolution from shared medium to high-performance switching

As LAN switches began to proliferate in the late 1990s, intelligent routing moved toward the edge of the LAN and remained as the primary WAN interface through IP. As LANs mature from Ethernet to 100-Mbps Fast Ethernet, and then to Gigabit Ethernet as the technology of choice, and reduce the number of hosts per LAN segment (sometimes down to a single host), the requirement emerged for a device that can provide fast, yet dumb switching of LAN traffic within the LAN at the MAC layer without complicated routing schemes. Thus, LAN switching hubs begin to dominate the LAN intraconnectivity and interconnectivity market, solving the problems of graceful LAN segmentation and growing capacity constraints with a somewhat scalable solution.

The Move to Distributed Routing

In summary, as LAN switching proliferates, the requirement for routing moves toward the periphery of the LAN as the primary WAN interface. LAN switching is performed in the workgroup environment, and more expensive routing can be performed at the periphery of the network. Distributing routing of traffic is still required from the LAN to the WAN, but complex routing functions are rarely required within a small LAN environment.

Merging of LAN and WAN: Free Bandwidth?

Two complementary phenomena are occurring simultaneously. Access and WAN circuit and packet-switched services are available in speeds that match LAN speeds, enabling users to buy bandwidth services that can provide virtual LAN connectivity across the WAN. The cost of WAN bandwidth is becoming less expensive, but will probably always be a factor larger than LAN bandwidth (primarily because WAN circuits need expensive transmission and restoral equipment and are capital intensive, whereas a LAN can be run over a cheap piece of copper wire). In addition, LAN bandwidth usage continues to accelerate, putting a continual strain on more expensive WAN bandwidth. The point may come where bandwidth in the WAN is as cheap as in the LAN. Many people believed this was the trend until the dot-com implosion at the turn of the century, where many providers that overbuilt their networks and offered low-cost WAN services went bankrupt, and WAN rates stabilized for a time. Evidence the advent of Wave Division Multiplexing (WDM) providing terabit speeds across a single fiber. In the WAN, transport service at WDM speeds is still brutally expensive, and fiber to the desktop and home has not achieved significant market penetration.

So where is the real cost element in data networking for the foreseeable future? Information is currency. The networking elements that cost the most money are people, tools, process, and information management. The price almost always follows the value, and with intelligent networks the value is in the control, management, security, and storage of information.

IP Virtual Private Networks: Building an Intranet Within the Internet

The Internet continues to be the most commonly used medium for computer communications. The Internet services market was estimated at $22 billion in 2000. IDC forecasts the Internet Services Market at $69 billion by 2005. The estimated number of Internet users is speculated at over 300 million. The Internet continues to be *the* public information superhighway—the Infobahn. Virtual Private Networks (VPNs) are being formed over public and private IP transport networks, and can also use the public Internet as the transport utility. We will discuss VPNs in much greater detail in Chapter 10.

The Goal of Seamless Protocol and Service Interworking

How do all these protocols tie together over a single network infrastructure? Most enterprise networks have multiple locations with a myriad of applications and networking protocols. When do we have a single protocol that can provide seamless protocol and service interworking? The original premise of Broadband ISDN (B-ISDN) was to provide the capability to serve voice, video, and data using the same technology. This concept has been dubbed "seamless interworking" across the LAN and WAN. Figure 1-24 illustrates this vision of seamless interworking using ATM. Voice, video, and data are converted to ATM at the user site, where they are interconnected to the WAN via ATM. Access to voice and other legacy services is shown in the WAN. MPLS is emerging as another alternative to ATM.

In the first few editions of this text, we predicted that ATM would likely assume the role of a backbone technology to optimize transport. This prediction came true as service providers worldwide adopted ATM as their backbone protocol of choice. Even the

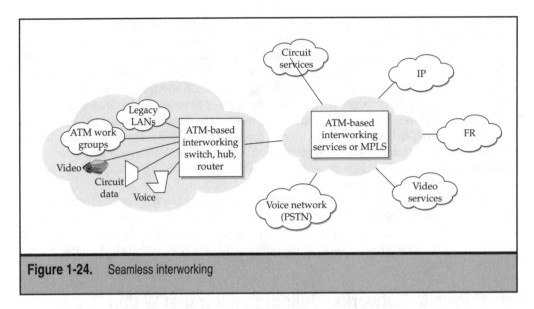

Figure 1-24.   Seamless interworking

public Internet and public service provider IP backbones used ATM as their trunking protocol of choice. But as times changed so did internetworking protocol requirements. Carriers moved to the MultiProtocol Label Switching protocol (MPLS) to provide the integration between circuit and packet-switched services like FR, ATM, and IP. ATM is still the protocol of choice for true integration of voice, data and video networks, but technology advances in IP have enabled many of ATM's QoS capabilities to be built into IP CoS capabilities.

Time will tell what platform will eventually become the dominant service platform, but until then we continue to have a conglomerate of separate voice, PL, FR, ATM, and IP networks that are tied together with gateways and internetworking devices to the best of our present capabilities.

This argument of seamless interworking also extends to the mobile computing world via wireless access services. Mobile communications and phone links that extend the mobile host from the car, train, meeting room, or hotel room to the corporate LAN are becoming commonplace as business travelers take with them mobile-communications-equipped wireless PCs and computing devices (such as PDAs). But we have yet to enter the world of broadband wireless access for the general computing community, as vendors and nations argue over standards and frequencies. The world of the seamless internetwork has yet to be realized.

THE DATA NETWORK OF THE TWENTIETH CENTURY

Have you ever wondered what the architecture of tomorrow's data network will look like? Every edition of this book has forecasted what the data network will look like in the twentieth century. Now that we have passed that century, we see that many of these forecasts have come true, while a few have not materialized. We predicted and saw static, predefined private communications networks migrate to dynamic, virtual networks—networks with ubiquitous access that can interwork past, present, and future protocols, and offer any-to-any communications. Witness carrier services that allow a single access port with virtual circuits to PL, FR, ATM, IP, and plain old telephone system (POTS) terminations. Virtual, public data networks have, as predicted, continued to add more and more intelligence in the backbone, in essence enabling the network to become the computer, through offerings like dedicated hosting, intelligent backup and disaster recovery services built into the network and routing protocols, SAN services, and network-resident applications.

And as the corporation becomes more and more dependent upon the network to run the day-to-day business, security becomes an increasingly important consideration. The war on technical obsolescence carries on, and is taken to new heights with IP technology. Today's Rosetta stone for protocol interworking that enables multiple protocols to be deciphered and understood would include PL, FR, ATM, and IP. But when will these networks provide ubiquitous, any-to-any access for all users? Time will tell.

Private and Virtual Private Networks (VPNs)

As broadband data services begin to emerge in force, there is a move from using expensive dedicated private networks to shared virtual private networks. This follows a pattern set by voice services. This section describes and compares two alternative approaches for very high-speed computer networking: dedicated circuits between computers, servers, routers, and workstations (with these systems also performing switching functions) versus shared-access lines connected to network switches, which provide virtual, on-demand capacity for workstation-to-computer communications.

Many users chose private networks more than ten years ago because the falling transport prices of long distance bandwidth and deregulation had created uncertainty of telephone company support. Divestiture caused these long-distance bandwidth prices to drop, making private networks a viable solution for voice and data. Many users built intelligent multiplexer networks to aggregate traffic and more efficiently use the carrier bandwidth (higher utilization). The monopoly carriers held back T1 offerings from customers until the new carriers offered T1 bandwidths and even AT&T was forced to provide T1 capabilities to the DoD as the first customer. Private networks provided efficient, reliable interoffice communications. Efficiencies in voice compression helped to keep costs down.

Long-distance carriers provided private virtual networks with voice services for years, allowing users to manage virtual private networks within the carriers' public voice network. This was creatively marketed as services over and above private line usage. Thus, virtual private data networks began to be offered in the same manner. The cheap voice rates offered by carrier voice VPNs made migration to carrier-based VPNs irresistible. The T1 multiplexer networks that were cost-justified a few years before saw voice bleeding off to VPNs while data remained to provide approximately 80 percent of the fill in T1 private multiplexer networks. Most private networks are now dominated by data.

Figure 1-25 illustrates the first alternative to a private network that traditionally has been comprised of dedicated circuits. Servers are shown connected to workstations and routers via Ethernet LANs. Each router has two dedicated links to two separate computers via the network Points of Presence (PoPs) to provide survivability in the event of link failures. When a router is not directly connected to the destination router, the intermediate routers must perform routing.

The advantages of this private network approach are full user control and simple, less expensive network technology. The disadvantages are nonproductive redundancy, dedicated link capacity, additional equipment costs to perform routing, and the need to engineer the private line trunks for peak capacity.

Figure 1-26 illustrates the same set of servers, workstations, routers, and network PoPs as in the private network, but as part of a shared, virtual network. A separate virtual video network shares the backbone, as shown in the figure. A VPN switch is placed at each network PoP that has access lines to each user. The VPN switches are highly inter-

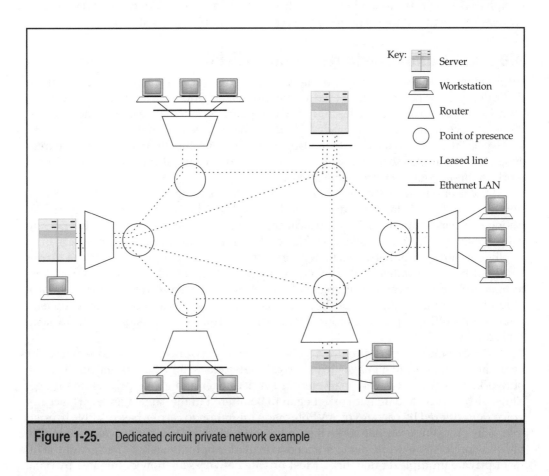

Figure 1-25.   Dedicated circuit private network example

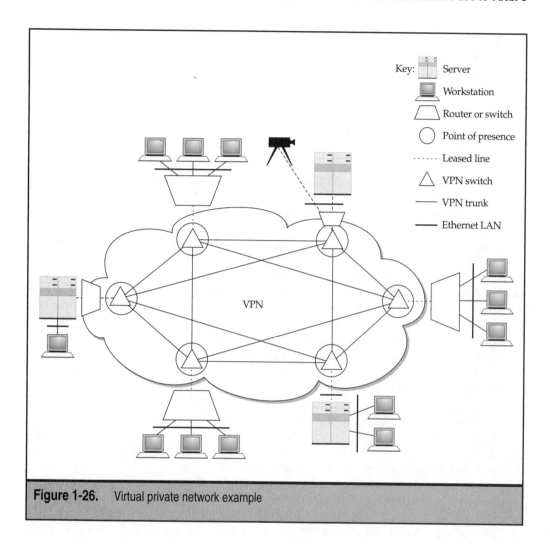

Figure 1-26.   Virtual private network example

connected by very high-speed links shared across multiple users, providing multiple services by dynamically allocating shared resources. Only a *single* access line is required for each user, thus halving the access cost when compared with the previous example. The reliability of access is identical to that of the dedicated network, assuming that the access circuits in the dedicated network take the same route to the network PoP. The VPN switches perform routing.

In summary, the advantages of the virtual network alternative are

▼   Reduced access and transport circuit charges

■   Capability to satisfy high peak bandwidth demands (particularly during low activity intervals for other services)

- ■ Cost impacts proportional to usage (versus cost proportional to peak rate in the dedicated network alternative)
- ▲ Enhanced availability and reliability

    Disadvantages include

- ▼ Less predictable peak capacity availability
- ▲ Less user control

A Virtual Private Network (VPN) is defined as a network partition of shared public network resources between multiple users to form a private network that *appears private to the users* but is still part of a larger public network. Carriers tout and advertise their VPN services to the user as having the benefits of a private network but also providing the economies and cost savings of switched services. The virtual network is a subset of the carriers' larger network, but provides the image of a complete data network to the user. Thus, VPNs offer multiple virtual networks within a single physical network. A corporate-wide frame relay network for client XYZ within a public frame relay service network is one example of a VPN. Shared network resources are assigned in fair proportion to the bandwidth required by customers.

In a virtual private network, a single access circuit from the site to the network is usually sufficient, because multiple virtual circuits can be provided between a user at a site to its destination. For example, each virtual circuit can be allocated a peak rate equal to the access circuit, but have a sum of average rates that is less than the access circuit. Figure 1-27 demonstrates this concept by showing how users A, B, C, and D at site 1 all have a single physical circuit into their premises FR or ATM device that converts these inputs to four FR or ATM virtual circuits (as indicated by the different line styles) and then transmits them over a *single* physical FR or ATM access circuit to the network switch. These individual user virtual circuits are logically switched across the FR or ATM network to the destination premises device where they are delivered to the physical access circuit of the end user, as illustrated in the figure. Note that while this single circuit provides good aggregation, it can also be a single point of failure for all users accessing the network.

The availability of switched broadband data services, with their bandwidth sharing capabilities through technologies such as FR and cell switching, has lured users away from private point-to-point networks and onto public networks. Thus, they attain the increased reliability of large public data network platforms and cost savings vis-à-vis private line operations due to the economies of scale of the larger backbone infrastructure and its high availability and resiliency to failure with built-in alternate routing. VPN alternatives to dedicated facilities can be provided in NxDS0, DS1 and DS3 speeds, and well into the gigabit speeds with services based on ATM, MPLS, SONET, and DWDM architectures.

An added advantage to public networks is for the user to tap the knowledge of the public network engineers and managers. Customers of public network services gain access to public network assets, such as engineering personnel, experience, resources, and network management. If done correctly, data consultation can be obtained to attract ad-

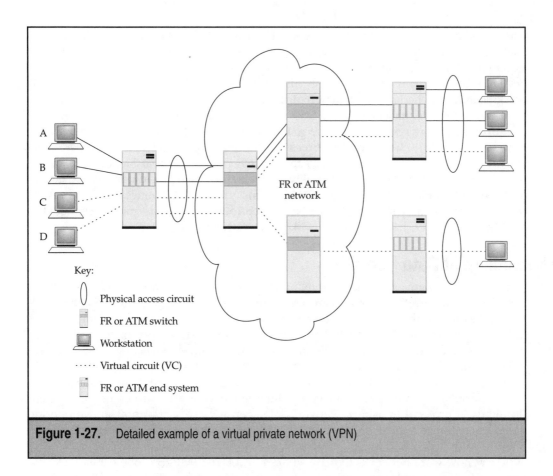

Figure 1-27.   Detailed example of a virtual private network (VPN)

ditional voice and data business. This is like having an in-house consulting service. But it is a two-way street. At the same time, the provider is allowed to learn the customer's business and applications and can sell into this customer base.

Virtual networking is in many ways a type of outsourcing. By providing advanced voice, data, and video services with customized network management, billing, and support systems to back these services, many data service providers offer a form of outsourcing. This outsourcing takes the form of resource reduction for systems and services which otherwise would have to be accomplished in house. Other benefits of virtual private networks that parallel outsourcing include carrier-provided network management, bandwidth management, fault tolerance, intelligent bridging and routing, security, order entry and order processing, and integration and standardization. Virtual data networks can also be used as an overflow technique or as a complete replacement for private networks. The network manager needs to decide what portion of the network resources to retain or replace, keeping in mind the costs of access to the public network, not just end-to-end circuits as in a private network. These advantages are additional bonuses of switched services. If anything, the network provider becomes a free consultant, offering experience, knowledge, and sometimes even manpower to potential or existing customers. The rules of outsourcing previously discussed also pertain to virtual private data networking and switched public data network services.

There are many challenges facing VPN providers. Users require an increased level of control over network resources, like the ability to offer the user the capability to modify the network on-the-fly without long lead times. One example of this is FR service, where users still need to submit orders and wait days to change Permanent Virtual Circuit (PVC). In the near future, users should have the capability to modify their own PVC routing almost instantaneously. The same is true for Virtual Paths (VPs) and Virtual Channels (VCs) in an ATM service, where not only should the user be allowed routing and adds/moves/changes but also the capability to change parameters like quality of service (QoS).

The Intelligent Data Network

Corporations and governments are moving toward using faster, larger, and more intelligent data communications networks where more routing, addressing, and switching intelligence lies *within* the network, rather than outside it. They are also moving to more intelligent network services, rather than simple, traditional private line or circuit switched data services. The term *intelligent network* connotes some level of *value-added* service provided by the network. Examples include address translation versus interpretation, intelligent routing decisions made within the network rather than predefined routes across the network, and protocol conversion and internetworking rather than just transparent (to the user) protocol transport. Network intelligence can also mean a service offering based on centralized, intelligent, network-based devices that serve as information servers offering voice, video, and imaging interpretation, routing, and online service features.

Users now want networks that are smarter and faster. MPLS is one technology that provides for this need by combining slow, intelligent routing with fast, dumb switching to achieve fast, intelligent switching and routing. Users want access to intelligent public data services so that they can better leverage the intelligence within their own network. Current and emerging data communication services are just now slowly adding this type of intelligence to their networks—intelligence that historically has resided in the customer premises. Now, network service providers offer alternative network intelligence that is extended to the user premises where significant intelligence may not be practical. And many service providers are extending capabilities and services that historically resided in their PoPs and placing it on the user premises.

There is thus a tradeoff between intelligent networks and intelligent user equipment. Many factors, driven by global industry standardization and the development of technology, along with cost factors, will influence decisions on where the network intelligence will reside. The market is both technology-driven and user-driven. For example, international providers want the network intelligence to reside in international gateway nodes. National carriers want intelligence to reside in carrier Points of Presence (PoPs). Local service carriers (legacy LECs) or Postal, Telegraph & Telephone Ministry/Administrations (PTTs) want intelligence mainly in the serving Central Office (CO). Customer Premises Equipment (CPE) vendors want the intelligence to reside at the premises. The profits of the next century lie in the intelligent functions, not the connectivity function, with all of the aforementioned groups recognizing this fact. This is why companies continue to control the content and interface as close to the end user as possible. The user needs to mix and match all of these options for the best cost and functional advantage—typically in a "hybrid" networking environment using a mixture of components to meet their need for an intelligent network. However, the network users and network providers must also work together to ensure that the mix and blend of technology being used produce products and services that allow businesses to achieve their objectives. This is critical for continued successful business operation. Relating the network responsibilities and capabilities to the strategic business objectives of the company will guarantee ongoing success.

Meeting the Needs of the Enterprise

Large enterprise networks typically have a few large locations that serve as major traffic sources and sinks. Typical environments can include large computing centers where mainframes or server or storage farms reside, large office complexes with many information workers, campuses requiring high-bandwidth communications, data or image repositories, or large storage area networks (SANs). These headquarter or hub locations have a significant community of interest among them; however, the enterprise usually also requires a relatively large number of smaller remote locations needing at least partial, lower performance access to this same information. These remote locations have fewer users, and generally cannot justify the higher cost of complex equipment or expensive networking facilities and staffs. Network costs generally increase as performance, number of features, and flexibility needs increase.

Hybrid networks with ATM interworking at the hub sites and FR or xDSL (running IP) access for the many smaller locations or IP access at all sites running on IP-VPN appear to be the normal configurations as of this printing. These lower-speed access sites require more efficient access rather than high performance, and thus FR access is often more cost-effective than ATM. This is because the cost per bit per second generally decreases as the public network access speed increases. For example, the approximate ratio of DS1/DS0 and DS3/DS1 pricing is approximately 8:1, while the speed difference is approximately 25:1. This means that a higher-speed interface can be operated at 40 percent efficiency at the same cost per bit per second. Conversely, the lower-speed interface costs 2.5 times as much per bit per second, and therefore efficiency can be important.

The War on Technological Obsolescence

Business users are concerned with maximizing their return on network investment (ROI), or as AT&T has coined the phrase, return on communications (ROC). Rapid advances in computing make an average technology lifetime of three to five years typical. Generally, the most expensive computer equipment is justified for only a small set of mission-critical applications. A similar situation exists in the area of data communications.

Currently, most intra-enterprise data communication networks are constructed from Customer Premises Equipment (CPE), interconnected by dedicated or packet-switched services at DS1/E1 speeds or less. The advent of public data network services such as FR, ATM, and IP along with their attractive cost efficiencies, has motivated some customers to migrate their bursty data applications from private lines to virtual private networks. Virtual private networks offer higher peak rates at affordable levels because there is normally no penalty for idle time, or equivalently, a low average rate for over usage (such as bursting above CIR with frame relay service). VPN technologies include FR, ATM, IP, and even the POTS.

FR and IP usually can be economically installed in most existing CPE with only a software upgrade. In addition to software upgrades, ATM usually requires new CPE, or an external CSU/DSU.

Ubiquitous Access and Any-to-Any Communications

Ubiquitous access to an intelligent data communications network with any day-to-day communications has become more important as corporate intercompany communications requirements increase. Users want to access the data network "cloud" as they do a utility, able to talk to any other user connected to that cloud without requiring any knowledge of the internals of the network cloud. A prerequisite to this capability is the assignment of a globally unique address to each user. The public voice network has these characteristics, with several lessons from that domain applicable to data networks. The experience of the Internet, which has different addressing characteristics, is a significant factor. If a user cannot reach any other user on the public data network, as is taken for granted in telephony and has become a *fait accompli* on the Internet, then the resulting data service will have little utility.

As Reliable as the Phone Network

Similar to the expectation of universal connectivity from telephony, data users expect public data networks to be as reliable as the telephone network, or—better yet—as reliable as their electrical utility. Intelligent network transport and switching services rely on their fiber transport to be both nearly error-free and nearly outage-free. Redundancy and restoration must be observed at every step in the design, with SONET technology typically providing this capability at the lowest layer, and TCP at the highest network layer (with potentially the same service provided at layers above TCP). Since many applications do not provide error correction or switching to alternate paths, the capability for any public service switched or routed network to guarantee nearly error-free transmission and continuous availability is important.

Successful service providers offer services with high and consistent network availability and performance as required by the corporations and government entities that build their enterprise networks on that virtual network. The move from conventional private lines to broadband-switched services is in full swing, but there will always be a need for dedicated private lines for specialized applications. The incremental reliability of the public data network, better performance, and the reduced price of switched data services based on the economies of scale inherent in the carrier frame and cell-based infrastructures make switched data services even more appealing in comparison to dedicated private line services.

Interoperability

Interoperability in data communications is defined as the communication and intelligent interaction between dissimilar network architectures, protocols, and systems linked by some common medium. This medium can take the form of an operating system, protocol, architecture, logical connection, or physical connection. The medium may even be as simple as network interface cards that support the same protocol.

Some difficulties encountered in providing interoperable networks include

▼   The large investment

■   Multiple standards and protocols to support and convert

■   Changing business requirements

■   Lack of network management and design tools

▲   Simple network inconsistencies

Open systems become increasingly important as the number of protocols and applications interacting in the wide-area network increase. The next chapter will cover the multiple industry standards through which the network designer achieves true interoperability.

REVIEW

In this chapter, we introduced the key application, technology, and infrastructure changes that are the shaping forces of networking for the beginning of the twenty-first century. Corporate and consumer applications are demanding high-speed multimedia bandwidth to the desktop. Broadband technologies such as ATM, SONET, and Dense Wave Division Multiplexing (WDM) offer protocol and transmission enhancements over today's communications superhighways and enable the cost-effective transport of these new applications. Finally, corporate infrastructures are shifting from legacy systems with hierarchical, centralized computing to more distributed, client-server environments that form the backbone of large communications networks to carry these broadband technologies and applications.

The landscape of data networking of the next century is that of constant change and virtualization of networking resources, and constant war with technological obsolescence. It is to that environment that we turn our study.

CHAPTER 2

Understanding the Standards and Their Makers

This chapter is designed to provide an overview of the primary standards organizations, committees, and forums and how they shape today's computer and communications industry standards. How standards organizations interface is even more fascinating than how standards themselves develop. The exponential rate of technology development and technological advancement presents an ever-increasing challenge to the players, and tests the standards and specifications process. An explosion of standards forums has occurred, primarily driven by vendors, users, and service providers. A few of the most recent forums are influencing many of the broadband services such as MPLS, optic switching and routing, and Voice Over packet. The Open Systems Interconnection Reference Model (OSIRM) is also introduced here, and some protocol architectures prevalent in the industry today are compared and contrasted to it.

CREATING STANDARDS: THE PLAYERS

Perhaps the single most important factor for successful standards and industry specifications is responsiveness to real user needs. Standards created for things with no real user need are rarely successful. Why are standards important? In the past, stand-alone systems (for example, CPU, terminal, printer, and so forth) worked well together for one application. In fact, at one time IBM had over 50 operating systems that worked just fine as stand-alone units. The interconnection of these systems by users created a de facto standard called *Systems Network Architecture* (SNA). In fact, ASCII was developed by non-IBM companies so as not to get locked into IBM's EBCDIC coding. Then ANSI blessed ASCII. Today, the exponential rate of technology development and technological advancement seems at times to outpace even the ratification of standards, and standards no longer always lead the deployment of technology. Witness frame relay where four companies banded together and built a de facto standard that years later was adopted by worldwide standards institutions.

Some of the most important questions a user can present to a vendor are, "Does it conform to industry standards and, if so, which ones and how?" Standards play a critical role in an age where standardized national and international interoperability is a key to successful data communications. Let's now look at the key players in the standards-setting process.

Vendors

Standards are a two-edged sword for vendors: On the one hand, they must consider the standards, while on the other hand, they must consider developing something proprietary to differentiate their products. The proprietary feature may increase the cost but add value, or remove some noncritical portion of the standard to achieve lower cost. Take MPLS—vendors have been concerned with meeting industry standards. Vendors who remain completely proprietary, or try to dictate the standards with their offerings, are confronted by users unwilling to risk their future business plans on proprietary systems.

Vendors can also drive standards, either by de facto industry standardization through formal standards bodies or through industry forums. De facto standardization can occur when a vendor is either an entrepreneur or the dominant supplier in the industry who wants to associate the new technology with its name, such as IBM with SNA. De facto standards in high-technology areas, however, do not last forever. Sometimes the dominant vendor is not the only one in the market with a product, but their product quality or market share makes it the de facto standard around which other vendors must design.

Users

Users do better when they purchase equipment conforming to industry standards rather than nonstandards-based products because they can competitively shop for products and services and be assured that there will be some level of interoperability. A certain comfort level exists in knowing that the equipment a company stakes its business communications on has the ability to interface with equipment from other vendors. Especially in the context of international interconnectivity, standards are of paramount importance. Also, users play a key role in developing standards since the use of standard equipment (as well as vendor acceptance) determines the success or failure of the standard.

Ubiquitous deployment is often required for standards success. Vendors say: "We will provide it when customers sign up." Customers say: "We will sign up when it is universally available at the right price, *unless* we see something else better and less expensive." ISDN was not ubiquitously available in North America for more than a decade but later saw success and wide availability due to an agreement of service providers to support "National ISDN," which is a subset of the original standard. ISDN marketability for high-speed access has been affected by higher-speed services such as cable modem and digital subscriber line (DSL), and IDSN has since become more popular as a disaster recovery technology. Users usually do not play an active part in the standardization and specification process but signal their approval with their purchases.

Network Service Providers

Network service providers also actively participate in the standard-making process; they are also users. Vendors often drive service providers, but service providers often select vendors that adhere to industry standards while still providing some (usually nonstandard) capability for differentiation. This does not lock them into one vendor's proprietary implementation and can facilitate the existence of a multiple vendor environment. Providers must not only make multiple vendor implementations interoperate within their networks, but they must also ensure the availability of industry standard interfaces to provide value-added services to users.

CREATING STANDARDS: THE PROCESS

In this section, the general standards and specification process is reviewed. Figure 2-1 illustrates the generic process of standardization and specification. The process begins by

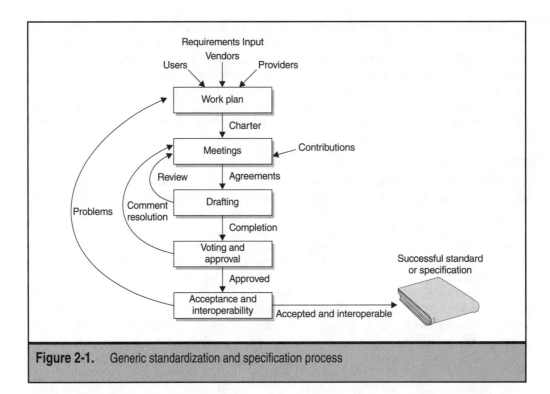

Figure 2-1. Generic standardization and specification process

reviewing a certain area through written contributions in technical meetings. The result is usually a document that is drafted and updated by the editor in response to contributions and agreements achieved in the meetings. The group reviews the drafts of this document, often progressing through several stages of voting and approval, eventually resulting in a final standard or specification. The standards process can be hindered by business and politics, with the final measure of success being user acceptance and interoperable implementations.

Work Plan

Most standards and specifications groups first agree on a work plan. A work plan defines the topics to be worked on, a charter for the activity, an organization for performing the work, and usually a high-level set of objectives. User input and involvement typically occurs at this stage, either indirectly or sometimes even through direct participation. This is the time when vendors and service providers often voice their requirements. The work plan for updating an existing standard almost always includes some changes resulting from user feedback or interoperability issues. Often, an approximate time frame is set for completion of the standard or specification.

Meetings and Contributions

The majority of the work occurs at technical meetings. A meeting can last from several days to several weeks. Participants submit written contributions that

▼ Propose specific text and drawings for the standard.

■ Present background information.

■ Present arguments for or against a particular approach.

▲ Serve as liaisons from other standards or specification bodies.

If the contribution proposes adding text to a baseline document, then a process is employed to determine whether the proposal is accepted, amended, or rejected. In formal standards bodies, there is usually an attempt to achieve consensus before agreeing to include a contribution's input or a straw vote in some industry forums.

If there is a large committee structure, then a meeting normally begins and ends with a plenary session where representatives from all subcommittees attend. After the plenary meeting, multiple subcommittee meetings usually occur in parallel. The subcommittees are granted some autonomy, however, since they usually must review major changes or key decisions in the plenary session. Meetings are also used to resolve issues that arise from the drafting, review, voting, or approval process described in the following section.

Drafting and Review

A key individual in the development of a standard or specification is the editor. The editor drafts text based upon the contributions, as amended in the meeting. The editor is often entrusted with researching related standards and specifications and aligning the document accordingly.

A key part of any standard or specification technical activity is the ongoing review, correction, and improvement of the *working* document or baseline text. Working documents, therefore, provide a major input to meetings and become the basis for contributions for the next meeting, which will further define the requirements in the document.

Voting and Approval

Once a particular document has reached *draft* status, it is usually distributed for a preliminary vote. Comments that members believe must be addressed in order to approve the document as a standard or specification are often addressed via a comment resolution process at meetings, resulting in more drafting for the editor.

The voting step of the process differs in various bodies in the number of members required to approve a change. If complete concurrence is the objective, then the process can be quite lengthy; if only a majority vote is required, then progress may be more rapid, but possibly increases risk.

Once the comment resolution process is completed, the standard or specification then goes to a final vote. Again, depending upon the rules governing the standards or specification body, anything from a simple majority to a certain percentage to unanimous approval is required for the body to release the document as an approved standard or specification. Often, there will also be a supervisory board that will review the proposed standard for consistency with the format, style, scope, and quality required by that body in the final approval stage.

User Acceptance and Interoperability

Since customers have business problems today that sometimes can only be solved by proprietary implementations *prior* to formal standards, waiting until the perfect standard is designed and approved may put them out of business; therefore, the user is caught in the dilemma of adopting an emerging standard now or waiting for it to become more mature. Users primarily determine the success of standards by creating the demand for specific capabilities and even technology, and by purchasing implementations from vendors and carriers supporting that standard.

The key technical measure of the success of a standard or specification is whether implementations from multiple vendors or carriers interoperate according to the details of the documentation. The documents should specify a minimum subset of interfaces, function, and protocol to achieve this goal. Additional documentation, testing, and industry interoperability forums may be required, such as those established for the Internet (IETF), FDDI (ANSI), and N-ISDN (ITU-T).

If customers do not accept a standard, or if significant interoperability issues arise, then this feedback is provided back into the standards process for future consideration. Acceptance by the vendor community also plays a key role in the success or failure of standards, since if no implementation of the standard is built, no user can buy it!

Business and Politics

Standards organizations and industry forums have had increased participation and scope in recent years. With this increased number of people working on a plethora of problems, comes the inevitable burden of bureaucracy. Service providers, vendors, and, to some extent users, view the chance to participate in the standard-setting process as an opportunity to express themselves and impress their views upon the industry.

This is a double-edged sword: While participation is necessary, biases are brought to the committees that can tie up decision making and bog down the process of making standards. One example in ATM standards is that of Generic Flow Control (GFC), where an agreement on a shared medium solution for ATM was never reached for this reason. The impact of this type of situation depends on whether the committee operates on a complete consensus basis or some form of majority rule. All too often a consensus-based approach ends up being a compromise with multiple, incompatible options stated in the standard. There is then a need to form a subset of a standard as an interoperability specification to reduce the number of choices and translate the ambiguities of the standard into specific equipment requirements.

Standards can also have omissions or holes that are undefined and left to vendor interpretation because they simply weren't conceived as issues. These holes may exist because no agreement could be reached on how the requirement should be standardized or because the standards committee moved on to a different area of the standard. Standards usually identify these items *for further study (ffs)* just to point out that there is an awareness of a need for a function or element that isn't standardized yet, but could be in the future.

Vendors can play the game of supporting their proprietary solution to make it a standard before their competitor's proprietary solution becomes a standard. This alone can delay and draw out a standards process for many months or even years. While standards organizations take their time to publish standards, some vendors try to take the lead and build equipment designed around a proposed standard or a partially issued standard, and then promise compliance with the standard once it is finally published. If they guess right, they can be well ahead of the pack; if they miss the mark, they could lose a significant investment.

Standards and Specification Bodies

Industry forums provide a vehicle for driving industry standards and the rallying points for standardization and interoperability. The actual industry standards are developed and approved by standards organizations. These standards bodies, along with users and vendors, play the most important part in deciding what actually becomes a standard. Users can also drive standards with the need for a specific technology and the desire to incorporate it as soon as possible. The standards organizations and forums provide common ground between users and vendors. They provide guidelines for the industry that define the interoperability requirements, not only between computer communications, but also between computer and user communications. While standards organizations are composed of both users and vendors, they attempt to remain objective about the standardization of technologies that could have a drastic impact on the businesses of both.

Currently, two classes of standards and specification bodies drive the technologies covered in this text: formal standards bodies and industry forums.

The leading formal international standards body is the International Telecommunications Union–Telecommunications Standardization Sector (ITU-T), formerly called the International Telegraph and Telephone Consultative Committee (CCITT). The ITU was formed in Western Europe in the late 1800s. The premier formal standards organization in the United States is the American National Standards Institute (ANSI) and its predominant communications committee, the T1 Standards Committee. The main formal standards organization in Europe is the European Telecommunications Standards Institute (ETSI).

Other key standards and specification bodies include the Institute of Electrical and Electronics Engineers (IEEE); international standards bodies include the International

Organization for Standardization (ISO) and International Electrotechnical Commission (IEC). Although the Federal Communications Commission (FCC) is not a standards-setting organization, it is a major regulatory power in the United States and also deserves mention.

International Telecommunications Union (ITU)

The International Telecommunications Union (ITU) was founded in 1948 and dates back as far as 1865; it is an international organization within the United Nations system. The ITU charter is to produce telegraphy and telephone technical, operating, and tariff issue recommendations. The ITU committee formerly known as the CCITT was renamed the Telecommunications Standardization Sector and is now referred to as the ITU-T. The ITU-T is a United Nations–sponsored treaty organization and one of the three ITU sectors. The U.S. voting member in the ITU-T is a representative of the U.S. State Department and includes technical advisors through the U.S. National Committee for the ITU-T. Only members may attend meetings. The standards produced by the ITU-T are identified as ITU-T recommendations in this book.

Until 1988, the ITU-T published approved recommendations once every four years in the form of a set of books that were often referred to by the color of their covers—red, yellow, blue, and so forth. After 1988, an accelerated standards process was adopted, where all subsequent recommendations are published when completed.

During a study period, which is now typically two years instead of four, a number of questions are assigned to one of 14 study groups. The study group then organizes into lower-level committees and produces working documents and draft recommendations. These study groups were once referred to by Roman numerals in the CCITT days, but in the new modernized ITU-T, the study groups are now referred to by decimal numbers. Study group 7, for example, is involved with data networks and open-systems communications, and study group 9 is responsible for broadband cable networks. To obtain further information about the ITU-T, you can go to the web site http://www.itu.int.

American National Standards Institute (ANSI)

The American National Standards Institute (ANSI) acts as the North American primary standards body, as well as the official interface to all international standards bodies. To ensure that standards sanctioned by ANSI are impartial to vendor, user, and service provider alike, contributions pending standardization are contributed from many voluntary nonprofit, nongovernmental organizations, including the Institute of Electrical and Electronic Engineers (IEEE), the Electronic Industries Association (EIA), and the Computer and Business Equipment Manufacturers Association (CBEMA). ANSI is the sole U.S. representative and member of the two major nontreaty international standards organizations, the International Organization for Standardization (ISO), and via the USNC and International Electrotechnical Commission (IEC).

ANSI standards define both electronic and industrial standards for the national and international communities. ANSI defines *national standards* such as American National Standards and promotes them internationally. These standards are published with the following number scheme:

ANSI/NNNN XXXX–20XX - Standard Name

NNNN is the name of the contributing organization (for example, IEEE); **XXXX** is a letter and/or number combination signifying the field of study and the reference number of the standard within that field; **20XX** is the date the standard was officially published; and **Standard Name** is the name of the standard. ANSI defines *international standards* sanctioned by the ISO in a similar manner:

ANSI/ISO XXXX–20XX - Standard Name

The fields are the same as for national standards. ANSI can be found at http://www.anis.org.

ATIS T1 Standards Committee

The T1 Standards Committee on Telecommunications is one of the most important standards bodies dealing with data communications and telecommunications in the United States. The committee, established in 1984, is sponsored by the Alliance for Telecommunications Industry Solutions (ATIS) and accredited by ANSI. T1 committee standards are developed in close coordination with the ITU-T, and address characteristics of technology that are unique to North America. Particular T1 subcommittees are involved with different aspects of standardization.

Established in February 1984, the mission of the Standards Committee T1 is to develop technical standards and reports supporting the interconnection and interoperability of telecommunications networks at interfaces with end-user systems, carriers, information and enhanced service providers, and customer premises equipment (CPE). The ATIS sponsors and provides the secretariat support for Standards Committee T1. Membership and full participation in its technical subcommittees is open to all parties with a direct interest in the T1 process and activities. Free of dominance from a single interest, this open membership and balanced participation safeguards the integrity and efficiency of the standards formulation process. ANSI due process procedures further ensure fairness.

Standards Committee T1 develops standards and technical reports related to interfaces for U.S. telecommunications networks, some of which are associated with other North American telecommunications networks. T1 also develops positions on related subjects under consideration in various international standards bodies. Specifically, T1 focuses on those functions and characteristics associated with the interconnection and interoperability of telecommunications networks at interfaces with end-user systems, carriers, and information and enhanced service providers. These include switching, signaling, transmission, performance, operation, administration, and maintenance aspects. Committee T1 is also concerned with procedural matters at points of interconnection, such as maintenance and provisioning methods and documentation, for which standardization would benefit the telecommunications industry.

Committee T1 currently has six technical subcommittees that are advised and managed by the T1 Advisory Group (T1AG). Each recommends standards and develops technical reports in its area of expertise. The subcommittees also recommend positions on matters under consideration by other North American and international standards bodies. The subcommittees are as follows:

▼ **T1A1** Performance and Signal Processing; Network Survivability; Multimedia Communications

■ **T1E1** Power Systems/ Power Interfaces; Analog Access; Wideband Access; Electrical and Physical Protection, DSL Access

■ **T1M1** Testing and Operations, Systems and Protocols; Internetwork Planning and Engineering; OAM&P

■ **T1P1** Personal Communications; Wireless Access and Terminal Mobility; Wireless/ Mobile Services & Systems

■ **T1S1** Architecture, Services and Control; Switching and Signaling Protocols; Number Portability

▼ **T1X1** Synchronization Interfaces; Metallic and Optical Hierarchical Interfaces

These technical subcommittees (TSCs), in turn, have established a number of working groups (WGs) and subworking groups (SWGs) to perform the detailed standards work associated with approved standards projects.

Alliance for Telecommunications Industry Solutions (ATIS)

The Alliance for Telecommunications Industry Solutions (ATIS), formerly the Exchange Carriers Standards Association (ECSA), sponsors the T1 Standards Committee, which is also responsible for SONET standards in North America. ATIS was originally incorporated as a not-for-profit association in 1983 and was called the Exchange Carriers' Standards Association (ECSA). Renamed in 1993, ATIS comprises members of the telecommunications industry to address exchange access, interconnection, and other technical issues that have resulted from divestiture. ATIS supports a number of industry forums on topics such as ordering and billing, network operations, bar code specifications, electronic data interchange (EDI), open network architecture, network reliability, and electrical protection. The ATIS can be reached at http://www.atis.org.

European Telecommunications Standards Institute (ETSI)

The European Telecommunications Standards Institute (ETSI) is primarily involved in the standardization of European telecommunications. The ITU-T develops recommendations for worldwide use, while the role of regional bodies (such as ETSI in Europe and ANSI in America) is to generate, on the basis of global standards, more detailed specifications adapted to the unique historical, technical, and regulatory situation of each region. To obtain further information about ETSI you can go to the web site http://www.etsi.org.

Institute for Electrical and Electronics Engineers (IEEE)

The Institute for Electrical and Electronics Engineers (IEEE) was formed in 1963 by a merger of the American Institute of Electrical Engineers (AIEE) and the Institute of Radio Engineers (IRE). It is now the world's largest professional engineering society. Standardization has always been a core activity of these two organizations. Through an international membership, the IEEE carries on that function by developing and disseminating electrotechnical standards that are recognized worldwide. Standard guides, practices, and reference manuals are developed by the IEEE to define these standards. The IEEE is truly a member-driven standards body that represents the engineering community. Anyone who is sponsored can become a member of the IEEE. Standards are approved through the IEEE Standards Board. Members put out many publications, journals, and newsletters under the IEEE title that contain various proposals and outline technology trends.

The primary IEEE standards discussed here are the IEEE 802.X standards, which include 802.1 through 802.19 and define such technologies as Ethernet (802.3), Token Ring (802.5), metropolitan area networking (MAN) (802.6), and Wireless LAN (802.11). The IEEE 802 standards are developed by the IEEE LAN Standards Committees.

International Organization for Standardization/International Electrotechnical Commission (ISO/IEC)

The International Organization for Standardization (ISO) is a voluntary international standards body made up of representatives of over 140 countries and chartered to cover many subjects. The organizational structure is based upon technical committees made up of subcommittees, which in turn are made up of working groups. Standards are published first as Draft Proposals (DPs) from working groups. Once approved, they become Draft International Standards (DIS) for ballot by the Technical Subcommittee. Upon approval, they become an international standard with the same DP number originally assigned by the Working Group.

Data communications standards, more commonly called information technology standards, are handled by the ISO Technical Committee 97. The International Electrotechnical Commission (IEC) and the ISO formed the Joint Technical Committee 1 (JTC 1) to produce joint ISO/IEC standards for information processing. The ISO/IEC JTC 1 includes participants of standardization bodies from 24 countries who submit standards to the ISO. It is interesting to note that ANSI administers the secretariat of the JTC 1, as well as four of its subcommittees. Subcommittees include data management, IT security technology, telecommunications, and Open Systems Interconnection, to name a few. The Open Systems Interconnectionreference model (OSIRM) that we discuss in the "Standard Protocols" section later in this chapter was developed by the OSIRM. See http://www.iso.ch for more information.

Federal Communications Commission (FCC)

The Federal Communications Commission (FCC) is not a standards organization, but it has served as the regulatory authority for radio, television, wire, and cable communications within the United States. The FCC has the charter to retain regulatory control over interstate and international commerce concerning communications. The FCC strives for competitiveness in these markets in relation to the public benefits of marketplace fairness, up-to-date and quality communications systems, and a broad range of communications offerings for the consumer. The FCC also has responsibilities for reviewing the rate and service change applications for telegraph and telephone companies, reviewing the technical specifications of communications hardware, and setting reasonable common carrier rates of return. These goals extend to the regional and national common carriers, and to any technical and regulatory policy issues that affect them.

Additional National Standards Bodies

The Computer and Business Equipment Manufacturers Association (CBEMA) sets standards for computer and business hardware. The Electronic Industries Association (EIA) and Telecommunications Industries Association (TIA) set standards on the communications, computers, and electronics fields, with an emphasis on interconnectivity between these fields. Both represent the manufacturing community, and the EIA is active as a trade organization and as an ANSI-accredited standards organization.

Additional International Standards Bodies

One additional international standards organization is the European Computer Manufacturers Association (ECMA), which establishes manufacturing computer standards and has members including Dell, IBM, Alcatel, Sony, and Siemens, to name a few.

The member body of the ISO and IEC include (but are not limited to)

- ▼ **The Netherlands**   Nederlands Normalisatie Instituut (NNI)
- ■ **Saudi Arabia**   Saudi Arabian Standards Organization (SASO)
- ■ **Sweden**   Standardiseringskommissionen i Sverige (SIS)
- ■ **China**   State Administration of China for Standardization
- ■ **Australia**   Standards Australia International Ltd.
- ■ **South Africa**   South African Bureau of Standards
- ■ **Chile**   Instituto Nacional de Normalizacion
- ▲ **Japan**   Japanese Industrial Standards Committee (JISC)

How Do They Interface?

Standards organizations and industry forums and committees interact on both a national and international level. Standards set by organizations that fail to anticipate all of the impacts can either be accepted or shunned by other rivals of nonnational organizations, causing dual standards to be implemented, thus defeating the purpose of standardization.

Figure 2-2 shows the standards organizations discussed and how they interact. The figure is layered, showing organizations that span the United States (national); a given geographic region, such as Europe (regional); and those that span the globe (worldwide).

Table 2-1 shows a summary of the standards organizations discussed, along with their areas of participation and influence.

In an age where global connectivity and communications is becoming the keystone for international business, the existence of global communication standards is imperative. The industries of both national and international business must drive these standards bodies to develop standards that are as consistent as possible. Interfaces, protocols, regulation, network management, and many other support technologies must become interoperable.

Heading down the road toward open systems, it is the responsibility of standards organizations to push for a global standard for telecommunications, and that standard seems to be open systems. From the music of the spheres in the seventh heaven, to Dante's rings of descending layers to the bottom-most depths of hell, people can relate to

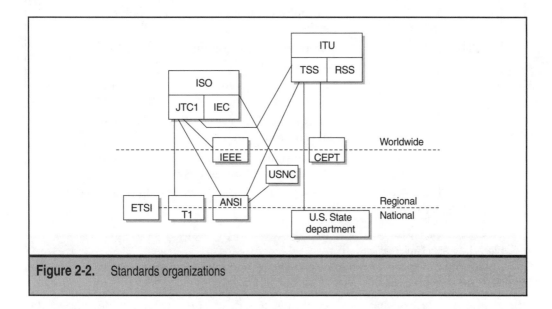

Figure 2-2.   Standards organizations

Standard Body	Standards Issues Covered	Sphere of Influence
ANSI	Electronics and industrial standards	Regional
T1 Standards Committee	Data communications	National
IEEE	General engineering, computer and communications, LANs and MANs	International
ISO/IEC	Data communications, NM, information technology	International
ITU-T	Telecommunications, data communications, telegraph and telephone	International
U.S. State Department	Telecommunications, data communications, telegraph and telephone	National
FCC	Regulatory for communications	National
CBEMA	Computer & business hardware	National
EIA/TIA	Communications, computers, electronic fields	National
ECMA	Manufacturers' computer standards	European
ATIS	Telecommunications, data communications	National
ETSI	Data communications, telecommunications issues	European
NNI, SASO, SIS, SACS, SAI, SABS, INN, JISC	Varies	International

Table 2-1. Standards Bodies

the degrees or layers that connect things together. Thus, we have developed the seven-layer OSI reference model (OSIRM). The OSIRM defines the development of hardware and software, systems and media, and communications services and processes. Vendors and service providers who define hardware and systems based upon these standards will gain a larger piece of the world data communications market share. Governments, IXCs, and PTTs can also play a major role in shaping these standards. But this global standardization process does not stop at organizations such as the ITU-T and JTC1, however. On the contrary, it typically starts at user group and forum levels. Following is a discussion of the user groups and forums helping to shape these standards both nationally and internationally.

CURRENT FORUMS

A new style of jump-starting the standards process emerged in the 1990s in the formation of industry forums. These are not formal standards committees, but independent groups formed by vendors, users, and industry experts who want to ensure standards for interoperability, but who do not want to add further implementation details to standards. Instead, specifications, or implementation agreements, are published by selecting an interoperable subset of requirements from standards, clarifying ambiguities, or, in some cases, specifying certain aspects in advance of standards. Sometimes these forums provide valuable contributions to the formal standards organizations (often as already implemented, and hence proven and not theoretical, approaches) like the LMI specifications developed by the Gang of Four for frame relay, speeding along the acceptance of an interface, protocol, or other aspect of a technology. Often, more than writing and publishing the standards is required for success. The multiple vendor and provider agreements developed in these industry forums are often essential to a standard's success.

One critical aspect influencing standards acceptance that is often overlooked is the development of services and applications to accompany the standards. An example of this is ISDN basic (BRI) and primary (PRI) rate interfaces, where the technology was fully developed but was still at a loss for applications for many years. ISDN was basically a PTT/telephone company standard used to upgrade, digitize, and put the latest technology into the utilities' networks for maximum efficiency—the end user was not a significant factor in the equation. Little wonder end users did not perceive its immediate value.

Acceptance by the vendor community also plays a key role in the success or failure of standards. The forum that keeps both the standard and the applications for that standard in mind will likely cause the standard to "live long and prosper," or at least live longer than those that concentrate primarily on the development of standards.

User trial communities and university test beds are other methods employed by these forums to help speed up the testing and acceptance of these new technologies. The Internet Protocol (IP) is one of the best examples of a standards process where the protocols that are standardized are proven to work first—the "rough consensus and working code" approach to standardization.

Some recent forums have made sizable impacts on technology development and standardization. Most of these forums provide training centers, seminars, and interoperability tests in test labs, and strictly adhere to parallel standards development by national and international standards bodies. Standards development seems to take place best in this free market of standards just as the free market of ideas has stimulated Western culture.

Three major industry forums currently active in our areas of study are the Frame Relay Forum, the ATM Forum, and the Internet Engineering Task Force (IETF) and the MPLS forum.

Frame Relay Forum

The Frame Relay Forum was formed in January 1991 as a nonprofit organization dedicated to promoting the acceptance and implementation of frame relay based upon national and international standards. The group originated when the "Gang of Four"—Cisco Systems, Inc., Digital Equipment Corporation, Northern Telecom, Inc., and StrataCom, Inc.— developed the frame relay Local Management Interface (LMI) specification which kick started frame relay services by allowing vendor interoperability instead of waiting on the formal standards' body. The coalition has global representation. The organization is divided into three groups: technical, organizational, and marketing. The Frame Relay Forum (FRF) submits all of its standards work to the international standards organizations, ensuring worldwide interoperability.

While the FRF is not a standards body, it is a forum for frame relay users to discuss implementation issues and drive the standards bodies such as ANSI and ITU-T to implement what the users (and vendors whose equipment relies on the user version of the standard) really require. One example of their efforts was their assistance to ANSI in implementing the LMI specifications. The committee also strives for interoperability between implementations of frame relay, and thus between users, as well as developing testing and certification standards.

Forums often corroborate closely in the production specifications. One example is the work between the Frame Relay Forum and the ATM Forum in the production of Frame Relay/ATM interworking specifications.

ATM Forum

The ATM Forum was formed in October 1991 by four companies: Northern Telecom (NorTel), Sprint, SUN Microsystems, and Digital Equipment Corporation (DEC). In January 1992, the membership was opened to the industry. Currently, the five categories of membership are principal, auditing, user, small business, and university affiliate. Only principal members can participate in technical and marketing committee meetings. Auditing members receive copies of the technical and marketing committee documents, but cannot participate in the meetings. Only user members may participate in End User Roundtable (ENR) meetings.

The three types of committees in the ATM Forum are Technical, Market Awareness, and End User. The Technical Committee produces implementation specifications and is organized into a number of technical subcommittees—subject matter experts. The Market Awareness and Education (MA&E) Committee produces tutorials, presentations, press releases, newsletters, and other informative material. Branches of this committee function in North America, Europe, and Asia. To obtain information about the ATM Forum you can go to the web site http://www.atmforum.com.

Internet Engineering Task Force (IETF)

The Internet Activities Board (IAB) was formed in 1983 by DARPA. By 1989, the Internet had grown so large that the IAB was reorganized, and the principal work of developing specifications to achieve interoperability was assigned to an Internet Engineering Task Force (IETF), split into eight areas, each with an area director (AD). The IAB and IESG are chartered by the Internet Society (ISOC) for these purposes. The General Area Director also serves as the chair of the IESG and of the IETF, and is an ex-officio member of the IAB. The Internet Assigned Numbers Authority (IANA) is the central coordinator for the assignment of unique parameter values for Internet protocols. The IANA is chartered by the Internet Society (ISOC) to act as the clearinghouse to assign and coordinate the use of numerous Internet protocol parameters. RFC 3160 gives a great overview.

The initial objective of the IAB/IETF was to define the necessary specifications required for interoperable implementations using the Internet Protocol (IP) suite. Specifications are drafted in documents called Request For Comments (RFC). These RFCs pass through a draft stage and a proposed stage prior to becoming an approved standard. Another possible outcome of a draft or proposed standard is that it is archived as an experimental RFC. Out-of-date RFCs are archived as historical standards. The archival of all approved—as well as historical or experimental RFCs—has created a storehouse of protocol and networking knowledge that is available to the world. To obtain more information about the IETF go to the web site http://www.ietf.org.

One spin-off from the IETF is the Internet Society. The Internet Society (ISOC) is chartered with speeding the evolution and growth of the Internet communications network as an international research network. Within this group is the IAB, comprising users of the Internet; it was the old governing board for the Internet. The Internet Activities Board has established such standards as TCP/IP. The Internet Society remains the administrative body for the Internet, providing functions such as database administration, user training, and Internet interoperability among its user community. The Internet Engineering Task Force (IETF) establishes the standards for Internet engineering, while the Internet Research Task Force (IRTF) pursues ongoing research.

MPLS Forum

The MPLS Forum is an international industry forum accelerating the adoption of multiprotocol label switching and its associated technologies. Formed in early 2000, it serves as a meeting ground for companies creating or deploying products that implement MPLS. The MPLS Forum works to promote nationwide and worldwide compatibility and interoperability, encourage input to appropriate national and international standards bodies, and create multiprotocol label switching implementation agreements drawn from appropriate national and international standards. The MPLS Forum views its role as entirely complementary to that of the existing standards bodies such as IETF, the ITU, and others. It only intends to develop implementation agreements in such areas of the technology where no other existing standards body has activity, and then with full collaboration with them. MPLS is a key development in Internet technologies that will assist in adding a number of essential capabilities to today's best effort IP networks, including Traffic Engineering, providing traffic with different qualitative Classes of Service (CoS) and Quality of Service (QoS), and providing IP-based Virtual Private Networks (VPNs). The MPLS Forum Technical Committee (TC) serves as a technical meeting ground for companies that are creating or deploying products that implement MPLS, or services that depend on the capabilities introduced by MPLS and its associated technologies. There are currently two working groups within the Technical Committee: the Applications & Deployment and Interoperability Working Groups.

STANDARD PROTOCOLS

Protocols are the standards by which we communicate. A *protocol* is similar to a language, conveying meaning and understanding through some form of communication. Computer communication protocols are defined as sets of rules and message exchanges. Protocol communications are modeled in a layered fashion, with lower-layer protocols providing services to the next higher layer. For one computer to talk to another, each must be able to understand the other's protocol. Protocols play an important role in data communications; without them, islands of users would be unable to communicate.

Protocols are defined through protocol architectures, the most well known being the seven-layer Open Systems Interconnection Reference Model (OSIRM). The concept of layered protocols is largely due to the OSI reference model; however, the protocol specifics of OSIRM are not widely implemented. Non-OSI standard and proprietary architectures have propagated a variety of protocols, many of which are used extensively today, such as TCP/IP and SNA. Still, each of these architectures has a similar layering structure. This concept of layering has enabled the entire industry of multiprotocol routing to dominate for over a decade.

Basic Protocol-layering concepts

A protocol is defined by Webster's New World Dictionary as "a set of rules governing the communications and the transfer of data between machines, as in computer systems." Communications and data transfer between machines takes place at many layers. These layers are defined within software or hardware, and the communications can be anything from software messages to the raising or lowering of voltage levels on the physical interface. Each layer, therefore, has a specific interface to the other layers, and these protocols interact either within their layer interface or between multiple layer interfaces. Figure 2-3 illustrates the basic concept of protocol layering that is relevant to the technologies discussed in this book. Let's now look at these protocol-layering concepts in detail.

Interfaces can be either physical or logical in nature. The term *interface* is used in two ways in different standards bodies. First, primarily in the ITU view, physical interfaces provide the physical connection between different types of hardware, with protocols providing rules, conventions, and the intelligence to pass data over these interfaces between peer protocol layers. Normally, the view is that bits flow over physical interfaces. In the OSI view, interfaces exist between protocol layers. Normally, the view is that Pro-

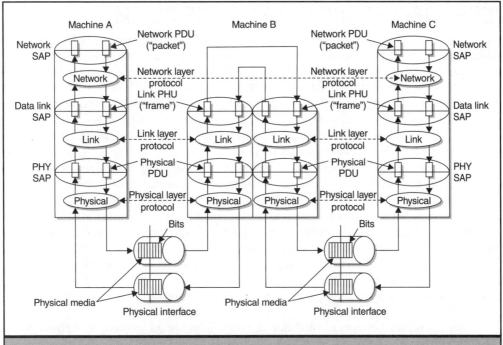

Figure 2-3.   Physical, data link, and network layers

tocol Data Units (PDUs), or *messages*, pass through protocol interfaces. These interfaces between layers are called Service Access Points (SAPs) because they are the points where the lower layer provides service to the higher layer. Stated another way, the physical interfaces provide the path for data flow between machines, while protocols manage that data flow across this path using protocol interfaces within the machines. Physical interfaces and protocols must be compatible for accurate data communications. Many network designs now incorporate multiple levels of protocols and interfaces, always starting at the physical layer.

The concepts behind the use of multiple protocol layers are important. The concepts of physical, data link, and network layer protocols can now be defined on a high level. Most technologies covered in this text have their roots in the physical, data link, and network layers of the OSI protocol model, which are covered throughout this book. Understanding the layering concept is important to network design. It enables you to distinguish your hardware components and protocol requirements by layer to determine exactly what your network will support.

If you work through the layers, ask yourself, "What do I need at Layer 1?" Determine everything you need at Layer 1, and then ask yourself the same question about Layer 2. As you work your way up or down the protocol stack (depending on your methodology), you will be less likely to leave out anything that could be critical to the operation of your network.

LAYERED REFERENCE MODELS: THE OSIRM

The Open Systems Interconnection Reference Model (OSIRM) was intended to define the functions and protocols necessary for any computer system to connect to any other computer system, regardless of the manufacturer. This model was developed by the International Organization for Standardization (ISO) beginning in 1977 with the formation of ISO Technical Subcommittee 97 (TC97), and Subcommittee 16 (SC16), and was officially documented in 1983 in ISO standard 7498. Figure 2-4 depicts the basic OSI reference model showing a source (A), intermediate (B), and destination (C) nodes and the protocol stack within each. Figure 2-4 shows an IP network.

The layers are represented starting from the bottom at the first layer, which has a physical interface to the adjacent node, to the top-most seventh layer, which usually resides on the user end device (workstation) or host that interacts with user applications. Each of these seven layers represents one or more protocols that define the functional operation of communications between user and network elements. All protocol communications between layers are peer-to-peer, depicted as horizontal arrows between the layers. Standards span all seven layers of the model. Although OSI has standardized many of these protocols, only a few are in widespread use. The layering concept, however, has been widely adopted by every major computer and communications standards body.

Many computer-networking architectures can be modeled by comparing them to the basic structure of the seven-layer OSIRM. Each layer of the OSIRM will now be covered in greater detail. The OSIRM outlines a layered approach to data transmission: seven layers, with each successively higher layer providing a value-added service to the layer below it.

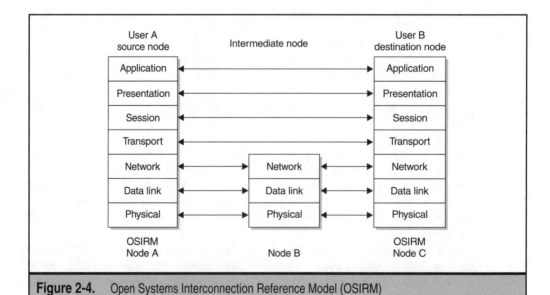

Figure 2-4. Open Systems Interconnection Reference Model (OSIRM)

Data flows down from Layer 7 at the originating end system to Layer 1 and onto the physical medium, where it is transmitted across a network of intermediate nodes over interconnecting physical media, and back up to Layer 7 of the destination end system. Not all seven layers need be used; this is dependent upon the application and user needs. The specific OSI protocols for each of the seven layers are not well defined in standards or widely adopted in practice, particularly the application, presentation, and session layers. The following sections summarize the generic functions of all seven layers starting with the physical layer, the one closest to the physical transmission medium.

NOTE: Think of the OSI reference model in terms of sending a letter to a friend. Let's say that you are in San Diego and your friend, Tom, is located in New York City and you want to get information through the mail system to Tom.

▼   **Application Layer**   The application layer represents the purpose for communicating and in our example is the actual letter you are sending to Tom.

■   **Presentation Layer**   The presentation layer determines how information is presented to the user. The information in the letter has to be presented to Tom in a way that he can understand. If either you or Tom can only read and understand the English language, then your choice is limited to writing the letter in English.

■   **Session Layer**   The session layer is where a session or dialog is created between applications. When your letter gets to Tom in New York and he opens the envelope, how does he know the letter is for him? The letter includes the salutation, Dear Tom. If he opens the letter and reads, Dear Mary, he knows the letter was intended for someone else.

■   **Transport Layer**   The transport layer determines how information is delivered from one location to another. Before mailing your letter to Tom, you have to determine how you want it delivered—certified mail or regular mail. Certified mail is similar to using a connection-oriented protocol. You want to ensure Tom gets the letter, so you make him sign for (acknowledge) receipt of the letter. Regular mail is much like using a connectionless protocol. You send the information into the network and hope it is delivered to Tom.

■   **Network Layer**   The network layer determines how we get information between networks or, in our example, between cities. To get your letter from San Diego to New York, you have to include a city, state, and ZIP code on the envelope. The postal worker looks at this information to make a routing decision, and then the letter is loaded into a truck, train, or airplane and delivered to the post office in New York City.

■   **Data Link Layer**   The data link layer determines how we get information between devices within a network. Your letter is now at the post office in New York City. The postal worker now uses the street address to determine where to deliver the letter locally.

▲   **Physical Layer**   The physical layer provides the transmission of a bit stream across the physical interconnection of network elements. In our example, the physical layer is the mail carrier actually carrying the letter to Tom's house.

Application Layer

The seventh layer (L7) encountered is the application layer. This layer manages the program or device generating the data to the network. The application layer is an equipment-dependent protocol and lends itself to proprietary vendor interpretation. Examples of standardized application-layer protocols include ITU X.400, X.420 X.500–X.520 directory management, ISO 8613/ITU T.411-419 Office Document Architecture (ODA), and the ISO 10026 distributed Transaction Processing (TP).

Presentation Layer

The sixth layer (L6) encountered is the presentation layer. The presentation layer determines how data is presented to the user. Official standards are now complete for this layer. Many vendors have also implemented proprietary solutions. One reason for these proprietary solutions is that the use of the presentation layer is predominantly equipment dependent. Some examples of presentation-layer protocols are video and text display formats, data code conversion between software programs, and peripheral management and control, using protocols such as ITU 8823 and ITU X.226 OSI connection-oriented protocol.

Session Layer

The fifth layer (L5) encountered is the session layer. The session layer is essentially the user's interface to the network, which may have some data transformations performed by the presentation layer. Sessions usually provide connections between a user, such as a terminal or LAN workstation, and a central processor or host. So-called peer-to-peer session-layer protocols can directly connect user applications. Session-layer protocols are usually rather complex, involving negotiation of parameters and exchange of information about the end-user applications. The session layer has addresses that are meaningful to end users. Other session-layer functions include flow control, dialog management, control over the direction of data transfer, and transaction support.

Some examples of the session layer are terminal-to-mainframe log-on procedures, transfer of user information, and the setup of information and resource allocations. The ISO standard for the session layer is the ISO 8327/ITU X.225 connection-oriented session protocol.

Transport Layer

The fourth layer (L4) encountered is the transport layer. The principal function of the transport layer is to interconnect session-layer entities. Historically, it has been called the host-to-host layer. Principal functions that it performs are segmentation, re-assembly, and multiplexing over a single network-layer interface. The transport layer enables a session-layer entity to request a class of service, which must be mapped onto appropriate network-layer capabilities. It is the fourth layer's responsibility to manage end-to-end flow control.

The transport layer may often perform error detection and correction as well, which has become increasingly more important since it provides a higher-level error correction and retransmission protocol for services such as FR, IP, and ATM. Often, frame relay users will ask what happens when DE frames are discarded. It is the responsibility of the transport layer to retransmit packets lost due to discarded and lost DE-marked frames.

One example of the transport layer includes the ITU X.224 OSI transport protocol TP4. Another widely used example of a transport type of protocol is the Transmission Control Protocol (TCP).

Network Layer

The third layer (L3) encountered is the network layer. The principal function of the network layer is to provide reliable, in-sequence delivery of protocol data between transport layer entities. In order to do this, the network layer always has an end-to-end global addressing capability. A unique network-layer address is assigned to each network-layer protocol entity. A network-layer protocol may communicate with its peer over a route of intermediate machines with physical, data link, and network layers. The determination of this route is called the *routing function*. Routing protocols and operation are covered later. Network layer PDUs are often called *packets*.

The network layer may also perform end-to-end flow control and the segmentation and reassembly of data. The network layer is the most protocol-intensive portion of packet networks. Some examples of protocols used in the network layer are the ITU X.25 and X.75 packet level and gateway protocols, the Internet Protocol (IP), CCITT/ITU-T Q.931, Q.933, Q.2931, and the OSI CLNP.

The network layer is used to define data call establishment procedures for packet and cell-switched networks in ISDN and B-ISDN. For example, ATM signaling uses a Layer 3 protocol for call setup and disconnection.

Data Link Layer

The data link layer is Layer 2 (L2) in the seven-layer OSI reference model, and the second layer in most other computer architecture models as well. The primary function of the data link layer is to establish a reliable protocol interface across the physical layer (L1) on behalf of the network layer (L3). This means that the link layer performs error detection and possibly even error correction. Toward this end, the data link control functions establish a peer-to-peer relationship across each physical link between machines. The data link layer entities exchange clearly delimited protocol data units, which are commonly called *frames*. The data link layer may use a limited form of addressing such that multiple data link layer protocol interfaces can be multiplexed across a single physical layer interface.

There may be a flow control function to control the flow of frames such that a fast sender does not overrun a slow receiver.

Computer communications via local area networks (LAN) utilize special functions of the data link layer called the media access control (MAC) and logical link control (LLC) layers. The MAC layer protocols form the basis of LAN and Metropolitan Area Network (MAN) standards used by the IEEE 802.X LAN protocol suite, which includes Ethernet, Token Ring, and Token Bus.

Examples of the link layer include ISO 7776, ITU X.25 link layer, ISDN LAP-D, ISO HDLC, and MAC-layer protocols such as the ISO 9314-2 FDDI Token Ring MAC. The 802.X protocol structures are covered in the next section, Standard Computer Architectures.

Some of the new services, such as FR and ATM, can be viewed as using only the first two layers of the OSI reference model, and rely heavily on reducing the link layer services to increase speeds at lower costs because of the resulting protocol simplification. A key difference between FR and ATM is that the addresses can take on an end-to-end significance, whereas in the OSI link layer addresses are only significant between nodes.

Physical Layer

The first layer encountered is the physical layer (L1), which provides for the transparent transmission of a bit stream across the physical interconnection of network elements. The intelligence managing the data stream and protocols residing above the physical layer are transparently conveyed by the physical layer.

The physical layer connections may be point-to-point or multipoint. The connection may be operated in full-duplex or half-duplex mode. Simplex means that transmission is in one direction only, while full-duplex means that transmission can occur in both directions simultaneously. Half-duplex involves the use of physical layer signaling to change the direction of simplex transmission. The bit stream may be transmitted serially or in parallel.

The physical layer includes specification of electrical voltages and currents, mechanical connector specifications, basic signaling through connections, and signaling conventions. The physical layer can also activate or deactivate the transmission medium and communicate its status through protocol primitives with the data link layer. The physical medium can either be an actual physical transmission medium or may be a satellite or wireless medium.

Examples of the physical layer include: EIA-RS-232-C, EIA-RS-449, ITU X.21/X.21bis, ITU V.35, IEEE 802 LAN, ISO 9314 FDDI, and the HSSI interface. One example of a wireless physical interface is a wireless LAN.

The terms *Data Termination Equipment (DTE)* and *Data Communication Equipment (DCE)* refer to the hardware on either side of a communications channel interface. DTE equipment is typically a computer or terminal that acts as an end point for transmitted and received data via a physical interface to a DCE. DCE equipment is typically a modem or communication device that has a different physical interface than that of the DTE. One commonly used type of DCE is called a Channel Service Unit/Data Service Unit (CSU/DSU); it converts the DTE/DCE interface to a telephony-based interface. Figure 2-5 shows a common end-to-end network configuration where DTE1 talks to DCE1, which in turn formats the transmission

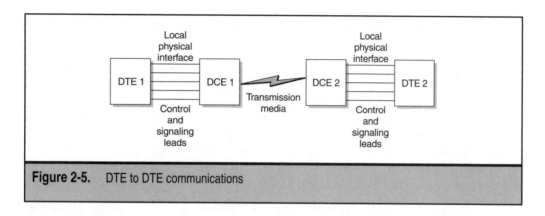

Figure 2-5.   DTE to DTE communications

for transfer over the network to the end DCE, which then interfaces to the end DTE. Also note that a single device can carry both a DTE and DCE designation, depending on its position and function in the network.

STANDARD COMPUTER ARCHITECTURES

Several major computer architectures have shaped and standardized the computer networking industry in the late twentieth century. These include the OSIRM; the IEEE LAN, MAN, and WAN 802.X standards; IBM's SNA; Novell's Internet Packet Exchange (IPX); and the TCP/IP protocol suite. This section explains each of these architectures.

IEEE 802.X Series (LAN/MAN/WAN)

Local, metropolitan, and wide area networks (LANs, MANs, and WANs) were defined in Chapter 1. The standards body that has played the greatest role in the development of LAN standards has been the Institute of Electrical and Electronics Engineers (IEEE).

The IEEE 802.X reference model defines three layers and two sublayers of operation. Figure 2-6 shows these three layers of the IEEE 802 model. Layer 1 is the physical layer,

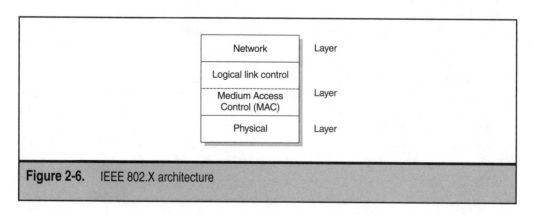

Figure 2-6.   IEEE 802.X architecture

Layer 2 is composed of the medium access control (MAC) sublayer and the logical link control (LLC) sublayer, and Layer 3 is the network layer. The standards for the network layer are still under development.

The logical link Layer 2 operates the same way for all LAN architectures, but not for the MAN architecture (a completely different beast!). The logical link control layer and physical layer operate differently for each of the local and metropolitan area network architectures. The LLC layer manages call establishment, data transfer, and call termination through three types of services: connection-oriented, unacknowledged connectionless, and acknowledged connection-oriented. All three are covered in Part II.

Three major LAN architectures are defined in the 802.X standards. Ethernet is by far the most common, and Token Bus is no longer used.

▼ **Ethernet**   IEEE 802.3 and Ethernet common specifications form what is called the Ethernet standard. The first Ethernet products appeared in 1981, and now sales for Ethernet outpace the other 802 architectures. There are four Ethernet frame formats, each mutually incompatible. Ethernet works primarily in the link layer where users contend for bus resources and send data through CMSA/CD and Token Passing. The interface is 10 Mbps. Fast Ethernet speeds are available in 100 Mbps and Gigabit Ethernet speeds are available at 1000 Mbps.

▲ **Token Ring**   IEEE 802.5 Token Ring architecture was developed by IBM development labs in Zurich, Switzerland. The first Token Ring products appeared in 1986. Token Ring initially gained on Ethernet as the popular LAN standard, but in the past five years has given ground to Ethernet. Token Ring operates on the 802.2 LLC layer with IEEE 802.2 Type 1 protocol and 802.5 MAC Token Passing Protocol.

IBM's Systems Network Architecture (SNA)

The introduction by IBM of Systems Network Architecture (SNA) in 1974 signaled the beginning of a vendor proprietary architecture that remains prominent in the computing industry even today. SNA has remained a dominant architecture through the 1990s. TCP/IP and SNA architectures and protocols are still competing today, so that many users of multiprotocol environments either retain separate networks for their IP traffic and SNA traffic, or encapsulate or translate their SNA traffic into a protocol that is more routable.

SNA was IBM's method of creating a computing empire through standardization and revolved around the mainframe and (distributed) front-end processors. The point of IBM attempting to standardize among its own products, and not other vendors' equipment and protocols, is sometimes forgotten. By providing a hierarchy of network-access methods, IBM created a network that could accommodate a wide variety of users, protocols, and applications, while retaining ultimate control in the mainframe host and front-end processors. The move from centralized to distributed processing has had pronounced effects on SNA. Advanced Peer-to-Peer Networking (APPN) using Advanced Peer-to-Peer Communications (APPC), otherwise labeled LU6.2, from IBM emerged as an attempt to save the homogeneous SNA networks from open standards.

The SNA architecture layers are similar to the OSI Reference Model. Figure 2-7 shows the SNA architecture model. The network control functions reside in the physical, data link, path, transmission, and data flow control layers. The physical and data link layers define functions similar to the OSIRM, with serial data links employing the SDLC protocol and channel attachments employing the S/370 protocol. The path control layer provides the flow control and routing between point-to-point logical channels on virtual circuits through the network, establishing the logical connection between both the source and the destination nodes. The path layer provides paths without addressing, which forces OSI protocols to *bridge* SNA traffic rather than to *route* or *switch*. The transmission layer provides session management and flow control over SNA sessions that it establishes, maintains, and terminates. The transmission layer also contains some routing functions. The data flow layer provides services related to the actual user sessions, with both layers operating at times in parallel. The network services functions reside in the presentation and transaction layers. These two layers combined are also called the function management layer. The presentation layer formats and presents the data to the users, as well as performing data translation, compression, and encryption. The transaction services layer provides network management and configuration services, as well as a fully functional user interface to the network operations.

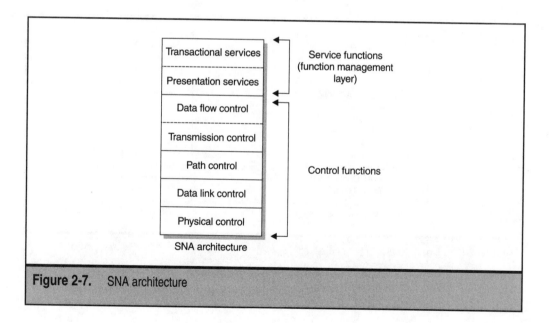

Figure 2-7.   SNA architecture

Novell's Internet Packet Exchange (IPX)

Novell NetWare was the most popular operating system with the leading market share in client-server implementations for many years. Microsoft Windows has now consumed a large portion of the NetWare market. Novell NetWare is a LAN workgroup operating system for client-server communications that has been adapted through Novell IPX into a wide area network (WAN) internetworking protocol. Its popularity is primarily due to its support of multivendor environments, specifically providing routing functions between the popular ARCnet, Ethernet, and Token Ring LAN protocols, interface cards and networks.

As shown in Figure 2-8, the Novell network layer uses Internet Packet eXchange (IPX) protocol (derived from XNS) and the transport layer uses the Sequence Packet Exchange (SPX) protocol. The architecture used by Novell is similar to XNS and is primarily a derivative of XNS. NetWare Core Protocol (NCP) client-server workstation shell software, Service Advertising Protocol (SAP), and Routing Information Protocol (RIP) operate above at the presentation and application layers. Note that IPX addresses include the MAC address and therefore use of the Address Resolution Protocol (ARP) is not necessary.

The Internet Packet Exchange (IPX) protocol is a standard defined within the Novell NetWare architecture. IPX formats the NCP data for transmission over the physical media and LAN access protocols (ARCnet, Ethernet, and Token Ring). The IPX packet is then inserted into the information (data) field on the 802.3 MAC frame, as shown in Figure 2-9.

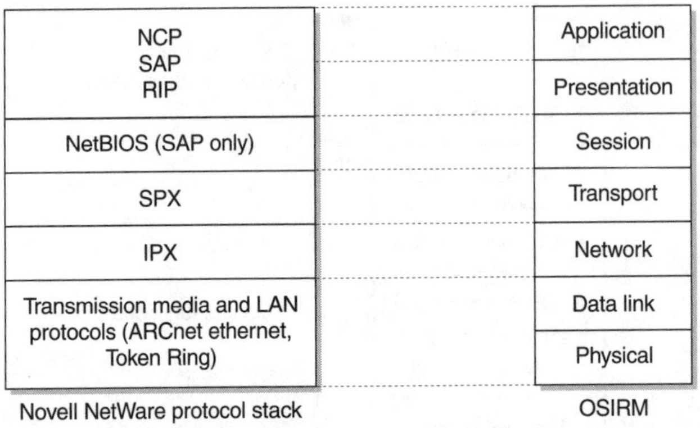

NCP SAP RIP	Application
	Presentation
NetBIOS (SAP only)	Session
SPX	Transport
IPX	Network
Transmission media and LAN protocols (ARCnet ethernet, Token Ring)	Data link
	Physical
Novell NetWare protocol stack	OSIRM

Figure 2-8. Novell NetWare protocol stack

Novell IPX supports encapsulation into ARCnet, Ethernet (including 802.3 with SNAP and 802.2), Token Ring, and Novell's proprietary data link protocol. IPX addressing and routing is similar to IP, and the SPX protocol performs packet sequencing similar to TCP. Novell made NCP independent of IPX and offered native TCP/IP as the default configuration for the NetWare products after version 5.0.

Transmission Control Protocol/Internet Protocol (TCP/IP)

The U.S. Advanced Research Projects Agency (ARPA) began development of a packet-switched network in 1969, and demonstrated the first packet switching capability in 1972. It was named the ARPANET. The ARPANET continued to grow, and in 1983 introduced the Transmission Control Protocol/Internet Protocol (TCP/IP), replacing the earlier Network Control Protocol (NCP) and Interface Message Processor (IMP) protocol.

Also in 1983, the ARPANET was split into a military network and a nonmilitary research network; the latter was the origin of the Internet. In 1986, the National Science Foundation (NSF) founded the construction of a 56 Kbps network connecting its six new supercomputer centers. It was upgraded to DS1 in 1988. In 1990, the National Science Foundation (NSF) embarked upon a program to upgrade the entire Internet backbone to DS3 speeds (45 Mbps) for supercomputer interconnection. In 1994, the NSF began upgrade of the Internet backbone for supercomputer communication to OC-3 speeds (150 Mbps). Internet II initiatives took these speeds into the gigabits.

The backbone speed continues to increase. Today, many of the Internet Service Providers (ISPs) connect or peer with each other using OC-48 and higher speeds. We will discuss TCP/IP in much greater detail in Chapter 10.

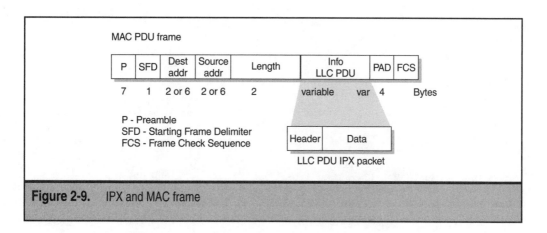

Figure 2-9.   IPX and MAC frame

REVIEW

This chapter identified the organizations that have taken an active role in standardizing and specifying many of the technologies introduced in this book. The standards-making process accelerates and improves every year, especially with catalysts like the industry forums. The role of the various players in the standards process—users, vendors, and service providers—was covered. The standards process was then described in terms of how standards are developed and finalized. Comments were provided on differences in approach between the various organizations and their efforts to cooperate to develop standards for faster deployment. This chapter also introduced some of the major architectures used in the late twentieth century and the concept of protocol layering. A brief description covered the OSIRM and its seven layers were described: physical, data link, network, transport, session, presentation, and application. The key architectures of IEEE 802.x, SNA, and Novell IPX were covered.

CHAPTER 3

Introduction to Transmission Technologies

This chapter provides an overview of common network topologies, circuits, connections, and transmission types, along with the fundamentals of bridging, switching, and routing. Five major network topologies are defined in this chapter and form the basis for most network designs. The presentation then covers the types of connections and circuits that interconnect these topologies. Each circuit type has characteristics, such as the direction of data flow, bit- or byte-oriented transmission, and physical characteristics. Finally, the major data communications hardware types that form the building blocks of today's data networks are discussed, including bridges, routers, hubs, switches, and gateways.

GENERAL NETWORK TOPOLOGIES

The five most commonly used network topologies for computer and data communications networks are point-to-point, multipoint (or common bus), star, ring (or loop), and mesh. The term *node* will be used to designate a network data communications element such as a router, switch, or multiplexer. The term *link* will be used to designate a circuit connection between nodes. A link may be either logical, such as a Permanent Virtual Circuit (PVC), or physical, as with a dedicated private line. Illustrated examples are provided for each network topology.

Point-to-Point

Point-to-point connectivity is the simplest topology, providing a single link between two nodes. This link can be composed of multiple physical and/or logical circuits. Figure 3-1 shows three examples of point-to-point links. The first example (A.) shows a single link between node A and node B with a single physical and logical (or virtual) circuit. Notice that communications can flow in both directions simultaneously over the same physical and logical circuit. The second example (B.) depicts a single link between node A and node B with multiple logical circuits riding over a single physical link. The third example (C.) depicts a single path between node A and node B with multiple (four to be exact) physical circuits, each one carrying multiple logical circuits.

Point-to-point configurations are the most common method of connectivity. Many data communications networks and the applications that ride them use point-to-point topologies in metropolitan area network (MAN) and wide area network (WAN) configurations. For example, almost every time a user accesses the many types of MAN or WAN network services (such as packet switching, Frame Relay (FR), or Asynchronous Transfer Mode, or ATM), some form of point-to-point topology is used. An example of the point-to-point topology is the private-line or dedicated circuit.

Common Bus (Multipoint)

A widely used function of multipoint is the common bus topology, where all nodes are physically connected to a common bus structure. Figure 3-2 shows the multipoint common bus topology, where nodes A through F communicate via a common physical and

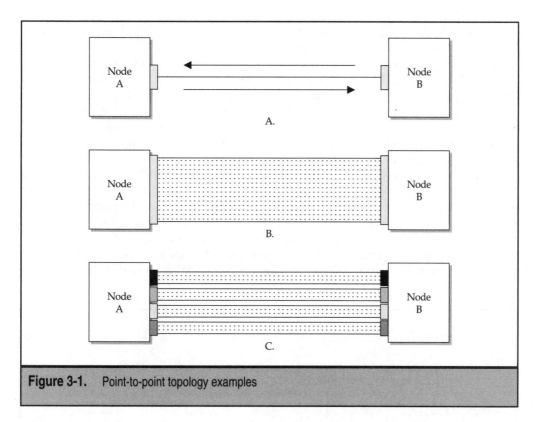

Figure 3-1. Point-to-point topology examples

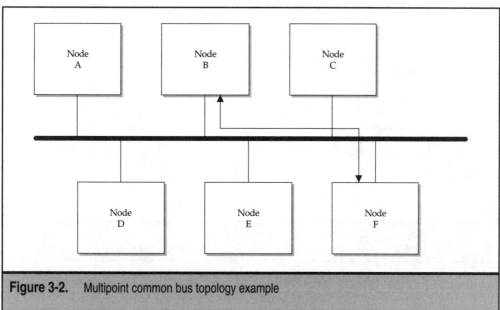

Figure 3-2. Multipoint common bus topology example

logical bus. The IEEE 802.3 Ethernet protocol uses a common bus topology. The common bus is also called a shared medium topology.

For many years, a multidrop analog line was commonly used for the Systems Network Architecture (SNA) Synchronous Data Link Control (SDLC) local loop access. In this example, an analog signal was broadcast from a primary station to all secondary stations. In the return direction, all secondary signals were added and returned to the primary. This was a very cost-effective mode of communication during the late twentieth century. The SNA SDLC protocol, which can use a multipoint circuit for access, was defined in great detail in Chapter 2.

Many companies are now using protocols such as the Internet Protocol (IP) and FR to transport their SNA traffic. Multidrop lines are predominately used in industries that need a small amount of bandwidth to many locations, such as banking (connections to automated teller machines, the other ATM) and gaming (connections to slot machines).

Other conceptual examples of the multipoint topology are illustrated in Figure 3-3. Another commonly used multipoint topology is that of broadcast, or point-to-multipoint, which is defined in the Broadband Integrated Services Digital Network (B-ISDN) standards

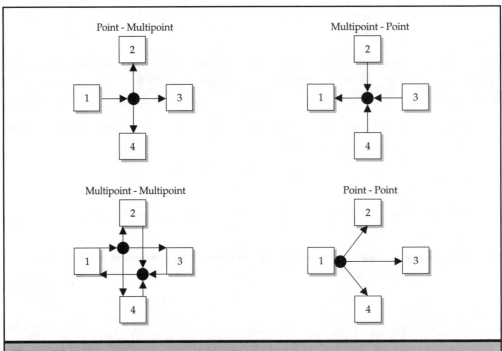

Figure 3-3. Conceptual illustration of multipoint topologies

as the case in which one sender's data is received by many other nodes. Yet another example is that of *incast*, or multipoint-to-point, where multiple senders' signals are received at one destination, such as in the secondary-to-primary direction. In this conceptual illustration, note that the multipoint-to-multipoint topology (that is, shared medium or multicast) is effectively the combination of a point-to-multipoint and a multipoint-to-point topology, as the name implies. The point-to-point topology is also illustrated for comparison purposes.

Star

The star topology was developed during the era when most computer communications were centrally controlled by a mainframe. It also has its analogy in the voice world where one central switch is connected to multiple remote switching nodes, each serving hundreds to even thousands of telephones. This network radiates in a star-like fashion from the central switch through the remote switches to the telephones on people's desks. All devices in the network are connected to the central (often headquarters site) node, which usually performs the processing and switching. Nodes communicate with each other through point-to-point or multidrop links radiating from the central node. The difference between this topology and that of the multipoint topology is that the central node only provides point-to-point connections between any edge node on either a physical or a logically switched basis.

Figure 3-4 shows a star topology, where node A serves as the center of the star and nodes B through E communicate with each other via connections switched through node A. Another example of a legacy star topology is many remote terminal locations accessing a centralized host processor. These terminals are often called *dumb* terminals since the processing power and intelligence are resident in the host.

The physical star topology is widely used to connect devices to a central hub. The central hub may logically organize the physical star as a logical bus or ring, as is commonly done in local area network (LAN) wiring hubs and switches. An example of this is having multiple personal computers connected to an Ethernet switch. The physical connections are organized as a physical star, but logically the devices communicate via a logical bus (Ethernet).

In some WAN designs, the central hub site is typically a headquarters location where the main applications reside and to which all remote sites are connected. This topology is also called "hub-and-spoke." Network designs based on the original SNA architecture resemble a star topology, where remote and local terminals directly communicate with communications controllers, which would then pass the information in a star fashion to front-end processors (FEPs) that pass the information to the host. Communications back to the remote users must follow the same hierarchy. Modern Application Service Provider (ASP) configurations also use a star design, as many remote locations access a central server where the application resides, but instead of this server residing at a separate headquarters location, it resides *within* the network typically on a service provider's hosted server.

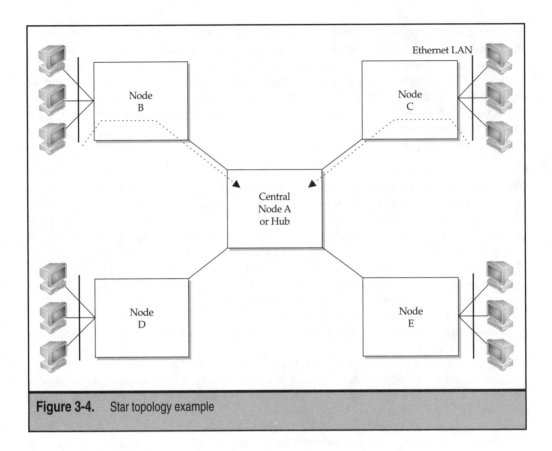

Figure 3-4. Star topology example

Ring

The loop, or ring, topology is used for networks in which communications data flow is unidirectional according to a particular protocol. A physical and/or logical ring is established, and each device attached to the ring passes information in the direction of the ring's traffic flow. In the example of the Institute of Electrical and Electronics Engineers (IEEE) 802.5 Token Ring protocol, each station has an opportunity to seize the token, pass data, and then release the token. The destination station [based on the Media Access Control (MAC) address] identifies the data as destined for it, strips the information off the ring, and then releases the token to pass more data. This method is referred to as a bandwidth reservation scheme, as opposed to the collision scheme used in Ethernet. The Token Ring protocol operates similar to a subway system where each car can be loaded with people, unloaded at the destination, and reused to carry more people.

Figure 3-5 shows a ring network where node A passes information (frame 1) to node C via the ring and through node D (steps 1 and 2). Node C then returns a confirmation

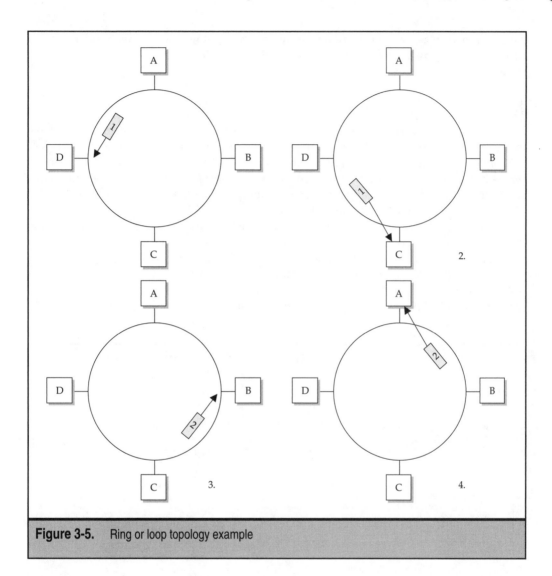

Figure 3-5. Ring or loop topology example

(frame 2) to node A via node B (step 3), at which point node A removes this data from the ring (step 4). There is a reuse of capacity in this ring example because the destination removes the information from the ring to make better use of capacity. Examples of the ring topology are the IEEE 802.5 Token Ring and the Fiber Distributed Data Interface (FDDI).

Note that the IEEE 802.6 physical topology is often drawn as a ring; however, its operation is logically a bus. Synchronous Optical Network (SONET) technology also uses a physical point-to-point architecture where the SONET-intelligent devices form logical ring architecture. SONET protection rings use a ring topology and are distinguished from a mesh topology by the difference in nodal switching action from that of a mesh of circuit switches.

Mesh

Most switched networks employ some form of mesh architecture. Mesh networks have many nodes that are connected by multiple links. Figures 3-6 and 3-7 show two types of mesh networks. Figure 3-6 shows a partial-mesh network where nodes B, C, D, E, F, and G have a high degree of connectivity by virtue of having at least three links to any other node, while nodes A and H has only two links to other nodes. Often, the number of links connected to a node is called its degree (of connectivity).

Figure 3-7 shows a full-mesh network where each node has a link to every other node. Almost every major computer and data communications network uses a mesh topology to give alternate routes for backup and traffic loads, but few networks use a full-mesh topology primarily because of high cost factors associated with having a large number of links. This is because a full-mesh n-node network has $n(n-1)/2$ links. For networks with n greater than 4 to 8 nodes, partial-mesh networks are usually employed.

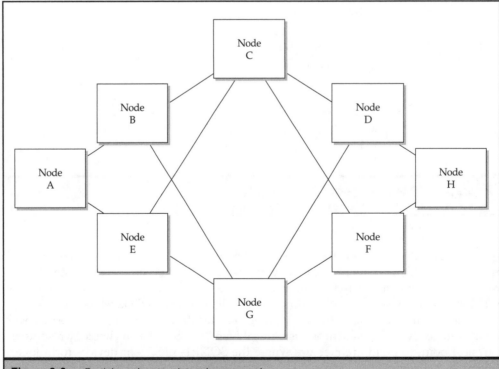

Figure 3-6. Partial-mesh network topology example

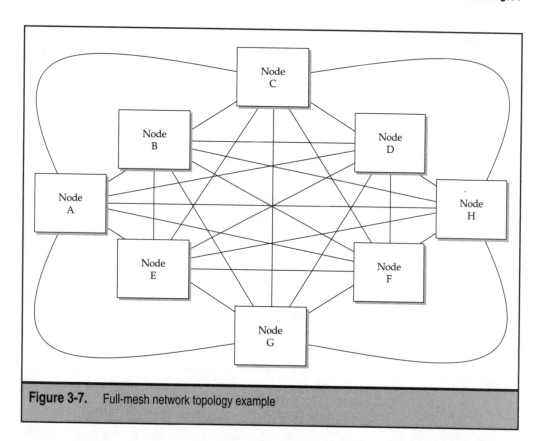

Figure 3-7.   Full-mesh network topology example

CONNECTION AND CIRCUIT TYPES AND SERVICES

This section takes a detailed look at the characteristics of the three major types of connections that define the data flows used in network topologies: simplex, half-duplex, and duplex. We next look at multidrop and private-line circuits, which form the fundamental components of connectivity for most types of data communications architectures. Additionally, most service providers, defined in legacy terms of Local Exchange Carriers (LECs), independent telephone and bypass companies, and inter-exchange carriers (IXCs), offer private lines and multidrop circuits as a tariff service. Finally, we look at a more recent type of high-speed local loop that has become very popular: the Digital Subscriber Line (DSL). Cable access will be covered later.

Connection Types: Simplex, Half-Duplex, and Duplex

Data terminal equipment (DTE) to data communications equipment (DCE) connections provide a local, limited-distance physical connection between DTEs or terminal equipment (TE), such as a computer, and DCEs, such as a modem or channel service unit/data service unit (CSU/DSU). The physical medium can be two-wire, four-wire, coaxial, fiber optic, or a variety of other interfaces.

The following illustration depicts a connection between a DTE and a DCE running simplex communications, which means that transmission is possible only in a single direction.

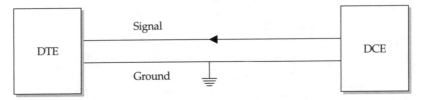

The following illustration displays a DTE/DCE connection using half-duplex communications, which means that a transmission can occur in either direction (as illustrated by the two-headed arrow), but only one direction is allowed at a time. The change of transmission direction is accomplished via the control leads between the DTE and DCE at the physical layer.

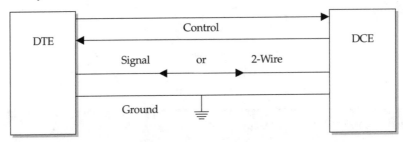

The next illustration depicts full-duplex communication, which means that transmission not only can occur in both directions, but can occur in both directions simultaneously.

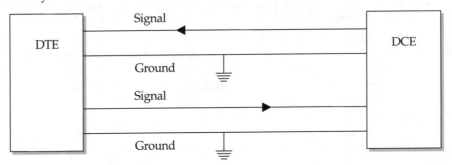

A separate ground lead is shown for each data signal, indicating a balanced interface that supports higher transmission speeds over longer distances on DTE-to-DCE connections. An unbalanced interface shares a ground lead between multiple signal leads and operates only over shorter distances. All of these examples demonstrate a point-to-point topology.

Multidrop Circuits

When one user, typically the originator of information, needs to communicate with multiple users over a shared facility, a multidrop circuit can be used. Figure 3-8 shows a two-wire multidrop circuit, and Figure 3-9 shows a four-wire multidrop circuit. In SNA multidrop networks, many remote users (B, C, and D) share a single, low-cost multidrop access circuit to a central site (A). Only one user (B, C, or D) may send data to the main leg of the circuit (A) at any one time. When using multidrop circuits, there is a primary-secondary relationship between the primary device, A, and the secondary devices, B, C, and D. A typical application is where the primary A is a cluster controller and B through D are dumb terminals connected to a host (either local or remote) to provide cost-effective access to a centralized host.

Note that when dealing with an SDLC loop operating on a two-wire multidrop circuit, only a half-duplex connection protocol can be used, as indicated by the two-headed arrow, while a full-duplex operation can be accommodated on a four-wire circuit, as indicated by the single-headed arrow on the path in each direction. In a half-duplex operation, the primary sends out data to the secondary devices and polls them for any response. The secondary device sets a "final" bit in its response, indicating the last frame to be returned. A full-duplex operation is similar, except now the primary can send continuously and uses this channel to poll the secondary devices.

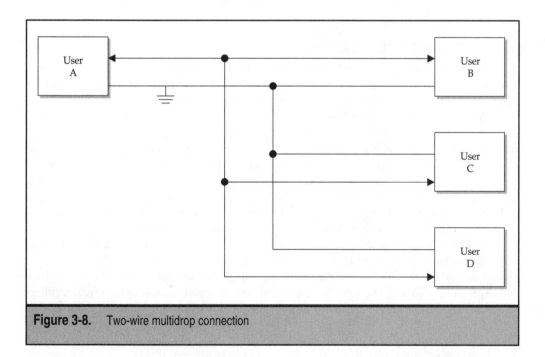

Figure 3-8.   Two-wire multidrop connection

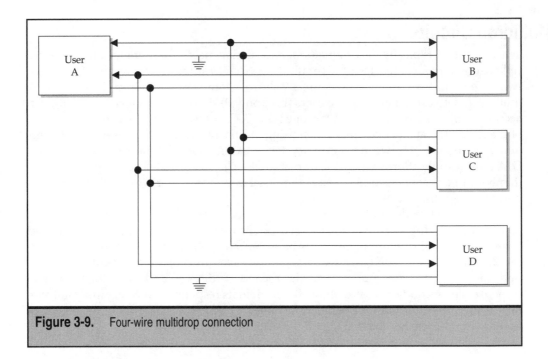

Figure 3-9. Four-wire multidrop connection

Private Lines and Local Loops

A private, or leased, line is a dedicated circuit leased from a service provider for a predetermined period of time, usually in increments of months or years. A private line may be upgraded by paying extra for a defined quality of service, such that conditioning is performed to ensure that a lower error rate is achieved, which makes a tremendous difference in data communications. When service providers installed all-fiber networks, digital private lines with much lower error rates are replacing the old voice-grade analog data circuits at the same or even lower cost. Although analog voice-grade lines are still available, most communications are carried on digital optical facilities. In the United States, there are very few private lines left that use microwave or analog circuits. This is especially true in major metropolitan areas. Service level agreements (SLAs) on private lines typically guarantee minimum availability, delay, throughput, and loss compliance.

When leased lines are used to access other services, they are called *access lines* or *local loops*. A local loop typically connects customer premises equipment (CPE) to the service provider's central office (CO). Leased access lines can be purchased through LECs, competitive access providers (CAPs), IXCs, or user-owned access arrangements. Access from these alternate sources is generally less expensive than the local telephone company prices. But, of course, the alternative access service provider usually "cream-skims" the lucrative traffic (metropolitan area services) and leaves the "skimmed milk" of the smaller, more remote, or occasional users for the LEC to serve. This is typically true for most high-speed Internet access Digital Subscriber Line (xDSL) services.

Private lines in Europe and Pacific rim countries are still very expensive, as is transoceanic fiber access. A service provider also must make an agreement with the party at the other side of a fiber to offer the transoceanic private-line service. A significant investment is required for a small amount of bandwidth. The high cost of international private lines may justify the cost of sophisticated, statistical multiplexers or statistical multiplexing services like FR to utilize the expensive bandwidth as efficiently as possible. New fiber-optic technologies like erbium-doping techniques are enabling long transoceanic fiber runs that do not require repeaters, thus significantly driving down the cost of transcontinental communications. The erbium-doping technique uses lasers to activate erbium ions in fiber to boost the optical signals transmitted through the fiber. Techniques like this create savings that eventually reach the consumer as lower private-line prices.

Digital Subscriber Line (DSL)

Another form of DSL rate signal, operating over four wires, is the HDSL. HDSLs eliminate the cost of repeaters every 2,000 feet, as in a standard T1 repeater system, and are not affected by bridge taps (splices). Users need to be within 12,000 feet of the serving CO, which covers over 80 percent of the DSL customers in the United States. ADSLs are also available and offer higher speeds (up to 640 Kbps) as well as better performance. The goal of ADSL technology is to deliver a video signal and telephone service over a majority of the existing copper twisted pairs currently connected to homes. Fiber-To-The-Curb (FTTC) and Fiber-To-The-Home (FTTH) have yet to see a wide-scale deployment. Both of these fiber implementations will enable services like ATM and higher-rate SDSL-like technologies to proliferate to the residential consumer. We will discuss more DSL options as well as other access technologies such as cable and satellite later in the book.

PRIVATE LEASED LINES VERSUS SWITCHED NETWORKS

In keeping with the discussion matter of this chapter, it is important to review the benefits and risks of private-line networks versus switched networks. There are three general options to data-transport networks today: private-line or dedicated leased-line networks, switched networks (including circuit and packet switched varieties), and hybrid designs incorporating a mix of both. Dedicated lines, also called private or leased lines, are dedicated circuits between two or more user devices. This type of circuit represents a dedicated private portion of bandwidth between two or more ports on the network, hence the term *private line*. A private line is dedicated to one customer; the opposite is a public service shared among multiple customers. This private circuit is available to a customer 24 hours a day, 7 days a week for a set fee (usually an initial nonrecurring fee and a monthly recurring fee). High volumes of traffic with frequent use justify this type of circuit. The only users of the circuit are the ports at both ends of the circuit. The bandwidth resources are in no way shared within the network. Although dedicated to a particular customer, these circuits are leased from the service provider, hence the term leased lines.

The second alternative is a switched network transport circuit. This can range from simple circuit switching, in which users dynamically select from a pool of multiple public service lines with fixed bandwidths, to intelligent, ubiquitous switched access networks where bandwidth is only allocated and used when needed, such as packet, frame, and cell relay networks.

Corporate communications usually comprise a hybrid network employing both solutions. The circuits requiring dedicated bandwidth to accommodate predictable volumes of constant-bandwidth traffic use *dedicated* circuits, while users requiring one-to-many connectivity, bandwidth-on-demand, and flexible or more dynamic access use *switched* network access. These decisions are also influenced by other factors such as the burstiness of data (burstiness is defined as the peak-to-average traffic ratio, where video traffic is less bursty and LAN-to-LAN TCP/IP traffic is typically very bursty), traffic patterns, bandwidth maximums, and minimum delay, to name a few. The three types of network services that match the previous access types include private-line services dedicated to one customer, virtual private services that look like private services but ride on a public or shared network platform, and public network switched services.

Private (Leased) Line Networks

Dedicated or private-line circuits are the simplest form of point-to-point communication. Circuits leased from a service provider (leased lines) are a form of private line. Private lines provide a dedicated circuit of fixed bandwidth between two points. Figure 3-10 shows three user devices connected via three private lines. User A has a dedicated 56-Kbps circuit to user B as well as a dedicated 1.544-Mbps circuit to user C. Users B and C have a dedicated 1.544-Mbps circuit between them.

Private-line bandwidths will vary, but typically follow standard electrical speed conventions of 56/64 Kbps (DS0), NxDS0 (56/64-Kbps increments) 1.544 Mbps, NxDS1 (1.5 Mbps increments), and optical speed conventions of OC-N where N is in increments of 51.83 Mbps. The digital and optical hierarchy (DS0, DS1, DS3, OC-N, and so on) will be explained in more detail in Chapters 4 and 5.

Users will generally lease a private line when the entire bandwidth will always be available between two points of choice whenever it is needed. They do not want to share this bandwidth with anyone else, nor do they want to contend with other users to establish the circuit (or wait during the delay time to establish it) to receive their required bandwidth. This bandwidth also affords the highest level of security and performance predictability.

Leased lines come in many grades and speeds. The most basic traditional service available consists of analog and digital leased lines having DS0, fractional DS1, DS1, fractional DS3, and DS3 speeds. These lines require a modem for digital-to-analog conversion and transmission over analog lines, or a CSU/DSU for line conditioning as well as proper framing and formatting for transmission over a digital line. This type of service ranges from economic analog circuits to higher-grade Digital Data Service (DDS) transmissions offered by the major IXCs and LECs, both inter-local access and transport area (LATA) and intra-LATA, respectively. Alternate access providers also offer DDS private-line connectivity. DDS is a private line digital service for data transmission and is generally more expensive and more reliable than analog leased lines.

The options for higher bandwidth access include SubRate Data Multiplexing (SRDM), fractional T1 (FT1), and dedicated T1, T2, and T3. SRDM offers the same access

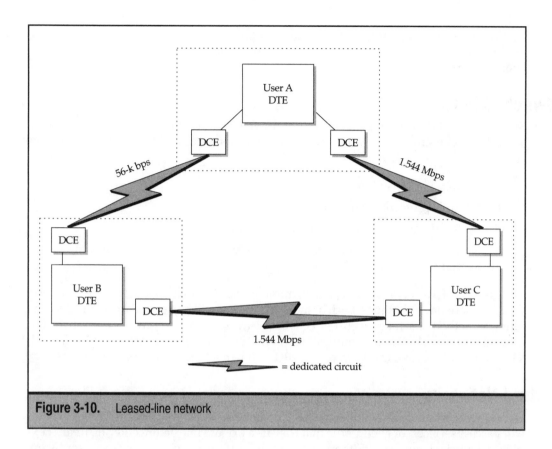

Figure 3-10. Leased-line network

speeds as DDS, but enables the aggregation of many low-speed channels into a single DS0 for cost savings. FT1 and FT3 offer the same type of service, but at a DS1 and DS3 level, respectively. Dedicated DS1 and DS3 offer just what they state: a single, dedicated high-bandwidth circuit to access the service provider. If a user wants additional functionality, reliability, and availability, switched services are the alternative. In later chapters, the emergence of SONET, WDM, and GbE, will show the technological quantum leap that is now moving cost-effective user access speeds into the gigabits.

Although dedicated private line circuits provide the benefit of guaranteed available bandwidth, they are typically nonredundant. At the network level, the digital cross-connects (DXCs) carrying private lines have network-layer disaster recovery, so the risk is at the access level, unless LEC/CAP access redundancy is ordered and routed. If the private line of any of its associated transmission equipment should fail or be taken out of commission (such as a fiber cut), the users on each end cannot communicate (unless they have some method of reconnecting or dialing around the failure). Thus, the user must decide which level of availability is needed for communications between facilities. A decision for switched services backup is predicated on these trade-offs. Most large service providers have SONET backbones that automatically reconfigure the user's private line to alternate facilities during a backbone circuit or node failure, but the local loop will not be restored if cut (unless alternate LEC facilities are provisioned). Many options are available for ensuring high availability in private lines. Some methods of routing traffic around physical network failures and using wireless access alternatives are discussed in later chapters.

Switched Networks

Switched networks can range from simple circuit switching to advanced packet, frame, and cell switching, and they can include technologies such as IP, FR, and ATM. The main characteristics of switched networks include

- ▼ Addressing capability
- ■ Multiple protocol and interface support
- ■ One-to-many, many-to-one, and many-to-many connectivity
- ▲ Network intelligence above the physical Open Systems Interconnection Reference Model (OSIRM) layer

Circuit and packet (including packet, frame, and cell) switching are the most common switched network techniques. Each of these techniques will be defined in detail later. The ultimate method of achieving cost-effective high availability and throughput is by using a switched network. Three examples of switched service offerings are FR, ATM, and IP VPNs. Examples of switched networks will be shown in later chapters.

Hybrid Networks

Hybrid networks consist of some measure or mixture of private line and switched network access services, or even traffic that transits a private line before entering or after exiting a switched network. Either way, the important considerations are hardware, software, and protocol compatibility (or transparency). Network management and support become more difficult when multiple network elements are crossed. Since switched networks offer significant cost savings and concentration benefits over dedicated lines, the driving factor should be to move from dedicated lines to switched network access as soon as possible where it makes sense. In some cases, a high-utilization, dedicated circuit bandwidth is required and a private line must be used. But in many cases, multiple traffic flows can be multiplexed together into switched access to achieve significant cost savings.

Today, the big choice in switched data is between switched services (including Switched 56/T1/T3), FR, and ATM. Routed services like IP will be covered in later chapters, along with combination switched and routed services like IP-FR and MPLS. Ubiquitous network access, quickly changing technologies with enhanced reliability, and the apparent economics of scale are driving many network designs to a switched network solution. Network support and management are also driving factors. Each of these decisions should be accompanied by a cost comparison of separate networks to a single network, or a dedicated line to a switched solution.

TRANSMISSION BASICS

Digital Data transmission methods are often characterized as being either asynchronous or synchronous. The terms *asynchronous* and *synchronous* are used in different contexts and have entirely different meanings. The most common use of these terms is in the comparison of asynchronous versus synchronous character or message transmissions. Since this text presents a study of ATM technology, it is important to review another use of these two terms, as in Synchronous versus Asynchronous Transfer Mode (STM and ATM). These two entirely different meanings of the same term can be confusing, which is why this section presents them together so that the reader can appreciate and understand the differences.

Asynchronous and Synchronous Data Transmission

Asynchronous character transmission has no clock either in or associated with the transmitted digital data stream. Characters are transmitted as a series of bits, with each character identified separately by start and stop bits, as illustrated in the example of ASCII characters in Figure 3-11. There will typically be a variable amount of time between each character transmission. Analog modem communication employs this method extensively. The baud rate defines a nominal clock rate, which is the maximum asynchronous bit rate. The stop bit can be greater than a baud interval in duration. Since at least 10-baud intervals are required to represent each character, the usable bit rate is no more than 80 percent of the baud rate (a good example of the overhead found even at Layer 1 of the OSIRM).

Asynchronous character transmission usually operates at low speeds (typically 9600 bps). Asynchronous interfaces include RS232-C and D, as well as X.21. Modern-day V.90 modems operate at an average of 56Kbps-capable throughput, but in actuality have lower throughputs.

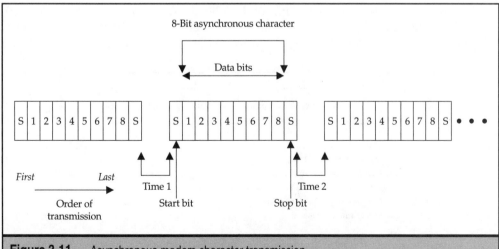

Figure 3-11. Asynchronous modem character transmission

Synchronous data transmission clocks the bits at a regular rate by a clocking signal either associated with or derived from the transmitted digital data stream. Therefore, sender and receiver must have a means to derive a common clock within a certain frequency tolerance. On a parallel interface there is often a separate clock lead. Data flows in character streams are called message-framed data. Figure 3-12 shows a typical synchronous data stream. The message begins with two synchronization (SYNCH) characters and a Start of Message (SOM) character. The Control (C) character(s) denotes the type of user data or message following. The user data follows next. The Cyclic Redundancy Check (CRC) character checks the data for errors, and the End of Message (EOM) character signals the end of the transmission stream. The equipment then looks for another two SYNC characters for the next piece of information.

Synchronous data transmission usually operates at speeds of 1,200 bps and higher. Synchronous data interfaces include V.35, RS449/RS-442 balanced, RS232-C and -D, and X.21.

Asynchronous Versus Synchronous Transfer Mode

Since this text pays particular attention to ATM, or asynchronous time division multiplexing, it is useful to compare this method to the commonly used STM, or synchronous time division multiplexing. Both of these methods have significant differences.

Figure 3-13 shows an example of STM and ATM. Figure 3-13 (A.) illustrates an STM stream where each time slot represents a reserved piece of bandwidth dedicated to a single channel, such as a DS0 in a DS1. Each frame contains n dedicated time slots per frame; for example, n is 192 in a DS1. Overhead fields identify STM frames that often contain operation information as well, such as the 193rd bit in a DS1 frame. Thus, if a channel is not transmitting data, the time slot remains reserved and is still transmitted, without any useful payload. In this case, if the other channels have more data to transmit, they have to wait until their reserved, assigned time slot occurs again. Frequent empty time slots result in low line utilization.

ATM uses a completely different approach. A header field prefixes each fixed-length payload, as shown in Figure 3-13 (B.). The header identifies the virtual channel. Therefore, the time slots are available to *any user* who has data ready to transmit. If no users are

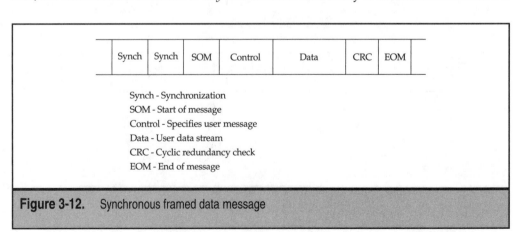

Figure 3-12.   Synchronous framed data message

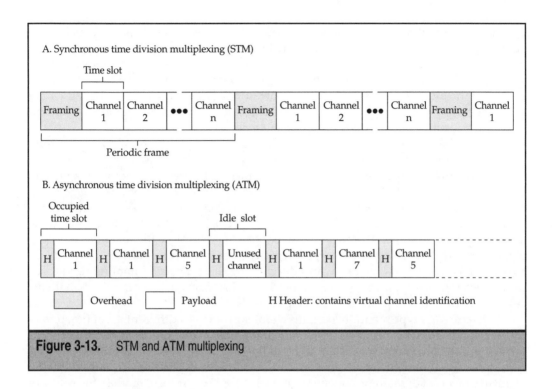

Figure 3-13. STM and ATM multiplexing

ready to transmit, then an empty, or idle, cell is sent. ATM as compared with STM usually carries traffic patterns that are not continuous much more efficiently. The current approach is to carry ATM cells over very high-speed STM transmission networks, such as SONET/Synchronous Digital Hierarchy (SDH). The match between high transmission speeds of SONET and SDH and the flexibility of ATM is a good one. We discuss the details of SONET/SDH in Chapter 5.

HARDWARE SELECTION IN THE DESIGN PROCESS

Data-networking circuit and packet topologies form the roads by which data can travel. We will now explore the wide variety of LAN and WAN devices that utilize these roads. The various types of equipment available now or under development for use in the local, metropolitan, and wide areas are reviewed in this section. The principal networking equipment categories in place today include hubs, switches, and routers. There are also a number of other (usually lower-level functions) that can be used in a building block manner, such as multiplexers, concentrators, CSU/DSUs, and bridging devices, that are summarized here. Multiplexers and switch access devices will be considered in Chapter 4.

Here is a critical item: Before bridges, LAN switches, and routers were available, the functions that these devices now serve were once performed in mainframes and FEPs. In fact, the FEP was the first true router. The migration was from cluster controllers and

FEPs to simple routing devices and then to router-based networks. This was a major paradigm shift in the last three decades of the twentieth century. As personal computing arrived on the scene, and as Millions of Instructions per Second (MIPS) moved to the desktop during decentralization, the bridging and routing functions traditionally accomplished at the FEP/host complex migrated toward the LAN and desktop. The advent of personal computing, along with local and wide area networking, made routing and switching outside the mainframe environment a necessity.

Perhaps the greatest driving factor was the multiple MAC and network-layer protocols operating within and between LANs as they moved into the WAN environment. Due to these diverse markets, technologies, and protocol suites, there evolved a need to make diverse LAN, WAN, and operating-system protocols speak one language (or at least provide a translation between similar languages on similar types of LANs). When bridges (predecessors to L2 switches) and routers (predecessors to L3 switches) first came along, they were designed to deal with lower-speed LANs. Now the functions of bridging, routing, and switching have merged in many cases into a single device. And with increased processor speeds, more advanced technologies, and concomitant reduced costs, these devices now support an extension of diverse LAN speeds over the WAN with access speeds from the Kbps up into the Gbps speeds.

Each hardware type mentioned in this chapter provides a different set of functionality, which can either be provided separately or together in one piece of equipment. Each provides protocol support for certain levels of the OSIRM as well as other proprietary architectures. For simplicity of discussion, and since the OSIRM seems to be the common architectural point of reference (along with the IEEE 802.X protocol model), the protocol support for each hardware device will be given in reference to the seven-layer OSIRM reference model. Repeaters and legacy bridges have come to play a reduced role, yielding to remote-access switches and routers and Small Office Home Office (SOHO) devices that require only a subset of their larger counterparts. Intelligent LAN hubs and switches that provide LAN connectivity and concentration, bridging, routing, and switching will also be covered in detail. Each of these new hardware technologies offers specific advantages and disadvantages depending upon user applications, protocols, addressing, and data transport needs. The network designer must understand each of these technologies to ensure successful LAN-MAN-WAN connectivity, interoperability, and integration. Starting with the simplest devices will allow us to work toward the most complex.

Repeaters

Repeaters are inexpensive distance-extension devices, providing physical distance extension through signal regeneration for point-to-point circuits. This enables a network to extend the distance between network devices, similar to an extension cord for electricity, while providing electrical isolation during problem conditions. Thus, repeaters offer the capability to extend an existing LAN or WAN segment at the L1 protocol interface. Repeaters possess very little intelligence. They are commonly used as signal regenerators, protecting against signal attenuation while improving signal quality. Due to this lack of intelligence, repeaters add value by maintaining the integrity of all data being passed, but they are completely transparent to all data content. Drawbacks to using repeaters include possible network congestion caused by the overhead they may add due to repeating and *jitter* imposed by signal delay. The effects of excessive jitter will be covered in later chapters. Repeaters form the core component of hubs and use only the physical layer of the OSIRM. Figure 3-14 portrays user A and user B communicating via a repeater in relation to the OSIRM. Note that while a repeater uses only the physical layer, it may operate electrically or optically.

Modems, Line Drivers/Limited-Distance Modems (LDMs)

A modem modulates outgoing digital signals from a computer or other digital device to analog signals and demodulates the incoming analog signal and converts it to a digital signal for the digital device. Signals are transmitted and received over unshielded twisted pair phone lines. Most modems today are 56 Kbps using the V.90 standard, which was derived from the x2 technology of 3Com (US Robotics) and Rockwell's K56flex technology. DSL services are accessed via the same medium, but use special DSL modems. DSL modems use various modulation techniques including Discrete Multitone Technology (DMT), Carrierless Amplitude Modulation (CAP), and Multiple Virtual Line (MVL). Broadband cable data services are also available that offer even higher bandwidth alternatives than traditional analog and DSL modems. Cable modems connect to both the computer or LAN and the Cable TV and offer bandwidth to both. Cable modems have a connection to the cable wall outlet and one to the PC (NIC card), router, switch, or set-top box. Cable modems modulate between analog and digital signals, and attach to the coaxial cable that communicates with a Cable Modem Termination System (CMTS) at the local cable TV company office. All cable modems can receive from and send signals only to

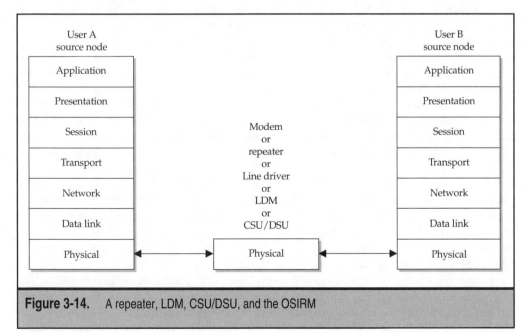

Figure 3-14.   A repeater, LDM, CSU/DSU, and the OSIRM

the CMTS, but not to other cable modems on the line. Some services have the upstream signals returned by telephone rather than cable, in which case the cable modem is known as a telco-return cable modem. Bandwidth can approach 27Mbps downstream and 2.5Mbps upstream, although current services offer much less bandwidth.

Line drivers, also called Limited-Distance Modems (LDMs), are used to extend the distance of a physical circuit. Basic telecommunications courses teach that modems provide modulation/demodulation between analog and digital data. LDMs provide the same functionality, but in the form of a repeater. Figure 3-14 shows the OSIRM layer used by line drivers and LDMs as Layer 1.

CSU and DSU

The terms *channel service unit (CSU)* and *data service unit (DSU)* are often incorrectly used interchangeably. Originally, the CSU was developed to protect CPE from voltage surges in the access line. Additional remote testing and monitoring capabilities such as bipolar violation and loop-back testing were later added. The DSU was typically the lower-speed device, providing signal format and protocol translation, timing recovery, and synchronous sampling, as well as acting as the termination point for DDS 56 Kbps and below. The CSU was a higher-speed device, used at DS1 rates, which could also be used at lower speeds. The CSU terminates digital circuits with the same features as a DSU, but it also provides many feature functions not provided by the DSU, such as filtering, line equalization, line conditioning, signal regeneration and amplification, circuit loop-back testing capabilities, and error control protocol conversion (that is, B8ZS) peculiar to DS1 service.

Today, a device is available that has merged CSU and DSU functionality. CSUs/DSUs have the capability for Extended Super Frame (ESF) monitoring and testing as well as advanced Simple Network Management Protocol (SNMP) monitoring functionality [with their own management information bases (MIBs)]. Some even have the capability to multiplex traffic from multiple input ports into a single point-to-point or multidrop circuit.

DSUs come in many speeds and with many different functions. There are six major categories of DSUs. First, fixed-rate DSUs operate at speeds of 19.2 Kbps and below (subrate) or at the fixed speed of 56 Kbps. Second, multirate DSUs can be purchased that operate at variable speeds at or below 56 Kbps. Third, these two types of DSUs can also be obtained with a secondary channel for network management. The fourth type of DSU is the switched 56-Kbps DSU, which operates with 56 switched digital services. T1 dedicated and switched DSUs are also available. Standard CSUs provide a T1 circuit interface and can have properties similar to the DSUs mentioned previously. Finally, CSUs and DSUs are capable of multiplexing multiple T1, V.35, and RS-232 user ports into a single data stream for "integrated access" into a LEC or IXC switch, where they can be demultiplexed and passed to the appropriate service. Some CDU/DSUs may even have management and reporting for higher-layer protocols that pass through their interfaces, or even provide part of the protocol functionality (such as FR CSU/DSU and ATM CSU/DSUs, respectively), as we will see in a minute.

Many CSU/DSU vendors also market DS-3/E-3 products, which provide the High-Speed Serial Interface (HSSI) for direct DS-3 connectivity. A few of the vendors, such as Quick Eagle Networks (formerly known as Digital Link), Visual Networks, and Kentrox offer SMDS and ATM support. But let the buyer beware, *caveat emptor*, for many of these SMDS and ATM support functions are proprietary between the CSU/DSU vendors and a particular hardware vendor.

With the emergence of broadband services such as SMDS and ATM Data Exchange Interfaces (DXIs), the CSU takes on an entirely new function apart from its normal functionality. Some SMDS and ATM CSUs actually perform some of the required protocol conversion and cell segmentation, going far beyond their original function as a power protector interface. For example, with SMDS DXI, special SMDS CSUs actually take the high-level L3_PDU frame and segment it into L2_PDU cells, performing part of the SMDS protocol function within the CSU. The CSU then interfaces to the SMDS network through a SMDS Interface Protocol (SIP). SIP will be reviewed in detail in Chapter 11.

Also note that many times a specific CSU or DSU setting or feature works best depending on the Layer 2 (L2) protocol being passed, such as with FR, where B8ZS is the option of choice for DS1 speeds using ESF.

DSU/CSU standard interfaces include 56-Kbps, FT1, and DS1 using EIA-232-C, V.35, and HSSI (on DS-3 models). CSU and DSU operation is similar to that shown in Figure 3-17 with repeaters, and the OSIRM layer used by CSUs and DSUs is shown in this same figure. Note that only physical Layer 1 is used by a CSU or DSU (except with the SMDS, ATM DSU, and some FR CSU/DSUs).

Hubs and LAN Switches

LAN hubs, also called concentrator hubs, are devices that connect multiple LAN segments (such as Ethernet and Token Ring) or single workstations (or servers) and combine them on a shared backplane. Thus, a hub can be used to combine multiple workstations or servers onto a single LAN segment, or multiple LAN segments onto a single LAN segment. The former case is the hub acting as a repeater for multiple LAN network interface cards (NICs); the workstations interface to the LAN media (that is, 10BASE-T). Larger hubs typically have multiple repeater cards and serve many workstations. In either case, these devices work as Layer 1 devices. Switching hubs, hubs combined with Layer 2 switching intelligence, can perform both the segment-joining functions as well as switching directly between workstations and servers or between LAN segments.

LAN hubs have been classified into four generations. Figure 3-15 illustrates each generation of LAN hub along with its LAN protocol support at each stage. Hub configurations tend to model the star topology, with the hub as the center and each LAN device (for multiple LAN) attached directly to the hub. The first-generation LAN hub appeared in 1984 and acted as a repeater for a single type of LAN connectivity (that is, an Ethernet homogeneous environment). These hubs provide the functionality of a LAN concentration point, supporting a single bus to provide physical connectivity for multiple ports on one or more LAN operating on the same architecture (later, different LAN types could be multiplexed, such as Ethernet and Token Ring). This function is similar to that of a combination patch panel and repeater, as shown in Figure 3-15 (A.). One example is IBM's Multistation Access Unit (MAU) wiring concentrator used for Token Ring coaxial hubbing. This architecture can now be purchased in stores in the form of a $30 four-port dumb hub and can be quite useful for small home area networks (HANs) sharing a single cable modem (the authors advocate a combination hub or switch with an integrated router/firewall to provide maximum security over a cable modem connection).

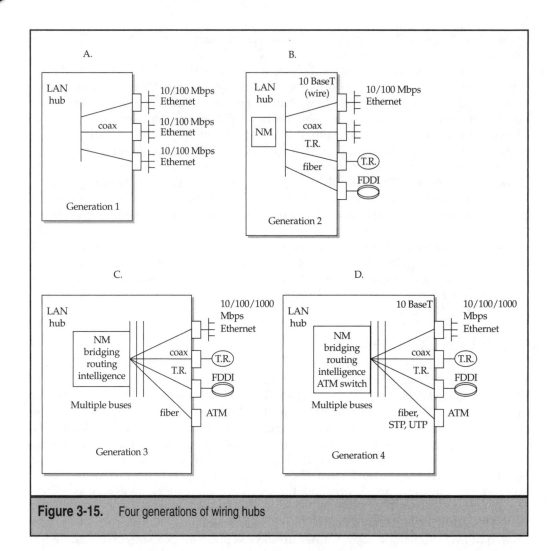

Figure 3-15. Four generations of wiring hubs

Second-generation LAN hubs provide the same bus architectures, but accommodate different LAN architectures over multiple ports, such as Ethernet and Token Ring. Additional features such as local and remote network management and configuration capabilities have also been added, as shown in Figure 3-15 (B.).

Third-generation LAN hubs/switches provide multiple buses for connectivity similar to the second generation, but also add L2 bridging [and occasionally Layer 3 (L3) routing] functions, now called a LAN or L2 switch. Vendors support a wide range of media and often multiple multimegabit or gigabit buses in the hub architecture. Third-generation LAN hubs/switches also have additional network management features and are sometimes called *smart hubs*. This generation also saw the appearance of ATM interfaces. These hubs are shown in Figure 3-15 (C.). Support for some form of network management protocol, like the SNMP, is a must.

Fourth-generation switching hubs appeared in the latter part of the 1990s. Switching hubs offer all the capabilities mentioned previously along with the addition of MAC-layer switching, transparent bridging, and standard wide area trunk interfaces. At times, these fourth-generation switching hubs offer simple routing and maybe even elementary firewall functions. These switching hubs are shown in Figure 3-15 (D.).

Figure 3-16 shows a building using a LAN switch to connect distributed LAN hubs of the same type or different types (Ethernet to Ethernet, Ethernet to Token Ring, Token Ring to Token Ring) from multiple floors. The following sections on bridges and routers will explain these techniques from the protocol and OSIRM point of view. Figure 3-17 shows the OSIRM layers used by LAN hubs and switches. Notice that hubs use the physical layer, while LAN bridges and switches use the data-link layer (DLL).

Hub and LAN switch designs are typically built in a hierarchical nature, as shown in Figure 3-18. Here we see the wiring collection, segmentation, and network management functions performed by hubs and LAN switches. Usually, many Ethernet or Token Ring twisted pair lines, FDDI, and ATM over twisted pair to individual workstations are run to a central hub or LAN switch often located in the wiring closet. Hubs enable administrators to assign individual users to a resource (such as an Ethernet segment), shown as an ellipse in the figure, via network management commands. Lower-level hubs are often connected in a hierarchy to higher-level hubs or LAN switches, sometimes via higher-speed protocols such as Fast Ethernet, Gigabit Ethernet, FDDI, or ATM over optical fiber and high-grade twisted pairs. These devices are often employed in a hierarchical manner to concentrate access for many individual users to a shared resource, such as a server or router, as shown in Figure 3-18. The highest-level hubs and LAN switches are candidates for collapsed backbone architecture based on protocols like Ethernet, FDDI, and ATM, which also support high-speed access to shared resources such as routers and other LAN switches. Stackable modular implementations are also available and provide an easy method of upgrade as the number of users increases.

Bridges

Bridges typically provide connectivity between LANs of similar architecture, such as Ethernet-to-Ethernet or Token Ring-to-Token Ring connectivity, forming one of the simplest of LAN and WAN connections. The exception to this rule is the translation bridge that translates from one media format to another. Many years ago, bridges were stand-alone boxes. Today, bridging can be performed in intelligent hubs, LAN switches, L3 switches or routers, or any device that runs bridging software. For the purposes of this discussion, we will refer to any device that performs bridging as a bridge.

A bridge uses a minimal amount of processing and thus is a less expensive way to link LANs having the same physical- and link-layer protocols. A hallway or an entire city can separate these LANs. Bridges can also connect devices using physical- and link-layer protocols to devices using the higher-level IEEE 802.X protocol suite (including FDDI). Since bridges are protocol transparent above Layer 2, they do not provide flow control or recognize higher-level protocols. They use only the physical and link layers of the OSIRM and support both the logical link control (LLC) and the MAC layers of LAN transmission. Modern-day LAN switches are in reality very fast multiport bridges.

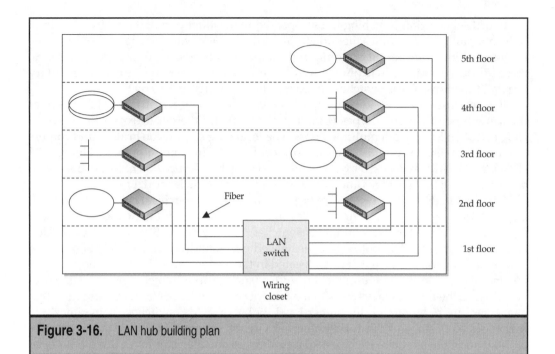

Figure 3-16. LAN hub building plan

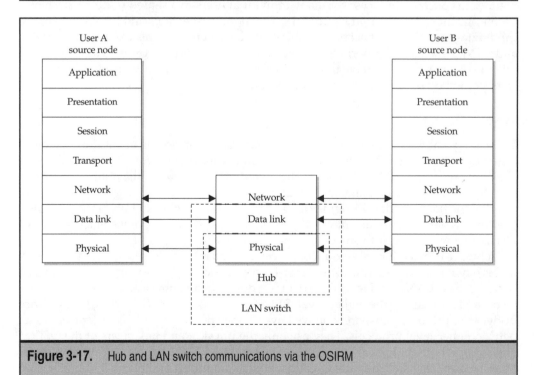

Figure 3-17. Hub and LAN switch communications via the OSIRM

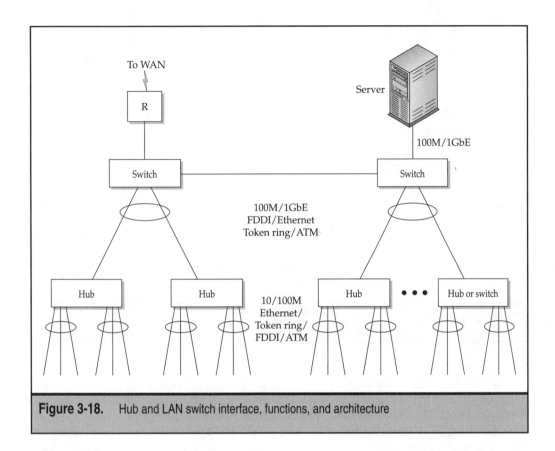

Figure 3-18. Hub and LAN switch interface, functions, and architecture

Figure 3-19 portrays user A and user B communicating via a bridge over the physical and link layers of the OSIRM. Bridges operate at the MAC layer of the OSI DLL. Both users are implementing the same protocol stack for Layers 1 and 2, and the bridge does not modify the information flow in any way (except a required MAC-layer conversion in translation bridging, depending on whether a header is included as part of the "information flow"). The bridge supports linking at the physical and link levels, but provides no addressing or switching functionality. Thus, the user provides all addressing and protocol translation. Bridges simply pass traffic from one network segment to another based on the destination MAC address of the packet being passed. If the destination address of the frame received by the bridge is not local to the bridge, the frame is obviously destined for another LAN and thus the bridge simply forwards the frame on to the next network device.

Bridges will store and forward packets between bridges as packet switches would, but the bridge cannot act as a switch. The exception to this rule is the LAN switch, which also performs bridging, in most cases. Bridges send each packet to a remote user based upon a destination address. Bridges can recognize either a fixed routing table scheme or, for more expensive bridges, a dynamic learning routing scheme. Bridges can "learn" the network through the use of intelligent bridging and routing protocols, and some bridges are able to dynamically update their forwarding tables. Bridging protocols will be discussed later.

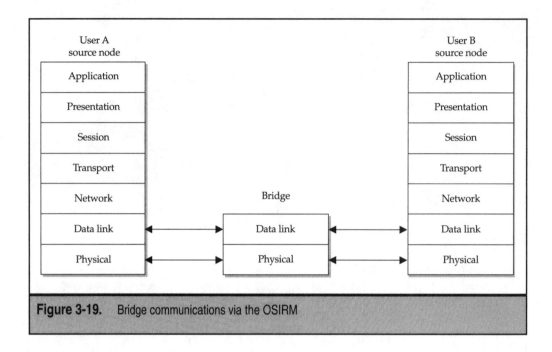

Figure 3-19. Bridge communications via the OSIRM

Another key function of bridges is their capability to filter data. But a major drawback to bridges is that they cannot forward data if operating at their maximum filtering rate. Bridges deployed in a network do not have advance knowledge of the network to which they are attached. They are blind to devices other than those that attach to their logical path structure. The flexibility of bridge connectivity will be discussed further when we cover bridge protocols in Chapter 7.

There are four major types of bridging: transparent, translating, encapsulating, and source route bridging. Each provides different functionality for the various LAN architectures.

When operating in *transparent* mode, bridges at both ends of a transmission support the same physical media and link-layer (MAC-level) protocols from the IEEE 802.X suite (or possibly FDDI), but transmission rates may vary. From the point of view of the network node, transparent bridges take no part in the route discovery or selection process. The higher-level protocols (OSI L3 and higher) need to be the same or compatible for all connected applications, because bridges are transparent to protocols at, or above, the network layer.

Figure 3-20 shows examples of transparent bridging between two local Ethernet LANs and two local Token Ring LANs. Encapsulation bridging between two Token Ring LANs is also shown, requiring CSUs or DSUs. In encapsulation bridging, the LAN frame is placed in a serial encapsulation [High-level Data Link Control (HDLC), Point-to-Point Protocol (PPP), or proprietary] over the point-to-point circuit and is then de-encapsulated without modification at the other end.

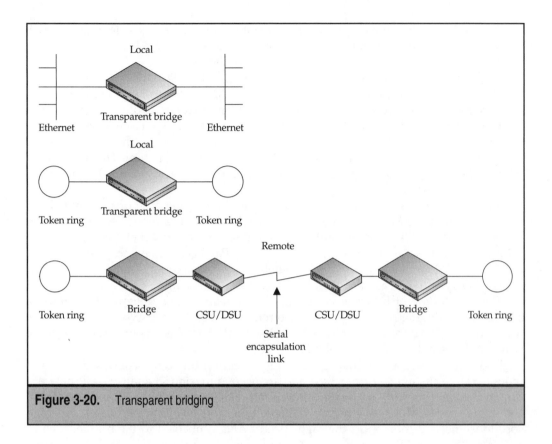

Figure 3-20.   Transparent bridging

Sometimes the bridge needs to send data between dissimilar LANs, such as from an Ethernet LAN to a Token Ring LAN. When operating in translation mode, bridges at both ends of the transmission can use different physical media and link (MAC-level) protocols. Translating bridges thus translate from one media format to another, manipulating the MAC-layer frame structure associated with each media type. Protocols in the network layer and higher must still be compatible.

The following illustration shows an example of translation bridging between dissimilar local Ethernet and Token Ring LANs.

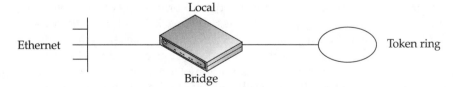

Translation bridges do not provide segmentation services, so the frame sizes of each LAN host must be configured for the same supportable length (usually a maximum of the largest allowable frame size of the limiting LAN technology).

When operating in *encapsulation* mode, bridges at both ends of the transmission must use the same physical and link-layer (MAC-level) LAN protocols, but the transmission network between the bridges can provide a similar or different physical media and MAC-level protocol. Encapsulating bridges provide a network interconnection or extension by placing received frames within a media-specific "envelope" and forwarding the encapsulated frame to another bridge for delivery to the destination. This is common when a Token Ring or FDDI backbone serves multiple Ethernet segments. The backbone protocol then serves as the WAN protocol.

Figure 3-21 shows two examples of encapsulation bridging. The first example illustrates two remote 10-Mbps Ethernet LANs being bridged via a metropolitan 100-Mbps FDDI network. The second example shows the same two Ethernet LANs, this time bridged over a 4- or 16-Mbps Token Ring network. Pay heed when encapsulating large MAC frames into smaller frame sizes. Remember that the maximum frame size for Ethernet is 1,500 bytes, whereas the Token Ring frame size can be up to 17,972 bytes.

The fourth type of bridging is through *source route bridging*. Figure 3-22 shows a source route bridging scheme between two remote Token Ring LANs and three source route bridges. The third Token Ring LAN is used only for transit. Source route bridging will be discussed in detail in Chapter 7.

Bridges are best used in small, geographically concentrated networks, which do not require a large customer address base and are needed to connect a fairly static network design. Bridging speeds vary, supporting subrate DS0 through T1 to T3, and even FDDI and Ethernet 100-Mbps and higher (gigabit Ethernet) bridging speeds. These high speeds are needed to support the high-speed LANs connected to the bridge, such as 10/100/1000-Mbps Ethernet and 4/16-Mbps Token Ring. Bridges provide local, remote, or both local and remote configuration support.

Careful future planning is required when deploying a bridged/switched network solution. The manager or engineer who employs a bridge solution may find that very soon his or her bridge solution will resemble the wood and stone bridge, built in 1850 and designed to accommodate a horse and carriage. Soon, there will be a need to drive not only a car, but also trucks over the bridge, but one year later rather than 150 years later. Thus, bridges can be good solutions for networks utilizing only one protocol and one architecture with no plans to change, or for very static network designs with multiple protocols and architectures that have close local control.

Some major disadvantages are associated with bridging. For example, bridges are susceptible to multicast or broadcast storms. For a packet with an unknown MAC address (one not associated with a port), a bridge floods that packet out all ports except the one on which it was received. Bridges in and of themselves do not create broadcast storms. Such storms occur when there is a bridging loop in the topology. Bridging problems increase with the size of the network and the number of users attached.

To minimize the problem, smart bridging/L2 switching techniques can provide some level of traffic isolation. Some bridges cope with broadcast storms by segmenting the bridged network into domains that restrict broadcast storms to a limited area. This con-

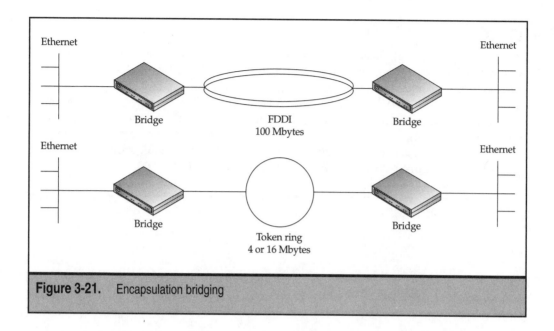

Figure 3-21. Encapsulation bridging

tainment method coupled with a multicast traffic ceiling effectively controls broadcast storms. Bridges are also limited in both address retention and memory. They are designed to retain a limited amount of information and can handle only limited network changes. The more changes occurring in the network, the greater is the traffic passing between routers to update routing tables; thus, an unstable network could occur.

Due to these disadvantages and limited capabilities, bridging should not be used in network designs calling for multiple protocol support, dynamic networks requiring frequent changes, or large networks of greater than 50 nodes. For networks with these requirements, more intelligent and robust devices will provide much of the bridging functionality and additional routing intelligence as well as eliminate the disadvantages of bridging. Enter the switch and router.

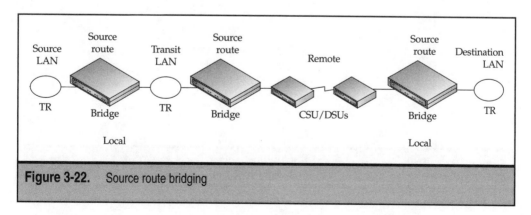

Figure 3-22. Source route bridging

Switches

There are four general classes of switches. *Workgroup* or *local switches* switch traffic within a workgroup, such as between workstations or local LANs. *Enterprise switches* connect multiple departments or workgroups. Both workgroup and enterprise switches are typically 100/1000-Mbps Ethernet or ATM. *Edge switches* serve as access or entry switches to a public data service and can be packet (X.25 or IP), frame (FR, Ethernet, or FDDI) or cell (ATM), or optical SONET/WDM switches. *Service provider backbone (CO) switches* (typically packet, frame, or cell switches) act as high-speed interconnects for edge switches. Figure 3-23 shows these four types of switches.

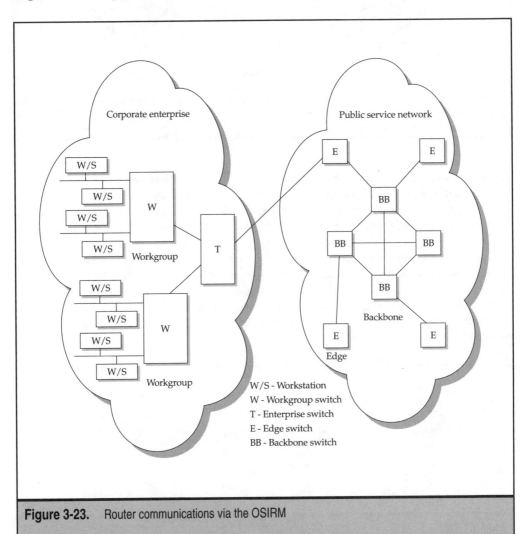

Figure 3-23. Router communications via the OSIRM

Usually, a private switched network is connected to one or more public switched networks. L2 switches are connection-oriented devices. The CPE interfaces to the service provider's switch and communicates the connection request information via a user-to-network interface (UNI) signaling protocol. An interswitch protocol may be used between switches. Networks are interconnected via a more complex network-to-network interface (NNI) signaling protocol. Signaling functions may be emulated by network management protocols where individual cross-connects are made. These switching fundamentals are illustrated in Figure 3-24.

There is much confusion as to which layers of the OSIRM are used when switching. There are basically two types of switches. L2 switches are commonly referred to as LAN switches, and as switch frames typically at the MAC layer (examples include Ethernet, Token Ring, FDDI, and ATM). Hybrid L2 and L3 switches are used when some form of packet, frame, or cell switching is being used, such as when routing IP or accessing FR or ATM services. Sometimes the function of the switch and other devices like routing will merge. For example, there are many backbone sites that place routing within ATM switches, as they can provide a better quality of service through protocol features specific

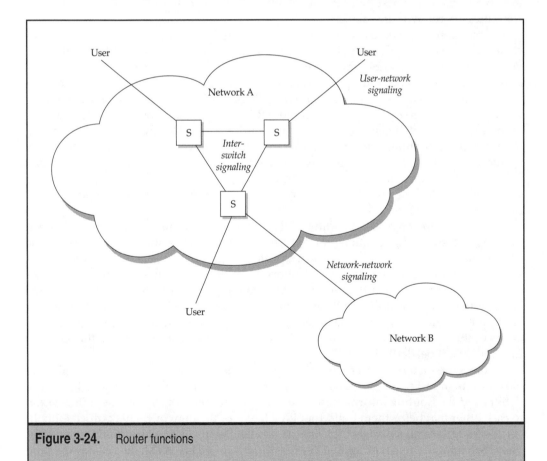

Figure 3-24.   Router functions

to ATM. But nothing is free and there is a trade-off: The virtual circuits (VCs) used in ATM are expensive network resources. With routing that uses quality of service, each router must maintain the state of every other switch in the network. The same is true for ATM switches that include routing and maintain quality of service. More on ATM switching will be covered in later chapters, and switching methods are covered in detail in Chapter 9. As you can see, once you have mastered the basic principles of networking, they will appear again and again—in technologies not yet invented.

Routers

Routers provide interconnectivity between like and unlike devices on LANs and WANs as well as extend the LAN into the metropolitan and wide area networking arena. Routers are protocol sensitive and can either bridge or route a large suite of network-layer and higher-layer protocols. Thus, they support various LAN devices that can employ a variety of networking protocols and addressing schemes. Routers understand the entire network, not just locally connected devices, and will route based on many factors to determine the best path. Routers have formed the core of the next generation of computer internetworking devices.

As mentioned previously, routers have subsumed many of the legacy functions of cluster-controllers-to-FEP-to-mainframe communications. Almost all Internet traffic traverses multiple routers. Routers emerged into the marketplace over the last two decades as the hottest thing since multiplexers [starting with the first-generation routers that appeared at the Massachusetts Institute of Technology (MIT), Stanford University, and Carnegie Mellon University (CMU) in 1983 and ARPANET predecessors three years earlier], with much more intelligence than bridges or multiplexers. Dozens of multiplexer vendors that did not anticipate nor adapt to the routing wave were quickly swept away within a few short years. Routing was a prime example of a technology that dramatically changed the vendor landscape, as evidenced by the rapid rise to fame and fortune of Cisco and Wellfleet (acquired by Bay Networks and later by NorTel Networks) based on routing technology.

Routers use the physical, data-link, and network layers of the OSIRM to provide addressing and switching functionality. Figure 3-25 shows the relation of the router to the OSIRM. Both users may exercise the same protocol stack up to L3. A router's main functionality resides in the data-link- and network-layer protocols, but it also uses the physical layer. Applications at both ends of the transmission do not need to support the same LAN protocol from the IEEE 802.X suite, or protocols up to OSI level 3 within the same architecture, but they do need to have the same protocol from the fourth through seventh layers of the OSIRM (or at least the intelligence at the user end to provide the gateway functionality, if needed).

Routers use their own internetworking protocol suite. Through the use of routing tables, as shown in Figure 3-26, and routing protocols, such as Open Shortest Path First (OSPF) and the Routing Information Protocol (RIP), routers constantly pass information to each other that helps them build topology tables of the network. This artificial intelligence, called *dynamic knowledge*, allows them to be globally aware of the entire network. They then interface to L1, L2, or L3 WAN services like PL, FR, ATM, or IP. These routing

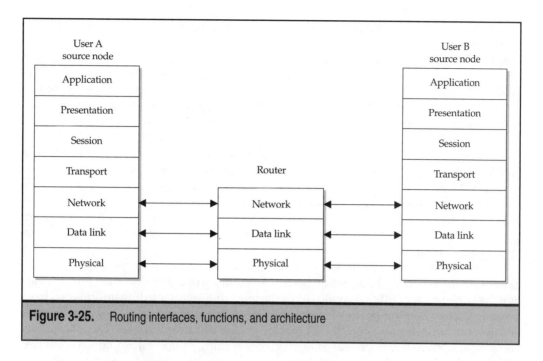

Figure 3-25.   Routing interfaces, functions, and architecture

protocols can discover network topology changes and provide rerouting based upon dynamically populated routing tables. For example, in OSPF each router keeps a map of the entire network. When changes in the network happen, only the change is propagated to other routers, versus RIP where the entire routing table is propagated.

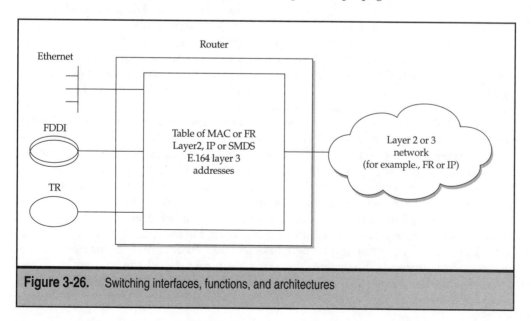

Figure 3-26.   Switching interfaces, functions, and architectures

Routers can limit the number of hop counts by their intelligent routing protocols. Hop count limits are determined by the routing protocols and the general protocol itself. For example, Internetwork Packet Exchange (IPX) RIP has a hop limit of 16, as defined in the IPX standard. IP has a hop limit of 255, as determined by the max value of the Time to Live (TTL) field. With the TCP/IP suite, different protocols have different values. RIPv1 is 15 hops, as defined in the standard. (E)IGRP is by default 100, but can be increased to 255. Again, the IP TTL limits itself. OSPF has no hop count limit per se, but an IP packet cannot "live" beyond 255 hops, as defined in RFC 1812, and thus in the TCP/IP suite itself.

Routers employ large addressing schemes, typically up to 4 bytes worth of addresses in a logical network [or more with Novell IPX or the OSI Connectionless Network Layer Protocol (CLNP)]. Routers also support large packet sizes in the many thousands of bytes. Internal bus speeds are also much higher, typically in excess of a gigabit per second. The other major advantage of routers is their capability to perform these functions primarily through the use of software, which makes future revisions and support for upgrades much easier.

Routers use routing protocols to route packets from node to node based on the packet-defined protocol information used by the routing protocols. Routing protocols are not the only means of placing routes into a routing table, or forwarding information base, as some call it. Routing protocols in and of themselves do not route. They are but one means of "path determination" (other means include static routes, directly connected interfaces, and the redistribution of routes between routing protocols). Routers route (or, as some say, forward) packets based on the routing/forwarding table. But routing protocols themselves are not part of this forwarding process. This information typically includes least-cost routing, minimum delay, minimum distance, and least-congestion conditions, depending upon the protocol and its support for features. Type of service (TOS) has never been implemented in TCP/IP OSPF, for example, because the Internet Engineering Task Force (IETF) could never figure out what it was they wanted to accomplish. Hence, the TOS bit is seldom used. Now with RSVP and QoS, particularly in conjunction with Voice over IP (VoIP), the TOS bits can and are manipulated and used.

Least-cost routing is an interesting term, which is usually seen used in conjunction with Private Branch Exchange (PBX) functionality for voice calls. How does this term work in a data network where the transmission cost is fixed? Multiprotocol routers can provide support for multiple protocols simultaneously.

Figure 3-27 illustrates the range of interfaces and the scope of routing. Physical or virtual circuits often connect routers. Routers have very sophisticated software, and are now being delivered with special-purpose firmware and hardware to increase packet-routing throughput. Current routers can forward in excess of 40,000,000 IP packets per second.

Routers automatically discover the addresses of devices connected to each router in an *internetwork*. They use an interior routing protocol (within their internetwork) and connect from their internetwork to outside networks using an exterior routing protocol. Static routing where the router is manually configured is also possible and not uncommon. Indeed, even the naming of networks as subnetworks of a larger network has proven to be a very scalable concept. Notice that the term network can be anything from a piece of cable that forms a LAN segment to many devices internetworked across a large geographic area that are managed by a single system and share a common addressing

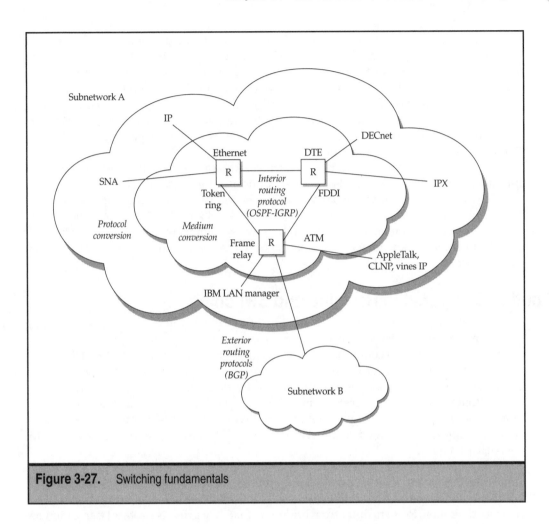

Figure 3-27.   Switching fundamentals

scheme. Packets are routed based upon the destination address, sometimes using the source address as well, or even an end-to-end route specification. Routers connect dissimilar protocols by way of routing and data protocol conversion. Routers can also handle both connection-oriented and connectionless network services, and can interconnect dissimilar media via media conversion.

Routing protocols continually monitor the state of the links that interconnect routers in an internetwork or the links with other networks through a variety of routing protocols. These protocols include RIP, OSPF, and Cisco's proprietary Enhanced Interior Gateway Routing Protocol (EIGRP) within their internetwork, as well as the Border Gateway Protocol (BGP) routing protocol, which is used to connect to other networks or the public Internet. Each of these routing protocols is covered in detail later. Through these protocols, routers can discover network topology changes and provide dynamic rerouting around link and node failures.

As access devices, routers accept multiple protocols and either route them to another local port on the router or convert them to a WAN protocol, such as IP, for transfer over a WAN link. When doing so, the router encapsulates, for example, IP traffic into FR frames, or ATM cells across a Layer 1 channel (such as a DS1) for transmission to or across a public network service. Routers can also switch WAN transport protocols between in-terface ports, such as switching frames or cells. When routers send data over a WAN using FR, SMDS, or ATM, they may need to look inside a sequence of frames, packets, or cells in order to perform the routing function.

Three prime examples of routers with these capabilities are the Cisco 7600 series Internet router, Nortel Network's Backbone Concentrator Node (BCN) router, and Juniper Networks' M-series Internet backbone routers. Many routers today support ATM interface and trunk cards, along with some form of ATM switching and LAN emulation. Routers typically are manageable through network management protocols such as IP and the Common Management Information Services/Common Management Information Protocol (CMIS/CMIP).

Routing Compared to Bridging and Switching

A great sage once wrote, "Route when you can, bridge when you must." Although routing is much more complex, it is also more feature-rich and has many advantages over bridging. Routers provide a level of congestion control not present in bridges, thus enabling the router to *dynamically* reroute traffic over, for example, the least cost path (where the cost metric can be the shortest path, the least cost ($) path, the lowest delay route, or a variety of other variables). Routers reduce broadcast storm danger by providing a segmentation capability within the network; that is, they do not forward broadcasts across segments, other than in certain specifically designated circumstances [such as Dynamic Host Configuration Protocol (DHCP) requests].

Thus, the network designer can build a hierarchical addressing scheme and design smart routing tables, which operate somewhat similarly to the filtering capabilities of bridges, but with the additional flexibility to define virtual network subsets within a larger network definition. Routers differ from bridges in that they provide protocol translation between users at the link level, while bridges just pass information in a store-and-forward mode between devices of similar protocol structures. Additionally, routers are required to access the public Internet, unless you are using a DSL L2 (usually ATM) access service where the service providers have the router that accesses the Internet, versus having the router on your customer's premise. Greater detail will be forthcoming when we discuss router access network design.

Routers that utilize IP routing schemes can solve packet-fragmentation problems caused by technologies such as X.25 and FDDI. Packet fragmentation is necessary whenever two media types with different sized packets are used. Routers have the capability to translate between MAC layers. Unlike bridges, routers can be isolated and routed around when network problems exist. Routers contain a level of investment protection over less intelligent (yet faster) switching and bridging devices.

However, there are also a few disadvantages to routers. Routing algorithms, discussed in great detail later, typically require more system memory resources than bridges and L2 switches and can be more complex to design and manage. Modern routing algorithms and implementations (IS-IS, OSPF, EIGRP, and BGP) are comparable to bridging in the amount of bandwidth overhead. This is because of the additional intelligence needed in the routing protocols and the various congestion-control techniques implemented.

Many router vendors have implemented multiple processors as well as faster platforms and processors [such as Reduced Instruction Set Computer (RISC) processor technology] to eliminate throughput problems caused by increased traffic loads of routing protocols. Table 3-1 shows a comparison of bridge and router uses and capabilities. Note that we use the term bridging and L2 switching interchangeably.

It is a good idea to *bridge/switch* when you need less overhead, have the same LAN media type across the entire network, have a small centralized LAN with a simple topology, or need to transport protocols that cannot be routed, such as the Network Basic Input Output System (NetBIOS) and the Compaq (formerly Digital Equipment Corporation) Local Area Transport (LAT). Spanning trees enable responses to topology changes, but they are slower than modern routing protocols.

Routing should be performed when you want to route traffic based upon network parameters like the least-cost route, have multiple MAC protocol environments, have large, dynamic networks with complex topologies, want dynamic routing around failed links over paths that run in parallel, or have network and subnetwork addressing requirements.

At present, Cisco still holds the largest share (over half) of the router market. In fact, most of the routers on the Internet backbone are Cisco. Every major router vendor supports bridging and routing capabilities. The prices of routers have dropped significantly,

Functionality	Bridging/Switching	Routing
Data sources	One source and destination	Multiple sources and destinations
Network addressing	No (MAC addressing is L2)	Yes (IP addressing)
Packet handling	Pass packet transparently	Interpret packet
Forward packets	Out all ports (except port on which packet received)	Out specific port to destination
Global network intelligence	Local only	Knows status of all devices
Priority schemes	Some (L2)	Yes
Security	Poor, based on isolating LAN segments or MAC filtering	Good, based on routing protocol combined with filtering or IP Security (IPSec)

Table 3-1.   Bridging to Routing Comparison

and many providers offer low-end remote access products that have a subset of protocol and memory resources from their larger counterparts. In fact, low-end SOHO routers can be purchased for a few hundred dollars or less today (and many at that cost with built-in firewalls and multi-port switching).

Many bridging and routing functions have been built into workstations, PCs, and servers. Although this offers the cost and management advantages of using only a single device, users should be aware of product support, scale, upgrade, and manageability limitations. Choose the right device that will grow with your network. Purchase a device that can support both routing and switching—you may not need routing today, but as your network grows you can upgrade without having to replace the device. It may be less expensive in the long run to purchase a router with a port expansion, rather than taking the network down and installing a larger or more feature-rich router later. Port sizing and traffic growth patterns will typically dictate the size of the switch and router.

Brouters

The term *brouter* is a conflated word formed by *bridge* and *router*. Brouters perform the functions of both bridges and routers; that is, they have the capability to route some protocols and bridge others. Some protocols need to be bridged (such as LAT and NetBIOS) rather than routed. Brouters were developed from the need to expand single-port bridges to multiple ports to support IBM's source route bridging and source route transparent bridging algorithms. The routing done by brouters is transparent to both the network-layer protocols and end stations, and is accomplished in the MAC address. Thus, brouters do not look at the network-level address. Rather, they route based on the MAC header. Router logical functionality is similar to that of bridges and routers, as shown in previous figures. The term brouter is rarely used anymore, and the more common form is in remote access routers that only require a subset of bridging and routing.

Gateways

Gateways provide all of the interconnectivity provided by routers and bridges, but in addition they furnish connectivity and conversion between the seven layers of the OSIRM as well as other proprietary protocols. Gateways can be performed in hardware, software, or both. Some applications use priority schemes not consistent between the OSI layers and proprietary protocol structures. Gateways are often application specific and, because of their complex protocol conversions, are often slower than bridges, switches, and routers.

One example of a gateway function is interfacing a device using SNA with a device using the OSI protocol stack. The gateway will convert from SNA to an OSI protocol structure (as well as the reverse conversion from OSI to SNA). Thus, the gateway's main functionality resides in its role of protocol translator for architectures such as SNA, IPX, TCP/IP, and OSI. It can also translate between IEEE 802.X architectures such as Ethernet to Token Ring LANs and vice versa. If protocol functionality is needed in excess of that found in routers, then the gateway is the device of choice. Gateways can reside within workstations, servers, minicomputers, or mainframes, and are considerably more expensive than routers. Some routers have limited built-in gateway functionality. Figure 3-28 portrays the same two users as the

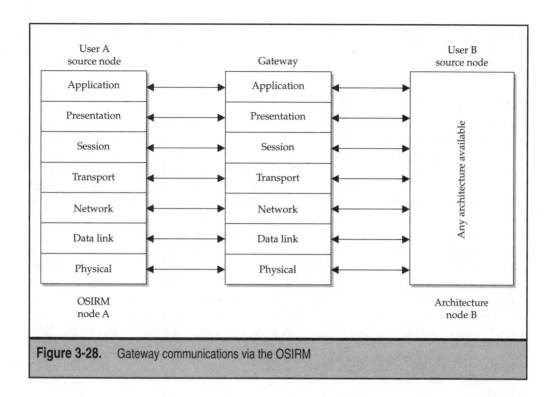

Figure 3-28.   Gateway communications via the OSIRM

last example, this time connected via a gateway. This figure also shows the relationship of gateways to the OSIRM. Both users may have different protocol stacks in any of the seven levels with both OSI and non-OSI protocol architectures.

There are three major disadvantages of gateways: low throughput during peak traffic conditions, user-to-gateway priority handling, and store-and-forward characteristics. During periods of peak traffic, a gateway may become the network's main congestion point, having to spend the majority of its time translating between many protocol suites. Gateways are often store-and-forward devices, forwarding only the information requested by the destination node. In spite of these drawbacks, and the high expense of gateways, there is a growing need for their functionality. Gateways will fill an important niche for many years to come in uniting disparate protocols. One key example is a voice gateway that acts as the intermediary node connecting a voice call between a packetized voice user (from an IP network) and a circuit-switched voice user [from the Public Switched Telephone Network (PSTN) network].

From Bridges to Routers to Hubs

Since the last edition of this book, routers and intelligent L2/L3 switches have predominated most major data internetworks. Bridge networks, on all but large SNA shops, have vanished in lieu of homogeneous router- and switch-based networks served by 100/1000-Mbps Ethernet switches. Switches are playing a key role in this shift because they aggregate many LAN segments much more cost-effectively and they provide greater flexibility. This change is pushing the routing function further toward the WAN. This is an important trend to understand. We discuss this trend in more detail in Chapter 7.

Private Branch eXchange (PBX)

For years, the PBX has been the key device that has separated the voice and data worlds. With the advent of ATM and IP technology, users, vendors, and service providers are adopting both ATM and IP switching approaches to PBXs. PBXs provide an automatic setup of circuits between telephone sets today, which most current ATM and IP switches do not plan to do. Traditional PBX call processing and call control are slowly being built into ATM and IP switching architectures. The PBX vendors do not see this happening; in fact, they see the opposite: ATM and IP-ready PBX products replacing ATM and IP LAN switches. One likely scenario will be a coexistence of ATM and IP-ready PBXs and ATM and IP switches with call-processing and control capabilities in both the campus and wide area. ATM and IP interfaces are now available for PBXs. One example is the Sphere Communications' Sphericall 3.x ATM Telephony System and 3Com's SuperStack 3 NBX Networked Telephony solution. The more probable scenario is that high-end ATM and IP network modules with front-end PBXs to the WAN as well as the feature-rich, call-processing software in the PBX will continue to handle the traditional voice traffic requirements.

REVIEW

In data communications, various topologies, circuit types, transmissions, and hardware types have evolved. The main topologies include point-to-point, multipoint, star, ring, and mesh. The three types of signal transfer are simplex, half-duplex, and duplex, as well as asynchronous and synchronous data transfers. The chapter concluded with a detailed discussion of each major type of network communications hardware and some L2 and L3 switching devices, such as bridges, switches, routers, and gateways, leaving a detailed discussion of multiplexers and switches to the next chapter.

PART II

Physical Layer Technologies

CHAPTER 4

Multiplexing and Switching Technologies: An Overview

This chapter provides an overview of multiplexer and switching technologies. Multiplexing takes many forms and makes up the core of many advanced data networks and services. We first cover multiplexing techniques based on space division, frequency division, time division, and addressing. We then review the major types of multiplexers used in voice and data communications networks and assist you with proper selection of these devices. We then turn our discussion to the plesiochronous digital transmission developed for the economic transmission of voice. Next, point-to-point, point-to-multipoint, space division, time division, address, and frequency or wavelength switching are covered, along with the hybrid matrix switch. Each section also reviews each specific type of switch. Next, we cover circuit switching and its implementation in digital cross-connect (DXC) devices. Finally, the origins and genealogy of packet switching are covered, focusing on the progressive introduction and definition of X.25, IP, frame relay (FR), Asynchronous Transfer Mode (ATM), and optical switching and network services. X.25, IP, FR, and ATM are discussed in detail in subsequent chapters. This chapter serves as the reference point for comparing multiplexing and switching technologies.

MULTIPLEXING TECHNOLOGIES

There is a close relationship between multiplexing and switching. Multiplexing defines the means by which multiple streams of information from multiple users share a common physical transmission medium, all of which might require some or all of the common yet shared bandwidth at any given time. This bandwidth sharing on the access reduces access costs for a user to get to the network, whether it is a dedicated digital network comprising private lines, a switched access service, or a genuine switched network service. Some multiplexing techniques assign fixed bandwidth to each user, while others use statistical multiplexing methods that make more efficient use of the transmission facilities that interface to the network. Multiplexing positions can be defined by space, time, frequency, or address.

This section defines multiplexing, summarizes multiplexing techniques, and discusses multiplexing methods.

Multiplexer Defined

A *multiplexer* is essentially a very simple switch composed of a multiplexing function and a demultiplexing function, as illustrated in Figure 4-1. The multiplexing function shares and combines many inputs to a single output. The demultiplexing function has one input, which must be distributed to many outputs. The multiplexing and demultiplexing functions can be implemented by any of the generic switching functions described in the previous section. Usually, a method from the same class is used for both the multiplexing and demultiplexing functions so that the multiplexing method used on each of the interfaces is symmetric in each direction. In most multiplexers, the overall speed or capacity on each access side interface is generally less than that on the trunk side. For example, the

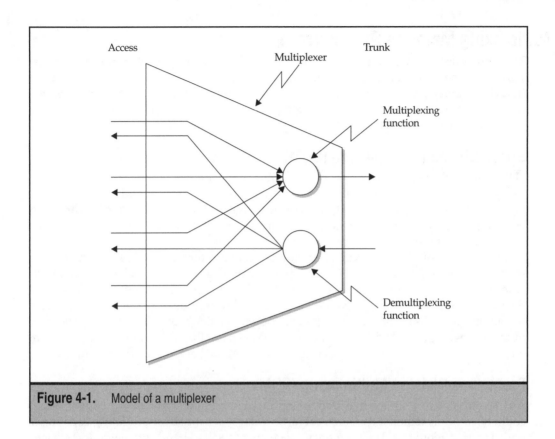

Figure 4-1.   Model of a multiplexer

speed or capacity often corresponds to different levels in the time division multiplexing (TDM) hierarchy, an example that we cover in some detail later in this chapter in the section "Digital TDM and the Digital Hierarchy."

The geometric symbol with the small end on the side of the single output (called the trunk side) and the large end on the side with multiple interfaces (called the access side) frequently denotes a multiplexer in block diagrams. It graphically illustrates the many-to-one relationship from the large side to the small side, and the one-to-many relationship from the small side to the large side.

Multiplexing techniques can be used to share a physical medium between multiple users at two sites over a private line, with each pair of users requiring some or all of the bandwidth at any given time. Some multiplexing techniques statistically assign fixed bandwidth to each user. Other multiplexing methods statistically assign bandwidth to users based on demand to make more efficient use of the transmission facilities that interface to the network. TDM is often used to reduce the effective cost of a private access line or international private line by combining multiple lower-speed users over a single, more economical higher-speed facility.

Multiplexing Methods Summarized

There are four basic multiplexing methods covered: space, frequency, time, and address. This is also the historical order in which these developed in data communications. Space, frequency, and time multiplexing all occur at the physical layer of the OSI reference model. Address switching occurs at higher layers, typically Layer 2 (for example, FR, ATM) and Layer 3 (for example, IP) of the OSI reference model.

Space Division Multiplexing (SDM)

SDM essentially reduces to the concept of cable management. Mechanical patch panels can facilitate this type of switching, or more appropriately, optical and electronic patch panels can perform the switching. To a large extent, SDM is falling out of favor and is being replaced by space division switching, discussed later in this chapter in the section "Switching Techniques," or other types of multiplexing.

An example of SDM is seen where multiple cables interconnect equipment. In other words, *space division* means physically separate cables. The original telephone network, where a pair of wires connected everyone who wished to communicate, is an example of the first use of SDM. The exclusive use of SDM quickly became impractical, as evidenced by old photographs of the sky of major metropolitan cities being blackened by the large number of wire pairs. Another example of SDM is from the early data communications era, where a separate cable was run from every terminal back to the main computer.

Frequency Division Multiplexing (FDM)

As transmission technology matured, it was discovered that many analog conversations could be multiplexed onto the same cable, or radio spectrum, by modulating each signal with a carrier frequency. The frequency spectrum of the baseband signal was then placed in separate frequency bands. This yielded a marked increase in efficiency and worked reasonably well for analog signals. The technology comprised analog electronics, and suffered problems of noise, distortion, and interference between channels that complicated data communications. Support costs were high.

FDM was widely used as an analog method of aggregating multiple voice channels into larger circuit groups for high-speed transport. FDM multiplexes 12 voice-grade, full-duplex channels into a single 48-kHz bandwidth group by translating each voice band signal's carrier frequency. These groups are then further multiplexed into a master group comprising 24 groups. Multiple master-group analog voice signals were then transmitted over analog systems. A lower-frequency analog microwave spectrum was used to frequency division multiplex a DS1 digital data stream in a technique called data under voice (DUV). Figure 4-2 shows an example of a frequency division multiplexer servicing ten 2400-bps user data channels and providing a single 56-Kbps network trunk.

One variation of FDM is wavelength division multiplexing (WDM). WDM on optical fibers is very analogous to FDM in coaxial cable and microwave systems. Optical fiber is *transparent* in two windows centered on wavelengths of 1300 and 1550 nanometers or nm

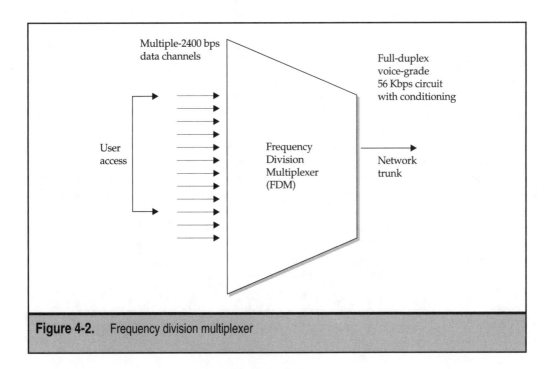

Figure 4-2.   Frequency division multiplexer

(10^{-9} meters), as shown in the plot of loss versus wavelength in Figure 4-3. The total bandwidth in these two windows exceeds 30,000 GHz. Here we see that one bps per hertz would result in a bandwidth of over 30 *trillion* bps per fiber!

The carrier frequency at the center of the 1300-nm window is 180 GHz and it is 125 GHz in the 1550-nm window. The sharp attenuation at 1400 nm is due to residual amounts of water (an OH radical) still present in the glass. Continuing improvements in optical-fiber manufacturing will likely make even more optical bandwidth accessible in the future. Systems currently exist that support 160 wavelengths per fiber, and the upper limit has yet to be reached. A new version of WDM called dense wavelength division multiplexing (DWDM) has moved to the forefront and is fundamentally different from WDM in only one area. DWDM spaces the wavelengths closer than WDM and therefore has a greater overall capacity than WDM. Both WDM and DWDM are discussed in more detail in Chapter 5.

Time Division Multiplexing (TDM)

TDM was originally developed in the public telephone network in the 1950s to eliminate FDM filtering and noise problems when many signals were multiplexed onto the same transmission medium. Later, there was a need to increase the multiplexing efficiency in crowded bundles of cables in large cities. This technique made use of emerging solid

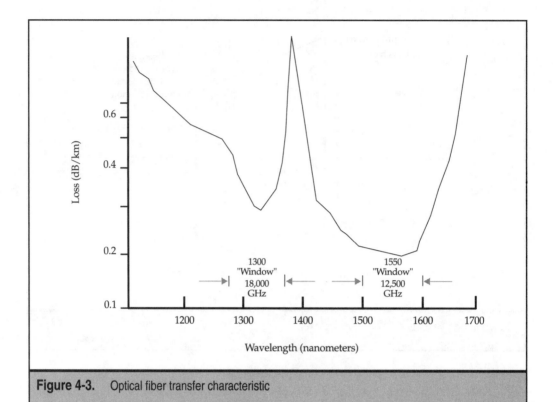

Figure 4-3.   Optical fiber transfer characteristic

state electronics, and was entirely digital. Analog information was first converted to digital information prior to transmission. The initial cost of this technique was high, but was less than the cost of replacing existing cables or digging larger tunnels. In the early 1980s, TDM networks using smart multiplexers began to appear in some private data networks, forming the primary method to share costly data-transmission facilities among multiple users.

In the last decade, TDM has matured and become the prevalent multiplexing method in most modern telecommunication networks. It is now taken for granted that every voice conversation is converted to digital data, transmitted an arbitrary distance, and then converted back to an audible signal. The consequence is that the quality of a voice call carried by digital TDM is now essentially very high and independent of distance. Data communications is more sensitive than digitized voice, but has reaped tremendous benefits from the deployment of TDM infrastructure in public networks. In theory, a TDM can also be applied to analog signals; however, this application was never widely used.

TDM allows multiple users to share a digital transmission medium by using preallocated time slots. Figure 4-4 shows a standard time division multiplexer with eight low-speed users sharing a single high-speed transmission line to a remote multiplexer. TDM assigns a specific time slot to each low-speed channel, in this case, slots one through eight.

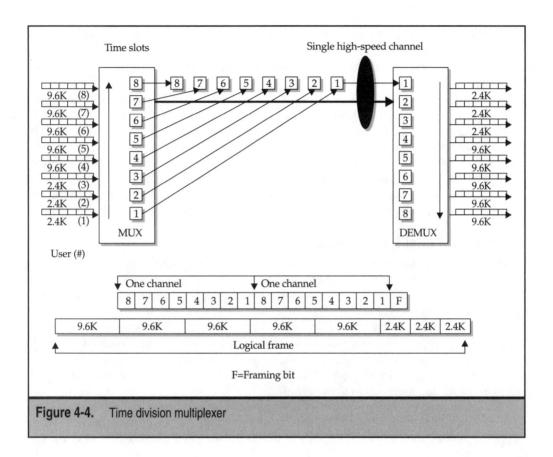

Figure 4-4.   Time division multiplexer

These eight synchronous time slots are then aggregated to form a single high-speed synchronous channel. In this example, five users are accessing the network with 9600-bps synchronous data circuits and three are 2400-bps low-speed users.

One channel contains eight time slots, which are preallocated and occupy a predetermined bit layout of the combined transmitted signal. Time slots are dedicated to a single user, whether data is being transmitted or the user is idle. The same time slots are dedicated to the same user in the same order for every frame transmitted. Thus, time slot 2 will always be dedicated to the same user, regardless of whether or not other users are transmitting data. Different time slots can be dedicated to different channel sources, such as voice channels, data, or video. Typically, multiplexer inputs simultaneously carry asynchronous and synchronous data, digitized voice, and even video. After the aggregate T1 or DS3 signal is transmitted across the network, it is received at the destination multiplexer node. Each channel is then demultiplexed at the receiving node. All transmissions between multiplexers are point-to-point.

A single T1 circuit can be configured for 24 to 196 allocated channels. The standard T1 1.544 Mbps data channel contains 8000 frames per second. Each frame is transmitted every 125 µs for a total of 24 multiplexed voice grade channels. Each frame contains eight bits for each of the 24 channels (8×24 = 192), plus one framing bit for a total of 193 bits per frame. Each channel uses 64,000 bps. The total T1 transmission can be seen in Figure 4-5, along with the frame format.

International circuits often use the CCITT E1 Conference on European Post and Telegraph (CEPT) standard, which supports a data transmission rate of 2.048 Mbps. Each E1 data channel contains frames with 30 or 32 multiplexed voice-grade channels. This allows 1.920M bps for voice channels and 128 Kbps for framing and synchronization. Multiplexers often use the DSX-1 standard for a physical interface with D4/ESF framing, while the CEPT/G.703 physical interface standard is commonly used for the E1 interface. For a user requiring access speeds from DS0 to T1 access, the cost breakeven point based on tariff structures is typically five to seven DS0s before going to a 24-channel T1 is cost-justified.

Address or Label Multiplexing

Address, or label, multiplexing was first invented in the era of poor-quality FDM analog transmission. A more common name for address multiplexing is asynchronous time division multiplexing (ATDM). Transmission was expensive, and there was a need to share it among many data users. Each "packet" of information was prefixed by an address that each node interpreted. Each node decided whether the packet was received correctly, and if not, arranged to have it resent by the prior node until it was received correctly. SNA, DECNET, and X.25 are early examples of address multiplexing and switching. More recent examples are FR and ATM. The remainder of this book covers various address multiplexing methods in great detail.

A widely used example of address multiplexing is found in statistical multiplexers. Statistical multiplexing, also called statistical time division multiplexing (STDM) or ATDM, operates similarly to TDM, except that it dynamically assigns time slots only to

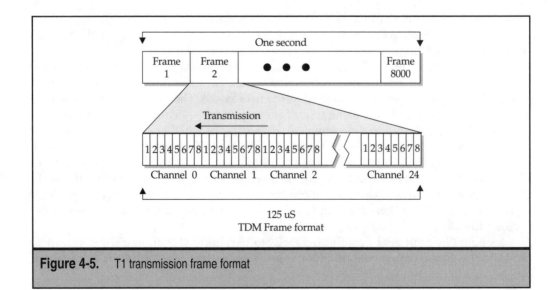

Figure 4-5. T1 transmission frame format

users who need data transmission. Efficiencies of up to 4:1 are gained for voice transmission by using available time slots rather than wasting them on users who are not speaking. Higher or lower statistical multiplex gains can be obtained for data traffic depending on the burstiness (peak-to-average statistics) of the data traffic. For example, aggregating multiple extremely bursty LAN traffic streams can achieve a very high rate of statistical multiplexing. The net effect is an increase in overall throughput for users since time slots are not "reserved" or dedicated to individual users—thus dynamic allocation of bandwidth achieves higher effective throughput. Figure 4-6 shows a statistical multiplexer that takes multiple low-speed synchronous (could also be asynchronous) user inputs for aggregation into a single 56-Kbps synchronous bit stream for transmission. The methods used to multiplex the various channels include bit-, character-, block-, and message-oriented multiplexing, each requiring buffering and more overhead and intelligence than basic TDM.

Figure 4-6 shows an excerpt from a statistical multiplexed data stream. In a statistical multiplexer, the output bandwidth is a 1:N output-to-input ratio less than the aggregate input bandwidth. This is done on purpose, assuming that not all input channels will be transmitting at the same time when each channel is sampled for transmission. Thus, the output synchronous data stream allocates bandwidth only to users who require it, and does not waste time slots by dedicating bandwidth to users who do not require it. Note in the example that channels 1, 2, 3, 4, and 6 are transmitting, and together use the 128-Kbps trunk bandwidth. Using the same example, if channel 5 were to also transmit data at the same instant, the total transmission requirements would exceed the available circuit transmission speed out of the multiplexer, and buffers would begin to store the information until space on the transmission circuit could become available.

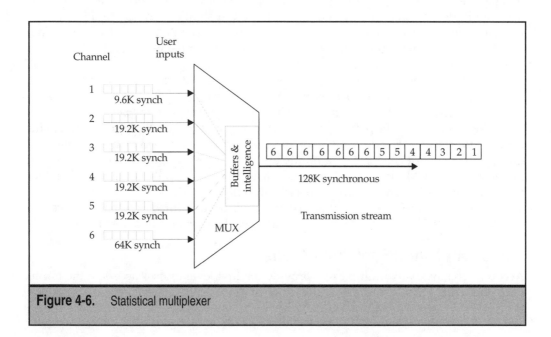

Figure 4-6.   Statistical multiplexer

One type of block-oriented multiplexer is the concentrator. Concentrators transmit blocks of information for each user as needed, adding an address to each block to identify the user and, in most instances, providing store-and-forward capabilities. This mode of transmission is similar to asynchronous block transmission, and multiplexers using this technique are called asynchronous time division multiplexers (ATDMs). This form of statistical multiplexing is similar to packet switching but operates over a single dedicated circuit between two points, as opposed to packet switching, which has multiple paths and destinations. The primary difference between concentration and multiplexing is that concentrators have additional intelligence to understand the contents of the data being passed and can route the information streams based on the data within them. A study of ATDM will be made when we study ATM in Chapter 9.

Another type of statistical multiplexing is statistical packet multiplexing (SPM). Statistical packet multiplexers combine the packet switching of X.25 and IP with the statistical multiplexing of STDM. SPM operates similarly to STDM in that it still cannot effectively transmit delay-sensitive information such as voice and video. There is still the overhead delay of guaranteed delivery of packets, but efficiencies are gained in dynamic bandwidth allocation and sharing by assigning active bandwidth to the channels that need bandwidth at any given time. Each multiplexer groups the user data into packets passed through the network, multiplexer to multiplexer, similar to packet switching.

Types of Multiplexers

Multiplexing is the process of aggregating multiple low-speed channels into a single high-data-rate channel. There are four major types of multiplexers used in data network designs: the access multiplexer (or channel bank), the network multiplexer, the drop-and-insert multiplexer, and the aggregator multiplexer. Capabilities and benefits of each type will be discussed. These multiplexers often contain the capability for demultiplexing. Demultiplexing is the segmenting of a single high-rate channel into multiple low-speed channels. This is also called "inverse multiplexing."

Most forms of multiplexing are protocol-transparent and protocol-independent. The user interface for multiplexing is typically at the physical layer and, with the exception of address multiplexing, all Layer 2 through Layer 7 protocols pass transparently to the network. Figure 4-7 shows the protocol stack operation of a typical multiplexer network. This provides for fast end-to-end transmission times since there is no need to interpret the data during transport. All channels on a multiplexer are either configured to take up certain time slots in the TDM channel or dynamically allocated to the available bandwidth. Either way, the bandwidth between the source and destination node is a "fixed" transmission speed. Any changes to the bandwidth allocation must be performed to both the source and destination nodes. We will see later how FR and ATM eliminates these restrictions.

Access or Channel Bank Multiplexers

Access or channel bank multiplexers provide the first level of user access to the multiplexer network. These devices typically reside on the user or customer premises and are

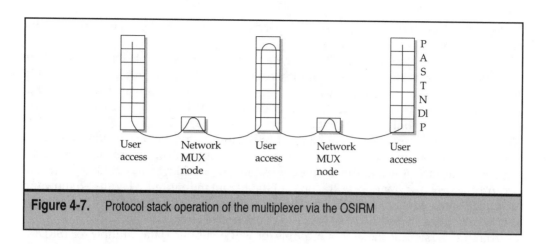

Figure 4-7.   Protocol stack operation of the multiplexer via the OSIRM

referred to as customer premises equipment (CPE) devices. These CPE devices are locally controlled and configured. Intelligent T1 access multiplexers are often used to combine voice and data signals into one high-speed data channel. These multiplexers can provide network access for a variety of user asynchronous and synchronous, low- and high-speed input devices and applications, including the following:

▼ Terminal

■ Data telephone

■ Front-end processor (FEP)

■ Personal computer

■ Host computer

■ Remote peripheral

■ Analog and digital Private Branch Exchange (PBX)

■ Transaction-oriented device

■ Local area network (LAN) transport

■ Imaging applications

■ Low-speed video transport

▲ Compressed voice and video transport

Access multiplexers usually provide one or more low-speed trunks to the next class of larger multiplexers, the backbone multiplexer. Access multiplexers are less expensive and less growth-oriented. They are best suited for static networks where there is little change, rather than dynamic networks where changes in network access are common. Access multiplexers can handle many of the circuit-switched interfaces (for example, FR,

ATM, X.25, SDLC/HDLC). The interface speeds of access multiplexers will vary and include DS0, fractional T1, DS1, and E1.

Two versions of the access multiplexer warrant further discussion. One version of the access multiplexer is the fractional T1 multiplexer. This multiplexer provides the capability for access speeds in fractions of a full T1. Fractional T1 (FT1) is a private line service that provides a capacity of one to 23 DS0 individual circuits in 56-Kbps or 64-Kbps increments. Some commonly used FT1 speeds include 56, 64, 128, 256, 384, 512, 768, and 1024 Kbps. Users who implement clear-channel B8ZS line coding can use contiguous bandwidth. Thus, the user accessing the fractional T1 multiplexer incurs only the cost of the bandwidth used. FT1 was one of the first steps toward providing bandwidth on demand, because the user pays for only a "fraction" of the T1, not the entire T1. Figure 4-8 shows an example of an access Fractional T1 multiplexer, with multiple fractions of T1 speeds for user access into a shared-T1 1.544 Mbps network access circuit.

Another version of the access multiplexer is the subrate data multiplexer (SRDM) shown in Figure 4-9. SRDMs provide multiplexing at the sub-DS0 level, aggregating multiple low-speed channels into a single DS0 channel. SRDM access speeds include 2400, 4800, 9600, and 19,200 bps. Again, the user accessing the SRDM multiplexer incurs only the cost of the bandwidth used. When we discuss FR access, a form of SRDM is used called the FR access device (FRAD). Both FT1 and SRDM optimize the use of access trunks for multiple low-speed users who, without these devices, would have to purchase a full DS0 or DS1 service even though they are using only a portion of its full bandwidth.

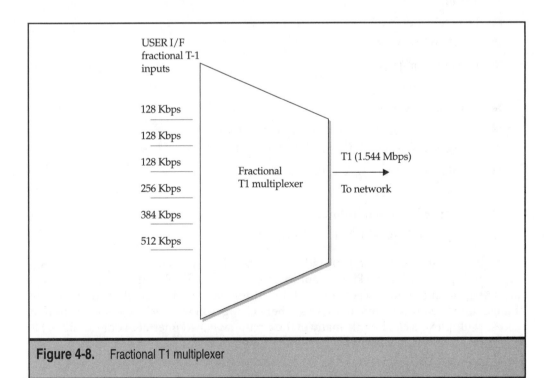

Figure 4-8.   Fractional T1 multiplexer

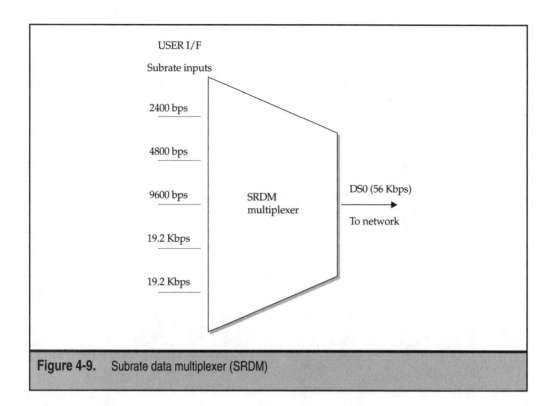

USER I/F

Subrate inputs

2400 bps

4800 bps

9600 bps   SRDM
                        multiplexer

19.2 Kbps

19.2 Kbps

DS0 (56 Kbps)

To network

Figure 4-9.   Subrate data multiplexer (SRDM)

Network Multiplexers

Network multiplexers accept the input data rates (and usually those much higher as well) of access multiplexers, typically supporting T1 on the access side and T3 or higher optical interfaces (OC-*x*) on the network side. Their trunk capacity is also much larger than access multiplexers, ranging from a dozen user trunks to hundreds of electrical or optical trunks, and supporting many more network trunks at higher speeds. Network multiplexers provide the additional functionality of network-management systems, have local and remote provisioning and configuration capability, and contain intelligent functions not found in less-expensive access multiplexers. Private and public data transport network backbones are built using network multiplexers. Network multiplexers also better position the backbone portion of the network for port growth and rapid expansion (that is, increased access and backbone circuit capacity).

Dynamic reroute capability is an important feature in network multiplexers. The multiplexer dynamic reroute capability can either be performed by predefined "routing tables" residing in software at each node or downloaded from the network management center, or through "routing algorithms," which update the network dynamically during changing network conditions. Algorithm control can also reside at either the individual nodes or at the centralized network-management center. Either way, it is important to fully understand these capabilities before deciding on a multiplexer vendor. Figure 4-10 shows an example of a network multiplexer and various multiplexer input possibilities.

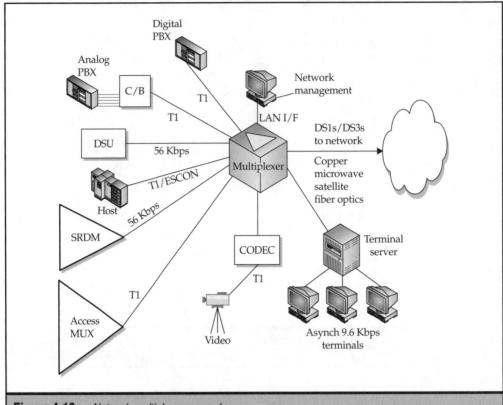

Figure 4-10. Network multiplexer example

Aggregator Multiplexers

Aggregator multiplexers combine multiple T1 channels into higher-bandwidth pipes for transmission. These multiplexers are also sometimes called hubs (not to be confused with LAN hubs). Aggregator multiplexers are labeled based on their aggregation and deaggregation rates. These labels include the following:

▼ **M12** Aggregates four DS1s to the rate of DS2 (or vice versa demultiplex)

■ **M13** Aggregates 28 DS1s to the rate of DS3 (or demultiplex). This is shown in Figure 4-11.

■ **M23** Aggregates seven DS2s to the rate of DS3 (or vice versa demultiplex)

■ **M22 and M44** Provides configuration management and rerouting capability of 22 and 44 channels, respectively

■ **MX3** Aggregates different combinations of DS1s and DS2s to the rate of DS3 (or vice versa demultiplex)

▲ **DWDM** Combines multiple optical signals into a single optical fiber and separates optical signals. Stated differently, it separates optical wavelengths into a single wavelength per fiber, but it can also separate into different DWDM that may have multiple wavelengths. More in Chapter 5.

It is also important to note that synchronization of the aggregate circuits within many of these multiplexers (even as the individual DS1s within the DS3 M13 multiplexer) is not supported by many vendors. This will have a major impact when services depending heavily on channel synchronization (such as Synchronous Optical Network, or SONET) are deployed and the multiplexer needs to be replaced with an optical multiplexer.

Some aggregator multiplexers also offer the capability for switched N×56/64-Kbps services. This provides the user with multiple dialup DS0 interfaces into a multiplexer, with the user impression of "bandwidth on demand" in 56/64 Kbps increments. Carriers offer this service through the variety of multiplexer devices mentioned above. These switched DS0, FT1, DS1, FT3, and DS3 services are the most cost-effective method of bandwidth-on-demand using a multiplexer, and are quite powerful when used by a statistical multiplexer. These switched services will be covered in detail when circuit switching is discussed. Aggregator multiplexers have been predominantly replaced by the drop-and-insert multiplexer, Digital Cross Connect (DXC), and optical cross-connect (OXC). All three types of hardware are covered in this chapter.

Drop-and-Insert Multiplexers

Drop-and-insert multiplexers are special-purpose multiplexers designed to drop and insert lower-speed channels in and out of a higher-speed multiplexed channel like a DS1, DS3, or OC-*n*. Channel speeds dropped and inserted are typically in these increments. For example, on a DS0 drop-and-insert, 56- or 64-Kbps channels are demultiplexed and remultiplexed for transmission.

Figure 4-12 shows a drop-and-insert multiplexer operation, where two 56-Kbps channels (channels 1 and 2) are dropped out and replaced by two new user 56-Kbps channels before the total 24 56-Kbps channels are multiplexed and retransmitted across a DS1 circuit. Some drop-and-insert multiplexers add circuit switching and network performance monitoring to their list of capabilities.

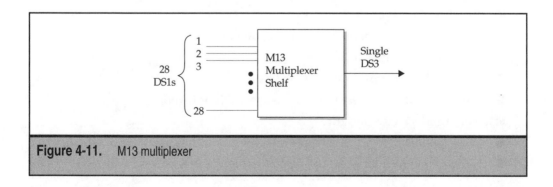

Figure 4-11. M13 multiplexer

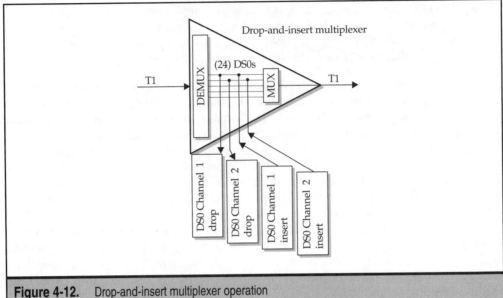

Figure 4-12. Drop-and-insert multiplexer operation

Selection of a Multiplexer

Since many options are available in multiplexers, each requirement must be analyzed to determine which type is the best fit for current and future applications. Some of the major decision criteria for all types of multiplexers are as follows:

▼ Level of intelligence required

■ Speed of access (from 9600 bps to OC-n speeds)

■ Speed of egress (from 56 Kbps to OC-n but typically DS3 and SONET OC-n speeds)

■ Capability of upgrading to LAN/WAN, T3, SONET, DWDM speeds/interfaces

■ Number of ports or cards per node

■ Maximum number of nodes in one logical network

■ Compatibility with existing CPE

■ Virtual network partitioning capabilities

■ Protocols and interfaces supported (such as FR or LAN)

■ Nonproprietary architecture

■ Voice quantization schemes supported (PCM 64 Kbps, ADPCM 32 Kbps)

■ Network media interfaces supported (that is, copper, fiber, or wireless)

- Physical interface standards supported (RS-232, V.35, ISDN, CCITT G.703)
- Types of framing and signaling (D4, ESF, B8ZS)
- Price versus functionality (cost versus feature function)
- Topologies supported (point-to-point, drop-and-insert)
- Network-management and network-diagnostic capabilities (terminal, graphical interface, proprietary or industry standard, SNMP manageable)
- Clocking restoration
- Event reporting
- Amount of circuit bandwidth available after multiplexer proprietary overhead (1.344 Mbps of user data out of 1.544 Mbps)
- Capability of selecting the primary and alternate routes
- Automatic fault isolation and reroute capabilities
- Degree to which the multiplexer offers dynamic bandwidth allocation of all data speeds
- ▲ Warranty available

The Future of Multiplexing

Technology advances continue to provide new methods to route and distribute data. Multiplexers of the 1980s yielded to the bridges, switches, and routers of the 1990s, which in turn are yielding to the high speed router/switch/firewall/optical networks of the early twenty-first century. Bandwidth requirements continue to increase. But as they increase, so does the demand for more intelligence to manage that bandwidth in an efficient and user-controllable manner, and the cost of that intelligence drops daily. Users no longer just want to aggregate their traffic into a single point-to-point circuit. Distributed, client-server computing and any-to-any communication requirements have driven users to more intelligent devices, such as routers, switching hubs, and soft switches. Multiplexer vendors have tried to keep pace by offering interface cards, additional interface options, and cost reductions, but the intelligent switching and routing vendors have stolen much of the data-transport market from the multiplexer vendors. The only true successes seem to be in the hybrid, multiplexer-switching products market and in the optical arena, especially when combined with Gigabit Ethernet alternatives.

Many traditional multiplexer vendors offer switching and routing electrical and optical protocol access cards for their multiplexer products. Some offer these capabilities in completely separate hardware and software that is interoperable with their existing multiplexer lines. Much more efficient platforms developed to handle LAN and WAN integration continue to replace the multiplexers. With LAN/WAN interface speeds increasing in leaps and bounds past the 100 Mbps range, and router vendors selling cost-effective CPE devices to transport these LAN speeds (some even natively) across the

WAN, it might not make sense to purchase T1 and T3 multiplexers whose proprietary interfaces are quickly becoming obsolete.

Multiplex vendors continue to modify existing product lines and build alliances to further their aging multiplexer product base. Multiplexers still have limitations compared to their routing and switching competition. Most of these deficiencies lie in the intelligence of the device, not in the speed. The user must clearly define short- and long-term requirements for varying types of traffic before deciding on a multiplexer solution. Interface and protocol options must be determined. This decision-making process will be covered later.

DIGITAL TDM AND THE DIGITAL HIERARCHY

Public networks developed plesiochronous digital transmission for economic transmission of voice, which was then used for data. More recently, SONET in North America and the Synchronous Digital Hierarchy (SDH) were developed in support of higher speed international transmission standard that offered better quality digital transmission. This section reviews some basics of the digital hierarchy. SONET and other optical technologies are discussed in detail in Chapter 5.

Plesiochronous Digital Hierarchy

The so-called plesiochronous (which means nearly synchronous) digital hierarchy was developed nearly 40 years ago by Bell Labs to carry digitized voice over twisted wire more efficiently in major urban areas. This evolved first as the North American Digital Hierarchy, depicted in Table 4-1. Each format is called a digital stream (DS) and is assigned a level in the hierarchy. The lower-numbered digital streams are multiplexed into the higher-numbered digital streams within a certain frequency tolerance. There is no fixed relationship in the data between levels of the hierarchy, except at the lowest level, called DS0, at a rate of 64 Kbps.

Signal Name	Rate	Structure	Number of DS0s
DS0	64 Kbps	Time Slot	1
DS1	1.544 Mbps	24×DS0	24
DS1c	-	2×DS1	48
DS2	-	2×DS1c	96
DS3	44.736 Mbps	7×DS2	672

Table 4-1. North American Digital Hierarchy

A transmission repeater system over a four-wire twisted pair was defined and called T1. The term "T1" is often used colloquially to refer to a DS1 signal. There is actually no such thing as a "T3" signal, even though it is often used to colloquially refer to a DS3 signal. The actual interfaces for DS1 and DS3 are called the DSX1 and DSX3 interfaces, respectively, in ANSI standards. The DSX1 is a four-wire interface, while the DSX3 interface is a dual coaxial cable interface.

Closely related hierarchies were also developed in Europe and Japan. These hierarchies are summarized in Table 4-2. All of these hierarchies have the property that multiplexing is done in successive levels to move between successive speeds, and that the speed of each of these levels is asynchronous with respect to the others within a certain tolerance.

An important consequence of these digital hierarchies on data communications is that only a discrete set of fixed rates is available, namely $n{\times}DS0$ (where $1 \leq n \leq 24$ in North America and Japan and $1 \leq n \leq 30$ in Europe), and then the next levels in the respective multiplex hierarchies. The North American SONET and the closely related international SDH were the next step in the evolution of TDM and are discussed in Chapter 5.

Digital Multiplexing Levels	Number of Voice Channels	Bit Rate (Mbps)		
		North America	Europe	Japan
0	1	0.064	0.064	0.064
1	24	1.544		1.544
	30		2.048	
	48	3.152		3.152
2	96	6.312		6.312
	120		8.448	
3	480		34.368	32.064
	672	44.376		
	1344	91.053		
	1440			97.728
4	1920		139.264	
	4032	274.176		
	5760			397.200
5	7680		565.148	

Table 4-2. Summary of International Plesiochronous Digital Hierarchies

SWITCHING TECHNIQUES

Switching takes multiple instances of a physical transmission medium, each containing multiplexed information streams, and rearranges the information streams between the input and output of the switch. In other words, information from a particular physical link in a specific multiplex position is switched to another output physical link, usually in a different multiplex position.

This section covers each of the major point-to-point switching functions and techniques: space, time, address, and frequency. Examples are provided for each, including the hybrid matrix switch. The examples chosen for this section define terminology and illustrate concepts that provide background for material in subsequent chapters.

Point-to-Point Switching Functions

Figure 4-13 illustrates the four basic kinds of point-to-point connection functions that can be performed by a multiplexer or switch.

▼ *Space* division switching delivers a signal from one physical (that is, spatial) interface to another physical interface. One example is a copper crosspoint switch.

■ *Time* division switching changes the order of time slots within a single spatial data stream, organized by the TDM method.

■ *Address* switching changes the address field in data packets, which can be further multiplexed into spatial, time, or frequency signals. This book focuses primarily on this switching method as it is applied to packet (IP), frame (FR), and cell (ATM) switching.

▲ *Frequency* (or wavelength) switching translates signals from one carrier frequency (wavelength) to another. Wavelength division multiplexing (WDM) uses this method over optical fibers.

Point-to-Multipoint Switching Functions

The concept of switching is extended from the case of point-to-point to the broadcast, or point-to-multipoint case, as shown in Figure 4-14. A space division broadcast switch replicates a single input signal on two or more outputs. A simple example is a coaxial television signal splitter. FDM broadcast switching replicates the same signal on multiple output carrier frequencies. TDM broadcast switching fills multiple output time slots with the data from the same input. Address broadcast switching fills multiple packets with different addresses with identical information from the same input packet.

Space Division Switching

Figure 4-15 illustrates a simple two-input, two-output crossbar network, using the crosspoint nodal function. The boldface lines and control inputs show an example connection. Notice that a total of four nodes are required. Classical space division switch fabrics have been built from electromechanical and electronic elements with the

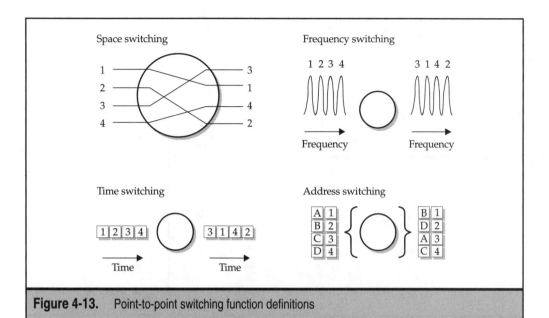

Figure 4-13. Point-to-point switching function definitions

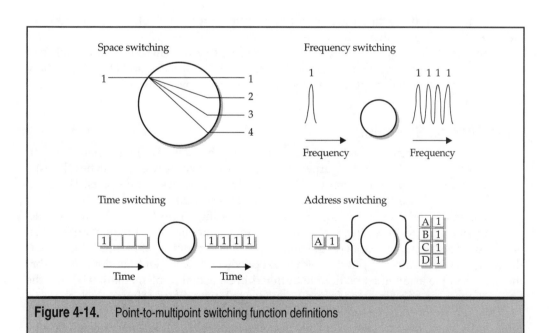

Figure 4-14. Point-to-multipoint switching function definitions

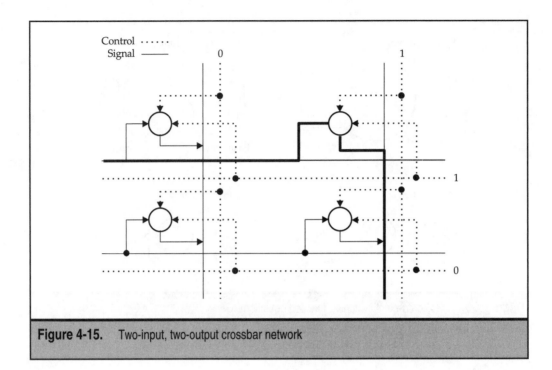

Figure 4-15.   Two-input, two-output crossbar network

crosspoint function. Technologies involving optical crosspoint elements with either electronic or optical control will be covered later.

Examples of space division switches are data terminal equipment (DTE) matrix switches, supercomputer high-performance parallel interface (HPPI) switches, and DXC 3/3s. Many space division switches employ multiple stages of crosspoint networks to yield larger switch sizes.

Time Division Switching

The operation of current digital telephone switches can be viewed as being made up of an interconnected network of special-purpose computers called time division switches (TDSs).

TDS operation is shown in Figure 4-16. Each TDM frame has M time slots. The input time slot m, labeled $I(m)$, is stored in the input sample array $x(t)$ in position m. The output address memory $y(t)$ is scanned sequentially by increasing t from 1 to M each frame time. The contents of the address array $y(t)$ identify the index into the input time slot array x that is to be output during time slot t on the output line. In the example of Figure 4-16, $y(n)$ has the value m, which causes input time slot m to be switched to output time slot n. Note that the input sample array must be double buffered in an actual implementation so that the time slot phase can be maintained for inputs and outputs with different frame clock phases.

This TDS function is performed for M time slots, that is, once every frame time. This must occur in less than $\tau =125$ μs (1/8000) for all slots, $n = 1,...,M$. The maximum TDS size

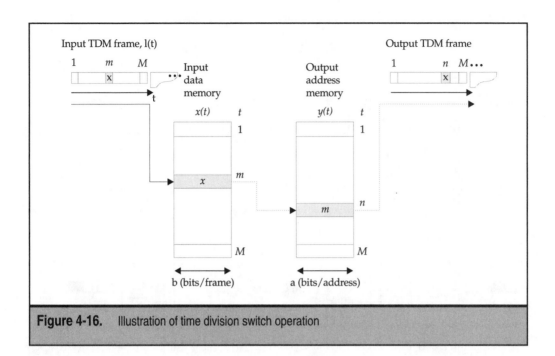

Figure 4-16.   Illustration of time division switch operation

is therefore determined by the TDS execution rate, I instructions per second (or equivalently I^{1} seconds per instruction); then the TDS switch size M must satisfy the inequality $M \leq \tau\, I$.

The TDS is effectively a very special-purpose computer designed to operate at very high speeds. For I ranging from 100 to 1000 MIPs, the maximum TDS switch size M ranges from 12,500 to 125,000. Larger TDSs can be constructed by interconnecting TDSs via multiple-stage crosspoint-type networks.

Usually, some time slots are reserved in the input frame to be able to update the output address memory. In this way, the update rate of the switch is limited by the use of some slots for scheduling overhead.

Address Switching

Address switching operates on a data stream in which the data is organized into packets, each with a header and a payload. The header contains address information that is used in switching decisions at each node. The address determines which physical port the packet is output to, along with any translation of the header address value. All possible connection topologies can be implemented within this switching architecture: point-point, point-to-multipoint, multipoint-to-point, and multipoint-to-multipoint. We illustrate these topologies in the following example.

Figure 4-17 illustrates four address switches, each with two inputs and two outputs.

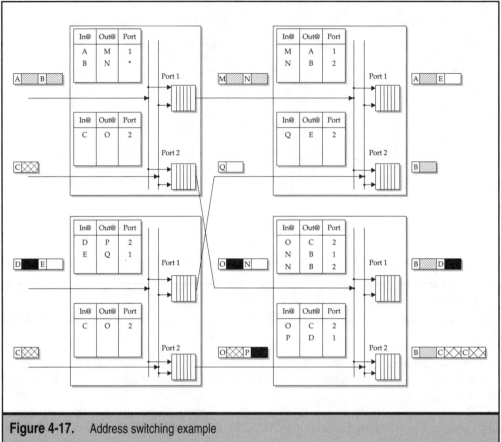

Figure 4-17. Address switching example

Packets (either fixed or variable in length) arrive at the inputs as shown on the left-hand side of the figure with addresses indicated by letters in the header symbolized by the square to the left of each shaded payload. The payload shading is carried through the switching operations from left to right to allow the switching result of the address switches to be traced visually. Then input address indexes into a table using the column labeled In@, which identifies the address for use on output in the column Out@, and the physical output port on which the packet is sent in the column labeled Port. For example, the input packet addressed as *A* is output on port 1 using address *M*. Conceptually, each switch functions as a pair of busses, which connect to the output port buffers. Packets destined for a particular output port are queued for transmission. Buffering is required because contention might occur for the same output port. At the next switch, the same process occurs until the packets are output on the right side of the figure.

The packets labeled A, D, and E form point-to-point connections. The packets labeled B form point-to-multipoint connections. The packets labeled C form multipoint-to-point connections. Address switching and multiplexing are at the heart of ATM, which we will cover in great detail in Chapter 9.

Frequency/Wavelength Switching

A more common option for large service provider backbones is the all-optical network. This network is made up exclusively of a shared media, all-photonic network that interconnects a number of end systems, as shown in Figure 4-18.

The optical end system nodes transmit on at least one wavelength λ and receive on at least one wavelength. The wavelengths for transmission and reception are currently tunable in a time frame on the order of milliseconds or microseconds. The end systems might also be capable of receiving on more than one wavelength. The wavelengths indicated by the subscripts on the character λ are used in the next example of a multiple-hop optical network.

If the end system cannot receive all other wavelengths, some means to provide inter-connectivity is required. One method is to use multiple-hop interconnections. In a multiple-hop system, each end system also performs a routing function. If an end system node receives a packet that is not destined for it, the node forwards it on the node's transmit wavelength. Eventually, the packet reaches the destination, as shown in the trellis drawing of Figure 4-19. For example, for station 1 to transmit to station 4, it first sends on wavelength $\lambda 1$, which is received by node 2. Node 2 examines the packet header and determines that it is not the destination, and retransmits the packet on wavelength $\lambda 2$. Node 3 receives the packet, examines the packet header, and forwards it on $\lambda 3$, which is received by the destination, node 4.

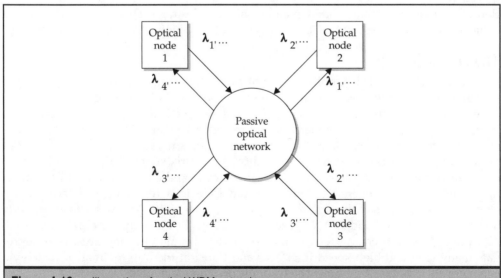

Figure 4-18.   Illustration of optical WDM network

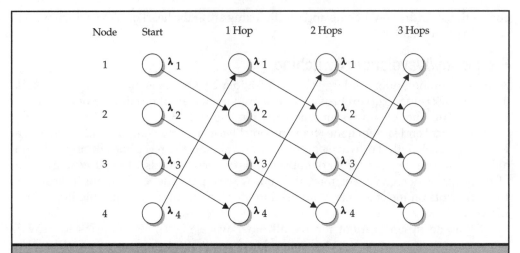

Figure 4-19. Illustration of multiple-hop WDM network trellis

This multiple-hop process makes inefficient use of the processing power of each node as the number of nodes grows large, and the alternative is the single-hop design. In these designs, the tunable transmitter and receiver are often employed. There is a need for some means to allocate and share the bandwidth in the optical network. Circuit- and packet-based signaling can be used, but packet switching, not circuit switching, is typically required due to the circuit setup time being unacceptable in circuit switching. Fixed allocation of bandwidth in a time-slotted manner is also not desirable. Dynamic scheduling and collision avoidance are solutions to the demands of very high-speed optical networking.

The Matrix Switch

Matrix switches provide a simplistic form of T1 multiplexing and offer the capability to switch ports similar to a cross-connect. They are composed of a high-speed bus for connection between ports. They are controlled and switched through a central network-management center, and can manage the entire network from a single point. This allows for centralized control and diagnostics, as well as quick network restoration in case of failure. The major drawback is the possibility of a matrix switch failure, which would bring down the entire network. Matrix switches can handle both DTE and DCE interfaces, and provide conversion from DTE and DCE to a four-wire interface. Matrix switches can be accessed through gateways or interface units. Matrix switches provide interfaces for all LAN and WAN speeds. Matrix switches usually support in excess of 4096 ports. A satellite chassis forms a method of distributing line interfaces. They aggregate many low- and high-speed interfaces and transmit them to the matrix switch via copper or fiber. Figure 4-20 shows an example of a matrix switch.

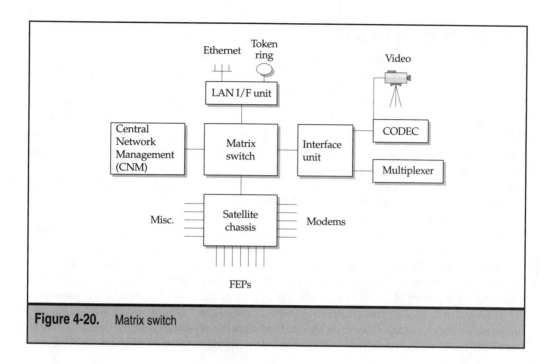

Figure 4-20.   Matrix switch

CIRCUIT SWITCHING METHODS

Circuit switching originated in the voice public telephone network. Let's look at the first telephone usage where each person had a dedicated circuit to every other person, which is essentially a permanent virtual circuit (PVC) service. This type of connectivity makes sense if you talk to very few people and very few people talk to you. Historically, this was how early telephone networks were constructed until the maze of wires began to block out the sun in urban areas, and before Strowger invented electromechanical switching. Now, let's move forward to the modern day, where the typical person makes calls to hundreds of different destinations, for business and pleasure. It is unrealistic to think that in this modern age each of these call origination and destination points would have its own dedicated circuit, since it would be much too expensive. Yet a person picks up the phone in one city and calls a person in another city. When this call goes through and both ends begin communicating, they are doing so over the equivalent of a switched virtual circuit (SVC). That virtual circuit is dedicated to the two people until they terminate the call. If they hang up and call back, another virtual circuit is established in the same manner, but not necessarily over the exact same physical or logical path as before. In this manner, common network resources (physical circuits) are shared among many users using logical bandwidth allocation.

Circuit Switching Illustrated

Figure 4-21 shows a simplified comparison of two communications networks connecting eight users, labeled user A through user H, which could be LANs, MANs, PBXs, routers, switches, or hosts. Network A shows dedicated circuits connecting each user, while network B shows circuit-switched access to a common, shared network with a single access line for each user. In network A each user has seven access lines into the network for dedicated circuits connecting to a distant access line for each possible destination. Data or voice is transmitted only via the physical layer. The data is not processed, but instead just passed across the network regardless of the content. The example in the circuit-switched network shows user A talking with user H, and user D talking with user E, where a dedicated circuit is only established for the duration of the call. Any user can communicate with any other user, although not simultaneously, just as in the telephone network.

Today, computers (hosts) need to "talk" to each other in the same manner. Computers can talk over the telephone network only if a modem is used to convert data signals to analog or digital signals that can be carried over the circuit-switched voice network. *Modem* is a contraction for modulator-demodulator. The modem presents a DCE interface to the computer equipment, and outputs a signal that is compatible with a standard phone line.

Data calls that use circuit switching operate in the same manner, but the transmission is not restricted to voice. A computer establishes a point-to-point telephone call whenever data communication is required and remains up for the duration of the "call." Either

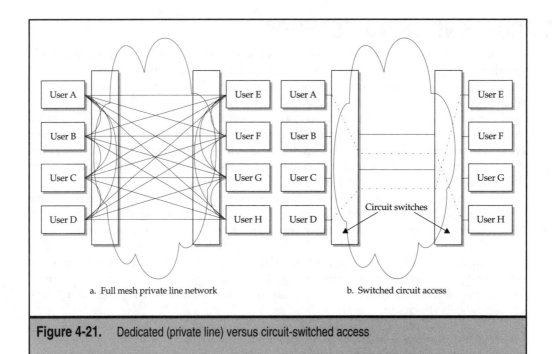

Figure 4-21. Dedicated (private line) versus circuit-switched access

the application or the end user disconnects the circuit when it is done. Since circuit switching is a form of connection-oriented service, the same factors apply. The entire circuit bandwidth is dedicated for the duration of the call. Circuit switching is an ideal technology for traffic that needs constant bandwidth but can tolerate relatively long call establishment and disconnection times.

Figure 4-22 illustrates this process between two users, A and B. Call setup delay associated with the call setup and confirmation is a major consideration with circuit switching for data communications. The call setup time and modem training time can often be as long as 30 seconds. Telephone switch routing usually does not minimize the propagation delay; however, this is usually not a critical factor for data applications operating at the lower speeds of the telephone network.

Circuit switching has yielded to packet/frame/cell switching as the leading public data service. Data circuit switching was much slower to emerge on the market than voice circuit switching, primarily because of the initial need to digitize switches. Also, the additional complexity of ISDN signaling requires software updates in switches as well as end-user equipment.

Circuit switching has been used historically as a backup for private line services. It remains the most cost-viable option for private network users, with most switched 56-Kbps data services selling at less than 20 cents per minute to less than 5 cents per minute depending on time of day, usage, speed, error-free rate, and other factors. This price is getting very close to that of voice service (which can average three cents per minute for

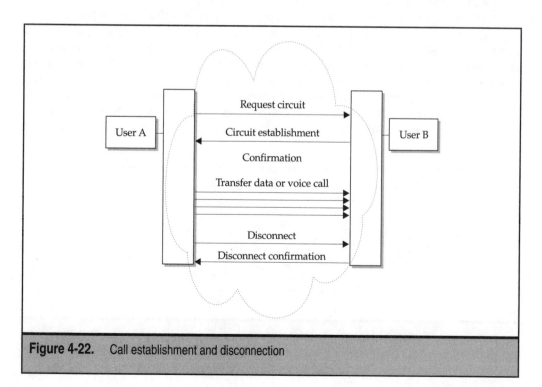

Figure 4-22.   Call establishment and disconnection

the average size enterprise), since that is basically what it is! This pricing makes it a very cost-effective option to leased-line services if the usage is less than several hours per day, or there are multiple destinations that require dynamic connectivity. The data communications user, however, needs up to three logical types of communication for one call: the data circuit, a signaling capability, and, optionally, a management capability.

High-speed circuit switching of subrate DS1, DS1, and DS3 speeds is now a ubiquitous service in the United States and is used for applications such as bulk data transport and/or those that require all the available bandwidth at predetermined time periods. Circuit switching can provide cost reductions and improve the quality of service in contrast to private lines, depending on application characteristics.

Switched n×56 Kbps and n×DS0

Since TDM uses 8000 samples per second per DS0 channel, a difference arises from the fact that 56 Kbps uses only seven bits per sample, while 64 Kbps uses all eight. The 56 Kbps rate resulted from the historical use by the telephone network of one bit per sample in what is called *robbed bit signaling* in digital transmissions.

Switched 56 Kbps, or simply switched 56, is a service offered in both the private and public networking environments. Often, a channel service unit data service unit (CSU/DSU) device is used via dedicated 56 Kbps or DS0 lines on the CSU side to access a switched 56 Kbps service. On the DSU side, a standard DCE interface is presented to the computer equipment, as was discussed at the beginning of this chapter.

Another important class of equipment comprises inverse multiplexers, which offer the capability to interface a high speed user-side interface to multiple lower speed network-facing interfaces, such as illustrated in Figure 4-23 where the 384 Kbps user-facing interface is inverse multiplexed into six DS0 64 Kbps network-facing WAN interfaces. In this example, the inverse multiplexer provides a DCE interface to the computer that aggregates the bandwidth available to the DTE in approximately 56/64 Kbps increments. The actual bandwidth provided to the DTE is slightly less than $n \times 56/64$ Kbps because the inverse multiplexer consumes some bandwidth in its operation. Many of these devices

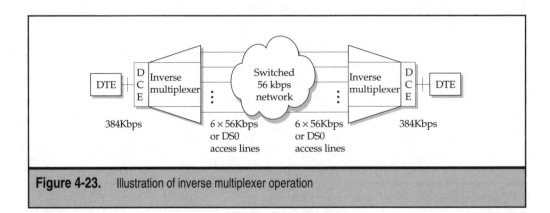

Figure 4-23.   Illustration of inverse multiplexer operation

allow 56/64 Kbps channels to be dialed up or disconnected on demand, offering a form of bandwidth-on-demand. Some router equipment has the intelligence to generate this signaling automatically based on traffic load. Some inverse multiplexers can even multiplex multiple DS1 or E1 lines into a DCE interface of approximately n×DS1 or n×E1 speeds for very high-speed connectivity. Early implementations of high speed FR and ATM required inverse multiplexed access (IMA) alternatives performed by the CSU/DSU.

The interface for switched services can be from the CPE directly to the interexchange carrier (IXC) point of presence (POP), or via a local exchange carrier (LEC) switched access service. Figure 4-24 shows these two types of access. Each type of access has its own merits and drawbacks, such as installation and usage charges, CPE costs, and reliability and availability, which must be weighed against each other.

Many users implement switched services as a backup for private lines or FR and to transport non-mission-critical data traffic. Others use it for infrequent high-data-rate constant-bandwidth data transfers. The typical traffic is long-duration, relatively constant bandwidth data transfers, such as batch file transfers, database backups, and highly aggregated, predictable data traffic.

Switched services span the DS0, FT1, DS1, and FT3 level, such as switched 384 Kbps used for video conferencing. Some carriers offer noncontiguous and contiguous fractional DS1 or n×DSX reconfigurable or switched services. Reconfigurable services often use a computer terminal to rearrange DXCs to provide a slower version of n×DSX switching. Video conferencing is one example where multiple 56-Kbps circuits are combined to form a single high-speed video conference channel at speeds such as 384 Kbps. Imaging and CAD/CAM file transfer are also good examples of high-bandwidth switched traffic. Some examples of switched DS1 and DS3 service traffic include video, imaging, and data disaster recovery.

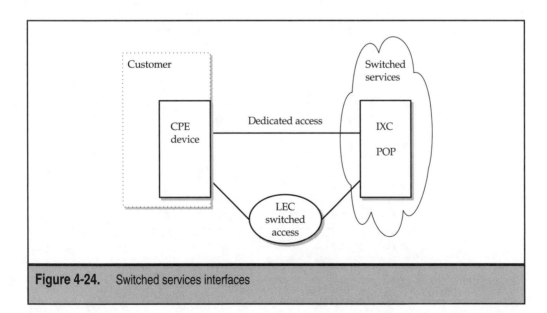

Figure 4-24.   Switched services interfaces

DXC

DXCs are central office devices capable of grooming multiple low-speed channels within a high-speed channel (for example, DS0s within a DS1, DS1s in a DS3). This provides a patch panel effect, where individual DS0s and DS1s can be mixed and matched between higher bandwidth aggregates. DXCs also perform reconfiguration, restoration and disaster recovery, circuit reroute, testing, and monitoring.

Figure 4-25 shows an example of a DXC 1/0, where 24 DS0 channels are groomed within one of the 28 T1s, which terminate at the DXC. DXCs also have the capability for network disaster recovery.

The major types of DXCs include:

▼ **DXC1/0** Supports subrate DS0s reroute capability within a DS1

■ **DXC3/1** Supports subrate DS1s reroute capability within a DS3

■ **DXC3/3** Supports multiple DS3s reroute capability

▲ **OXC** Acts as an optical cross-connect (similar to an electrical DXC) providing efficient network management of wavelengths at the optical layer

Figure 4-26 shows a network where both DXC 3/1 and DXC 3/3s are deployed.

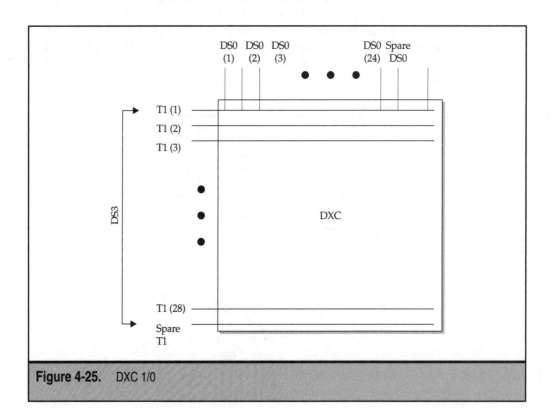

Figure 4-25. DXC 1/0

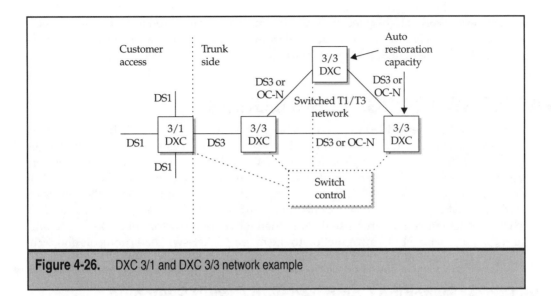

Figure 4-26.   DXC 3/1 and DXC 3/3 network example

Dialup Lines

Dialup lines represent low-speed dedicated point-to-point circuits that are established for a fixed period of time and then disconnected, similar to making a phone call. This type of circuit switching uses the Plain Old Telephone Service (POTS) for access, with access speeds typically now at 56 Kbps (V.90 modems). Figure 4-27 shows a user who accesses remote router resources via a 56 Kbps dialup line. A dialup modem is used to access the

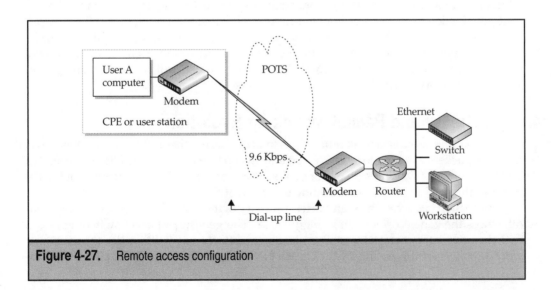

Figure 4-27.   Remote access configuration

telephone network. High-speed circuit switching can be compared to dialup lines, where bandwidth is "dialed up" as needed. N-ISDN dialup access offers a 16-Kbps (D-channel), 64-Kbps (B-channel), or 128-Kbps (2B) circuit.

PACKET-SWITCHING TECHNOLOGIES

This section has been added to provide a brief overview of packet-switching technology before delving into detail in subsequent chapters. *Packet switching* is a broad term that began with X.25 packet-switching services. It is now used in one form or another to represent FR, SMDS ATM, and IP services. Thus, the study of packet switching actually spans frame-, cell-, and packet-switching technologies. It is important to clear up the confusion with associating these diverse technologies with packet switching. First, we look at packet switching versus circuit switching, then move to the history of packet switching, and conclude with a brief introduction to the major packet-switched protocols and technologies discussed in this text.

X.25 Packet Switching Compared with Circuit Switching

Packet switching is much different from circuit switching. It allows multiple users to share data-network facilities and bandwidth, rather than providing specific amounts of dedicated bandwidth to each user. The traffic passed by packet-switched networks is "bursty" in nature, and therefore can be aggregated statistically to maximize the use of on-demand bandwidth resources. While there is much more overhead associated with packet switching as compared to circuit switching, error checking and correcting overhead guarantees error-free delivery by the use of addressed packets that transit the network. Each packet switching technology has tradeoffs of additional overhead to provide additional capabilities. Due to the connectionless characteristic of packet switching in contradistinction to connection-oriented circuit switching, the intelligence of the network nodes will route packets around failed links, whereas in circuit switching, the entire circuit would need to be switched, leading to service interruption. Some technologies we will see, such as with FR, ATM, and MPLS, have characteristics of both circuit and packet switching, but have virtual versus physical circuits.

Darwin's Theory and Packet Switching Evolution

Charles Darwin took nearly as much time to arrive at his theory of evolution as it has taken for packet switching to be conceived and sweep the world of data communications. The basic tenets of Darwin's theory of evolution are natural selection, survival of the fittest, and the need to adapt to a changing environment.

This section takes you through a brief summary of the history of packet switching that references the genealogy shown in Figure 4-28. The genesis of packet switching began with the proprietary computer communication architectures by IBM called Systems Network Architecture (SNA) and DEC's Digital Network Architecture (DNA). The Synchro-

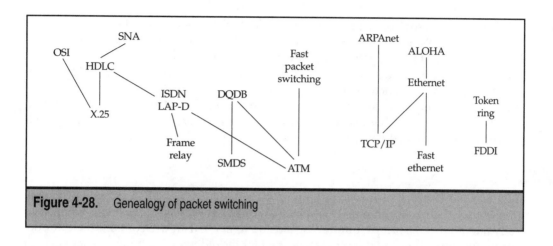

Figure 4-28. Genealogy of packet switching

nous Data Link Control (SDLC) protocol from SNA was refined and standardized as the High-level Data Link Control (HDLC) protocol, which begat X.25 and Link Access Protocol D-channel (LAP-D) within ISDN. FR evolved as basically a leaner, meaner LAP-D protocol. OSI adopted the X.25 protocol as the first link and packet layer standard. IP matured in parallel, as did ATM and newer technologies to merge the switching and routing world like MPLS.

Around the same time that OSI was being developed, the United States Advanced Research Projects Agency (ARPA) was working on a network with universities, think tanks, and industry that resulted in the suite of applications and high-level protocols based on IP. Ethernet also sprung up about this time as a result of experiments on packet radio communication in Hawaii. Ethernet has now evolved into Fast Ethernet or 100 Mbps Ethernet and Gigabit Ethernet, with further speed increases on the horizon. Token Ring was also developed by IBM shortly after Ethernet, and has evolved into the higher-speed FDDI. In the early to mid 1990s, the concepts of fast packet switching (FPS) and the distributed queue dual bus (DQDB) resulted in the Switched Multimegabit Data Service (SMDS) and Asynchronous Transfer Mode (ATM) technologies, both of which were surpassed by FR and IP technologies and services—again by the technology that was cheapest and easiest to implement and manage versus the best technology.

Packet switching played an increasingly important role in the rapidly changing environment of distributed processing in the 1990s. Several environmental factors drove the direction of data communications evolution. There emerged an accelerating need for more bandwidth driven by increasing computing power, increasing need for interconnectivity, and the need to support larger networks where any user or application can communicate with any other (ubiquity of communications). The low error rate of modern fiber-optic and wireless communications enabled more cost-effective implementation of higher-speed data communications. The same technology that increases computer power was used to increase packet switching performance.

This changing environment created new opportunities for new species of data communications protocols. The improved quality of transmission facilities alone was a major force in the evolution of IP, FR, and ATM—streamlined protocols in that they do not perform error correction by retransmission within the network, thus relying on higher-layer protocols to perform this function more efficiently. The fixed slot and cell size and efficiency of ATM have also enabled cost-effective implementation of switching machines. The increasing capabilities of high-speed electronics have been an essential ingredient in advanced packet switched devices.

X.25

X.25 was the first protocol issued defining packet switching. Access speeds originally ranged up to 56 Kbps, and now DS1 speeds. Trunks between network nodes were originally limited to 56/64 Kbps, but now speeds up to DS3 exist. X.25 contains the error detection and correction and flow control needed for the older analog transport networks of the 1980s. But much of this overhead and the processor-intensive operations are not needed in today's fiber-optic networks environment. X.25 Packet switching is solely a connectionless service using connection-oriented virtual circuits, and is good for time-insensitive data transmission but poor for connection-oriented and time-sensitive voice and video. Packet switches pass data through the network, node to node, employing a queuing scheme for buffering and transmitting data. Data is received and passed if bandwidth is available. If it is not, data is stored in the queue until bandwidth is available (to the extent of the memory buffer). Each node is responsible for error detection and correction and to initiate error recovery. The newer fast packet services do not perform this queuing function at each switch, rather they drop the extra traffic that cannot be transmitted over a congested network and force the end hosts (application) to do the error checking at higher layers.

X.25 allows numerous virtual circuits on the same physical path, and can transport packet sizes up to 4,096 bytes. Both PVCs and SVCs are supported in X.25, and the addressing scheme allows any user to send or receive data from any other user. Traffic can also be prioritized. Chapter 11 covers X.25 packet switching in detail.

FR

FR is most commonly referred to as a connection-oriented public data service employing PVCs and SVCs similar to packet switching. Frames can vary in size and bandwidth is allocated on demand based on conformance to a committed information rate (CIR). Multiple sessions (up to 1000 PVCs) can take place over a single physical circuit, and these access circuits can range from DS0, through fractional T1 speeds, and up to a DS3 (minus the overhead). Thus, FR exhibits a similar statistical multiplexing feature as X.25. FR is only a transport service (although integrated Internet access can be achieved through a FR access circuit), and does not employ the packet processing of X.25, which guarantees end-to-end error and flow control. Instead, FR relies on the user to implement higher-level protocols in the upper layer of the OSIRM (Layer 3 and above) for flow control and error correction [such as Transmission Control Protocol (TCP)]. FR must be transmitted over reliable fiber-optic transmission media with low bit-error ratios. Errored or excess (blocked) data is simply discarded at the ingress, within the network, or at the egress, since error detection and correction is not built into FR because of the assumption of the reliability of the fiber-optics. Chapter 8 provides a detailed explanation of FR. FR design is considered in Chapter 17.

There are seven functions provided by FR that are also provided by X.25. These include address translation, discard of incorrect frames, fill of interframe time, FCS checking and generation, flag recognition and generation, recognition of invalid frames, and transparency. The concept of PVCs and SVCs is also similar. Together this constitutes about one-fourth of the services provided by X.25, and FR can be viewed as a subset of X.25 packet-switching technology and functions. It can be seen that while the scaling down of services contributes to a less intelligent network, the benefit is a reduction in overhead, and thus greater throughput and lower latency can be achieved if clean transmission media and proper traffic engineering are used. FR also provides much higher transmission speeds than X.25. Still, FR is not a replacement for X.25 packet switching or TCP/IP, especially if poor transmission facilities are inescapable and guaranteed delivery is a must. This is especially true in many third world countries.

Fast Packet

Fast packet is a term for a data transmission technique, trademarked by Stratacom (now Cisco). It is not a defined standard, protocol, or service. Fast packet is a *backbone* technology (as opposed to FR *access* technology) that combines attributes of both circuit switching and packet switching. Fast packet can accommodate both (time) delay-sensitive traffic (for example, voice and video) as well as data traffic not affected by variable delay. It also offers low network delay and high network resource efficiency. Fast packet resembles a circuit switch for constant-bandwidth traffic such as voice and video (isosynchronous) and a packet switch for "bursty" data traffic such as local and wide area network traffic, dynamically increasing the bandwidth for high-bandwidth requirements and decreasing it for low-bandwidth requirements.

Fast packet switching speeds up packet transfer and delivery through reduction of overhead since error detection and correction is not done in the intermediate nodes. The packets or cells passing through the network use the data-link layer instead of the network layer. These packet or cell sizes can either be *fixed* (cell switching and ATM) or *variable* (FR). Fast packet can also provide protocol transparency. This causes minimal node delay, while providing addressing and routing capabilities. Fast packet technologies typically use advanced fiber-optic transport media, such as T3, SONET, and WDM.

Fast packet multiplexing (FPM) is a general term for providing the capabilities of fast packet switching through multiplexing various types of traffic onto the transmission medium. FPM is characterized by a combination of both TDM and SPM, where packets of fixed or variable size, of fixed or variable delay-sensitive traffic, are statistically multiplexed over a network high-bandwidth circuit. Packets pass *through* network devices rather than into and out of them, thus providing minimal nodal delay. FPM can also dynamically reallocate bandwidth on any packet, regardless of whether it is within the multiplexer or partially in transit. This leads to variable or fixed packet or cell sizes based on the transmission medium being used. The most common form of FPM is ATM technology, which uses a fixed cell switching form of fast packet multiplexing. We will discuss this technology in great detail in Chapter 9.

ATM

ATM is one form of fast packet switching. ATM packetizes voice, data, and video and then "statistically multiplexes" the packets onto the same high-speed data channel. ATM provides two types of connection: virtual *channel*, which provides logical packet connection between two users, and virtual *path*, which defines a source to destination route for users.

ATM is a technology that allows for the transmission of data, voice, and video traffic simultaneously over high-bandwidth circuits, typically on the order of hundreds of Megabits per second (Mbps) to Gigabits per second (Gbps), while defining specific service classes that guarantee quality of service (QoS) at the virtual circuit and path level. ATM hardware and software platforms form a communications architecture based on the switching and relaying of small units of data called *cells*. The primary differentiator between ATM-based services and other existing data communications services, such as FR, SMDS, and FDDI, is that it is the first technology and protocol structure to effectively integrate voice, data, and video over the same communications channel at speeds in excess of DS3 (45 Mbps) and E4 (140 Mbps). Chapter 9 covers ATM in detail, and a discussion on SONET can be found in Chapter 5.

IP

The Internet Protocol (IP) is the most popular of all the packet switching protocols. This is due in large part to the explosive growth of the Internet. IP is the protocol supported to transfer information over the Internet.

IP provides a connectionless datagram network service. The IP datagrams are packets that contain a header, data, and a trailer. The header contains delivery information, such as the source and destination addresses. The data is the information being transported, and the trailers typically contain a checksum value to ensure that the data is not modified in transit. Because IP is a connectionless datagram network service, it does not support any concept of a session or connection. If a connection is required, IP relies on higher-layer protocols to set up and maintain the connection. Once a packet is transmitted or received, IP maintains no memory of the communication. IP expects the protocols above it, generally the transport layer, to understand what has or has not been delivered. If the IP service on a device receiving an IP datagram detects an error during transmission, it simply ignores the packet without notifying the receiving entity. We will learn much more about IP in Chapter 10.

Integrated Circuit/Packet Switches

Switches are available that combine both circuit- and packet-switching capabilities within the same unit. These devices can combine X.25, IP, FR, or ATM packet/frame/cell switching with TDM techniques, and can even include DXC and channel bank functions.

Thus, a large variety of traffic—from bursty LAN to dedicated DS1 and DS3 data streams—can be handled in the most efficient manner required, with the added capabilities offered by a DXC. X.25, IP, and LAN routed traffic can be *packet* switched, while LAN bridged, SNA, voice and video, and other delay-sensitive traffic can be *circuit* switched. The primary advantage is seen when using this switch as a hub concentrator for many types of traffic through dynamic allocation of available bandwidth. It allows an integrated platform for both data transport and network management. Thus, the network designer can design one network, and not multiple networks for both circuit and packet switching, thus consolidating equipment and operating costs of both. But one must also ask, "Can a Volkswagen beat a drag racer in a race if you need speed, or can a drag racer enter a miles-per-gallon race?" The point is that this solution is not without the drawbacks of both technologies, as we have discussed previously.

One such technology is multiprotocol label switching (MPLS). MPLS was derived from the Cisco label switching standards and label distribution protocol (LDP). The essence of MPLS is that it combines slow yet intelligent routing (packet) with fast yet dumb switching (circuit) for an integrated circuit/packet switching/routing backbone protocol. We discuss MPLS in more detail in Chapter 10.

DEFINITION OF NETWORK SERVICES

Data network services are categorized in the OSIRM as being either connection oriented or connectionless. Connection-oriented services involve establishing a connection between physical or logical end points prior to the transfer of data. Examples of connection-oriented network services (CONSs) are private line, FR, and ATM.

Connectionless services, on the other hand, provide end-to-end logical connectivity and do not require the establishment of a connection prior to data transfer. Examples of connectionless network services (CLNSs) are IP and SMDS. Ethernet can also be viewed as a CLNS. Historically, connection-oriented services were generally used in WANs, while connectionless services were primarily used in LANs. ATM (and its associated adaptation layers) is one example of a CONS that provides the capability to support both connection-oriented and connectionless services.

CONS

CONS require establishment of a connection between the origin and destination before transferring data. Usually, the connection is established as a path of links through intermediate nodes in a network. Once established, all data travels over this same path in the network. The requirement that data must arrive at the destination in the same order as sent by the origin is fundamental to all connection-oriented services.

If the connection is established by network management or provisioning actions and is left up indefinitely, then it is called a PVC. If control signaling of any type is used to establish and take down the connection dynamically, then it is called an SVC.

When a PVC is used, a permanent connection is made between two or more physical or logical interfaces. Physical wiring, equipment configuration commands, service provider provisioning procedures, or combinations of these actions can establish the connection. These actions might take several minutes to several weeks, depending on exactly what is required. Once the PVC is established, data can be transferred over it. PVCs are usually established for long periods of time and remain static. Examples of physical PVCs are analog private lines, DTE-to-DCE connections, and digital (dedicated) private lines. Examples of logical PVCs are the X.25 PVC, FR PVC, and ATM VP/VC. One of the simplest CONS examples is a phone call over the Public Switched Telephone Network (PSTN).

In the case of an SVC service, only the access line and address for the origin and each destination point need to be provisioned beforehand. The use of a control-signaling protocol plays a central role in SVC services. Via the signaling protocol, the origin requests that a connection be made by the network to one or more destinations. The network determines the physical (and logical) location of the destination(s) and attempts to establish the connection through intermediate node(s) to the destination(s). The success or failure of the attempt is indicated back to the originator. There might also be a progress indication to the originator, alerting for the destination, or other handshaking elements of the signaling protocol as well. Often, the destination(s) also use signaling to allow them to either accept or reject the call. In the case of a failed attempt, the signaling protocol usually informs the originator of the reason the attempt failed. Once the connection is established, then data can be transferred over the connection. Usually, SVCs are used so that resources can be shared by allowing users to dynamically connect and disconnect using the signaling protocol. The signaling protocol usually allows either the originator or destination(s) to initiate a disconnect action.

Furthermore, a failure in the network or of the originator or destination(s) usually results in an automatic disconnect. Examples of SVCs are telephone calls, ISDN and X.25 calls, FR SVCs, and ATM SVCs. MPLS networks can act like large SVC networks.

The above description might sound complicated, but it isn't. There is a direct analogy to each of the above terms in the steps of establishing and taking down an SVC connection-oriented service and a normal telephone call, as illustrated in Table 4-3. In fact, much of the complexity of ISDN is introduced by having a more complicated signaling protocol with new names as summarized below. ISDN can support voice calls since the required signaling primitives are part of the signaling protocol.

In the case of a switched connection, data is transferred over a connection established through the network, and this same connection is then disconnected, or taken down, after it is no longer needed. The advantage of this additional complexity is that resources can be shared in time, and in some cases the charges for use of a public service can be significantly less for an SVC than they would be for a comparable set of PVCs. In the case of physical SVCs, the entire bandwidth of the connection is available to the end points. In the case of logical SVCs, the network might be doing some statistical sharing of bandwidth in the switches interior to the network. Connection-oriented services are therefore best used if the required data transfer is intermittent, but lasts quite a bit longer than the time required by the signaling protocol to establish it. Also, SVCs can be used to control bandwidth allocation or access to a shared resource, such as a dialup database service.

General Signaling Protocol Terminology	Voice Telephone Call Example
Provision access/address	Order service from phone company
Handshaking	Dial tone
Origin request	Dialing the number
Successful attempt indication	Ringing tone
Unsuccessful attempt indication	Busy tone
Destination acceptance	Answering the phone
Data transfer	Talking on the phone
Disconnect request	Hanging up the phone

Table 4-3.   General Signaling Comparison to Voice Call

Most of the technologies introduced earlier in this chapter are based on connection-oriented services. Private lines and circuit switching are a few examples of connection-oriented services provided by the telephony-oriented carriers, whose primary service is based on connection-oriented services. Many carriers and service providers also offer FR and ATM services, and more recently MPLS services that rely on IP and ATM as transport service protocols.

CLNS

In CLNS, no prior establishment of an end-to-end connection is required for data transmission. Thus, there is no predetermined path that data must take through the network. Therefore, in some connectionless services, data might arrive at the destination in a different order than it was sent from the origin. In contrast to connection-oriented services, which might be physical and/or logical, connectionless services are always logical. Another key attribute of many connectionless services is that there is no need for provisioning; you simply plug in the end station equipment, and you are connected! This is often called "plug and play" in data communications.

In connectionless services, the originating node transmits packets to the destination via the best path from that node, and typically "hop by hop" over each node. As other nodes receive these packets, they interpret the address information in the packet and process it based on this node's position in the network and its selection of the best path to the destination as determined by a routing algorithm. The node then switches packets destined for other nodes onto a trunk, and delivers those packets destined for users connected to this node. In a connectionless service, the delivery of the packet or cell is not guaranteed; therefore, applications must rely on higher-level protocols to perform the end-to-end error detection/correction, data integrity checking, flow control, loss detection and retransmission. Flow control is usually minimal (if any), and the service often does not provide for error detection or correction. Bandwidth efficiency and message sequencing are sacrificed for high performance through fast switching of packets, avoiding the overhead incurred through call establishment and management. Connectionless service is sometimes referred to as datagram service.

The dynamic, automatic determination of which node to select when switching a packet in the above process is, in general, a complicated problem. The generic term for protocols that determine this next hop-selection mechanism is *routing protocols*. Chapter 10 reviews some aspects of routing protocols.

Connectionless service is the predominant mode of communications in LANs because it is well suited to the intermittent, bursty traffic found on applications that use LANs. LANs also take key advantage of the "plug and play" property. Low-level logical LAN connectivity is usually established automatically simply by plugging in the wiring to the LAN adapter interface on the end system. Besides the common LAN technologies such as Ethernet, Token Ring, and FDDI, the largest CLNS in the world is the Internet based on the IP. By virtue of the routing protocols, IP also has the plug-and-play property that simply attaching (a properly configured) computer (host) to the Internet allows data communication to occur. This is done by the other nodes in the network discovering the added node through routing messages, and adding this to their next hop decision tables. Some connectionless data services technologies such as IP have seen wide scale acceptance, whereas others, such as SMDS, have found much more limited acceptance and have almost disappeared from the data services world.

REVIEW

The capabilities of and differences between multiplexing and switching are important. There are many methods of multiplexing, such as space division, frequency division, time division, and addressing multiplexing, and each has multiple hardware devices to satisfy the various user needs for traffic aggregation. We found that address multiplexing was the most common form found in modern data communications networks. The coverage then moved to digital TDM, originally designed to provide more cost-effective telephone calls, and which represented the foundation for the beginnings of high-performance digital data communications. Circuit-switching services and technologies are quite valuable to constant data-rate traffic, as well as valuable for dedicated circuit backup. Packet-switching technologies span from the older X.25 packet switching to newer techniques in fast packet and cell switching such as FR, SMDS, ATM, and various forms of IP. After understanding the advantages and disadvantages of each type of technology, it is apparent that many network designs require a "hybrid" of both dedicated and switched technologies, which is offered through MPLS-based services. Definitions were given of connection-oriented and connectionless services.

CHAPTER 5

Optical Networking

Optical networking is rapidly changing the landscape of communications and has thrown a whole new light on the future of networking. Optical technology advances in lasers and fiber optics media have greatly reduced costs, which simultaneously has increased capacity. Aggressive optical deployments have enabled optical Ethernet offerings in the metropolitan area networks (MANs) and optical routing in the backbone of private and public network infrastructures. Advances in optical components and systems over the last five years have taken the industry into the terabit transport continuum, but optical amplification and optical techniques in current development will create even greater economies of scale, revolutionizing the networking industry. As some industry experts have stated, the bandwidth capacity of fiber optics is increased by a factor of four every 18 months. Put another way, it is Moore's Law squared. (Moore's Law states that the number of transistors per integrated circuit doubles every 18 months.) Leading-edge vendors are now testing technology that breaks this law and will probably be in production by the time this book is published.

The optical networking area is continuing to evolve, slightly hampered by the dot com bust at the turn of the century. Despite the economic downturn, companies continue to have a voracious appetite for bandwidth, so optics are here to stay. In this chapter, we will discuss the Synchronous Optical Network (SONET)/Synchronous Digital Hierarchy (SDH) standards and dense wavelength division multiplexing (DWDM) techniques for increasing the capacity of an optical network. Optical Ethernet/gigabit Ethernet and optical routing, now available in the LAN, MAN, and WAN as a technology and public service, will be covered in Chapter 20.

HISTORY OF OPTICAL NETWORKING

The renaissance of optical communication dates back over 200 years. The optical telegraph was invented in the 1790s and over 100 years later (in 1880) Alexander Graham Bell patented the optical telephone system. Alexander Graham Bell's telephone invention revolutionized the world and the optical telephone system was ahead of its time. It is also interesting to note that true optical communications were used by the Greek and Roman empires. Fire signals were given from mountain to mountain or from tower to tower at night.

Modern optical communication dates back to the 1950s and 1960s with the development of pulsing-laser technology (light) across fiber (glass or plastic) with low loss rates to achieve high-speed data and voice communications transfer. In 1977, optical technology began passing live telephone traffic in the United States and the United Kingdom, and the amount of telecommunication traffic on optical networks hasn't stopped since. At the turn of the century, 10 gigabits per second (Gbps) fiber-optic systems were operational and 1 terabit per second (Tbps)—across a single fiber!—systems were operational in labs.

In 1984, the Exchange Carriers Standards Association (ECSA) began work to establish a standard for connecting one fiber system to another, which produced the Synchronous Optical Network (SONET) standard. Following the development of SONET, the International Telecommunication Union Telecommunication Standardization Sector (ITU-T) published a world standard, Synchronous Digital Hierarchy (SDH), in 1989. SONET/SDH standards define the basic transmission rates and characteristics, frame formats and testing, and an optical interface-multiplexing scheme—as well as defining operation, administration, maintenance, and provisioning (OAM&P).

As SONET/SDH had been the main WAN transport technology deployed through the 1990s, the turn of the century brought deployments using dense wavelength division multiplexing (DWDM). DWDM allows 160 wavelengths to be supported per fiber with higher numbers possible, where each wavelength can support anywhere from 2.5 to 10 Gbps. Most communications originate in the digital world (DS0 and DS1 circuits and services) and optical systems typically convert the end-user electrical signals to optical for transport across the network and then back to an electrical signal at network egress. In the optical transport networks today, the switching, adding, dropping, or regenerating of an optical signal requires the optical signal to be converted to an electrical signal for manipulation and then back to optical again. This process is called optical-electrical-optical (OEO). Future systems will be all-optical and will process the signal in the optical domain, thus eliminating the OEO process and greatly reducing network delay (latency)—the enemy of network systems.

SONET/SDH STANDARDS

SDH is the international standard for fiber transmission and is based on ITU specifications. As standards are continually being changed and updated, you can refer to the ITU web site at http://www.itu.int for a complete and current list of standards.

SONET is the North American standard for fiber transmission and is based on American National Standards Institute (ANSI) specifications. For the most current information on the SONET specifications, the ANSI web site address is http://www.ansi.org.

SONET/SDH

SONET and SDH are U.S. and international standards, respectively, for optical telecommunication transport. The SONET/SDH comprehensive standards will continue to define the world's telecommunication transport infrastructure for the foreseeable future.

As the standard for network transport, protocol, and architecture, SONET/SDH has eliminated the different transmission schemes and rates of North America, Europe, and the Pacific Rim through a common international rate structure. It also provides a technology that enables the major service providers to internationally standardize and control broadband network transport media through a common fiber interface called a *midspan meet*. Probably the greatest benefits of SONET/SDH lie in its in-band OAM&P, which will be discussed in this chapter. SONET/SDH systems provide increased configuration flexibility and bandwidth availability over older telecommunication systems, thus providing major advantages, such as

▼ Reduction of equipment needed and increased network reliability and availability

■ Centralized fault isolation and management of payload (traffic carried)

- Synchronous multiplexing formats for DS1 and E1 allowing easy access for switching and multiplexing

- International vendor interoperability

▲ Flexible architecture able to accommodate future requirements

Before diving into SONET/SDH specifics, we will define synchronous, plesiochronous, and asynchronous:

▼ **Synchronous**   All clocks are traceable to one Stratum 1 primary reference clock (PRC). All digital transitions in the signals occur at exactly the same rate.

- **Plesiochronous**   Clocks are extremely accurate and almost exact, but a small difference exists between them. An example is a connection between two different carriers, each using different Stratum 1 clock sources.

▲ **Asynchronous**   The clocks don't have to match or be equal.

So, why was synchronous chosen as the method of transmission for SONET? Transmission systems before SONET were dominated by DS1 and DS3 circuits and operated asynchronously. To adjust for clock variation, extra bits were added to adjust for the variation (bit-stuffing). In synchronous networks, bit-stuffing isn't required due to the accuracy of the clocks, reducing complexity. If SONET is used between two networks in a midspan meet configuration, SONET has a *pointer* function to allow for adjustments in timing.

The SONET architecture has four layers: physical (or photonic), section, line, and path. These layers can be seen in Figure 5-1. Three of these layers—section, line, and path—roughly correspond to the layers of overhead present in the SONET frame. First, the physical layer defines the physical fiber type, path, and characteristics. The more common examples of the physical interface include 1550-nanometer (nm) dispersion-shifted fiber (DSF) and 1310-nm conventional glass fiber. The physical layer also includes the many electrical interfaces, which become virtual channels within the Synchronous Transport Signal-1 (STS-1) frame—the base level building block of SONET.

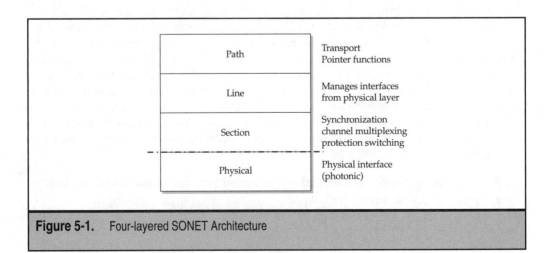

Figure 5-1.   Four-layered SONET Architecture

Second, the section layer builds the SONET frames from either lower SONET interfaces or electrical interfaces. Third, the line layer provides synchronization, channel multiplexing, and protection switching. This layer provides the communications channel between line-terminating equipment (LTE) at the point of STS-1 multiplexing to higher rates, as well as providing management between LTE and section-terminating equipment (STE). The path layer manages the actual data transport across the SONET network, as well as the pointer function.

The following list refers to Figure 5-2 and provides descriptions of the equipment and functions of the layers:

▼ **Path**   Information carried end-to-end.

■ **Line**   Information carried for STS-*n* signals between multiplexers.

■ **Section**   Information carried for communication between adjacent network equipment, such as regenerators.

■ **Path-terminating equipment (PTE)**   Typically the user interface at the CPE.

■ **Line-terminating equipment (LTE)**   Typically a terminal, switch, add/drop multiplexer, or cross-connect.

▲ **Section-terminating equipment (STE)**   Primarily a regenerator.

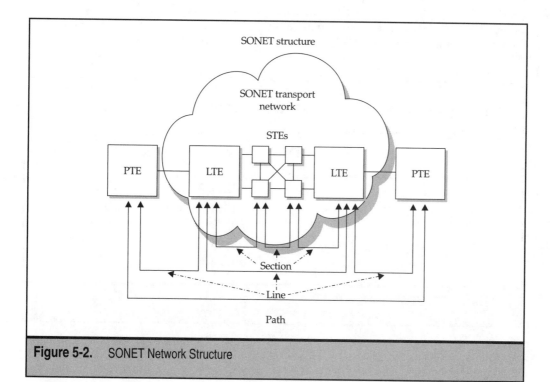

Figure 5-2.   SONET Network Structure

Since we are primarily focusing on SONET specifics versus SDH specifics, it is important that we discuss the convergence of SONET and SDH as well as a few differences. SONET and SDH converge at SONET's STS-1 (51.84 Mbps) level, which is known as Synchronous Transport Module-0 (STM-0 in SDH terminology). As SONET's base level is STS-1, SDH's base level is STM-1, which is equivalent to SONET's STS-3. The SONET standard was changed from bit interleaving to byte interleaving, allowing SDH standards to accommodate both transmission hierarchies. Table 5-1 shows both hierarchies, but it should be noted that SDH's STM-1 and SONET's STS-3 utilize different frame formats.

SONET Structure

The SONET structure follows a strict definition and hierarchy, which maps to the electrical hierarchies of many nations. The SONET structure is then multiplexed to form higher-speed transport circuits that range today into the gigabits and provide an alternative to aggregating multiple DS1 and DS3 transmission facilities. SONET solves many of the network management problems associated with DS3 transmissions. To help with understanding SONET, we will discuss its basic structure and frame formats.

The structure of SONET is built around a STS-1 building block, which is an aggregate 51.84 Mbps STS-1 bit stream. This stream, when converted from electrical to fiber optic, is called optical carrier-1 (OC-1). The STS-1 is comprised of a specific sequence of 810-byte frames sent at a rate of 8,000 per second (125 microseconds). A STS-1 payload has the capacity to transport 28 DS1s, 1 DS3, or 21 E1s (2.048 Mbps). All SONET rates are multiples of the STS-1 basic structure, as shown in Table 5-2, along with the number of DS0s (a typical voice channel), DS1s, and DS3s that can be transported.

SONET Signal	Bit Rate	SDH Signal	SONET Capacity	SDH Capacity
STS-1, OC-1	51.84 Mbps	STM-0	28 DS1s or 1 DS3	21 E1s
STS-3, OC-3	155.52 Mbps	STM-1	84 DS1s or 3 DS3s	63 E1s or 1 E4
STS-12, OC-12	622.08 Mbps	STM-4	336 DS1s or 12 DS3s	252 E1s or 4 E4s
STS-48, OC-48	2488.32 Mbps	STM-16	1344 DS1s or 48 DS3s	1008 E1s or 16 E4s
STS-192, OC-192	9953.28 Mbps	STM-64	5376 DS1s or 192 DS3s	4032 E1s or 64 E4s

Table 5-1. SONET/SDH Hierarchies

STS Level	Bit Rate (Mbps)	DS0s	DS1s	DS3s
1	51.84	672	28	1
3	155.52	2,016	84	3
12	622.08	8,064	336	12
24	1,244.16	16,128	672	24
48	2,488.32	32,256	1,344	48
192	9,953.28	129,024	5,376	192

Table 5-2.   SONET STS-*n* Speed Hierarchy

Frame Format

When looking inside the 810-byte frame that makes up the STS-1 building block, you see that the frame is broken into two parts: payload and overhead. Because manageability is a key advantage of SONET architectures, understanding the capabilities of overhead provides a view of the key SONET capabilities.

The SONET STS-*n* frame format is shown in Figure 5-3. Notice that the frame composes the transport overhead that includes the section and line overhead, and the Synchronous

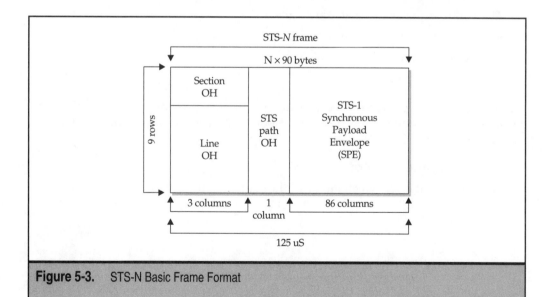

Figure 5-3.   STS-N Basic Frame Format

Payload Envelope (SPE) includes the data and path overhead. The frame size for an STS-1 SPE is 9 rows × 90 columns (one byte per column) or 810 bytes. The total STS-1 frame of 810 bytes is transmitted each 125ms, resulting in the basic SONET/STM rate of 51.84 Mbps.

STS-1 Overhead

The SONET overhead structure parallels the existing telephone network, with three layers to match section, line, and path segments. The first three columns of the frame are the transport overhead, which is divided into the section overhead composing the first three rows, and the line overhead composing rows four through nine. The fourth column contains the path overhead, as shown in Figure 5-3.

Section Overhead   The section overhead contains nine bytes that are accessed, generated, and processed by STE—such as a regenerator. This overhead supports functions of

- ▼ Performance monitoring
- ■ Framing
- ■ Messaging communication between STEs for control, monitoring, administration, and other communication needs
- ▲ Voice communication between STE

Line Overhead   The line overhead contains 18 bytes that are accessed, generated, and processed by LTE—such as multiplexers. This overhead supports functions of

- ▼ Locating the SPE in the frame
- ■ Multiplexing or concatenating signals
- ■ Performance monitoring
- ■ Automatic protection switching
- ▲ Line maintenance

Path Overhead   The path overhead contains nine bytes, providing communication between the creation point of the SPE and the point where it is dissembled. This overhead supports functions of

- ▼ Performance monitoring of the SPE
- ■ Path signal label, which indicates the content of the SPE

- Path status, which conveys status and performance back to the originating terminal

▲ Path trace, which allows verification of continued connection with the originating terminal

STS-1 Synchronous Payload Envelope (SPE)

The payload is defined as the actual data to be transported across the SONET path. Payloads can take many forms, such as typical T-carrier channels (such as DS3), or virtual tributaries (VTs) of various sizes, which we will discuss. Payloads are backward compatible with the North American, European, and Pacific Rim standard transport technologies. The SPE is defined as 783 bytes and is shown as 87 columns × 9 rows. The first column of the SPE is the path overhead and columns 30 and 59 are not used for payload, but designated as the fixed stuff columns, which leaves 84 columns × 9 rows (or 756 bytes) for payload.

To support services that require a payload larger than STS-1, SONET offers the flexibility of concatenating STS-1s together to support higher bandwidth requirements. If you see STS-3c shown, the c refers to a concatenated payload of a full STS-3.

Pointers

The SONET answer to frame synchronization is the use of pointers. SONET can easily identify subchannels down to the DS0 level within a SONET transmission using pointers. These pointers are located within the line overhead portion of each frame. The SPE is allowed to "float" anywhere within the SPE-allocated portion frame, and often overlaps multiple frames. The pointer number (pointers H1, H2, and H3) indicates the start of the SPE frame. If the frame experiences jitter or wander, the pointer shifts within the frame parallel to the SPE shift, thus maintaining its pointer integrity. The H1 and H2 pointers are then updated at each terminal across the network.

Figure 5-4 illustrates an example of an SPE that spans two STS-1 frames. In this figure, the H1, H2, and H3 pointers in the line overhead identify the start of the SPE-3 frame. In the next STS-1 frame, H1 and H2 identify the beginning of another STE, but the H3 octet holds the value of the last byte in SPE-3. This continues through the transmission. Pointers are also used to identify VTs within an SPE.

Virtual Tributary (VT)

VTs are the building blocks of the SPE. The label VT*xx* designates VTs of *xx* Mbps. These VTs are labeled as VT1.5 for DS1, VT2 for E1 (CEPT1), VT3 for DS1C, and VT6 for DS2. Table 5-3 shows these VTs and their respective equivalents.

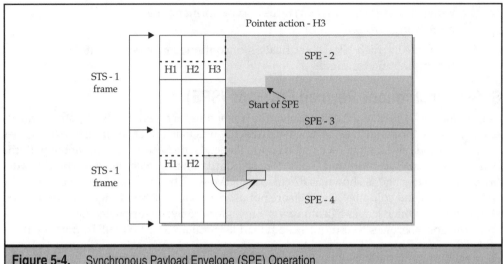

Figure 5-4.   Synchronous Payload Envelope (SPE) Operation

VTs are combined to form VT groups. These VT groups consist exclusively of four VT1.5s, three VT2s, two VT3s, or one VT6 within a 9-row × 12-column portion of the SPE. A complete SPE is then comprised of seven VT groups, 2 bit-stuffed unused columns, and the path overhead column, as shown in Figure 5-5. These VT groups can be mixed to make up an STS-1, which can either contain multiple VTs or a single DS3. VTs can either operate in *locked mode*, which fixes the VT structure within an STS-1 and is designed for channelized operation, or in *floating mode*, which allows these values to be changed by cross-connects and switches and is designed for unchannelized operation.

Multiplexing

SONET provides direct multiplexing of both SONET speeds and current asynchronous and synchronous services into the STS-*n* payload. Payload types range from DS1 and DS3

VT*xx*	Data Rate (Mbps)	Electrical Channel Equivalent
VT1.5	1.544	DS1
VT2	2.048	E1 (CEPT1)
VT3	3.152	DS1C
VT6	6.312	DS2

Table 5-3.   VT Classes with Equivalents

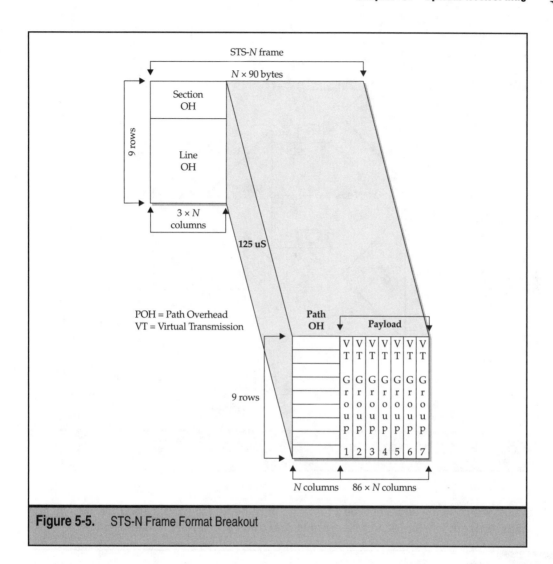

Figure 5-5.   STS-N Frame Format Breakout

to OC-3c and OC-12c payloads. For example, STS-1 supports direct multiplexing of DS1 and DS3 clear channel into single or multiple STS-1 envelopes, which are called VTs. Multiple STS-1 envelopes are multiplexed into an STS-n signal.

Figure 5-6 shows the method of multiplexing, where users 1 through 28 represent individual DS1, DS2, DS1C, and CEPT2 VT user access circuits. Each of these inputs is first adapted to an STS-1 stream. These streams are then combined with OC-1 and DS3 streams into a SONET multiplexer, where they are converted to an OC-3 stream. Finally, they are converted to an OC-12 trunk and transmitted across the WAN. This figure also shows an M13 multiplexing 28 DS1s into a single DS3, which the SONET multiplexer converts to an OC-n format. Five Mbps worth of overhead is bit-stuffed into the signal to

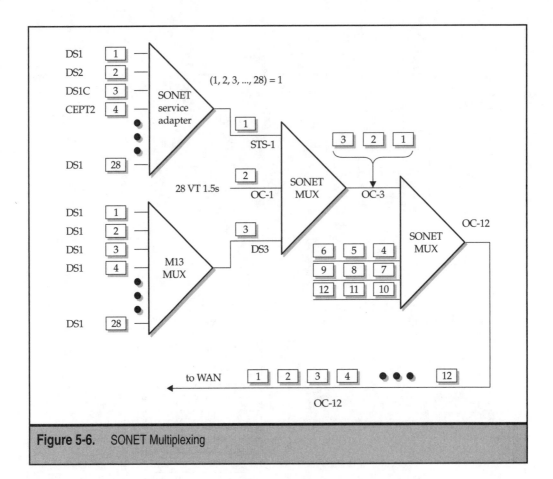

Figure 5-6. SONET Multiplexing

boost the contents and meet the STS-1 rate of 51.84 Mbps. Notice also that the synchronous order in which the subrate channels are transmitted remains constant.

NOTE: We teach students that the best way to remember the optical carrier speed is to read the OC speed, that is OC-12; remember that an OC-12 has the capacity of about 12 DS3s. In actuality, an OC-1 (51.84 Mbps) has more bandwidth than a DS3 (45 Mbps).

The other major advantage of SONET is that each individual signal down to the DS1 level can be accessed without the need to demultiplex and remultiplex the entire OC-*n* level signal. This is commonly accomplished through a SONET digital cross-connect (DXC) or multiplexer.

It is important to note that SONET multiplexing requires an extremely stable clocking source with a stable reference point. Thus, the frequency of every clock within the network must be the same as or synchronous with the others. This central clocking source is typically a Stratum 1 source, which has an atomic or radio clock directly attached, for greatest accuracy.

SONET Hardware

SONET hardware distinctions are possibly the most difficult aspect of SONET to understand. The most common equipment term used is the SONET terminal. The word *terminal*, or terminal *adapter*, is used at times to represent a SONET multiplexer, DXC (or more appropriately, optical cross-connect [OXC]), and even a switch. More often, there is a DXC/OXC interface or terminal adapter to lower-speed interfaces and protocols, and these devices are combined through a SONET terminal or switch. OC-*n*–OC-*n* SONET devices, those that provide an interface from OC-12 and OC-48 to higher-speed tributaries, like OC-192, are most often called terminals as well.

The primary benefit of SONET Central Office (CO) terminal equipment—terminals, multiplexers, terminal multiplexers, DXCs, and switches—is the reduction of equipment required for DS1, DS3, and OC-*n* connectivity and interswitch trunking. SONET terminal equipment is pushing the envelope to increase the bandwidth-to-fiber ratio even higher, using DWDM to achieve what is now a common emerging terminal speed of OC-192 (9.6 Gbps). DWDM will be discussed more later. We will now study the many types of SONET termination equipment.

SONET Terminating Multiplexer

Terminating multiplexers provide user or customer premises equipment (CPE) access to the SONET network. Terminating multiplexers—also called terminal adapters, edge multiplexers, or just terminals—operate similarly to the M13 multiplexer, and allow lower-speed access to the SONET backbone. Terminating multiplexers, also called PTE, turn *electrical* interfaces into *optical* signals by multiplexing multiple DS1, DS3, or E1 VTs into the STS-*n* signals required for OC-*n* transport. These devices are arranged in point-to-point configurations, which can be represented by the simplest SONET link (a section, line, and path all in one link).

SONET Add/Drop Multiplexer (SADM)

The current system of electrical transport and multiplexing is asynchronous at DS3 and lower speeds. This requires a huge investment in asynchronous equipment (multiplexers, DXCs). This method not only involves extensive overhead, but also the need for large numbers of multiplexers and DXCs. Multiple back-to-back M13 multiplexers and patch panels are used to break out low-speed channels from the aggregate DS3 signal. SONET eliminates these multiple equipment implementations and requirements with the use of a SADM.

SADMs work in a similar manner to their electrical equivalents, but enable the provider to drop and add not only the lower SONET rates, but also electrical interface rates down to the DS1 level. Drop-and-insert, drop-and-continue, and broadcast mode are standard features. Current SADM equipment converts the optical signal to electrical (and these functions are performed electrically), but the future might hold purely optical SADM equipment.

Figure 5-7 shows a comparison of the asynchronous and SONET methods of add/drop multiplexing. Notice that the asynchronous digital method requires the M13 multiplexer to break down a DS3 into 28 DS1s, which are then placed into a cross-connect or patch panel for drop-and-insert capability. The SONET digital cross-connect (SDXC) allows the direct drop-and-insert of any DS3 through DS1 VT within the OC-n signal (in this case an OC-12). Note that SADMs require point-to-point connectivity to both LTE terminal devices. Also, notice the reduction in equipment with additional functionality.

SADMs are generally used for distributed point-to-point network connectivity. They are CO devices, forming the building blocks of the SONET network. SADMs enable easy expansion and are often used in SONET ring architectures. They generally operate at the higher transmission speeds of OC-3 through OC-192.

SONET Digital-Loop Carrier Systems (DLCs)

DLCs are used to concentrate multiple DS0 traffic from remote terminals into a single OC-3 signal. These devices are typically situated at local service providers and handle both voice and data traffic, providing a SONET network interface for non-SONET equipment. DLCs also have many of the capabilities typically found in service providers' voice systems, such as operational and maintenance capabilities, and can handle access for many of the integrated voice and data services, such as N-ISDN and B-ISDN. These devices are also used when a remote terminal cannot transmit an OC-n signal to another service provider.

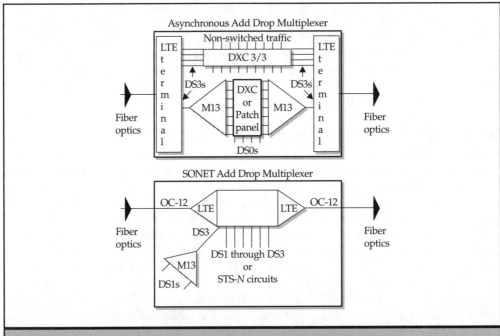

Figure 5-7.   Comparison of Asynchronous Add/Drop Multiplexing and SONET

SONET Digital Cross-Connects (SDXCs)

SDXCs operate like standard DXCs in that they enable switching and circuit grooming across all levels of the transmission, down to the DS1 level—including those that interface to the SDXC without being on the incoming or outgoing transmission. In fact, SDXCs originated as simple SONET STS-1 interfaces on a non-SDXC. SDXCs provide SONET OC-n level cross-connect provisioning capabilities and can also act as SONET hubs to provide both asynchronous and synchronous user or network access. Thus, they can reside on either the user-line interface side or the trunk side of a SONET terminal. SDXCs have helped migrate existing legacy service providers' asynchronous networks to SONET. Most grooming and routing of SONET circuits is done through SDXCs. (Figure 5-8 shows an example of a SDXC.) SDXCs can also provide interfaces to other switched architectures such as Ethernet/IP, ATM, wireless, and voice switches.

SDXCs come in two flavors: broadband (BDXC) and wideband (WDXC). The lower-speed device is the WDXC, which provides cross-connect capability for floating VTs within an STS-n. WDXCs can also provide a transparent connection between multiple DS1 interfaces and DS3 or OC-n termination. The higher-speed device is the BDXC. The BDXC can both cross-connect at DS3 (asynchronous or synchronous) and STS-1 signals, and provide concatenation of multiple STS-1 signals to STS-n levels. SDXCs and ATM DXCs are similar and can coexist in the same network, but SDXCs can provide restoration for ATM switches that do not have restoration features. In this case, the ATM switch would provide the network access and conversion to ATM over optical OC-n channels, and the SDXC would serve as an optical DXC. SDXCs can also act as international SONET gateways.

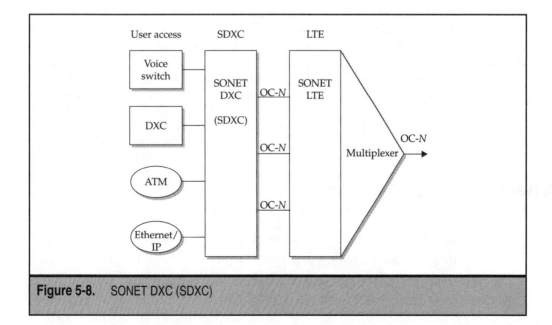

Figure 5-8. SONET DXC (SDXC)

SONET Regenerators and Optical Amplifiers

SONET regenerators and optical amplifiers work in the same manner as the signal repeaters covered in an earlier chapter, but they work through optical signal regeneration over fiber optics. Where optical amplifiers just amplify the signal and noise, regenerators reshape, retime, and retransmit signals that have incurred dispersion or attenuation over long transmission distances.

SONET Network Configurations

SONET networks can be implemented in the following configurations:

▼ **Point-to-point**   Two PTE pieces of equipment are connected directly together or with a STE/regenerator in line.

■ **Point-to-multipoint**   The PTE equipment is connected to a LTE/SADM that enables circuits to be added or dropped along the way.

▲ Ring architecture.

SONET rings are deployed in most large-scale service provider networks, so let's look at their architectures in a little more detail.

SONET Ring Architecture

SONET terminals are typically connected via point-to-point fiber connections, but through the SONET protocol they form logical rings, with each device connected to another through a minimum of a two-pair fiber configuration. Two-pair fiber configurations typically have each pair geographically and diversely routed, when diverse routes are available. A route that is not diverse is called a *spur*. When running a ring architecture, one fiber pair acts as the full-time working transmission facility while the other fiber pair acts as the full-time protection pair, remaining idle and empty while the primary pair is functioning. If a problem is detected, the SONET terminal automatically (in milliseconds) reroutes the traffic to the idle pair.

Figure 5-9 shows an example of SONET four-fiber, bidirectional line-switched fiber ring connectivity, (a) demonstrating normal operation, (b) showing automatic reconfiguration during outage on the working pair, and (c) illustrating automatic reconfiguration during fiber cut of *both* working and protected fiber pairs. To extrapolate further, the failure of either a single node or span, or both, would not take down the entire ring. Nonintrusive in-band maintenance can also be performed on the spans.

Advantages and Disadvantages

Some of the many advantages provided by SONET include the following:

▼ Reduced network complexity and cost through SADM and SDXC capabilities

■ Ability to transport all forms of traffic: voice, data (ATM, IP), and video

■ Capability to build optical interconnects between carriers

- Efficient management of bandwidth at the physical layer

- Aggregation of low-speed data transport channels into common high-speed backbone trunk transport

- Standard optical interface and format specification providing vendor interoperability

- Increased reliability and restoration over electrical systems

- Increased bandwidth management through logical path grooming

▲ Smart OAM&P features with uniformity

Some of the challenges and drawbacks of SONET deployment include the following:

▼ Strict synchronization schemes required

- Complex and costly SONET equipment contrast to cheaper optical Ethernet and other alternate MAN technologies

- High percentage of SONET protocol overhead

- Fiber laying unutilized in a ring architecture, waiting on a failure

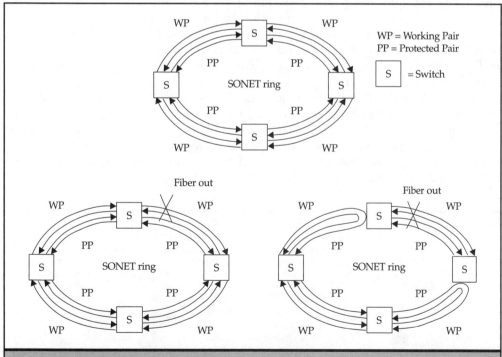

Figure 5-9.   SONET Four-fiber Protected Ring Connectivity

Overall, network synchronization is one of the greatest challenges to running a SONET network. Network management runs a close second. Despite these drawbacks, the benefits have won out in most service provider networks, where SONET continues to be the backbone Layer 1 optical transport technology of choice, with increased acceleration of DWDM augmentation on core long-haul routes.

DENSE WAVELENGTH DIVISION MULTIPLEXING (DWDM)

As telecommunication carriers are challenged with requirements for a dramatic increase in network capacity, they have three methods for relieving the capacity shortage:

▼ Increase the bit rate of existing systems, such as moving OC-48 systems to OC-192 systems.

■ Install new fiber.

▲ Optimize the use of existing fiber using methods like increasing the number of wavelengths (and thus bandwidth available) per fiber.

This section addresses the third option of increasing the number of wavelengths on a fiber, which is known as wavelength division multiplexing (WDM). Figure 5-10 shows multiple wavelengths being multiplexed onto and transmitted over a single fiber optic strand, then demultiplexed at the terminating end back into the individual wavelengths.

As this section is titled DWDM, we first need to address the question of differences between WDM and DWDM. WDM and DWDM differences are fundamentally only one of degree. DWDM spaces the wavelengths closer than WDM and therefore has a greater overall capacity than WDM.

So, DWDM and WDM are techniques that enable more than one wavelength to be added to a single-mode fiber, thus increasing the capacity of that transmission path by a factor equal to the number of wavelengths added. Systems currently exist that support 160 wavelengths per fiber and the upper limit has yet to be reached. The term wavelength is often used interchangeably with *lambda* and *channel*, but for purposes of this book we will utilize the term wavelength.

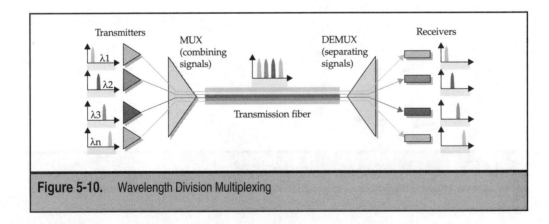

Figure 5-10. Wavelength Division Multiplexing

Understanding Colorful DWDM

Here, we discuss the number of crayons in crayon boxes to help understand DWDM.

Take my six-year-old, Alexander, who has a crayon pack of five colors. Alexander's crayon box would represent the initial WDM systems. Each wavelength can be represented by a color. If you have eight colors, you can have eight wavelengths. Each color has the capacity of OC-48 to OC-192 (10 Gbps), so the system could have a maximum bandwidth capacity of 80 Gbps!

Now take my younger son, Cameron, who comes to class with a crayon pack of 128 colors and ultra-thin crayons. These are the big boxes of all the colors I have never even heard of (chartreuse crayons?!). The crayon box takes up the same size, but because the crayons are smaller they are bunched closer together. Just like in the previous discussion, each color represents a wavelength. So, Cameron's crayon box represents a DWDM system using 128 closely packed wavelengths, where each wavelength has the capacity of OC-48 to OC-192, and therefore the system would have a maximum bandwidth capacity of 1.28 Tbps (1.28 trillion bits per second)!!!

A major advantage of DWDM is that every wavelength is independent of the others. Stated differently, you could use one wavelength to transport SONET, the second wavelength to transport optical gigabit Ethernet, and the third wavelength to transport native ATM. As discussed in the previous section, SONET has a large amount of overhead or inefficiencies that DWDM doesn't require, but DWDM is primarily a point-to-point technology whereas SONET uses the overhead for OAM&P and ring redundancy. Usually, service provider networks have a combination of both technologies.

Another advantage of DWDM technology is that optical amplifiers can act on all wavelengths, thus providing cost savings over requiring a traditional single amplifier per fiber. If you had 160 wavelengths on a DWDM fiber, this would equate to a savings of 160:1.

DWDM Hardware

DWDM equipment typically works *only* in the optical domain. Here is a quick summary of DWDM equipment types:

▼ **DWDM multiplexer/demultiplexer**   Combines multiple optical signals into a single optical fiber and separates optical signals. Stated differently, it separates optical wavelengths into a single wavelength per fiber.

■ **Optical add/drop multiplexer (OADM)**   Acts like a SADM, except that it functions exclusively in the optical domain. It allows wavelengths to be split or added to a DWDM fiber.

■ **OXC**   Acts as a cross-connect between *n*-input ports and *m*-output ports. It provides efficient network management of wavelengths at the optical layer.

The functions that can be performed are signal monitoring, restoration, provisioning, and grooming (similar to an electrical DXC).

■ **Optical amplifier** Amplifies the optical signals so that the signaling strength can travel over long distances.

▲ **Regenerator** Provides the functionality of an optical amplifier with resharing and retiming capabilities.

Note that the goal of SONET and DWDM designers is to use new technologies that reduce or eliminate the need for amplification and regeneration—thus greatly reducing the cost and increasing the availability of building and operating optical networks. We explore some of these advanced technologies in Chapter 20.

Optical Amplifiers/Regenerators

An understanding of the differences between regenerators and optical amplifiers, along with some current design rules, is important to designing cost-effective optical networks.

To demonstrate the difference between regeneration and amplification, Figure 5-11 shows that amplification only increases the size (power) of the original (yet badly degraded) signal, whereas regeneration reproduces the original signal. Amplification does not discriminate between signal (good) and noise (bad). As amplification is performed on both the original signal and the noise, the signal noise is amplified. As the signal noise accumulates, the optical signal-to-noise ratio (OSNR) is negatively impacted, and overall signal quality degrades. It is logical that if a signal (original signal *and* noise) is amplified a number of times, the original signal (without noise) might eventually become distorted to the point that it cannot be recognized and interpreted. So, why not always just regenerate only the signal?

An optical amplifier is a cost-effective method for extending the distance between end devices, or regenerators. Typically, optical amplifiers are placed in line every 80 to 120km, but a signal regenerator is required every 600 to 1,000km. With respect to cost, an optical amplifier works in the optical domain and can amplify all the wavelengths. A regenerator must convert the optical signal to electrical to perform the reshape, retime, and

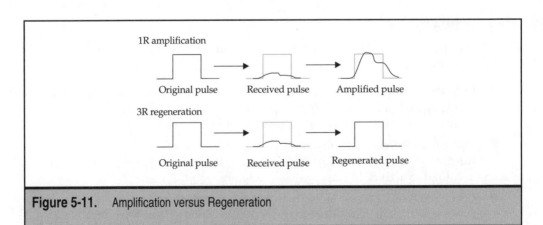

Figure 5-11.   Amplification versus Regeneration

retransmit functions, and the conversion back to optical. This optical-to-electrical-to-optical process can create excessive signal delay—our enemy in long haul transport. In addition, a regenerator is required per wavelength. Cost-effective and low-power optical regenerators are a continual target for optical component design companies.

Interfaces

Because DWDM is not as interface specific as, say, SONET, DWDM can support many different types of interfaces. DWDM equipment can support the following interfaces:

▼ SONET

■ Ethernet (1 Gbps, 10 Gbps, and fast)

■ Fibre channel

▲ ATM

Most industry studies show that a majority of the traffic on today's service providers' fiber backbones is data. That data traffic is predominately Internet protocol (IP) packets, frame relay frames, ATM cells, or LAN frames (that is, Ethernet) transporting a public SONET backbone, which is designed to transport voice. This protocol layering creates a significant amount of overhead. For example, many IP backbones utilize an ATM core over SONET, which results in an IP over ATM over SONET protocol stack. Taking a quick look at the overhead in this example, SONET contributes a 6 to 7 percent overhead. A 500-byte data packet transmitted using TCP/IP over ATM contributes another 21 to 22 percent overhead for a grand total of 28 percent overhead! Be thankful we had a big packet. If the data packet had been 100 bytes, TCP/IP over ATM overhead would have been 53 percent for a total of 60 percent overhead!!! (Remember that overhead/protocol efficiency is only one design objective and can be less significant as it relates to other efficiencies that can be achieved by integrating voice, video, and data traffic over a single backbone architecture.)

The last overhead calculation points out protocol independence as one advantage of DWDM. In MAN designs, many implementations are utilizing DWDM to transport gigabit Ethernet directly without SONET or a fiber channel connection between hospital campuses. Remember that DWDM is a technique to add capacity to the fiber physical layer on point-to-point implementations, and does not provide the reliability and flexible bandwidth management that SONET does.

DWDM Network Configurations

DWDM network configurations are based on many factors, including applications and protocols, distances, usage, network access, and the legacy network. Before beginning a design, it is important to understand the architecture and topology options. The topology of the architecture can be any one of the following:

▼ Point-to-point

■ Ring

▲ Mesh (partial or full)

Point-to-Point

This architecture can be as simple as two locations directly connected or a configuration that utilizes an OADM to break the network into multiple point-to-point segments. These networks have the characteristics of ultra-high-speed channels (10–40 Gbps), high signal integrity and reliability, and fast path restoration. The distance between transmitters and receivers can be several hundred kilometers with less than 10 amplifiers.

Ring

As rings are utilized in many SONET networks, many MAN networks utilize ring architectures with OADM to add and drop wavelengths. When rings are used in MAN networks, they typically span less than 50km and utilize a small number of wavelengths and nodes. In long-haul networks, SONET rings can be built in combination with DWDM. Because SONET can be transported across a DWDM span, congested routes such as Chicago to LA might utilize DWDM, split off the SONET wavelength's at the end points, and build local SONET rings. Protection schemes like unidirectional path-switched ring (UPSR) or bidirectional line-switched ring (BLSR) can be used in ring configurations that utilize SONET.

Many MAN networks transport protocols transparently instead of utilizing SONET to reduce overhead and costs. In utilizing DWDM networks in the MAN without SONET, the DWDM architecture doesn't support ring protection schemes that SONET supports, decreasing reliability.

Mesh

Some industry experts argue that the future architecture will be meshed. Meshed architectures connect all-optical nodes together with two routes, and implement intelligence in the nodes to reroute wavelengths on faults. A meshed architecture can be thought of as a router network where every router in the network has a direct connection to every other router. If a problem is detected, the traffic is routed to another path. This type of configuration can be extremely expensive to implement and manage, which points to one of the key benefits of SONET ring architectures.

Advantages and Disadvantages of DWDM

Advantages of DWDM include the following:

▼ The capability to support 160 Wavelengths means that over 1 Tbps of traffic can be carried.

■ Each wavelength can be a different traffic type such as SONET, gigabit Ethernet, or IP over PPP, and can operate at different speeds. This provides bandwidth and protocol flexibility with payload efficiency.

▲ Optical amplifiers provide cost savings by amplifying all wavelengths instead of requiring an optical amplifier for each fiber.

Disadvantages of DWDM include the following:

▼ Some fiber plants are not suitable for DWDM and do not support DWDM.

■ DWDM systems can be extremely difficult to troubleshoot, manage, and provision. Service providers typically run SONET over DWDM to utilize SONET's network management capabilities, but the DWDM-specific equipment still needs to be managed.

■ Vendor interoperability issues exist.

▲ Ring architecture protection schemes are not supported and point-to-point, 1 for 1 protection is used, which wastes bandwidth.

PERFORMANCE AND DESIGN CONSIDERATIONS

In designing an optical network, it is important to understand the following areas:

▼ **Applications and protocols**   What traffic is going to be transported on the network?

■ **Current network**   Will new fiber or the existing fiber plant be used?

■ **Optical power budget**   Determine your loss plan.

▲ **Interoperability**   A safe rule is not to mix equipment from different vendors on a per-leg basis. Whereas SONET is more mature and interoperability is more predominant, DWDM has a number of areas of non-standard contention between vendors, ranging from the spacing of wavelengths to the wavelength number scheme. Today, almost all DWDM implementations are single vendor.

Design the network to carry the traffic. In looking at applications, are you transporting voice, data, or a combination of both? Is the data ATM, Ethernet, frame relay, and so on? Are you transporting LAN-to-LAN traffic in a MAN or designing for long-haul WAN transport? Asking these questions should enable you to determine whether SONET transport, or a native type of transport such as gigabit Ethernet, is the right choice. If you have a combination of voice and data, SONET is the best solution for voice transport that is not packetized, but on a pure MAN for Ethernet, native transport might be the right choice. Remember not to over engineer your solution by supporting both because as you design for savings in protocol efficiency, your costs of supporting two different transport technologies could skyrocket. Put another way, keep it simple stupid (KISS). Understand that order provisioning and network management costs are real and the complexity of a system forces large amounts of money to be spent supporting these activities.

For legacy network providers, understand your current network. If you have existing fiber, can it support optical techniques like SONET and/or DWDM? The following is a list of the three principle types of single-mode fiber and their ITU specifications:

▼ Non-dispersion-shifted fiber (NDSF), G.652

■ Dispersion-shifted fiber (DSF), G.653

▲ Non-zero-dispersion-shifted fiber (NZ-DSF), G.655

NZ-DSF is optimized to support DWDM, but DSF is not suitable for DWDM. NDSF, also referred to as Standard single mode (SM) fiber, accounts for the majority of the installed fiber in the MAN that can support DWDM.

Optical power budgets are a critical part of planning an optical network. Equipment vendors must provide engineering rules. Many factors can result in optical signal loss—from the distance your fiber travels, to the number of devices such as OADMs. A rule of thumb is to use a span budget of 25dBm (a dBm is the signal power level in relation to one milliwatt). The span budget is the sum of the following:

Total system loss + (fiber length × 25) + fiber aging margin + connector/splice losses

▼ **Connector splice loss**   0.2db if connectors are modern, single mode, and from the same vendor, and 0.35db if connectors are from different vendors

■ **Fiber loss**   0.25db/km due to attenuation

▲ **Fiber aging**   2db over the life of the system

If the sum is less than 25, we are within budget. If the sum is more, we need to look at including amplifiers or reducing the number of loss-inducing elements on the span.

REVIEW

Advancements in optical networking continue to shape telecommunications. Service providers have launched new services such as gigabit Ethernet in the MAN, and implemented new equipment to increase bandwidth and reduce costs. In designing or upgrading networks, service providers have three methods to increase capacity:

▼ Increase the bit rate

■ Install new fiber

▲ Increase the number of wavelengths

We covered the first method in our discussion of SONET and SDH. In this discussion, we covered the different layers of SONET and SONET equipment as well as the SONET frame structure. In the discussion of the frame structure, we saw the OAM&P capabilities that are built into the overhead of SONET.

We then covered DWDM, which addresses increasing the number of wavelengths. In this discussion, we provided a definition of DWDM and DWDM equipment and explored the differences between regenerators and optical amplifiers.

We concluded the chapter with a discussion of performance and design considerations, specifically discussing the optical power budgets.

As optical networking is changing rapidly, we will cover additional topics of optical networking in Chapter 20.

CHAPTER 6

Physical Layer Protocols and Access Technologies

As introduced in Chapter 2, a protocol is similar to a language, conveying meaning and understanding through some form of communications. A protocol is a set of rules governing communications between two devices or between two protocol layers. The definition of protocol also implies documentation, negotiation, and the establishment of rules. For one computer to talk to another, each must be able to understand and translate the other's protocols. Protocols can be defined as fitting into one or more layers of a standard seven-layer model, which includes the physical layer, data link layer, network layer, transport layer, session layer, presentation layer, and application layer. Each of these is defined in Chapter 2 in the OSIRM. But protocols can also be grouped by communication pattern or device type, such as physical interface protocols (RS-232, V.35), link layer protocols (frame relay, ATM), LAN or switching protocols (EthernetToken Ring), or routing protocols (OSPF, BGP), transport protocols (TCP), session protocols (SNA), and upper- or user-layer protocols (X.400). These protocol groupings are the more commonly used terms. This chapter discusses both interfaces and protocols at the physical layer and those used in the most common network access technologies. Interface protocols play an important part in network design by providing the physical and logical connectivity between the user and the network. Transport protocols play a very important part in data transmissions, for without them, islands of users would be unable to communicate. Let's first take a look at the protocol and interfaces at the physical layer.

PHYSICAL LAYER PROTOCOLS AND INTERFACES

There are several major types of physical interfaces that primarily reside within the physical layer of the OSIRM. The more commonly known interfaces include RS-232C; EIA-449; EIA-232E; EIA-530; International Telecommunication Union (ITU-T) Recommendations V.24/V.28, X.21, X.21bis, I.430, I.431, T1/E1, and D4/ESF; high-speed serial interface (HSSI); high-performance parallel interface (HIPPI); ESCON; FICON; and Fibre Channel. Some physical interfaces are integrated with link and network layer protocols such as the IEEE 802.X LAN standard interfaces. Selected standards will be discussed. Physical wiring interfaces and transmission protocol framing standards such as T1/E1 and D4/ESF will also be discussed.

Physical Media

There are three major types of physical media. Copper (unshielded copper wire and shielded copper wire) and fiber optics (one or more fiber-optic strands) compose the two most common forms. Air can also form part of the transmission media, such as with point-to-point wireless, wireless LAN, cellular wireless, microwave, or satellite.

Unshielded copper wire is found in most buildings in the form of unshielded twisted pair (UTP). UTP is the least expensive of all cabling types. Unfortunately, UTP has high error rates and is subject to crosstalk, noise, and interference.

Shielded copper wire can be present as shielded twisted pair (STP) coaxial (coax), twin-axial (twin-ax), and broadband (used in CATV). The shielding protects the cable from the interference and high error rates experienced by UTP. All forms of shielded copper wire are more expensive than UTP.

Fiber optics is fast becoming the standard for all new facilities transmission cabling. The price of fiber optics and its connection devices continues to drop, and for new builds, can be close to that of copper alternatives. Fiber optics has the added advantage of resistance to electromagnetic signals and is not affected by crosstalk, interference, or the elements. But the cable requires more protection than older, sturdier copper media.

In most cases, each progressive transmission medium has a better error rate and can carry much more high-bandwidth and high-speed protocols and applications. In fact, new technologies such as wavelength division multiplexing (WDM) can push a single strand of fiber-optic cable to transmit more than 40 billion bits of data per second, while UTP is limited to the range of 10 million bits per second over long distances (at short distances, even 155 Mbps ATM or 1 Gbps Ethernet are possible, based on a trade-off of distance for speed).

In IBM cabling terms, Type 1 cabling is two-wire STP, Type 2 cabling is two-wire STP or four-wire UTP, Type 3 cabling is four-wire UTP, Type 5 cabling is fiber, and Types 6, 8, and 9 cabling are braided large-gauge two-wire copper.

EIA-232-C and -E, EIA-449, and ITU-T V.24/V.28

RS-232-C and EIA-232-E are defined by the Electronic Industries Association (EIA) as synchronous interface standards for use with the physical layer of the OSIRM. Adopted at a time when analog transmission was the prevalent industry standard, RS-232-C is probably the most common interface standard, and provides a D-shaped 25-pin connector DTE interface to voice-grade modems (DCE). The EIA-232-E is a more recently adopted standard, which though offering a significant upgrade to the RS-232-C standard, has had limited acceptance.

The ITU-T V.24/V.28 standard is very similar to RS-232-C and provides the international version of the RS-232-C standard. ITU-T V.24 defines the physical interface and V.28 defines the electrical interface. Many of the EIA standards parallel multiple ITU-T standards. For example, the RS-232-C standard contains the electrical, mechanical, and signal definitions for physical connectivity. The ITU-T V.24 (signal definition), V.28 (electrical), and ISO mechanical standards are required to define a similar interface.

Since the 232 standards are more than 35 years old and are based on the technology of that time, limitations show up on implementation, such as a maximum distance of 15 meters (50 feet) and a speed of 19.2 Kbps on standard RS-232-C. RS-449 was adopted later to alleviate these distance and speed restrictions and improve performance by using a 37-pin connector. This provides balanced signaling and tighter cabling and electrical specifications.

Two other standards were developed to further extend the distance and speed of the RS-232-C interface. The RS-423A offers speeds up to 300 Kbps and operates in "unbalanced" transmission mode, while the RS-422A offers speeds up to 10 Mbps and operates in "balanced" transmission mode. Note that EIA-449 is a mechanical interface and uses a 423/422 electrical interface. EIA-530 is also mechanical and uses a DB-25 interface instead of EIA-449 DB-37 or DB-9.

ITU-T X.21 and X.21bis

The ITU-T developed the X.21 standard in 1972 as a physical interface specification for digital networks using digital transmission facilities (unlike RS-232-C, which was designed during the analog network era). X.21 also eliminates the restrictions imposed by RS-232-C by using balanced signaling and two wires for each circuit (as opposed to two wires total for transmit and receive in RS-232). This allows for full duplex transmission of user data and control and circuit status information. X.21 also adds more logic at the DTE and DCE interfaces. X.21 spans the gap between the physical and data-link layers of the OSIRM, at times even touching on the network layer for circuit-switched networks. X.21 uses a 15-pin connector and operates only in synchronous transmission. It provides an unbalanced or balanced mode of operation. The major capabilities present in RD-232-C but lacking in X.21 are the ability to pass control information during data transfer and the separation of transmit and receive signal-element timing circuits and signal rate selectors. The X.21bis interim standard was developed as a migration from the RS-232-C, EIA-232-D, and V.24 standards to X.21.

T1/E1 and D4/ESF Framing and Formatting

A T1 circuit (a colloquial term for a DS1 circuit) operates at a speed of 1.544 Mbps. This is called the *circuit capacity*. Accounting for overhead, a DS1 will generally offer less than 1.536 Mbps to the user for data transfer, called *throughput*. T1 technology derives from the use of digital processing. With the advent of the *transistor effect* and the development of *integrated circuits*, the large-scale telephone utilities began to move this new technology into the telephone transmission network many decades ago. T1 took two twisted wire pairs and accommodated 24 voice conversations instead of only one. It was little thought of at the time to offer this capability to the end users. When the T1 capability was extended to the end user by the advent of CPE multiplexers, private lines from the service providers were used. Even today, T1 circuits (and their close cousins, the FT1 and FT3) remain the bestseller of digital private line services.

A T1 consists of 24 channels with 8 bits per channel over a time frame of 125 μs. This adds up to 192 bits per T1 frame, with a framing bit added for a total of 193 bits per frame. The transmission rate of the T1 is 8000 frames per second, and includes an 8-Kbps overhead channel. E1 is the European standard of the T1, and differs by offering 2.048-Mbps bandwidth. The 8-Kbps framing overhead on each T1 channel can be used to great advantage, depending on what framing protocol is used. The D4 12-frame superframe concept allows the 8-Kbps overhead on each T1 channel to be used for frame synchronization and signaling. The physical T1 port (often called a *T1 framer port)* is a DS1 channel as defined under the DSX-1 standard. Framed T1 runs at 1.544 Mbps over a DSX-1 interface. D4 framing formats can provide nonchannelized or channelized (as in DS0) circuits. D4 framing can also be used to access fractional T1 and DXC services.

There exists an alternative method of using the 8-Kbps overhead channel. Extended super frame (ESF) is an enhancement to D4 framing. The ANSI standard for ESF is T1.403. With ESF, both the carrier and the user can "nonintrusively" monitor and test the performance of private lines. The ESF divides the 8-Kbps overhead channel into three network-management and reporting functions: 2 Kbps performs the frame synchronization and signaling, 2 Kbps provides a cyclical redundancy check (CRC-6) code for providing error detection of end-to-end format and logic errors, while the last 4 Kbps is the facility data link (FDL) used as an open control channel.

The obvious advantage to ESF is the capability for remote monitoring and problem detection, without having to take the circuit out of service to test (as in D4 framing). This is called *nonintrusive* monitoring and testing. If ESF is implemented in conjunction with intelligent network equipment, errors affecting performance can be detected and corrected transparently to the user. ESF has played a valuable role with services, such as frame relay (FR), in which network management information provided by ESF can supplement and, in some instances, make up for existing deficiencies or lack of capabilities.

Fractional T1 (FT1) is a service offered by many providers. FT1 is used as a cost-effective interim step for purchasing a few (usually around a half dozen) dedicated circuits that cost less than a full T1 (24 channels). Thus FT1 (and its big brother, FT3) offers a cost tradeoff at speeds of 128 Kbps, 192 Kbps, 256 Kbps, and so on. DS3 service is available in most large metropolitan areas and offers an upgrade to DS1 service. FT3 rates are also available usually in increments of DS1 speeds (3 Mbps, 4.5 Mbps, 6 Mbps, and so on). Currently, the average price breakpoint for T3 seems to be the need for enough bandwidth for five to nine T1s to justify the DS3 facility. This varies widely based upon pricing and distance.

DS3 circuits can either use asynchronous or synchronous protocol multiplexing. The asynchronous transmission protocols are defined in ANSI T1.107 and the synchronous transmission protocols (SYNTRAN) are defined in ANSI T1.103. Timing is usually derived by the CPE from the network elements, and is often referred to as *loop* timing.

AMI and B8ZS Line Coding

Line coding varies depending on the speed of access. DS0 channels can be configured as either 56 Kbps or 64 Kbps. 56-Kbps channels use a technique called alternate mark inversion (AMI). A process called *bit stuffing* is used to set the least significant bit (LSB) in every byte to 1, and thus it is not available for user traffic. Bipolar eight zero substitution (B8ZS) is used in the case of 64-Kbps, or clear channel, service. B8ZS allows the entire bandwidth of 64 Kbps to be used. This is a requirement for 64-Kbps FR network access.

HSSI

HSSI is a physical interface operating at speeds up to 52 Mbps. Cisco Systems and T3Plus Networking (acquired by 3Com) were the primary developers of the HSSI interface. This high-speed interface was designed to become the standard interface between the DS3 rate of 45 Mbps and the OC-1 SONET interface of 51.84 Mbps for everything from WAN connectivity to a DTE-to-DCE direct-channel interface. It can be used to extend 45-Mbps DS3 mainframe channels to remote devices, providing a valuable high-speed interface between computer and communications equipment and, in effect, extending the WAN with larger bandwidth pipes.

HIPPI

HIPPI is a high-speed broadband parallel point-to-point channel (interface) for supercomputer networking. A few scientists at the Los Alamos National Laboratory who required high-speed parallel transfer speeds for graphic-intensive applications designed HIPPI. HIPPI is standardized in ANSI X3T9.3/90-043, 1990. The ANSI X3T9.3 HIPPI working group drafted the following four standards:

▼ **HIPPI-PH**   The physical and electrical specification

■ **HIPPI-FP**   The framing protocol of a point-to-point interface

■ **HIPPI-LE**   The encapsulation of IEEE 802.2 LLC data packets

▲ **HIPPI-SC**   The control of HIPPI physical layer switches

The standard defines HIPPI data transfer speeds of 100 MBps or 20 MBps over 50 twisted-pair copper cable with a maximum distance of 25 meters. Serial-HIPPI specifications can reach baud rates of up to 1.2 Gbps over fiber-optic media. HIPPI circuits can be connected through multiple circuit switches in a crossbar topology.

Enterprise Systems Connection (ESCON) Architecture

ESCON is IBM's fiber-optic technology for connecting mainframes using IBM channels that provide high-speed direct-channel connectivity for VM- and VSE-based system processors, direct-access storage devices (DASD), and peripherals. ESCON is the name for a set of IBM and vendor products that interconnect S/390 computers with each other and with attached storage, locally attached workstations, and other devices using optical fiber technology.

ESCON transfers data through synchronous, variable-length frames as opposed to the older byte-by-byte, bus-and-tag parallel interface. In the early '90s, ESCON replaced a much slower and more cumbersome system of interconnecting mainframes and attached devices known as the bus-and-tag cable. Bus-and-tag cable was copper, used a parallel bit attachment, and is usually referred to as a parallel environment in comparing it to the ESCON environment, which uses serial bit-by-bit technology. ESCON data rates can reach 200Mbps but are usually much less. ESCON operates over fiber-optic cable, rather than the copper wire used in bus-and-tag. ESCON uses both device and link-level framing protocols, and can operate in either a cached or noncached mode. Cached transfer operates at 10- or 17-Mbps channel speeds. Noncached data transfers will operate at the full device speed.

ESCON also uses a device called a *director*. ESCON's fiber-optic cabling can extend the local-to-the-mainframe network, also known as the channel connection, up to 60 kilometers (37.3 miles) with chained directors. A director acts as a high-performance switch and router for all attached devices. ESCON topology, when using the director switch/router, resembles a logical star. This configuration is shown in Figure 6-1.

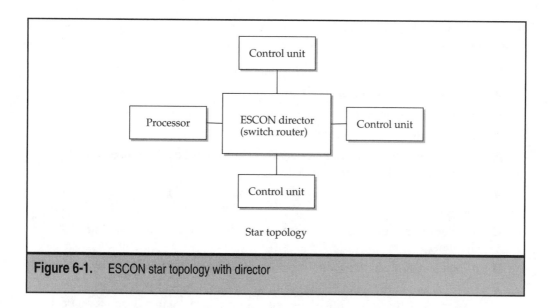

Figure 6-1.   ESCON star topology with director

The advantages of ESCON over legacy connectivity include

▼   Enables data center local or remote connectivity

■   DASD extension (9-kilometer versus 400-foot maximum distance between peripherals)

■   Improved application and resource availability

■   Increased transfer speed of data

■   Increased control of data transfer

■   Increased network and system performance

■   Improved network management across all DASD and peripherals

■   Easy configuration

■   Enables electronic vaulting of critical data—disaster recovery

■   Provides user transparency to system reconfiguration

▲   Uses Fiber-optic cables versus copper

Fibre Connection (FICON) Architecture

A newer standard called FICON made some performance improvements such as providing higher speeds at longer distances than ESCON. With native FICON attachment, IBM storage area network (SAN) switches and tape controllers can provide improved performance over greater distances compared with ESCON attachments. FICON channels increase I/O capacity through the combination of a new architecture and faster physical link rates to make them up to eight times more efficient than ESCON. Other benefits of FICON include

▼ Improvement in application performance through increased throughput

■ Enhances network performance over long distance connections

■ More flexibility in terms of network layout, because of the greater distances

■ Requires only one channel address

■ Support for full-duplex data transfers, which enables simultaneous reading and writing of data over a single link

■ Centralized and proactive management capabilities with a single point of control

■ Smaller cabling infrastructure associated with the consolidation of ESCON channels

■ Bridge feature, which enables support of existing ESCON control units

▲ Uses packet-switched technology allowing multiple I/Os from different systems to actively execute at the same time at each switch destination port

IBM products have adopted the ESCON and FICON standards as their primary high-end interfaces. Converter devices are required to convert between parallel bus-and-tag to ESCON channels, and thus make ESCON and FICON implementations more cost-effective. Cisco routers can connect directly to IBM devices through an ESCON or FICON interface.

For more information on ESCON and FICON, see the IBM Redbook at http://www.redbooks.ibm.com.

Fibre Channel *Standard (FCS)*

FCS defines a high-speed data-transfer interface for connecting and transferring data between computing devices ranging from workstations to supercomputers. FCS supports full-duplex data rates from 133–1062 Mbps over distances up to 10 kilometers, and works over both electrical and optical media. Topologies include point-to-point, loop, and switch matrix. FCS also has a built-in sliding window protocol for end-to-end delivery of data. FCS supports a variety of higher-level protocols such as HIPPI, IP, IEEE 802.2, and SCSI. Details on this technology can be found in ANSI X3.230-1994, Fibre Channel Physical and Signaling Interface (FC-PH). The Fibre Channel Industry Association (FCIA) was formed in 1999 as a result of a merger between the Fibre Channel Association and the Fibre Channel Community. FCIA is a not-for-profit corporation with more than 150 members that include manufacturers, systems integrators, developers, systems vendors, industry professionals, and end users organized to support and drive the fibre channel market.

Fibre channel is a technology for transmitting data between computer devices at a data rate of up to 1 Gbps. The FCIA has proposed a data rate of 10 Gbps. Fibre channel is especially suited for connecting computer servers to shared storage devices and for interconnecting storage controllers and drives. Since fibre channel is three times as fast, it has begun to replace the small computer system interface (SCSI) as the transmission interface between servers and clustered storage devices. Fibre channel is more flexible; devices can be as far as 10 kilometers (about six miles) apart if optical fiber is used as the physical medium. Optical fiber is not required for shorter distances, however, because fibre channel also works using coaxial cable and ordinary telephone twisted pair.

Fiber channel offers point-to-point, switched, and loop interfaces. It is designed to interoperate with SCSI, the Internet Protocol (IP) and other protocols, but has been criticized for its lack of compatibility—primarily because (as in the early days of SCSI technology) manufacturers sometimes interpret specifications differently and vary their implementations. Standards for fibre channel are specified by the Fibre Channel Physical and Signaling standard, and the ANSI X3.230-1994, which is also ISO 14165-1. Fibre channel allows concurrent communications among workstations, mainframes, servers, data storage systems, and other peripherals using SCSI and IP protocols. It provides interconnect systems for multiple topologies that can scale to a total system bandwidth on the order of a terabit per second. Fibre channel delivers a new level of reliability and throughput. Switches, hubs, storage systems, storage devices, and adapters are among the products that are on the market today, providing the ability to implement a total system solution. The ambitious requirements given the standards group are

▼ Performance from 266 Mbps to more than 4 Gbps

■ Support for distances up to 10 kilometers

■ Small connectors

■ High-bandwidth utilization with distance insensitivity

■ Greater connectivity than existing multidrop channels

■ Broad availability (that is, standard components)

■ Support for multiple cost/performance levels, from small systems to supercomputers

▲ Ability to carry multiple existing interface command sets, including IP, SCSI, IPI, HIPPI-FP, and audio/video

Fibre channel is being provided as a standard disk interface. Industry leading RAID manufacturers are shipping fibre channel systems. Soon, RAID providers will not be regarded as viable vendors unless they offer fibre channel.

In a fibre channel network, legacy storage systems are interfaced using a fibre channel to SCSI bridge. IP is used for server-to-server and client/server communications. Storage networks operate with both SCSI and networking (IP) protocols. Servers and workstations use the fibre channel network for shared access to the same storage device or system. Legacy SCSI systems are interfaced using a fibre channel to SCSI bridge.

Fibre channel products have defined a new standard of performance, delivering a sustained bandwidth of more than 97 Mbps for large file transfers and tens of thousands I/Os per second for business-critical database applications on a Gigabit link. This new capability for open systems storage is the reason fibre channel is the connectivity standard for storage access. The installed base of fibre channel technology (and by extension, SANs) has been growing at a rate of 85 percent CAGR for several years and is expected to be one of the major growth areas in the information technology (IT) marketplace over the next several years. See http://www.fibrechannel.com for more information.

IEEE 802 Physical Interfaces

The three most common MAC physical interfaces for the IEEE 802 architecture model are Ethernet (802.3), Token Ring (802.5), and wireless LAN (802.11).

10-Mbps (Legacy) Ethernet

The physical interface for IEEE 802.3 and Ethernet provides more than just the synchronous interface standard provided by RS-232 or V.35. Recognition of the presence or absence of the control of the carrier sense multiple access with collision detection (CSMA/CD), data transport, collisions, and the translation of signaling from physical to MAC layer (Layer 2 sublayer) is provided by the physical layer of Ethernet. These are discussed in Chapter 7.

There are many different physical types of Ethernet access: 1Base5, 10Base2, 10Base5, 10BaseT, 10Broad36, 10BaseF, 100BaseT, 100BaseFX, and fiber-optic inter-repeater link (FOIRL). Each type defines both the wiring and the device terminating the end of the wiring. 10Base5 was the thick-cable Ethernet with the drop cable needed by each user to access via a tap. The *10* refers to 10-Mbps Ethernet, while the *5* refers to the 500-meter maximum length of a segment. The *Base* stands for baseband, which refers to the signaling. Baseband signaling indicates that Ethernet signals are the only signals carried over the media system. 10Base2 was introduced in the '80s as thin-wire Ethernet (or "Cheapernet"), offering a thinner coaxial cable with the same method of access. The 2 refers to 200-meter cable length. The physical connectors are called BNC and AUI, respectively. The 10BaseF and the FOIRL are physical Ethernet types that require fiber. The 100BaseT supports UTP, and the 100BaseFX supports fiber.

The most common connectivity is via twisted-pair wiring using the 10BaseT or 100BaseT standards, where users access the medium through their telephone's wall jack, which is wired no more than 100 meters from the central hub or switch. The *T* stands for twisted-pair cable. Both baseband coaxial and broadband coaxial were designed to operate at 10 Mbps, while unshielded twisted-pair (UTP) was designed to operate at 1 Mbps. A transceiver module might be needed to adapt to the 10Base2 thin-wire or 10BaseT twisted-pair Ethernet connection. Hubs are used to concentrate the star distributed twisted-pair cable connections. Other Ethernet proprietary implementations might require an external radio frequency modem or fiber-optic inter-repeater link. Another standard used quite often is the 10BaseF. The *F* stands for fiber. These standards specify fiber optics with Ethernet networks and backbone Ethernet. The distance for Ethernet could be extended to 2 kilometers, the same as for FDDI. The 10BaseF standard comes as three separate options (10BaseFB, 10BaseFL, and 10BaseFP) based on specific requirements and distances. All three options use 62.5/125 μm fiber-optic cable with ST connectors to connect to the equipment on both ends and a 800–910-nm (infrared) light source. The 10Base-FB option has a feature to detect jabbering transmitters and can automatically enable a backup link. Table 6-1 identifies the intended use and characteristics of some of the 10-Mbps Ethernet specifications.

Name	Intended Use	Characteristics
10Base-FP (fiber passive)	Workstation-to-repeater and repeater-to-repeater links	Organizes computers into star topology, segments can be up to 500 meters long
FOIRL (fiber-optic inter-repeater link)	Repeater-to-repeater links	1 km maximum segment length, 4 repeater maximum cascade
10Base-FL (fiber link)	Workstation-to-repeater and repeater-to-repeater links, designed to replace the FOIRL	2 km maximum segment length, able to interoperate with FOIRL
10Base-FB (fiber backbone)	Allows additional segments and repeaters to be connected to the network	2 km maximum segment length, 15 repeater maximum cascade, must be built into repeater
10Base2 (thinnet)	Connect user stations	50-ohm thin coaxial cable, distance limit of 185 meters per segment
10Base5 (thicknet)	Connect user stations	50-ohm baseband coaxial cable, distance limit of 500 meters per segment
10BaseT	Connect user stations	Uses two pairs of twisted-pair cabling, has a distance limit of approximately 100 meters per segment
10Broad36	Attaching devices to a broadband local network	Uses broadband coaxial cable, has a distance limit of 3600 meters per segment

Table 6-1.   Comparisons of Ethernet Cabling Specifications

Fast Ethernet

Fast (100-Mbps) Ethernet is now the new preferred standard, and most new purchases of an Ethernet NIC are typically for a 10/100-Mbps autosensing card. Compared with the 10-Mbps specifications, the 100-Mbps system results in a factor of 10 reduction in the bit time, which is the amount of time it takes to transmit a bit on the Ethernet channel. This produces a tenfold increase in the speed of the packets over the media system. However, the other important aspects of the Ethernet system including the frame format, the amount of data a frame can carry, and the media access control mechanism are all unchanged.

The Fast Ethernet specifications include mechanisms for autonegotiation of the media speed. This makes it possible for vendors to provide dual-speed Ethernet interfaces that can be installed and run at either 10 Mbps or 100 Mbps automatically. The autonegotiation function allows the devices to perform automatic configuration to achieve the best possible mode of operation over a link. Autonegotiation provides automatic speed matching for multispeed devices at each end of a link. The autonegotiation protocol includes automatic sensing for other capabilities such as autonegotiation of duplex operation.

There are three media varieties that have been specified for transmitting Fast Ethernet signals:

▼ **100BaseTX**   Uses 2-pair Category 5 UTP cable

■ **100BaseFX**   Uses fiber-optic cable

▲ **100BaseT4**   Uses 4-pair Category 3, 4, or 5 UTP cable

The third part of the identifier determines the segment type. The TX segment type is a twisted-pair segment that uses two pairs of wires and is based on the data grade twisted-pair physical medium standard developed by ANSI. The FX segment type is a fiber-optic link segment based on the fiber-optic physical medium standard developed by ANSI and that uses two strands of fiber cable. The T4 segment type is a twisted-pair segment that uses four pairs of telephone-grade twisted-pair wire.

Gigabit Ethernet

Because it increases performance by building on a company's current investment, Gigabit (1000-Mbps) Ethernet is ideal when budgets are tight but there is a requirement for higher bandwidth. Technicians are familiar with the technology, so retraining is not needed. Costly protocol and hardware and cabling changes can be avoided, and any disruption to the network is usually minimal. Gigabit Ethernet employs all the same specifications defined by the original Ethernet standard, including the same Ethernet frame format and size. 1-Gbps Ethernet is now available in mass quantities, and 10-Gbps Ethernet products are on the planning boards. Benefits of Gigabit Ethernet include

▼ Supports quality of service (QoS) services such as IEEE 802.1p traffic prioritization "tagging" of Ethernet packets and Resource Reservation Protocol (RSVP).

■ RSVP supports the ability to request a service level from the network to support a particular application.

■ Widespread deployment of Gigabit is possible over the existing copper infrastructure.

■ Fully compatible with the large installed base of Ethernet and Fast Ethernet nodes, which makes it easy to scale.

▲ Supports full-duplex operations, which offers virtually twice the bandwidth and maximizes performance.

The 1000BASE-T physical layer standard provides 1-Gbps Ethernet signal transmission over four pairs of Cat-5 UTP cable. It transmits at 125 Mbaud, the same symbol rate as Fast Ethernet. But by using more sophisticated five-level (PAM-5) coding along with four wire pairs, it is able to transmit much more data. To simplify, each wire pair sends and transmits simultaneously, for 250 Mbps per pair (125 Mbaud × 2 bits). Multiplying 250 Mbps by four pairs yields the nominal rate of 1000 Mbps. The standard covers cabling distances of up to 100 meters, or networks with a diameter of 200 meters. The 100-meter cabling distance is the safe limit for reliable transmission, and the diameter assumes 100 meters in two directions from a switch. Most implementations of Gigabit Ethernet are supported using fiber-optic cabling because of the benefits provided by fiber optics such as greater distance and higher performance. Gigabit Ethernet is supported by the following options:

▼ **1000BaseT** Uses four pairs of CAT-5 balanced copper cabling and a 5-level coding scheme

■ **1000BaseCX** Uses 150-ohm shielded copper cable and supports a maximum length of 25 meters

■ **1000BaseF** Uses fiber-optic cable

■ **1000BaseFX** Uses 62.5/125 multimode fiber and supports a maximum distance of 412 meters

■ **1000BaseSX** Uses 50/125 or 62.5/125 multimode fiber and supports a maximum distance of 550 meters

■ **1000BaseLX** Uses 9/125 single-mode, 50/125 multimode, or 62.5/125 multimode fiber and supports a maximum distance of 5 kilometers

■ **1000BaseZX** Uses 9/125 single-mode fiber and supports a maximum distance of 100 kilometers

▲ **10-Gbps Ethernet** Uses only fiber-optic cable

Wireless LAN (IEEE 802.11)

The IEEE 802 standards committee formed the 802.11 Wireless Local Area Networks Standards Working Group in 1990. The IEEE 802.11 wireless standards specify connectivity between LAN devices using radio-based equipment. The standard allows us to connect our computers together and to the Internet at a very high speed without any cabling infrastructure or the costs associated with this infrastructure. The 802.11 standards are similar to the IEEE 802.3 Ethernet standard for wired LANs. The IEEE 802.11 specifications address the physical (PHY) and media access control (MAC) layers. Instead of using the Ethernet 802.3 collision detection protocol, the MAC protocol supported by 802.11 is Carrier Sense Multiple Access with Collision Avoidance (CSMA/CA). Collision detection cannot be used for the radio frequency transmissions because when a node transmits over the air it cannot hear other nodes on the network. This is due to its own signal drowning out any signal that might arrive.

The 802.11 standards support the stations operating in two different configurations. The first configuration is called the independent or ad-hoc configuration. This allows stations to communicate directly with each other without having to access a central point. This option is limited in coverage area. The second option is called the infrastructure configuration and requires the stations to communication with access points. The access point acts as a distribution system much like a bridge in a wired LAN and offers an extended coverage area. The access point is generally some form of a bridge or router. In Figure 6-2, the access point is a cable or DSL router that supports both wired and wireless connections. This is very common today for home area networks. The user can roam from room to room with their laptop and stay connected to the Internet. With a wired solution, they would have to unplug from the LAN as they moved between rooms (or have a very long Ethernet cable).

The 802.11 standard supports the interoperability of manufactured wireless LAN radio equipment but does not specify the technology to use or how to implement it. The wireless LAN standards provide only the specifications for the physical layer and MAC layer. Currently, the two predominate physical layer standards are the 802.11a and 802.11b, as detailed in Figure 6-3. Each specification operates in a different radio band and uses a different transmission technology. The 802.11a specification operates in the 5 GHz range and uses a transmission technology called orthogonal frequency division multiplexing (ODFM). Like FDM (discussed in Chapter 4), ODFM divides the radio signal and then transmits multiple data streams simultaneously at different frequencies to the receiver. The advantage of ODFM is the ability to reduce the amount of disturbance caused by electromagnetic interference through the cable infrastructure. The 802.11b specification operates in the 2.4 GHz range and uses a transmission technology called direct-sequence spread spectrum (DSSS). With DSSS, the data signal at the transmitting station is combined with a higher data rate bit sequence that separates the user data according to a special spreading ratio. The bit sequence is a redundant pattern for each bit that is sent.

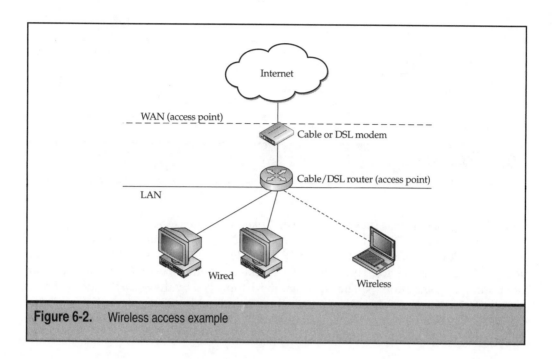

Figure 6-2.   Wireless access example

Because of the redundancy built into the bit stream, original data can be recovered even if bits in the pattern are damaged. This process helps the signal resist interference that could normally disrupt the communication.

One of the issues facing the wireless LAN market is that of security. Any wireless network adapter within range of another wireless adapter can instantly join the wireless network (whether you want them to or not). One way around this is to enable the wired equivalent privacy (WEP) algorithm. WEP is somewhat secure, but has some inherent flaws and is not secure enough for critical data or data that needs to remain private. It is more suitable for home area networks that don't entice the serious hackers. Security and encryption protocols have a tendency to slow a network down, sometimes as much as 50 percent, due to the processing and protocol encapsulation taking place. New 802.11 standards are being developed to address some of the current limitations of the specifications such as security, QoS, and the support for more physical layer options. Currently, vendors offer proprietary implementations for these limitations. But, buyers beware: the problem with implementing proprietary solutions is that it limits your options to a single vendor.

Token Bus and Token Ring

Physical interface for IEEE 802.4 Token Bus and IEEE 802.5 Token Ring is the DB connector, interfacing the IBM Type 1 shielded twisted-pair cable. Coaxial cable connections are also available. Token Ring wiring is usually run in Type 1 (2-pair STP), Type 2 (4-pair STP),

IEEE standard	Standard completed	Nickname	Radio band	Number of channels	Link rate per channel	Transmission technology
802.11a	1999	WiFi5	5 GHz	8	6 to 54 Mbps	OFDM
802.11b	1999	WiFi	2.4 GHz	3	11 Mbps	DSSS

Figure 6-3.   802.11a and 802.11b specifications

Type 3 (UTP), and Type 5 (fiber-optic cable). Token Ring interfaces at either 4 Mbps or 16 Mbps through an IEEE 802.5 interface, and uses 802.2 Type 1 LLC support. It also can interface via shielded twisted pair at 1, 4, and 16 Mbps. Figure 6-4 shows an example of Token Ring physical connectivity. The IEEE 802.4 Working Group is currently inactive and not supporting ongoing projects. The latest standard approved by the 802.5 Standards Board was the 802.5z Gigabit Token Ring standard approved in May 2001.

Table 6-2 shows a comparison of some of the LAN physical media we've discussed in this section based on speed, maximum distance, and signaling.

ACCESSING THE NETWORK

The way corporations and consumers access the network has changed dramatically over the last few years. The two general categories of access methods we cover here are corporate and consumer or residential. The consumer access market has seen significant improvements. Just a few short years ago, we were limited to accessing the Internet from home with dialup connections using 56-Kbps modems. Through rapid advancements in technology, today we have multiple options including "legacy" dialup, Integrated Services Digital Network (ISDN), Digital Subscriber Line (DSL), cable, and wireless, all of which we discuss in this chapter. The average access speed of DSL and cable modems, albeit shared access, now averages 1 Mbps—close to a DS1! Corporate access types have also changed, mostly in the speed of access. Corporations typically can use most con-

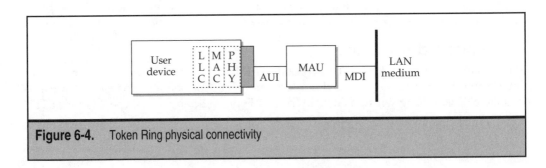

Figure 6-4.   Token Ring physical connectivity

Physical Media	Standard Name	Speed Mbps	Max Distance, m	Signal Mode
50-ohm coaxial	10Base5	10	500	Baseband
Thin coaxial	10Base2	10	200	Baseband
UTP	10BaseT	10	100	Baseband
STP	Token Ring	4/16	100 (lobe)	Baseband
Broadband coaxial	10Broad36	10	3600	Broadband
STP (data grade)	Token Ring	16	700 (lobe) + 800 inter-MAU	Baseband

Table 6-2. Physical Media Comparison

sumer methods of access (such as DSl to FR) plus have additional service options enabled by fiber access to corporate locations. With fiber comes the ability to have significantly more bandwidth and a plethora of new service options such as metro Ethernet, IP over SONET, and ATM.

Consumer or Residential Alternatives

Consumers are generally limited to copper, cable, or wireless infrastructure, as shown in Figure 6-5, which minimizes their choice in access technologies. Home offices and small business offices generally use one of the following access alternatives:

▼ Existing copper phone line:
- Plain old telephone service (POTS)
- Dialup
- ISDN
- Basic rate interface (BRI)
- DSL
- Cable Line:
- Cable modem
▲ Wireless:
- Direct broadcast satellite (DBS)
- Very small aperture satellite (VSAT)

Line type	Cable type	Speed
56 Kbps	Copper/UTP	56 Kbps
ISDN—BRI	Copper/UTP	128 Kbps
Wireless	No cable	2Mbps
ADSL	Copper/UTP	9 Mbps
Cable	Coaxial cable	30 Mbps
DS3/T3	Fiber/coaxial/copper/UTP	45 Mbps

Figure 6-5.   Consumer access methods and speeds

Corporate or Business Access Alternatives

Corporate business locations have access to most of the consumer alternatives plus technologies offered over fiber-optic infrastructures. Depending on how many people are located in a building, a medium size office generally chooses between a private line service (full T1, FT1, or DS0 service), ISDN (both BRI and primary rate interface [PRI]), or DSL. With fractional T1 service, the customer buys all the networking equipment purchased for a full T1 service, but pays a fraction of the monthly T1 cost, depending on the actual bandwidth required (more than 56 Kbps, but less than 1.544 Mbps). Large sites would generally require a minimum of T1 speeds, with some customers purchasing OC-12 access circuits today. Medium and large business offices generally use one of the following access alternatives:

▼ Copper:

   ■ All consumer methods

   ■ DS1, FT3, DS3

   ■ ISDN

▲ Fiber:

   ■ DS3

   ■ SONET OC-N

To help understand why the access speed is so important, Table 6-3 shows the transfer times to send a 10-megabyte file across access circuits of varying speeds.

Medium	Speed	Transfer Time
OC-12	622 Mbps	<1 second
DS3/T3	45 Mbps	1.8 seconds
ADSL	4 Mbps	20 seconds
DS1/T1	1.544 Mbps	52 seconds
Cable	1 Mbps	1.3 minutes
ISDN/IDSL	128 Kbps	10.4 minutes
56K	53 Kbps	25 minutes

Table 6-3.   File Transfer Times

COPPER ACCESS TECHNOLOGIES

Most homes and businesses today have copper transmission facilities available. A standard telephone line in the United States consists of a pair of copper wires that is provided by a local phone company. Up until the last five years, these copper wires supported primarily voice calls, but they can handle a much greater range of frequencies to provide more bandwidth and carry more than just phone conversations. Wide-scale use of these copper facilities for data was not exploited until the Internet explosion in the '90s. First ISDN was deployed, but cost and ubiquity limitations hampered wide-scale user adoption. Later in the 90s, xDSL and cable modems came on the scene and true broadband access was available at a cost-effective price. The copper access technologies we discuss in this section include dial access via legacy analog and digital modems, ISDN, DSL, and cable. We start by defining the most common form of copper access: the UTP cable.

UTP

We discussed the digital hierarchy in Chapter 4. A transmission repeater system over a four-wire twisted pair is defined and called *T1*. The signal and service is referred to as a *DS1*. A DS1 consists of 24 DS0s. T1 is a very popular access method to the Internet and to the wide area network for medium to large organizations. The price for an Internet access T1 has been drastically reduced over the last few years (less than $1,000 monthly in the U.S. for a few hundred miles), making it popular even for remote sites. In the mid to late '90s, companies would use T1 circuits at their headquarters location and 56-Kbps circuits at their remote locations. In the late '90s, many customers transitioned their remote locations to T1 speeds. T1 circuits are brought to the customer location via either copper or fiber.

UTP is the most popular type of copper wiring. The copper wiring that connects homes to the telephone network consists of two insulated copper wires that are twisted around each other. Twisting the wires reduces the electromagnetic induction and crosstalk. In some situations, multiple pairs are installed in a single cable. UTP is very common because it is very inexpensive compared with shielded copper and fiber alternatives, plus it is flexible and thinner and therefore easier to install. Although twisted pair is often associated with home use, a higher grade of twisted pair is often used for horizontal wiring in LAN installations because it is less expensive than coaxial cable. The EIA/TIA cabling standards specify the following ratings for UTP cable:

▼ Category 1 is used for voice and low-speed data transmission up to 56 Kbps.

■ Category 2 is equivalent to IBM's Type 3 cabling. It's ideal for 4-Mbps token ring, RS-232, RS-422, and AS/400.

■ Category 3 supports up to 16 MHz. It is ideal for telephone, 4-Mbps token ring, and 10BaseT applications.

■ Category 4 supports up to 20 MHz and is generally used for 16-Mbps token ring.

■ Category 5 supports up to 100 MHz, which makes it suitable for 100BaseT Ethernet, 16-Mbps token ring, and OC-3 ATM. This is the most common UTP cabling in the market today.

■ Category 5e supports up to 200 MHz. It supports throughput speeds up to 1.2 Gbps and is typically used for Gigabit Ethernet.

▲ Category 6 (TIA/EIA-568-B.2-1) is a newly ratified standard designed to support Gigabit Ethernet and future applications. It is rated up to 350 MHz or 155 Mbps.

The widespread use of twisted pair wiring has made 10BaseT the most popular version of Ethernet. 10BaseT supports a 10-Mbps transmission rate over two pairs of Category 3 or better telephone twisted pair cabling, also known as *voice grade* twisted pair. 10BaseT uses one pair of wires for transmitting data, and the other pair for receiving data. The two pairs of wires are bundled into a single cable that might often include two additional pairs of wires, which are unused for 10BaseT. Each end of the cable is terminated with an 8-position registered jack-45 (RJ-45) connector.

100BaseT deployments have quickly overtaken legacy 10BaseT, and most NIC cards are now sold as 10/100-Mbps autosensing. Both technologies use the same media.

Dialup or Legacy Analog Modem

Dialup or legacy analog modem access is supported by the use of a modulator/demodulator (modem). The sending modem translates a digital signal from the computer to an analog signal (modulates) to send over the service provider's telephone network. Once the signal arrives at the receiving end, the receiving modem translates the analog signal back to digital (demodulates). The newest standard, 56 Kbps, was developed in the mid '90s and became a standard around 1998. The current standard for 56-Kbps modems is V.92.

It was long thought that the theoretical limit on modem speed over an ordinary phone line was 33.6 Kbps, but 56-Kbps modems achieve their speed by avoiding a conversion from digital to analog lines in the connection between user and the service provider. Ordinary connections begin over an analog line; they are then converted to digital by the phone company and are converted back to analog in the final segment before arriving at the service provider, as shown in Figure 6-6.

Connections of 56 Kbps begin as analog, are converted to digital, and are not converted back to analog at the service provider. This requires the service provider to have a direct digital connection, and avoids one conversion of the signal. By avoiding this second conversion, speeds of 56 Kbps and faster are possible. Therefore, modem users need to know that they can achieve 56 Kbps only if their service provider supports it. Remember that just because 56 Kbps is possible, it doesn't mean that every user will achieve it. Poor local phone lines, the modem speed of your Internet service provider, and other conditions might limit speed. Also, Federal Communications Commission (FCC) regulations limit the speed to 53 Kbps.

Prior to 56-Kbps modems, the best speed you could get between two modems was 33.6 Kbps. With 56-Kbps technology and V.90 standards, connection speeds can exceed 50 Kbps. The data speeds are different when you connect in V.90 mode; the download speeds are up to 54 Kbps, and the upload speed is limited to 33.6 Kbps. The ITU-T documented an improved ITU-T 56K modem standard: V.92. Though the top speed for downloads is still 56 Kbps, V.92 has a number of enhancements:

▼ **Upload speed increased to 48 Kpbs**   The maximum upload speed has been increased from 33.6 to 48 Kbps, which should improve video conferencing and general file uploading.

■ **Startup time reduced from about 20 seconds to about 10 seconds**   The startup time—the time needed to establish a connection—has been reduced, making hopping on and off the Internet much easier. Reports from months ago claimed that startup time had been reduced from around 20 seconds to about 5 seconds, though more recent reports put the figure at 10 seconds. (One difference in the figures might be whether or not dialing time is included, or if the figures cover only the time when the two modems are screeching at each other during the connection phase.)

▲ **Internet call waiting**   V.92 uses this feature, which provides a standard method of disconnecting the modem long enough to let you know that someone is trying to call you without losing the connection.

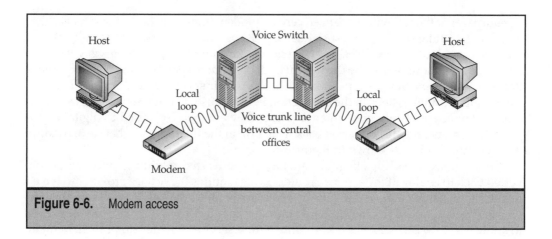

Figure 6-6.   Modem access

ISDN

The ISDN standard was designed to provide a next generation consumer and corporate broadband access service. ISDN's original development and deployment goes back for decades when 56 Kbps was a broadband access speed. Today, ISDN BRI provides one of the best disaster recovery alternatives (along with dial modem access) for services such as FR and IP (VPNs and Internet access), and serves a variety of other consumer and corporate uses. We now turn our attention to the original ISDN standards, where most of the frame-and cell-switched protocols discussed in this book have their roots. First, the ISDN BRI and PRI services are described. Next, the basic ISDN protocol and framing structure are covered. Subsequent to the definition of broadband ISDN (B-ISDN) used in protocols such as ATM, the ISDN standards are now referred to as the narrowband ISDN (N-ISDN) standards.

ISDN Basics

ISDN was built on the time division multiplexing (TDM) hierarchy developed for digital telephony, as defined in previous sections. The ITU-T defines two standards for the physical interface to ISDN: BRI, or basic rate interface access, as defined in ITU-T ISDN I.430, and Primary Rate Interface (PRI), as defined in ITU-T ISDN I.431. Both standards define the electrical characteristics, signaling, coding, and frame formats of ISDN communications across the user access interface (S/T) reference point. The physical layer provides transmission capability, activation, and deactivation of terminal equipment (TE) and network termination (NT) data (D)-channel access for TE, maintenance functions, and channel status indications. The basic infrastructure for these physical implementations and the definition for the S and T reference points, TE, and NT, are contained in ITU-T Recommendation I.412. ISDN functional groups and reference points (as defined in ITU-T Recommendation I.411) are shown in Figure 6-7.

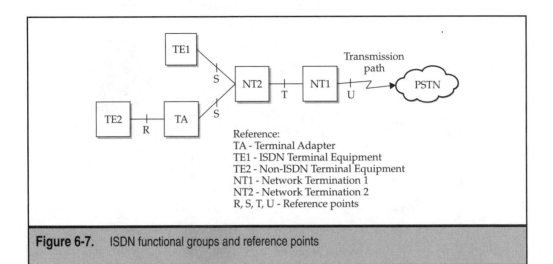

Figure 6-7. ISDN functional groups and reference points

The physical interface in ISDN is one part of the D-channel protocol, and defines a full-duplex synchronous connection between the TE Layer 1 terminal side of the basic access interface (TE1, TA, and NT2 functional group aspects) and the NT Layer 1 terminal side of the basic access interface (NT1 and NT2 functional group aspects).

Figure 6-8 shows both a point-to-point configuration with one transmitter and one receiver per interchange circuit, as well as a multipoint configuration with multiple TE, both for BRI. Note that only one TE can use the line at the same time. Both bus distances cannot exceed 1000 meters, except when using a short passive bus, when the limitation is 180 meters, as opposed to an extended passive bus in multipoint mode. The bit rate in both directions is 192 Kbps. Figure 6-9 shows some of the typical options for accessing an ISDN network.

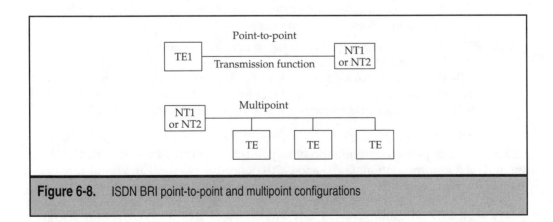

Figure 6-8. ISDN BRI point-to-point and multipoint configurations

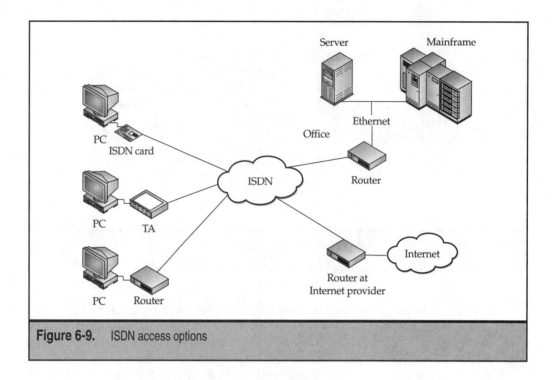

Figure 6-9.   ISDN access options

BRI and PRI Service and Protocol Structures

BRI service configurations are defined as follows:

▼ **BRI**   Provides two 64-kbps bearer (B)-channels for the carriage of user data and one 16-Kbps control, messaging, and network management D-channel. This interface, shown in Figure 6-10, is commonly referred to as 2B + D. BRI was intended for customer access devices requiring voice, data, and video communications, albeit low video rates.

▲ **PRI**   Provides 23 64-Kbps bearer (B) channels and one 64-Kbps data (D) signaling channel referred to in North America as 23B + D. Internationally, 30 B-channels are provided in a 30B + D configuration, as shown in Figure 6-11. The PRI was intended for use by higher bandwidth or shared customer devices such as the private branch exchange (PBX), personal computer, and LAN.

The ISDN PRI provides a single 1.544-Mbps DS1 or a 2.048-Mbps E-1 data rate channel over a full-duplex synchronous point-to-point channel using the standard TDM hierarchy. ITU Recommendations G.703 and G.704 define the electrical and frame formats of the PRI interface, respectively. Sending 8000 frames per second with each frame containing 193 bits accomplish the 1.544-Mbps rate. The DS1 stream comprises 24 DS0 channels of 64 Kbps each, containing 23 B-channels at 64 Kbps each and one D-channel at 64 Kbps.

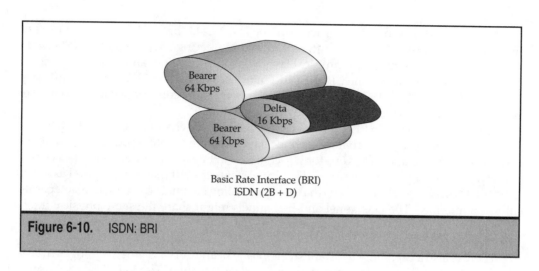

Basic Rate Interface (BRI)
ISDN (2B + D)

Figure 6-10. ISDN: BRI

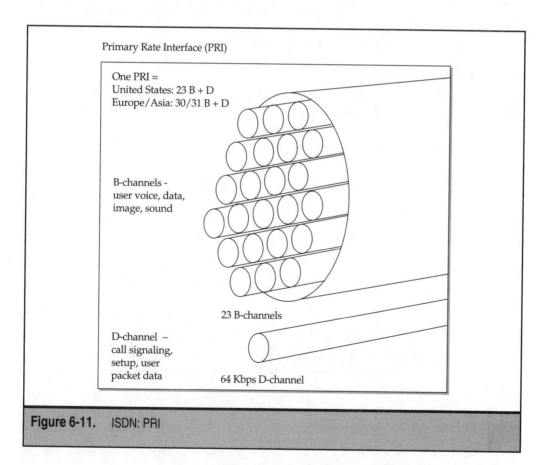

Figure 6-11. ISDN: PRI

Figure 6-12 shows the frame structure of the DS1 1.544 Mbps PRI. The CEPT E1-based PRI frame structure is somewhat different from this, offering 30 B-channels, one D-channel, and a channel reserved for physical layer signaling, framing, and synchronization.

The frame structure for the CEPT E1 PRI interface is shown in Figure 6-13. A primary attribute distinguishing ISDN service from telephony is the concept of common channel signaling, or out-of-band signaling using the D-channel.

H-channels are used in PRIs. Two types are defined: H_0-channel signals, which have a bit rate of 384 Kbps, and H_1-channels, which have a bit rate of 1536 Kbps for H_{11}-channels in the United States and 1920 Kbps for H_{12}-channels in Europe. These channels (except for the H_{12}-channel implementation) use B-channel slots on a PRI that is configured as either 24×B or 30×B. Note that this means that the D-signaling channel is provided on a separate physical interface. The D-channel and B-channels might share the same physical interface, or the D-channel on one interface might control the B-channels on several physical interfaces.

There is also a capability to establish an nxDS0 bearer service, where n ranges from 1 to 24 (or 30 at the European channel rate) via ISDN signaling. The nxDS0 service uses n contiguous time slots or a bit-map-specified set of DS0 time slots in the DS1 or E1 frame. This is called the multirate circuit mode bearer service (MRCMBS). Also, ISDN signaling can establish a frame mode bearer service (FMBS) or a switched X.25 connection.

ISDN Protocol Model

ISDN standards were first developed by the ITU in 1972, with the first standards documents published in 1984. The original intent of ISDN was to provide a conversion of tele-

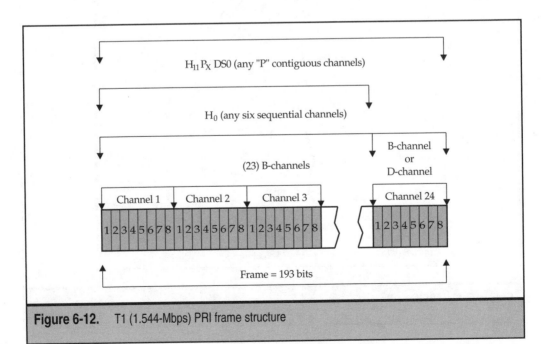

Figure 6-12. T1 (1.544-Mbps) PRI frame structure

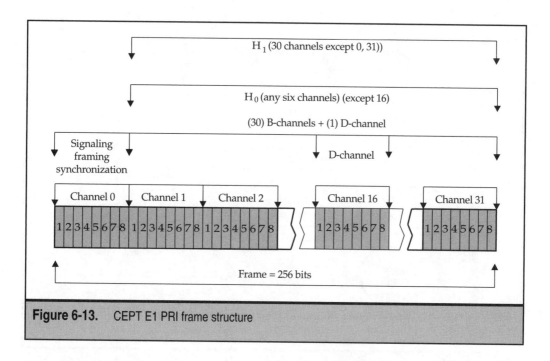

Figure 6-13. CEPT E1 PRI frame structure

communications transmission and switching techniques to a digital architecture, providing end-user-to-end-user digital service for voice, data, and video. But ISDN standards have been used for much more. ISDN standards are also at the root of ATM (previously B-ISDN) standards.

The primary ISDN architecture concept consists of multiple devices connecting through an ISDN network termination device (called a TE) into the central office environment where information services are provided, as shown in Figure 6-14. ISDN introduced the notion of multiple planes: the bearer service (or user plane), the control plane, and the management plane. A different OSI layer-structured protocol suite for each plane was defined in ISDN, as described next.

The ISDN protocol architectural structure is composed similar to the OSIRM, as shown in Figure 6-15. While all seven protocol layers are the same as the OSIRM, the physical, data link, and network layers define the lower-layer functions, which include the bearer services. These layers define physical connectivity and transmission as defined in ITU-T Recommendations I.430, I.431, and I.432; data-link management, flow, error, and synchronization control, as defined in ITU-T Q.921(LAP-D); and network addressing, congestion control, end-to-end call establishment, routing or relaying, and switching, as defined in Recommendations Q.931/I.451, Q.932/I.452, and Q.933/I.453. The transport, session, presentation, and application layers define the higher-layer functions, including the teleservices, which define services such as messaging, telephone, and telex. Standards for these layers are host-to-host and application-specific.

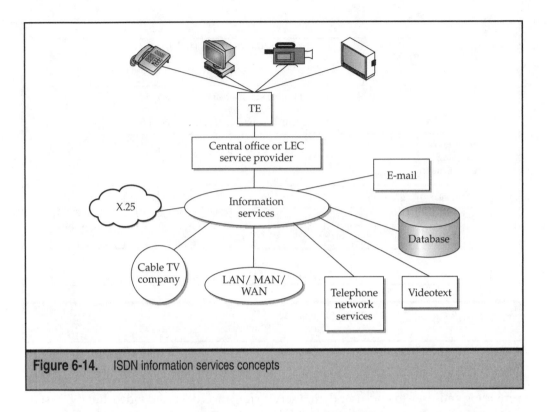

Figure 6-14. ISDN information services concepts

The ISDN architecture of the user, control, and management planes is shown in Figure 6-16. The user protocol (or bearer service) is Layer 1 for circuit-mode, Layer 2

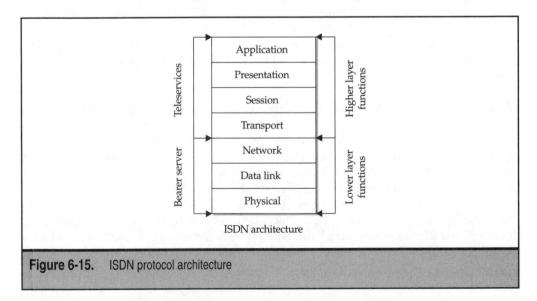

Figure 6-15. ISDN protocol architecture

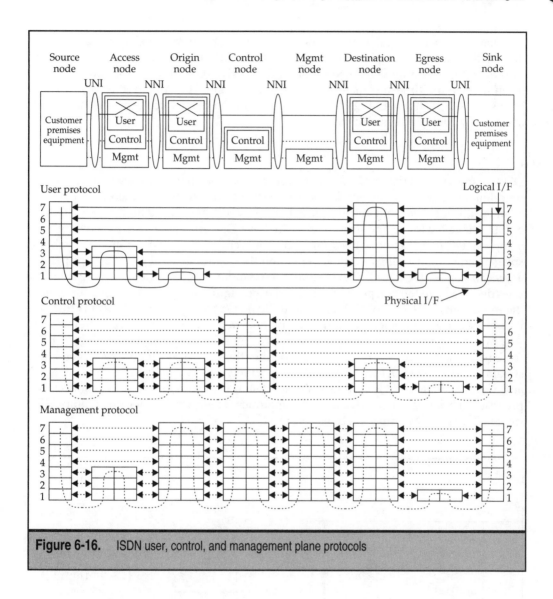

Figure 6-16. ISDN user, control, and management plane protocols

for frame-mode, and Layer 3 for packet-mode services. Teleservices and value-added services are modeled as higher layers. Intermediate nodes might provide only physical connectivity. User network interfaces (UNI) and network-to-network interfaces (NNI) are explained later. Conceptually, another application runs the control, or signaling, plane. The purpose of the control plane protocols is to establish, configure, and release the user plane (bearer) capabilities. Finally, the management plane is responsible for monitoring the status, configuring the parameters, and measuring the performance of the user and control planes.

One ISDN feature that is particularly useful for achieving higher aggregate channel bandwidth rates than 64 Kbps within a single PRI is the Bandwidth-on-Demand Interoperability Group (BONDING) standard. BONDING enables an ISDN device to act as an inverse multiplexer function by splitting a single data stream (that is, 384 Kbps) over six 64-Kbps channels. BONDING has the required delay calculating mechanisms to assure equal delay across all channels.

DSL

DSL, as shown in Figure 6-17, is a newer access method that competes with cable for a predominant portion of the nondial access market share. xDSL has taken business away from the ISDN market, but more accurately the low bandwidth and high expense failings of ISDN have led to the opportunity exploited by xDSL and cable. DSL supercharges existing twisted-pair telephone lines and allows subscribers to gain downlink transmission speeds higher than 1 Mbps over copper circuit they could drive at only 56 Kbps per legacy technologies. The *x* in xDSL determines the standard upstream and downstream data rates defined from the perspective of the end user. Figure 6-18 provides a chart of some of the more common forms of DSL offered in the market today. The upstream is from the user to the service provider. The downstream is from the service provider to the end user. At a minimum, DSL supports simultaneous transmissions of at least 64 Kbps in both directions. Note that every service provider defines these services differently, so actual upstream and downstream DSL rates could vary widely. It is generally faster than ISDN BRI and analog modems, but is limited to shorter distances. The xDSL customer connects to a premises distribution network via service modules. These service modules employ STM (that is, TDM), ATM, or packet transport modes.

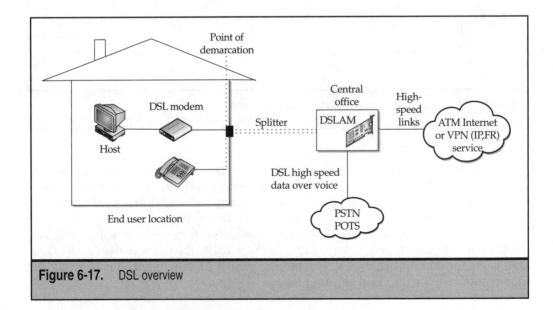

Figure 6-17.   DSL overview

Acronym	Full name	Upstream rate	Downstream rate	Example
HDSL (DS1)	High Data Rate Digital Subscriber Line	1.544 Mbps	1.544 Mbps	North American T1 Service
HDSL (E1)	High Data Rate Digital Subscriber Line	2.048 Mbps	2.048 Mbps	European and International E1
SDSL	Single-Line Digital Subscriber Line	1.544 Mbps	1.544 Mbps	North American T1 Service
SDSL	Single-Line Digital Subscriber Line	2.048 Mbps	2.048 Mbps	European and International E1
ADSL	Asymmetric Digital Subscriber Line	16 to 640 Kbps	1.5 to 9 Mbps	Video on demand, LAN and Internet access
VDSL	Very High Data Rate Digital Subscriber Line	1.5 to 2.3 Mbps	13 to 52 Mbps	High-quality video, high-performance Internet/LAN
IDSL	ISDN-like	144 Kbps	144 Kbps	ISDN lool-alike
ADSL Lite	ADSL Lite	128 Kbps	1 Mbps	Lower BW applications
RADSL	Rate Adaptive DSL	16 to 640 Kbps	7 Mbps	Same as ADSL
UDSL	Universal DSL	2 Mbps	2 Mbps	Any

Figure 6-18. DSL types

XDSL rates are typically a flat monthly fee. XDSL is most often used as the access media to the public Internet, although it is becoming more popular as a lower-cost access method for core data services such as FR. xDSL offers a cost-effective FR access solution for remote sites. However, there are tradeoffs in SLAs (limited versus standard FR), MTTR (days versus hours), and issues with the local exchange carrier that can frustrate users. The bottom line is that xDSL services are predominantly still not on par with corporate access services.

XDSL modems are available from most legacy modem providers and xDSL services are available in most metropolitan areas. The distance limitations of xDSL make it difficult to offer service in urban areas.

The existing copper telephone line connects the customer's xDSL modem to a service provider modem in the public network. The xDSL modem can create the following three channel types:

▼ High-speed downstream channel ranging from 1.5 to 52 Mbps

■ Medium-speed duplex channel ranging from 16 Kbps to 2.3 Mbps

▲ POTS channel

DSL Equipment

DSL uses modern equipment that sends digital signals through the copper infrastructure instead of analog signals. Therefore, DSL can enable a higher capacity use of the existing analog telephone line. At the customer location, a computer or networking device is connected to a DSL modem generally through a USB or 10 base-T Ethernet port. The DSL modem sometimes supports routing, switching, or firewall functionality. The DSL modem is then used to connect across the local loop to the service provider's DSL access multiplexer (DSLAM).

The DSLAM uses a statistical multiplexing technique to combine many DSL lines from many customers in the same geographical area into a single, high-capacity circuit to the service provider's backbone and ultimately to the Internet or other VPN services. DSLAMs typically support different types of DSL in a single central office and in most cases support additional features such as IP routing or DHCP for dynamic IP address assignment. The DSLAM provides each customer with a shared connection to the service provider's network.

Advantages and Disadvantages of xDSL

Here are some advantages of xDSL over legacy dial access:

▼ You can leave your Internet connection open and still use the phone line for voice calls.

■ The speed is much higher than a "legacy" V.92 modem (1.5 Mbps and higher versus 56 Kbps).

■ xDSL doesn't necessarily require new wiring; it can use the phone line you already have.

▲ The company that offers xDSL will usually provide the modem as part of the installation and recurring monthly fee.

But there are disadvantages:

▼ The connection is faster for receiving data than it is for sending data over the Internet (usually not a problem for typical Internet use).

■ The service is not available everywhere—the closer you are to a metropolitan area, the greater the chance DSL is available. A DSL connection works better when you are closer to the provider's central office. DSL is very distance sensitive.

▲ Distance limitations exist

■ ADSL, ADSL Lite, IDSL, RADSL, UDSL: 18,000 feet

■ HDSL, HDSL 2: 12,000 feet

■ SDSL: 10,000 feet

■ VDSL: 4,500 feet

NOTE: All displayed distances are upstream distances; downstream rates are typically much less.

Even if the service provider's central office is physically close to the customer location, there is no guarantee that the customer can be supported by DSL. The achievable high-speed downstream data rate depends on

▼ Length of twisted-pair line

■ Wire gauge

■ Presence of bridged taps (repeaters) and load coils (filters) from the old party-line days

▲ Cross-coupled interference from other lines

Many circuits contain bridge taps, which are repeaters between the customer and the central office that extends service to other customers. Bridge taps are not noticeable in normal phone service, but might affect DSL service by extending the total length of the circuit beyond the distance limits of the service provider. The wire gauge also affects the DSL support. Figure 6-19 summarizes speed and distance limitations for 24-gauge twisted pair. The double-headed arrows in Figure 6-19 are placed vertically at the maximum speed for the DSL technology, with their horizontal dimension indicating the range of feasible operation.

Most Common Type of DSL

The most common type of DSL offered today is asymmetric (ADSL). Many homes and small business users are connected to the Internet through an ADSL connection. ADSL divides up the available frequencies with more being supported for the download (web page, music, movies, and online games) than the upload (request packet the users send).

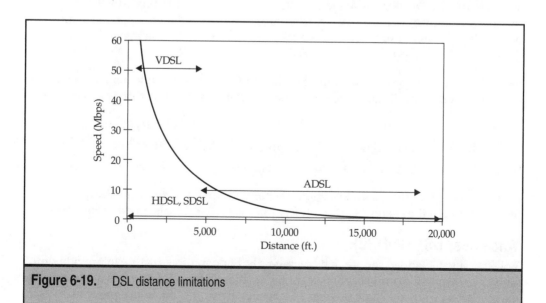

Figure 6-19.   DSL distance limitations

What speed a customer receives is dependent on their service provider. ADSL will support downstream (DSLAM to customer) speeds of up to 9 Mbps and upstream (customer to DSLAM) speeds of up to 640 Kbps.

Like other forms of DSL, ADSL is distance sensitive. The limit for ADSL service is 18,000 feet (5,460 meters). Many ADSL providers will place even a lower limit on the distances for the ADSL service to account for speed and quality of service. As the connection's length increases, the signal quality decreases and the connection speed goes down. In practice, the best speeds widely offered today are 1.5 Mbps downstream, with upstream speeds varying between 64 and 640 Kbps.

DSL Standards

DSL uses advanced digital signal processors and specialized algorithms to get large amounts of bandwidth out of the existing twisted pair cabling infrastructure. The DSL modems use special standards to divide the signals into separate channels. The official ANSI standard for ADSL is discrete multitone (DMT). DMT is a form of frequency division multiplexing (FDM) that divides the data into 256 downstream and 32 upstream channels, each 4-KHz wide. The data stream is split into a number of channels having the same bandwidth but different frequencies. This allows the channels to become independent of each other. Each channel is continuously monitored and, if the quality begins to disintegrate, the signal is shifted to another channel. The DMT system constantly searches for the best channels for transmission and reception and shifts the signals between the different channels.

Other modulation standards include quadrature amplitude modulation (QAM) and carrierless amplitude/phase (CAP).

QAM   QAM uses phase and amplitude modulation to create 16 different channels. QAM supports two carriers that have the same frequency but differ in phase by 90 degrees. At the source of transmission, the two carriers are combined and then separated again at the destination. Because it supports the two carriers, QAM enables data transmission at twice the rate of standard pulse amplitude modulation.

CAP   CAP is a version of QAM and an earlier and more easily implemented ADSL standard that operates by dividing the signals on the telephone line into three distinct bands:

▼ Voice conversations are carried in the 0 to 4 KHz (kilohertz) band.

■ Upstream channel is carried in a band between 25 and 160 KHz.

▲ Downstream channel is carried in a band between 240 KHz and 1.5 MHz.

CAP keeps the three channels widely separated to minimize the possibility of interference between the channels on one line, or between the signals on different lines.

Voice over DSL (VoDSL)

VoDSL is a value-added service that leverages the copper infrastructure to provide simultaneous transmission and reception of multiple voice lines and data applications (such as Internet access) over the same existing DSL access circuit. VoDSL is just one of many technologies to support convergence from the customer location. Service providers use VoDSL to combine multiple services on one circuit in areas where the availability of cooper loops is limited and at a premium. VoDSL requires the same DSL equipment as stated earlier in this section with additional equipment, as shown in Figure 6-20, to handle the requirements specifically related to voice services. The additional equipment includes

▼ Customer voice equipment such as telephones, fax machines, and PBXs

■ Integrated access device (IAD) is a device that interfaces between the customer's voice equipment and the DSL network service. The customer's equipment is responsible for prioritizing the voice packets over the data packets to ensure toll-quality voice delivery, and then sends the packets over the DSL line. The IAD is responsible for the packetization of voice traffic.

■ Data switch separates the data traffic from the voice traffic it receives from the DSLAM. The data traffic is forwarded to the data network, and the voice traffic is forwarded to the voice gateway.

■ Voice gateway depacketizes the voice packets and converts the voice traffic to a format deliverable to a class-5 voice switch.

▲ Class-5 voice switch provides the dial tone and call routing in the PSTN, as it would a normal voice call.

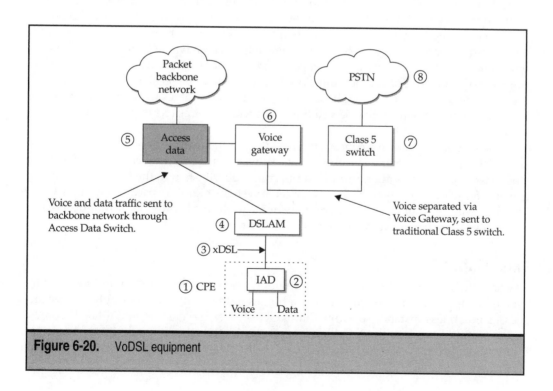

Figure 6-20.   VoDSL equipment

It is important to note that VoDSL is an access service that allows the user to originate service on a private voice or data network, use DSL as a data access media, and have the service provider perform a class-5 voice switch gateway function to terminate the voice calls on the PSTN.

In the service provider network ("the cloud"), VoDSL traffic is usually transported by FR, ATM, or the Internet protocol (IP). Current analysis indicates that approximately 90 percent of those installed based on DSLAMs use ATM as the transport mechanism. What makes DSL so attractive is its ability to enhance existing copper lines to transport voice and data services simultaneously at very high speeds. Because of this, many standards organizations including ANSI, ETSI, Digital Audio Video Council (DAVC), ATM Forum, the ITU, and the ADSL Forum are working fast and furious to develop standards for our next-generation DSL services. The continuing goal is to have the next-generation switching products handle the integrated voice and data traffic at the first point of switching and continue to enhance the functionality of VoDSL services.

CABLE ACCESS TECHNOLOGIES

Many people who are able to get access to cable television can now get a high-speed connection to the Internet from their cable provider over the same (coax cable) access circuit. John Walson is credited as the inventor of cable access. Mr. Walson owned an appliance store in the late '40s that sold television sets in a small town outside Mahanoy City, Pennsylvania. Selling television sets was difficult because the town was separated from the city by a mountain, so it was outside the range of the Pennsylvania television stations and consumers in Mahanoy City could not get good reception. Mr. Walson purchased an antenna and installed it on a mountain close to town, where he received television signals via the antenna and then transmitted the signals through cables from the antenna to his appliance store. When people viewed the clear picture he was receiving, his sales on televisions sets increased.

Today, we use this same concept to provide broadband cable access, as shown in Figure 6-21. Traditional one-way cable networks were used for broadcasting signals from the master headend location through a programmable system to the home. But, cable is not just for television anymore. Two-way cable systems today are used to simultaneously send and receive high-speed data from the home to the cable provider through a flexible and programmable network, as shown in Figure 6-21.

Coaxial Cable

At one time, coaxial cable was the most widely used network cabling and today is installed in approximately 60 percent of all homes in the United States. Cable Internet access is much less distance sensitive than DSL, so over the past decade it has become a more popular access method. Cable access is considered a broadband system due to the

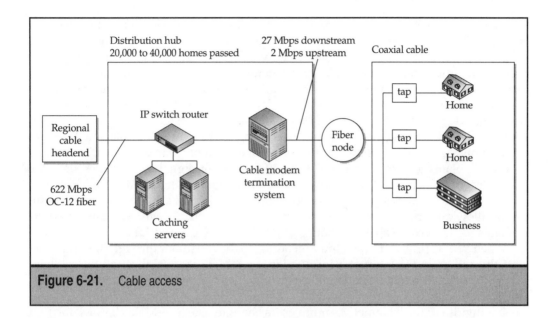

Figure 6-21. Cable access

bandwidth available over the cable access circuit. Broadband systems use analog signaling and a range of frequencies to achieve this bandwidth. With analog transmission, the signals are continuous and nondiscrete. Signals flow across the physical medium in the form of electromagnetic or optical waves. With broadband transmission, signal flow is unidirectional. A broadband device transmits information within an assigned frequency. This information gets multiplexed with other information over a single wire. The advantages of a broadband system are its ability to support multiple users over a long distance and that it can carry voice, video, and data simultaneously.

In its simplest form, coaxial cable consists of a core made of solid copper surrounded by insulation, a braided shielding, and an outer cover. The core is surrounded by a dielectric insulating layer, which separates it from the wire mesh. The braided mesh acts as a ground and protects the core from electrical noise and crosstalk, defined as signal overflow from an adjacent wire.

Coaxial cable is more resistant to interference and attenuation than twisted-pair cabling. Attenuation is the loss of signal strength, which begins to occur as the signal travels further along a copper wire.

Two-Way Cable Operation

The coaxial cable used today in the cable television system can carry hundreds of megahertz of signals. Each television signal is supported by a 6-MHz (millions of cycles per second) channel on the cable and transmitted down the cable to the consumer, as shown in

Figure 6-22. A few years ago, high-end coaxial cable supported 550 MHz, which allowed cable providers to support approximately 75 television channels to each household.

Because of competition from satellite providers, cable service providers began upgrading the imbedded coaxial cable infrastructure with fiber optics and upgrading the headends (cable distribution points) with digital technology. The fiber-optic cable is installed from the cable company's headend location to a neighborhood location. The fiberoptic is terminated in the neighborhood location and then the signals are distributed from coaxial cable to individual homes. According to the National Cable and Telecommunications Association, cable operators have invested more than $55 billion to upgrade their cable plants to take advantage of the efficiencies of digital technologies since the 1996 Telecommunications Act. Cable providers have replaced thousands of miles of cable with fiber optics and many providers now support 750-MHz cable systems. These upgrades allow cable providers to offer their customer base more television channels as well as high-speed Internet, cable telephony, and interactive video services.

When a cable provider offers Internet access to the consumer through their cable access, the data from the Internet is inputted into a 6-MHz channel through the cable infrastructure. On the cable, the data looks just like another television channel. The first user to connect to the Internet through a specific 6-MHz channel can use almost the entire bandwidth of that channel. As more users begin to use the 6-MHz channel, the first user might begin to notice a drop in performance. Cable service providers are aware of

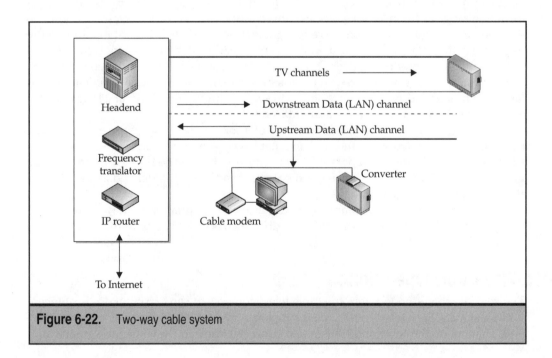

Figure 6-22. Two-way cable system

this issue and resolve performance degradation by adding a new channel and splitting the number of users on each channel. Average throughput is typically about 1 Mbps.

Equipment Associated with Cable Access

Transporting data over a legacy cable television system requires two types of equipment: a cable modem on the customer end and a Cable-Modem Termination System (CMTS) at the cable provider's end.

A cable modem provides users with high-speed Internet access through a cable television network on average of 3–50 Mbps and a distance of up to 100 kilometers and, in some cases, more. Cable modems connect to a home or small business LAN or computer at one end and the coaxial cable infrastructure on the other end. The cable modem can be external to the computer or internal as a component of the computer (in most cases, they are external). In some cases, the cable modem is a set-top device that supports Internet access, cable television programming, and telephone access to the PSTN. The cable modem operates using a tuner to separate the data channels from the cable television programming, a demodulator to convert analog signals to digital on/off pulses, and a modulator to convert the computer's digital information into analog signals for transmission.

The CMTS is located at the cable provider's headend location. The CMTS is similar to the DSLAM described earlier in the DSL section of this chapter. The CMTS acts as a multiplexer combining traffic from multiple customers onto a single channel and is used to connect the cable television network to the Internet. A CMTS can support up to as many as two thousand connections to the Internet through a single 6-MHz channel. This is dependent on how the cable provider implements the system internal to their network. The CMTS supports both upstream and downstream data. The upstream data is transferred from the customer to the CMTS in a separate division of time not used or seen by other customers sharing the CMTS. The downstream data, on the other hand, is supported much like an Ethernet LAN. The data is sent from the CMTS to the cable bus and each individual network connection determines if the data is for that particular network.

Cable Modem Standards

Until recently, many cable modems installed in the United States and Canada were proprietary products. This forced users to use a cable modem provided by their cable provider. The Institute of Electronic and Electrical Engineering (IEEE) formed the 802.14 Cable TV Media Access Control and Physical Protocol Working Group in May 1994. As of 1996, the 802.14 standard was not published. A group of cable operators tired of waiting for the IEEE 802.14 standard formed a limited partnership called Multimedia Cable Network System Partners Ltd. (MCNS) to research and publish their own cable modem system specifications. In 1996, the MCNS consortium published an open standard for cable modem products called Data Over Cable Service Interface Specification (DOCSIS).

DOCSIS defines the technical specifications for both the cable modem and the CMTS. As with standards in general, DOCSIS was developed to ensure the compatibility of cable modem equipment built by different manufacturers. DOCSIS is the dominating cable modem standard in the United States. The International Telecommunications Union (ITU) accepted DOCSIS as a cable modem standard in March 1998. The ITU DOCSIS is called ITU J.112. DOCSIS generally supports data services over a cable television network using one 6-MHz channel in the 50–750 MHz spectrum range for the downstream traffic and a second channel in the 5–42 MHz band for the upstream traffic. CableLabs, a nonprofit research and development consortium, began managing the testing and certification process to ensure cable modems are DOCSIS compliant in 1998. Products that pass the rigorous testing process are labeled "CableLabs Certified."

In Europe, there are two competing data over cable standards. The first developed was DVB-RCC, sometimes referred to as ETS 300 800. This standard is based on ATM, which we discuss in detail in Chapter 9. DVB-RCC has not been heavily implemented due to some initial security issues and now is sharing the European market with the other standard, EuroDOCSIS. EuroDOCSIS is essentially the same as DOCSIS except that it is Digital Video Broadcasting (DVB)–compliant at the physical layer. The European Telecommunications Standards (ETSI) publishes the DVB standards.

FIBER ACCESS TECHNOLOGIES

Fiber is the preferred cable media for servicing access rates at DS3 and above. There is a wide range of fiber access solutions and technologies offered today including SONET/SDH, ATM, MPLS, and Ethernet/IP/PPP networks. These solutions are supported using a wide array of products including multiservice access nodes, ATM/IP/MPLS equipment, fiber-optic modems, rate/media converters, and multiplexers. In the United States, residential broadband access is supported using fiber-to-the-curb (FTTC) and fiber-to-the-home (FTTH) services. Traditional fiber-optic networks then link metropolitan areas and cities with other countries. The *last-mile* is a term commonly used to describe the connection or circuit from the customer location (customer premises equipment, CPE) to the location the customer connects to the service provider network (point of presence, POP). Bandwidth-challenged legacy copper wires have traditionally served the last mile and remain so because of the complexity, cost, and difficulty of physically engineering and deploying fiber-optic networks directly into buildings and homes. The market is just now supporting vendors offerings of high-speed Internet access services up to 100 Mbps and Gigabit Ethernet over optical fiber. Here are just some of the services offered today via fiber access:

▼ **ATM passive optical network (APON)**   APON systems began large-scale deployment in the technology boom of the late '90s, but since have slowed considerably. The goal of APON equipment is to lower the cost of access networks by extending optical bandwidth without using more expensive "active" components such as lasers or amplifiers. APON works by means of a passive star. Multiple optical network units share a single feeder and line termination. It allows traffic from different APONs to be segregated and transferred to their respective core networks.

- **DS3 service**   DS3 service is a high-capacity channel for the transmission of 44.736 Mbps of voice, data, video, and/or switched services. It is well suited for organizations requiring very high capacity Internet connection or whose full-time requirements surpass the capabilities of a few T1s.

- **SONET/SDH access**   Service providers offer SDH/SONET extension over fiber-optic cable at rates from T1/E1 to OC-12/ STM-4. SONET/SDH access is supported with a wide range of modems, multiplexers, multiservice access nodes, and converters. Most SONET access is sold as Internet access, except when it is forming the local access portion of a point-to-point private line.

- ▲ **Metro Ethernet**   Metropolitan Ethernet comes in 1-Mbps and 10-Mbps increments, which allows customers to buy only what they need. This service is often sold at 50–75 percent less than comparable SONET private lines. Customers can also save on CPE because they can purchase Ethernet cards for the CPE routers at approximately $300 instead of SONET cards, which run closer to $5,000 for the same router. The key forum resource for metro Ethernet is the Network Ethernet Forum (MEF).

AIR ACCESS TECHNOLOGIES

Millions of people around the world are accessing data networks and the Internet every day. They use these networks to work while on the road, communicate with others back at the office, keep up with the day-to-day news, check the weather, check their flight schedules, make travel plans, shop, and train. Staying connected to work, family, and friends has become a major requirement and almost second nature. Most people can't handle being away from their personal computer and laptops for more than a few hours. Because of our need to stay connected and the fact that we are becoming a more mobile and global society, many people are beginning to use mobile or air access technologies. In this section, we divide air access technologies into two groups: mobile and fixed wireless.

- ▼ Mobile wireless technologies include cellular and wireless LAN
- ▲ Fixed wireless technologies include point-to-point, fixed radio, and satellite

Mobile wireless technologies offer access to data networks and the Internet, as shown in Figure 6-23.

Mobile Wireless

Requirement for access to the Internet and corporate resources over the Internet "anytime" and "anywhere" has forced a mobile wireless explosion in both technology and use. This move is accelerating this century. Gartner indicated that "the mobile phone will be the most numerous Internet access device in the world, the total number of installed mobile phones will exceed a billion some time after 2003." IDG predicted that by the time this book is published "the world will have more wireless subscribers capable of Internet access than it will wired users." Until recently, the market for mobile wireless access to

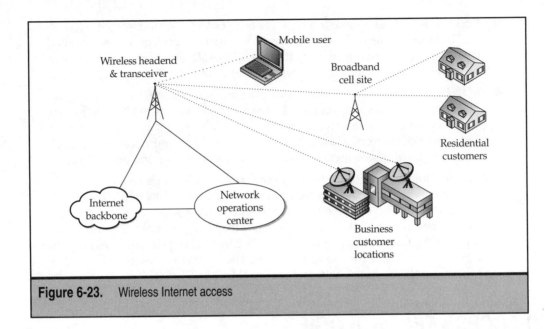

Figure 6-23. Wireless Internet access

data communications has not grown as rapidly as wireless voice communications. Part of this is due to the low bandwidth achievable on handheld portable wireless devices, on the order of 9.6 or 19.2 Kbps. Since Internet access, or more specifically access to key information on the Internet (stock quotes, company e-mails, and so on) are the key drivers of mobile wireless access, these low bandwidth limitations have limited ubiquitous usage. New technologies are emerging that are moving this barrier to 56 Kbps, but even that might not be enough given the insatiable demand for graphic-intensive applications and information. The most successful mobile wireless solutions have been for specific functions such as instant stock quotes for the Blackberry.

Cellular analog and digital networks work using a hierarchical model, as shown in Figure 6-24, that consist of base stations and antennas that cover a large area. The area a base station covers is called a cell. Macro cells are the largest of the cells and provide extensive coverage to wider areas and is often the first built to provide coverage. Macro cells work best for fast-moving subscribers. The micro cells support selected outdoor areas and slow-moving subscribers and controls the cells laid beneath it. The pico cells are the smaller of the cells and are built to provide capacity. Pico cells generally cover the interior of buildings.

Cellular wireless technology began in 1895 when the Italian inventor Guglielmo Marconi built equipment that could transmit electrical signals through the air. The FCC is the organization responsible for U.S. radio spectrum regulations and licensing. The cellular technologies have evolved from first generation, such as FDMA, to third generation, such as CDMA2000, as shown in Figure 6-25.

Analog cellular service operates using Frequency Division Multiple Access (FDMA), which allows only one conversation per each designated radio frequency. With FDMA,

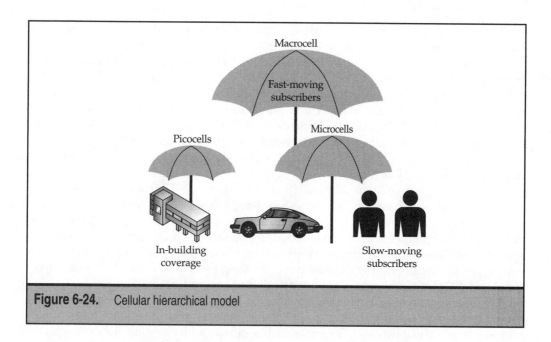

Figure 6-24.   Cellular hierarchical model

each channel can be assigned to only one user at a time. FDMA divides the frequency band into 30 channels, each of which can carry a voice conversation. FDMA is the basic technology in the analog Advanced Mobile Phone Service (AMPS), the first and most widely-installed cellular phone system installed in North America, and is also used in the Total Access Communication System (TACS). The problems related to the first generation systems are capacity and quality.

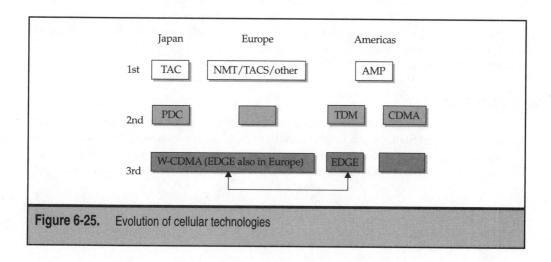

Figure 6-25.   Evolution of cellular technologies

The second generation cellular wireless systems implemented were based on digital technology. There are various noncompatible types of digital cellular around the world. TDM access (TDMA) is one digital methodology of aggregating multiple simultaneous transmissions over a single high-speed channel by allocating unique time slots to different users. Multiple users are each assigned individual time slots on a common frequency, which allows multiple users to share a single frequency. The Digital-Advanced Mobile Phone Service (D-AMPS) uses FDMA discussed earlier but adds TDMA to get three channels for each FDMA channel, tripling the number of calls that can be handled on a channel. Cellular digital packet data (CDPD) is a mobile wireless packet switched data service that overlays over a TDMA network and supports 19.2-Kbps data transfer.

A second digital cellular wireless technology is Code Division Multiple Access (CDMA), which was commercially introduced in 1995. CDMA is a method of using a coded modulation technique to aggregate multiple transmissions over a single channel. A conversation is tagged with a special frequency code. With this method, multiple users spread their energy over a common wide-frequency band using an assigned code. The receiving device deciphers only the data corresponding to a particular code to reconstruct the signal. CDMA is also referred to as spread spectrum radio technology.

Third-generation cellular wireless systems are based on new international standards. These new services will have more capacity, higher bit rates, and are designed to be worldwide standards to make it easier for someone to commute with a single cellular phone. One example of this is the Universal Mobile Telecommunications System (UMTS), which is being developed within the ITU IMT-2000 framework. The basis of UMTS was formed from a migrated version of CDMA called wideband CDMA. Wideband CDMA supports mobile voice, data, and video communications at up to 2 Mbps, depending on the distance. Another new technology is enhanced data rates for global evolution (EDGE). It's an air interface that, along with another network technology, or general packet radio services (GPRS), will let GSM and TDMA networks achieve 3G throughput rates. Global System for Mobile Communications (GSM) is another protocol used to multiplex mobile wireless network traffic. It dominates the European market but has a very limited share in North America. One of the most important factors related to next generation wireless is access to the Internet. We've already seen a proliferation of digital cell phones in the last few years related to mobile wireless Internet access. Estimates indicate that there are more than 50 million cell phones in use today that can access the Internet.

Fixed Wireless

Local loop diversity and alternative access are the keys drivers of fixed wireless access services. In the United States, the wireless local loop (WLL) approach, which uses radio technology, is being implemented for places too expensive to wire such as mountain, swamp, and rural cluster areas. WLL is used to provide a wireless alternative to wired local loop, to a local switch, and to deploy telecommunications services rapidly for developing countries and remote and/or sparsely populated areas. Some examples of WLL include

▼ **Multichannel multipoint distribution service (MMDS)**   Uses microwave channels to distribute a varied range of telecommunications services to subscribers. MMDS is a line-of-sight service that operates in the 2.1–2.7 GHz frequency range. Historically, it has been called wireless cable and has been used to provide up to 133 channels to neighborhoods using a single antenna. Much like cable television, MMDS can support 6-MHz channels. In a flat area, MMDS can reach up to 70 miles. Since 1997, MMDS has also been used to provide two-way data services as well as television channels.

▲ **Local multipoint distribution service (LMDS)**   In the United States, the FCC has allocated the 27.5–29.5 GHz band to LMDS, a radio-based service developed to provide two-way wireless cable television and high-speed data service. Similar to MMDS, but uses higher frequencies and has a transmission capacity that is many times larger. Because of the higher frequency, the antennas are only about 6 inches in diameter—but the antennas must be within about 3–5 miles of the subscriber's house.

Satellite

Satellites are used for data, voice, and television communications all over the world. This technology allows users to access networks from areas where no terrestrial services exist. Signals are transmitted from an uplink location to the satellites, which then broadcast the signal back down over a target area. The first active communications satellite was launched by the United States in 1958 and commercial satellites began deploying in 1963 with the founding of the Communications Satellite Corporation (COMSAT). In 1964, the International Telecommunications Satellite Organization (INTELSAT) was formed and now includes more than 100 nations. INTELSAT owns and manages a constellation of communications satellites that support international broadcast services. Today, popular satellite systems generally fall into two areas: geosynchronous (GEO) and low earth orbit (LEO).

Geosynchronous satellites orbit at an altitude of 22,300 miles above the Earth and remain fixed over the Earth's equator. The advantages of the geosynchronous systems are their wide coverage and their longer lifespan. The major disadvantage of these systems is the round-trip delay that can be more than half a second. An example of a geosynchronous satellite system used for access is the International Mobile Satellite Organization (Inmarsat) system that can allocate frequencies in the 6 GHz band. Inmarsat was activated in the early '80s, and today is the number one global mobile satellite communications network. An example of a company that supports services using Inmarsat is France Telecom. France Telecom offers services such as voice, fax, telex, data, video conferencing, e-mail, ISDN service, and LAN/WAN-access up to 64 Kbps. Another company, Internet Express (IE) offers Internet connectivity throughout the United States and Mexico using a geosynchronous satellite-based system that supplies a 540-Kbps/150-Kbps connection speed. Cidera is yet another provider of geosynchronous satellite service. Cidera focuses on the service provider market and delivers up to 45 megabits a second directly to the edge of their network.

The new direct broadcast satellite (DBS) services offered today are provided by geosynchronous satellite systems and offer a number of advantages over cable. The audio is CD quality, the video is a higher quality because of digital transmission, and more programs are available because of the higher capacity. DBS systems have until recently provided only a one-way connection, the downlink. You could receive data from the Internet, but the uplink connection to the Internet was provided via a standard phone line and modem. Today, service providers are now offering two-way access to the Internet. The StarBand system offers two-way connectivity to the Internet and satellite television service from EchoStar's DISH Network using a single dish antenna. An example of the StarBand system is shown in Figure 6-26.

LEO satellite systems are also gaining in popularity today. LEO systems address the delay problem associated with geosynchronous satellite systems. LEO satellite systems follow elliptical orbits, allowing them to provide better coverage and reduce the delay. The disadvantage of LEO satellite systems is that they require a larger number of satellites to provide adequate coverage. Also, the satellites must be replaced more often than the geosynchronous orbiting satellites. The Orbcomm System is a LEO system that provides packet data only, allowing users to track, monitor, and manage remote locations. Orbcomm is ideal for short, daily messages and requires only minimum amounts of power to operate. The Orbcomm system requires 34 satellites for reliable, full-world coverage, and provides 2400 bps on the uplink and 4800 bps on the downlink. The LEO systems have

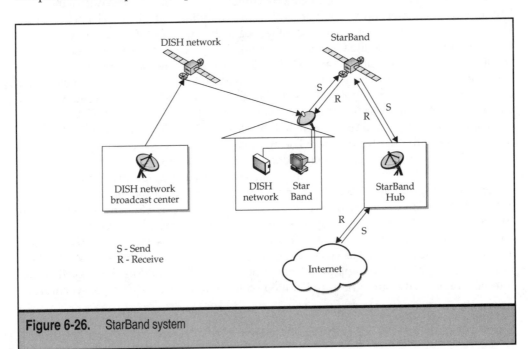

Figure 6-26.   StarBand system

had some bad press over the last few years. Iridium, probably the most well known LEO system, went bankrupt in 1999. The major problems associated with Iridium were that the handsets were large, bulky, and expensive (averaging around $1,200), and the service charges were as much as $3 per minute. Another LEO satellite system, Globalstar, which supports a constellation of 48 satellites that operate over 80 percent of the Earth's surface and provides 9.6-Kbps linkup speeds for data-filed bankruptcy in February 2002. Neither system could compete with the rapid growth of land-based cellular systems being provided at a tenth of the cost.

REVIEW

This chapter completes a discussion on the physical layer protocols and access technologies spanning the data communications market place. It is clear that there are many different physical interfaces, but there is a central logic and progression of speeds and capabilities exhibited among them. Our discussion included an overview of the interfaces and protocols at the physical layer and those used in the most common network access technologies. The more commonly known interfaces included: RS-232C; EIA-449; EIA-232E; EIA-530; ITU-T Recommendations V.24/V.28, X.21, X.21bis, I.430, I.431, T1/E1, and D4/ESF; HSSI; HIPPI; ESCON; and Fibre Channel. We discussed options for both corporate users and residential users for accessing intranets, extranets, and the Internet.

The access technologies we discussed were divided into three major categories: copper, fiber, and air. We began our copper discussion with an overview of UTP and 56-Kbps modem access. Upon this foundation, construction of the ISDN protocol model was built. Our access discussion also included the big push for high bandwidth services such as cable and DSL. We then covered the major corporate access methods available through fiber. Because of the research and development push toward the wireless market place, we spent time discussing some of the newest developments in cellular, radio, and satellite data services.

For one computer to talk to another, each must be able to understand and translate the other's protocols even at the lowest layer. When dealing with LANs, the physical interface protocols are intricately tied to the data link layer protocols. New protocols such as 100-Mbps and 1000-Mbps Ethernet have provided a tenfold increase in available bandwidth. We detail the more popular Layer 2 LAN protocols in Chapter 7.

PART III

Protocols and Interfaces: Layer 2

CHAPTER 7

Common Protocols and Interfaces in the LAN Environment

This chapter focuses on the data-link layer, which is Layer 2 (L2) in the seven-layer OSI reference model and the second layer in most other computer architecture models as well. It discusses some of the primary functions of the data-link layer, including establishing a reliable protocol interface across the physical layer (L1) on behalf of the network layer (L3). We begin with concepts related to the data-link layer, including flow control, error detection, and framing. From there we discuss some of the more popular data-link layer protocols such as Binary Synchronous Control (BSC), Digital Data Communications Message Protocol (DDCMP) Synchronous Data Link Control (SDLC), and High-level Data Link Control (HDLC).

Some of the more popular protocols sitting at the data-link layer include Ethernet, Token Ring, and Fiber Distributed Data Interface (FDDI). We take an in-depth look at each of these protocols and discuss how they exchange data. This chapter then discusses how the IEEE 802.X protocol standards divides the data-link layer into two sublayers, Logical Link Control (LLC) and Media Access Control (MAC), and how these two sublayers differ.

A quick review of bridging shows how bridging schemes such as the IEEE 802.1 Spanning Tree Protocol (STP) and IBM Source Routing Protocol (SRP) allow the bridges to dynamically change packet relaying based on network topology changes. The chapter ends with a discussion of LAN switching and virtual LANs (VLANs).

BACKGROUND: DATA-LINK LAYER CONCEPTS

The data-link layer is L2 in most computer architecture models, including the seven-layer OSIRM. The data-link layer interfaces between the first physical layer and the third network layer protocols, interpreting the data flow across the physical media and feeding the network layer protocols information on the outcome of these services. The primary function of the data-link layer is to establish a logical link across the physical medium, manage data flow across this medium, and terminate the link after completion of accurate data flow. The data-link control functions establish a peer-to-peer relationship across the network. This layer can also provide functions and services such as error control, detection, and correction; flow control; framing and character formatting; synchronization; sequencing for proper delivery; connection control; and management functions. This means that the link layer performs error detection and possibly even error correction. Toward this end, the data-link control functions establish a peer-to-peer relationship across each physical link between machines. The data-link layer entities exchange clearly delimited protocol data units, which are commonly called frames or cells. The data-link layer can use a limited form of addressing such that multiple data-link layer protocol interfaces can be multiplexed across a single physical layer interface. There can be a flow control function to control the flow of frames such that a fast sender does not overrun a slow receiver.

Some services provided by service providers today, such as frame relay (FR) and ATM, can be viewed as using only the first two layers of the OSI reference model, and rely heavily on reducing the link layer services to increase speeds at lower costs because of the resulting protocol simplification. Other examples of link layer protocols include ISO 7776, ITU X.25 link layer, ISDN LAP-D, ISO HDLC, and MAC-layer protocols such as the ISO 9314-2 FDDI Token Ring MAC.

Data-link functions and protocols use many circuit topologies, including point-to-point, multipoint, switching, and broadcast. Since computer communications via LANs use special functions of the data-link layer, both the MAC and LLC sublayers are emphasized. The MAC layer protocols form the basis of LAN and MAN standards used by the IEEE 802.X LAN protocol suite, which includes Ethernet, Token Ring, and Token Bus. The 802.X protocol structure are covered in the "LLC and MAC Sublayer Protocols" section later in this chapter.

DATA-LINK LAYER PROTOCOLS

Data Link Control (DLC) protocols have two forms: asynchronous and synchronous. The synchronous data-link layer protocols are the primary focus of this section. Character-oriented protocols such as BSC use control characters from character sets such as ASCII or EBCDIC as the control fields set within frames of variable formats. Byte-count-oriented protocols such as DDCMP from Digital Equipment Corporation (DEC, now Compaq) are similar to the character-oriented protocols but use count fields to indicate the number of bytes being transmitted. Finally, bit-oriented protocols such as SDLC, HDLC, ISDN BRI and PRI, and X.25 use specific bit patterns for frames. The individual bits define the protocol specifics and control the transmission. Bit-oriented protocols are of the most interest to us, because they represent the primary DLC protocols. Data-link layer functions specific to FR and ATM are discussed in Chapters 8 and 9.

BSC Protocol

The BSC protocol, or Bisync, was introduced by IBM in the mid-1960s as an asynchronous, half-duplex, point-to-point or multipoint, character-oriented protocol for bidirectional transmissions of character-oriented data. Each variable-sized frame consisted of control codes such as start-of-text (STX) and end-of-text (ETX) to manage transmission of character-coded user information. All codes are derived from a single character set, EBCDIC, the model for the American Standard Code for Information Interchange (ASCII). Figure 7-1 shows a typical BSC text frame consisting of the following characters: a frame pad (PAD), two synchronous idles (SYN), a start-of-header (SOH), header information, STX, non-transparent data (denoting a fixed- or variable-bit pattern), an ETX, a block check count (BCC), and another PAD. Note that when using BSC, every block sent requires a receipt acknowledgment, drastically limiting throughput.

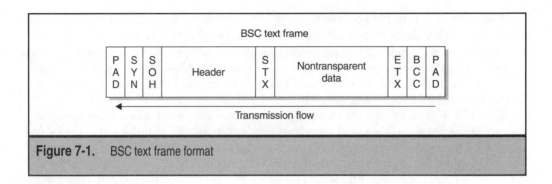

Figure 7-1. BSC text frame format

DDCMP

The DDCMP developed by DEC provides a byte-count-oriented protocol transmitted either asynchronously or synchronously over half- or full-duplex circuits on point-to-point or multipoint topologies. This protocol is similar to BSC, and uses a count field to indicate the number of bytes in the body. The count must be received properly for the sender and receiver to stay in frame synchronization. The header, which includes the flag, response, sequence number, and address fields, is protected with a separate error control checksum, generally 16 bits long. Figure 7-2 shows a standard DDCMP frame showing placement of these fields. DDCMP also provides for supervisory and information frames, where this information would replace the information field. No single coding scheme was standardized because each vendor had self-interest to "proprietize" the coding for its unique products, lock in users, and protect its customer base.

SDLC Protocol

In 1973, IBM was the first vendor to produce a bit-oriented protocol, called Synchronous Data Link Control (SDLC). This de facto standard has been modified and adopted by the International Standards Organization (ISO) as the HDLC or ISO4335 protocol and by the American National Standards Institute (ANSI), as the Advanced Data Communications Control Procedure (ADCCP) or ANSI X3.66. The ITU-T also has developed two standards based on SDLC.

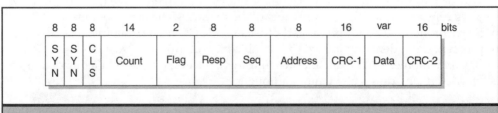

Figure 7-2. DDCMP standard frame format

The ITU-T Link Access Procedure Balanced (LAPB) is the X.25 implementation of SDLC, and the ITU-T Link Access Procedure-D (LAPD) is the ISDN and FR (LAPF) HDLC-based implementation of SDLC. Since LAPB and LAPD are subsets of HDLC, this section centers on HDLC. HDLC has spawned a variety of HDLC-like protocols, including LAP, LAPB, LAPD, LAPF, LAPM, and LAPX. Figure 7-3 shows the relations and progression of various DLCs derived from SDLC. The framing of the SDLC frame is very similar to the HDLC framing covered in the next section.

The present version of IBM's SDLC primarily uses the unbalanced normal response mode of HDLC together with a few proprietary commands and responses for support of loop or ring topology polling. SDLC operates independently on each communications link, and can operate in multipoint or point-to-point, switched or dedicated circuit, and full- or half-duplex operation. The primary difference between SDLC and HDLC is that SDLC does not support the extended address field or the extended control field.

SDLC has largely replaced the less-efficient BSC protocol. Some improvements of SDLC over BSC include the ability to send acknowledgments, addressing, block checking, and polling within every frame rather than in a separate sequence; the ability of handling long propagation delays; no restrictions to half duplex; no susceptibility to missed or duplicated blocks, no topology dependence, and no character-code sensitivity.

HDLC Protocol

HDLC protocol is not only one of the most popular protocols for data-link control implementations (L2), but it also forms the basis for ISDN and FR protocols and services. HDLC is an international standard, adopted under ISO TC97. HDLC is a bit-oriented simplex, half-duplex, or full-duplex and synchronous protocol passing variable-bit length streams over either a point-to-point or multipoint configuration. HDLC can also operate over either dedicated or switched facilities.

There are two types of point-to-point link structures: a primary station in "balanced mode" transmitting commands to and receiving responses from the secondary station, as in Figure 7-4; and a combined transmitting and receiving station in "unbalanced"

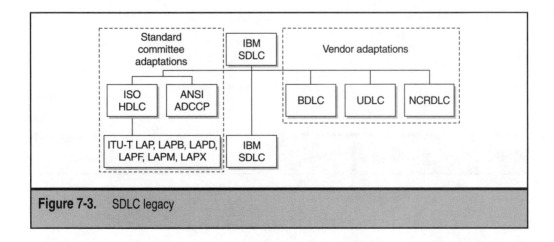

Figure 7-3. SDLC legacy

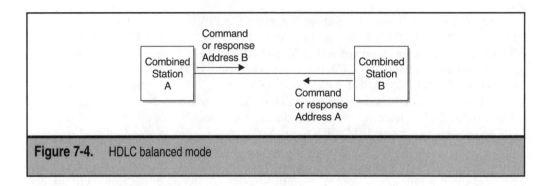

Figure 7-4.   HDLC balanced mode

mode acting as a primary and secondary station, with the capability of sending either a command or a response, as in Figure 7-5. The multidrop link structure with one primary and multiple secondary stations is also shown in Figure 7-5. Both configurations can be configured over switched or nonswitched facilities.

HDLC has three types of data-transfer modes. The two most common types are "unbalanced" Normal Response Mode (NRM) and Asynchronous Balanced Mode (ABM). NRM is used in multidrop and point-to-point links with the secondary station awaiting a poll from the primary one. ABM is used in the "balanced" configuration between combined stations, and allows only one secondary station to be active at any time. A third type or

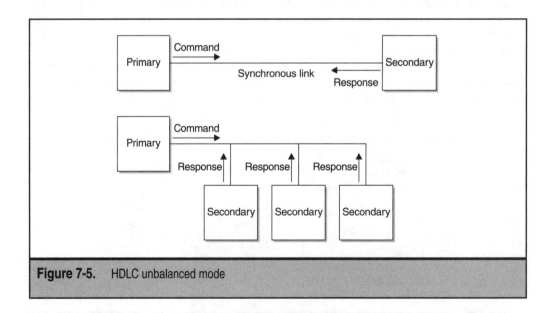

Figure 7-5.   HDLC unbalanced mode

method is via "unbalanced" Asynchronous Response Mode (ARM), which requires the secondary stations in an "unbalanced" mode to have explicit permission from the primary station to initiate transmissions.

A standard HDLC frame format is used for both information exchange and transmission control. This frame format is represented in Figure 7-6. This frame format supports both basic and extended control-field formats. Two flag fields of proprietary bit patterns encapsulate the frame; an address field provides the address of the secondary station (but is not needed for point-to-point configurations); the information field, of course, contains the data being transmitted; and the frame check sequence (FCS) verifies the accuracy of the fields within the frame. Also included in this frame is a *control field* to identify one of three types of frames available. The first bit (or 2 bits with supervisory and unnumbered frames) of each control field is used to identify the type of frame: *information, supervisory,* or *unnumbered.* These basic control field formats in an 8-bit version are found in Figure 7-7. The 16-bit version of the information, supervisory, and unnumbered frames is found in Figure 7-8.

The *information* frame is used to transport user data between stations. Within this frame, the N (S) and N (R) fields designate a modulo 8 send-and-receive count for the number of frames to be sent (S) and received (R), respectively. The P/F field designates a poll requesting transmission from the secondary station or a final bit indicating the end frame in the transmission sequence. The *supervisory* frame manages flow control and error control through positive and negative acknowledgments using four modes of operation: Receive Ready (RR), Receive Not Ready (RNR), Reject (REJ), and Selective Reject (SREJ). *S* bits establish one of these modes, and all other fields operate the same as before. The actual bit transmission order is also shown in Figures 7-7 and 7-8.

The *unnumbered* frame specifies a variety of control functions through the mode-setting commands just discussed: NRM, ARM, and ABM. The *M* modifier bits specify which type of unnumbered frame to use.

Other implementations of HDLC are also used. It is interesting to note that HDLC is often used in satellite transmissions, because the window can open from 2 to 127 frames before an acknowledgment is needed. This is important due to the 500-milliseconds turn-around times for up- and down-link transmissions.

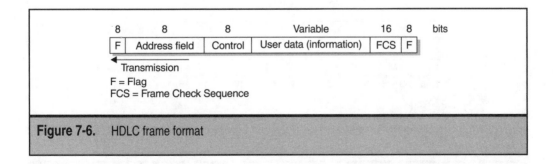

Figure 7-6.   HDLC frame format

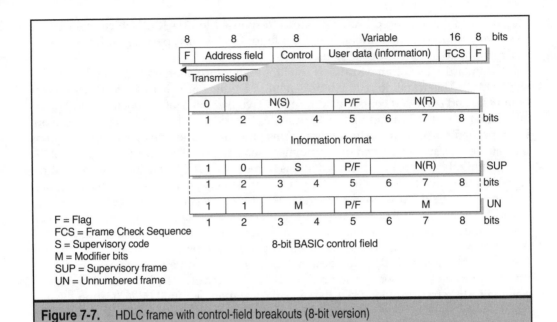

Figure 7-7. HDLC frame with control-field breakouts (8-bit version)

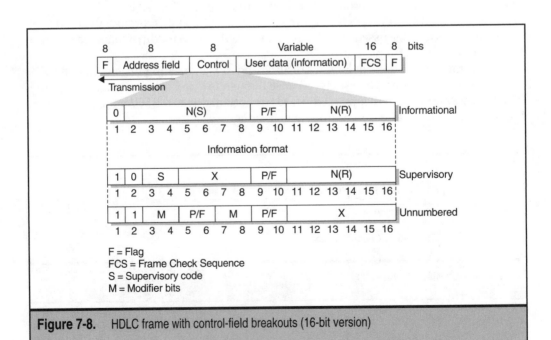

Figure 7-8. HDLC frame with control-field breakouts (16-bit version)

Link Access Procedure (LAP) Protocols

There are three types of Link Access Procedure (LAP) protocols. LAP was the first ISDN protocol and was designed based on the HDLC Set Asynchronous Response Mode (SARM) command used in "unbalanced" connections. This mode formed the basis for Link Access Procedure Balanced (LAPB), an HDLC implementation that uses balanced asynchronous mode with error recovery to form the basis of the X.25 packet-switching protocol.

The third extension of HDLC and LAP was Link Access Protocol over D-channel (LAPD), standardized by the ITU-T in Recommendations Q.920/Q.921 and I.440/I.441 as the Digital Subscriber Signaling System No.1 (DSS1) data-link layer. This implementation of HDLC uses either the basic or extended asynchronous "balanced" mode configuration and provides the basis for both ISDN and FR services. Figure 7-9 shows a comparison of LAPB (X.25), LAPD (ISDN), and LAPF (FR) frame structures. ISDN and FR protocols and standards span the first three layers of the OSIRM: physical, data link, and network.

Point-to-Point Protocol (PPP) and Serial Line Interface Protocol (SLIP)

Point-to-Point Protocol (PPP) differs from the previously mentioned router protocols in that it was developed for serial-line communications between routers, often multiprotocol routers of different vendor origins. PPP is a data-link layer protocol designed to encapsulate IP inter-network data. Created by the Internet Engineering Task Force (IETF) in 1988, it has superseded the older asynchronous Serial Line Interface Protocol (SLIP), which was theoretically limited in both speed (56 Kbps maximum) and protocol support (TCP/IP only). PPP can support the configuration and management of links between multiple multiprotocol routers via a serial interface in both synchronous and asynchronous mode.

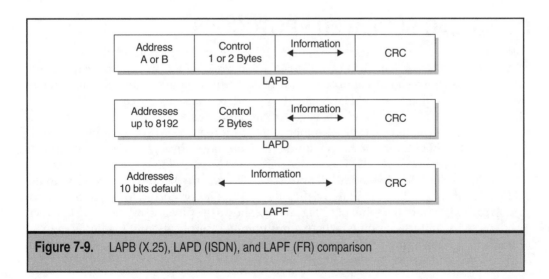

Figure 7-9.   LAPB (X.25), LAPD (ISDN), and LAPF (FR) comparison

Both HDLC and PPP can be used on any leased line for point-to-point connections between two routers not supported by FR or ATM. The T1 or 56 Kbps circuit acts as the L1, while HDLC, PPP, FR, and ATM are all L2 encapsulation options. All routers support using either PPP or HDLC encapsulation on the serial links. PPP seems to have more management capability. HDLC appears to be simpler in terms of how the router processes data frames. IPX and IP are both supported over HDLC encapsulation with no issues whatsoever as long as both routers are made by the same vendor. With PPP sometimes issues arise, depending on how and when the L3 information or the bridging or switching information is configured. PPP tends to be reserved for dialup or a mixed-vendor environment, while HDLC, at least in the Cisco world, is the default for T1 serial connections. FR, obviously, is a different story, but it is still a type of encapsulation that sits on top of a T1 infrastructure.

PPP can support communications between routers using many protocols in addition to TCP/IP, such as DECnet and OSI Internet protocols such as CLNP, IPX, and AppleTalk. PPP has many advantages, such as employing data-compression techniques, providing link-quality monitoring via the Link Quality Monitoring (LQM) protocol, and offering levels of encryption. Its security features allow the network to check and confirm the identity of users attempting to establish a connection. PPP operates like many of the services and protocols that rely on clean, reliable transmission media: it discards any packets received in error, letting the higher-level protocols sort out the retransmission. PPP does not have to tie up the entire physical circuit. It can be shared with other serial-line protocols only on a session-by-session basis. Two encapsulations (for example, SLIP, PPP, and FR) cannot be used simultaneously. PPP defines both a Link Control Protocol (LCP) for link establishment, configuration, and testing as well as an Internet Protocol Control Protocol (IPCP, specifically, IPXCP for IPX, ATCP for AppleTalk and so on) for network control. PPP has been adopted by hub and router vendors alike and is often the protocol of choice for remote-switched access.

LLC AND MAC SUBLAYER PROTOCOLS

Now let's take a closer look at the LLC and MAC sublayers in preparation for bridging and LAN switching discussion. The LLC and MAC sublayers roughly associate to the upper and lower layers of the data-link control layer (L2) of the OSIRM. Figure 7-10 shows this relationship. Together with the physical layer, data-link standards make up the core IEEE 802.X protocol standards. The MAC layer manages communications across the physical medium, defines frame assembling and disassembling, and performs error detection and addressing functions. The LLC layer interfaces with the network layer through service access points (SAPs), as shown in Figure 7-11. This section defines the MAC and LLC sublayer functions.

While the IEEE 802.2 standard defines the LLC layer, further developments with the IEEE 802.3 through 802.6 standards define the MAC layer protocols. Multiple MAC protocols can exist under the same LLC. Figure 7-12 shows the physical relationship between LLC and MAC interface points, where a multiple-host application LLC interfaces to an Ethernet LAN via a single MAC address. A network interface unit (NIU) also provides a single MAC address to the same Ethernet LAN.

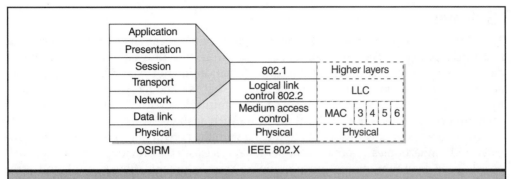

Figure 7-10.   LLC and MAC layer protocol stack of IEEE 802.X compared with the OSIRM

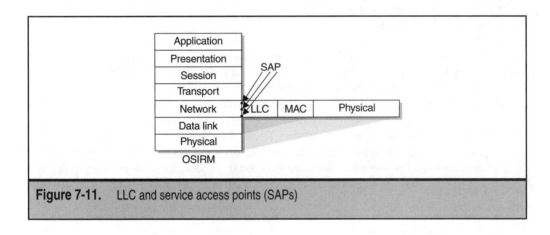

Figure 7-11.   LLC and service access points (SAPs)

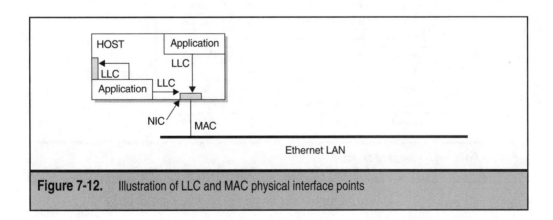

Figure 7-12.   Illustration of LLC and MAC physical interface points

LLC Sublayer

The LLC protocols are designed for peer-to-peer communications over multipoint bus and ring topologies. The IEEE 802.2 standard defines the LLC sublayer within the L2 data-link layer. In LLC, primary and secondary stations do not exist. All stations are *common* to the transmission medium, with no intermediate switching. The LLC sublayer protocol allows an 802.3, .4, or .5 protocol to carry multiple, logical, subnetwork traffic of each protocol over the same physical medium, such as the LAN.

The two major modes of service interfacing with the network layer are connection-oriented and connectionless. Connection-oriented service uses the previously mentioned SAP peer-to-peer communications, and provides acknowledgments, flow control, and error recovery. There are two classes of connectionless services provided in the LLC: class 1, or *unacknowledged* connectionless, which requires both the sending and receiving station address to be contained in each packet; and class 2, or *acknowledged* connectionless, which requires the acknowledgment of each individual frame. Both types of connectionless services provide no acknowledgments, flow control, or error control, but rely on higher-level protocols to perform these functions.

The LLC and MAC sublayers of the L2 data-link layer, along with the other layers of the OSIRM, are shown in Figure 7-13. From this reference, it is clear that the LLC sublayer serves a peer-to-peer protocol function between end users, and that the MAC and physical layers interface to the LAN transport media.

When the logical data-link layer receives user data in the form of an information field, it adds a header to this field and forms a PDU. Figure 7-14 shows the formation of the LLC PDU. The information field can vary in size. The PDU header contains both a destination address and a source address of the origination port for a network hardware device or application for network software. Both are referred to as service access points (SAPs). It is important to note that the size of these address fields determines the number of possible

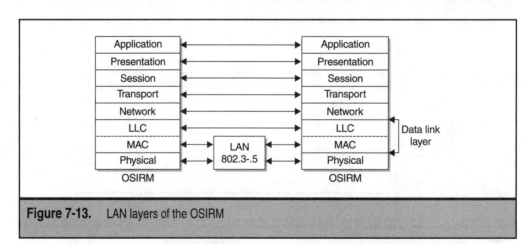

Figure 7-13.   LAN layers of the OSIRM

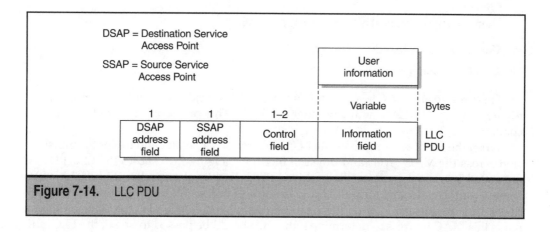

Figure 7-14.   LLC PDU

addresses on the network. There are two options: a 2-byte or a 6-byte address field, with each defined as individual or group, with universal or local authority.

The physical and logical link layers of many vendor-proprietary LAN standards follow those of the 802.X standards. As a final note, IEEE 802.1 is defined by the ISO and ITU-T as the Higher Level Interface (HILI) standards. These standards are focused on bridging protocols, and one example, the Spanning Tree Protocol (STP), is defined later in this chapter in the "Bridge Protocols" section.

MAC Sublayer

The MAC sublayer in the OSIRM data-link layer (L2) manages and controls communications across the physical media, manages the frame assembling and disassembling, and performs error detection and addressing functions. It is the point where distributed processing begins. The four most common MAC layers include

▼ **802.3**   CSMA/CD Ethernet

■ **802.4**   Token Bus

■ **802.5**   Token Ring

▲ **802.6**   MANs

Other completed standards include

▼ **802.9a**   isoEthernet

■ **802.10**   LAN Security Working Group

■ **802.11**   100BaseVG

▲ **802.12**   Wireless

There are two technical advisory groups (TAGs):

▼ **802.7** Broadband

▲ **802.8** Fiber-optic

There is also one MAC layer bridge protocol, 802.1d bridge (Spanning Tree), designed to interface any 802 LAN with any other 802 LAN. This protocol is covered later in this chapter.

When the MAC layer receives the LLC PDU, it adds a header and trailer for transmission across the MAC layer (and physical medium). Figure 7-15 shows the LLC PDU as formatted into a new frame called a MAC PDU. Each of the specific IEEE 802.X MAC frames conforms to this format, and is described in the following sections. MAC addresses are unique and identify physical station points on the local network. Each station reads this MAC address to determine if the call should be passed to one of the LLC entities. Each network user interface (NUI), discussed in the "LLC and MAC Sublayer Protocols" section, has its own SAP and address.

Since there are many potential combinations of Ethernet types and protocols, the LLC control header was extended. The IEEE defined an extension to the 1-byte SAP field to allow more than 64 SAP values to be identified. In a normal MAC frame, the LLC DSAP and SSAP would be 1 byte, and the LLC control 1 to 2 bytes. When the DSAP and SSAP val-

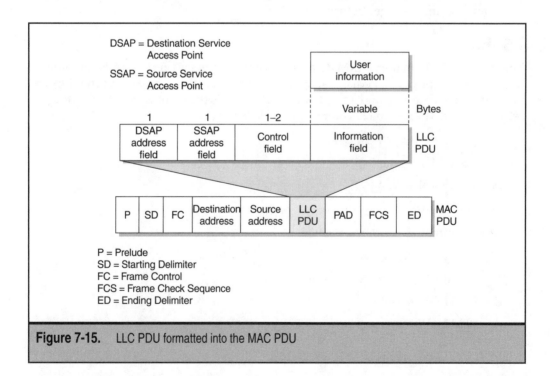

Figure 7-15. LLC PDU formatted into the MAC PDU

ues equal 0×AA (hexicimal), and the LLC control field equals 0×03, then there are two fields added to the MAC frame header—an organizationally unique identifier (OUI) for defining an organization that will assign a protocol identifier (PID) for the type of Ethernet. One example would be an Ethertype frame running DECnet Phase IV protocol, where the OUI and PID values would be 0x00000 and 0x6003, respectively. Figure 7-16 illustrates the SNAP structure. The list of available LLC1/SNAP header types is published in RFC 1340. Use of the SNAP is shown in later chapters where many Ethertypes and protocol types are identified as they are transported over packet, frame, and cell-switched services such as SMDS.

ETHERNET, TOKEN RING, TOKEN BUS, AND FDDI

As stated in Chapter 1, almost every major corporate location today has one or multiple local area networks (LANs). A LAN generally covers a range of 0.1 kilometer (350 feet) and provides local connectivity for workstations, printers, servers, and other "host" devices that are all typically within a building, floor, or room. A LAN segment can be shared among many users, or as few as a single dedicated host. The most common LANs supported today are Ethernet/IEEE 802.3, Token Ring/IEEE 802.5, and FDDI. Although rarely seen in networks today, for the sake of history, this section also discusses Token Bus/IEEE802.4. LAN protocols function at the physical and data-link layers of the OSI reference model.

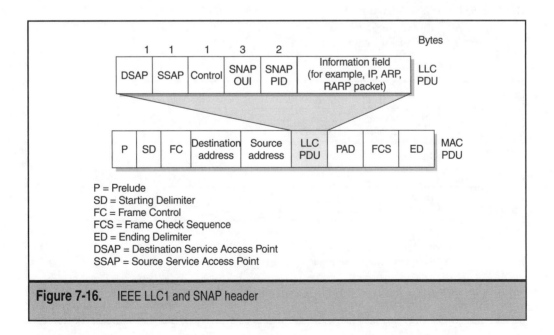

Figure 7-16.   IEEE LLC1 and SNAP header

802.3 CSMA/CD (Ethernet)

Dr. Robert M. Metcalfe invented Ethernet in 1973 at the Xerox Palo Alto Research Center. The multivendor consortium of DEC, Intel, and Xerox (DIX) published the first Ethernet specifications in 1980, and the first products for Ethernet appeared in 1981. This standard used a MAC protocol called Carrier Sense Multiple Access with Collision Detection (CSMA/CD) within a standard Ethernet frame across a common physical medium bus with channel-attached MAC-addressed stations. The IEEE later adopted Ethernet as the IEEE 802.3 standard. This is a classical case of vendor-driven standards development. The use of CSMA/CD allows the LLC sublayer to send data (given a collision does not occur) at rates theoretically reaching 10 Mbps. In actuality, it can reach about 3.5 Mbps under maximum load conditions (unless switched).

CSMA/CD allows for stations to both transmit and receive data in a "best-effort" data delivery system. No guarantee of data delivery is made. During a collision, the end stations initiate a "backoff" algorithm and follow a mathematical formula to randomize each station's next attempt to retransmit. The medium can be either baseband or broadband. The specific data-link functions of Ethernet include encapsulation and de-encapsulation of user data, media access management (such as physical layer and buffer management), collision detection and handling, data encoding and decoding, and, finally, channel access to the LAN medium. Each station on the network can attempt transmission, and if the medium is idle, gain the right to transmit. If they receive a busy signal, they transmit when the medium becomes idle. If the station encounters a collision, it stops transmitting and sends out a jamming signal to notify all other stations of a collision. The station then waits a random period of time and again attempts retransmission.

Figure 7-17 shows the IEEE 802.3 CSMA/CD MAC protocol data unit (PDU) frame (A) compared with an Ethernet frame (B).

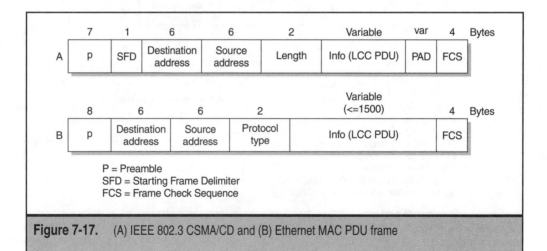

Figure 7-17. (A) IEEE 802.3 CSMA/CD and (B) Ethernet MAC PDU frame

The preamble field provides synchronization. It is the "carrier" that is detected by other stations, which in turn stops them from transmitting. The Starting Frame Delimiter (SFD) is a "start-of-frame" character. The destination and source address provide the MAC-layer destination and source address. Each address is created by combining a 24-bit OUI from the manufacturer of the Ethernet interface card with a 24-bit unique address to form a 48-bit hardware-coded MAC address. The length field identifies the length of the data field in bytes. The information field is the LLC PDU. The pad provides extra characters to achieve a minimum frame-length value. Finally, the FCS is the standard CRC-32. The maximum size of the 802.3 frame is 1500 bytes. This is an important number to remember when we start segmenting MAC frames into IP packets.

802.4 Token Bus

The IEEE 802.4 Token Bus standard defines the MAC protocol for a token-passing bus topology. A logical ring is formed on the physical bus, and each station knows only the preceding station on the bus. A token is passed down the bus, from station to station in logical ring sequence and by descending station address. This token contains the destination address of the next station. When the destination station receives the token, it can use the medium to transmit information for a limited time before having to turn the token over to the next station on the bus (in sequence). Figure 7-18 shows the Token Bus token-passing routine. Token Bus is the least-used MAC protocol today.

Figure 7-19 shows the IEEE 802.4 Token Bus MAC PDU. This is similar to the Ethernet MAC PDU, with the omission of the PAD functionality and the addition of both a frame control (FC) character to identify the frame type and an end delimiter (ED), which indicates the end of a frame.

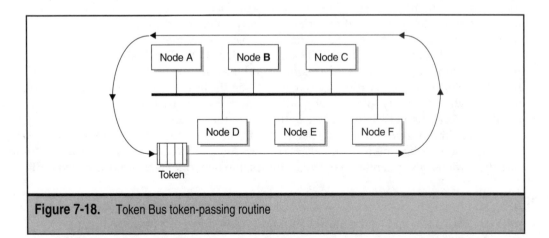

Figure 7-18.   Token Bus token-passing routine

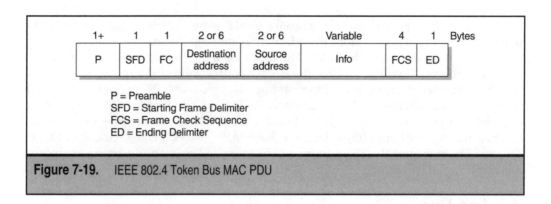

1+	1	1	2 or 6	2 or 6	Variable	4	1	Bytes
P	SFD	FC	Destination address	Source address	Info	FCS	ED	

P = Preamble
SFD = Starting Frame Delimiter
FCS = Frame Check Sequence
ED = Ending Delimiter

Figure 7-19. IEEE 802.4 Token Bus MAC PDU

802.5 Token Ring

The Token Ring protocol was developed by IBM development labs in Zurich, Switzerland, in the late 1960s, with the first products appearing in 1986. The IEEE has adopted Token Ring as IEEE Standard 802.5, which works on the IEEE 802.2 logical control layer with IEEE 802.2 Type 1 protocol and 802.5 MAC Token Passing Protocol. Basic operation consists of a token, which circulates around the physical "hub" and logical "ring" topology and provides "priority access" to the network medium. The token is either free or busy. As a free token circles the ring, each station is able to seize the token, modify it, load data onto the bus, and send it on to the destination station. If the token is busy (the token contains data destined for a different station), the station regenerates it and passes it on to the next station without modification. Thus, only one station on the ring can transmit data over the common medium at a given time. Priorities can be assigned to the token for specific stations on the ring. At heavy load conditions, the Token Ring protocol is much more bandwidth-efficient than other LAN protocols (because there are fewer idle tokens—as opposed to Ethernet, which experiences many collisions during heavy load conditions). Figure 7-20 shows the Token Ring token-passing routine.

Figure 7-21 shows the IEEE 802.5 Token Ring MAC PDU. This is similar to the Token Bus PDU, with the omission of the preamble and the addition of the access control (AC) field, for priority and reservation access control, and the frame status (FS) character. Also, note that when an empty token is sent, only three characters are needed: the start delimiter (SD), AC, and an ED field in place of the rest of the Token Ring PDU.

The maximum frame size for a Token Ring frame using the 4-Mbps medium is 4000 bytes; for the 16-Mbps medium, it is 17,800 bytes. Again, this number is important in future discussions of segmentation of MAC frames into network layer protocols such as IP.

FDDI

FDDI was designed to provide either a high-performance LAN or a campus backbone. Shared FDDI MANs can be connected via DS3 or OC-3 SONET pipes to form a wide area network, subject to distance constraints. FDDI is a LAN and MAN standard defined by

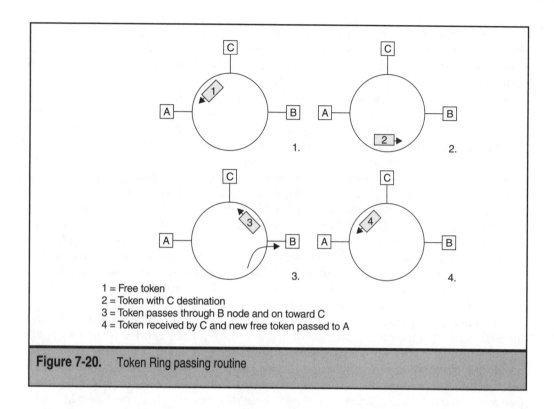

1 = Free token
2 = Token with C destination
3 = Token passes through B node and on toward C
4 = Token received by C and new free token passed to A

Figure 7-20.   Token Ring passing routine

ANSI (and CBEMA Committee) as X3T12. It is also recognized as an ISO standard. FDDI operates over both physical- and MAC-layer protocols, providing a 100-Mbps transmission over a dual, counter-rotating optical fiber ring between nodes. Although the band-

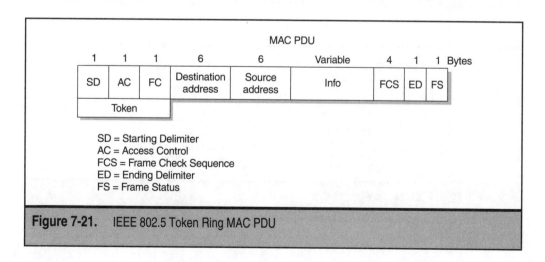

SD = Starting Delimiter
AC = Access Control
FCS = Frame Check Sequence
ED = Ending Delimiter
FS = Frame Status

Figure 7-21.   IEEE 802.5 Token Ring MAC PDU

width provided on the ring is 100 Mbps, the actual throughput is usually much lower. Still, this makes FDDI a high-speed LAN technology. Up to 500 dual-attachment connection devices can interface to the FDDI ring in series. FDDI rings support a maximum of up to 1000 stations, with a maximum distance between stations of 2 kilometers and a maximum ring total circumference (path) of 100 to 200 kilometers. Many more network stations can be supported by FDDI than lower-speed LAN technologies, leading to better performance curves and less LAN degradation per user. There is also a standard for FDDI protocol over copper: Copper Distributed Data Interface (CDDI).

In an OSIRM comparison, the FDDI protocols cover the same territory as the Token Ring protocol. In fact, FDDI operation is very similar to Token Ring protocol operation, and Token Ring can be credited with providing the basics of FDDI. This FDDI ANSI standard X3T12 specifically defines the Physical Medium Dependent (PMD) (X3.166) layer for single or multimode operation through full-duplex connectors, optical transceivers, and optional bypass switches. The physical layer of FDDI consists of a class A dual attachment physical interface via the PMD sublayer. The Physical Protocol (PHY) (X3.148) layer implements a Nonreturn to Zero Inverted 4-bit-to-5-bit (NRZI-4B/5B) encoding/decoding algorithm and also performs handshaking between each station's PHY protocols. Physical interfaces to the transmission medium are via multimode or single-mode fiber.

The MAC (X3.139) layer serves as peer-to-peer communications for the LLC layer and the SMT layer over the ring, as well as routing and traffic allocation. The Station Management (SMT) (X3T12/84-48) layer provides addressing, bandwidth allocation, fault isolation and ring reconfiguration, and initialization of station control functions. This important layer provides the means of inserting and removing stations from the ring. SONET interface and transport exists. Figure 7-22 shows these differences, where the Layer Management (LMT) layer provides the station interaction management between physical and MAC layer protocols.

PDUs similar to those used in Token Ring are formed in the same manner as other LAN protocols, and use the FDDI MAC layer frame format found in Figure 7-23 FDDI fields are labeled in symbols, which represent four bits each, and all fields shown in this

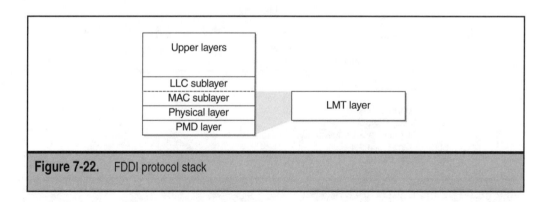

Figure 7-22.   FDDI protocol stack

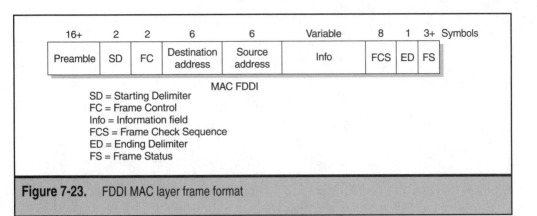

Figure 7-23.   FDDI MAC layer frame format

figure have been discussed. The information field (data packet) ranges from 128 to 4500 bytes. The address fields conform to the Token Ring standard. The maximum frame length is 9000 bytes.

Basic FDDI operation is similar to that described in the "802.5 Token Ring" section, with the exception of free-token seizing and the release of the token after transmission. Each idle station on the FDDI ring has a chance to seize a passing free token. Figure 7-24 shows an example of FDDI token passing. If there is a free token passing by station A, the station can (1) seize the token and (2) transmit a frame to station C. The original token will be taken off the ring, and a new token not released until station A has transmitted its full frame. This is the major difference between FDDI and Token Ring. A new token will be released onto the ring (3) after the completion of frame transmission from station A, even though the destination station C has not received the full frame (4). In this manner, high-speed transmissions can be accomplished without the need for the transmitting station A to clear the original token. The frame that was transmitted by station A will eventually come back around (station C reads the frame as it passes) and station A must purge the frame from the ring (5).

Two classes of stations use the FDDI ring. Figure 7-25 shows both types of stations and their use of the FDDI ring. Class A stations (stations 1, 2, 3, and 4) are classified as *primary stations* and use both the inner and outer fiber rings. They are called dual attachment stations (DAS) since they attach to both fiber rings. Class A stations can route around network failures by using a combination of both primary and secondary rings. These stations can also use a bypass switch, which enables the ring to remain intact even though the station has lost power. Class B stations (stations 5 and 6) cannot provide rerouting, and use only the *primary (outer) ring*. They are called single attachment stations (SASs). Each SAS attaches to the ring via only two fibers, and can be isolated by the hub during failure conditions. These stations are shown connecting to the FDDI LAN through a wiring hub, also called a dual attachment station (DAS) concentrator. Under normal operation, stations use the primary ring for data transfer.

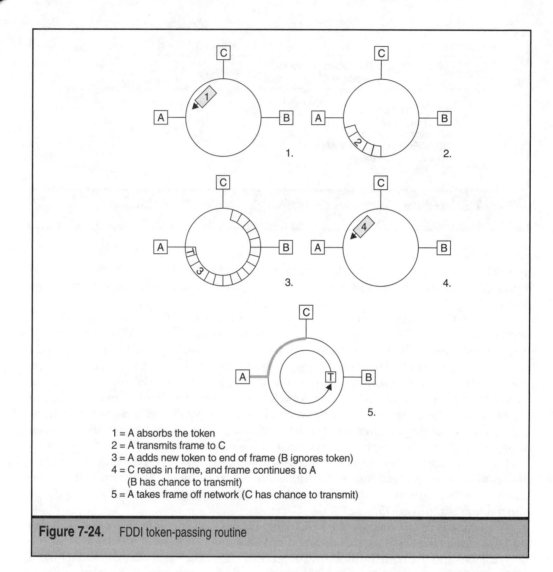

1 = A absorbs the token
2 = A transmits frame to C
3 = A adds new token to end of frame (B ignores token)
4 = C reads in frame, and frame continues to A
    (B has chance to transmit)
5 = A takes frame off network (C has chance to transmit)

Figure 7-24. FDDI token-passing routine

During a link failure (shown in Figure 7-26), all class A stations can automatically reconfigure to use the secondary ring. This capability is called *self-healing*. Class B stations will be offline because the primary ring they use is inactive during a failure condition. Any station on the link can be taken down without affecting the FDDI ring.

The secondary (inner) ring acts as an online backup to the primary (outer) ring. This is due to physical connections on the dual FDDI ring that share a single MAC layer and a single MAC address. FDDI networks can also be configured in a star-wiring arrangement, where a patch panel is used for concentration of workstations. FDDI concentrators are available that can aggregate multiple single attachment devices into a single FDDI ring attachment. Each of these devices must be within 2 km of the FDDI ring.

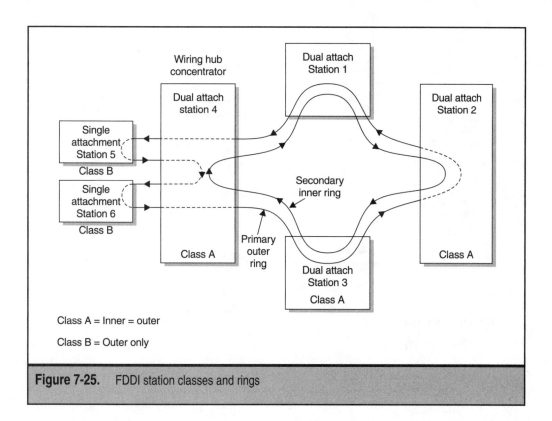

Figure 7-25.   FDDI station classes and rings

FDDI can be implemented with either single mode or multimode fiber-optic cable. During multimode operation, a 1300-nm (nano-meter) bandwidth LED light source is transmitted over ANSI-specified 62.5/125 micron (core/cladding diameter) multimode fiber, with a 2-kilometer maximum between stations. During single-mode operation, a laser is used in place of the LED to increase distance.

FDDI can be transmitted over shielded and unshielded twisted-pair distances up to about 100 meters. This is with data grade, not voice grade, UTP wire limited to 50 meters. The Unshielded Twisted Pair Forum (UTF) has developed the shielded twisted-pair standard called Copper Distributed Data Interface (CDDI). FDDI using CDDI can still use the fiber-optic backbone, but can provide twisted pair to the desktop. This is then used n conjunction with 32-bit FDDI PC interface cards.

WAN attachment is accomplished through both encapsulating and translating dual-attached bridges. Encapsulating bridges are designed to perform encapsulation of the MAC LAN packet into an FDDI packet. This new packet is then forwarded through the router network. This is a proprietary approach. Translating bridges bond the MAC LAN packet address to a SubNet Access Protocol-Service Access Point (SNAP-SAP) packet. This packet is then routed between FDDI devices, and is universally understood among many FDDI vendors. Figure 7-27 shows an example of an FDDI campus WAN, where a workstation communicates with a remote server across an FDDI WAN.

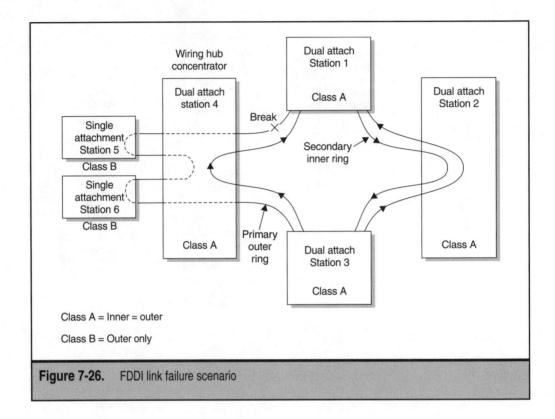

Figure 7-26. FDDI link failure scenario

The many advantages of implementing a FDDI LAN include

▼ Accommodate large numbers of users on a single LAN segment

■ 100 Mbps shared bandwidth with high utilization potential

■ Extend geographic LAN coverage (long-distance LAN)

■ High reliability through self-healing

■ Fiber immune to copper cable interference—high transmission quality

■ Supports more stations than standard LAN protocols

■ Built-in network management (SMT)

▲ Support for multimedia services on LAN

There are also a few disadvantages to FDDI LANs:

▼ Expensive to install (cost of hardware and fiber runs)
versus 100/1000 Mbps Ethernet

▲ Potential speed-conversion problems with Ethernet

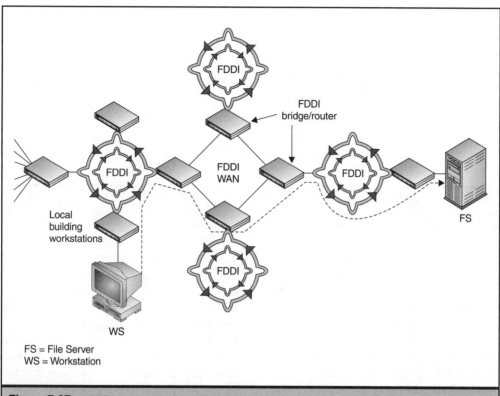

Figure 7-27.   FDDI campus backbone or WAN

FDDI-II

FDDI-II is a protocol supported by a mechanism called Hybrid Ring Control (HRC), which allows FDDI LANs to transport multiplexed asynchronous packet data and isochronous circuit-switched data. Figure 7-28 shows the FDDI-II protocol structure. The physical layer will probably change to SONET, but, as of now, it still uses the old FDDI-I 100-Mbps interfaces. There is now a hybrid multiplexer layer between the physical and MAC sublayer. The MAC sublayer has been split into a packet-processing MAC sublayer (from the old FDDI-I standard) and a new isochronous MAC sublayer. Frames are now called cycles. The PMD layer passes a cycle onto the FDDI-II ring every 125 μs (microseconds). The hybrid multiplexer layer strips off the header and the cycle to the appropriate MAC layer. The station management remains to be worked out for compatibility between different vendor hardware.

Multiple 6-Mbps portions of data can be dynamically allocated to DS1 channels to support voice, data, and video. This 6-Mbps (actually 6.144-Mbps) chunk of data consists of multiple 64-Kbps channels. Each cycle can carry up to 16 channels, and each channel up to 6.144 Mbps. Isochronous traffic can also use the 6.144-Mbps channels. This service

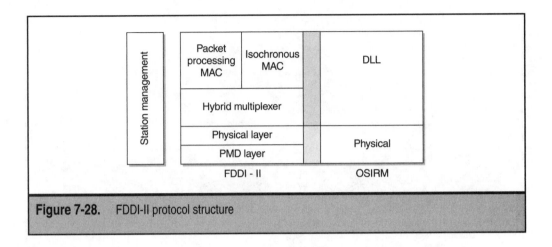

Figure 7-28.   FDDI-II protocol structure

is good for interconnection of PBX equipment to the LAN and WAN, and combines tele-communications and data communications mixed media on the same fiber. Other planned enhancements include the WBS subchannels, dedicated packet groups, and cycle formatting. Future protocol support might include XTP, HCR, and HIPPI. To date, the deployment of FDDI-II has been stalled by the majority of network managers turning to Fast Ethernet (described in the next section). FDDI does not provide address screening and security features such as those found in SMDS. FDDI also contains some distance limitations. When using multimode fiber, the distance is limited to 2 km. Using single mode fiber, which supports distances up to 60 km, can solve the distance limitations.

FDDI-II might eventually correct the lack of FDDI isochronous service capability and allow FDDI to compete more effectively with ATM and fast Ethernet speeds. But it does seem that these technologies will coexist for some time. In fact, FDDI, ATM, and Ethernet can be viewed somewhat as competing technologies, but can also coexist.

100-Mbps Ethernet: 100BaseT and 100VG-AnyLAN

Ethernet (10 and 100 Mbps version) is clearly the most popular LAN technology in use today. It provides low-cost hardware and an IEEE standard that is very common. Two IEEE approaches that offer 100 Mbps Ethernet have emerged: 100BaseT and 100VG-AnyLAN. 100BaseT has become the more prevalent of the two, with 100VG-AnyLAN being almost nonexistent as of this edition.

▼ **100BaseT Fast Ethernet** speeds up the existing CSMA/CD media access control mechanism of common 10 Mbps Ethernet to 100 Mbps. Thus, the time to transmit a bit on the medium is reduced by a factor of 10. 100BaseT is an IEEE 802.3 standard. Frame format, data content and size, and media access control mechanism are all the same, and it is fully compatible with 10 Mbps Ethernet. Three major segment types exist: T4, TX, and FX. T4 segment type uses four-pair twisted wiring. TX uses two-pair twisted media. FX uses two-strand fiber-optic cable. Both the TX and FX ANSI physical media standards are referred to as the 100Base-X standard, which was the standard originally developed for FDDI. All three use a 40-pin MII connector.

▲ **100VG-AnyLAN** is also called VG, Fast Ethernet, Fast Token Ring, and Demand Priority. 100VG-AnyLAN uses a new media access control mechanism, which uses a switching hub device that controls access to the medium by a "demand priority" mechanism. The IEEE standard for 100VG-AnyLAN is 802.12, while 100BaseVG is an IEEE 802.11 standard. The 10 Mbps Ethernet frame format remains the same, and the standard also supports Token Ring frame types. 100VG-AnyLAN can operate over four-pair UTP (up to 100 meters), two-pair STP (up to 200 meters), and fiber-optic cable (up to 2000 meters). A deterministic demand priority scheme is used to create a predictable order by which nodes share the network. A round robin polling scheme is used, along with a dual priority system that distinguishes between high or normal priority.

100BaseT is best used as an upgrade to existing 10-Mbps Ethernet when cabling permits but continued interoperability is required. The IEEE 100VG-AnyLAN standard allows an easy migration from existing Ethernet speeds of 10 Mbps and Token Ring speeds 4 and 16 Mbps. As of the writing of this book, Fast Ethernet (100BaseT) has dominated this market including the migration from Token Ring.

There also exists a proprietary standard called 100Mbps TCNS developed in 1990 as a 100-Mbps extension to ANSI standard 878.1 ARCNET. Here a token bus passing access method is used. UTP, STP, coaxial, and fiber-optic cable are supported, but typically at less than 100 meters. The IEEE had been working on a standard that would specify a 16-Mbps isochronous Ethernet (IEEE 802.9a) designed to support multimedia, something which the current Ethernet cannot do well, but this version never caught on.

The Fast Ethernet standards above have become the new wave for workstation LAN attachment. 100BaseT standard equipment outsold 100VG-AnyLAN by a long shot since their inception and is currently the most popular migration path for 10BaseT networks that have higher bandwidth requirements. LAN Emulation (LANE) helps with ATM integration.

Gigabit (1000-Mbps) Ethernet

Because of the popularity of Ethernet due to its low-cost hardware and ease of use, research and development dollars have been poured into making it better and faster. Gigabit Ethernet is an example of this and builds on top of the existing Ethernet protocol. Gigabit Ethernet increases the speed of Fast Ethernet tenfold to 1000 Mbps (1 Gbps). The first Gigabit Ethernet protocol was standardized in 1998, and has proven to be a major player in high-speed local area network backbones and server connectivity. Gigabit Ethernet offers a simple and painless upgrade from Ethernet or Fast Ethernet because it uses the existing set of rules (CSMA/CD), is backward-compatible with the installed media, and offers the use of either full-duplex or half-duplex operation.

802.3z was the first Gigabit Ethernet standard to be ratified, and was a combination of two existing standards: Ethernet/IEEE 802.3 and FibreChannel/ANSI X3T11. The 802.3z standard maintains the original 802.3 link layer protocol, frame format, and maximum frame size, and includes the FibreChannel/ANSI X3T11 for the physical layer interface. The 802.3z supports the following specifications:

▼ **1000BaseCX (copper physical interface)**   Supported over 150-ohm shielded copper cable with a maximum segment length of 25 meters

■ **1000BaseFX**   Supported over 62.5/125 multimode fiber-optic cable with a maximum segment length of 412 meters

■ **1000BaseLH (long-haul)**   Supported over 9/125 single-mode fiber-optic cable with a maximum segment length of 10,000 meters

■ **1000BaseLXz (long-wave)**   Supported over either 9/125 single-mode fiber-optic cable with a maximum segment length of 5000 meters, or 50/125 or 62.5/125 multimode fiber-optic cable with a maximum segment length of 550 meters

■ **1000BaseSX (short-wave)**   Supported over 50/125 multimode fiber-optic cable with a maximum segment length of 550 meters, or 62.5/125 multimode fiber-optic cable with a maximum segment length of 275 meters

▲ **1000BaseZX**   Supported over 9/125 single-mode fiber-optic cable with a maximum segment length of 100,000 meters

A second task force, 802.3ab, was formed in 1997 to work on a copper-based solution for Gigabit Ethernet. This task force adopted 1000BaseT, which is supported over Category 5 or 5E unshielded twisted pair (UTP) cable with a maximum segment length of 100 meters.

Gigabit Ethernet is a viable technology that allows Ethernet to scale in the LAN. Today, many organizations are using Gigabit Ethernet in their server farms or for specialized graphic intensive applications with high bandwidth requirements. Network managers do not need to train their staff on new technology to provide support for Gigabit Ethernet if they have an existing Ethernet or Fast Ethernet environment. Between Fast Ethernet and Gigabit Ethernet, ATM and FDDI have seen dramatic decrease in popularity. Some of the advantages that Gigabit Ethernet has over ATM are lower cost, higher bandwidth (155 Mbps versus 1000 Mbps), and familiarity with the technology (more support staff understand and have experience with Ethernet). Gigabit Ethernet has also had major effect on the metropolitan area network (MAN) market. Many service providers are now selling some kind of gigabit-MAN product (1000baseT over fiber in a metro area), and 10-gigabit MAN products are already appearing.

BRIDGE PROTOCOLS

The IEEE 802.1 Spanning Tree Protocol (STP) and IBM's Source Routing Protocol (SRP) are the two major protocols for network bridging. These protocols operate at the physical (L1) and MAC sublayer (L2) to provide a limited form of relaying packets over the local and wide area network media. True bridging protocols operate as relay points only. They provide a LAN extension similar to the repeater function but with limited additional intelligence. Some bridges used fixed (static, or manually configured) tables to make forwarding decisions, while others, such as the IEEE 802.1 Spanning Tree Protocol, employ dynamic, forwarding tables capable of updates. Bridging schemes such as these allow the bridges to dynamically change packet relaying based on network topology changes. Ethernet relies on the spanning tree approach when scanning for address destinations on the WAN. Token Ring almost always uses SRP to accomplish the same, but not 100 percent of the time.

IEEE 802.1 Spanning Tree Protocol (STP)

The IEEE Standard 802.1 Spanning Tree Protocol (STP) is a bridging protocol based on the IEEE 802.1 Transparent Spanning Tree algorithm. STP was developed to prevent bridging loops in a network and offer some path redundancy. To provide redundancy, STP creates a tree-like environment that includes all the bridges or switches in the LAN network. To prevent loops in a bridged environment, only a single path can be active between two end points. STP acts to disable any secondary paths by putting them in a standby or blocked condition unless the primary path is deactivated for any reason. The LAN switches and bridges use bridge protocol data units (BPDU) to exchange information with each other to remove any loops in the network. This STP process also includes electing a root bridge or switch and building the tree topology. The shortest distance to the root bridge is then calculated for each bridge in the network and a designated bridge, the bridge closest to the root bridge, is selected. Some vendors implementing this protocol accommodate load sharing across multiple physical links, but beware of these implementations, as they are purely proprietary and are difficult to implement in mixed vendor networks.

STP is a true bridging protocol and is inefficient and disadvantageous when used in a large internetwork. STP is better used when the network is made of many point-to-point circuits. STP does have a few disadvantages. STP elimination of loop paths ties up expensive leased-line resources. Also, building spanning tree tables after network failures takes considerable time and introduces long application traffic delays.

IBM's Source Routing Protocol (SRP)

The IBM SRP allows LAN workstations to specify their routing for each packet transmitted. Thus, each packet transmitted by a workstation on the LAN to the bridge contains a complete set of routing information for the bridge to route on. The workstation learns this optimal path routing from the discovery packet it broadcasts throughout the bridged network. Thus it becomes a combination of bridging and routing, but the distinction is that the routing is performed at the data-link layer, not the network layer. The connection is built at OSIRM L2, and thus the connection must be reestablished if there is a topology change in the source routes. The addressing scheme is hierarchical in nature. Each device makes its ring number part of the data-link address, thus creating a hierarchy of addresses for each level of devices. The bridge then routes according the packet instruction, and routing is performed at the data-link layer (L2) rather than the network layer (L3).

The information for source routing to perform its function is contained in the routing information field (an extension of the source address field) within the MAC sublayer frame. Figure 7-29 shows the structure of this field, which starts with a 2-byte control header, and then contains consecutive ring and bridge numbers, each 12 bits and 4 bits long, respectively, to identify the path towards the destination ring. The maximum size of the address field is 230 bits, which would allow up to 14 ring or bridge numbers. Since most implementations require the use of two ring/bridge numbers per "hop," there is a maximum of 7 bridges or "hops." IBM's Token Ring implementation of source routing has a seven-hop count maximum. The more uncommon IEEE 802.5 standard states a maximum of 14 or 15 hops, but this is almost never used. If the routing information field is zero, the bridge does not pass the frame (performs filtering). Any frame with the routing information indicator (RII) bit in the address header set to 1 is routed to the next bridge in sequence.

Source Route Transparent (SRT) Bridging

There is also a standard called Source Routing Transparent (SRT) bridging defined by the IEEE. IEEE SRT marries the IEEE STP and the IBM SRP into one bit-selective bridging protocol. The selective bit is transmitted to the router within the MAC-frame information field. SRT can then interact with the source route bridging of token ring while performing transparent bridging to other LAN implementations. Many bridge rates are over 14,500 frames per second sustained over a long period of time using this technique. STP is used primarily for LAN-to-LAN and LAN-to-WAN connectivity, but should be used with caution, as performance and response time are much poorer than with routing protocols. Note that SRP has more overhead than SRT, but the processing is reduced for each bridge it traverses. SRT can also allow SNA source routing into Ethernet TCP/IP networks and DECnet networks.

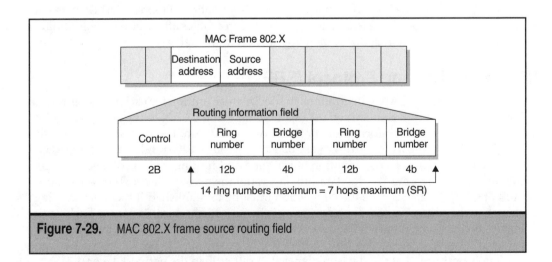

Figure 7-29.   MAC 802.X frame source routing field

Source Routing Extensions

Many vendors such as Nortel and Cisco have implemented extensions to the SRB protocol. These routers, while providing bridging capability, can transmit bridged traffic across an entire WAN composed of multiple routers, and still the entire network will count as only a single hop. Network end stations can support both local source route bridging and inter-network routing, while eliminating the seven-hop count restriction on source route bridging. Routing tables are built dynamically through use of the source route explorer packets. Each router is able to reset the hop count to zero as it passes the source route packet on to the next router. While this method is just another form of encapsulation of the token ring packet, it improves reliability of transmission, eliminates the hop count restriction, and can decrease response time across the network.

SWITCHING IN THE LAN ENVIRONMENT

There is no question that Ethernet is the king of the LAN today. It is extremely cost-effective, with 10/100 Mbps adapter cards typically priced at less than $50. The Ethernet 10-Mbps and 100 Mbps limit, or realistically 3 to 4 Mbps or up to 45 Mbps when the medium is shared, is not a limit for some communities of users. But workstation client-server and multimedia applications continue to push the envelope, requiring greater amounts of bandwidth every day, thus creating a situation of *media constraint.* Add to this the fact that many LANs carry traffic that does not originate nor terminate on their segment. As more users are added to the LAN, or each user requires more bandwidth, the network load or number of collisions increases and network performance begins to suffer. We note that when the average user's bandwidth requirements begin to exceed 100 Kbps on a regular basis, then the number of users per LAN should be less than 50. When this number goes to greater than 500 Kbps, the number of users is further decreased to less than 10. Users that require more than 500 Kbps on a regular basis are good candidates for a single-segment LAN.

Traditional passive or repeater hubs provide a common back-plane for LAN aggregation and are less expensive than switching hubs. Unfortunately, they provide only L1 repeater functionality. Their shared bandwidth efficiency decreases quickly as the individual user bandwidth requirements and amount of LAN segmentation increases. Now the requirement to switch traffic between LAN segments and dedicate bandwidth to each user segment requires a more dynamic device and methodology. Enter the LAN switch and VLAN.

Ethernet and Token Ring LAN Switch

How do you get more bandwidth to each user? Segmenting the LAN to have fewer users per shared medium can accommodate power users, workgroups with bandwidth-intensive applications, and servers. The term used for segmenting a LAN with many users into small or single-user LANs is *microsegmentation.* A LAN switch can take multiple segments with much fewer users and act as an aggregation and switching backbone. LAN switching of traffic only between source and destination LAN segments can save much bandwidth, rather than routing traffic across multiple LAN segments that serve as neither source nor destination segment. This switching function is performed at L2 (the MAC sublayer), and is similar to the transparent bridging discussed earlier. LAN switching allows the manager to preserve his or her strategic investment in legacy LAN speed devices while adding the elements of scalability and control. The LAN switch offers its own high-speed back-plane, much higher than 10 Mbps, and can offer multiple LAN segments to smaller workgroups or even to single-user segments. In this manner, each LAN segment or port is its own collision domain. This is a sharp contrast to the traditional LAN hub, where the entire hub served as a single collision domain.

When Should You Use a LAN Switch?

Network scaling issues accompany any network growth, and routed networks are no exception. Routing protocols must constantly be analyzed for design efficiency. Routing protocols broadcast information across the network to all other routers in an attempt to discover network services and to update their neighbors through distributing routing information. They interact with protocols such as ARP and SAP used for address resolution. Routers communicate via routing protocols such as OSPF, RIP, BGP, IGRP, E-IGRP, IS-IS, NLSP, RTMP, AURP, MPLS, and PNNI. Their communications multicast and broadcast information that, if misconfigured, can cause a lot of overhead across a large inter-network. Excessive broadcasts, or *broadcast storms,* are typically caused by misconfigured or defective systems (routers, hosts, and so on) and can take entire networks out of commission. The goal of the designer is to limit the propagation of broadcasts without denying the benefits they afford.

How can you design the network to reduce the amount of routing required, yet control the amount of contention for MAC layer (LAN) bandwidth? LAN segments can be placed first into LAN switches—devices that will segment and switch local traffic at the MAC (L2) layer and reduce WAN routing requirements. LAN switches rarely have WAN interfaces. At the higher end, you can certainly purchase WAN interface cards for LAN switches—see the Cisco, the Extreme, and the Foundry catalogues. Up to OC12 is available, and with the higher-end products, you can get OC192. This gets us into the "Layer 3 switching" arena, which has been a major push over the last few years. Generally, routers are used to provide the broadcast function across the WAN, but the LAN switches now allow the network to scale much larger. LAN switches allow the broadcast domains of a network to scale much larger than with shared hubs, while routers provide the ability to scale the WAN.

When should you consider a LAN switch (versus a router)?

▼ When workstation-to-workstation and workstation-to-server traffic is no longer mostly local

■ With large routed networks where the router update protocols are generating high levels of overhead

■ When scalability is required as the number of users and switches increases (much more complex in router-based networks) to avoid LAN bottlenecks

- As the number of users per router port increases (assuming delivery of constant user bandwidth)

- If mission-critical applications are moving to LANs, increasing throughput and availability requirements

- When client-server technology is stretching boundaries of LANs (inter-LAN)

- If workgroups are becoming more dynamic—enter the VLAN

- When higher-speed and performance LAN segments with fewer users per segment (more available bandwidth per user) are needed

- If increased manageability of each LAN port through SNMP is needed

- When port, protocol, and address flexibility is required

- If support for mobile roaming users to access shared server resources is required

- If current Ethernet and Token Ring investments need to be preserved

▲ When the bandwidth requirements of the individual user cannot be accommodated in a shared media environment

LAN switches are not roses without thorns. Beware: these devices can be difficult to manage and administer configurations, and hard to troubleshoot when there are problems. Make sure each device is fully manageable and experts are performing the administration and management. Explore the creation of zones where the server is placed on its own segment and operates as a centrally located resource to all other segments. Also beware that as the bandwidth available to users increases, so too does the bandwidth they require.

LAN Switching Operations

Ethernet switching typically employs application-specific integrated circuits (ASICs) to aggregate multiple single-segment LAN users onto a single-switched (typically bus or cross-bar) back-plane that can run at speeds in excess of 20 Gbps. Thus, each client or server can transmit at the entire wire rate of 10 Mbps or 100 Mbps Ethernet for an entire segment's worth of bandwidth, and the LAN switch filters and forwards the traffic. Local traffic is switched to the destination LAN segment and remote traffic is switched out a port to another device (typically a router) via a protocol such as ATM, FDDI, or 100 Mbps Ethernet. Each LAN switch acts as a multiport bridge. When a LAN switch port receives a L2 MAC PDU, it

▼ Examines the source and destination address

- Learns where the source resides (so that when another destination tries to send frames to that source the switch remembers where it is)

▲ Either *forwards* the data out to the destination address or *filters* it out if it goes back out the same interface it was received on (if the destination address is on the same LAN segment as the source address)

If the destination address is unknown, the LAN switch, such as a bridge, will forward the packet to all interfaces other than the source interface.

Servers can be connected via multiple single-user Ethernet segments when more bandwidth is needed. Thus, Ethernet switching allows better throughput and extends the life cycle and investment of the existing LAN and wiring structure.

Ethernet switch designs use either symmetric or asymmetric switching. Symmetric switching provides switching between like-bandwidth LANs (for example, 100 Mbps to 100 Mbps). Asymmetric switching provides rate adaptation switching between unlike bandwidth LANs (that is, 10 Mbps to 100 Mbps). Here, the entire packet is held until bandwidth is available to transmit to the destination (LAN segment) address. There are two general types of Ethernet switches: cut-through and store-and-forward. Cut-through switches act as cell switches; they start to forward the MAC frame to the destination address before receiving the end of the frame. This technique is good for minimizing delay but bad for propagating errors. Store-and-forward switches read in the entire MAC frame before forwarding it to the destination address. They also perform error checking on packets and discard erred packets. This method is used when moving frames from a lower-speed LAN to a higher-speed LAN as with asymmetric switching, and is the more common and more expensive approach.

Token Ring switches offer similar benefits to Ethernet switches. Token Ring switches mostly use either transparent bridging or source route bridging (SRB).

VLANs and LAN Emulation

VLANs (VLANs) are defined by switching devices that group users into a virtual community in which it appears that all users within that community share a local LAN segment. VLANs allow networks to be segmented logically without having to be physically rewired. Virtual communities can be software-defined workgroups, cross-functional teams, and cross-departmental project teams—any group that needs to communicate in a virtual shared environment independent of physical limitations. VLANs are also used to segregate traffic by protocol, and/or by application, in order to reduce the size of broadcast domains, thus limiting the numbers of broadcasts on a network. VLANs allow logical networks to be formed independent of where each device is physically located. In this manner, administrative changes can be made dynamically without reassigning IP addresses or changing physical wiring structures. One example of a VLAN feature is the capability for automatic address registration across the VLAN.

The IEEE VLAN standard, 802.1Q, adds four bytes to each Ethernet frame to identify the frame as belonging to a specific VLAN group. The switch reviews these bytes to determine where the frame should be delivered. Figure 7-30 shows an example of the 802.1Q frame with the additional bytes. The first two bytes (TPI) indicate the frame is an 802.1Q VLAN frame. The second two bytes (TAG) determine the priority, bit order, and where the frame belongs.

There are three methods of implementing VLANs: ATM LAN emulation (LANE), IEEE 802.10, and proprietary implementations. VLANs tend to require that all ports in the VLAN use the same media. Mixed media VLANs imply translation functions (trans-

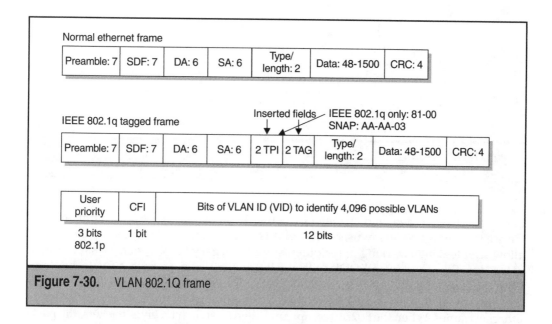

Figure 7-30. VLAN 802.1Q frame

lation bridging ala IEEE 802.1) being performed by the LAN switch or router. ATM LANE is performed with four components. A LAN emulation client (LEC) provides a translation bridge from the LAN protocol to ATM. A LAN emulation server (LES) acts to resolve unknown and broadcast addresses by maintaining and replying to known address resolution requests. The broadcast and unknown server (BUS) maintains all ATM addresses and handles all point-to-point and point-to-multipoint addressing, emulating the LAN broadcast and multicast functions absent from ATM technology. The LAN emulation configuration server (LECS) provides the address of the LES and BUS to every LEC when they initially attach to the ATM network (emulated LAN management and address registration functions).

IEEE 802.10 VLANs can use the standard 802.10 PDU frame header originally designated for secure data exchange (SDE). The VLAN ID is carried within the IEEE 802.10 header, specifically within the Security Association IDentification header (SAID) field, as shown in Figure 7-31. This approach offers a low-latency packet-tagging approach as pioneered by Cisco.

There are also many proprietary methods of implementing a VLAN. One of the more popular is Cisco's Inter-Switch Link (ISL). All frames are tagged with a proprietary VLAN identifier and all trunking between VLAN devices is proprietary.

Most VLANs are application specific today, but this is changing. ATM technology is actually one of the best enablers of VLANs, and vice versa. The capability for newer ATM networks to emulate many desirable features of existing LANs is often a key requirement. Terminal equipment (TE) should be able to interface to ATM LANs and be automatically recognized. Equipment configurations and connection should be capable

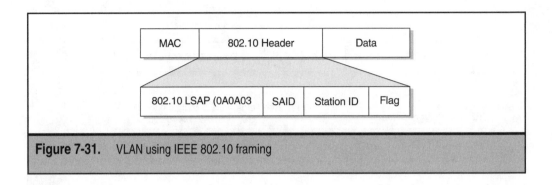

Figure 7-31.   VLAN using IEEE 802.10 framing

of being moved, added, and changed by network management, or even automatically. Only a few years ago, many users viewed ATM as the unifying technology that would allow seamless interworking of the older, so-called legacy LAN systems (that is, Ethernet, Token Ring, and even FDDI) with the latest, high-performance ATM technology. With the onset of both Fast Ethernet and Gigabit Ethernet LAN markets, fewer companies are moving to ATM in the LAN. 802.1Q is the standard for implementing VLANs on Ethernet frames. When the 802.1Q compliant Ethernet switch receives packets, the packets are tagged with VLAN information based on the port or the MAC address of the sending machine. The tagged frame is then forwarded based on the destination MAC address and the VLAN identifier.

REVIEW

We have covered many of the common protocols that function at the data-link layer, which is L2 in the seven-layer OSI reference model. The data-link control functions establish a peer-to-peer relationship across the network that manage reliable data flow across this medium and terminates the link after completion of accurate data flow. Some of the more popular protocols sitting at the data-link layer include Ethernet, Token Ring, and FDDI.

When dealing with LANs, the physical interface protocols are intricately tied to the L2 data-link layer protocols. For LAN data transport, the data-link protocol layer is divided into MAC and LLC sublayers, performing local media access and managing end-to-end data transport, respectively. Protocols such as FDDI , Fast Ethernet, and Gigabit Ethernet have increased the available bandwidth, and Ethernet switching has emerged to play a key role in rapid expansion of multiple LAN environments and single-segment users with an eye toward preserving existing infrastructure. VLANs play an important part in some LAN designs. Routing and higher-layer protocols will be explained in the next chapter.

CHAPTER 8

Frame Relay

Frame relay (FR) exploded on the data communications scene in the early 1990s, driven by the need for speed and previously unseen industry-wide vendor cooperation. FR provides higher speed access and reduced network latency over legacy X.25. FR operates at the data-link layer of the OSIRM, and thus removes the retransmission capability of the network found previously in X.25. The retransmission capability was removed due to improved transmission media such as fiber optics. FR services provide users with equipment and bandwidth cost savings over building private-line networks.

Many experts projected early on that FR was the death knoll to private lines, but time has shown that the markets for both FR and private lines have grown and that each technology continues to solve different networking requirements. The sales of FR equipment and services are expected to exceed $18 billion in 2002, making FR the dominant WAN technology for corporate data designs and the primary data service sold by service providers (the traditional IXCs, LECs, and RBOCs).

BACKGROUND

Why did the industry need a new public data service in the early 1990s? As LAN deployments accelerated and supported speeds of 10 Mbps for Ethernet and 16 Mbps for Token Ring, connecting LANs required higher throughput and lower latency than X.25 services could provide. Deploying routers connected by private lines became the standard design for connecting LANs, but as networks grew and connectivity patterns meshed, private lines remained expensive and prone to single point-of-failure outages. As new fiber-optic transport infrastructures reduced overall error rates from thousands down to ten errors per billion bits, the requirement for network retransmission, which was a staple of X.25, was no longer required. The fiber-optic infrastructure enabled the opportunity to make retransmission the sole responsibility of the application, which in turn allowed less expensive network switch platforms to be deployed.

The ITU-T published the original description of FR in I.122 in 1988, but had six pages laden with a more than usual "for further study" prose. The original description envisioned running an FR service over ISDN D or B channels. In 1990, four vendors known as the "Gang of Four" (StrataCom, Cisco, Northern Telecom, and DEC) wrote a specification for the local management interface (LMI), which defined access to a FR network. These four vendors also formed the Frame Relay Forum, an association of vendors, carriers, users, and consultants committed to the education, promotion, and implementation of FR, which has helped push standards bodies such as ITU-T and ANSI and interoperability of FR equipment.

In March of 1991, WilTel launched the first FR service using StrataCom (now part of Cisco) switches, which was followed by services from most carriers within the next two years. AT&T launched a FR service in late 1992, along with the other leading IXCs, to protect a large base of their private-line customers from switching to other providers' FR services, hence a new age of modern day data services was born.

Overview

FR enables each location to provide one or more physical-access circuits into the network, and within these physical circuits, create multiple logical connections between locations called permanent virtual circuits (PVCs) or switched virtual circuits (SVCs). These PVCs and SVCs are then transported over a switched network service efficiently and quickly via a streamlined frame transmission technique. A switched network service such as FR will automatically reroute traffic (PVCs and SVCs) around the failure of a network circuit or switch, thus increasing network availability to the end user. PVCs operate similar to voice calls over the PSTN.

FR supports access speeds from DS0 (56/64 Kbps) up to DS3 (45 Mbps) rates. FR service can give the impression that each device on the network is logically connected to every other device through a fully or partially meshed logical design. The amount of connectivity (meshing) required is a design trade-off of price versus functionality/traffic patterns. FR service provides a cost-effective solution for LAN interconnection between multiple sites.

In addition to LAN interconnection, FR can be used to transport legacy mainframe traffic using devices called FR access devices or assemblers/disassemblers (FRADs), legacy voice traffic as packetized voice (VoFR), as well as many other legacy applications. A FR network will typically have higher round-trip delay compared with a private-line network (but lower compared to an IP) due to network switch buffering and latency, which can affect performance of applications that are delay sensitive. Data networks are typically either bandwidth-limited (a lack of LAN or WAN bandwidth limits the application throughput and thus performance) or application-limited (even if there were more bandwidth in the LAN/WAN, the application could not go fast enough to use the extra bandwidth). FR focuses on eliminating the bandwidth constraint, while it is up to the user to eliminate the application constraint.

FR has become a dominant access interface/protocol for broadband carrier or private networks due to its simplicity and enormous coverage of bandwidth speeds and supported vendors. The technology used between FR switches is important to the end user only in how it affects the performance, reliability, and predictability of the virtual circuit. In the "Performance and Design Considerations" section, we will discuss the different options that are available in public FR offerings, why all FR network architectures are not equal, and what to look for in an FR service offering.

FR technical specifications provide for transport and signaling protocols.

▼ The transport protocol is based on the ISDN LAP-D specification that is an HDLC-based frame. FR is a data-link layer protocol, which is Layer 2 of the OSIRM, and uses an address known as a data-link connection identifier (DLCI) to signal to the FR network switch where ingress frames are destined.

▲ The signaling protocol is known as local management interface (LMI). LMI communicates between the FR customer premises equipment (CPE) device and the FR network switch providing a heartbeat or hello messages. In most FR implementations, the FR CPE devices send a frame every 10 seconds and the FR network switch responds that it received the frame. Every sixth frame, or 60 seconds, the FR CPE sends what is known as a Full Status message, in which the FR network switch provides the status of all PVCs that are configured on that port.

Figure 8-1 shows a typical network configuration of two sites with Ethernet LAN segments connecting workstations (A and B), a router at each site, and FR service connecting the two sites. FR is a Layer 2 WAN protocol, and Ethernet is a Layer 2 LAN protocol. A router is a Layer 3 (network layer) device. Internet Protocol (IP) is the most common Layer 3 protocol. Note that Layer 3 IP communications remain at the edge of the network (within the CPE) in this example. In the "MPLS Frame" section, we cover a new version of FR service which supports IP routing in the FR network.

Workstation A (also called a "host" in IP terminology since it has a unique IP address) sends an IP packet, which is encapsulated in an Ethernet frame and sent to the router. The router then strips off the Ethernet frame and looks at the destination IP address to determine the next hop IP address. Once the next hop IP address is determined, the router passes the IP packet down to the FR software, which determines the destination DLCI. The IP packet is then re-encapsulated in an FR frame and sent out the FR interface toward the FR network and ultimately, the destination FR port and PVC address. For each FR frame transmitted, the router appends a frame check sequence (FCS), which is also known as a cyclical redundancy check (CRC). A FCS or CRC is a mathematically commuted value that can be calculated on the receive end of the connection to determine if any bits in the frame have been corrupted.

Note that if the frame has been corrupted (which rarely happens) it is immediately dropped, and it is up to the transmitting application (for example, TCP) to retransmit lost packets, which are again encapsulated into frames. Once the FR switch receives the frame, it switches the frame across the switch network or "cloud" based on the DLCI address. At the terminating FR switch, the DLCI is changed to the DLCI that points to the source, which in our example is DLCI 17, and then forwarded to the customer router.

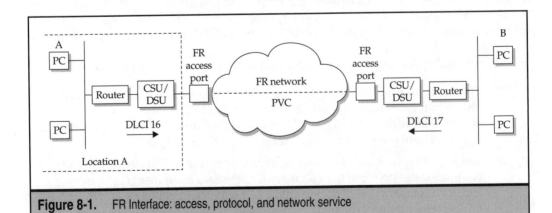

Figure 8-1. FR Interface: access, protocol, and network service

The customer destination router strips the FR frame header, inspects the destination IP address, and determines the next hop for the IP packet. The router then passes the IP packet to the Ethernet module, which in turn determines the source and destination Ethernet address, encapsulates the IP packet into an Ethernet frame, and forwards it to the destination host.

FR SPECIFICATIONS

FR specifications are based on a number of ITU-T, ANSI, and industry implementation documents published by the Frame Relay Forum.

The ITU-T specifications to reference for FR are as follows:

▼ Recommendation I.122, Framework for providing Additional Packet Mode Bearer Services, ITU, Geneva, 1988

■ Recommendation Q.922, ISDN Data Link Layer Specification for Frame Mode Bearer Services, ITU, Geneva, 1993

■ ITU-T Recommendation Q.921, ISDN User Network Interface Data Link Layer Specification ITU, Geneva, 1997

■ ITU Recommendation Q.933, ISDN Signaling Specifications for Frame Mode Switched and Permanent Virtual Connections Control and Status Monitoring, ITU, Geneva, 1995

■ ITU-T Recommendation Q.931, ISDN User-Network Interface Layer 3 Specification for Basic Call Control, ITU, Geneva, 1993

▲ ITU Recommendation I.370—Congestion Management for the ISDN Frame Relaying Bearer Service, 1991

Teaching the Network

When teaching classes, an instructor should explain the process of walking a packet through the network. This process is helpful for students to understand the process and steps involved. Make a point to discuss that a router strips off the data link protocol such as Ethernet and then looks at the network layer destination address (that is, destination IP address) and determines the next hop. Once the next hop is determined, the IP packet is passed to the egress port of the router and the data link protocol such as FR is added. If the egress port is a FR port, the router must determine the FR DLCI that will reach the next hop IP address. It also helps to discuss what protocol is being used at L1, L2, and L3 along each hop to show how some protocols are locally network significant, like Ethernet, and some globally network significant, like IP.

The ANSI specifications to reference for FR are as follows:

▼ ANSI T1.617-1991 (R1997), Digital Subscriber System No. 1 DSS1 Signaling Specification for Frame Relay Bearer Service

▲ ANSI T1.618-1991 (R1997), Digital Subscriber Signaling System No. 1 (DSS1)— Core Aspects of Frame Protocol for Use with Frame Relay Bearer Service

This section is divided into three subsections:

▼ **Frame format**   Provides the protocol specifications and defines all the fields of FR

■ **User-to-network interface (UNI)**   Provides definition of PVC, SVC, CIR/EIR, and LMI

▲ **Network-to-network interface (NNI)**   Used to connect different FR networks together

Frame Format

The frame format used by FR services is a derivative of the ISDN Link Access Protocol D-channel (LAP-D) framing structure, as shown in Figure 8-2. Figure 8-3 shows the standard FR frame structure with a two-octet address based upon the ITU-T/CCITT Recommendation Q.922 including the ANSI T1.618 Address Field. Data is transmitted across the network using this frame structure.

In Figure 8-2, the address field contained within the frame is based on the ANSI standard. The first and last one-octet fields (labeled Flag) serve as HDLC flags for frame delimiting. HDLC zero stuffing is performed to avoid mistaking user data for a flag. The second field is the address field, taking up two octets. Although Figure 8-3 depicts a two-octet address field, there are also three- and four-octet address formats (see Figures 8-5 and 8-6). The third field is for user data. The user data field can be up to 4092 or 8188 octets (either 4096 or 8192 minus 2 bytes each for the address and FCS field). The total packet length is limited to 4096 in most cases due to the integrity of the FCS. The Frame Relay Forum Implementation Agreement FRF 1.2 states that all implementations shall support a maximum frame size of 1600 octets. The FCS field is two octets long, and is the same used in HDLC, X.25, and a number of other protocols.

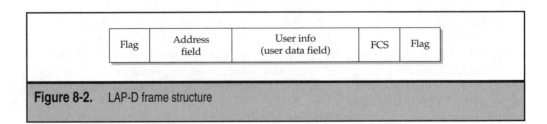

Figure 8-2.   LAP-D frame structure

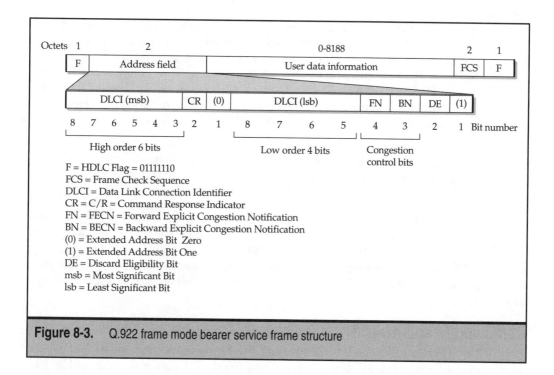

Figure 8-3. Q.922 frame mode bearer service frame structure

The address field resides within the frame, as shown in Figure 8-3. A description of each field follows.

DLCI

The DLCI is the Layer 2 address for FR. For transmitted frames, the DLCI is the destination address, and on receiving frames it is the source address. The DLCI is split into two fields, together forming a 10-bit DLCI that identifies up to 1024 virtual circuits per interface.

NOTE: In most network implementations, there are less than a handful of PVCs per physical interface per remote site, and many PVCs per HQ site.

This DLCI identifies the logical channel connection within the physical channel or port for a predetermined destination. The DLCI might have local significance on an access circuit or global significance to the specific service provider's FR network. A point-to-point FR virtual circuit might have different or similar DLCIs on each end. Figure 8-4 displays the difference between a local and global DLCI design.

▼ **Global DLCI**   Each CPE device attached to the frame network is assigned a DLCI number and remote sites use the DLCI value assigned to a CPE to reach that CPE. A global addressing scheme can be used for the whole network, as in a private FR network or per customer in a public network (for example, each customer has 100 assigned to a single CPE but across the network there are many DLCI 100s assigned). In Figure 8-5, a customer has sites A, B, and C (Site A, DLCI 100; B, DLCI 200; and C, DLCI 300). At Site C, if we want to reach A, we send an FR frame with DLCI 100. At Site B going to A, we send with DLCI 100. Service providers using a global DLCI assignment scheme and supporting only a two-octet address field limits the size of an FR network to approximately 1000 nodes.

▲ **Local DLCI**   DLCI values only have meaning when it is related to the port that it is assigned within. In this manner, DLCI numbers can be reused on each FR access port across the network. (See Figure 8-4.)

Each FR access circuit can contain up to 1024 PVCs using two-octet addressing. Table 8-1 shows which DLCI values are reserved and which can be assigned. When using LMI types Annex D or Annex A, the management PVC always uses DLCI = 0. Always check with the CPE and switch vendor to see how many PVCs are supported per physical port. It might be much less than 992. The extended address (EA) bit enables this number to be increased.

Command/Response (C/R)

The C/R bit is required to be passed through the FR network unchanged and can be used by end devices. Most FR devices do not employ the C/R bit, but some devices like an IBM 3745 do.

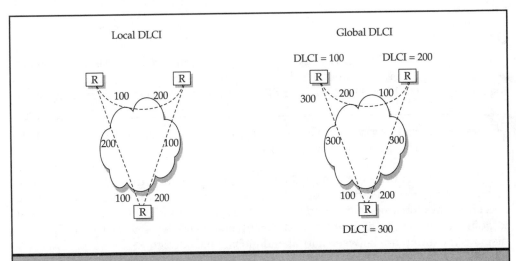

Figure 8-4.   Local and global DLCI assignments

Two-Octet DLCI Value	Three-Octet DLCI Value	Four-Octet DLCI Value	Function
0	0	0	In-channel signaling or management with Annexes A, D, and NNI
1-15	1-1023	1-131071	Reserved
16-1007	1024-64511	131072-8257535	Assigned using FR procedures
1008-1022	64512-65534	8257536-8388606	Reserved
1023	65535	8388607	In-channel LMI

Table 8-1.   DLCI Addressing Structures and Assignments

Forward-Explicit Congestion Notification (FECN)

The FECN bit is a toggle that tells the remote *user* that network congestion was encountered by the frame transmitted across the physical media and that the user should take action to prevent data loss. FECN is set in frames traversing the network from sender to receiver that encounter congestion. FECN can be used in receiver-based flow control protocols.

Backward-Explicit Congestion Notification (BECN)

The BECN bit works the same as FECN, but notifies the *sender* of congestion in the data on the returning path. An increase in the frequency of FECN and BECN bits received is a good indication of the congestion throughout the network.

Unfortunately, FECN and BECN bits might not be implemented in the FR device you are using and if implemented, are often not supported by most FR service providers, and even if supported might indicate a congestion problem within the network that will resolve before the CPE device attempts to react to it.

Discard Eligibility (DE)

The DE bit, when set at 1, indicates that the frame should be discarded during congestion conditions, as opposed to discarding other frames with a higher priority (those set at 0). The DE bit can be set by the user CPE devices or can be set by the FR switches when traffic exceeds the committed information rate (CIR). See the CIR subsection under the "UNI" section for more discussion of CIR.

EA

EA bits act as address field delimiters, set at 0 and 1, respectively. These bits are used to extend the DLCI addressing range to three- and four-octet formats.

NOTE: Per the Frame Relay Forum Implementation Agreement FRF 1.2, the three-octet address format is not supported.

Each user CPE device with multiple logical and physical ports must have a separate DLCI for each destination on the egress port it wants to transmit to. These DLCIs are built into the switching/routing tables of each CPE and switching device on the network. Networks that require more than 1000 DLCI values at a frame port can expand the number available, as shown in Table 8-1 with Extended Addressing. An NNI port will typically see four-octet addresses.

The majority of the public FR services support only two-octet address fields, as shown in Figure 8-3, whereas FR standards have defined options for three- and four-octet address fields. A representation of the three-octet extended addressing is shown in Figure 8-5. A representation of the four-octet extended addressing is shown in Figure 8-6.

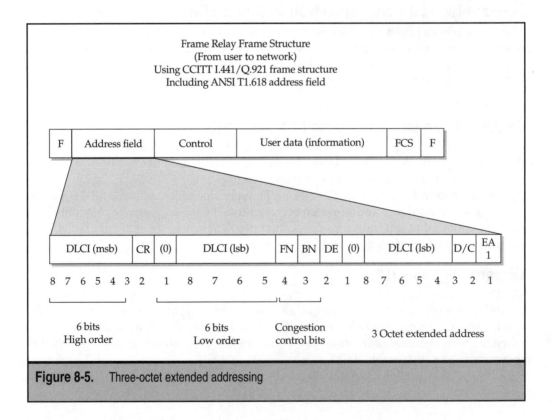

Figure 8-5. Three-octet extended addressing

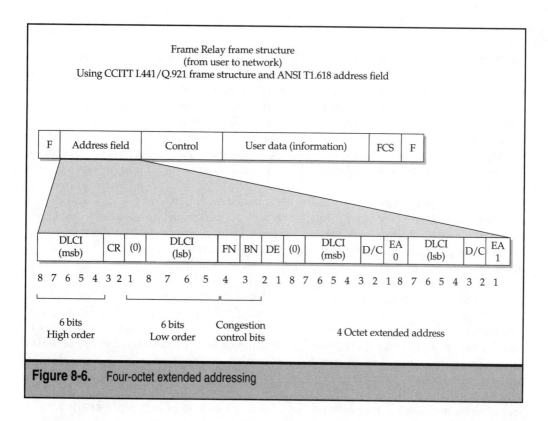

Figure 8-6.   Four-octet extended addressing

The DLCI/control indicator (D/C) indicates whether these address bits are used as part of the DLCI address or control bits.

Information Data Field

The information data field or *payload* can vary in size up to 4096 or 8188 octets long. This number varies by service provider, but the limit of 4096 is the most common, driven by the integrity of the FCS only up to 4096 octets. The Frame Relay Forum Implementation Agreement FRF 1.2 states, "Maximum frame relay information field size of 1600 octets shall be supported by the network and the user."

The data can be pure data when FR is terminating directly to a native device, or it can be higher layer protocols such as IP, IPX, or SDLC (SNA).

FCS

The FCS field assures data integrity of the frame. If there is an error, the frame in error is discarded. The sending device's upper layer protocol (typically TCP) is responsible for recognizing that one or more frames—or, more accurately, one or more IP packets within one or more frames—has been discarded and retransmit/resend the discarded packets and, subsequently, frames. Note that in TCP/IP over FR, lost frames will result in lost packets, which in turn need to be retransmitted by TCP. The FCS is defined in ANSI Standard T1.618 as a 16-bit CRC (CRC-16).

UNI

The FR UNI is defined as between the CPE (typically a router) and the FR network switch, as depicted in Figure 8-7. The UNI defines how the CPE equipment communicates with the FR network and has three main components of access, port, and virtual circuit(s).

The access circuit is defined as the transmission media between the CPE and the FR network switch. In the United States, this is typically referred to as the *local loop*. In the United States, FR can use 56 Kbps, T1 (1.544 Mbps), multiple T1 (*nx*DS1), or DS3 (45 Mbps) local loops today, while support for OC-3 (155 Mbps) local loops is in the works. In Europe, E1 (2.048 Mbps) and E3 (34 Mbps) connections from the CPE to Network Switch are supported.

The FR access port is defined as the used bandwidth between the CPE and the FR network switch. The customer might have a T1 access circuit but use only two channels of the T1 or 128 Kbps as the FR access port. Thus, the user could order a DS1 loop and a 128-Kbps FR access port. The design section discusses integrated access that enables the remaining channels on the T1 to be used simultaneously for other applications such as voice.

FR access port speeds range from 56/64 Kbps at the low end up to 1.536 Mbps in 56/64 Kbps increments and then can range from 1.536 Mbps to 45 Mbps in 1.536 Mbps increments either by using a DS3 access, or multiple T1 access circuits using a hardware device known as an inverse multiplexer, or multilink FR as specified in the Frame Relay Forum Implementation Agreements. FR port implementations on both the user-side CPE and the network-side switch supports LMI for PVC management. PVC management provides a heartbeat protocol for link status plus communication of the status of the PVCs from the Network. PVC management or LMI has a couple of different versions and a number of optional capabilities.

The virtual circuits are defined as logical connections between end points. As a private line is a physical connection between two end points, FR sets up logical connections between two logical end points within FR ports. There can be multiple logical/virtual cir-

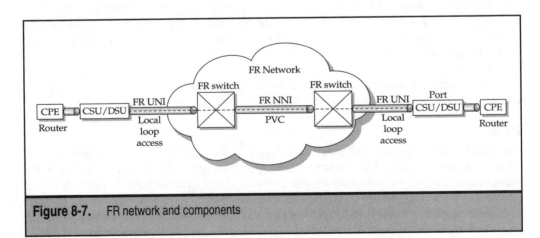

Figure 8-7.　FR network and components

cuits defined over a single physical port and access providing cost savings and increased efficiencies. Two types of virtual circuits are used to transfer data over FR:

▼   **Permanent virtual circuit (PVC)**   A logical representation between two points that does *not* change. This is by far the most common form of VC for FR.

▲   **Switched virtual circuit (SVC)**   A logical representation between two points, but the connection is set up on-demand when data is transferred and then disconnected when data transfer is complete. SVC is similar to a telephone call in that a call is made, data/words are transferred, and then the connection is broken or taken down.

A connection called an "enterprise PVC" can also be found in IP-enabled FR implementations, whereas only one PVC is required per FR access port. This implementation will be covered later in this chapter.

Since virtual circuits are true logical connections, virtual circuits have speed and throughput characteristics that are defined as the Committed Information Rate (CIR) and excess information rate (EIR).

PVC

Each FR UNI supports one or more PVCs. PVCs are virtual circuits, or virtual private lines, provisioned point-to-point from one FR access port to another FR access port. This virtual private line is similar in connection characteristics to a dedicated private line. Any data transmitted over this virtual circuit arrives in the exact sequence as it was sent; end-to-end security of the virtual circuit is virtually the same as with a physical circuit. In actuality, these PVCs might be switched many times by FR switches within the FR network transparent to the user. PVCs are provisioned and then remain static until changed by the user or provider via administrative changes.

Imagine a single physical FR access circuit (UNI) as the highway, with three PVCs (1, 2, and 3) as the lanes that cars travel down. Now, let's say that the FR UNI is a DS0 (56 Kbps) physical access circuit (UNI). Three PVCs are provisioned within that 56 Kbps physical access circuit (UNI), and each is assigned a throughput "rate" of 16 Kbps. This rate will later be defined as a CIR. The combined *simultaneous* transmission speeds of all three PVCs cannot exceed the physical limitation of 56 Kbps. PVCs can be oversubscribed so that the aggregate CIR rate of all PVCs exceeds the physical port speed, as this could lead to congestion as over-provisioned on-ramps to highways can become congested at times.

Obviously, one of the benefits of FR is statistical multiplexing, and we will see later how a user can assign CIR rates to attain high levels of statistical multiplexing, especially for LAN-to-LAN traffic that is bursty in nature. Remember that the total bandwidth available to all PVCs within an access circuit at a specific instant in time is still no greater than the port connection speed of the physical circuit. Also, note that a PVC does not consume bandwidth when it is not transmitting data, but can consume some router resources. Figure 8-8 shows a representation of multiple PVCs per FR access circuit.

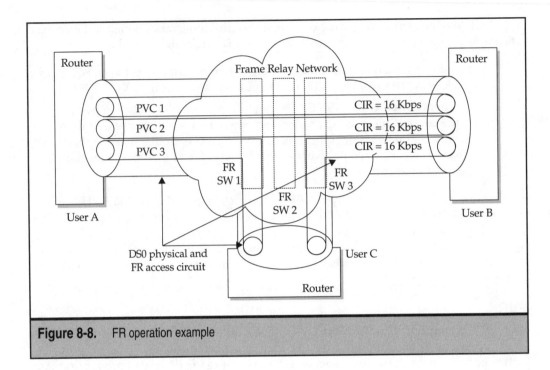

Figure 8-8. FR operation example

SVC

An SVC is a dynamically set up virtual circuit between two end-user CPE devices. An SVC is set up like a phone call—specifically like an ISDN telephone call. When data transfer between the two end CPE devices is completed, the virtual circuit is disconnected just like a phone call is disconnected when one of the user phones is placed back on the hook. SVC signaling is defined in ITU-T Recommendation Q.933 and the Frame Relay Forum implementation agreement FRF4.1.

SVC service offers an excellent opportunity to users requiring the following:

▼ Short connect, low volume, and transfer times with infrequent connectivity and traffic patterns (such as video conferencing)

■ VoFR

■ Connectivity provisioned on the fly

▲ Backup for PVC failures to FR switch

SVCs enable a sending DTE to transmit the address of the receiving DTE along with the data at call setup time. When the first switch receives this address and data, it establishes the connection-oriented, virtual path to the receiver. This method eliminates the need for preconfigured PVCs. Some of the functions available on SVCs include DLCI control and addressing scheme assignments, user channel negotiation, and service parameters negotiation (maximum frame size, throughput, transit delay) all on a switched service offering.

SVCs never reached wide deployment, and most service providers who originally supported SVCs do not support them now. Instead, a new service based on multiprotocol label switching (MPLS) called IP-enabled FR has emerged, eliminating the need for SVCs and hooking FR directly to the IP routing protocols within the user CPE routers. Thus, SVC-like connections are dynamically created between a single IP-PVCs ("enterprise PVC") per FR port based on routing requirements, making the old FR SVC standard obsolete. This capability also eliminates the need for expensive meshed and backup/disaster recovery PVCs.

CIR and EIR

FR defines the transmission rate of each PVC in terms of a CIR. The CIR, in strict terms, is a quality-of-service measurement that provides a statistically guaranteed minimum rate of throughput to its PVC at any one period in time. It provides a method for sizing your bandwidth on a per PVC basis and comes close to ensuring a minimum throughput (and thus end-to-end bandwidth) for protocols and applications. CIR rates are typically unidirectional or simplex, in that each PVC has a CIR rate for *each direction*, but some providers support only bidirectional PVCs, which have the same rate in both directions. The term *16k PVC* typically means a PVC with a 16-Kbps CIR in both directions, but not always!

In addition to CIR, FR defines EIR, which is the maximum allowed throughput on a PVC. All data above the EIR is discarded. When the data exceeds the CIR but hasn't exceeded the EIR, the network typically marks the frame's DE bit. Thus, if congestion occurs, the FR switch will discard this frame over frames that don't have the DE bit marked.

The CIR is computed as the number of bits in a committed burst size (Bc) that can arrive during an averaging interval (T) such that CIR = Bc/T. If the number of bits that arrive during the interval T exceeds Bc but is less than an excess threshold (Bc + Be), then the subsequent frames are marked as DE. The EIR is defined as (Bc + Be)/T. The bits that arrive during the interval T in excess of Bc + Be are discarded by the access FR node. Figure 8-9 shows the representation of CIR and EIR.

The value of T varies per FR network with a large value of T (say 60 seconds) being advantageous to the user because the amount of burst can be high, while a small T value

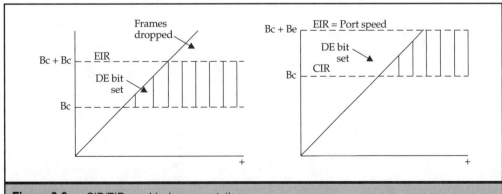

Figure 8-9.   CIR/EIR graphical representation

would be advantageous to the service provider. It should be noted that FR network switches include methods for crediting users if they send traffic with the DE bit set or, stated differently, the DE set traffic is not used against the CIR calculation. How CIR is managed by different network architectures is discussed in the "Performance and Design Considerations" section.

PVC Management, or LMI

PVC management, or LMI, is the control signaling between a CPE device and a FR network switch, as shown in Figure 8-10. The PVC management/LMI provides link status indication by performing a heart beat protocol typically initiated by the CPE to the network (for example, Q. Are you there? A. Yes I am.) and configuration and PVC status. The three versions of PVC management include:

▼ ITU-T Recommendation Q.933 Annex A

■ ANSI T1.617 Annex D

▲ Frame Relay Specification with Extensions (also known as the Gang of Four specification)

Annex A and Annex D use DLCI 0 to communicate PVC Management information between the CPE and network while the Gang of Four used DLCI 1023 for its communication.

Each of the PVC management versions supports status enquiry messages and full status Enquiry Messages. As Annex A and Annex D specifications allow for either device to initiate the status enquiry messages, the normal implementation is for the CPE device to send a status enquiry message to the network switch every 10 seconds and a full status message every six status enquiry messages or every 60 seconds. The interface is declared down if three out of four status enquiry messages don't hear back from the network. Each status enquiry message has a sequence value that the network increments and returns the incremented response in the return status message.

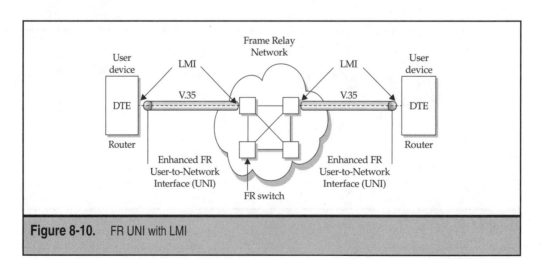

Figure 8-10. FR UNI with LMI

The full status enquiry receives a full status message from the network with the status of all PVCs configured on the port. The number of PVCs that can be supported by Annex A for example is limited by the maximum frame size that can be on that interface. If 1600 bytes is the maximum frame size, only 317 PVC Status information elements can be encoded, thus limiting the number of PVC per interface. In the Frame Relay Forum Specification Agreement FRF 1.2, Annex A defines an enhancement that increases the number of PVCs supported.

As a summary of PVC management/LMI, the following functions are supported:

▼ Notify user of PVC status (active/inactive state of a configured PVC).

■ Notify user of additions and deletions of PVC.

▲ Link integrity verification (physical link keep-alive signal).

NNI

The FR NNI is defined by the standards as a method for two FR networks to interconnect, pass FR traffic, and manage the logical connections (PVC and SVC) that originate on one FR network and terminate on another.

Figure 8-11 illustrates an NNI network example. User A interfaces to RBOC 1 FR network via an FR UNI. RBOC 1 interfaces to the IXC FR network with an FR NNI. The IXC also interfaces to RBOC 2 FR network with an FR NNI. Finally, RBOC 2 FR network interfaces to the destination user B with an FR UNI. Users A and B view their connection as a single PVC between their CPE. Each FR provider should have visibility, query capability, and bidirectional polling of the end device or switch in the adjacent FR network through the NNI interface. NNI circuits are also used to connect dissimilar switch types, as is usually the case between different FR services, providing multivendor interoperability.

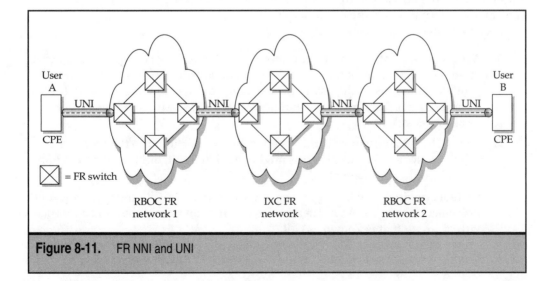

Figure 8-11. FR NNI and UNI

FR NNI standards/implementation agreements include:

▼ ITU Recommendations X.76 NNI between public data networking providing the FR data transmission service

■ Frame Relay Forum FR NNI implementation agreement FRF 2.1

▲ FR forum SVC NNI implementation agreement FRF 10.1

FR interconnectivity between service providers has become commonplace today but there are issues that you should be aware of when comparing total solutions being proposed by different service providers:

▼ **Different network fundamentals**   For example, how CIR is managed. See the section "Performance and Design Considerations" for differences between open- and closed-loop congestion algorithms.

■ **Trouble isolation**   If the problem is between the providers, resolution of the problem could be delayed.

▲ **Reliability and congestion**   NNI points can be a single point of failure and a congestion point.

FR DESIGN

As FR is the dominant data transport service provided by service providers throughout the world, the list of features supported and enhancements can vary widely. Chapter 12 covers the process of determining requirements, which is required to make decisions on architecture and port sizing. The dominant architecture of FR networks is "star" or "hub and spoke," designed around the corporate communications pattern in which all remote sites typically connect back to the headquarters site. If the remote sites are to communicate, they communicate via the headquarters site.

There are three components of FR:

▼ **Access**   The local loop from the customer site to the FR service provider's point of presence (POP) or central office. A local loop is ordered from the local service provider (this was traditionally the exchange carrier (LEC) or a Competitive Local Exchange Carrier (CLEC), but now legacy IXCs also provide cost-effective local access services).

■ **Port**   The FR access port is the speed of the connection into the FR service providers switch. The local access might be a T1 circuit, but the FR access port might be only two channels of the T1 or 128 Kbps.

▲ **Virtual circuit(s)**   Of the two types of virtual circuits (PVC and SVC), most FR implementations use PVCs. There is also a minimum throughput speed for each virtual circuit that is known as CIR.

Access

The access circuit is the local loop that runs from each customer site to the network switch. The domestic choices are a 56-Kbps circuit, a T1 circuit, multiple T1 circuits, or a DS3 circuit. As the cost of T1 circuits has come down (T1 breakeven can be less than the cost of five DS0s), make sure that the additional cost of a T1 circuit over a 56-Kbps circuit is understood, because a T1 circuit provides easier future expansion and growth versus another implementation cycle and potential downtime.

Some service providers do *not* provide multiple T1 circuit connections (also known as N × T1 FR interface) or DS3 connectivity in their FR offering. This might force you to design an ATM connection at the headquarters site to get either N × T1 or DS3 connectivity and use the service provider's service interworking between ATM and FR.

FR Port

The FR port is the speed that the connection is running between the CPE devices (router and CSU/DSU) and the Network Switch port. The lowest speed that is typically used is 56 Kbps with increments of 56/64 Kbps up to T1 (1.536 Mbps). An example of a port speed is 384 Kbps, which uses six of the 24 T1 channels. The free channels can be configured to simultaneously support other services from the service provider such as voice, which is covered in the integrated access subsection. Port speeds above T1 are based on T1 speed multiples such as 3 Mbps and 4.5 Mbps, up to typically 8 T1s, which would be 12 Mbps. If a speed in excess of 12 Mbps is required, some providers support a DS3 (45 Mbps) port speed. As a rule of thumb, the cost of a DS3 circuit is equal to about 6 to 8 T1s purchased separately.

The port needs to be sized to support the aggregate of PVC CIRs both in and out, assuming asymmetrical PVCs. A full T1 has 1.536 Mbps upstream and 1.536 Mbps downstream, so asymmetrical PVCs could cause a problem in one direction and not the other. Most FR providers allow oversubscription, which means that the sum of the aggregate PVC CIRs is greater than the port speed. The odds are that all PVCs won't require the CIR rate all at the same time. If you reduced your combined CIR below the port speed and one remote site needed to get more bandwidth than the smaller CIR value is, it might not get the network bandwidth, which could cause a throughput problem even though the port was not the congestion point.

So the port speed is determined partially (and often minimally) by the CIR rates to each remote site. Headquarter sites are often T1 or higher speeds, while remote sites are typically 56 Kbps or sub-512 Kbps. If you have over 10 remote sites, it usually justifies a T1 port at the HQ.

Virtual Circuits

FR access circuits and FR ports form a connection from the CPE equipment to the network switch, and over these is provisioned one or more virtual circuits as a connection between two FR sites.

Network architecture is determined based on traffic flows and pricing. As hub-and-spoke designs are the most frequent, partially meshed and full meshed PVC designs are also options. A star/hub and spoke design is shown in Figure 8-12. As regional offices increase communication, connectivity can be added between the offices creating a partially meshed design. If every site needs to talk to every other site, then you should consider a fully meshed topology, or better yet, an MPLS-based IP-enabled FR service.

The network architecture trend is toward partially meshed as distributed communication and many-to-many traffic patterns continue to increase. A star network allows communication between remote sites, but all the traffic goes through the HQ sites. As more remote-to-remote traffic grows, the bandwidth requirement at the HQ site increases (traffic in and then out) and network delay can increase and throughput decrease. There are, of course, additional design considerations that drive hub-and-spoke versus meshed topologies—such as security, cost, and network control.

CIR rates are chosen based on perceived traffic throughput minimums and peak maximums. CIR rates are determined based on the type of traffic and protocol being transmitted and the time required (delay and throughput being two key calculations here) to get information from origin to destination. Figure 8-13 illustrates the example where two 32-Kbps CIR rate PVCs are provisioned through a single router and over a single 56-Kbps physical access circuit.

A PVC is assigned between user A and user C, and one between user B and user D. Users A and B need to send a 200,000 byte file using TCP/IP to users C and D, respectively. If user A is the only one transmitting a 200,000-byte file in a given time period, say 1 minute, it will take approximately 25 seconds if user A can burst above its 32-Kbps CIR to the full 64-Kbps port speed. Now, say both users A and B are bursting 200,000-byte files simultaneously. Since their PVCs share the same FR access circuits, each has maximum available bandwidth of only their CIR rate of 32 Kbps, and both files take a minimum of 50 seconds to

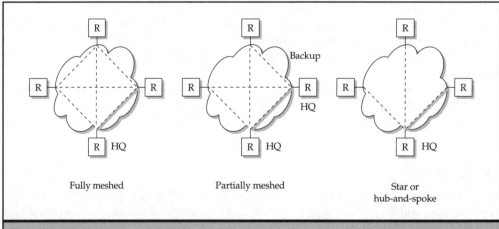

Figure 8-12.   FR network architectures

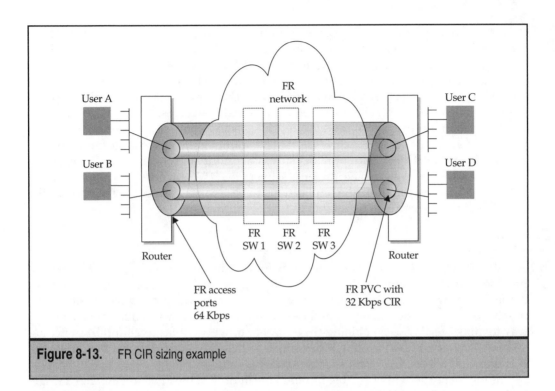

Figure 8-13.   FR CIR sizing example

reach their destinations. These transmission times don't take into account the delay due to the transmission media, propagation delay, switching and routing delay, higher protocol windowing delay, and DE bit setting. Loss of frames due to congestion (most often if DE traffic is used) would increase the total transmission time even further.

$$\frac{200\ kbyte}{} * \frac{8\ bits}{1\ byte} * \frac{1\ second}{64\ kbits} = 25\ seconds$$

$$\frac{200\ kbyte}{} * \frac{8\ bits}{1\ byte} * \frac{1\ second}{32\ kbits} = 50\ seconds$$

As you can see, it is best to size your CIR to attain the minimum throughput you can stand under congestion conditions for your mission-critical traffic. This is like a "threshold of pain" you will experience in end-to-end throughput and thus transmission time for traffic to travel from users A to C and users B to D. If you are not achieving the average throughput required for user satisfaction or minimum application performance, try either tuning your transport protocol and application or increasing the size of your CIR. Also note that end-to-end latency also affects this calculation. Many service providers allow PVC CIR rates to be different in each direction; these are referred to as *unidirectional, asymmetrical,* or *simplex* CIRs. Based on traffic patterns and service provider pricing, adjusting the CIR rates to match asymmetrical traffic patterns could improve performance and save money.

Some service providers offer optional utilization and performance reports that provide per PVC information such as peak and average traffic loads. These reports provide a valuable resource for sizing FR access ports and PVC CIR rates.

As the requirement to support multimedia traffic such as real-time voice and video continues to rise, the design might require a PVC to be implemented for specific applications to allow quality of service (QoS) setting to be different across multiple PVCs. A separate PVC for multimedia applications might allow some control to the designer over the prioritization of traffic from the egress port of the frame cloud, which is the typical bottleneck of QoS traffic. One service provider supports priority egress queuing (PEQ), which allows one PVC's packets to have preference over other PVCs at an egress point in the FR network. This allows multimedia applications to be prioritized into the network by the CPE and out of the network based on PEQ.

MPLS Frame

As MPLS has emerged as the key technology for routing and switching IP traffic, service providers are now offering MPLS-enabled FR or IP-enabled FR services. MPLS is a technique that provides the advantages of Layer 3 routing/switching while reducing the number of network routing points and keeping network latency to a minimum. Another way to think of MPLS is combining the best of both worlds—fast (yet dumb) switching and intelligent (yet slow) routing into a single switched/routed protocol that offers the best of both worlds—intelligent and fast switching and routing.

MPLS can be thought of as a big router in the middle of the FR cloud that has a single PVC connection to each CPE device—in this case, an IP router. MPLS-enabled (also called IP-enabled) FR is a perfect choice for networks that require partial or fully meshed connectivity between sites because MPLS-enabled frames provide full meshed connectivity at a portion of the cost of standard PVC meshing and without the complexity of FR SVCs. In addition to the fully meshed connectivity, MPLS reduces the requirements on the CPE device for routing by moving the routing determination into the network and can offer attractive and automatic disaster recovery scenarios to backup HQ FR sites. See Chapter 20 for additional information on MPLS.

FRAD

One device as unique to FR as the packet assembler/disassembler (PAD) is to X.25 packet switching is the FRAD. Figure 8-14 shows FRAD aggregating multiple network access devices (SNA/SDLC, bisynchronous [BSC], asynchronous, X.25, and 2780/3780 RJE terminals), hosts, and other various network elements into a single FR access circuit. The FRAD performs the framing function, encapsulating the user protocol into an FR frame. The FRAD then provides the connectivity to a private or public switched FR network. Access speeds are via DS0, fractional T1 (FT1), or full T1. A FRAD can also provide an interface for LAN protocols such as Token Ring or Ethernet.

FRADs contain the powerful capability to carry SNA and LAN traffic over a single interface or network access circuit, and typically provide spoofing or some level of PU4/PU5

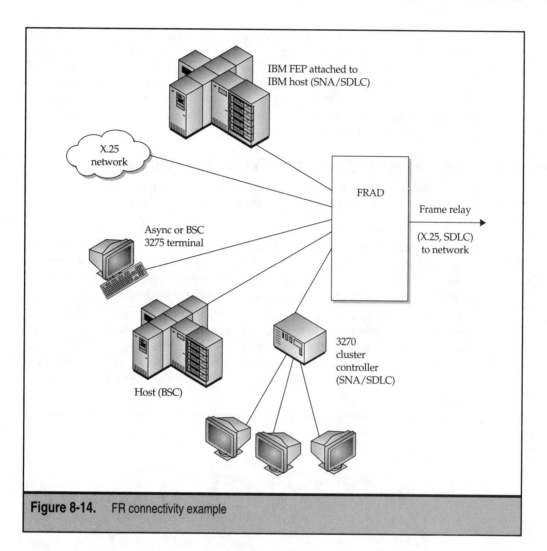

Figure 8-14.   FR connectivity example

emulation. FRADs can interface directly to an FR-capable front-end processor (FEP), AS400, or through a Token Ring LAN.

FRADs can perform a level of congestion control outside the FR network through SDLC congestion-control techniques. By generating and acknowledging the polls of each individual session, the FRAD can reduce or eliminate polling from being transmitted across the FR interface and thus drastically reduce the congestion caused by polling on each session. Conversion from legacy networking equipment to a FRAD configuration can enable you to keep much of your existing legacy infrastructure in place. This conserves much of your current investment and minimizes change to the users. FRADs can make the replacement of multipoint and private lines almost transparent.

Figure 8-15 shows a FRAD providing access to many of the devices listed in this section. The network access side shows a FR access circuit with X.25 and SDLC transparent protocol passing. Typical network side interfaces are RS-232, RS-449, V.35, and DS1. Trunk side interfaces are typically DS0, FT1, DS1, and DS3 using ESF, SF, and B8ZS formatting. When shopping for a FRAD, valuable options include SNMP manageability (with support for standard MIBs), built-in CSU/DSU, basic routing capabilities, Voice over FR (VoFR), and LAN interfaces.

Fault-Tolerant Design and Disaster Recovery Options

Data network reliability continues to be critical to business operations so it is important to understand some methods of increasing reliability. Some common configurations include the following:

▼ **Main site protection with a backup site**   SVC can be defined to connect to a disaster recovery site if a main site is isolated or a service provider's disaster recovery PVC option, which can provision PVCs to a backup site in under an hour. Extra PVCs to each site can also be set up to the backup site.

■ **Access circuit/equipment at HQ**   Two access circuits that are redundantly routed can be terminated into the HQ site and into two different CPE devices. This design requires twice the number of PVCs but protects against a local loop problem to the HQ site. Note that redundantly routed local loops can be expensive but redundancy options are increasing with wireless local loop deployment.

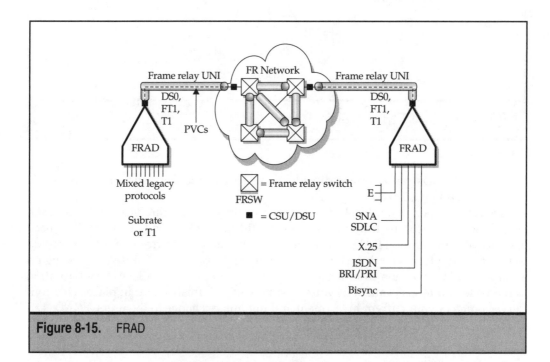

Figure 8-15.   FRAD

▲   **MPLS automated redundancy option**   IP-FR services based on MPLS offer
the ability for the service provider's intelligent platform to automatically reroute
PVC connectivity from one site to a backup site, transparent to the end user,
at the IP-address level. In IP-FR, each site provisions only one "enterprise
PVC" per FR access circuit. Each site's router then shares its IP routing with the
FR switch (through Border Gateway Protocol (BGP) or static routes). So if the
primary HQ site goes down, the CPE routing protocol will recognize that that
HQ IP address has disappeared and start sending all data to a backup HQ site
automatically (versus having the SP reconfigure PVCs). This is the cleanest and
most readily available disaster recovery option for FR as of print time.

Dial Access

Many networks have users that require either infrequent or mobile access to corporate resources. These users are typically located at remote sites that do not need continuous connectivity and cannot justify the expense of a dedicated private line. In this case, dial
access can provide a cost-effective alternative to dedicated access. Dial access can also be
used as a backup to dedicated access.

Dial access provides the capability to dial into a dedicated network device, such as the
FR switch and terminal server, as shown in Figure 8-16. When access is required, the
FRAD dials a phone number (over POTS) of the dedicated FR switch port within the FR
network service. Once the link is established, data is transmitted. When no data communications are required, the link is terminated.

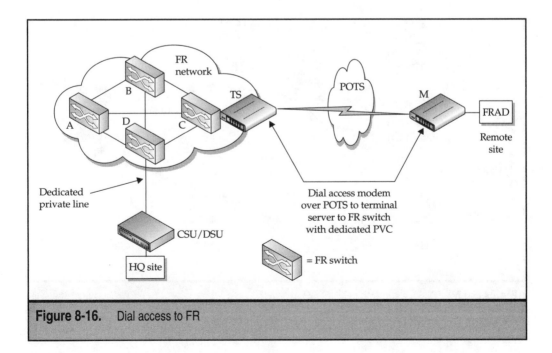

Figure 8-16.   Dial access to FR

There are three forms of dial access to FR services:

▼ Standard analog dial (ranging from 28.8 Kbps to 56 Kbps)

■ Digital switched 56 Kbps and T1

▲ Digital ISDN (BRI and PRI)

Dial access can also provide dial backup should a primary, dedicated link fail or something else goes wrong (such as the connection between the FR CPE and FR network switch). Dial backup is the capability for the remote site to dial up an alternate circuit for disaster recovery should the primary access circuit fail (via the router or a dial backup modem or CSU/DSU). Dial backup outside the FR network is shown in Figure 8-17.

Integrated Access

Integrated Access is defined as a single local loop from the carrier to the customer location, typically sharing both voice and data. In a static setup, specific individual channels on a T1 connection are assigned to voice and others are assigned to data connectivity. Figure 8-18 shows a static configuration where the service provider employs a digital cross-connect (DXC) function at the serving POP to split off the non-FR portion of the T1 and connect the FR DS0 or Fractional-T1 (FT1) circuit to the FR switch. A multiplexer—also known as a drop and insert device—is required at the customer site to split the

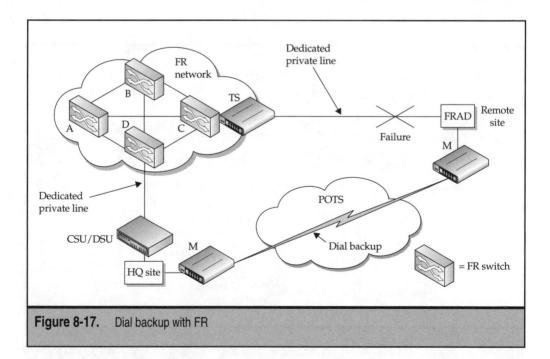

Figure 8-17. Dial backup with FR

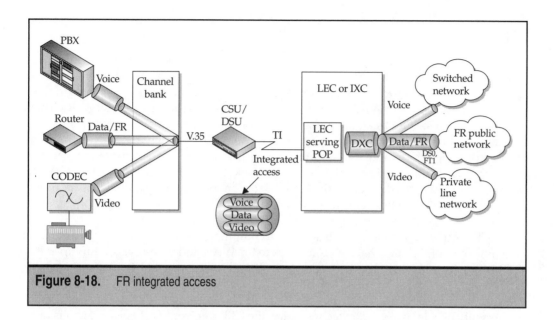

Figure 8-18.   FR integrated access

channels of non-FR out and the FR channels to the CPE device. Many vendors offer these multiplexing services to save access costs and combine service access methods. Occasionally Internet access is also available within Integrated Access services.

Pricing

Pricing for FR is typically broken into each of the components of access circuit (local loop), FR port, and virtual circuit CIR rate. There are a few variances:

▼ **Standard CIR**   Service providers offer their PVCs based on CIR rates. The primary variance is in the cost of a 32k PVC, which means a bidirectional 32-Kbps CIR rate on a single PVC versus buying PVCs asymmetrically based on CIR rate. Either way, the CPE must match the CIR rate to the minimum bandwidth required in both directions.

■ **Zero CIR**   One pricing scheme available is Zero CIR. If you decide to price Zero CIR, it is important to evaluate apples to apples, so make sure that each of your service providers gives you a Zero CIR and then your projected CIR rates. Some describe Zero CIR as "pump and pray" because there is no guaranteed throughput as with CIR. If slow throughput at times, or possibly for long periods of time, won't cripple your business, Zero CIR might be a cost-effective solution.

▲ **Service matching**   With enhanced services such as MPLS-based FR and IP-based VPN, selecting the best service for your needs will be based on security concerns as it relates to IP-based VPN and network architecture as it relates to MPLS-based FR.

VOFR

Voice over packet technologies such as Voice over IP (VoIP), Voice over DSL (VoDSL), Voice over ATM (VoATM), and VoFR have matured to the point that billions of voice minutes are being transmitted across voice over packet technologies. VoFR provides an efficient protocol for transmitting voice between devices that are connected by FR virtual circuits. Voice over FR has an advantage over VoIP in that the overhead is considerably less and VoFR can guarantee a minimum throughput through the CIR. Minimum throughput might be extremely important for highly compressed voice over packet traffic. Overhead on all methods of voice over packet technologies is calculated as the amount of protocol header versus the actual data containing voice samples. In an implementation of G.729 (8 Kbps compressed voice) using a 20-millisecond sample of voice per frame/packet, VoIP is around 25 Kbps while VoFR is around 10 Kbps.

VoFR requires a virtual circuit between all communication end points (typically, CPE routers). The VoFR routers have FR interfaces to the WAN and time-division multiplexing (TDM), or telephony interfaces to connect to a PBX or Public Switched Telephone Network (PSTN) and LAN ports. The requirement of a virtual circuit terminating on the CPE device reduces the uses to PBX-to-PBX connectivity or PSTN Gateway-to-PSTN Gateway.

As with all voice over packet technologies, the CPE receives TDM voice either via analog or digital telephony ports and then converts the constant stream of voice into frames. The frames are transmitted across the data network to the remote CPE, which converts the frames back to a constant stream of voice. Here are a few terms to understand:

▼ **Vocoder/codec** is the compression algorithm used to compress the 64-Kbps standard voice stream into a lower amount of bandwidth to conserve network bandwidth. Note that a voice call uses 64 Kbps in each direction or 128 Kbps of total network bandwidth. Some of the vocoders or codecs use G.729 (8 Kbps), G.723.1 (5.3/6.3 Kbps), and G.726/ADPCM (32 Kbps) standards.

■ **Jitter buffer** is an algorithm that compensates for frames/packets being received late based on network delay. As voice is a constant 64-Kbps stream, jitter buffer algorithms delay the play out at the start of the conversation and then manage a buffer to keep the play out stream constant.

▲ **Silent suppression or voice activity detection (VAD)** are algorithms that require packets to be transmitted only when there is voice energy, thus reducing the network bandwidth requirements by 50 percent. This can occur because most people on a phone conversation aren't speaking and listening at the same time. In addition, Silent Suppression and VAD algorithms support inter-syllabic savings for pauses between sentences and words.

An understanding of telephony and data networking is required when designing VoFR solutions. For additional specifics on VoFR, you can refer to the Frame Relay Forum's Implementation Agreements FRF.11 and FRF.12. To verify that voice transport across the FR network is going to be acceptable quality to the end users, you need to verify the following:

▼ **End-to-end delay** Verify that round-trip ping delays between the end devices is less than 200 milliseconds so that the total vocoder delay, end-to-end delay, and jitter buffer (check CPE equipment for jitter buffer size; Cisco devices are typically 70 milliseconds) is less than 200 milliseconds in one direction. If the ping delay is greater than 200 milliseconds, the voice will still work but the users might begin getting satellite effect, which is excessive delay causing the two people in the conversation to verbally step on each other.

▲ **Jitter or delay variation** When pinging between the end devices, does the ping end-to-end delay change or stay constant? The jitter should be less than 40 milliseconds but can be controlled by settings in the CPE devices. If the jitter is coming from the FR service providers network, you won't be able to control the jitter. If you run your test when you are not transmitting traffic across your FR network, the jitter can be isolated to the service provider. To control and reduce jitter, you can prioritize the voice packets over the data packets.

PERFORMANCE AND DESIGN CONSIDERATIONS

All FR networks are not created equal, so the reader must understand the advantages and disadvantages of different architectures. The switching architecture used in FR networks will determine the characteristics of end-to-end delay (latency), jitter (delay variation), and handling of CIR/DE traffic that has an effect on higher-layer protocols (such as TCP/IP and IPX) and ultimately, the performance and availability of applications.

FR access and backbones are designed to be *statistically multiplexed*, which is defined as a network that shares the network bandwidth for all customers and has designed the amount of access bandwidth to far exceed the network backbone bandwidth. Based on probability, the input bandwidth for all customers will not be used completely all at the same time; in fact, rarely more than a fraction of the time. Statistical multiplexing designs are part of our everyday life in that the PSTN (Public Switched Telephone Network) doesn't design a port on the Class 5 switch for every home in a neighborhood. If everyone in your neighborhood went off hook at the same time, probably only one in four would get a dial tone, which is a 4:1 design ratio. Said differently, this network was designed so that statistically only one user out of four will be using the network at the same time. In FR networks, the design ratio can near 1:1 for CIR traffic but can exceed 10:1 for DE-based traffic. On international networks where bandwidth is expensive, the burst above CIR typically is minimal, which means the ratio for DE traffic can exceed 100:1.

FR network backbones usually fit into two categories:

▼ **Cell-switching** The FR switch supports FR as an access protocol and then translates or encapsulates the FR traffic into cell-switching technology, which is usually based on Asynchronous Transfer Mode (ATM). The FR variable length frame, which can vary in size from 64 to 8196 bytes, is chopped or sliced based on your cooking style into fixed-length cells (ATM uses a 53-byte cell). Conversion between the FR DLCI address and cell-switch technology, such as a VPI/VCI address of ATM, is performed at the ingress and egress switches. The cells are transported across the network at high speeds and recombined at the terminating (egress) FR port into a frame egress port and delivered to the end CPE device. This method could also include MPLS.

▲ **Frame-switching**   The FR switch supports FR as an access protocol, uses an internal network address scheme (for example, IP or DLCI), and then switches the frame to another switch using FR, PPP, or another variable-length data-link protocol. When the frame makes its way to the terminating switch, the frame is delivered to the end CPE device.

A major enhancement to cell-switching architectures is the ability to implement cut-through. Cut-through is when the FR switch begins chopping or slicing the frame into cells and forwarding those cells to the destination before the whole frame has been received into the FR switch and the FCS verified. The cut-through technique reduces serialization delay, which reduces overall latency and also provides a constant jitter. A lower overall latency equates to higher throughput, especially on low speed FR access circuits.

To better understand performance and design considerations of the select FR architectures, there are two areas that require some additional discussion:

▼ **Congestion control architectures**   How the network operates when traffic is sent into the network above the CIR, and how FECN/BECN is used from the network perspective and the user perspective.

▲ **Enhanced network features**   Enhanced services and the delivery of them can be driven by the network architecture. Some of the enhanced features are FR to ATM interworking, IP-enabled FR (using MPLS), DSL Access to FR, and priority egress queuing.

Congestion Control Architectures

Congestion control architectures control how and when the network will drop packets. There are two different schools of thought known as open-loop and closed-loop architectures.

Open-Loop Architecture

In an open-loop architecture, as shown in Figure 8-19, each user (PVC) is allocated a committed burst size or CIR. Users can transmit all their traffic and not mark any frames DE if the committed burst (CIR) is not exceeded. If the CIR is exceeded in a period of time t, the frames that exceed CIR are marked DE by the service provider. The first frames to be discarded during congestion are those marked with the DE bit. If EIR is implemented, frames received after EIR is exceeded are immediately discarded and the application is responsible for transmission.

Serialization Delay Savings

An example of serialization delay savings is when a 1000-byte frame is being transmitted across a 56-Kbps access port speed. In this example, each frame serialization delay would be (1000 bytes × 8 bits/byte)/56 Kbps, which equals 143 milliseconds. If you had a short local loop, the number of serializations to get into the network equals about 1. On a long local loop, the number of serializations is closer to 2. A short local loop has about 1 serialization because the first bit that is sent is almost immediately received by the network switch. In a long local loop of, say, 1000 miles, the first bit takes 8 milliseconds to reach the network switch due to propagation delay. If the network uses cut-through, even on long local loops, the number of serializations is about one. What does that mean to the user? Say the total round-trip delay is one second without cut-through but 800 milliseconds with cut-through. With a window size of one, throughput with cut-through equates to a 25 percent increase to 10 Kbps from 8 Kbps. Note that when the window size is increased, the delay dependence is reduced.

All traffic that has been discarded has to be retransmitted from the originating host (typically, workstation or server on the LAN), along with new traffic requiring transmission. Applications that react by retransmitting lost packets and thus frames will cause congestion to intensify even further. Window-sizing flow-control protocols such as Transmission

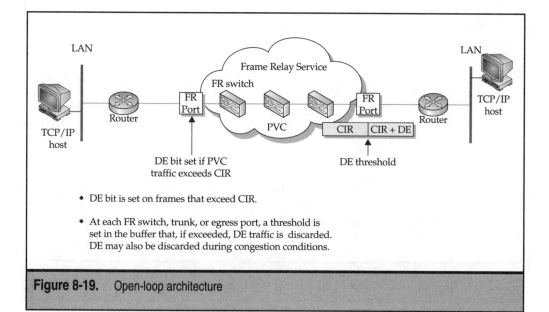

- DE bit is set on frames that exceed CIR.

- At each FR switch, trunk, or egress port, a threshold is set in the buffer that, if exceeded, DE traffic is discarded. DE may also be discarded during congestion conditions.

Figure 8-19. Open-loop architecture

Control Protocol (TCP) can be used to scale down the volume of retransmissions and spread the load over a greater time period, but at a potential negative impact to the application. This can slow the effective offered load and decrease the throughput gracefully until congestion clears.

In open-loop architectures, the ingress port on the FR service provider backbone is the meter point for the carrier. It watches the data over a time period t; computes the CIR, giving credit to frames that the CPE marked DE; and then marks all frames above CIR in time period t, DE frames, dropping all frames above EIR in time period t. After the ingress port, all trunk and egress buffers typically have a threshold mark for the buffer signaling that traffic is backing up. When this threshold mark is met, all DE traffic received is dropped and only CIR traffic is put in the remaining free buffer. But open-loop architectures do not notify the originating and terminating hosts of DE setting or discarded frames, and thus these hosts must identify the congestion or lost frames and retransmit that data. Thus, the true metering of application transmission and throughput is incumbent upon the end user hosts.

Closed-Loop Architecture

Closed-loop architecture, as shown in Figure 8-20, uses a protocol algorithm running on all the carrier backbone network switches to create a closed environment, where every switch within the carrier's FR network fabric knows the congestion condition from origin (ingress backbone port) to destination (egress backbone port). This congestion preven-

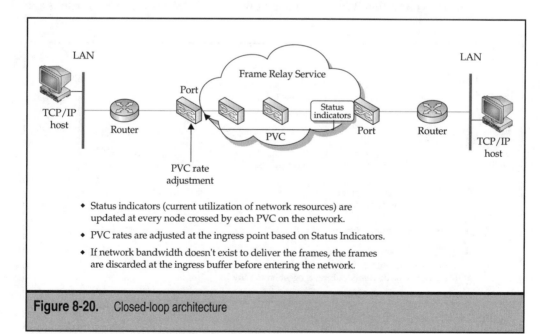

- ◆ Status indicators (current utilization of network resources) are updated at every node crossed by each PVC on the network.
- ◆ PVC rates are adjusted at the ingress point based on Status Indicators.
- ◆ If network bandwidth doesn't exist to deliver the frames, the frames are discarded at the ingress buffer before entering the network.

Figure 8-20.   Closed-loop architecture

tion is used in place of allowing the user to continue to burst and marking DE frames, knowing that discard and retransmission of some frames is inevitable (effectively providing congestion avoidance versus congestion control and recovery used in open-loop architectures). Closed-loop algorithm signals to the ingress ports that congestion has been detected and the ingress ports decrease the amount of frames entering the network but never below CIR. Closed-loop algorithms typically provide less delay and jitter (variations in delay) in the network due to controlling the amount of buffering at the ingress port. Closed loops rarely ever discard packets; rather, they throttle back traffic at the ingress port to prevent the dropping of packets that would never have made it across the network due to congestion. This is ultimately better for applications because they can see a limit in throughput early enough to gracefully adjust to it instead of continuing to send frames into the network that will surely be discarded and need to be retransmitted, and thus further increase delay to queued data.

This method also allows the FR provider to attain a much greater usage of network resources than by the open-loop method. Another side benefit is easier capacity and growth planning. The real advantage to the user is that it achieves a somewhat predictable QoS delay level to every user. This implementation is better for constant bit rate (CBR) traffic that is jitter sensitive, such as packetized voice, TCP/IP, and legacy session-oriented applications.

Summary of Open Versus Closed

As the argument between open- and closed-loop architectures has raged for almost ten years, here are some arguments on both sides.

Arguments for open over closed:

▼ Closed designs don't scale in a worldwide environment. With the fastest transfer of information being the speed of light, that is, 8 milliseconds per 1000 miles, notification of a problem could take more than 40 milliseconds, in which time, congestion might have been resolved. Closed-loop service providers have solved this problem by regionalizing their closed-loop algorithm decisions.

■ Open-loop networks typically have more buffers throughout the network, which could mean that bursting above CIR will be allowed more, but the tradeoff to additional buffers is increased latency. This is the reason open-loop FR networks almost always have greater delay than closed-loop ones.

▲ Less complexity. Closed designs require software-signaling logic between all switches. Open designs use buffer thresholds throughout the network. This also increases the cost of closed vs. open-loop architectures and services.

Arguments for closed over open:

▼ A closed design is fairer to all customer traffic due to limiting the number of customers who could load the network and cause congestion. A closed network would slow down the flow of all traffic thru a congested route, but not lower than the CIR rate.

- ■ A closed design along with a cut-through algorithm can provide superior QoS because the network has only one buffer point at the ingress port that reduces the jitter and end-to-end delay.

- ▲ A closed design can produce better TCP throughput due to a controlled mechanism of adjusting drops. In open, if a problem is encountered, a large number of packets could be dropped causing greater adjustments to the TCP window size and overall a drop in application throughput.

One of the primary differences is that closed loop networks deliver a congestion avoidance methodology, whereas the open loop network delivers congestion control and recovery.

Enhanced Network Features

Since FR networks have become a dominant technology in most service providers offerings, enhancements to the offerings are required to allow frame to better compete against new technologies and to allow graceful upgrade paths for FR users. MPLS-enabled-FR or IP- FR has been discussed and will be covered more in Chapter 20.

X.25 to FR Service Internetworking

Since FR was an upgrade to X.25 switching—or, as some say, X.25 on steroids—X.25 to FR interworking was an early connectivity choice. To define interworking, one customer would have an X.25 connection in Europe while another customer would have a FR connection in the United States. The traffic from the X.25 PVC format would get translated to the FR PVC format somewhere in the network.

ATM to FR Internetworking

ATM offers a speed and QoS upgrade to FR. Most service providers support FR PVC to ATM PVC interoperability. As FR speeds today have a maximum speed of 45 Mbps (DS3), ATM interfaces run up to 622 Mbps (OC-12) and beyond. In addition, ATM has more flexibility in managing different traffic types by supporting five different PVC types that include CBR for circuit emulation. FR-ATM interworking allows a single seamless network that supports some sites that require the added functionality of ATM while providing seamless interworking with remote sites that might not require ATM and where FR might solve their functionality requirements. The FR PVC with CIR is matched to an equivalent ATM "PVC" with "CIR" that is equivalent to an ATM service class, but the end-to-end QoS defaults to the lowest common denominator: CIR.

Dial/DSL to FR Internetworking

In addition to FR/X.25 and FR/ATM interworking, FR service providers support xDSL to FR, dialup to FR, and FR-to-IP interworking functionality.

On xDSL to FR interworking, xDSL networks use ATM as the L2 access protocol. An ATM access switch in the xDSL world is known as a Digital Subscriber Line Access Multiplexer (DSLAM). In xDSL to FR interworking, CIR is not always supported due to the maturity of xDSL networks and the point that many xDSL networks are oversubscribed with 100:1 and higher statistical multiplexing ratios. Also note that while xDSL access might be much cheaper than a dedicated FR port, the tradeoffs are in the service level agreements, such as mean time to repair (MTTR) of one to two days versus two to four hours, no CIR versus CIR, management visibility (could lead to lower availability), and lack of managed services support.

IP to FR Internetworking

On the FR to IP interworking functionality, a FR customer can get Internet access from a PVC within the same port as their intranet corporate PVCs, thus sharing the same local access costs for circuits and equipment. One potential downfall to supporting an integrated FR PVC to the Internet is security, but that can be addressed through various network-based firewall solutions now being offered in conjunction with public FR services.

ADVANTAGES AND DISADVANTAGES OF FR

FR has the following benefits over a private line network design:

▼ Cost savings

■ More efficient circuit use

■ Higher network availability

■ Extended technology life duration

■ Higher performance

■ Virtual circuits versus physical circuits

■ More granular QoS allocation

■ Cost-effective for network management services

▲ True international standard

Let's investigate a few of these benefits further.

Cost Savings

Most FR public pricing rates and tariffs are not mileage-sensitive, while private line rates are.

FR offers a reduction of physical local loops over a private line network because frame uses a virtual circuit for each separate connection versus two dedicated ports for each new PL connection. Figure 8-21 shows the number of FR local loops versus private line local loops required in a meshed network environment. Note that the majority of deployed FR networks are star or hub and spoke topology. For a cost savings measurement, each local loop can cost between $200 and $500 for a T1 access. The number of circuits required to support a fully meshed network can be computed by this formula where n is the number of sites:

$$Fully\ meshed\ network\ (\#\ of\ circuits\ required) = \frac{(n)(n-1)}{2}$$

> **NOTE:** The number of local loops for frame is typically equal to *n* or the number of sites, and (n)(n − 1) for private line networks that are fully meshed.

Based on the reduction of physical local loops, the CPE requires fewer ports on the equipment, which can provide savings of hundreds of dollars per port.

Higher Circuit Utilization

FR makes maximum use of physical circuit bandwidth by statistically multiplexing multiple PVCs over a single physical circuit. The total utilization is improved by more effectively making use of the bandwidth at a more granular level. This quality can drive the price/performance ratio of FR very low.

Higher Network Availability

FR networks employ switches that support automatic rerouting of PVCs around circuit failures. This capability gives FR a higher inherent availability over private lines, al-

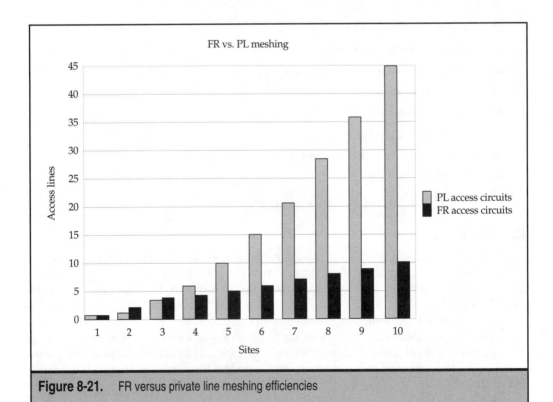

Figure 8-21.   FR versus private line meshing efficiencies

though many private line vendors are offering SONET-based services that automatically route around failures. MPLS-based FR services offer additional disaster-recovery benefits.

Extended Technology Life Duration

FR is an access protocol/interface that enables FR to have a long life span. FR is backwards compatible with older technologies like X.25, and forward compatible with newer technologies such as ATM and MPLS. It also can interwork with IP services.

Performance

FR service offers higher speeds with lower delay as compared to X.25, dedicated QoS vs. CoS offered by IP networks, lower protocol overhead as it relates to new technologies such as ATM, and can provide higher bandwidth opportunities for the same costs as private lines in long-haul requirements.

NOTE: FR networks do have an inherently higher end-to-end latency (delay) than private line networks (this can be from a few to hundreds of milliseconds across a 1000 miles), in most cases due to increased buffering and switch delays not present in digital and optical cross-connect networks.

Once a user has established a port to the FR network, it is easy to provision additional PVCs or increase/decrease the CIR, which is the speed of the PVC. The standard intervals of adding or changing PVCs is usually three to five days versus changing or adding a new dedicated circuit being 30 to 60 days. Eventually, it will be commonplace for users to make PVC changes on demand.

Protocol Independence

FR supports a wide variety of application transports and meets the throughput requirements of both advanced and legacy computing applications and platforms. Higher layer protocols can be transported transparently. In other words, FR does not care what Layer 3 through 7 protocols it is transporting; however, FR performance can have an effect on these protocols. Transport frame sizes can vary, with standards-specified minimums and maximums depending on FR service provider switching equipment and CPE.

Cost-Effective for Network Managed Services

As FR service providers now have managed solutions that extend from their backbone network through the CSU/DSU through the routers and into the LAN, FR technology provides flexibility to provision a virtual circuit to a network management center versus ordering a private line. In this manner, service providers can manage the customer premises through SNMP or a proprietary solution. Also as discussed, FR has LMI that monitors circuit health in-band through a heartbeat protocol (for example, Question. Are you there? Answer. Yes I am!).

True International Standard

The acceptance of FR around the world has been phenomenal. The ITU-T (CCITT) originally developed FR standards, and FR service is available worldwide in hundreds of countries. Due to the success of the Frame Relay Forum, compatibility problems between vendors are rare.

REVIEW

This chapter began by reviewing why FR has quickly become the dominant WAN protocol in the last decade. We showed how FR provided both the need for additional speed at a cost-effective price for the new generation of statistically multiplexed bursty LAN traffic. We reviewed the technology and standards origins of FR and how it was one of the first technologies to increase the speed of standards development. In the overview section, we described how FR is a data-link layer protocol and the basic function including the DLCI address flip by the network.

The specification section provided details of the frame format including definitions of all the fields, CIR/EIR, and PVC management/LMI. The design section discussed FR architectures and the three components of FR that must be ordered in access, port, and virtual circuits. The design section also covered FRADs, integrated access, disaster backup/fault tolerant designs, and service provider pricing structures.

The VoFR section covered definitions and high-level discussion of VoFR design. The performance and design consideration section discussed different network architectures and congestion control systems (open versus closed) along with recent advances in FR to X.25/ATM/IP interoperability and previewed the new standard for IP and FR interoperability using MPLS, or IP-enabled FR. The chapter concluded with advantages and disadvantages of FR over legacy technologies.

CHAPTER 9

Common WAN Protocols: ATM

Asynchronous Transfer Mode (ATM) appeared on the public service provider scene in the early 1990s, offering a boon to service providers and enterprise customers: a single protocol that could statistically multiplex and prioritize voice, data, and video traffic in a single interface, protocol, and public service at DS3 speeds and above. It could also offer these advanced traffic control services through software and over common physical and link layer access protocols. At one point, it seemed that ATM was the natural successor to frame relay (FR) and private lines as the WAN service of choice, and had a promising future of taking quality of service (QoS) down into the LAN and even to the desktop. Application Programming Interfaces would then be written between ATM LAN and key applications, enabling a true end-to-end QoS network protocol for the 21st century.

Alas, this dream did not entirely come true. The ubiquitous and cheap tag-team duo of Ethernet (10 Mbps, 100 Mpbs, and now 1 Gbps Ethernet) and IP (private network and public Internet) won in a world where fast and cheap continue to rule. The Internet craze of the mid-to-late 1990s had enterprises around the world chasing less expensive FR and IP solutions, and ATM floundered. ATM continues to play the role as the dominant WAN optimization backbone technology for most leading service providers networks, and ATM WAN services deployed hand-in-hand with FR networks, taking up the slack where FR left off. And many enterprises running multimedia environments where end-to-end QoS was critical to the business did indeed see the value of and deployed ATM networks. The DSL revolution used ATM as its Layer 2 control layer, and FR to ATM interworking became a standard use when the FR WAN demanded higher than DS1 speeds at a site. But alas the ATM LAN market never truly materialized and while there are multithousand node ATM LAN and WAN networks in existence, they are few and far between. ATM WANs have fared much better, but still hold a minority market share to FR networks.

In this chapter, we discuss ATM as an architecture, technology, and service.

MARKET SIZE AND GROWTH

ATM can take the form of a transport or networking protocol and technology, a physical and logical interface, a method of integrated access, and a virtual private network (VPN) service and infrastructure. The B-ISDN standards model defines the ATM protocol structure. This chapter defines the terms and standards that create the framework for ATM protocol, products, and services. ATM operational theory from cell structure through asynchronous multiplexing techniques will be discussed. This coverage begins with the building blocks of ATM: transmission paths (TPs), virtual paths (VPs), and virtual channels (VCs). Next, the ATM cell and its transmission and switching will be examined through a series of simple examples.

We briefly cover ATM theory as it forms the foundation of the entire ATM-based B-ISDN protocol stack. The primary layers of the B-ISDN protocol reference model are the physical layer (PHY); the ATM layer, where the cell structure occurs; and the ATM Adaptation Layer (AAL), which provides support for higher-layer services such as circuit emulation, LAN emulation (LANE), FR, and other packet, frame, and cell services. The PHY layer corresponds to OSI Reference Model (OSIRM) Layer 1; the ATM user-plane layer and the AAL correspond to OSIRM Layer 2; while other layers, for example, the control-plane layer used in ATM signaling, correspond to OSI Layer 3 and above. It is logical to start at the bottom with the PHY layer, and then move to the ATM layer, which defines VPs and VCs.

Traffic contracts and QoS parameters are covered, including how they relate to specific applications. Many of the details concerning the AAL and all higher-layer functions of the protocol model are left for further study in references such as McDysan and Spohn's *ATM: Theory and Applications* (McGraw-Hill, 1998). All layers of the ATM protocol stack will be briefly defined, along with the many methods of user and network connectivity with a focus on ATM WAN services. We also include the performance, benefits, and design considerations of ATM.

BACKGROUND: ATM DEFINED

ATM is a cell-based switching and multiplexing technology designed to be a general-purpose, connection-oriented transfer mode for a wide range of services. ATM has also been applied to LAN and private network technologies as specified by the ATM Forum for Token Ring, Ethernet, and FDDI LANE.

Cell relay historically defined two major technology platforms: 802.6 distributed queue dual bus (DQDB) and ATM, over which a variety of services such as Switched Multimegabit Data Service (SMDS) and broadband ISDN (B-ISDN) were to be offered. Today, we find ATM primarily in the WAN through public ATM VPN service offerings.

ATM transports and switches both connection-oriented (for example, private line emulation, video, voice traffic) and connectionless (for example, IP, Ethernet LAN) traffic. Connection-oriented traffic is handled directly (cell-based) or through adaptation layers, and connectionless traffic is handled through the use of adaptation layers. ATM uses virtual connections or channels (from this point on we will use circuits for FR and channels for ATM) and VPs similar to FR permanent virtual circuits, but with much more bandwidth granularity and QoS options. ATM virtual connections operate at either a constant bit rate (CBR) or a variable bit rate (VBR), with unspecified bit rate (UBR) and available bit rate (ABR) variations. Each ATM cell sent into the network contains addressing information that achieves a virtual connection from origination to destination. All cells are then transferred, in sequence, over this virtual connection. ATM provides two modes for the establishment of virtual connections: permanent virtual circuit (PVC) and switched virtual circuit (SVC). ATM is asynchronous because the transmitted cells need not be periodic as time slots for data are required to be in Synchronous Transfer Mode (STM). So ATM is viewed as a connection-oriented service that can transport and switch connection-oriented *and* connectionless services—over the same physical access!

ATM offers the potential to standardize on one network architecture defining the multiplexing and switching method for WAN and LAN, and even has API hooks to higher layer software architectures. ATM uses SONET/STM to provide the basis for the physical transmission standard at very high speeds. SONET/STM was defined in Chapter 5. ATM supports multiple QoS classes over these VPs and VCs to support simultaneous transport and switching of differing application requirements for delay and loss performance. Thus, the vision of ATM is that an entire network can be constructed using

ATM and AAL switching and multiplexing principles to support a wide range of all services, such as

▼ Voice
■ Packet data (IP, FR, SMDS)
■ Video
■ Imaging
■ Circuit emulation
■ LANE
▲ LAN Emulation (LANE)

ATM provides true bandwidth-on-demand through the use of SVCs or ABR services, and also supports LAN-like access to available bandwidth across the WAN.

THE MANY FACES OF ATM

ATM technology takes on many forms:

▼ Serving as the core architecture technology for the network backbone infrastructure
■ Providing a technology that performs software and hardware multiplexing, switching, and cross-connect functions and platforms
■ Serving as an economical, integrated network access method
▲ Providing a WAN transport service that provides speed and QoS upgrades to FR

Let's now explore each.

ATM as an Architecture and Technology

ATM has served as the core technology of many Internet and Service Provider's network access and backbone infrastructures. ATM hardware and associated software together have provided the Layer 2 (data-link layer) intelligent statistical multiplexing and QoS switching required by today's advanced communications networks.

ATM also provides a very scalable infrastructure, from the campus environment to the central office. Scalability is available in the dimensions of interface speed, available bandwidth, number of ports (that is, port density), switch size, network size, and addressing.

ATM as an Interface and Protocol

ATM is defined as an interface and protocol designed to switch variable bit-rate and constant bit-rate traffic statistically, based on virtual channel (VC) configurations, over a common transmission medium. ATM protocols are based on the B-ISDN protocol stack.

ATM's technology and protocol structure enables the user to use existing and extend capabilities such as LAN, TCP/IP, conferencing, FTP, and many other applications in a more cost-effective and efficient manner than with separate networks and access facilities.

ATM is often referred to as a technology comprising hardware and software that conform to ATM protocol standards, which provides multiplexing, cross-connecting, and switching functions in a network. ATM technology takes the form of a network interface card, multiplexer, cross-connect, or switch. Today, ATM is most prevalent as a WAN interface on the network-facing switch or router. ATM LANs and end systems that access user applications through APIs have never materialized in mass quantity. Some unique applications have emerged, especially in the government and military arenas, but are not covered here.

ATM as Economical, Integrated Access

Many experts originally viewed an ATM-based architecture as the future platform for data and voice convergence. While it is true the ATM platform continues to offer a superior solution, this integration has typically taken place at the enterprise premises.

Public ATM service providers have offered ATM-based integrated access services for a few years now (see AT&T's INCS) that enable enterprises to capitalize on a basic advantage of ATM: integrated physical and service access to reduce cost. The flexibility of bandwidth and QoS allocation make ATM the technology of choice for true integrated, dynamic access.

ATM as a WAN Transport Service

ATM uses the AALs to offer five classes of service that offer the user a myriad of configurations to achieve a desired level of prioritization and QoS per application: CBR, real-time VBR (rt-VBR), non-real-time VBR (nrt-VBR), UBR, and ABR. ATM also offers true QoS as opposed to attempted QoS or class of service (CoS) found in other packet services such as IP.

ATM PROTOCOL OPERATION: ATM CELL AND TRANSMISSION

The primary unit in ATM is the fixed-length cell. This section defines the ATM cell and presents several examples used to illustrate the basic concepts of ATM protocol operation.

ATM Cell

ATM standards define a fixed-size cell with a length of 53 octets (or bytes) comprising a five-octet header and a 48-octet payload, as shown in Figure 9-1. The figure also shows a caption of the standard block cell format as defined in the standards. The bits in the cells are transmitted over the Transmission Path (TP) from left to right in a continuous stream. Cells are mapped into a physical TP, such as the North American DS1, DS3, or SONET (that is, STS-3c/OC-3, OC-12); European, E1, E3, and E4; or ITU-T STM standards; and various local fiber and electrical transmission payloads.

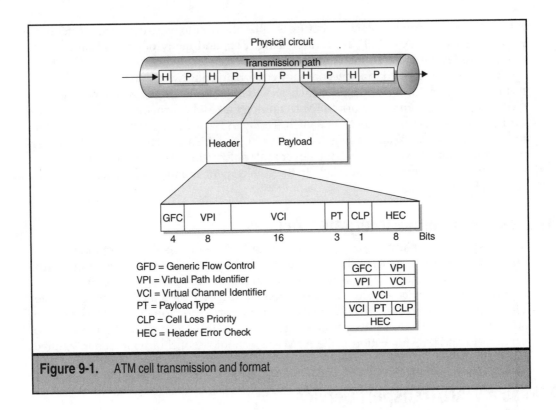

Figure 9-1.   ATM cell transmission and format

All information is switched and multiplexed in an ATM network in these fixed-length cells. The cell header identifies the destination, cell type, and priority. The VP identifier (VPI) and VC identifier (VCI) hold local significance only, and identify the destination address. The VPI and VCI act similar to the data-link connection identifiers (DLCIs) in FR, identifying the end points of the VCs and VPs. The generic flow control (GFC) field allows a multiplexer to control the transmission rate of an ATM terminal. While the GFC has been defined, there has been no ATM Forum implementation of the standards or agreements produced on how to actually use or implement it (similar to the fate of the FECN and BECN bits in FR). The payload type (PT) indicates whether the cell contains user data, signaling data, or maintenance information. The cell loss priority (CLP) bit indicates the relative priority of the cell similar to discard eligible (DE) bits in FR service. In fact, CLP is used to map ATM VP/VCs to FR PVCs. Lower-priority cells may be discarded before higher-priority cells by the usage parameter control (UPC) at the ingress if cells violate the predetermined user contract, or by the network if congestion is experienced. For further definition on the usage of these bits, refer to McDysan and Spohn's *ATM: Theory and Applications* or *Hands-on ATM*.

Because of the critical nature of the header, the cell header error check (HEC) detects and corrects errors in the header. The payload field is passed through the network intact, with no error checking or correction. ATM relies on higher-layer protocols to perform error checking and correction on the payload. The fixed cell size simplifies the implementation of ATM switches and multiplexers and enables implementations at very high speeds.

When using ATM, longer packets cannot delay shorter packets as in other packet-switched implementations because long packets are chopped up into many cells. This enables ATM to carry CBR traffic such as voice and video, in conjunction with VBR data traffic potentially having very long packets, within the same network and the same physical medium (PM), for example, a single router port running ATM and accessing the ATM WAN.

Cell Segmentation Example

ATM switches take a user's data, voice, and video, then chop it up into fixed length cells, and multiplex it into a single bit stream that is transmitted across a PM. An example of a multimedia application is that of a person needing to send an important manuscript for a book to his or her publisher. Along with the letter, this person would like to show his or her joy at receiving a contract to publish the book.

Figure 9-2 illustrates the role of ATM in this real-life example, where Jeanne is sitting at her workstation. Jeanne's workstation has an ATM interface card, sound card or software with microphone, and video camera. The workstation is connected to a local ATM switch, which in turn is attached to a public ATM-based wide area network service, to which the publisher is also connected.

Jeanne places a multimedia call to the publisher, begins transmitting the data for her manuscript, and begins a conversation with the publisher, with Jeanne and the publisher able to see each other, providing text, voice, and video traffic, respectively, in real time. The publisher is looking through the manuscript at her workstation, all the while having an interactive dialogue with Jeanne. Let's break this scenario down into its working ATM components.

Video and voice are very time-sensitive; the information cannot be delayed for more than a blink of the eye (users will notice delays of 100 milliseconds or more), and the delay

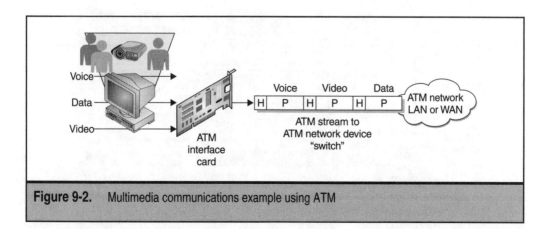

Figure 9-2.   Multimedia communications example using ATM

cannot have significant variations (less than 50 milliseconds). Disruption in the video image of Jeanne's face or distortion of the voice destroys the interactive, near real-life quality of this multimedia application. Data, such as a file transfer using TCP/IP, can be sent in either connection-oriented or connectionless mode. In either case, the data is not nearly as delay-sensitive as voice or video traffic. Data traffic, however, is very sensitive to loss. Therefore, ATM must discriminate between voice, video, and data traffic, giving voice and video traffic priority with guaranteed and bounded delay, while simultaneously assuring that data traffic has very low loss.

Examining this example in further detail, a VP is established between Jeanne and the publisher, and over that VP three VCs are defined for text data, voice, and video. Figure 9-3 shows how all three types of traffic are combined over a single ATM VP, with VCs being assigned to the text data (VCI = 51), voice (VCI = 52), and video (VCI = 53). In this example, then the VP has the QoS required for the most stringent VC. Note that VCIs 0–31 are typically reserved as specified by the ATM Forum standards, and that all three of these VCs could have been on separate VPs.

ATM Cell Sizes

ATM uses a 53-byte cell size, chosen as the optimal solution in the tradeoff between efficiency and packetization delay versus cell size and illustrated in Figure 9-4. Efficiency is computed for a five-octet cell header. Packetization delay is the amount of time required to fill the cell at a rate of 64 Kbps, that is, the rate to fill the cell with digitized voice samples. Ideally, high efficiency and low delay are both desirable, but cannot be achieved simultaneously. As seen from the figure, better efficiency occurs at large cell sizes at the expense of increased packetization delay. To carry voice over ATM and interwork with two-wire analog telephone sets, the total delay should be less than about 12 milliseconds, otherwise echo cancellation must be used. Two time-division-multiplexing-to-ATM conversions are required in the round-trip echo path. Allowing four milliseconds for propagation delay and two ATM conversions, a cell size of 32 octets avoids the need

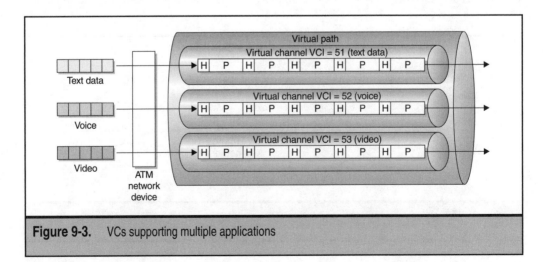

Figure 9-3.　VCs supporting multiple applications

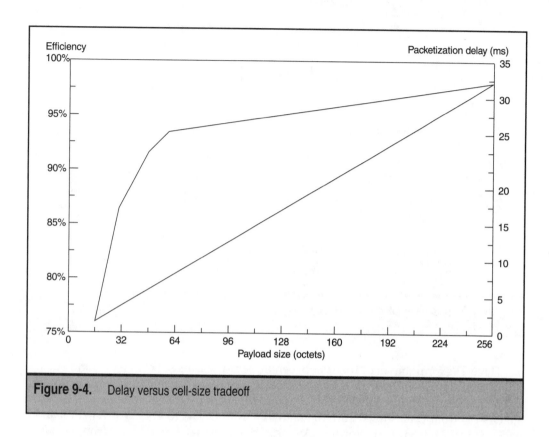

Figure 9-4. Delay versus cell-size tradeoff

for echo cancellation. Thus, the ITU-T adopted the fixed-length 48-octet cell payload as a compromise between a long cell sizes for time-insensitive traffic (64 octets) and smaller cell sizes for time-sensitive traffic (32 octets).

ATM NETWORKING BASICS

Three major concepts in ATM are the TP, the VP, and, optionally, the VC. These form the basic building blocks of ATM. Note that in ATM service terminology the VP and/or the VC equate to a PVC, and the TP equates to an ATM (logical) port. The final component is a physical circuit over which all these transit.

TP, VP, and VC Analogy

Let us look at a simple example of these concepts in relation to vehicle traffic patterns. These analogies are not intended to be exact, but to introduce some concepts that are elaborated on later in this chapter. Think of cells as vehicles, TPs as roads, VPs as a set of directions, and VCs as a lane on the route defined by the VP. Figure 9-5 illustrates the example described in this section.

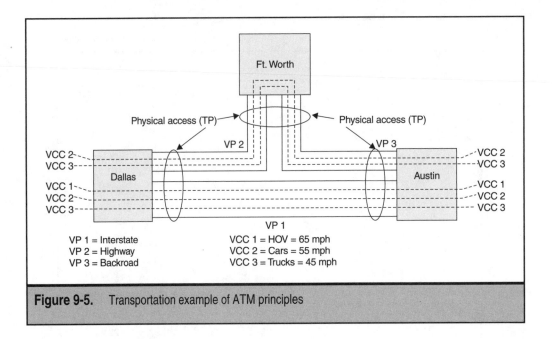

Figure 9-5. Transportation example of ATM principles

Three TPs form the set of roads between three cities: Dallas, Fort Worth, and Austin. There are many interstates, highways, and back roads between any two cities, which creates many possibilities for different routes; but the primary routes, or VPs, are the interstate (VP1) from Dallas to Austin, the highway from Dallas to Fort Worth (VP2), and a back road (VP3) from Fort Worth to Austin. Thus, a car (cell) can travel from Dallas to Austin either over the highway to Fort Worth and then the back road to Austin, or take the direct interstate. If the car chooses the interstate (VP1), it has the choice of three lanes: car pool or high-occupancy vehicle (HOV, VCC1), car lane (VCC2), or the truck lane (VCC3). (Note that the Virtual Channel Connections [VCC] are subvirtual connections within each virtual channel, and will be defined later in this chapter.) These three lanes have speed limits of 65 mph, 55 mph, and 45 mph, respectively, which will cause different amounts of delay in reaching the destination. In our analogy, vehicles strictly obey this lane discipline (unlike on real highways).

In our example, the interstate carries high-speed traffic: tractor trailers, buses, tourists, and business commuters. The highway can carry car and truck traffic, but at a lower speed. The back roads carry locals and traffic avoiding backups on the interstate (spill-over traffic), but at an even slower speed.

Note that our example of automotive traffic (cells) has many opportunities for missequencing. Vehicles might decide to pass each other, there can be detours, and road hazards might cause some vehicles (cells) to arrive out of sequence or vary in their delay. This is evident in normal transportation when you always seem to leave on time, but traffic causes you to be delayed. Automotive traffic must employ an Orwellian discipline where everyone follows the traffic routes exactly (unlike any real traffic) for the analogy to apply.

The routes also have different quality of service. When you get a route map from the American Automobile Association (AAA), you have a route selected based on many criteria: least driving (routing) time, most scenic route, least cost (avoids most toll roads), and avoid known busy hours. The same principles apply to ATM.

Now, let's give each of the road types (VPs) and lanes (VCCs) a route choice. A commuter from Dallas to Austin in a hurry would first choose the VP1, the interstate. A sightseer would choose the highway to Fort Worth (VP2) to see the old cow town, and then the back road to Austin (VP3) to take in Granbury and the Dinosaur Valley Park on the way. When commuters enter the interstate toward Austin, they immediately enter the HOV lane (VCC1) and speed toward their destination.

Figure 9-6 adds a railroad (VCC4) running from Dallas to Austin along the same interstate route (VP1) in the previous example. Assuming no stops between Dallas and Austin, the railroad maintains the same speed from start to finish, with one railroad train running after another according to a fixed schedule. This is like the STM or TDM discussed in Chapter 4. Imagine there are passengers and cargo going between Dallas and Austin, each having to catch scheduled trains. The arriving passengers and cargo shipments originating at Dallas must wait for the next train. Trains travel regardless of whether there are any passengers or cargo present. If there are too many passengers or cargo for the train's capacity, the excess must wait for the next train. If you were a commuter, would you want to rely on the train always having capacity, or would you prefer to have a car and statistically have a better chance of making it to Austin in even less time using ATM? We make these same decisions for each application we place over the ATM network, and assign the VPs and VCs accordingly.

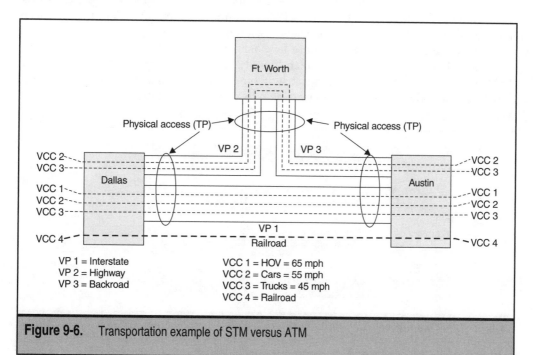

Figure 9-6.   Transportation example of STM versus ATM

Studying this analogy, observe that the private vehicles (and their passengers) traveling over VCC1, VCC2, or VCC3 have much more flexibility (ATM) than trains (STM) in handling the spontaneous needs of travel. The trains are efficient only when the demand is accurately scheduled and very directed, such as during the rush hour between suburbs and the inner city.

Note that the priorities, or choice, of each VCC can vary throughout the day, as can priorities between VPs in ATM. An additional VCC can be configured on a moment's notice (it would be labeled VCC5) and assigned a higher priority, as in the case of an ambulance attempting to travel down the median during a traffic jam to get to the scene of an accident. No analogy is perfect, and therefore extensions or comparison of other aspects of transportation might not be valid.

TP, VP, and VC

Bringing our analogy forward into ATM transmission terms, Figure 9-7 depicts graphically the relationship between the physical TP, VP, and VC. A TP contains one or more VPs, while each VP contains one or more VCs. Thus, multiple VCs can be trunked within a single VP. Switching can be performed on a TP, VP, or VC level.

This capability to switch down to a VC level is similar to the operation of a private or public branch exchange (PBX) or telephone switch in the telephone world. In the PBX/switch, each channel within a trunk group (path) can be switched. Figure 9-8 illustrates this analogy. Devices that perform VC connections are commonly called VC switches because of this analogy with telephone switches. Transmission networks use a cross-connect, which is basically a space-division switch, or effectively an electronic patch panel. ATM devices that connect VPs are commonly often called VP cross-connects in the literature by analogy with the transmission network.

These analogies are useful for those familiar with TDM/STM and telephony to understand ATM, but should not be taken literally. There is little technical reason for an ATM cell-switching machine to restrict switching to only VCs and cross-connection to only VPs, and today's ATM switches are able to do both simultaneously.

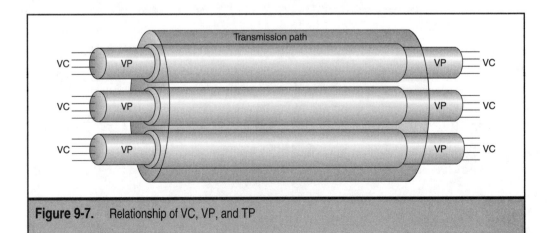

Figure 9-7. Relationship of VC, VP, and TP

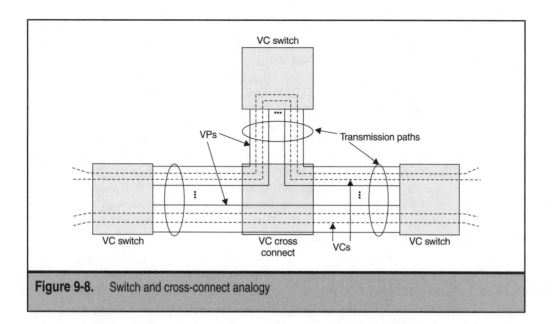

Figure 9-8.   Switch and cross-connect analogy

VP Connections (VPCs) and VC Connections (VCCs)

At the ATM layer, users are provided a choice of either a VPC or a VCC, defined as follows:

▼   **VPCs** are switched based on the VPI value only. The users of the VPC may assign the VCCs within that VPI transparently since they follow the same route.

▲   **VCCs** are switched based on the combined VPI and VCI value.

Both VPIs and VCIs are used to route cells through the network. Note that VPI and VCI values must be unique on a specific TP. Thus, each TP between two network devices (such as ATM switches) uses VPIs and VCIs independently. This is demonstrated in Figure 9-9.

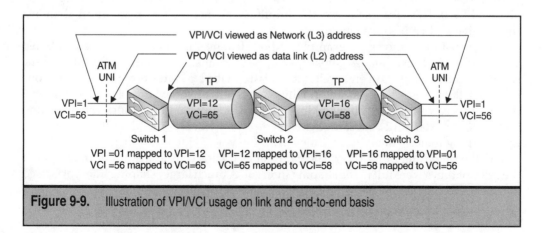

Figure 9-9.   Illustration of VPI/VCI usage on link and end-to-end basis

Each switch maps an incoming VPI and VCI to an outgoing VPI and VCI. In this example, switch 1 and switch 2 have a single TP between them. Over this TP there are multiple VPs. At the ATM User Network Interface (UNI), defined as the access circuit from the user ATM premises device to the network ATM access/edge device, the input device to switch 1 provides a video channel over VPI 1 and VCI 56. Switch 1 then assigns the VCI 56 to an outgoing VCI 65, and the incoming VPI 1 to outgoing VPI 12. Thus, on VPI 12 switch 2 specifically operates on VCI 65. This channel is then routed from switch 2 to switch 3 over a different path and channel (VPI 16 and VCI 58). Thus, VPIs and VCIs are tied onto each individual link across the network. This is similar to FR, where DLCIs address a FR virtual circuit at each end of a link. Finally, switch 3 translates VPI 16 into VPI 1, and VCI 58 on VP 16 to VCI 56 on VP 1 at the destination UNI. The destination VPI and VCI need not be the same as at the origin. The sequence of VPI/VCI translation across the switches can be viewed as a network address in an extrapolation of the OSI Layer 3 model. VPIs and VCIs switched internal to network TPs are transparent to the user on the UNI.

THEORY OF OPERATION

This section presents two examples of how user traffic is segmented into ATM cells, switched through a network, and processed by the receiving user.

A Simple ATM Example

Let's look in more detail at the last example, where Jeanne is simultaneously transmitting text, voice, and video data traffic from her workstation. The workstation contains an ATM interface card, where the "chopper" slices and dices the data streams into 48-octet data segments, as shown in Figure 9-10 (A.) In the next step, the "postman" addresses the payload by prefixing it with the VPI, VCI, and the remaining fields of the 5-octet header. The result is a stream of 53-octet ATM cells from each source: voice, video, and text data. These cells are generated independently by each source, such that there might be contention for cell slot times on the interface connected to the workstation. The text, voice, and video are each assigned a VCC: VCI = 1 for text data, VCI = 2 for voice, and VCI = 3 for video, all on VPI = 0. This example is greatly simplified, as there can be many more than just three active VCI values on a single VPI.

Figure 9-10 (B.) shows an example of how Jeanne's terminal sends the combined voice, video, and text data. A gatekeeper in her terminal shapes the transmitted data, sending a cell at intervals of eight cells (about 80 µs at the DS3 rate), normally allowing one voice cell, then five video cells, and finally what is left—two text data cells—to be transmitted. This corresponds to about 4 Mbps for high-fidelity audio, 24 Mbps for video, and 9 Mbps for text data. All data sources (text, voice, and video) contend for the bandwidth, each shaping interval of eight cell times, with the voice, video, and then text data being sent in the preceding proportion. The gatekeeper retains cells in the buffer in case all of the cell slot times were full in the shaping interval. A much larger shaping interval is used in practice to provide greater granularity in bandwidth allocation.

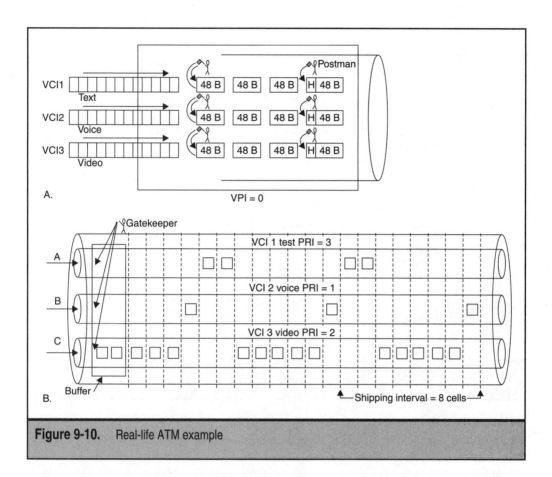

Figure 9-10.   Real-life ATM example

An ATM Switch Example

An illustration of an ATM switch is shown in Figure 9-11. A continuous video source is shown as input to a *packetizing* function, with logical destination VPI/VCI address D. The continuous bit stream is broken up into fixed-length cells composed of a header and a payload field (indicated by the shading). The rate of the video source is greater than the continuous DS3 bit stream with logical destination address A, and the high-speed computer directly packetized input addressed to B. These sources are shown time-division multiplexed over a TP, such as SONET or DS3.

The initial function of the ATM switch is to *translate* the logical address to a physical outgoing switch port address and to an outgoing logical VPI/VCI address. This additional ATM switch header is prefixed to every input ATM cell as shown previously. There are three point-to-point virtual connections in the figure. The DS3 has address A that is translated into C destined for physical port 1. The video source has address D, which is translated into address E, destined for port 2. The computer source has address B, which is translated to address F, destined for port 1.

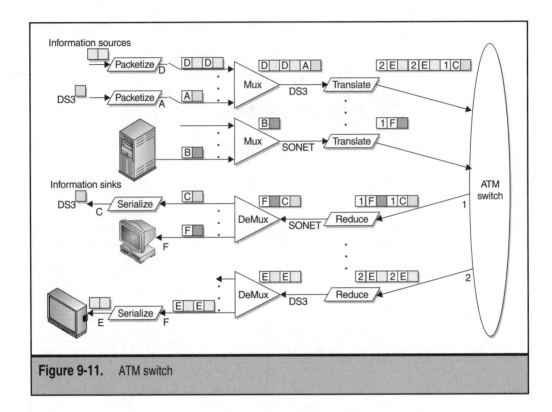

Figure 9-11. ATM switch

The ATM switch uses the physical destination address field to deliver the ATM cells to appropriate physical switch port and associated transmission link.

At the output of the ATM switch, the physical address is removed by a *reduce* function. The logically addressed ATM cells are then time-division multiplexed onto the outgoing transmission links. Next, these streams are demultiplexed to the appropriate devices. The CBR connections (that is, video and the DS3) then have the logical addresses removed, and are reclocked to the information sink via the *serialize* function. Some devices, such as workstations with an ATM interface card, can receive ATM cells directly.

B-ISDN PROTOCOL REFERENCE MODEL

This section describes the protocol model for B-ISDN that is built on ATM. Figure 9-12 depicts the B-ISDN protocol reference model from ITU-T Recommendation I.321, which is used to structure the remaining recommendations. A significant portion of the architecture exists in this protocol dimension. This subsection introduces the B-ISDN protocol reference model.

The top of the cube illustrates the planes, which are defined on the front and side of the cube. The user plane and control plane span through the higher layer, down through

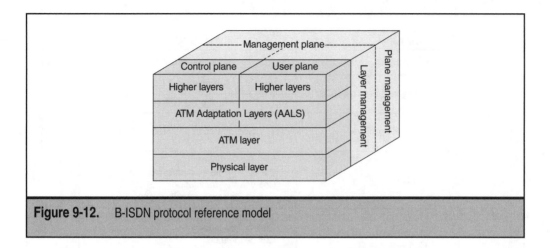

Figure 9-12. B-ISDN protocol reference model

the AALs (which can be null), to the ATM layer and PHY layer. Therefore, the PHY layer, ATM layer, and AALs are the foundation for B-ISDN. The user and control planes may make use of common ATM and PHY layer protocols; however, the end purpose differs in the AALs and higher layers.

The management plane is further broken down into layer management and plane management. As shown in the figure, layer management interfaces with each layer in the control and user planes. Plane management has no layered structure and is currently only an abstract concept with little standardization at this point. It can be viewed as a catchall for the things that do not fit into the other portions of this model, by having the role of overall system management.

THE PLANE-LAYER TRUTH: AN OVERVIEW

If the front and right sides of the B-ISDN protocol cube were unfolded, they would yield a two-dimensional layered model like that shown in Figure 9-13.

Figure 9-13 lists the functions of the four B-ISDN/ATM layers along with the sublayer structure of the AAL and PHY layer, as defined in ITU-T Recommendation I.321. Starting from the bottom, the PHY layer has two sublayers: transmission convergence (TC) and PM. The PM sublayer interfaces with the actual PM and passes the recovered bit stream to the TC sublayer. The TC sublayer extracts and inserts ATM cells within the plesiochronous or synchronous time-division multiplexed (TDM) frame and passes these to and from the ATM layer, respectively. The ATM layer performs multiplexing, switching, and control actions based on information in the ATM cell header and passes cells to, and accepts cells from, the AAL. The AAL has two sublayers: the segmentation and reassembly (SAR) sublayer and the convergence sublayer (CS). The CS is further broken down into common-part (CP) and service-specific (SS) components. The AAL passes

Layer name		Functions performed	
Higher layers		Higher layer functions	Layer management
AAL	Convergence Sublayer (CS)	Common Part (CP)	Layer management
AAL	Convergence Sublayer (CS)	Service Specific (SS)	Layer management
AAL	SAR sublayer	Segmentation and reassembly	Layer management
ATM		Generic flow control Cell header generation/extraction Cell VCI/VPI translation Cell multiplexing/demultiplexing	Layer management
Physical	Transmission Convergence (TC) sublayer	Cell rate decoupling Cell delineation Transmission frame adaptation Transmission frame generation/recovery	Layer management
Physical	Physical Medium (PM)	Bit timing Physical medium	Layer management

Figure 9-13.   B-ISDN/ATM layer and sublayer model

protocol data units (PDUs) to and accepts PDUs from higher layers. PDUs may be of variable length, or may be of a fixed length different from the ATM cell length.

How does this model fit into the OSIRM? The PHY layer corresponds to Layer 1 in the OSI model. The ATM layer and AAL correspond to parts of OSI Layer 2, but the address field of the ATM cell header has a network-wide connotation that is similar to OSI Layer 3. A precise alignment with the OSI layers is not necessary, however. The B-ISDN and ATM protocols and interfaces make extensive use of the OSI concepts of layering and sublayering as we shall see. Figure 9-14 illustrates the mapping of the B-ISDN layers to the OSI layers and the sublayers of the PHY, ATM, and AALs that we describe in detail later.

It is interesting to look at the number of instances of defined standardized protocols or interfaces that exist for each layer, and whether their target implementation is in hardware or software. Figure 9.15 depicts the number of instances at each layer by boxes with the arrows on the right side showing how the layers are either more hardware- or software-intensive. The arrows illustrate the fact that ATM implementations move from being hardware-intensive at the lower layers (PHY and ATM) to software-intensive at the higher layers (AALs and higher layers). This shows how ATM is the pivotal protocol, for which there is only one instance, for a potentially large number of PMs, several AALs, and an ever-expanding set of higher-layer functions. The inverted pyramid on the left

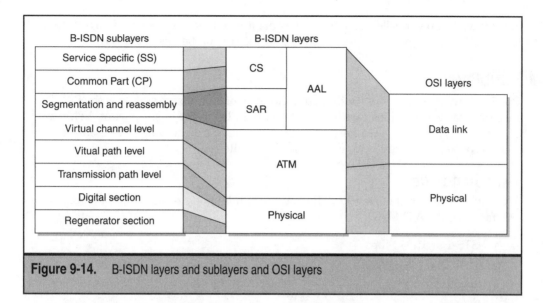

Figure 9-14. B-ISDN layers and sublayers and OSI layers

side of Figure 9-15 illustrates this concept. In other words, ATM allows machines with different physical interfaces to transport data independently of the higher-layer protocols using a common, well-defined protocol amenable to high performance and cost-effective hardware implementation.

Now the journey begins up through the layers of the B-ISDN/ATM protocol model, starting with the PHY and ATM layers.

PHY LAYER

This section covers the key aspects of the PHY layer. The PHY layer provides for transmission of ATM cells over a PM that connects two ATM devices. The PHY layer is divided into two sublayers: the PM-dependent (PMD) sublayer and the TC sublayer. The TC sublayer

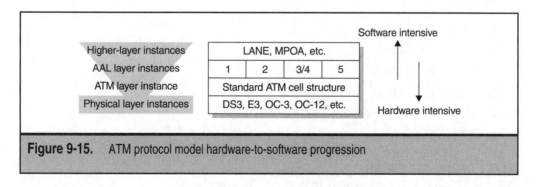

Figure 9-15. ATM protocol model hardware-to-software progression

transforms the flow of cells into a steady flow of bits and bytes for transmission over the PM. The PMD sublayer provides for the actual transmission of the bits in the ATM cells.

PMD Sublayer

The PMD sublayer provides for the actual clocking of bit transmission over the PM. There are three standards bodies that have defined the PHY layer in support of ATM: ANSI, CCITT/ITU-T, and the ATM Forum. Each of the standardized interfaces is summarized in terms of the interface clocking speed and PM following.

ANSI Standards

ANSI standard T1.624 currently defines three single-mode optical ATM SONET-based interfaces for the ATM UNI:

▼ STS-1 at 51.84 Mbps

■ STS-3c at 155.52 Mbps

▲ STS-12c at 622.08 Mbps

ANSI T1.624 also defines operation at the DS3 rate of 44.736 Mbps using the Physical Layer Convergence Protocol (PLCP) from the 802.6 DQDB standard.

CCITT/ITU-T Synchronous Digital Hierarchy (SDH) Recommendations

CCITT/ITU-T recommendation I.432 defines two optical SDH-based physical interfaces for ATM that correspond to the ANSI rates mentioned in the last section. These are

▼ STM-1 at 155.520 Mbps

▲ STM-4 at 622.08 Mbps

Since the transport rates (and the payload rates) of the SDH STM-1 and STM-4 correspond exactly to the SONET STS-3c and STS-12c rates, interworking is simplified. ITU-T standardizes additional electrical, physical interface rates of the following type and speeds:

▼ DS1 at 1.544 Mbps

■ E1 at 2.048 Mbps

■ DS2 at 6.312 Mbps

■ E3 at 34.368 Mbps

■ DS3 at 44.736 Mbps using PLCP

▲ E4 at 139.264 Mbps

ATM Forum Interfaces

The ATM Forum has defined four PHY layer interface rates:

▼   DS3/44.7 Mbps

■   100 Mbps

▲   155 Mbps

Two of these are interface rates intended for public networks and are the DS3 and STS-3c standardized by ANSI and the ITU-T. The SONET STS-3c interface may be supported on an OC-3, either single-mode or multimode fiber. Rates of 25 Mbps and 51 Mbps are also available, as well as ATM frame UNI (FUNI). The following three interface rates and media are for private network application:

▼   FDDI-based at 100 Mbps

■   Fiber channel–based at 155.52 Mbps

▲   Shielded twisted pair (STP) at 155.52 Mbps

The FDDI-based PMD and fiber channel interfaces both use multimode fiber, while the STP interface uses type 1 and 2 cable as specified by EIA/TIA 568. The ATM Forum also specifies ATM cell transmission over common building wiring, called unshielded twisted pair (UTP) types 3 and 5.

TC Sublayer

The TC sublayer converts between the bit stream clocked to the PM and ATM cells. On transmit, TC basically maps the cells into the TDM frame format. On reception, it must perform "cell delineation" on the individual cells in the received bit stream, either from the TDM frame directly, or via the HEC in the ATM cell header. Generating the HEC on transmit and using it to correct and detect errors on receive are also important TC functions. Another important function that TC performs is cell rate decoupling by sending idle cells when the ATM layer has not provided a cell. This is a critical function that allows the ATM layer to operate with a wide range of different speed physical interfaces.

Two examples of TC mapping of ATM cells will be covered: direct mapping to a SONET payload and the PLCP mapping to a DS3. The use of the HEC and why it is so important will be shown. The description of the TC sublayer will be completed with an illustration of cell-rate decoupling using unassigned cells.

Examples of TC Mapping

In this section, we give an example of direct and PLCP mapping by the TC sublayer of the PHY layer.

SONET STS-3c Direct Mapping

The SONET mapping is performed directly into the SONET STS-3c (155.52 Mbps) synchronous payload envelope (SPE), as defined in Chapter 5 and as shown in Figure 9-16. ATM cells fill in the STS-3c payload continuously since an integer number of 53-octet cells do not fit in a single STS-3c frame. This results in better efficiency than carriage of M13-mapped DS3s, or

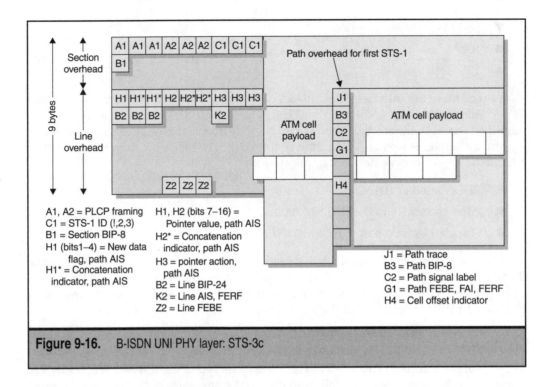

A1, A2 = PLCP framing
C1 = STS-1 ID (!,2,3)
B1 = Section BIP-8
H1 (bits1–4) = New data
    flag, path AIS
H1* = Concatenation
    indicator, path AIS

H1, H2 (bits 7–16) =
    Pointer value, path AIS
H2* = Concatenation
    indicator, path AIS
H3 = pointer action,
    path AIS
B2 = Line BIP-24
K2 = Line AIS, FERF
Z2 = Line FEBE

J1 = Path trace
B3 = Path BIP-8
C2 = Path signal label
G1 = Path FEBE, FAI, FERF
H4 = Cell offset indicator

Figure 9-16.   B-ISDN UNI PHY layer: STS-3c

even VT1.5 multiplexing over SONET. Not all the SONET overhead is supported by the standards or implementers. The ATM layer uses the HEC field to delineate cells from within the SONET payload. The cell transfer rate is 149.760 Mbps. The mapping over STS-12c is very similar in nature. The difference between SONET and SDH is in the TDM overhead bytes.

DS3 PLCP Mapping

Figure 9-17 illustrates the DS3 mapping using the PLCP defined in IEEE 802.6. The ATM cells are enclosed in a 125-µs frame defined by the PLCP, which is defined inside the standard DS3 M-frame. The PLCP mapping transfers 8 kHz timing across the DS3 interface, which is somewhat inefficient in that the cell transfer rate is only 40.704 Mbps, which uses only about 90 percent of the DS3's approximately 44.21-Mbps payload rate. Note that the PLCP does not use ATM's cell delineation because the PLCP frame indicates the exact location of each cell. Some ATM switch vendors allow the user to disable PLCP in favor of using cell delineation to achieve better efficiency and usage of the DS3 frame.

TC HEC Functions

The HEC is a 1-byte code applied to the 5-byte ATM cell header. The HEC code is capable of correcting any single-bit error in the header. It is also capable of detecting many patterns of multiple-bit errors. The TC sublayer generates HEC on transmit and uses it to determine if the received header has any errors. If errors are detected in the header, then the

PLCP framing		POI	POH	PLCP payload	Definitions
A1	A2	P11	Z6	ATM cell 1	PLCP = Physical Layer Convergence Protocol
A1	A2	P10	Z5	ATM cell 2	A1 = 11110110
A1	A2	P9	Z4	ATM cell 3	A2 = 00101000
A1	A2	P8	Z3	ATM cell 4	P0-p11 = Path Overhead Identifier (POI)
A1	A2	P7	Z2	ATM cell 5	POH = Path Overhead
A1	A2	P6	Z1	ATM cell 6	Z1-Z6 = Growthoctets - 00000000
A1	A2	P5	X	ATM cell 7	X = Unassigned
A1	A2	P4	B1	ATM cell 8	B1 = PCLP Bit Interleaved Parity -8 (BIP-8)
A1	A2	P3	G1	ATM cell 9	G1 = PLCP path status
A1	A2	P2	X	ATM cell 10	= AAAAXXXX = FEBE B1 count
A1	A2	P1	X	ATM cell 11	= XXXXAXXX = RAI
A1	A2	P0	C1	ATM cell 12	C1 = Cycle Stuff Counter
					Trailer nibbles = 1100
					Trailer
1 Octet	1 Octet	1 Octet	1 Octet	53 octets	13 or 14 nibbles
			Object of BIP-8 calculation		

Figure 9-17.   B-ISDN UNI PHY layer: DS3

received cell is discarded. Since the header tells the ATM layer what to do with the cell, it is very important that it not have errors; otherwise, it might be delivered to the wrong user or an undesired function in the ATM layer might be inadvertently invoked.

The TC also uses HEC to locate cells when they are directly mapped into a TDM payload. The HEC will not match random data in the cell payloads when the 5 bytes that are being checked are not part of the header. Thus, it can be used to find cells in a received bit stream. Once several cell headers have been located through the use of HEC, then TC knows to expect the next cell 53 bytes later. This process is called *HEC-based cell delineation* in standards.

TC Cell Rate Decoupling

The TC sublayer performs a cell-rate decoupling, or speed-matching function, as well. PMs that have synchronous cell time slots (for example, DS3, SONET, SDH, STP, and the fibre channel–based method) require this function, while asynchronous media such as the FDDI PMD and Ethernet do not. As we shall see in the next section, there are special codings of the ATM cell header that indicate that a cell is either *unassigned* or *idle*. All other cells are *assigned* and correspond to the cells generated by the ATM layer. Figure 9-18 illustrates this operation between a transmitting device and a receiving ATM device. The transmitter multiplexes multiple VPI/VCI cell streams, queuing them if an ATM slot is not immediately

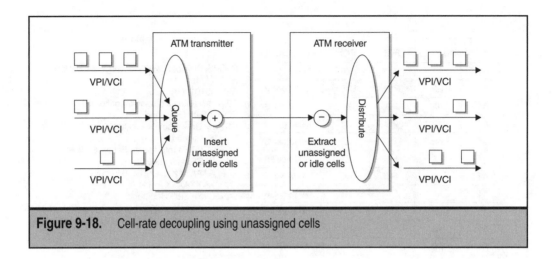

Figure 9-18.   Cell-rate decoupling using unassigned cells

available. If the queue is empty when the time arrives to fill the next synchronous cell time slot, then the TC sublayer inserts an unassigned or idle cell. The receiver extracts unassigned or idle cells and distributes the other, assigned cells to the destinations.

ITU-T Recommendation I.321 places this function in the TC sublayer of the PHY layer and uses idle cells, while the ATM Forum places it in the ATM layer and uses unassigned cells. This might present a potential low-level incompatibility if different systems use different cell types for cell-rate decoupling. Look for ATM systems that support both methods to ensure maximum interoperability. The ITU-T model views the ATM layer as independent of whether or not the PM has synchronous time slots.

ATM LAYER: PROTOCOL MODEL

This section moves to the focal point of B-ISDN, the ATM layer. First, the relationship of the ATM layer to the PHY layer and its division into a VP and VC level are covered in detail. This is a key concept, which is the reason that several analogies were presented earlier in the chapter. Several examples are provided in this section portraying the role of end and intermediate systems in a real-world setting rather than just a formal model. This is accomplished by explaining how the ATM layer VP and VC functions are used in intermediate and end systems in terms of the layered protocol model. An example is then provided showing how intermediate systems perform ATM VP or VC switching or cross-connection, and how end systems pass cells to the AAL.

Physical Links and ATM VPs and VCs

A key concept is the construction of ATM VPs and VCs. Figure 9-19 illustrates this derivation based on ITU-T Recommendation I.311. The PHY layer is composed of three levels: regenerator section, digital section, and TP, as shown in the figure. At the ATM layer, we

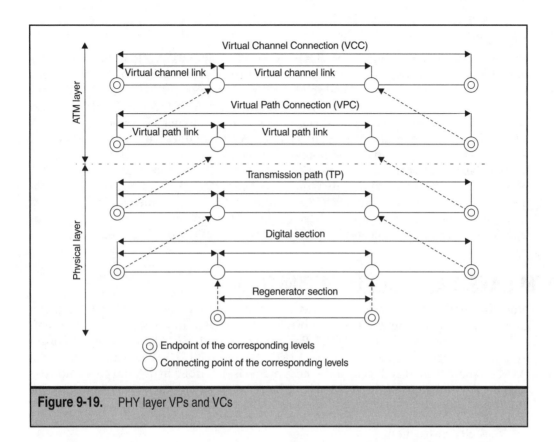

Figure 9-19.   PHY layer VPs and VCs

are concerned only about the TP because this is essentially the TDM payload that connects ATM devices. Generically, an ATM device may be either an endpoint or a connecting point for a VP or VC. A VPC or VCC exists only between endpoints, as shown in the figure. A VP link or a VC link can exist between an endpoint and a connecting point or between connecting points. A VPC or VCC is an ordered list of VP or VC links, respectively.

VC Level

The VCI in the cell header identifies a single VC on a particular VP. Switching at a VC connecting point is done based on the combination of VP and VCI. A *VC link* is defined as a unidirectional flow of ATM cells with the same VCI between a VC connecting point and either a VC endpoint or another VC connecting point. A VCC is defined as a concatenated list of VC links. A VCC defines a unidirectional flow of ATM cells from one user to one or more other users.

A network must preserve cell sequence integrity for a VCC; that is, the cells must be delivered in the same order in which they were sent. A QoS is associated with a VPC or VCC.

VP Level

VPs define an aggregate bundle of VCs between VP endpoints. A VPI in the cell header identifies a bundle of one or more VCs. A VP link provides unidirectional transfer of cells with the same VPI between VP endpoints or connecting points. Switching at a VP connecting point is done based on the VPI; the VCI is ignored. A VP link is defined as a VP between a VP connecting point and either a VP endpoint or another VP connecting point. A VPC is defined as a concatenated list of VP links. A VPC defines a unidirectional flow of ATM cells from one user to one or more other users.

Standards do not require a network to preserve cell sequence integrity for a VPC; however, the cell sequence integrity requirement of a VCC still applies. A QoS is associated with a VPC. If a VPC contains VCCs in different QoS classes, then the VPC assumes the QoS of the VCC with the highest quality. Thus, in our example with the author-to-publisher communication, a VCC rather than a VPC would be used for QoS.

ATM LAYER AND CELL: DEFINITION

Now for a detailed look inside the ATM cell header and the meaning of each field. The user-to-network and network-to-network interfaces (UNI and NNI) are defined first, followed by a summary of the ITU-T Recommendation I.361, ANSI, and ATM Forum definitions of the cell structure at the ATM UNI and NNI. The basic functions of the ATM layer are then introduced, and each function is described in detail. This section details the key functions of the ATM layer. The ATM layer provides many functions, including

- ▼ Cell construction
- ■ Cell reception and header validation
- ■ Cell relaying, forwarding, and copying using the VPI/VCI
- ■ Cell multiplexing and demultiplexing using the VPI/VCI
- ■ Cell PT discrimination
- ■ Interpretation of predefined reserved header values
- ■ CLP processing
- ■ Support for multiple QoS classes
- ■ UPC
- ■ Explicit forward congestion indication (EFCI)
- ■ GFC
- ▲ Connection assignment and removal

The most important of these functions will be covered in this chapter.

ATM UNI and NNI Defined

Figure 9-20 defines the ATM reference configurations at the UNI and NNI. The ATM UNI occurs between the user equipment or end system (ES) or broadband terminal equipment (B-TE), and either the terminal adapter (TA) or network termination (NT) or intermediate system (IS) like a service provider ATM switch.

The ATM Forum terminology of private and public UNIs is mapped to the ITU-T reference point terminology in this figure. The ATM UNI may be a private ATM UNI, which would occur at the R or S reference points in ITU-T Recommendation I.413 and ANSI T1.624, or a public ATM UNI, which would occur at reference points T or U, as shown in Figure 9-20. The NNI defined in ITU-T Recommendation I.113 is normally thought of as the standard interface between networks, which will most likely also be the interface used between nodes within a network. The ATM Forum distinguishes between an NNI used for private networks and public networks, as shown in the figure.

Two standardized coding schemes exist for cell structure: UNI and NNI. The UNI is the interface between the user or customer premises equipment (CPE) and the network switch. This is typically the ATM service offering interface. The NNI is the interface

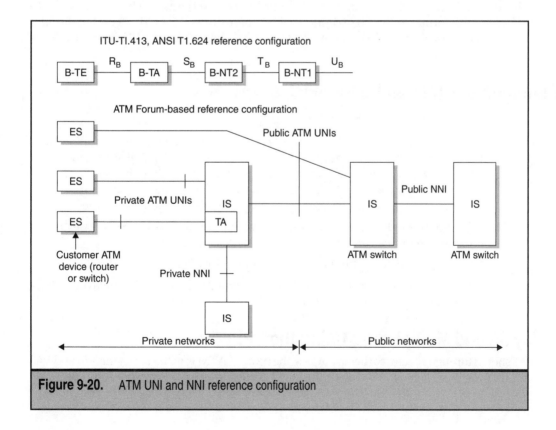

Figure 9-20.   ATM UNI and NNI reference configuration

between switches or between networks. UNI and NNI coding schemes are introduced and each field is defined in this section. ITU-T Recommendation I.361 is the basis of these definitions, with further clarifications given in ANSI T1.627 and the ATM Forum UNI and broadband intercarrier interface (B-ICI) specifications.

ATM UNI Cell Structure Detailed

Figure 9-21 illustrates the format of the 53-byte ATM cell at the UNI. The cell header contains a logical address in two parts: an 8-bit VPI and a 16-bit VCI. The cell header also contains a 4-bit GFC, 3-bit PT, and a 1-bit CLP indicator. The entire header is error-protected by a 1-byte HEC field. This section details the meaning of each header field. A fundamental concept of ATM is that switching occurs based on the VPI/VCI fields of *each* cell. Switching done only on the VPI is called a VPC, while switching done on both the VPI/VCI values is called a VCC. VPCs and VCCs may be either provisioned as PVCs, or established via signaling protocols as SVCs.

ATM NNI Cell Structure Detailed

Figure 9-22 illustrates the format of the 53-byte ATM cell at the NNI. The format is identical to the UNI format with two exceptions. First, there is no GFC field. Secondly, the NNI uses the 4 bits used for the GFC at the UNI to increase the VPI field to 12 bits at the NNI as compared to 8 bits at the UNI.

Definition of ATM Cell Header Fields

This section provides a description of each header field.

▼ **GFC** A 4-bit field intended to support simple implementations of multiplexing. In the early 1990s, GFC was being specified to implement a DQDB-like, multiple-access-type protocol. However, the current standards define the *uncontrolled* mode, where the 4-bit GFC field is always coded as zeroes. If too many nonzero GFC values are received, layer management should be notified.

■ **PT** A 3-bit field that discriminates between a cell payload carrying user information or one carrying management information

■ **CLP** A 1-bit field that indicates the loss priority of an individual cell

▲ **HEC** Provides error checking of the header for use by the TC sublayer of the PHY layer as defined earlier

Relaying and Multiplexing Using the VPI/VCI

As shown through several earlier examples, the heart of ATM is in the use of the VPI and VCI for relaying or switching. ATM also effectively performs multiplexing and demultiplexing

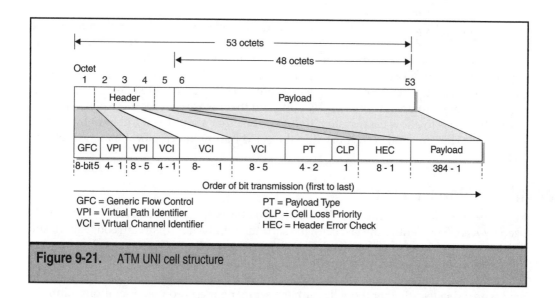

Figure 9-21.   ATM UNI cell structure

of multiple logical connections with different quality requirements using the fixed-length ATM cell.

The number of bits allocated in the ATM cell header limit each physical UNI to support of no more than $2^8 = 256$ VPs and each physical NNI to support of no more than $2^{12} = 4096$ VPs. Each VP can support no more than $2^{16} = 65,536$ VCs on the UNI or the NNI.

Although the UNI and NNI cell formats specify 8 and 12 bits for the VPI, respectively, and 16 bits for the VCI on both interfaces, based on current ESs and applications not need-

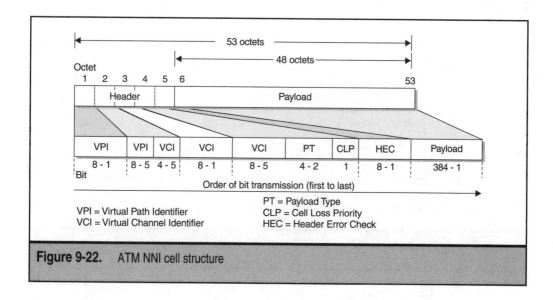

Figure 9-22.   ATM NNI cell structure

ing that many VCs, an implementation need only support a smaller number of the lower-order bits in the VPI and VCI. Thus, a real ATM application might differ markedly from the preceding maximums. This means that the number of VPs and VCs actually supported in a live ATM network might be far less than the maximum numbers defined earlier. This has important implications in interoperability if one ATM device expects the next ATM device to operate on VPI/VCI bits, but that device ignores these bits. One way to handle this is to allow each system to query the other about the number of bits that is supported. This function is supported in the ATM Forum interim local management interface (ILMI).

Meaning of the PT Field

Figure 9-23 depicts PT encoding. We see the first bit is an AAL indication bit (currently used by AAL 5 to identify the last cell), the second bit indicates upstream congestion, and the third bit discriminates between data and operations cells. Payload types carrying user information might also indicate whether congestion was experienced by EFCI or whether the cell contains an indication to the AAL protocol. The management information payload type indicates whether the cell is either a segment or end-to-end operations administration and maintenance (OAM) cell for a VCC or resource management (RM) cell.

Meaning of the CLP Field

A value of 0 in the CLP field means that the cell is of the highest priority, or in other words, it is the least likely to be discarded. A value of 1 in the CLP field means that this cell has low priority, or in other words, it may be selectively discarded during congested intervals to maintain a low loss rate for the high-priority CLP = 0 cells. The value of CLP may be set by the user or by the network as a result of a policing action. The ATM CLP bit is similar to the DE bit in FR.

PT coding	PT coding
000	User Data Cell, EFCI - 0, AAL_indicate = 0
001	User Data Cell, EFCI - 0, AAL_indicate = 1
010	User Data Cell, EFCI - 1, AAL_indicate = 0
011	User Data Cell, EFCI - 1, AAL_indicate = 1
100	OAM F5 segment associated cell
101	OAM F5 end-to-end associated cell
110	Resource management cell
111	Reserved for future functions

EFCI = Explicit Forward Congestion Indication
AAL_indicate = ATM-layer-user-to-ATM-layer-user indication

Figure 9-23.   PT encoding

TRAFFIC DESCRIPTORS AND PARAMETERS

The traffic descriptor is a list of parameters, which captures intrinsic source traffic characteristics. ATM traffic descriptors include the following key contract parameters, as shown in Figure 9-27:

▼   PCR = $1/T$ in units of cells per second, where T is the minimum intercell spacing in seconds (that is, the time interval from the first bit of one cell to the first bit of the next cell).

■   CDV tolerance = τ in seconds. This traffic parameter normally cannot be specified by the user, but is set instead by the network. The number of cells that can be sent back-to-back at the access line rate is $\tau/T+1$, as shown in the figure.

■   SCR is the maximum average rate that a bursty, on-off traffic source that can be sent at the peak rate, such as that depicted in Figure 9-24.

▲   MBS is the maximum number of cells that can be sent at the peak rate.

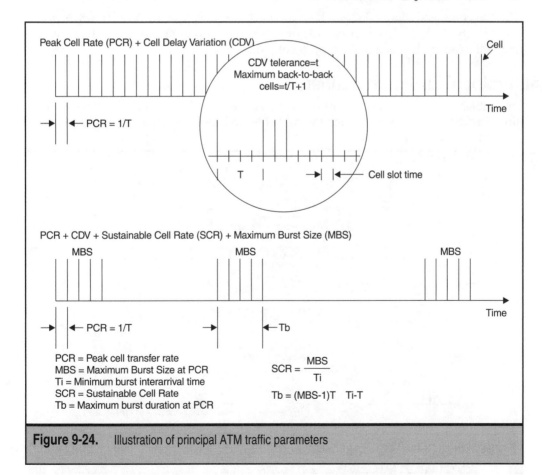

Figure 9-24.   Illustration of principal ATM traffic parameters

More information on traffic descriptors and parameters can be found in *ATM: Theory and Application*.

TRAFFIC AND CONGESTION CONTROL DEFINED

Traffic control details are left for further study. Traffic control provides the means that allow a user to ensure that the offered cell flows meet the rate specified in the traffic contract, and the means for networks to ensure that the traffic contract rates are enforced such that the QoS performance is achieved across all users. There are two predominant types of UPC and traffic-shaping implementations. One standardized means for handling priority is that of selective cell discard based on the CLP bit in the ATM cell header. Another is that of EFCI. A third is fast resource management. Details on each of these schemes can be found in *ATM: Theory and Application*.

AAL: PROTOCOL MODEL

ITU-T Recommendations I.362 and I.363 define the next layer of the ATM/B-ISDN protocol stack, the AAL. AAL service class attributes and example applications will be covered first, followed by the generic AAL protocol model.

AAL Protocol Structure Defined

The B-ISDN protocol model adapts the services provided by the ATM layer to those required by the higher layers through the AAL. Figure 9-25 depicts the structure and logical

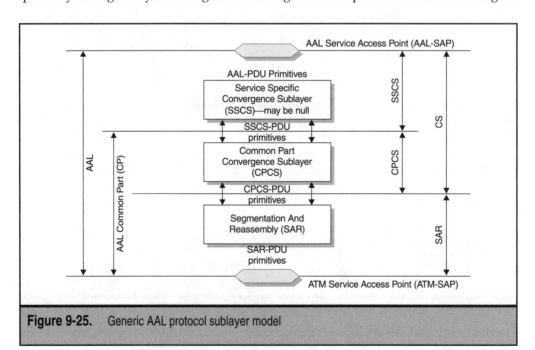

Figure 9-25.   Generic AAL protocol sublayer model

interfaces of the AAL. Services provided to higher layers by an AAL SAP are shown at the top of the figure, across which primitives regarding the AAL PDUs are passed. The AAL is divided into the CS and the SAR sublayers. The CS is further subdivided into SS and CP components. The SSCS may be null, which means that it need not be implemented. The CPCS must always be implemented along with the SAR sublayer. These layers pass primitives regarding their respective PDUs among themselves as labeled in the figure, resulting in the passing of SAR-PDU primitives (which is the ATM cell payload) to and from the ATM layer via the ATM-SAP.

AAL Service Attributes Classified

ITU-T Recommendation I.362 defines the basic principles and classification of AAL functions. The attributes of the service class are the timing relationship required between the source and destination, whether the bit rate is constant or variable, and the connection mode is connection-oriented or connectionless. Figure 9-26 depicts the four AAL service classes, labeled A through D, summarized as follows:

▼ **Class A**   CBR service with end-to-end timing, connection-oriented

■ **Class B**   VBR service with end-to-end timing, connection-oriented

■ **Class C**   VBR service with no timing required, connection-oriented

▲ **Class D**   VBR service with no timing required, connectionless

These service classes approximately map to AALs, and then AALs map to QoS classes used by service providers. The next section indicates the AAL(s) that can support the attributes of the defined AAL service class and also gives several application examples for each service class and AAL.

Attribute	Service class			
	Class A	Class B	Class C	Class D
Timing relation between source and destination	Required		Not required	
Bit Rate	Constant	Variable		
Connection mode	Connection-oriented			Connectionless
AAL(s)	AAL1	AAI2	AAL3/4 or AAL5	AAL3/4 or AAL5
Exanoke(s)	DS1, E1, n×64 Kbps emulation	Packet Video, Audio	Frame Relay, X.25	IP, SMDS

Figure 9-26.   ATM ITU ATM/B-ISDN service classes

AAL: Definition

AAL1 through AAL4 were initially defined by the CCITT to directly map to the AAL defined service classes A through D. ITU-T Recommendation I.363 states the standards for the AALs. AAL1 has been defined by the ITU-T and further clarified in the ANSI T1.630 standard for CBR applications. The CPCS and SAR sublayer for each of the currently standardized CP AALs are defined as

▼ AAL1 supports CBR traffic, specifies how TDM-type circuits can be emulated over an ATM network. Circuit emulation is specified in detail for DS1, DS3, and nxDS0 support in ANSI T1.630.

■ AAL2 specifies ATM transport of connection-oriented circuit and VBR high-bit-rate packetized audio and video (like the Motion PhotoGraphic Experts (MPEG) video encoding standard).

▲ AAL3/4 supports VBR traffic, both connection-oriented and connectionless.

AAL5 supports lightweight VBR traffic, both connection-oriented and connectionless, for example, signaling SSCS protocols, FR, and multiple protocols (including IP) can be operated over AAL5.

TRAFFIC CONTRACT AND QOS

A traffic contract is an agreement between a user and a network regarding the QoS that a cell flow is guaranteed—if the cell flow conforms to a set of traffic parameters defined by the leaky bucket rule. The principal QoS parameters are: average delay, variation in delay, and loss ratio. The traffic parameters define at least the peak cell rate (PCR), and may optionally define a sustainable cell rate (SCR) and maximum burst size (MBS). A cell delay variation tolerance (CDVT) parameter is also associated with the peak rate, but is not usually specified by the user. A leaky bucket algorithm in the network checks conformance of a cell flow from the user by pouring a cup of fluid for each cell into a set of buckets leaking at rates corresponding to the PCR, and optionally the SCR. If the addition of any cup of cell fluid would cause a bucket to overflow, then the cell arrival is considered *nonconforming,* and its fluid is not added to the bucket. Additional considerations in setting the depth of the leaky buckets to account for tolerances in the traffic parameters are also described.

ITU-T Recommendation I.371 and the ATM Forum UNI Specification version 3.1 define the formal concept of a traffic contract. The traffic contract is a sort of contract with the user. In essence, a separate traffic contract exists for every VPC or VCC. The traffic contract is an agreement between a user and a network across a UNI regarding the following interrelated aspects of any VPC or VCC ATM cell flow:

▼ The QoS that a network is expected to provide

■ The traffic parameters that specify characteristics of the cell flow

- ■ The conformance checking rule used to interpret the traffic parameters
- ▲ The network's definition of a compliant connection

The definition of a compliant connection allows some latitude in the realization of checking conformance of the user's cell flow. A compliant connection can identify some portion of cells to be nonconforming, but no more than the portion that the ideal conformance checking rule would identify as nonconforming.

Reference Model

The basis of the traffic contract is a reference configuration, which in the standards is called an *equivalent terminal reference model*, as illustrated in Figure 9-27.

ATM cell traffic is generated by a number of cell sources, for example, a number of workstations, which each have either a VPC or VCC connection endpoint. These are all connected to a cell multiplexer, which in a distributed implementation could be a local ATM switch, router, or hub. Associated with the multiplexing function is a traffic shaper, which ensures that the cell stream conforms to a set of traffic parameters defined by a particular conformance-checking algorithm. The output of the shaper is the PHY layer service access point (SAP) in the OSI layered model of ATM.

After the shaper function, some PHY layer (and other) functions may change the actual cell flow emitted over a private ATM UNI (or S_B reference point) so that it no longer conforms to the traffic parameters. This ATM cell stream may then be switched through other CPE, such as a collapsed ATM backbone, before it is delivered to the public ATM UNI (or T_B reference point).

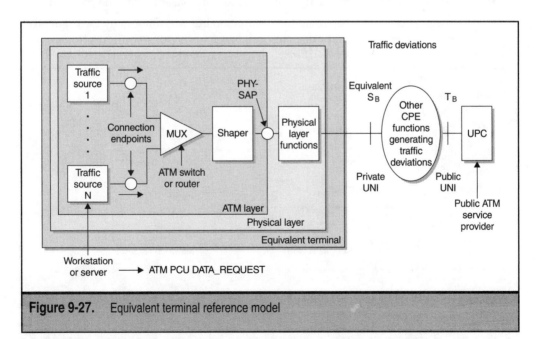

Figure 9-27. Equivalent terminal reference model

The end-to-end QoS reference model may contain one or more intervening networks, each with multiple nodes (ATM switches) as depicted in Figure 9-28. Each of these intervening networks may introduce additional fluctuations in the cell flow due to multiplexing and switching, thereby impacting QoS. In principle, the user should not have to be concerned about how many intervening networks there are and/or what characteristics they have, but should always be provided the guaranteed end-to-end QoS for all configurations. However, this principle and reality have not yet been aligned in standards or interworking of multiple networks (but usually stands true within a single service provider's ATM network).

QoS Parameters

QoS is defined by specific parameters for cells that are conforming to the traffic contract. To simplify a user's request for a certain QoS, certain classes are defined.

QoS is defined on an end-to-end basis—a perspective that is actually meaningful to an end user. The definition of *end user* can be the end workstation, a customer premises network, a private ATM UNI, or a public ATM UNI.

QoS is defined in terms of one of the following measurement outcomes. The measurement is done with respect to cells sent from an originating user to a destination user.

▼ A transmitted cell from the originating user

■ A successfully transferred cell to the destination user

■ A lost cell that does not reach the destination user

■ An errored cell that arrives at the destination but has errors in the payload

▲ A misinserted cell that arrives at the destination but was not sent by the originator. This can occur due to an undetected cell header error or a configuration error.

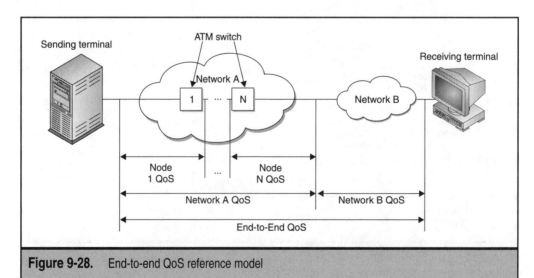

Figure 9-28.   End-to-end QoS reference model

Cell transfer delay can be affected by coding and decoding, segmentation and reassembly, and end-to-end nodal and transmission delay, the components of which are illustrated in Figure 9-29.

Delay can occur on the sending and receiving sides of the end terminal, in intermediate ATM nodes, and on the transmission links connecting ATM nodes.

Cell delay variation (CDV) is currently defined as a measure of cell clumping, which is heuristically how much more closely the cells are spaced than the nominal interval.

QoS classes are defined primarily in terms of the following parameters defined by ITU-T Recommendation I.350 for each ATM VPC or VCC:

▼ Average delay

■ Cell delay variation

■ Loss on CLP = 0 cells for ATM

■ Loss on CLP = 1 cells for ATM

▲ Error rate

For those connections that do not (or cannot) specify traffic parameters and a QoS class, there is a capability defined by the ATM Forum as *best effort* where no QoS guarantees are made and no specific traffic parameters need be stated. This traffic can also be viewed as "at risk" since there are no performance guarantees. In this case, the network admits this traffic and allows it to use capacity unused by connections that have specified traffic parameters and have requested a QoS class. It is assumed that connections using the best-effort capability can determine the available capacity on the route allocated by the network.

QoS Classes

To make things simpler on users, a small number of predefined QoS classes are defined, with particular values of parameters (defined earlier) prespecified by a network in each of a few QoS classes. The ATM Forum UNI Specification version 3.1 defines the five numbered QoS classes and example applications summarized in Table 9-1.

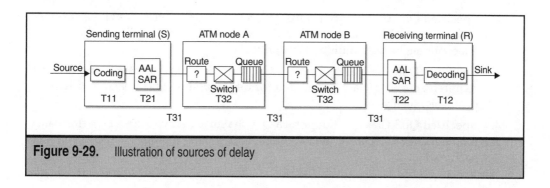

Figure 9-29.   Illustration of sources of delay

QoS Class	QoS Parameters	Application
0	Unspecified	"Best Effort," "At Risk"
1	Specified	Circuit Emulation, CBR
2	Specified	VBR Video/Audio
3	Specified	Connection-Oriented Data
4	Specified	Connectionless Data

Table 9-1.   ATM Forum QoS Classes

A specified QoS class provides performance to an ATM virtual connection (VCC or VPC) as specified by a subset of the ATM performance parameters. For each specified QoS class, there is one specified objective value for each performance parameter, where a particular parameter may be essentially unspecified, for example, a loss probability of 1. Initially, each network provider should define the ATM performance parameters for at least the following service classes from ITU-T Recommendation I.362 in a reference configuration that might depend on mileage and other factors:

▼ **Service class A**   Circuit emulation, constant bit-rate video

■ **Service class B**   Variable bit-rate audio and video

■ **Service class C**   Connection-oriented data transfer

▲ **Service class D**   Connectionless data transfer

These QoS classes are currently defined by the ATM Forum:

▼ **Specified QoS Class 1**   Supports a QoS that meets service class A performance requirements. This class should yield performance comparable to current digital private line performance.

■ **Specified QoS Class 2**   Supports a QoS that meets service class B performance requirements. This class is intended for packetized video and audio in teleconferencing and multimedia applications.

■ **Specified QoS Class 3**   Supports a QoS that meets service class C performance requirements. This class is intended for interoperation of connection-oriented protocols, such as FR.

▲ **Specified QoS Class 4**   Supports a QoS that meets service class D performance requirements. This class is intended for interoperation of connectionless protocols, such as IP.

ATM Service Translations of QoS Classes

When an enterprise purchases ATM service, they will select specific service classes. Service providers have taken the QoS classes defined in the standards earlier and defined five categories that guarantee a particular QoS:

▼   CBR

■   rt-VBR

■   nrt-VBR

■   UBR

▲   ABR

Each of these are defined as follows.

CBR

CBR QoS was designed to support real-time applications requiring a fixed amount of bandwidth defined by PCR. These include applications that cannot tolerate variations in delay (TDM-like). The primary QoS parameter limitations include tightly constrained CTD and CDV. Example applications include voice, CBR video, and circuit emulation services (CES).

rt-VBR

rt-VBR QoS supports applications that are time-sensitive, require constrained delay and delay variation, and transmit at a time varying rate constrained to a PCR and an average rate defined by the SCR and MBS. The primary QoS parameter limitations include PCR, SCR, and MBS. rt-VBR offers the worst-case source traffic pattern for which the network guarantees a specified QoS. Example applications include bursty, delay-variation-sensitive sources, conforming to the traffic contract, such as voice and variable-bit-rate video; and sources that may be statistically multiplexed.

nrt-VBR

nrt-VBR QoS supports applications that do not require any constraints on delay and delay variation, and have variable-rate, bursty traffic characteristics. The traffic contact includes PCR, SCR, and MBS. nrt-VBR also offers the worst-case source traffic pattern for which the network guarantees a specified QoS. Example applications include packet switched data transfers such as FR, LAN, and IP traffic; terminal sessions; file transfers; and sources that may be statistically multiplexed.

ABR

ABR QoS supports applications that require sophisticated congestion control. The protocol cooperates with sources that can change their transmission rate in response to rate-based network feedback (the only ATM QoS category providing this) used in the context of closed-loop congestion management. ABR can dynamically provide application access to bandwidth currently not in use by other service categories. ABR provides a network service that offers very low cell loss, but does not bound delay variation. ABR is used by applications that specify a maximum transmit-rate bandwidth (PCR) and minimum required cell rate (MCR). Example applications include LAN interconnection, high-performance file transfers, database archival, non-time-sensitive traffic, and web browsing.

UBR Best-Effort Service

UBR, also called *best effort*, supports applications with no tightly constrained delay and delay variation, no specific QoS requirements, and no guaranteed throughput. All traffic is considered at risk. There are no performance guarantees. Example applications include LANE, IP over ATM, and nonmission-critical traffic. This service offers the equivalent to the airline industry's flying standby. One component of the best-effort service is that the user application is expected to adapt to the time-variable, available network resources.

USER PLANE OVERVIEW

This section covers the general purpose and function of the user plane. The control and management planes exist to support the user plane, which contains the SSCS and higher layers of the user plane. The higher planes area of higher-layer protocol support for ATM includes standards like the IETF RFC 1483—multiprotocol encapsulation over ATM, for which an explanation can be found in McDysan and Spohn's *ATM: Theory and Application*. Also defined is a detailed specification for packing MPEG into AAL5, IP over ATM, and the ATM Forum private NNI (P-NNI).

FR and SMDS over ATM

FR and ATM interworking are specified in ITU-T Recommendation I.555, the ATM Forum B-ICI specification, and the FR Forum Implementation Agreements (IAs) Network Interworking (FRF.5) and Service Interworking. FR interworking over ATM is defined in detail in McDysan and Spohn's *ATM: Theory and Application*.

The FR-SSCS supports multiplexing through the use of the DLCI field, with the ATM layer supporting connection multiplexing using the VPI/VCI. There are two methods of multiplexing FR connections over ATM: many-to-one and one-to-one. Many-to-one multiplexing maps many FR logical connections identified by the DLCIs over a single ATM VCC. One-to-one multiplexing maps each FR logical connection identified by DLCI to a single ATM VCC via VPI/VCIs at the ATM layer.

Appendix A of the ATM Forum B-ICI specification maps these FR traffic parameters like access line rate (Ra), committed burst size (Bc), excess burst size (Be), and measurement interval, which define a committed information rate (CIR) and an excess information rate (EIR) in T1.617 to the ATM traffic parameter in terms of PCR, SCR, and MBS.

The ATM QoS class for the VCC must also be selected. Usually, QoS class VBR would be used.

CONTROL PLANE AAL

The control plane handles all virtual connection–related functions, most importantly the SVC capability. The control plane also performs the critical functions of addressing and routing. The higher-layer and service-specific AAL portions of the signaling protocol have been translated by service providers into the five Service Classes defined earlier.

Control Plane Overview

The control plane provides the means to support SVC and PVC connections on behalf of the user plane. SVCs and PVCs can be either point-to-point, point-to-multipoint, or multipoint-to-point VPCs or VCCs, as defined earlier. A VPC or VCC provides a specified QoS with a certain bandwidth defined by traffic parameters in an ATM-layer traffic contract.

Control Plane Addressing and Routing Defined

There are two capabilities that are critical to a switched network: addressing and routing. Addressing occurs at the ATM VPI/VCI level and at the logical network level, just as it does at the DLCI level in FR. Since the VPI/VCI is unique only to a physical TP, there is a need to have a higher-level address that is unique across at least each network. Ideally, the address should be unique across all networks to provide universal connectivity. Once each entity involved in switching virtual connections has a unique address, there is another even more onerous problem of finding a route from the calling party to the called party. Using routing solves this problem.

ATM Layer VPI/VCI Level Addressing

The signaling protocol automatically assigns the VPI/VCI values to ATM addresses and physical ATM UNI ports based on the type of SVC requested according to the following set of rules: either point-to-point or point-to-multipoint. A physical ATM UNI port must have at least one unique ATM address. An ATM UNI port may also have more than one ATM address.

Recall that a VCC or VPC is defined in only one direction; that is, it is simplex. A point-to-point SVC (or a PVC) is a pair of simplex VCCs or VPCs: a forward connection from the calling party to the called party, and a backward connection from the called party as illustrated in Figure 9-30. The forward and backward VCC or VPC can have different traffic parameters. A point-to-point SVC is defined by the forward and backward

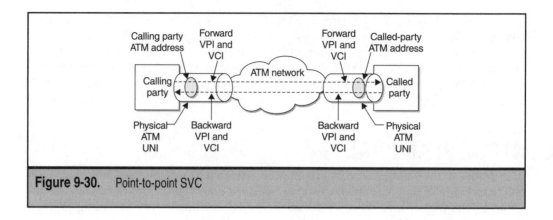

Figure 9-30.   Point-to-point SVC

VPI (and VCI for a VCC) as well as the ATM address associated with the physical ATM UNI ports on each end of the connection. The VPI and VCI assignment can be different for the forward and backward directions of a VPC or VCC at the same end of the connection as well as being different from the other end of the connection. A convention where the VPI (and VCI for a VCC) is identical at the same end of a connection may be used, and is the most common implementation method.

A point-to-multipoint SVC (or PVC) is defined by the VPI and the ATM address associated with the physical ATM UNI port of the root node, and the ATM address and VPI and VCI for each leaf node of the connection, as shown in Figure 9-31.

There is essentially only a forward direction because the backward direction is allocated zero bandwidth. Note that more than one VPI/VCI value and ATM address can be assigned to a physical interface as part of the point-to-multipoint connection. This means that the number of physical ATM UNI ports is always less than or equal to the number of logical leaf endpoints of the point-to-multipoint connection. The implementation of a point-to-multipoint connection should efficiently replicate cells within the network. A minimum spanning tree is an efficient method of constructing a point-to-multipoint connection.

ATM Control Plane (SVC) Addressing

There are two types of ATM control plane (SVC) addressing plans defined in the standards bodies to identify an ATM UNI address: the network SAP (NSAP) format defined in ISO 8348 and CCITT X.213, and the CCITT E.164 standards. Details on both can be found in *ATM: Theory and Application.*

Basic Routing Requirements and Attributes

Cells from the same VPC or VCC must follow the same route, defined as the ordered sequence of physical switch ports which the cells traverse from source to destination.

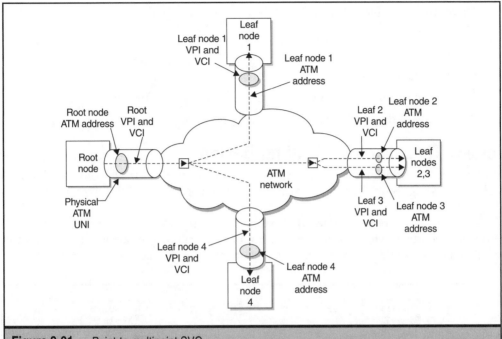

Figure 9-31. Point-to-multipoint SVC

A route is established in response to the following events:

▼ A PVC is newly provisioned.

■ An SVC connection request is made.

▲ A failed PVC is being automatically reestablished.

A route is cleared in response to the following events:

▼ A PVC disconnect order is processed.

■ A failure is detected on a restorable PVC.

■ An SVC disconnection request is made.

▲ Call clearing is done in response to a failure.

The route traversed should minimize a cost function including, but not limited to, the following factors:

▼ Delay

■ Economic expense

▲ Balance use (when multiple links are present between a node-pair)

There are desirable attributes to follow when designing an ATM layer routing scheme. Attributes of the routing scheme include at least the following:

▼ Simplicity

■ Automatic determination of least-cost route(s)

■ Ease of managing changes in the network in terms of new links and nodes

▲ Scaling of the routing scheme to a large network

A Simple ATM Layer VCC Routing Design

A simple routing design for VCCs uses routing based on the VPI value only. Each physical node is assigned a VPI value, which means that it is a VPC endpoint, as illustrated in Figure 9-32.

Every node can route traffic to a destination node using a VPC connecting point with the VPI corresponding to the destination node number. Each node—knowing that the tandem nodes will connect this VPC through to the destination node—accomplishes this routing.

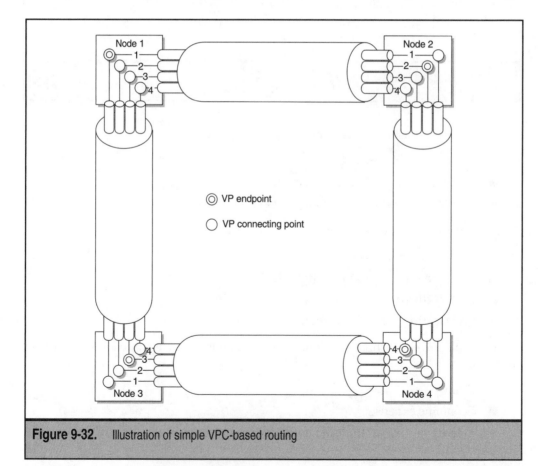

Figure 9-32.   Illustration of simple VPC-based routing

The principal advantage of this method is that it is very simple: no VPI or VCI translation is required. This method has two main disadvantages: it is inefficient since VPIs are allocated on routes that are not used and it limits the number of VPCs that can be assigned to user applications.

Control Plane Protocol Model

Figure 9-33 illustrates the protocol model for the signaling AAL (SAAL). The CP AAL was previously defined. The SSCS portion of the SAAL is composed of two protocols: the Service-Specific Coordination Function (SSCF) and the Service-Specific Connection-Oriented Protocol (SSCOP). More details on control plane architecture and signaling, and information on the signaling messages and their key parameters and the basics of the signaling protocol can be found in *ATM: Theory and Applications.*

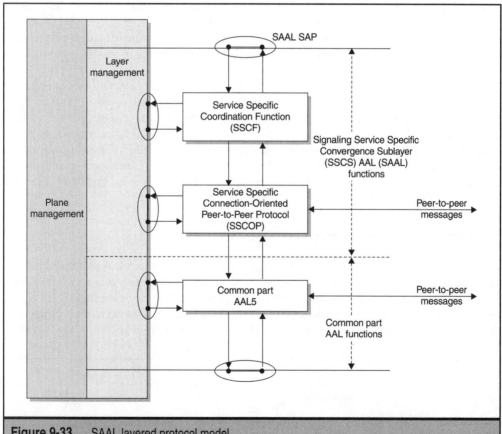

Figure 9-33.   SAAL layered protocol model

MANAGEMENT PLANE

The management plane covers the layer management and plane management functions. Layer management interfaces with the PHY, ATM, AAL, and higher layers. Plane management is responsible for coordination across layers and planes in support of the user and control planes through layer management facilities. This ensures that everything works properly.

SUB-DS3 ATM

Some users require lower speed access rather than use a full DS3 or OC-3 access line. One option is the ATM Forum specified ATM data exchange interface (DXI), which supports either the V.35, RS449, or the HSSI DTE-DCE interface at speeds from several Kbps up to and including 50 Mbps. ATM DXI specifies the interface between a DTE, such as a router, and a DCE, usually called an ATM CSU/DSU, which provides the conversion to an ATM UNI, as illustrated in Figure 9-34. The ATM DXI is normally thought of as a DTE-DCE interface specification. The FUNI Protocol was defined for longer distance access over nxDS0, DS1, and nxDS1 access lines. The ATM DXI is an example of relatively simple network interworking with ATM.

The FUNI specification was developed by the ATM Forum as a method for standard CPE, such as a router, to interface to an ATM network with little software and no hardware reconfiguration or change. FUNI was designed to provide low-speed ATM access protocol rates of nxDS0, DS1, and E1. FUNI CPE send FUNI HDLC frames to a network-based ATM switch at speeds up to and including 2.048 Mbps. The network switch then performs a SAR function on the HDLC frames and converts them into standard ATM cells. This is a protocol encapsulation segmentation into cells, but FUNI does not provide interoperability between ATM and FR end users.

ATM PUBLIC SERVICES

There are many factors to consider when choosing a public network ATM-based service: the type and speed of access, the CPE support, the QoS classes offered, interworking support, network management support, and billing options. The decision factors for choosing an ATM-based service will now be covered. First, public ATM network architectures are examined, and then public network ATM services are reviewed.

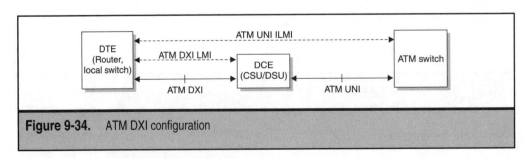

Figure 9-34.   ATM DXI configuration

Public ATM Network Architectures

ATM services have taken on the primary role of providing an evolutionary path from lower-speed FR and, in some cases, traditional TDM architecture networks. An architecture based on ATM technology uses ATM switches in both the central office (CO) and on the CPE. ATM can also be employed in cross-connects, routers, gateways, workstations, and IWFs. Also, most public ATM-based service provider networks employ a SONET or SDH backbone. Figure 9-35 shows a network example where users either interface to the ATM network directly via an ATM UNI, an ATM DXI interface, or an FR interface, achieve access to an IP connectionless server or the public Internet, or interface through multiple other protocols through a multiprotocol interworking function.

ATM Service Suite

Most enterprises that purchase ATM service buy a transport service. But there are a whole slew of service names on the ATM service market. The suite of ATM services includes

▼ ATM cell relay service (CRS)
■ Transparent LAN service (TLS)
■ FR network and service interworking with ATM
■ IP, VPN, and Internet access over ATM
■ Multiprotocol (for example, IP) interworking over ATM—IP-enabled ATM
■ X.25 interworking over ATM
▲ Voice over ATM

A few of these deserve mention in further detail:

ATM Interworking Service   It is also possible to order ATM Interworking service, where an enterprise can order an ATM port at one site and a FR port at another, and interwork them together with a shared ATM-FR PVC. Note that the PVC defaults to the lowest common QoS parameter, which is the equivalent of a CIR rate (PCR in ATM, typically translated for the user as an ATM PVC CIR rate when in actuality it is a PCR). This configuration is typical for large FR implementations where ATM is used at the HQ site.

IP-Enabled ATM   A new version of FR and ATM has appeared at the turn of the century, driven by the IP revolution. IP-enabled FR was defined in Chapter 8. IP-enabled ATM operates similarly in that only one enterprise VP/VC (or ATM E-PVC in ATM service terminology) is required per physical/logical ATM port, and the service provider network switch performs the routing using IP and a routing protocol between the switch and the customer CPE. The edge-routing protocol is usually Border Gateway Protocol (BGP). Thus, in many aspects IP-ATM works the same as IP-enabled FR, but the service also offers all the QoS class methods of ATM. IP-ATM offers the most current version of internetworking IP over ATM.

IP VPN and Internet Access over ATM   Many ATM Services allow integrated PVC access to IP VPN sites within that corporation's intranet, or integrated access to the public Internet. This access method can achieve significant cost savings and improve security.

ATM Service Components

When purchasing ATM service, an enterprise will typically order a physical port (for example, DS3), a logical ATM port (for example, 3 Mbps), and one or more VP/VCs per location. Larger locations may have multiple ATM physical and logical ports, and hundreds or thousands of VP/VCs. Note that many service providers change the name of ATM VPs and VCs to just PVC to match their service descriptions to FR.

Public ATM Services and Providers

Commercial ATM service offerings continue to be offered by the leading data communications service providers including AT&T, MCI Worldcom, BT, Qwest, Sprint, SBC, Verizon, and BellSouth.

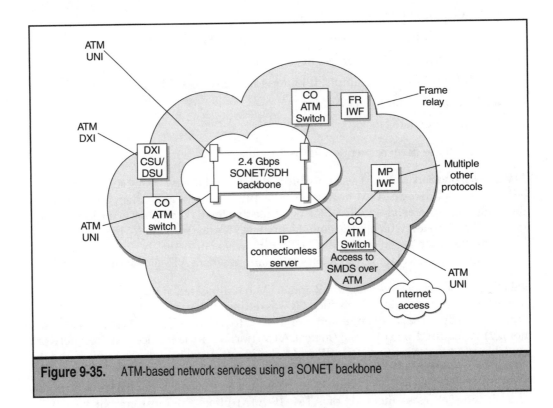

Figure 9-35.   ATM-based network services using a SONET backbone

THE FUTURE OF ATM

ATM LAN services have not deployed nearly as much as planned, and ATM WAN transport services still lag FR and IP deployments. Some of this is due to the complexity of ATM. Some is due to the challenges faced by ATM, including

▼ Interworking between ATM QoS and IP RSVP

■ Aggressive, low-cost 100Mbps and GbE metro offerings

▲ Migration of users toward IP and SONET transport

The ATM Forum continues work on these efforts and more.

Some of the greatest challenges that lie ahead for ATM remain in the area of networking and applications. These are probably the least understood and least standardized—yet most critical—areas to the success of ATM. Applications must be written that interface directly to AAL and QoS classes are a key to ATM success, such as multimedia and IP support for multiple QoS classes. Application programming interfaces (APIs) for ATM exist, but are not in widespread use.

In summary, ATM networks will offer many capabilities that might yield success:

▼ **Collapsed backbone**   The ability to collapse multiple LANs on the back-plane of an ATM switch

■ **Integrated access**   The circuit emulation capabilities that allow circuit-based voice, video, and data to share expensive access lines

■ **Virtual private networking and public connectivity**   Carrier-provided virtual networks built on ATM architectures that are more cost-effective than private networks

■ **High-performance internetworking**   An alternative to or hybrid with routers for high-speed and channel extension connectivity

■ **Protocol internetworking**   With ATM, FR, and IP interfaces via a portfolio of interworking services

■ **High-performance server connections**   Moving ATM to the desktop and providing true competition for FDDI, Switched Ethernet, and Fast Ethernet

■ **ATM work groups**   ATM adapter cards in high-end workstations and servers

▲ **Video over ATM**   Seamless integrated video-conferencing over ATM using the CBR service.

It is forecast that ATM networks will coexist with existing STM based networks for a long time. ATM seems to be the next step in the evolution of universal public networking technologies. ATM should be the star in the ever-evolving multiprotocol network, probably for at least the next five years. ATM also continues to play a dominant role in service-provider backbones.

Look for each of these capabilities to play a key role in the future success of ATM.

REVIEW

The chapter began with definitions of ATM terminology and concepts. Examples were presented throughout the chapter in an attempt to compare ATM concepts to everyday life examples. The presentation then moved on to define the basic building block of ATM—the cell—and the method of constructing cells by assigning VPI and VCI addresses to a header field, which prefixed the user payload. With these basics in hand, the chapter progressed through two examples of ATM protocol operation. ATM has many facets, and is referred to as an interface, a technology, integrated access, a network infrastructure, and even a service. Each of these aspects was summarized to set the stage for the rest of the book. The building blocks of ATM networking—the TP, VP, and VC—were covered. The concepts of both VPCs and VCCs were then introduced.

The foundations of B-ISDN are in the PHY layer, the ATM layer, and the CP AALs. The chapter started with an overview of how these layers fit into the overall B-ISDN protocol model, and went on to investigate the sublayer structure of the PHY and AALs. The PHY layer broke down into PMD and TC sublayers. Examples of how the PMD supports different PMs and interface rates and how the TC sublayer effectively makes the PHY layer appear as a pipe that can transfer cells at a maximum rate to the ATM layer were covered.

The ATM layer protocol model was covered, including an explanation of VP and VC links, connections, and concepts complete with network examples from several points of view. The ATM cell was dissected, clearly defining every field in the header, reviewing some of the basic functions, and identifying where to reference detailed treatment of particular aspects of ATM in other areas of this book. The chapter next introduced the concepts of traffic and congestion control and indicated where these would occur in user equipment or networks.

The notion of congestion as demand in excess of resource capacity was defined. The degree of congestion impacts contention for resources, which can reduce throughput and increase delay, as occurs in vehicular traffic jams. Congestion can occur at multiple levels in time and space. In time, congestion can occur at the cell level, the burst level, or the call level. In space, congestion can occur at a single node or multiple nodes. Congestion-management attempts to ensure that congestion never occurs, which may be done at the expense of reduced efficiency. Congestion-avoidance schemes attempt to operate in a region of mild congestion to obtain higher efficiency at nearly optimal performance, while congestion recovery is tasked with moving the network out of a severely congested state in the event that the previous two philosophies fail, sometimes using rather drastic measures.

This chapter also introduced higher layer ATM protocol functions. A high-level study of AALs 1 through 5 was provided along with an overview of the higher layers of the AAL. Overviews were provided for the user plane, along with the control and management planes, which support the services provided by the user plane. FR to ATM interworking and access to SMDS via ATM were also described. Finally, we discussed current ATM public-service offerings and the future of ATM.

PART IV

Protocols and Interfaces: Layer 3

CHAPTER 10

Common Protocols and Interfaces in the Upper Layers (TCP/IP)

We began our discussion is this book with the beginning of telecommunications and worked our way up through the years of analog communications to digital communications to optical communications and discussed the way each has been used. We have discussed multiplexing and the origination of switching as well as computer networks of today and yesteryear. Through all of those changes, we can see the need for open communications and how compatibility is very important for computer networks to communicate and transmit data from one location to the next. Now let's take a look at the way computer networks of today communicate through a common language known as Transmission Control Protocol/Internet Protocol (TCP/IP). We will also cover other key higher-layer protocols, including UDP, FTP, and SNMP

INTRODUCTION: LAYER 3

In the last few chapters, we discussed the physical and data-link layers and how frames of information are built and placed onto the physical medium. This chapter moves up the OSI reference model and focuses primarily on the network layer, but also includes in less detail the remaining upper layers. The most common network layer protocol today is the Internet Protocol (IP), one of many protocols included in the TCP/IP suite. The TCP/IP suite is the most widely implemented multivendor protocol suite in use today. This is due in large part to IP being the protocol that fuels the Internet engine. Almost all vendors today support at least a portion of the TCP/IP suite of protocols. Because of this, we will use the TCP/IP protocol suite to guide us through the remaining layers. This chapter describes technical aspects of IP, TCP, and other protocols associated with the TCP/IP suite.

BACKGROUND: ROUTING PROTOCOLS

As networks increase in size and protocol complexity, they almost always implement some form of routing. As previously discussed, routers perform both *routing* and *bridging* functions (and can support switching). A router is considered a Layer 3 devise because that is the highest layer it can operate. A router also supports functions of Layers 1 and 2. Both methods require that the router perform address resolution. There are multiple routing protocols that build forwarding tables using different metrics. Some perform routing based on the shortest path to the destination node, some use least-cost routing, and others are based on complex algorithms. Routers use a series of algorithms to perform the task of routing, along with dynamic routing tables to manage this routing. Almost all routers support bridging protocols, as it is preferable to perform translation bridging with a router as opposed to encapsulation bridging with a bridge. An example of a translation bridge is a bridge that translates Ethernet frames to token ring frames and vise versa. An example of encapsulation bridging is when there are two Ethernet LANs separated by a FDDI ring. The bridge will encapsulate the Ethernet frames into FDDI frames and then reverse the procedure on the receiving end back to Ethernet frames. Routers can also support Layer 2 (LAN) and Layer 3 switching.

Routing Protocols Defined

Routers perform router-to-router communications via routing *protocols*. The forwarding process to determine output interfaces uses routing tables built inside the routers. Communications can take place between autonomous systems (Exterior Gateway Protocol [EGP]) and within autonomous systems (Interior Gateway Protocol [IGP]). We will cover RIPv1, RIPv2, IGRP, EIGRP, EGP, BGP, OSPF, and IS-IS.

Gateway protocols are actually used once the destination address is resolved. Routers then need to determine the best way to reach that address through a network of nodes. This determination is made based on a variety of parameters. One example is to assign a specific *cost* to each link in a network. It is then the job of the routing protocol to find the least-cost route. This cost might or might not be economic, and might reflect some performance information such as the delay or latency of the link.

Routing algorithms generally exchange information about the topology, that is, the links that are connected and their associated costs, in two generic methods: distance vector and link state.

Distance vector algorithms use neighbor nodes to periodically exchange vectors of the distance to every destination in the network. This process eventually converges on the optimal solution. Distance vector algorithms employ the Bellman-Ford algorithms; each device builds its table, and then sends an update, and eventually everyone will agree.

Link state algorithms have each router learn the entire link state topology of the entire network at startup. Once the devices on the network understand the topology, only changes to the link state topology are forwarded through the network. This process involves copying the message from one node to other nodes in the network in a tree-like fashion such that every node receives only one copy of the message. Link state algorithms flood all router tables until each device agrees they have the same one. Then each device builds its own forwarding table from its own perspective. The link state approach is more complex, but converges much more rapidly. *Convergence* is the rate at which a network goes from an unstable state to a stable state. Stable in that all devices have a "complete" routing table, and no more changes need be accommodated (for the moment). When the topology of the network changes due to a link or node failure, or the addition of a new node or link, this information must be updated at other nodes. The amount of time required to update all nodes in the network about the topology change is called the convergence time.

Distance-Vector Routing Protocols

The first routing protocols to emerge on the market were based on distance vectors. The distance vector method was used in the initial data communication networks such as the ARPANET and is used by the Internet's Routing Information Protocol (RIP). A key advantage of the distance vector is its simplicity. A key disadvantage is that the topology information message grows larger with the network (depending on the addressing scheme used and the ability to do address summarization), and the time for it to propagate through the network increases as the network grows. Convergence times on the order of minutes are common. Some examples of address summarization are

▼ IP RIP automatically summarizes at the edges of a class (A, B, C) network.

■ OSPF can be configured to summarize on more arbitrary area boundaries.

▲ IPX RIP doesn't do any summarization at all.

Figure 10-1 shows an example of the use of distance vector routing determination for routing table exchange.

Distance vector protocol allows router A to talk to its nearest neighbors, namely routers B and C, periodically (for example, every 30 seconds). Router A will constantly exchange its routing tables with routers B and C, and vice versa. Thus, router A in effect broadcasts its status to router C who, in turn, broadcasts to routers D and E, and so forth throughout the network.

Problems can arise due to convergence, where the transfer of these routing tables between nodes takes 30 seconds or more per hop. In a large network, this can amount to a multiple-minute delay, causing a different network status at multiple locations throughout the network.

There are many implementations of the distance-vector routing protocols. One of the first developed was RIP, developed for the XNS protocol suite. There are currently two versions of RIP. RIP version 1 (RIPv1) is the most basic and operates in a connectionless mode at the application layer, interfacing with transport layer protocols through UDP. Its decision for routing is based on hop count only, where each router is one hop. RIPv1 computes this hop count while ignoring the length of the hop and the capacity available in that and other hops. This can cause problems when a higher-bandwidth path is available and desirable for transport, as in Figure 10-2. Here, a host on router A would like to send a 500KB file to a host router E. Since the path through router D requires only two hops, it will be chosen (regardless of distance) instead of the higher-bandwidth path (and three

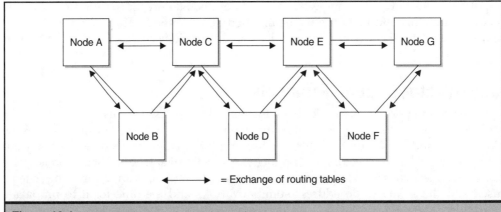

Figure 10-1. Distance vector routing table exchange

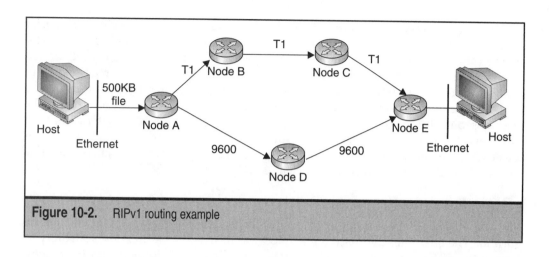

Figure 10-2.   RIPv1 routing example

hops) through routers B and C. RIPv1 also requires an abundant amount of overhead to update neighboring routing tables every 30 seconds. Rather, this is not just an update, for each router in the network transmits its entire routing table to each of its neighbors every 30 seconds. This problem obviously compounds as the network becomes larger. RIPv1 protocol also has a hop-count restriction of 16 hops, and is prone to routing loops (nodes stuck transmitting back and forth to each other because each believes the other has the shortest path to the destination) if misconfigured. RIP version 2 (RIPv2) added several features and is the default on many router RIP implementations today.

▼   External route tags

■   Subnet masks

■   Next-hop router addresses

■   Authentication

▲   Multicast support

The use of split horizons and poison reverse can improve performance and reduce the chance for loops, and hold-downs can be tweaked per the environment. Split horizon is a technique used to ensure information is not sent back in the direction in which it was received. With poison reverse, the router sets a table entry that keeps the network state consistent while other routers gradually converge correctly on the topology change.

IGRP is another type of routing protocol proprietary to Cisco Systems routers. This protocol operates similar to RIPv1, but is superior because it understands bandwidth limitations between hops, as well as time delays. IGRP is tunable to make it faster than RIPv1 if desired (that is, no use of hold-downs). This is the classic distance vector trade-off of network stability versus time. While this protocol improves on RIPv1, it also triples the transmit time (RIP is 30 seconds; IGRP is 90 seconds) of information between nodes, amplifying the opportunity for a convergence problem. E-IGRP (enhanced IGRP) is the most recent version of this protocol.

Exterior Gateway Protocol (EGP) and Border Gateway Protocol (BGP) are exterior routing protocols, that is, they are used between separately administered networks. Internet service providers (ISPs) use BGP to share routing information between their networks, and in situations where it matters, such as where sites are dual homed (most singly homed Internet subscribers are statically routed, and since it is a binary decision, the route is either there or not there and no path selection occurs). EGP (the protocol, not the class of protocols including BGP) is deprecated. The OSI version of an exterior routing protocol is *IDRP*, and like other exterior routing protocols, specifies how routers communicate with routers in different domains. IDRP is based on BGP but is designed to operate seamlessly with other OSI protocols such as CLNP, ES-IS, and IS-IS.

Link-State Routing Protocols

More recently developed and even more efficient as a routing protocol is the *link state* algorithm. The link state advertisement method was designed to address the scalability issues of the distance vector method. Routers using link-state routing protocols request changes in link states from all nodes on the network. Routing tables are exchanged with neighbors, but every device on the network must be a neighbor to at least one other device. In this manner, each router will eventually be updated with everyone else's routing tables. This makes good use of the routing process and eliminates having various network states running simultaneously throughout the network. When a link is added or deleted from the network, an advertisement of its cost is flooded through the network. Each node has complete knowledge of the network topology in time t (usually tens of milliseconds to seconds) after any change and computes the least-cost routes to every destination using an algorithm such as the Dijkstra algorithm. Link state updates are sent using 64-byte packets (depending on the specific protocol) in a multicast mode, and require acknowledgments. The actual neighbor reachability exchanges are small, with the actual link state updates potentially larger. This protocol will also notify users if their address is unreachable. This method is more memory intensive for the router, and requires large amounts of buffers and memory space. More router CPU cycles are also needed, as more complex algorithms must be used.

There are three major implementations of link-state routing protocols on the market:

▼ The Internet's Open Shortest Path First (OSPF) Protocol

■ The OSI Intermediate System to Intermediate System (IS-IS) Routing Protocol

▲ Novell's Netware Link Services Protocol (NLSP)

OSPF, a standard IGP developed by the OSPF Working Group of the IETF and identified under TCP/IP (DARPA), provides a much more comprehensive view of the network. OSPF uses the Dijkstra algorithm for packet routing. OSPF routing is based on many parameters, including shortest path, bandwidth available, congestion, interface costs, and time delay combined into a single manually configured metric. All costs for links are designated on the outbound router port. Routers are sectioned into "areas," with each area maintaining its own topological database. These areas are then connected to a backbone area.

OSPF routing supports multiple types of networks: point-to-point, broadcast, Nonbroadcast Multi-Access (NBMA), virtual links, and point-to-multipoint. Point-to-point networks join a single pair of routers. Broadcast networks attach more than two routers, with each router having the ability to broadcast a single message to multiple routers through a single address. Nonbroadcast networks, such as X.25 and frame relay (FR), attach more than two routers but do not have broadcast capability. Point-to-multipoint is another mode of NBMA that treats the nonbroadcast network as a collection of point-to-point links and virtual links are a special case of demand circuit configured through nonbackbone areas to establish or maintain connectivity of the backbone.

OSPF also supports subnetting and filtering, which we will discuss later in the "Addressing and Routing Design" section. OSPF is useful only with TCP/IP networks. OSPF also supports bifurcated routing: the ability to split packets between equal paths.

The International Organization for Standardization (ISO) developed the IS-IS protocol. The original intent was to route within ISO Connectionless Network Protocol (CLNP) networks. IS-IS is the OSI standard equivalent to OSPF, and provides similar benefits. There is also a Cisco version of the IS-IS standard that has been around since 1992 and is very similar to OSPF. A version of IS-IS, Integrated IS-IS (it also referred to as Dual IS-IS), was created to support both CLNP and IP networks. Several fields are added to IS-IS packets to allow Integrated IS-IS to support additional network layers.

The End System to Intermediate System (ES-IS) protocol is used to route between end nodes and intermediate nodes, while the IS-IS protocol is used to route between network nodes. ES-IS protocol is complimentary to IS-IS, and comparable to ARP for IP. Another analogy is to compare OSPF to IS-IS, as ARP is to ES-IS. An extension of IS-IS, Integrated IS-IS (also called Dual IS-IS, as proposed by DEC), can support both OSI and TCP/IP networks simultaneously. This protocol helps TCP/IP users migrate to the OSI platform. IS-IS is used by many major ISPs because it scales better and is apparently more stable than OSPF. OSI IS-IS standards are popular in the international community, where OSI maintains some market share. IS-IS standards do not have a hop-count limit. In fact, there is no concept of a hop count in OSPF or IS-IS. The interface costs build up cumulatively throughout the network. There is one real distinction between the protocols: OSPF provides a wider range of interface costs than IS-IS.

Another routing protocol that should be mentioned is Cisco's proprietary Enhanced Interior Gateway Routing Protocol (EIGRP), which integrates the capabilities of link-state protocols into distance vector protocols. It takes some of the better attributes of both protocol categories and combines them to make a more operationally efficient protocol. EIGRP uses a special algorithm developed at SRI International by Dr. J.J. Garcia-Luna-Aceves called Diffusing Update Algorithm (DUAL). The advantages of using DUAL is that is can determine whether a path advertised by a neighbor is loop-free or not and affords routers some path alternatives without waiting on updates from other routers. Cisco offers seamless interoperation between EIGRP and IGRP routers. As with IGRP, EIGRP is a proprietary protocol and is supported only on Cisco routers.

Routing Protocols Comparison

Table 10-1 shows a comparison matrix between communications protocols and their native routing protocols.

TCP/IP SUITE

The TCP/IP suite allows computers of all sizes, from many different computer vendors, running totally different operating systems, to communicate with each other. It is quite amazing because it has far exceeded its original estimates many times over. What started in the late '60s as a government-financed research project into packet-switching networks, has in the 2000s, turned into the most widely used form of networking between two or more computers. It is truly an open system in that the definition of the protocol suite and many of its implementations are publicly available at little or no charge. It forms the basis for what is called the World Wide Web or Internet, a wide area network of millions of computers that literally span the globe.

Origins of TCP/IP

The U.S. Advanced Research Projects Agency (ARPA) began development of a packet-switched network in 1969, and demonstrated the first packet-switching capability in 1972. It was named the ARPANET. The ARPANET continued to grow, and in 1983 introduced TCP/IP, replacing the earlier Network Control Protocol (NCP) and Interface Message Processor (IMP) protocol. Also in 1983, the ARPANET was split into a military network and a nonmilitary research network; the latter was the origin of the Internet. In 1986, the National Science Foundation (NSF) founded the construction of a 56 Kbps network connecting its six new supercomputer centers. It was upgraded to DS1 in 1988. In 1990, the NSF embarked on a program to upgrade the entire Internet backbone to DS3 speeds (45 Mbps) for supercomputer interconnection. In 1994, the NSF began upgrade of the Internet backbone for supercomputer communication to OC-3 speeds (150 Mbps).

Communications Protocols	Native Routing Protocols
OSI	ES-IS, IS-IS, IDRP
TCP/IP	BGP, RIPv1, RIPv2, OSPF, integrated IS-IS, IGRP, EIGRP
XNS, Novell IPX	RIP, NLSP for IPX
AppleTalk	RTMP

Table 10-1.   Communications and Routing Protocols

The backbone speed continues to increase. Many of the major ISPs support OC-192 today. The Internet has its own standards body, called the Internet Engineering Task Force (IETF), which is described in Chapter 2.

Structure of TCP/IP

Figure 10-3 illustrates the TCP/IP suite in comparison to the OSI reference model. The major difference between the OSI model and the TCP/IP suite is that the OSI model was published as a set of "open" international standards. Today, the OSI reference model is comprised of hundreds of standards, each of which has taken years to develop, agreed on and finally published in its final OSI form, with the TCP/IP protocol suite being more restricted to a geographic and technical scope (meaning the United States). TCP/IP developers adopted a very pragmatic approach to its standardization. The standardization of the TCP/IP protocol suite was based on the Request for Comments (RFC), a flexible and fast standardization process using electronic mail to publish and exchange comments and ideas as well as update drafts. It didn't take long before the government demanded TCP/IP for all systems, thereby ensuring that every U.S. government computer supplier provided it. They also funded universities to implement these standards. In the United States, such publicly funded work and ideas enter the public domains freely to all citizens as long as they are not specifically of a military nature.

Service Aspects of TCP/IP

TCP/IP implementations typically constitute a router, TCP/IP workstation and server software, and network management. TCP/IP protocol implementations span UNIX, DOS, VM, and MVS environments. A majority of UNIX users employ TCP/IP for internetworking. Many network operating system (NOS) vendors integrate TCP/IP into their NOS platforms. Examples include Novell's NetWare and Microsoft's Windows. TCP/IP is used internationally.

The User Datagram Protocol (UDP) Internet Control Message Protocol (ICMP) routing control protocols, and the Transmission Control Protocol (TCP) interface directly with IP.

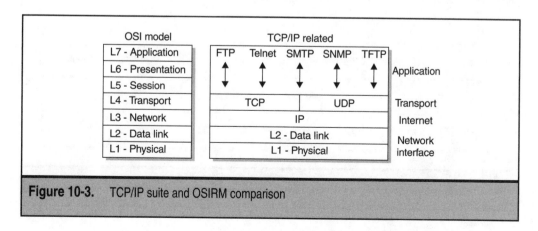

Figure 10-3. TCP/IP suite and OSIRM comparison

Both TCP and UDP provide the capability for the host to distinguish among multiple applications through port numbers. TCP provides a reliable, sequenced delivery of data to applications. TCP also provides adaptive flow control, segmentation, and reassembly, and prioritized data flows. UDP provides only an unacknowledged datagram capability. A number of applications interface to TCP and UDP, as shown in Figure 10-4. The File Transfer Protocol (FTP) application provides for security log-in, directory manipulation, and file transfers. TELNET provides a remote terminal log-in capability. The Simple Network Management Protocol (SNMP) supports configuration setting, data retrieval, and alarms. The Trivial FTP (TFTP) protocol provides a simplified version of FTP, which is intended to reduce implementation complexity. The Remote Procedure Call (RPC) and Network File Server (NFS) capabilities allow applications to interact over IP. Domain Name Services (DNS) provide a centralized name service, and can run over UDP or TCP.

Routers send error and control messages to other routers using ICMP. ICMP also provides a function in which a user can send a PING (echo packet) to verify connectivity to an IP-addressed host. The Address Resolution Protocol (ARP) directly interfaces to the data-link layer, for example, Ethernet. The purpose of ARP is to map a physical address (for example, an Ethernet MAC address) to an IP address.

NETWORK LAYER (INTERNETWORK LAYER)

The OSI network layer is called the internetwork layer in the TCP/IP suite. The network layer is responsible for defining the Internet addressing scheme, delivering packets between networks, fragmentation and reassembly of datagrams, and routes datagrams to remote hosts.

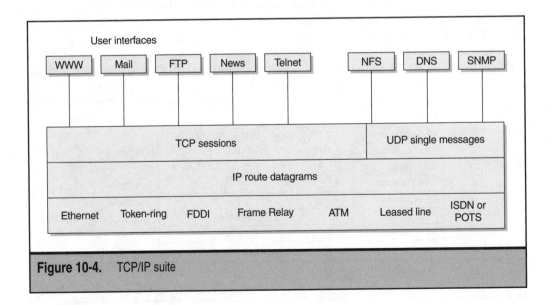

Figure 10-4.   TCP/IP suite

IP

IP was standardized with RFC 791. IP provides a datagram network service. The *datagrams* are packets that consist of a header, data, and a trailer. The header contains delivery information, such as the source and *destination addresses*. The data is the information being transported and the trailers typically contain a *checksum value* to ensure that the data is not modified in transit. IP is a connectionless protocol; therefore, does not support any concept of a session or connection. Once a packet is transmitted or received, IP maintains no memory of the communication. It expects the protocols above it, generally in the transport layer, to understand what has or has not been delivered. If the IP service on a device receiving an IP datagram detects an error during transmission, it simply ignores the packet without notifying the receiving entity.

IP Packet Formats

Figure 10-5 illustrates the format of the IP packet. The Version field specifies the IP protocol version. The header length field specifies the datagram header length in units of 32-bit words, the most common length being 4 words, or 20 octets. Use of the Type of Service (TOS) field varies across the industry. Either each bit is treated as an individual flag (a 3-bit precedence of 1 to 7: 1 bit to indicate delay sensitivity, 1 bit to indicate high throughput, and 1 bit to indicate a request for high reliability), or a 3-bit field is used with values of 0 through 7 (or 1 through 8, even) and 8 levels of precedence or service qualities. The total length field specifies the total IP datagram length for the header and the user data. The

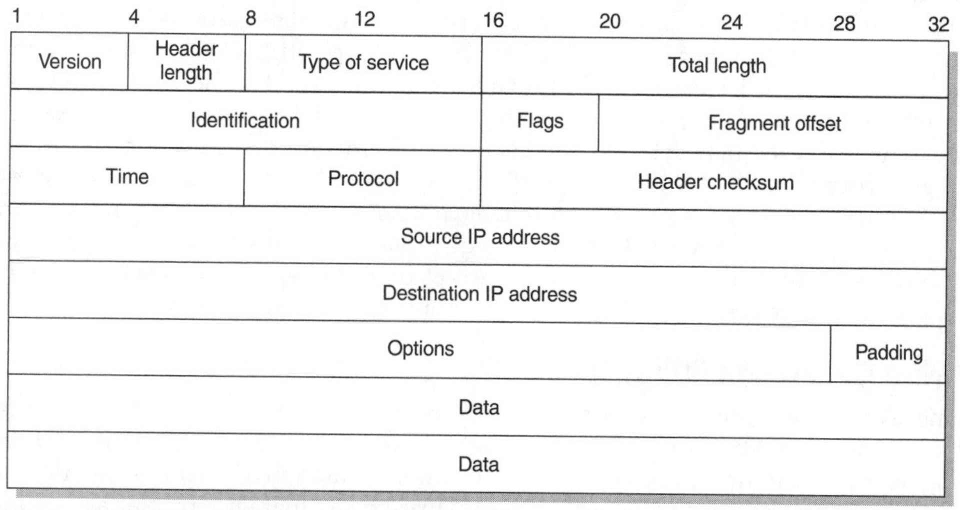

Figure 10-5. IP datagram format

identification, flags, and fragment offset fields control fragmentation (or segmentation) and reassembly of IP datagrams. The Time to Live (TTL) field specifies how many routers the packet can pass through in the Internet before it is declared "dead." Intermediate nodes or routers decrement TTL, and when it reaches zero, the packet is discarded. The protocol field identifies the higher-level protocol type (for example, TCP or UDP), which identifies the format of the data field.

The header checksum ensures integrity of the header fields through a calculation that is easy to implement in software. Source and destination IP addresses are required, and the user data is placed in the data field. The nonmandatory fields for options and padding can specify routing and time-stamp information.

IP Addressing

The Internet is a huge worldwide network that uses IP version 4 (IPv4), 32-bit IP addresses as a global network addressing scheme. Each user, or "host" in Internet parlance, is assigned a unique IP address of 32 bits, or 4 octets, represented in the following dotted decimal notation:

XXX.XXX.XXX.XXX

where XXX ranges from 0 to 255 decimal, corresponding to the range of 00000000 to 11111111 binary. There are 2^{32}, or more than 4 billion, IP addresses.

IP addresses are grouped into classes A, B, and C, as shown in Figure 10-6, where the class determines the maximum network size for publicly assigned addresses, and is measured in number of hosts. A class A address supports a network of up to 16 million host addresses (2^{24}), a class B address supports up to 64,000 (2^{16}) hosts, while a class C address supports up to 256 (2^{8}) host addresses. Internet addresses are assigned and managed by a central authority, the Internet Assigned Numbers Authority (IANA), to ensure that they are unique. A network may assign the host addresses however it wishes, as long as the assignment is unique. If unique addresses are not maintained, problems with address conflicts can arise when networks are interconnected. More on IP address assignment and design is covered in the "Addressing and Routing Design" section later in this chapter.

IP works with TCP for end-to-end reliable transmission of data across the network. TCP will control the amount of unacknowledged data in transit by reducing either the window size or the segment size. The reverse is also true, where window or segment size values can be increased to pass more data if error conditions are minimal.

IP Next Generation (IPng): IPv6

Some users claim, "The Internet is out of addresses!" While it is difficult to obtain a large block of addresses (that is, class B or C), it is not impossible. With more rational address assignment policies now in place, and with the implementation of Classless Interdomain Routing (CIDR) and the availability of routing protocols that support variable-length subnet masks, the IPv4 address space should last a few more years. CIDR is discussed in detail in the "Addressing and Routing Design" section later in this chapter. The frugal use of address space (that is, RFC 1597) and network address translation, while clearly not agreed on universally, also helps with address conservation.

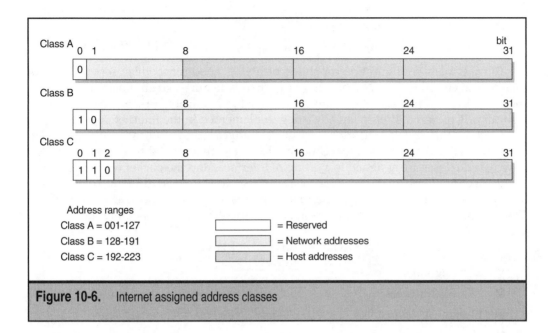

Figure 10-6.   Internet assigned address classes

In July 1994, the IETF issued RFC 1752, the Recommendation for the IP next-generation protocol: IPng. IPng supersedes IPv4, and is formally referred to as IPv6. Some of the "formal" RFCs for IPv6 include

▼ **RFC 2460 (obsoletes 1883)**   IP Version 6 (IPv6) Specification

■ **RFC 2373 (obsoletes 1884)**   IP Version 6 Addressing Architecture

■ **RFC 2463 (obsoletes 1885)**   Internet Control Message Protocol (ICMPv6) for IP Version 6 (IPv6) Specification

▲ **RFC 1886**   DNS Extensions to support IP version 6

IPv6 contains the following additions and enhancements to IPv4:

▼ Expands the address size from 32 to 128 bits

■ Simple dynamic auto-configuration capability

■ Easier multicast routing with addition of "scope" field

■ Any cast feature—send packet to any cast address and it is delivered to one of the nodes that allows nodal routing control

■ Capability to define quality of service to a traffic flow added

■ Reduction of overhead—some header fields are optional

■ More flexible protocol design for future enhancements

■ Authentication, data integrity, and confidentiality options

■ Easy transition and interoperability with IPv4

▲ Support for all IPv4 routing algorithms (for example, OSPF, RIPv1, and so on)

The automatic configuration capability of IPv6 is good for mobile users that do not want to use virtual LANs (VLANs). It is also a handy feature that eliminates the requirements for LAN administrators to constantly reconfigure the network. Some manual configuration is required. IPv6 is already being implemented in the Internet.

There are three types of IP addresses: unicast, anycast, and multicast. All addresses in IPv6 are assigned to an interface. Unicast addresses are assigned to a single interface. Anycast addresses are assigned to a group of interfaces and the packet will be delivered to at least one of these interfaces. Multicast addresses are assigned to a group of interfaces such that when a packet is sent all interfaces receive it. Space is also reserved for NSAP, IPX, and neutral addresses. With 128-bit addressing there is the possibility for 340×10^{36} individual addresses.

IPv6 is designed to accommodate traditional applications such as

▼ IP datagram service

■ FTP file transfers

■ E-mail

■ X-windows

▲ Gopher

It also accommodates new applications such as

▼ Nomadic computing

■ Wireless

■ Network-available entertainment

■ 500-channel TV

■ Video on demand

▲ Home device control (electrical and mechanical)

The header format for IPng is shown in Figure 10-7. Notice that the version field value equals 6. The priority field allows eight values (0, 1, 2, 3, 4, 5, 6, and 7) for prioritizing traffic that can back off during congestion, and eight values (8, 9, 10, 11, 12, 13, 14, and 15) that can be assigned to traffic that does not back off in response to congestion (for example, "real-time" constant bit-rate traffic such as video). The flow label field works in concert with the priority field to determine quality of service. The payload length field specifies the length of the payload. The next header field identifies the type of header immediately following this header (same values used as with IPv4). The hop limit field is a count that decrements by one each time the packet is forwarded. If the count reaches zero, the packet is discarded. The source and destination addresses are the same as for IPv4, except that there are 128 bits. Variable-length extension headers may be added up to a total of 40 bytes.

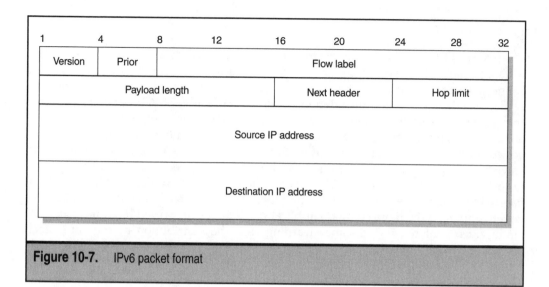

1	4	8	12	16	20	24	28	32

Figure 10-7.   IPv6 packet format

ICMP

IP does not provide for error reporting back to the source when routing anomalies occur. This task is left to the Internet Control Message Protocol (ICMP). ICMP was established with RFC 792 and is part of the Internetwork layer. ICMP uses the IP datagram delivery mechanism to transmit control, error reporting, and informational messages. ICMP is used to report errors and send messages about the delivery of a packet. It can also be used to test TCP/IP networks and is often used for troubleshooting problems. Some examples of ICMP messages include

▼ **Echo message** (PING) is sent to determine if a remote computer's IP is available.

■ **Source quench message** is transmitted back to a sending station to instruct the source to stop sending datagrams temporarily when the datagrams are arriving faster than the receiving station can process them.

■ **Destination unreachable message** is sent to the source of a datagram when a router cannot locate the destination.

■ **Redirect message** is sent by a gateway device to tell a host to use another gateway, generally because it is a better option.

▲ **Time exceeded message** is sent to the source host when the TTL of a packet reaches zero which indicates it has exceeded its allocated time to exist within an Internet. The router will discard the packet and send a warning message back to the source host.

IGMP

The Internet Group Management Protocol (IGMP) is a network layer protocol defined by RFC 966 used by IP hosts to register their dynamic multicast group membership and by connected routers to discover these group members. Multicast is the communication between a single sender to multiple defined receivers on a network. A broadcast message is transmitted to every host on a network. With multicasting, the receivers of the message are defined. A multicast datagram is delivered only to the members of its destination host group. The membership of a host group is dynamic, which allows devices to join and leave the group as required. IP multicast addresses are assigned by IANA using the class D address space of 224.0.0.0–239.255.255.255. The purpose of multicasting is to conserve bandwidth and reduce traffic by delivering a single stream of information to multiple recipients. Some of the more common applications that are supported by multicasting include video conferencing, distance learning, and the distribution of software, stock quotes, and news.

ARP

As stated earlier, ARP directly interfaces to the data-link layer, for example, Ethernet. The purpose of ARP is to map a physical address (for example, an Ethernet MAC address) to an IP address. ARP is based on RFC 826. ARP is required because the network layer is not aware of the data-link layer's addresses (and vice versa). ARP is responsible for obtaining hardware addresses and matching them to their IP address when the destination computer is on the same network.

IP addresses are dynamically discovered on IEEE 802.X LANs through the use of ARP and Reverse ARP (RARP). ARP sends out a broadcast message to find the hardware address (MAC address) corresponding to a particular network-layer address. RARP, based on RFC 903, sends out a broadcast message to locate the network-layer address associated with a particular hardware address. RARP is used predominately with diskless nodes in which network-layer addresses are not known when they are initialized.

TRANSPORT LAYER

The protocol layer just above the network layer is the *transport layer*, also known as the *host-to-host layer*. This layer provides the communication between the source and destination computers, and breaks application layer information into packets. Principle functions that it performs are segmentation, reassembly, and multiplexing over a single network-layer interface. It is responsible for initiating and terminating the connection, providing end-to-end data integrity, and for providing a highly reliable communication service for entities that want to carry out an extended two-way conversation. The transport layer allows a session-layer entity to request a class of service, which must be mapped onto appropriate network-layer capabilities. It is the transport layer's responsibility to manage end-to-end flow control. When a process sends a message to another process the size of the message might be larger than what is supported on the network at one time. Therefore, these packets need to be fragmented, or divided into smaller chunks, for data transmission and then recomposed at the receiving end.

The two protocols that reside in the transport layer for the TCP/IP suite are Transmission Control Protocol (TCP) and User Datagram Protocol (UDP). TCP is a connection-oriented protocol that provides reliable data delivery by the receiving station acknowledging that it received the data. TCP is used to guarantee end-to-end delivery of data, to ensure data arrives in the proper sequence, and to check for transmission errors. UDP is a connectionless protocol designed to provide fast transfer of information and low overhead. Unlike TCP, UDP relies on the upper layer protocols to provide error checking and delivery of data. Application programmers choose the service that is most appropriate for their specific applications.

With both TCP and UDP, there are 65,534 ports available for data transmission on each protocol. Both TCP and UDP identify applications using 16-bit port numbers, as shown in Figure 10-8, which means that services are normally identified by their well-known port numbers. An example of this concept would be that every FTP server provides its service on TCP port 21 for transmitting data and port 20 for receiving. Every Telnet server is on TCP port 23. Every implementation of TFTP is on UDP port 69. Those services can be provided by any implementation of TCP/IP and have well-known port numbers between 1 and 1024. The Internet Assigned Numbers Authority (IANA) manages the well-known ports. You can locate the IANA at http://www.iana.org.

A socket is a software function that connects an application to a network protocol. An application creates a socket by specifying three items:

▼   IP address of the host

■   Type of service (TCP or UDP)

▲   Port the application is using

An application can create a socket and use it to send connectionless traffic to remote applications. An application can also create a socket and connect it to another application's socket. Data can then be reliably sent over this connection. Sockets are also commonly referred to as Application Program Interfaces (API).

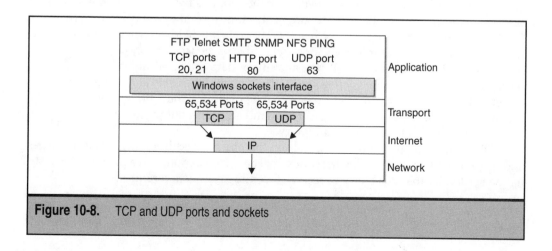

Figure 10-8.   TCP and UDP ports and sockets

TCP

TCP is a connection-oriented transport protocol that sends data as an unstructured stream of bytes and allows hosts to maintain multiple, simultaneous connections. TCP provides full-duplex connections and reliable service by ensuring that data is reintroduced when the initial transmission results in an error. TCP is used by applications that require reliable data delivery. By using sequence numbers and acknowledgment messages, TCP can provide a sending node with delivery information about packets transmitted to a destination node. Where data has been lost in transit from source to destination, TCP can retransmit the data until either a timeout condition is reached or until successful delivery has been achieved. TCP can also recognize duplicate messages and will discard them appropriately. If the sending computer is transmitting too fast for the receiving computer, TCP can employ flow control mechanisms to slow data transfer. TCP communicates delivery information to the upper-layer protocols and applications it supports through ports and sockets. Instead of using the term "session," TCP/IP uses the terms "socket" and "port" to describe the path over which applications communicate. A TCP port provides a specific location for delivery of messages. Port numbers below 256 are defined as commonly used ports.

Port Number	Description
21	FTP
23	Telnet
53	DNS
139	NetBIOS session service

TCP Frame Format

Figure 10-9 illustrates the TCP frame format. The source and destination TCP port numbers identify a specific application program in the source and destination hosts. The sequence number field identifies the position of the sender's byte stream in the data field. The acknowledgment number field identifies the number of the next octet to be received. The HLEN provides the length of the header. The code bits field determines the use of the segment contents (for example, SYN for synchronize sequence numbers and RST for reset connection). The window field tells the amount of data the application is willing to accept. The checksum is applied across the TCP header and the user data and is used to detect errors. The urgent pointer field specifies the position in the data segment where the urgent data begins if the code bits indicate that this segment contains urgent data. The options and padding fields are not mandatory.

TCP is a connection-oriented protocol and therefore has additional, specific messages and a protocol for an application to request a distant connection, and a means for a destination to identify that it is ready to receive incoming connection requests.

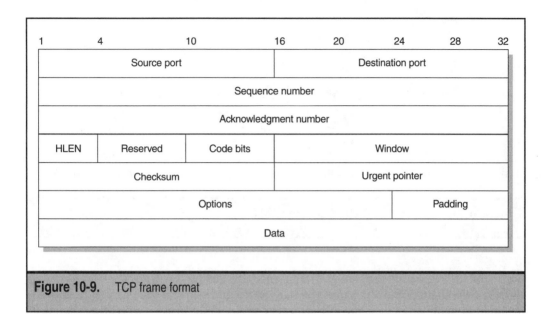

1	4	10	16	20	24	28	32

Figure 10-9.   TCP frame format

TCP/IP Functions

IP provides a connectionless datagram delivery service to the transport layer and, in this case, to TCP. IP does not provide end-to-end reliable delivery, error control, retransmission, or flow control; it relies on TCP to provide these functions.

A major function of IP is in the routing protocols, which provide the means for devices to discover the topology of the network, as well as detect changes of state in nodes, links, and hosts. Thus, IP routes packets through available paths around points of failure. IP has no notion of reserving bandwidth; it only finds an available path. Most of the routing algorithms will minimize a routing cost, as discussed previously.

Example of TCP/IP Operation

Figure 10-10 shows an example of a TCP/IP network transferring data from a workstation client to a server. Both TCP and IP are built on the principle that the underlying network is a connectionless datagram network that can deliver packets out of order, or even deliver duplicate packets. TCP handles this by segmentation and reassembly using the sequence number in the TCP header, while IP does this using the fragment control fields in the IP header. Either method, or both, may be used. A user's data ABCD is segmented into four TCP segments on the left side of the figure. A router is initially routing this traffic via an IP network and sends datagram A via that route. The router then becomes aware of a direct connection to the destination router, and routes the remaining datagrams via the direct route. This routing action causes the datagrams to arrive at the

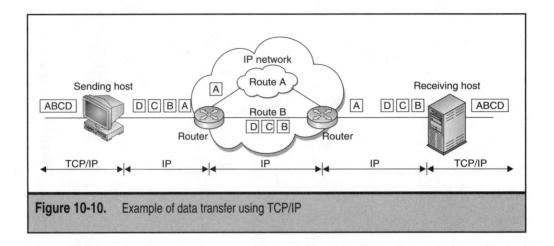

Figure 10-10. Example of data transfer using TCP/IP

destination server out of order, with datagram A traversing the IP network and arriving significantly later. TCP resequences the datagrams and delivers the block of data to the destination in the original order. IP performs a very similar process using fragmentation and reassembly. IP does no reordering or retransmission, and reassembly occurs only at the final destination host.

This operation by TCP/IP of accepting datagrams out of order, and being able to operate over an unreliable underlying network, makes it quite robust.

Traffic and Congestion Control Aspects of TCP/IP

TCP works over IP to achieve end-to-end reliable transmission of data across a network. TCP flow control uses a sliding window flow-control protocol, such as X.25; however, the window is of a variable size, instead of the fixed window size used by X.25. X.25 is discussed in more detail in Chapter 11. Figure 10-11 illustrates a simplified example of key concepts in the dynamic TCP window flow-control protocol between workstation and a server. The sender starts with a window size equal to that of one TCP segment. The IP datagrams are delivered to the destination workstation, resulting in a delivered segment, which is acknowledged. The sender then increases the window size to two segments. When these two segments are received, they are both acknowledged, and the sender increases the window size to three segments. The network has become congested at this point, and the third segment is lost. The sender detects this by starting a timer whenever a segment is sent. If the timer expires before the acknowledgement of reciept is recieved, then the segment is resent. On such a retransmission time-out, the sender resets its window size to one segment and repeats the above process. Specific implementations will vary, and there is constant fine-tuning of the algorithms and their implementation. Fortunately, the architecture permits the sender and receiver to use different algorithms so improvements can actually be deployed.

The tuning and refinement of the TCP dynamic window flow control protocol has been the subject of a great deal of research. The above operation is often referred to as the Van Jacobson "Slow Start" TCP protocol.

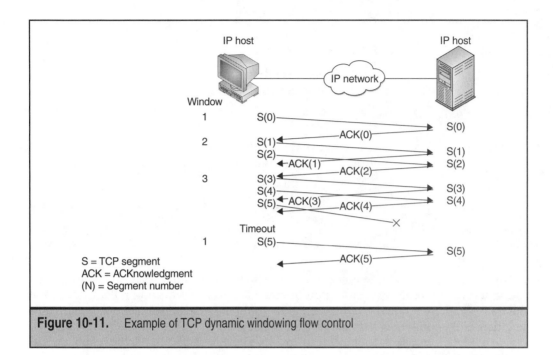

Figure 10-11.   Example of TCP dynamic windowing flow control

User Datagram Protocol (UDP)

UDP is another transport layer protocol. Unlike TCP, UDP is an unreliable, connectionless datagram protocol. UDP offers "best effort" delivery, which means that the arrival of datagrams is not guaranteed, nor is the correct sequencing of delivered packets. UDP is used by applications that do not require an acknowledgement of receipt of data and that typically transmit small amounts of data at one time. UDP offers no solution for verifying that the data reached the receiving end of the network correctly, which allows applications to exchange messages over the network with a minimum of protocol overhead. UDP is very useful if the amount of data being transmitted is small. When there is a need to transfer a small amount of data, the additional overhead used to create a connection and ensure reliable delivery might create more work than required by the application or more work than allowing the application layer to just retransmit the entire data packet if required. Another application that works well with UDP is a query-response application. This is an application that is sending a query to receive a positive response. If a response is not received within a certain amount of time, the application just sends another query. SNMP, which is used for managing devices by sending out requests for configuration settings and alarm reporting, is an example of a query-response application.

Field	Function
Source Port	UDP port of sending host—the sending port value is optional. If not used, it is set to 0.
Destination Port	UDP port destination host—this provides an endpoint for communications.
Message Length	The size of the UDP message—the minimum UDP packet contains only the header information (8 bytes).
Checksum	Verifies that the header is not corrupted.

Table 10-2.   UDP Header

Many applications are designed to provide their own techniques for reliable data delivery and do not require a connection-oriented service, so requiring reliable service at the transport layer would be redundant and would result in additional overhead. Table 10-2 details the components of the 8-byte UDP header.

To use UDP, the application must supply the IP address and UDP port number of the destination application. The port provides a location for sending messages. A port functions as a multiplexed message queue, meaning that it can receive multiple messages at a time. A unique number identifies each port. UDP ports are distinct and separate from TCP ports even though some of them use the same port number, as shown in the following example:

Port	Description
15	NETSTAT—Network Status
53	Domain Name Server
69	TFTP
137	NetBIOS-Name Service
161	SNMP monitor

APPLICATION LAYER

The application layer handles the details of the particular applications and is the layer in which user-access network processes reside. This layer provides functions for users or their programs, and it is highly specific to the application being performed. There are many common TCP/IP applications that almost every implementation provides. We discussed these items in the last section, but let's review for clarity.

▼ Telnet, terminal emulation for remote login

■ FTP, for file transfer

■ TFTP, for file transfer

■ SMTP, for electronic mail

▲ SNMP, for network management

The application layer supports encryption, decryption, compression and decompression and can manage sessions between cooperating applications. The TCP/IP application layer incorporates the three upper layers of the OSI reference model, which include the session, presentation, and application layers. As described in Chapter 3, the application layer represents the purpose for communicating, the presentation layer determines how information is presented to the user, and the session layer is where a session or dialog is created between applications.

ADDRESSING AND ROUTING DESIGN

Now that we have established the topology, it is necessary to go into great detail on network addressing. Multiple techniques will be explored. The examples used take this exercise into a brief discussion of IP address design. The most widely used WAN protocol remains IP. Since IP networks are so predominant, this network design section will focus on the IP address structure and design. There are many books available on addressing, and specifically IP address design. This section is just an introduction to some basic principles of IP address design.

Overview of Addressing

Ubiquitous access to an intelligent data-communications network that spans the globe has become a rallying cry of many users. Users want to access the data network as a large "cloud" and thus be able to talk to any other user connected to that cloud without requiring any knowledge of the internals of the network cloud. A prerequisite to this capability is the assignment of a globally unique or network-recognized unique address to each user. The public voice network has these characteristics, with several lessons from that domain applicable to data networks, such as with the Internet. If a user cannot reach any other user on the public data network, as is taken for granted in telephony and has become a *fait accompli* on the Internet, then the resulting data service will have little utility.

Addresses are used to direct traffic from an origination point to a single or multiple destination point(s). Addresses differ from names in that addresses form a data structure in a communications system that defines the specific physical or logical location of an entity, device, or single access point, whereas *names* provide a humanly readable symbol of a network entity or device. Addresses can be assigned to entities or devices, and a route defines the other devices with which a given address can be reached (thus specifying from and to). Routes can be created to define the other devices or entities from which a given address can be reached. Addressing schemes should be nonproprietary when possible and should be used consistently across the network. In this section, we will discuss various types of common addressing schemes and how they influence the network design.

Levels of Addressing

Addresses can be assigned in either a flat or a hierarchical scheme corresponding to the access and backbone style of design. For example, IP addresses are arbitrary in nature within the scheme of the Internet address classes, while E.164 SMDS addresses are hierarchical with geographic significance (individual IP address assignments can also be hierarchical with geographic significance). It is obviously much easier to control and filter hierarchical addresses, but there is also the disadvantage of requiring change of addresses every time a user changes his or her location.

Types of Addresses

Throughout the technology chapters, many types of addressing have been discussed. A summary is found in Table 10-3.

Each network architecture has its own type of addressing. These architecture-specific addressing schemes must be mapped to any network-addressing scheme (such as network IP address design, which is discussed next) to eliminate any addressing discrepancies. The other architectures have similar address designs.

Address Assignment and Resolution

A key requirement in any communications network is that unique addresses be assigned to each of the entities that want to communicate. This is the case in the telephone network

Technology	Type	Size
Circuit switching	None	None
X.25 packet switching	LCI	12 bits
X.121	LCI	14 BCD digits
Frame relay (ANSI)	DLCI	2 octets (4 for ITU)
802.6	E.164/D15	16 or 48 bits
802.6/SMDS	E.164/D15	Individual 60 bits, group bits, or NPA/NXX
802.X LAN	MAC	16 to 48 bits
ATM	VPI/VCI	8/16 bits

Table 10-3. Addressing by Technology

where every public network–attached phone in the world has a unique number, and in the 48-bit IEEE 802.3 Media Access Control (MAC) assignments that are built into every Ethernet interface card. Every user or "host" in the Internet is assigned a unique IP address.

Ensuring that the address assignments are unique and that they efficiently administer an address space presents some challenges. Not only must addresses be handed out, but also a means for users to return addresses and request blocks of addresses is also required. Furthermore, if there is more than one administrative authority, then the scope of assignments allocated to each administration must be clearly defined. It is sometimes difficult to predict the demand for addresses. For example, area codes have been realigned because the demand differs from what was forecast years ago. If an administrative authority hands out blocks of addresses too freely, then the network can run out of unique addresses well before the limit determined by the number of bits in the addresses, as has occurred with many of the IP address blocks.

Once you have your own address and the address of someone that you wish to communicate with, how do you resolve the address of the desired destination into information about how to get it there? First, consider the following simple analogy. Let's say that you have spoken to an individual on the telephone for the first time and have agreed to meet him or her at a party to which you both have been invited by the same host. Once you arrive at the party, you can find the individual (resolve the address) in one of two ways: you can jump up on stage, grab the microphone, and broadcast your presence, or you can locate the host and ask to be introduced to the individual. Broadcast is commonly used in shared-medium LANs to resolve addresses. A problem arises when the volume of broadcast traffic begins to approach the level of user traffic. The concept of having someone who has the information (the host) resolve the address (match an address with a user) is called a *Domain Name Server (DNS)*.

IP Address Design

IP is by far the most common WAN addressing scheme. The design of an IP network based on the addressing format is a critical issue. A network might have a large number of hosts. If every router in a network needed to know the location of every host, then the routing tables could become quite large. A key concept used in routing IP is that of "subnetting." Subnetting allows the host address space to be broken down into multiple subnetworks by masking the bits in the host address field to create a separate subnetwork for each physical network.

The Internet assigns 32-bit numbers to each user employing an organizational hierarchy. Entire blocks of numbers, which need not have any geographic meaning whatsoever, are assigned to an organization. A user might move geographically, and it becomes the job of the intelligent network to find him or her using a routing discovery protocol. The organization may structure its block of addresses however it chooses, geographically, organizationally, or in some other manner. The Internet has achieved worldwide nearly ubiquitous access and addressing.

IP Address Design Primer

An IP address is a 32-bit integer. This integer is divided into four integers, each 8 bits long. Each of these 8-bit integers is separated by a dot. For example, 198.62.193.32 is a single address. Each of these 8-bit integers can be represented by a decimal (0 through 255), hexidecimal (0 through FF), or binary (00000000 through 11111111) number. Thus, an IP address "A.B.C.D" has one of these three formats:

▼ **Binary** 00000000.00000000.00000000.00000000 through
  11111111.11111111.11111111.11111111

■ **Decimal** 0.0.0.0 through 255.255.255.255

▲ **Hex** 0.0.0.0 through FF.FF.FF.FF

The ranges can also be expressed as

▼ **Binary** 00000000-11111111.00000000-11111111.00000000-11111111.00000000-
  11111111

■ **Decimal** 0-255.0-255.0-255.0-255

▲ **Hex** 0-FF.0-FF.0-FF.0-FF

Classes and Mask

There are five classes of IP addresses, each defined by a mask. These are labeled A, B, C, D, and E. The most common are classes A, B, and C. Network masks divide the network portion from the host portion. An IP address class can be identified by the value in the first octet.

Class A 1–126 = 255.0.0.0

Class B 128–191 = 255.255.0.0

Class C 192–223 = 255.255.255.0

▼ The class A mask has an address structure that allows a possibility of 126 networks (0 is unusable and 127 is reserved for loopback testing), each with greater than 16 million nodes (or hosts).

■ The class B mask has an address structure that allows a possibility of 16,384 networks (or nets), each with 65,534 nodes (or hosts).

▲ The class C mask has an address structure that allows a possibility of more than 2 million networks (or nets), each with 254 nodes (or hosts).

Class A addresses are assigned by IANA for very large corporate networks or to service providers such as AT&T, Sprint, and Bellsouth. Class B addresses are assigned to midsize networks or providers, and class C addresses are for smaller networks. IP address space is controlled by IANA, and domain-name registration is done through numerous organizations with oversight performed by ARIN (which is a Government-registered trademark) that has been leased to ICANN. When address space changes, that is IANA. Most address space requests are made to service providers, since they control the large blocks.

As an example, a class C address of 198.62.193.0-255 would have a network mask of 255.255.255.0.

Let's take an example network where our design calls for four routers (one headquarters and three remote sites), and each site requires up to 10 hosts per router. Figure 10-12 illustrates this network. Our network mask of choice might be a .240 mask. How many networks and hosts does a 240 mask provide? The mask would be represented by .11110000 or 128+64+32+16+0+0+0+0=240. Separating the 1's and the 0's gives us 1111=8+4+2+1=15 less 0 all 1's=14 networks (all 0's and 1's are not used). This leaves four bit positions left for the number of hosts, so the same calculation gives us 14 hosts per network.

16 networks less all 0's and all 1's = 14 networks

16 hosts less all 0's and all 1's = 14 hosts per network

Total hosts throughout = 14×14 = 196 maximum hosts

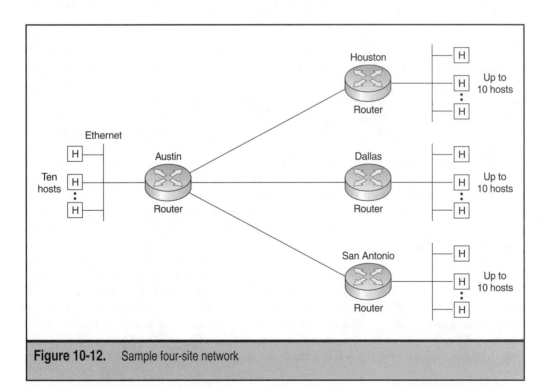

Figure 10-12.   Sample four-site network

Types of hosts include

▼ PCs

■ Workstations

■ Router ports (LAN and WAN)

■ Print servers

▲ Terminal servers

Note that all 0's and all 1's conditions are defined as the network and broadcast address and are not accepted by some router manufacturers, and in some cases will not route these addresses.

Therefore, since we need only a maximum of 10 hosts per site, we can use the mask of 240, since it will allow us to assign up to 14 hosts per site. A mask of 248 would have allowed us only up to 8 hosts per site—11111000 where hosts were 16+8+4+2+1=31−1=30 with 4+2+1=7+0=eight hosts per site. So, if we have a class C address of 198.63.193.0 we can add a mask of 255.255.255.0 and a subnet mask of 255.255.255.240.

There are two main rules to using masks: the mask always moves from left to right in bit order, and every mask needs to contain contiguous 1's (no 0's between 1's). Thus, a mask of 11111111.11111111.11111111.11000000 (or 255.255.255.192) would be correct, but a mask of 11111111.11110000.11111111.11000000 (255.240.255.192) would be incorrect.

IP Address Topologies

There are many methods of implementing an IP address scheme. The first determination is whether the network will follow a hierarchical or matrix topology. With a matrix topology, each user (workstation, host, server) will be assigned a single IP address. Communications will be peer-to-peer. As discussed previously, this style of addressing scheme would be fine for a small network with few users, but becomes unmanageable with large networks.

For larger networks, a more manageable design is the hierarchical topology. IP addresses are assigned in blocks based on geographic region and where (by level) the user resides in the hierarchy. Boundaries are drawn by what are called masks and subnet masks. These masks provide a method of segmenting and reducing the number of network addresses that network devices (access and backbone) need to know and advertise.

For example, the matrix IP addressing would resemble the old style of sending mail, where the sender would simply place a person's name, address, city, and state on the letter. Each post office or stop would pass the mail along to the city, where the person would then be located by name and address. This was fine for a small number of cities with few people where everyone knew each other, but would not work today. The hierarchical mail scheme adds a ZIP code. Today, each city has a minimum of one ZIP code, and larger cities have several ZIP codes. In fact, some companies have their own ZIP codes (XXXXX-YYYY). Now each city can sort mail based on ZIP code (XXXXX), and filter out any mail not destined for that city. Then, each post office in any area of a city can sort based on the last four digits of the code (YYYY) and is able to filter all addresses for that given ZIP code extension. The (XXXXX) portion of the ZIP code acts as the subnet mask, and the (YYYY) acts as the specific user ZIP code extension. This is an example of what masking does for IP addressing. Let's look at some specific examples.

Addresses Based on Topology

Now that the style of topology for the network has been determined and we understand the fundamentals of IP addressing, it must be determined how many addresses will be allocated at each site for each level of the hierarchy. For example:

▼ Each workstation receives one host address

■ Each LAN segment receives 64 host addresses

■ Each floor receives 256 host addresses

▲ Each building receives 1024 host addresses

These numbers indicate a sample number of host addresses per unit of measure. This allocation would be accomplished, along with segmentation and hierarchical design practices, through the use of subnet masks. OSPF routing, one of the more common IGPs, can be used in an autonomous system where subnet masks are required. Routers forward and filter traffic based on subnet addresses. They can forward or filter traffic by mapping the IP destination host address to the router's subnet address. Now we will discuss subnet masks.

Subnet Masks

Once you have identified what network mask you will use (class A, B, or C), and decided on the number of networks and hosts required, it is time to assign addressing within the network. Subnet masks further divide single Internet Assigned Numbers Authority (IANA) registered class A, B, and C network masks into multiple hosts and "subnetworks." Subnet masks are used in conjunction with network masks as follows:

Take the class B address 108.10.0.0. The network portion of this number is actually 108.10. The network mask of 255.255.0.0 defines two positions, .0.0 to .255.255, to use for host addressing. This allows your 108.10.0.0 network to define up to a total of 255.255.0.0. This identifies that 16 bits belong to the network portion, and 16 bits belong to the host portion. With 16 bits in the host portion, we can support $2^{(16)}-2$ or 65,534 hosts.

Let's go back to our first example. We are building a network with four sites and up to 10 hosts per site. The class C address we are assigned is 198.62.193.0. Using the cross-reference table in Appendix C, we use a 240 subnet mask to further divide this class C mask into usable chunks of addresses that accurately reflect our mix of subnets and hosts. This allows us to have up to 14 nets with 14 hosts each (two nets and two host addresses are reserved). The 14 network addresses we have available are

■ 198.62.193.16 to 198.62.193.31

■ 198.62.193.32 to 198.62.193.47

■ 198.62.193.48 to 198.62.193.63

■ 198.62.193.64 to 198.62.193.79

■ 198.62.193.80 to 198.62.193.95

■ 198.62.193.128 to 198.63.193.143

■ 198.62.193.144 to 198.63.193.159

■ 198.62.193.160 to 198.63.193.175

■ 198.62.193.176 to 198.63.193.191

■ 198.62.193.192 to 198.63.193.207

- 198.62.193.96 to 198.62.193.111
- 198.62.193.112 to 198.62.193.127

- 198.62.193.208 to 198.63.193.223
- 198.62.193.224 to 198.63.193.237

We keep 198.62.193 through .15 and 198.62.193.238 through .255 reserved. We start by assigning a block of 14 network addresses available to each subnet or site. We first assign the subnet 198.62.193.10 through 198.62.193.31 to the Austin site. We see in the upper right of the Figure 10-13 the assignment of the 198.62.193.32 through 198.62.193.47 subnet to Houston. We continue on with the assignment of .48 through .63 to Dallas and .64 through .79 to San Antonio. We next assign subnet masks to each network circuit. Austin to Houston is assigned the .80 to .95 subnet, Austin to Dallas the .96 subnet mask, and Austin to San Antonio the .112 subnet mask. The subnet mask for each of these is 255.255.255.240. Note that each network point-to-point circuit is now a subnet unto itself. Since each end of the subnet requires only one address, with our subnet masking scheme of 14 addresses per subnet, 12 addresses are

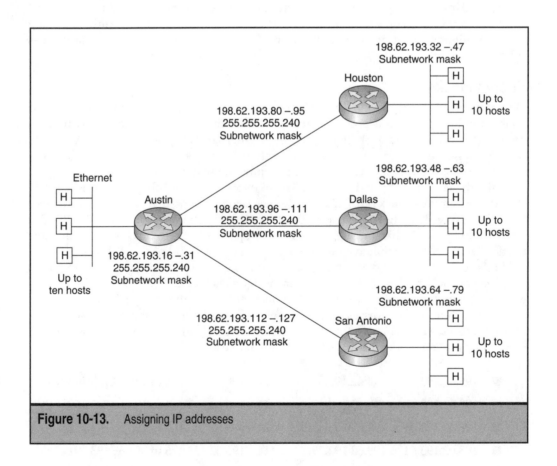

Figure 10-13.   Assigning IP addresses

wasted per WAN link subnet. We will see later how variable-length subnet masking can help us reclaim some of these addresses. Also note that we already used up seven of the total 14 subnets.

We next assign specific addresses within each subnet to the hosts within that subnet, as shown in Figure 10-14. Remember that a host can be a workstation, server, or a LAN or WAN router port. We reference our same network example illustrated now in Figure 10-14. We first take the WAN circuit between Austin and Houston. Within this 198.62.193.80 subnet, we have 14 addresses we could assign: 198.62.193.81 to 198.62.193.94 (.80 and .95 are reserved). The port on the Austin end is assigned the address 198.62.193.81. The port on the Houston end is assigned the address 198.62.193.82.

We continue to assign the other two WAN circuits their respective addresses. Note again how wasteful this address assignment is. We lose 12 out of the 14 addresses available across each of the three WAN links, for a total of 36 wasted addresses.

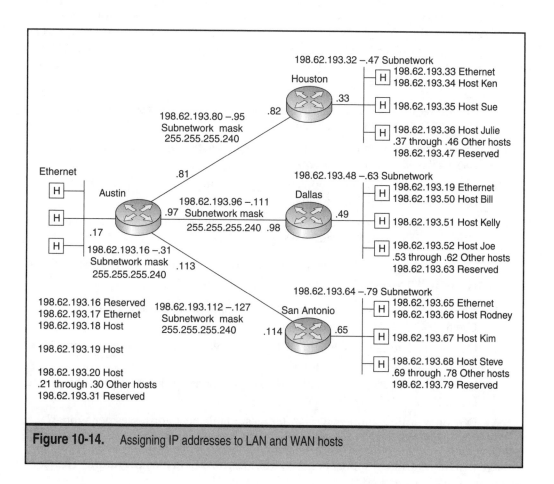

Figure 10-14. Assigning IP addresses to LAN and WAN hosts

We next assign addresses to our workstation hosts. We start in the Houston LAN subnet. We assign the first address in our block of 14 (within *this* subnet mask) 198.62.193.33 to the Ethernet LAN port. We continue to assign three more addresses, .34, .35, and .36, to the three hosts (Ken, Sue, and Julie) attached to that Ethernet segment. Note that we have the potential to add up to 10 more addresses within this subnet. We then move to the next subnet, Dallas, where we assign .49 to the Ethernet segment and .50, .51, and .52 to Bill, Kelly, and Joe hosts, respectively. Finally, we assign addresses within the San Antonio subnet to the Ethernet segment (.65), Rodney (.66), Kim (.67), and Steve (.68). The same address assignment process would be performed at the Austin location.

This design works well over private line networks or when the size of the network remains under 14 routers. But what happens when the network grows larger? Or is placed over a WAN service such as FR? Larger network masks can be used, or you can resort to other subnet options.

Optimal mask and subnet mask design depends on the type and size of your network. One method of assigning masks is based on location of devices. For example, assign one network mask for the entire network, one subnet for each device and WAN link, and an individual address to each WAN port, LAN port, and workstation. A subnet could be an entire network, or an individual site with X workstations. Let's look at some examples using a class C network mask:

▼   Do you require 64 subnets with four assignable host addresses per subnet? Use a 255.255.255.252 subnet mask.

■   Do you require 32 subnets with eight assignable host addresses per subnet? Use a 255.255.255.248 subnet mask.

■   Do you require 16 subnets with 16 assignable host addresses per subnet? Use a 255.255.255.240 subnet mask.

▲   Do you require two subnets with 128 assignable host addresses per subnet? Use a 255.255.255.128 subnet mask.

What if you are running a much larger network with many more users per subnet? Try using a class B network mask with the following subnets:

▼   Do you require 64 subnets with 1024 assignable host addresses per subnet? Use a 255.255.252.000 subnet mask.

■   Do you require 32 subnets with 2048 assignable host addresses per subnet? Use a 255.255.248.000 subnet mask.

■   Do you require 16 subnets with 4096 assignable host addresses per subnet? Use a 255.255.240.000 subnet mask.

▲   Do you require 2 subnets with 32,000 assignable host addresses per subnet? Use a 255.255.128.000 subnet mask.

Are you running out of subnet or host addresses, now or in the near future? Then look at variable-length subnet addressing.

Appendix D shows all available subnet masks and their corresponding number of assignable addresses per subnet for class A, B, and C network masks. This table should come in handy when you are designing IP networks and subnetworks.

Variable-Length Subnet Masks

Variable-length subnet masks (VLSMs) are used for dividing subnets into variable-size subnets for more efficient use of available addresses. For example, VLSMs break up a class C address into uneven pieces to gain more optimal address assignment. In this manner, greater granularity can be imposed *between nets* on a restricted number of addresses within the entire class C mask.

Using the last example, we now want to reclaim some of the addresses we lost to the WAN links (remember we lost 12 addresses within each WAN link subnet mask). To review, we started with a 198.62.193.0 network mask. From there, we used a subnet mask of 255.255.255.224. This subnet mask gave us 14 subnets with 14 hosts per subnet. We then proceeded to assign the .80 through .95 subnet mask addresses to the Houston-to-Austin link and determined we would lose 12 addresses in the process. If we now take that 198.62.193.80 through .95 subnet, we can assign it a "stubnet" mask of 255.255.255.252. In doing so, we split a .240 subnet mask supporting 14 hosts into .252 subnets (also called "stubnets") supporting four networks with four hosts each. The addressing structure to accomplish this is shown in Figure 10-15. We now can use the .84, .88, and .92 stubnets for *three* WAN links instead of just *one*, using the .89, .90, .93, and .94 host addresses for two other WAN links. In this manner, we just saved ten addresses per WAN link over the previous .240 subnet scheme. This is compared with using just the .240 subnet mask in Figure 10-14. Variable subnet masking is valuable for designs using FR because each PVC's DLCI requires its own subnet mask number, and this is one way of extending a limited number of addresses.

Design Rules: Subnets and FR

Routing protocols such as RIPv1 and IGRP allow only one network address per link. Therefore, there is a problem when trying to use a single network mask across a WAN that allows multiple virtual circuits within a single physical circuit. For example, in FR, a router has multiple virtual ports aggregated within a single physical port. To IP, each of the virtual circuit (PVC) ports looks like a single physical port (no difference between a physical and logical circuit to IP). The other problem is the overhead incurred when RIPv1 broadcasts across a FR network. If using a FR network in this above design scenario, both split horizons and poison reverse (as covered earlier in the "Distance-Vector Routing Protocol" section) must be used.

Subnet masking is not allowed when using RIPv1. RIPv1 views and understands addresses only from its nearest neighbor. It does not understand subnet mask addresses, because the subnet mask is not part of its limited protocol header. If subnet masks are used in conjunction with RIPv1, there is a high probability that hosts will not be able to reach certain other hosts. The subnet mask is assumed from the mask assigned to the interface receiving the RIPv1 packet. It is best to avoid using RIPv1 in a network with subnet masks. The alterna-

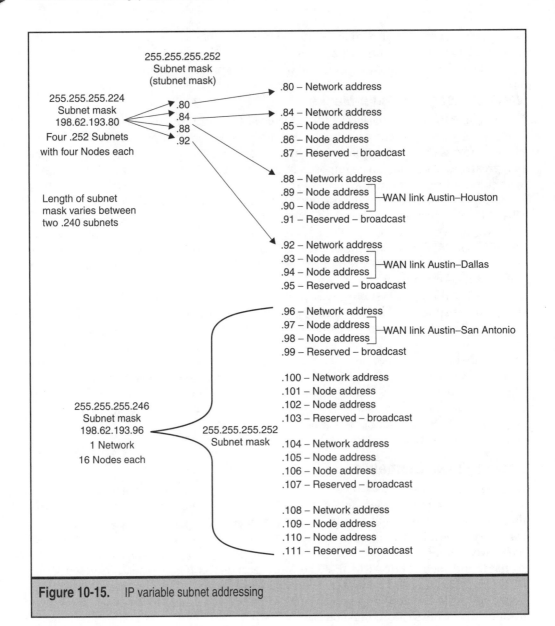

Figure 10-15. IP variable subnet addressing

tive is to use a routing protocol, such as OSPF or IGRP, that uses a packet structure that comprehends both destination host address and network (or subnetwork) address.

Subnetwork masks that have many subnets, such as .252 and .240, are typically used when designing large, point-to-point networks with hub or star topologies. Larger masks such as 255.255.255.0 (class C subnet masks) are typically used in fully meshed networks.

OSPF versus RIPv1 and Default Gateways

Every IP addressing scheme should be designed in conjunction with the routing protocol. Note that it is more efficient to use RIPv1 routing protocol in the local area subnets and OSPF in the WAN. The fact that summaries have been used in OSPF reduces the amount of address updates which transit the network. RIPv1 is an acceptable routing protocol to use in the local area network because LANs have a lot of bandwidth and can tolerate the periodic RIPv1 updates. Also, most LAN-attached devices support RIPv1 (OSPF is not implemented on most hosts). Many network administrators do not support routing protocols on local segments to reduce the reachability and problems associated with advertising multiple devices as routers. If a single router is the only interface to the LANs within an area, and if there is only one interface per LAN, RIPv1 routing is not required. A default workstation gateway entry will allow the workstations to find problems with the network through a default gateway address (in our example, the router port to which the LAN connects).

If the packet has a remote destination, the device will send it to a specified IP address on the router (default gateway IP address). Note that the network mask must be the same across the entire network. If all networks and hosts are directly attached to the same router a routing protocol is not required. The default gateway function can be used in cases where each LAN attached to the router has only one interface. Remember that with RIPv1, each LAN device can both send and receive RIPv1 updates.

IP routes effectively between subnets, but not *within* a subnet. Thus, a network may have different routing protocols within the subnet than those used outside the subnet. Try not to use RIPv1 over the IP backbone, because it generates too much overhead (and the larger the network, the more the overhead) due to transmission of entire routing tables as updates every 30 seconds. Also, RIPv1 does not have password authentication and does not work well if you are using a variable subnet mask within the network. OSPF uses filtering or subnet masking to filter out what addresses are broadcast to the entire network. Filtering can be used on RIPv1 as well. Effective filtering and masking can create efficiencies in the network design.

Global addressing varies based on the service, technology, and protocol being used. In a mixed environment, IP addresses are individually mapped to each technology's specific addressing scheme (such as to DLCIs for FR).

Mask Effect on Higher-Layer Protocols

Network and subnet masks are transparent to higher-layer protocols. If TCP is running on two hosts connected by one or more local and/or wide area subnets using IP, IP does not really care about the masks employed. The subnet is, in effect, transparent to it. It is up to the routing protocols such as OSPF to understand where each IP address is located within its network and subnet.

Address Management

Accurate address management is key to the effective running of a network. The roles of address management include

▼ Assign network, node, and host addresses

■ Maintain an up-to-date database of all addresses

■ Track addresses as they move around the network

■ Troubleshoot IP address conflicts

■ Reassign inactive addresses

▲ Maintain each user with a unique address

Address management works best when its policies are centrally administered. Thus, there are also protocols such as Dynamic Host Configuration Protocol (DHCP) and BootP that automate the process of assigning addresses on-demand. Every user device typically does not use an IP address at the same time. These tools are good for mobile workers and telecommuting and for the conservation of addresses.

CIDR

CIDR (pronounced "cider") provides the network designer a method to slow down large scale address allocation and limit routing table overflow in large networks. The following RFCs define the various aspects and implementations of CIDR:

▼ **RFC 1467**   Status of CIDR Deployment in the Internet

■ **RFC 1517**   Applicability Statement for the Implementation of CIDR

■ **RFC 1518**   An Architecture for IP Address Allocation with CIDR

■ **RFC 1519**   CIDR: an Address Assignment and Aggregation Strategy

■ **RFC 1520**   Exchanging Routing Information Across Provider Boundaries in the CIDR Environment

▲ **RFC 1817**   CIDR and Classful Routing.

CIDR is a means of expressing networks in terms of prefix length. Protocols that support CIDR are referred to as *classless* protocols, as opposed to a *classful* protocol such as RIPv1 and IGRP, because there are no class boundaries imposed on the address scheme. OSPF, RIPv2, IS-IS, and (with certain caveats) EIGRP are classless protocols because they do not care about network prefixes that are shorter than their "classful" position would indicate. For example, 192.1.0.0 with a mask of 255.255.0.0 is a CIDR classless notation while 192.1.0.0 with a mask of 255.255.255.0 is classful notation. CIDR replaces the address class requirement with an *IP prefix*. This prefix is used to perform route aggregation, where one route in effect summarizes many original IP network numbers. This allows allocation of addresses in bite size chunks rather than large classes to reduce wasting addresses. The benefits to CIDR include

▼ Continuous, uninterrupted growth of the Internet

■ Lesser requirement to update external routing tables

■ Saves routing table space

■ Reduces rapid changes in routing

■ Reduces CPU load of transit nodes

■ Helps the Internet reduce routing overload

▲ Increases likelihood that your routes will be carried by all ISPs

REVIEW

This chapter completes a discussion on the physical through transport layer protocols spanning both telecommunications and data communications. This chapter focused on bridge, router, and higher-level protocols. Bridge and router protocols are used to determine how information is transferred. We examined many of the more popular routing protocols in detail, showing their advantages and disadvantages. The predominant network and transport protocols associated with the TCP/IP suite were discussed such as ARP, IP, TCP, and UDP. Several techniques for network addressing were covered, including a detailed example of IP address design using a network mask and subnet masks. Details on non-IP protocols addressing were previously covered in their respective technology chapters.

CHAPTER 11

Mature Packet Switched Protocols

This chapter covers mature packet switched protocols, or what some would refer to as "old" or "legacy" packet protocols. History is a great teacher, and history often tends to repeat itself—and it has quite often in packet switching protocols. X.25 packet switching was the packet solution for the late '70s and '80s and the precursor to modern packet technologies such as frame relay (FR) and ATM. X.25 packet switching is still used today throughout the world, especially in countries that have legacy copper infrastructures, but is rarely seen in the United States due to the predominance of low-error fiber infrastructure. In fact, FR has been referred to as "X.25 on a diet," as many of the overhead error-correction, retransmission, and flow-control functions inherent in X.25 are no longer required (or have already been performed by higher-layer protocols) when transporting packets over a fiber-optic infrastructure.

In addition to X.25, Switch Multimegabit Data Service (SMDS) is covered. SMDS was the initial cell-switching offering and used some strengths of X.25 in supporting public addressing and network-to-network interfaces. SMDS in many ways was IP grown up—sporting security, reliability, and access classes not available in native IP networks. SMDS today still has some geographic strongholds but the service never achieved a fraction of the traction of FR and has been left in the dust by the new packet/frame/cell-switching standard of FR, ATM, and private IP network service offerings that provide QoS, class of service (CoS), and security.

BACKGROUND: EARLY REASONS FOR PACKET SWITCHING

Several factors created the need for packet switching: the need to extend reliable transmission of voice and data over unreliable and noisy transmission facilities, the need to create standard interfaces and protocols for communications between computing devices, the more efficient use of expensive transmission (WAN) bandwidth, and the efficient interconnection of a large number of computing devices.

The early days of computing saw the development of a new interface and data-communication protocol with each computer. Large computer manufacturers, such as IBM and DEC, developed protocols that were standardized across, yet proprietary to, their products (generally speaking). One of the goals of the Open System Interconnection (OSI) standardization effort was to enable standard computer communication interfaces and protocols in a multiple-vendor environment.

We will consider any form of communication—video, voice—to be data. It was first decided to break data into some form of protocol data unit (PDU), and in this case a "packet" was chosen. Each packet was designed to include a cyclical redundancy check (CRC) field that detected bit errors. If a packet was received in error (as measured by an unsuccessful CRC), then the packet switching protocol was defined to continue to resend the packet(s) in error until each one was successfully received. An ingress and egress buffering system was used to queue packets until acknowledgment of successful receipt or failure notification was received. If failure notification was received, the packet was requeued. This process was performed on every packet and by every switch in the network. This queuing system, while providing reliable transmissions, could cause excessive application delay. The advent of low bit-error-rate digital and fiber-optic transmission media greatly reduced the number of transmission errors and allowed this function to be performed more cost-effectively in the end systems rather than in each WAN packet switch.

Early packet switching systems were designed for terminal-to-host communications. The typical transaction involved the user's typing a few lines, or even just a few characters, and then sending a transaction to the host. The host would then return anywhere from a few lines to possibly an entire screen's worth of data. This terminal-to-host application traffic pattern was very bursty; that is, the peak transmittal rate of each terminal was much greater than its average rate. In a department with many users on terminals, rarely would all users/terminals be transmitting at exactly the same time (maybe 25 percent at the same time). This statistical nature would further add to the burst ratio across the WAN. Packet switching allows many such bursty users to be statistically multiplexed onto expensive transmission facilities.

As the number of computers, applications, and people using computers increased, the need for interconnection increased, and the bandwidth usage per application increased, the need for bandwidth accelerated. Similar to the growth in telephony, it quickly became absurd to have a dedicated circuit to connect every pair of computers that needed to communicate. Packet switching and routing protocols were developed to connect terminals to hosts and hosts to hosts, where a host could range from a mainframe computer to a personal computer running IP.

History of Packet Switching

The history of packet switching reads like a who's who of networking icons. It includes names such as Paul Baran, Lawrence Roberts, Leonard Kleinrock, Robert Kahn, and Vinton Cerf, two of whom the authors had the pleasure of working with at MCI.

Packet switching as described by Paul Baran in 1962:

> "Packet switching is the breaking down of data into datagrams or packets that are labeled to indicate the origin and the destination of the information and the forwarding of these packets from one computer to another computer until the information arrives at its final destination computer. This was crucial to the realization of a computer network. If packets are lost at any given point, the message can be resent by the originator."

In 1957–1958, Dwight D. Eisenhower formed the Advanced Research Projects Agency (ARPA) in response to the USSR's launching of Sputnik, the first artificial earth satellite. In July 1961, Leonard Kleinrock at MIT published the first paper on packet switching theory, followed by the first book on the subject in 1964.

In 1965, Larry Roberts and Tom Merrill connected a computer in Massachusetts to a computer in California with a low-speed dial-up telephone line, creating the first wide-area computer network ever built (where was broadband when you needed it?). This experiment concluded that the circuit-switching telephone system was totally inadequate for the job and confirmed Kleinrock's conviction of the need for packet switching.

In 1967, Larry Roberts, who was now the chief scientist at ARPA, presented his plan for the ARPANET (a data network connecting various ARPA-funded universities and research facilities) at a conference and learned about two other parallel paths of packet switching development that he was unaware of:

▼ "A Digital Communications Network for Computers" published in 1967 by Donald Davies and Roger Scantlebury of National Physical Laboratory (NPL)

▲ "On Distributed Communications: I. Introduction to Distributed Communications Network" published in 1964 by Paul Baran of RAND group

In 1968, Roberts and the ARPA-funded community had refined the overall structure and specification for the ARPANET and released a Request for Quote (RFQ) for the packet switch called Interface Message Processor (IMP). Bolt, Beranek, and Newman (BBN) won the RFQ, delivering and installing the first IMP in 1969 at UCLA, where Leonard Kleinrock was now a professor and Vinton Cerf was a graduate student. Robert Kahn, who is the coauthor of the original TCP/IP protocol with Vinton Cerf, played a major role in the development of the IMP while at BBN.

In 1972, the first e-mail program was created by Ray Tomlinson of BBN and ARPA was renamed Defense Advanced Research Projects Agency (DARPA). In 1973, Larry Roberts left DARPA to become the CEO of Telenet, which was the first packet switching carrier.

In 1976, X.25 was the recommended protocol by the International Telegraph and Telephone Consultative Committee (CCITT), which was renamed the International Telecommunications Union (ITU) in 1993.

X.25 is still in use today in many parts of the world, as are derivatives of X.25 such as FR that removed the network retransmission capabilities. Furthermore, in developed countries, the low error rates of the transmission media underlying modern packet switching networks eliminates the need for network retransmission. X.25 continues to be a service offering throughout the world but is rarely seen in the United States. Figure 11-1 shows an X.25 packet switched network.

History of SMDS

The story begins in 1982 when the IEEE was working on standards for transmission of voice, compressed video, LAN interconnectivity, and bulk-data transfer within metropolitan areas. A metropolitan area network (MAN) is roughly defined as being within a the diameter of a city. These ideas for a MAN were presented to the cable television (CATV) community, which didn't tune into the idea. Burroughs National and Plessey initiated a second effort in 1985 with the slotted ring concept. This effort died when the leveraged buyout of Sperry Univac cut required funding, and again MAN technology waited. The next effort began with a Bell Labs MAN standard proposal and was developed in parallel with the ex-Burroughs FDDI venture called MST (multiplexed slot and token). This new Bellcore MAN standard became the IEEE Project 802.6 in the late '80s.

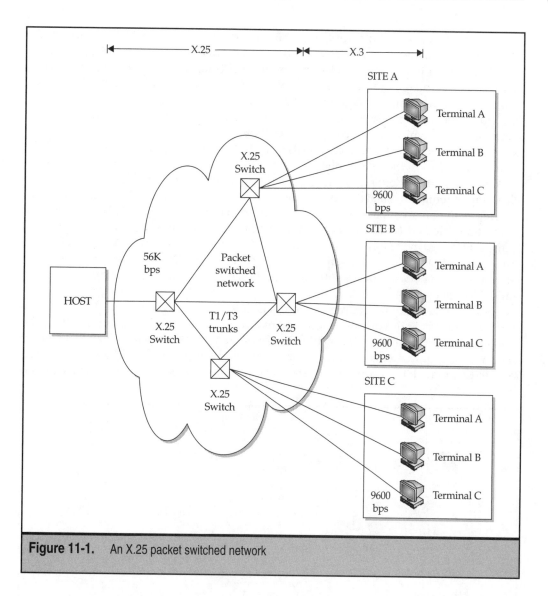

Figure 11-1.   An X.25 packet switched network

The IEEE 802.6 standard is based on the distributed queue dual bus (DQDB) technology. The DQDB architecture (which resembles the Bell Technology Lab's dual coax with reservation MAN architecture, called Fastnet) was invented at the University of Western Australia, and hardware was first produced by QPSX LTD (a University of Western Australia and Telecom Australia spin-off). The IEEE 802.6 DQDB standard defines connectionless data-transport service using 53-byte slots to provide integrated data, video, and voice service over a MAN.

Bellcore developed SMDS service definitions based on the IEEE 802.6 standard. The SMDS definitions detailed service definition and carrier-to-carrier interfaces as well as switch-to-switch interfaces. An example of an SMDS network supporting these traffic types is shown in Figure 11-2. This cell-switching architecture combines the best of two worlds: (1) connectionless datagram public data-transfer services similar to packet switching and (2) speeds in excess of 155 Mbps. SMDS also provides some ingress and egress security features, which are covered in the "Source Address Validation and Address Screening" section later in this chapter. The SMDS implementations based on the IEEE 802.6 standard were the first public services to use ATM-like cell-switching technology.

Cell switching is defined in terms of standards, underlying architectures, initial services implementation (such as SMDS), and protocols. Cell switching has since taken two development paths: connectionless data transport in the form of IEEE 802.6 (DQDB), and connection-oriented (which can offer connectionless and connection-oriented protocol transport classes) in the form of Asynchronous Transfer Mode (ATM). SMDS services use the IEEE 802.6 DQDB CL (connectionless) service. While SMDS provides LAN/WAN interconnection, a network design offering SMDS service over a DQDB architecture is not limited to a geographical area.

SMDS deployment had minimal success isolated to a few geographical areas due to the rapid success and worldwide implementations of FR and ATM services hitting the market soon after SMDS was available. FR provided a simpler (yet less flexible) protocol that met the requirements for quality of service and speed yet could be provided at a lower cost and with nonproprietary hardware and software. Many would also agree that

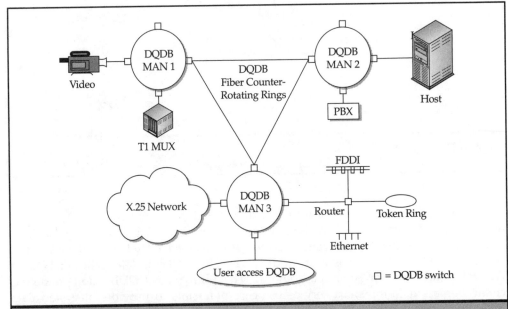

Figure 11-2.   An SMDS network supporting carrier-to-carrier and switch-to-switch interfaces

SMDS pricing schemes were too complex for many users that turned to the simplicity of FR and IP. As history repeats itself, we find that the best protocol rarely wins, and in the SMDS-FR battle, FR and IP proved to be easier to implement, more cost-effective, and in retrospect, marketed more effectively than SMDS. And, as history shows, FR and IP were much more successful despite its functionality inferiority to SMDS.

ITU RECOMMENDATION X.25

In the beginning, there were proprietary protocols, then the CCITT (now ITU) standardized upon the first international layered protocol: X.25. The ITU X.25 packet switching standard, along with a number of other "X dot" standards, was developed to provide a reliable system of data transport for computer communications over the noisy, unreliable analog-grade transmission medium. The early packet switches topped out at 56 kbps with packet size limits, while today's switches provide networking speeds of DS1 and E1 (and, in some cases, DS3 trunking), with packet sizes up to 4096 bytes.

The ITU set of "X dot" standards for the physical, link, and packet level protocols shown in Figure 11-3 are known collectively as X.25. The three levels of X.25 structure maps to the first three layers of the OSIRM. This is an important concept, in that X.25 provides the protocol functions of physical transport for bit flow, creating a managed link

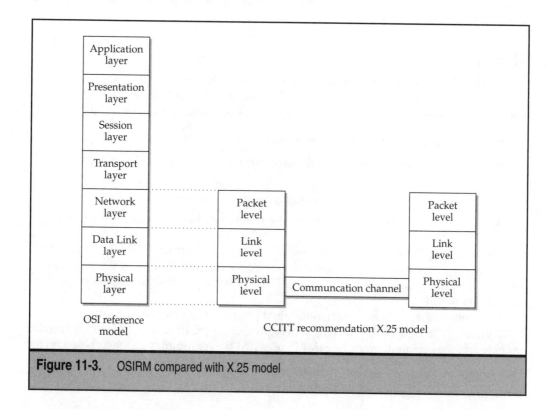

Figure 11-3. OSIRM compared with X.25 model

layer protocol for reliable transfer, having an international network-layer addressing scheme, and even contains some Layer 4 functionality in the packet ordering and retransmission functions at each X.25 switch (services today performed for IP networks by the Layer 4 TCP protocol).

Before covering the three levels, we need to define X.25 network devices, as shown in Figure 11-4:

▼ **Data Terminal Equipment (DTE)** is the end-user equipment. DTE can be terminals, personal computers, or network hosts and are typically located on the premise of individual subscribers.

▲ **Data Circuit-terminating Equipment (DCE)** is the carrier equipment. DCE equipment is typically the packet switch.

NOTE: A modern-day analogy of a DTE in the IP world is a personal computer (also called a "host") or a router. A modern-day analogy of a DCE in the IP world is a modem or a CSU/DSU.

Physical Level

The physical level of X.25 deals with the electrical, mechanical, and functional interface between the DTE and the DCE. The physical layer includes several standards such as X.21, X.21bis, V.24, V.35, and RS-232.

Link Level

The link level ensures reliable transfer of data between the DTE and the DCE by transmitting the data as a sequence of frames. Each frame is an independent unit with an address, control information, and data. The link level performs the following functions:

▼ Transfer of data in an efficient and timely fashion

■ Synchronization of the link to ensure that the receiver is in step with the transmitter

■ Detection of transmission errors and recovery from such errors

▲ Identification and reporting of procedural errors to higher levels, for recovery

The link level is based on the High-level Data Link Control (HDLC) ISO standard. X.25 modified this and initially called it a link access procedure (LAP), subsequently revising it again to align with changes in HDLC resulting in the link access procedure, balanced (LAPB).

X.25 network access can be accomplished over a single circuit or multiple circuits between the DTE and DCE. The single link procedure (SLP) uses standard ISO HDLC framing and the multilink procedure (MLP) uses LAPB over multiple channels based on the

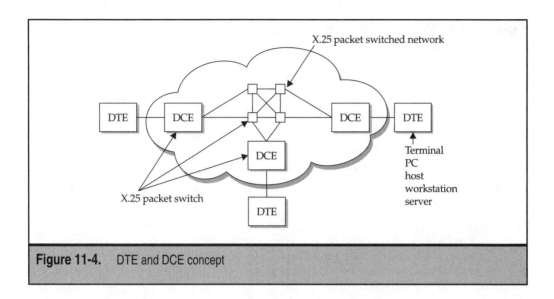

Figure 11-4. DTE and DCE concept

ISO MLP standard. An example of the SLP frame (HDLC frame structure) is shown in Figure 11-5. A breakout of the multilink procedure (MLP) frame differences is also shown. Note that this is the same frame structure defined in the ANSI ADCCP specifications.

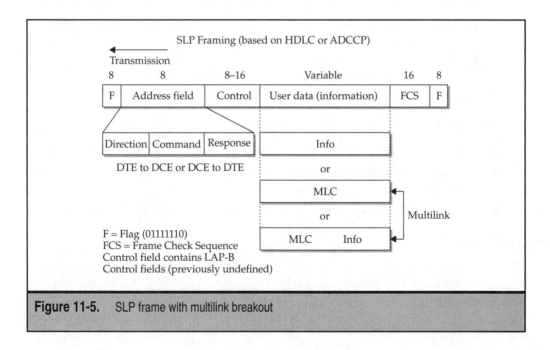

Figure 11-5. SLP frame with multilink breakout

Link Access Protocol, Balanced (LAPB)

The LAPB protocol uses the following frame structure as defined in Figure 11-6.

▼ The Flag fields indicate the start and end of the frame.

■ The Address field contains the address of the DTE/DCE; it is most important in multidrop lines, where it is used to identify one of the terminals.

■ The Control field contains sequence numbers, commands, and responses for controlling the data flow between the DTE and the DCE. The field length is one or two octets in length in the extended mode.

■ The User Data field is the X.25 (which contains the user's higher-level protocol info and application data).

▲ The Frame Check Sequence (FCS) field indicates whether or not errors occur in the transmission. The FCS is computed by the sender and is recomputed by the receiver to detect if there were any bit errors in the received LAPB.

There are three kinds of frames:

1. **Information**   This kind of frame contains the actual information being transferred. The control field in these frames contains the frame sequence number.

2. **Supervisory**   There are various types of supervisory frames:

   ■ **Receive ready**   Acknowledgment frame indicating the next frame expected

   ■ **Reject**   Negative acknowledgment frame used to indicate transmission error detection

   ■ **Receive not ready (RNR)**   Operates similar to receive ready but tells the sender to stop sending due to temporary problems

3. **Unnumbered**   This kind of frame is used only for control purposes.

LAPB also provides the following commands:

▼ **Disconnect (DISC)**   Allows the machine to announce that it is going down

■ **Set normal response time (SNRT)**   Allows a machine that has just come back on line to announce its presence

▲ **Frame reject (FRMR)**   Used to indicate that a protocol violation has been detected

Packet Level

The packet level standard is called the X.25 Packet Layer Protocol (PLP), which resides at the network layer of the OSIRM. The packet level provides procedures for handling the following services:

▼ **Switched virtual circuit (SVC)** is a temporary association between two DTEs. The DTE signals to the network to set up a connection to the other DTE. Once the connection is established, data is passed. When the data is completed, the connection is taken down. SVCs are like the DTE devices making phone calls, having a conversation, and then one of the DTE devices hanging up.

NOTE: SVCs compare with phone calls over the Public Switched Telephone Network (PSTN), where the DTE is the phone receiver, and calls are virtual circuits created across multiple voice switches.

- **Permanent virtual circuit (PVC)** is a permanent association between two DTEs. No connection setup is required, as the connection is always up.

- **Datagrams (DGs)** are self-contained user data units, containing sufficient information to be routed to the destination DTE without establishing a call. The data units are transmitted one at a time with no guarantee of final or orderly delivery. Each datagram must contain complete address and control information to enable it to be delivered to the proper destination DTE.

- **Fast select** is a service that enables control packets to carry data as well as setting up the connection/virtual circuit.

- ▲ **The other services** level/layer provides the call setup and clearing procedures required for virtual circuit service and deals with flow control to ensure that a DTE does not overwhelm the other users with packets to send and maintains timely and efficient delivery of packets.

Each packet to be transferred across the DTE/DCE interface is carried or packaged within the data link layer HDLC (LAPB) frame information field, as shown in Figure 11-6.

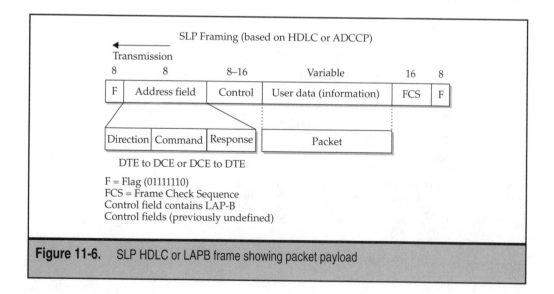

Figure 11-6.   SLP HDLC or LAPB frame showing packet payload

The SLP HDLC or LAPB frame (Layer 2) has the (Layer 3) protocol of X.25 in the User Data/Information field of the Layer 2 LAPB frame.

X.25 Level 3 Packet Format

The X.25 packet level (OSIRM Layer 3) is composed of a header and a user data, or information, field, as shown in Figure 11-7. The qualifier (Q) bit allows the transport layer to separate control data from user data. The D bit is used in delivery confirmation during call setup. The next two bits indicate the packet type, with *01* indicating a data packet with three-octet header. A four-octet header is also standardized. The X.25 packet level address has a 4-bit group number and an 8-bit logical channel number, together forming a 12-bit logical channel number (LCN), or virtual circuit number. Virtual circuit zero is reserved, and therefore there can be up to $2^{12} - 1 = 4095$ virtual circuits. The packet layers receive and send sequence numbers (RSN and SSN) that provide packet level flow control. The more (M) bit supports segmentation and reassembly by identifying packet segments with a value of one, with the last segment having a value of zero.

USER CONNECTIVITY

ITU-T Recommendations X.3, X.28, and X.29 are defined as link-level protocols that provide DTE with asynchronous terminal interfaces to X.25 networks. These standards are for interactive DTE, which do not support X.25 synchronous capability and can communicate only via low-speed asynchronous mode. X.25 also provides synchronous user connectivity, and X.32 provides synchronous dial-up capability. Figure 11-8 shows three

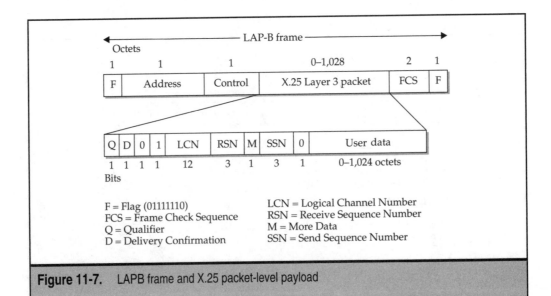

Figure 11-7.   LAPB frame and X.25 packet-level payload

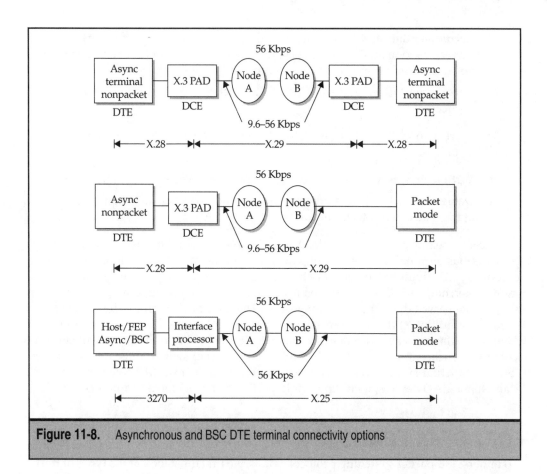

Figure 11-8.   Asynchronous and BSC DTE terminal connectivity options

examples of asynchronous and BSC DTE terminal connectivity options to an X.25 packet switching network. Each of the interface protocols is defined as follows:

▼ **Recommendation X.121**   Defines the international numbering plan for packet switching networks.

■ **Recommendation X.28**   Defines the operational control of these functions between the (nonpacket mode) character mode terminal DTE device and the DCE packet assembler/disassembler (PAD). Through the use of X.28 protocol, the DTE (through the PAD) establishes a virtual circuit, initializes the service, and exchanges the control and data packets. The X.28 protocol manages these controls and exchanges of data flows between the DTE and PAD through a terminal-user command language.

■ **Recommendation X.29**   Defines the same controls, but for the host computer destination (or origination). Information exchange can happen at anytime over the virtual call. X.29 uses machine commands that identify packets between the host and the PAD.

■ **Recommendation X.3** Defines a PAD concentrator function for start-mode or character-mode DTE devices. These terminal management functions include the bps rate, terminal specifics, flow control, and escape sequences.

▲ **Recommendation X.32** Defines X.25 synchronous dial-up mode for DTE services.

There are two types of user-to-network interfaces, each of which span all three OSIRM layers:

▼ **Virtual circuits** include PVC and SVC and ensure sequencing of user data.

▲ **Datagrams** are messages unto themselves and do not ensure sequencing of the data as virtual circuits do.

Packet assembler/dissembler (PAD) is defined by X.3 as taking asynchronous inputs from various terminals and assembling their individual transmissions into a single, synchronous X.25 circuit to the packet network. The PAD acts as a point-to-point statistical multiplexer, and PAD buffers are used to accumulate and accommodate the information streams not passed due to network congestion. The same device can also be used to disassemble (demultiplex) the X.25 synchronous channel into individual asynchronous user interfaces. Many packet switches have the PAD functionality built into them, and provide for asynchronous user ports directly into the packet switch, thus, the switch performs a function similar to the front-end processor and host. More common are the stand-alone PAD devices, including single-port cards for personal computers.

THEORY OF OPERATIONS

To understand packet switching protocol details, we first must look at the types of traffic best suited for transport over a packet switch network and their characteristics. We can then discuss the basic operation of switching packets between DTE.

Traffic Characteristics

Most data transmissions have a duration of less than five seconds, attributable to what is called *bursty traffic*. This bursty traffic often travels predominantly in one direction, rather than equally in both. A good example is modern-day web HTTP browsing, where an end user has a low-bandwidth request to a remote web site, and the reply of multiple web pages with graphics uses a large amount of bandwidth. When packet switching networks were first built, they provided an ideal transport for the typical terminal user who had many pauses between transmissions, causing the data to be bursty in nature. Packet switching networks also best accommodate traffic that is not delay-sensitive, therefore, the two primary requirements that best suit packet networks are *burstiness* and *delay-insensitive* traffic. Because of the dynamic allocation of bandwidth techniques used by packet switches, bursty delay-insensitive traffic is ideal for transport over a packet switching network.

Figure 11-9 shows 3 low-speed terminal users at sites A, B, and C communicating simultaneously with a single high-speed user host through a packet switching network. The terminals could use low-speed X.3 circuits to request information downloads from the host, or possibly X.32 synchronous dial-up access through a modem. Terminal traffic *to* the host is very light (low-bandwidth use) compared with the data traffic received *from* the host (high-bandwidth use). For instance, a small inquiry to the host can generate a long response back to the terminal. Also, there is a high probability that not all of the terminals will be requesting information at the same time. In fact, they will probably be transmitting and receiving less than 10 percent of the time. The single 56 Kbps multiplexed

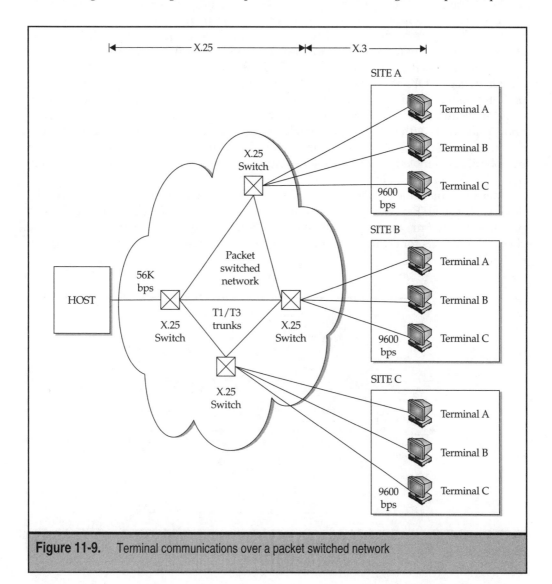

Figure 11-9.   Terminal communications over a packet switched network

X.25 line from the host into the packet switching network shows the efficiencies of asymmetrical traffic patterns where the host will transmit to terminals much more traffic than it receives.

X.25 Packet Switching: Basic Operation

Figure 11-10 shows a sample packet switching network with six nodes (1–6), each with three users (terminals A, B, and C). Typically, there would be many more users on this network, but we have shown only nine total for simplicity of the example. Each user device is acting as a DTE, and each network node is acting as a DCE. User A on Node 1 wants to transmit a message of size 1024 bytes to user B on Node 3. User A begins this process by transmitting the message to node 1. Node 1 breaks the message into four packets of 256 bytes (ignore the overhead associated with transmission). These packets are then routed across the network toward node 3 based on routing tables predefined in the packet switches. Observe that the second packet, as well as both the third and fourth packets, were transmitted via a different route to node 3. This alternative path routing could have automatically been determined by increased traffic loads between node 1, node 5, and node 3 (the original path packet 1 took), or a variety of other network conditions, such as failed circuits in either of those two paths. The packets are then received by node 3, reassembled into the 1024-byte original message with the packets in their original order, and passed on to user B.

This example shows users accessing the packet switching network through DTE devices. These DTE devices transmit data to the network via synchronous mode X.25 protocol through the use of packets. As packets flow through the network, each node checks the packets for errors and then retransmits if necessary. All operations are transparent to the user.

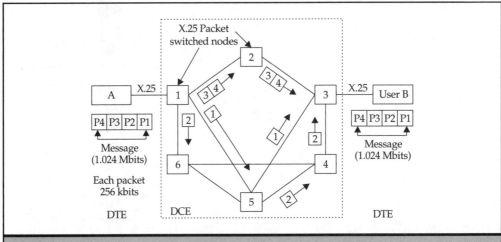

Figure 11-10.   Sample X.25 packet switching network

An elaborate acknowledgment and retransmission scheme is provided in packet switching, primarily because of the large amount of errors, which could be experienced when using voice-grade analog lines. This scheme provides flow control and error detection and correction, and limits the traffic flow by buffering to prevent congestion. Since packet switching was built on the premise of using voice-grade (nondigital or nonoptical) lines for transport, much overhead, error correction, and buffering were built into the X.25 protocol. Since the advent of digital and later fiber transmission facilities, many of these capabilities are no longer needed.

NETWORK LAYER FUNCTIONS

Now let's look at the packet switching protocols from the network layer perspective. Each physical interface can establish one or multiple virtual circuits to remote physical interfaces. Each of these logical circuits is then assigned LCNs similar to phone numbers, but with only local significance. Local significance refers to the address—in this case, a logical channel number—having significance only to the local physical port, whereas the same LCN can be used on different physical ports throughout the network. Virtual circuits ensure sequence integrity in the delivery of user data, established either administratively and statically as a PVC, or dynamically as an SVC through call control procedures. Over these PVCs and SVCs flow both normal data and call control packets. An X.25 "call" is set up using a global X.25 address, and an SVC channel number is negotiated and allocated between each switch. The X.25 global address is present only in call setup and tear-down, and all data in between is identified by its SVC channel number; thus, the X.25 address is globally significant (defined as being unique across all physical ports in the network), and the SVC channel number is locally significant. This section describes the X.25 protocol as it defines the network layer features and functions. These same concepts of local and global significance to addresses will be found in all other packet-switched network protocols.

PVCs and Virtual Calls

The network layer provides the user with up to 4095 logical channels designated either as PVCs or virtual calls (VCs) over one LAPB physical channel. PVCs are virtual circuits permanently established between a source and destination node. This is similar to having a private or leased line dedicated at all times between two specific users. These PVCs guarantee a connection between two points when demanded by the user. The user always sees the virtual circuit as a dedicated circuit for his or her use only, whereas the network provides the same circuit as a shared resource to multiple users upon demand.

Figure 11-11 illustrates three users of a public X.25 packet switching network. Each user has a single physical DS0 access circuit to the network, labeled 1, 2, and 3. Within each access circuit there are multiple PVCs, labeled 12, 23, and 13, that allow each site to communicate with the other two. Each of these PVCs is static, thus, their end points are predefined. Each PVC carries traffic in both directions. SVCs operate in the same manner, but are established and terminated on demand.

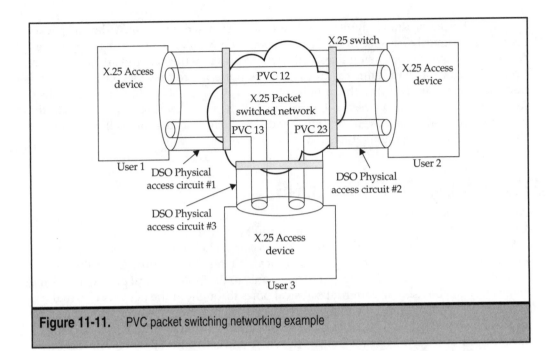

Figure 11-11.   PVC packet switching networking example

Figure 11-12 shows the transfer of data between users A and B. Notice that the virtual circuit remains established and only data (with the proper protocol information) is sent across the network between DTE devices. While the end points of the PVC or SVC remain fixed, the actual network path might vary.

VCs and SVCs act as circuit-switched calls, with the characteristic of being connected and disconnected after the data has been sent between the source and destination node; therefore, one source can connect to many destinations at different times, as opposed to

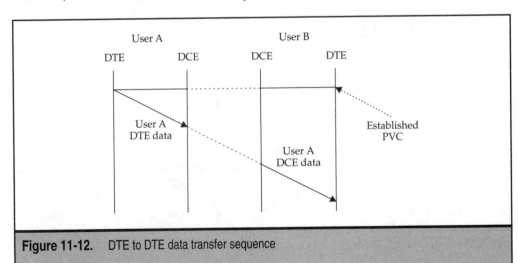

Figure 11-12.   DTE to DTE data transfer sequence

always being connected to one destination. This is similar to the method of making a tele-phone call, with the phone off the hook, and talking during the duration of the call. Each time a call is made, regardless of the destination, it is re-established through the entire network. Figure 11-13 shows a standard packet sequence for the establishment of an SVC virtual call, data transfer, and then call clearing. Note that the data transfer stage can last any amount of time.

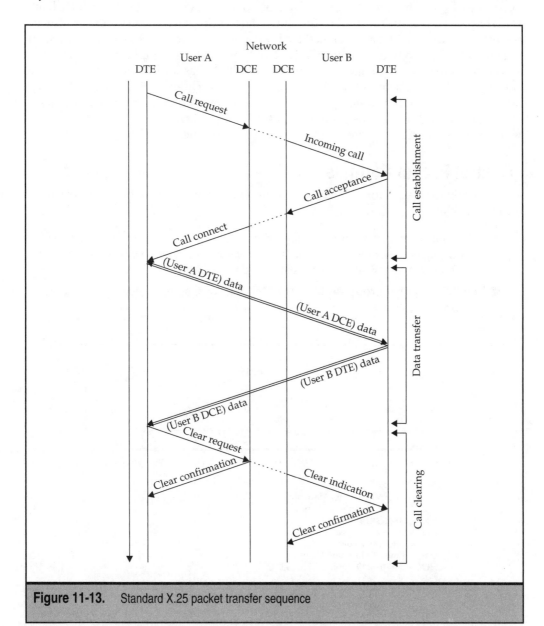

Figure 11-13.   Standard X.25 packet transfer sequence

Using SVCs can add even more delay than using PVCs. SVCs, in addition to encountering connection blocking and connection delay, can encounter queuing and retransmission delays. These delay factors must be taken into account during the design.

VCs and LCNs

LCNs are assigned to each of the incoming and outgoing virtual calls for each DCE and DTE, respectively, as well as to all PVCs. Out of the 4095 logical channel numbers available per physical circuit, PVCs are assigned the lowest numbers, followed by one-way incoming virtual calls, then two-way incoming and outgoing calls. The highest numbers are reserved for one-way outgoing VCs. Figure 11-14 illustrates an interpretation of logical channel administration as defined in the X.25, Annex A. These LCNs hold only local significance to that specific physical port, but must be mapped to a remote LCN for each VC.

Figure 11-15 shows the assignment of LCNs between two users. Note that the network layer of the OSIRM performs the relaying and routing of packets via the LCNs.

X.25 Control Packet Formats

Control packets are used for VC setup and termination. Figure 11-16 shows the format for a control packet.

▼ **General format identifier** indicates the general format of the rest of the header, indicating whether the packet will be a call setup, clearing, flow control, interrupt, reset, restart, registration, diagnostic, or data packet.

■ **Logical channel group number (LCGN)** has local significance for each logical channel.

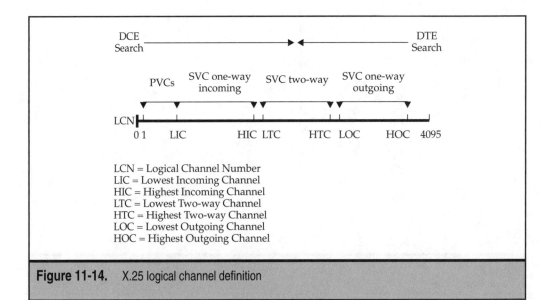

Figure 11-14.   X.25 logical channel definition

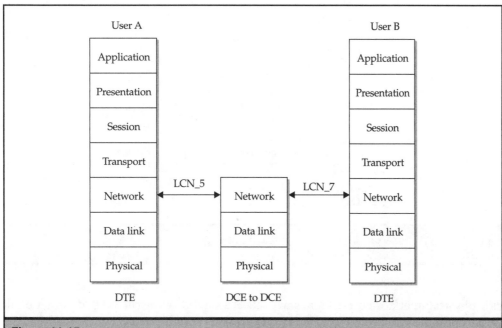

Figure 11-15. User logical channel number assignment

■ **LCNs** are assigned to each incoming and outgoing virtual circuit for each DCE and DTE.

■ **Control packet type identifier** relates the packet type (indicated in the general format identifier) from DCE to DTE and from DTE to DCE.

▲ **Additional bytes** contain information that is packet-type specific. Control packets perform many functions, including: call request and incoming call packets; call accepted and call connected; clear request and clear indication; DTE and DCE clear confirmation, data, interrupt, interrupt confirmation, RR, RNR, reset confirmation, and restart confirmation; reset request and reset indication; restart request and restart indication; diagnostic; DTE reject (REJ), registration request, and registration confirmation.

A quick explanation of these control packets is in order. Clear packets are used to clear the user-to-user session (DTE-to-DTE). Interrupt packets are used when the user wants to bypass the normal flow control protocol. Interrupt packets are used for single-priority packet transmissions where the DTE must accept the packet. RR and RNR packets manage flow control and are initiated by user terminals. These packets work in a manner similar to their HDLC counterparts, and provide a level of flow control above the normal HDLC functions through the use of LCNs. Reset packets reset the entire PVC or SVC during data transfer. Restart packets reset all the PVCs and clear all SVCs on a spe-

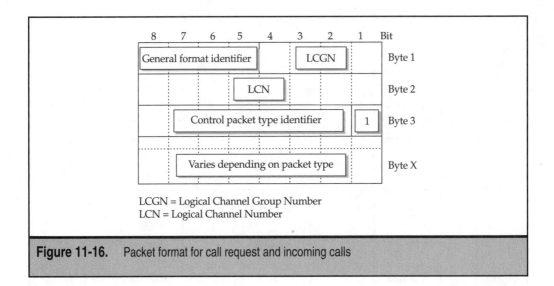

Figure 11-16. Packet format for call request and incoming calls

cific physical interface port. Diagnostic packets are used as the catch-all identifier of all error conditions not covered by the other control packets. Reject packets reject a specific packet and retransmission occurs from the last-received packet.

Normal Data Packet Formats

Normal data packets are transferred *after* call setup and *before* call termination. PVCs require only normal packet formats, as the virtual circuit is permanent and does not need to be set up or terminated. Figure 11-17 shows the format of a normal data packet. The qualified (Q) data bit distinguishes between user data and a user device-control data stream. The data (D) bit is set to *0* if the flow control and acknowledgments have local significance, and set to *1* to designate end-to-end significance. The LCGN and LCN together provide the 12 bits needed to form the VCN. The P(R) and P(S) fields designate the receive and send sequence count, respectively. The more (M) data bit is set to 0 throughout the length of the message, and is set to *1* on the last packet of the message, indicating the end of the message. The M bit is used to chain packets together, which serve as a single message, such as a 737-byte message that gets segmented into many 128-byte packets. The data field is specified to a maximum size (such as 16, 32, 64, 128, 256, 512, 1024, 2048, or 4096 bytes) and contains the actual user data (or padding).

Flow Control and Windowing

The send and receive sequence numbers in the X.25 packet level are also used to provide flow control between the packet level source and sink. Figure 11-18 illustrates a simple example of X.25 packet level flow control where the source is a transmitting device and

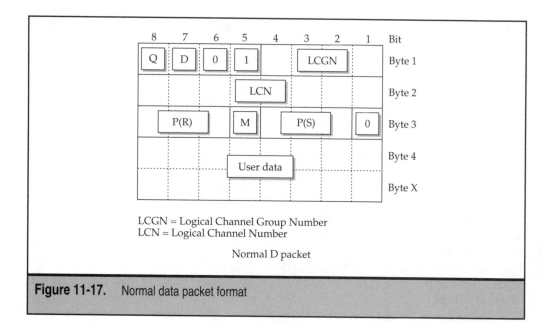

Figure 11-17.   Normal data packet format

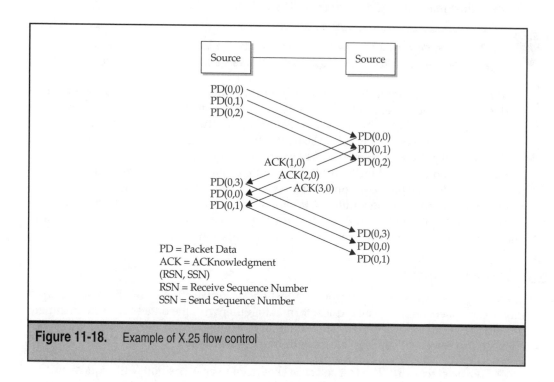

Figure 11-18.   Example of X.25 flow control

sink is a device that receives. The send sequence number is a sequential number for the current packet. Numbers are incremented modulo the maximum window size. This example uses a modulo of 4, which means that sequence numbers are incremented in the order 0, 1, 2, 3, 0, 1, 2, 3, 0, and so on.

The RSN in the acknowledgment indicates the next SSN expected in the next packet from the other end of that virtual circuit. Therefore, the RSN acts as an acknowledgment for all packets up to one less than the RSN.

The transmitter can send no more packets than modulo – 1 without acknowledgment; otherwise, the sender could become confused as to which packets the receiver was acknowledging. As shown in the example, the sender transmits three packets and then waits for the acknowledgment before sending any additional packets.

This is called a *sliding window* flow control protocol. This process allows the receiver to control the maximum rate of transmission over a virtual circuit, and is therefore a form of traffic control. This is still an essential function for a slow receiver (such as a printer) to control a fast transmitter (a computer) in many data communications applications today. The RSN acknowledgment can be "piggybacked" in the packet header for a packet headed in the opposite direction on a virtual circuit, or can be sent in a separate acknowledgment packet.

Window size is directly proportional to traffic load on the logical channel, so resources should be used wisely, balancing the cost of providing more logical channels and bandwidth against maintaining performance. The default window setting is 2.

NOTE: The more error-free the transmission facility, the larger the window size and, thus, the greater the application throughput is achieved. This is very similar to the protocol operation of TCP.

While this method operates at both the data-link and network layers, it allows the network to throttle individual logical channels rather than an entire physical circuit. Some protocols, such as TCP/IP, are programmed to reduce the window size during network congestion and increase the window size after the congestion has been relieved.

The control packet forms the basis of the flow control element of X.25. These packets operate between DTE and DCE and limit the rate of packet acceptance by updating the packet data (RSN). This flow control is negotiated separately in each direction, in the form of opening and closing windows. RR and RNR play an important role in postponing or closing and opening the DTE window during problem DCE conditions. Out-of-band interrupt packets can also be used to control transmissions.

Fast Connect Option

There also exists a fast connect option for fast packet transactions in X.25. In fast connect mode, each packet has the call request format together with the data so the establishment of a virtual circuit is not required. This is similar to a datagram. There are two types of fast connect: fast select call and fast select with immediate clear.

▼ **Fast select call** The fast select packet from user A has both call request and user data (up to 128 bytes of data), and user B can respond with a call-accept packet that also contains user data from user B. The rest of the call connection and disconnect works the same as an SVC call. This operation can be seen in Figure 11-13.

▲ **Fast select with immediate clear**   This option is similar to the fast select, with the call request packet establishing the connection and the clear indication packet terminating the connection. Data flows for the fast select with immediate clear can be seen in Figure 11-19. This mode is similar to the datagram and is designed for single transaction-based services, in addition to remote job entry (RJE) and bulk data transfer.

X.75 INTERNETWORKING PROTOCOL

ITU-T Recommendation X.75 defines the protocol structure and procedures for internetworking multiple X.25 packet switching private data networks (PSPDNs). Such might be the case when two service providers want to link their networks to provide seamless networking between users on both networks; thus, the access of any user to an individual X.25 network is extended across multiple X.25 networks, providing the capability to

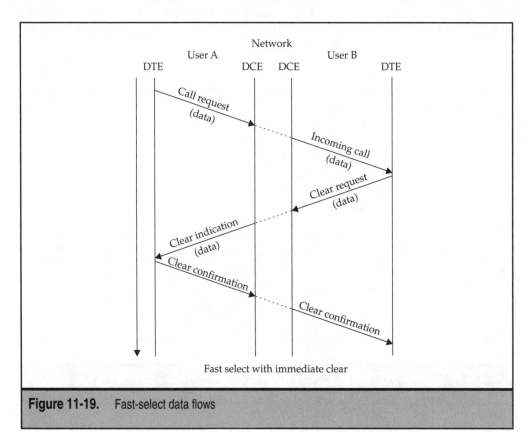

Fast select with immediate clear

Figure 11-19.   Fast-select data flows

share network resources and data across the international or multiprovider arena. X.75 can also be used to connect the larger backbone packet switches to one another. X.75 provides address translation in conjunction with the X.121 addressing protocol standard. X.75 functions reside in the network layer above X.25 functions. All functions of the X.75 protocol are similar to the X.25 protocol (such as LCGNs, LCNs, PVCs, or SVCs). X.75 also supports the multilink procedures to support multiple links between signaling terminal exchange (STE). The STE acts as the internetwork interface point and performs both packet transfer procedures and packet signaling.

Figure 11-20 shows DTEs from two separate X.25 networks located in the United States and the U.K. communicating via the X.75 protocol. The actual communication still takes place over the X.28 and X.29 protocols, and the X.75 network protocol is transparent to the end users. The DCE in this case is part of network node functionality, and communicates X.25 protocol directly, or native X.25, into the X.25 network. This is an example of X.75 being used as an international packet switching service. The links between these STEs can either be an A1 link, which is used between two adjacent nodes, or a G1 link, which is used between a source STE (United States) and a destination STE (U.K.). Many countries have some form of private and public packet switching networks and use X.75 to link these networks. Most vendors and X.25 networks implement different versions of the X.75 standard, changing or supporting one or more of the options available. One cannot assume that just because the network supports X.75 that it will be able to communicate with another X.25 network supporting X.75.

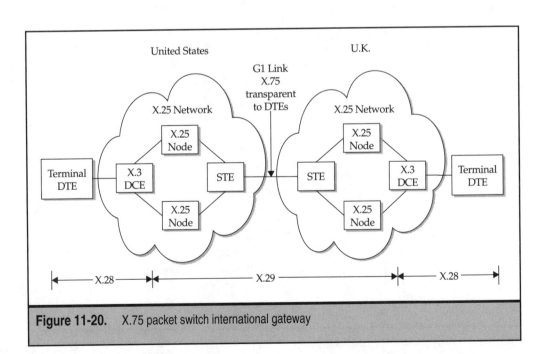

Figure 11-20.   X.75 packet switch international gateway

Performance and Design Considerations

Regardless of how fast the packets enter the network switch, they go into a queue before being switched through each node. If the queue is full, the node will buffer a certain amount of packets until they can pass through the queue and bandwidth is available. The amount and length of queuing is directly related to the blocking delay through the network. Some packet switches degrade in throughput as their queues fill up and, thus, throughput decreases. More buffering causes greater delay and congestion. Errors in the network transport can also cause more queuing and delay. Overhead is also a major consideration. The overhead incurred per packet is anywhere from 64 to 256 bits per packet. Since typical messages are 256 to 1028 bits, overhead would account for 25 percent of the total transmission bandwidth in this example. This directly reduces efficiency.

Performance in a packet switching network is measured in packets per second throughput in relation to the delay incurred from switch ingress to egress. These figures calculate to throughput and delay characteristic curves, which should be supplied by any prospective vendor. Packet delay through a typical packet switch node is 50 to 200 milli-seconds due to packet processing. Typical packet processing per node is anywhere from 300 packets per second up to hundreds of thousands of packets per second. Switches should be favored that have constant packet per second processing at all levels of traffic throughput. Also, the switch performance should be constant, irrespective of packet size. Some packet switches drastically degrade performance and packet processing as the packet size increases above 128 or 256 kilobits. These larger packets are characteristic of batch processing, which uses packet switching networks because it cannot justify dedicated or leased-line circuits. This type of traffic absolutely requires good performance and constant throughput, regardless of packet size.

Another consideration is protocol conversion. The amount of protocol conversion performed by a switch or PAD reduces throughput and performance. In addition, as PAD operations increase, the actual data throughput degrades due to the increased processing power.

ADVANTAGES AND DRAWBACKS

Advantages of X.25 packet switching include

▼ Performs format, code, and speed conversions between unlike terminal devices

■ Inherent secure transmission scheme

■ Fault-tolerant technology (routes around failures)

■ Packetizes long messages and short messages, which do not interfere with each other

■ Supports rapid exchange of short messages, and consistent delay of long messages under steady load

■ Performs network functions transparently to users

- Efficient transport for small batch files
- Supports both asynchronous and synchronous interfaces including dial or lease lines
- Supports transmission speeds from 150bps to E1 (2.048Mbps)
- Provides better circuit use than circuit switching
- Can reduce access costs for multiple users (versus dedicated access)
- ▲ Supports international connectivity with lower-cost circuits

Primary drawbacks of X.25 packet switching include

- ▼ Low-speed access limitations
- High delay potential
- ▲ High overhead, which reduces effective throughput

SWITCHED MULTIMEGABIT DATA SERVICE (SMDS)

Switched MultiMegabit Data Service (SMDS) is a public, connectionless, cell-switched data service, which allows data to be switched between multiple public-addressed subscribers at multimegabit-per-second speeds based on the IEEE 802.6 standard. SMDS offers a method of high-speed LAN and MAN interconnection across a WAN that, through the aggregate of a single physical network interface per subscriber, is more economical and efficient than using a dedicated (private line) network. SMDS offers the capability to virtually extend the LAN, at direct-connect LAN speeds, across a MAN and WAN. SMDS, along with other modern packet protocols, does not support network error correction and thus requires retransmission over low-loss digital and fiber-optics networks.

SMDS has limited pockets of deployment with no announced deployments on the horizon. FR's explosive growth, regulatory battles between carriers, and the arrival of ATM effectively killed future prospects for SMDS. Due to the reduced influence of SMDS, we will provide a high-level overview and description of the interface protocols, and not dive into DQDB architectures, which haven't been discussed in years.

SMDS AND IEEE 802.6

IEEE 802.6 is part of the IEEE defined 802.X suite of LAN and MAN protocols. The IEEE 802.6 MAN protocol spans both the physical layer (Layer 1) and media access control (MAC) sublayer (Layer 2) of the OSIRM. It also interfaces to the logical link control (LLC) sublayer. Figure 11-21 depicts how the IEEE 802.X standard (Layer 2) and other 802.X IEEE protocols relate to the OSIRM layers.

SMDS and the IEEE 802.6 DQDB protocol have a one-to-one mapping to each other, as illustrated in Figure 11-22. The SMDS Interface Protocol (SIP) has protocol data units

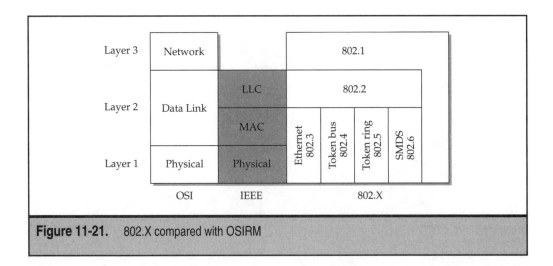

Figure 11-21.   802.X compared with OSIRM

(PDUs) at levels 2 and 3. These PDUs are labeled L2_PDU and L3_PDU for level 2 and level 3, respectively. The level 2 SIP PDU is a 53-byte cell that corresponds to the DQDB MAC PDU of the IEEE 802.6 standard. The level 3 SIP PDU can contain one customer data packet of up to 9188 bytes and is treated the same as the upper layers in IEEE 802.6. SMDS protocols work independently of network and higher-layer protocols, yet their operation can have an effect on these higher-layer protocols.

SMDS/802.6 PDU Formats

Figure 11-23 illustrates the relationship between the user data, the level 3 SMDS PDU, and the level 2 SMDS PDU. The user data field might be up to 9188 octets in length. The level 3 protocol adds a header and a trailer field, padding the overall length to be on a

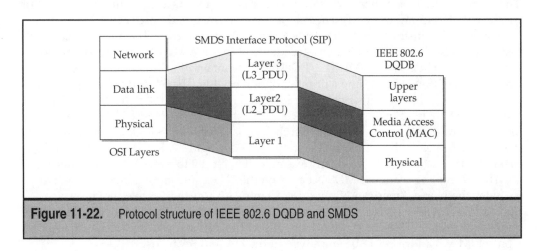

Figure 11-22.   Protocol structure of IEEE 802.6 DQDB and SMDS

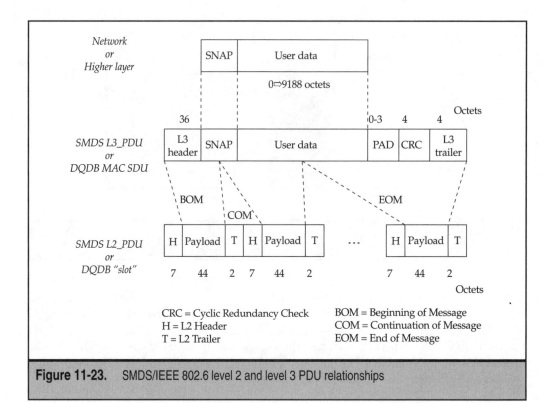

Figure 11-23.   SMDS/IEEE 802.6 level 2 and level 3 PDU relationships

four-octet boundary. Level 2 performs a segmentation and reassembly function, transporting the level 3 payload in 44-octet segments. The level 2 PDU has a seven-octet header and two-octet trailer resulting in a 53-octet slot length, the same length as an ATM cell. The level 2 header identifies each slot as being either the start, continuation, or end of message (SOM, COM, or EOM). The cells are then transmitted header first.

Figure 11-24 illustrates the SMDS level 3 PDU (L3_PDU) format. The first two octets and last two octets of the SMDS L3_PDU are identical to the AAL3/4 common part convergence sublayer (CPCS). The SMDS L3_PDU header contains the SMDS source and destination addresses (SA and DA) and a number of other fields. The SA and DA are populated by the CPE. Most of these other fields are included for alignment with the IEEE 802.6 protocol and are not used in the SMDS service. When the SMDS level 3 PDU is segmented by level 2, all information needed to switch the cell is carried in a single segment message (SSM, which means the whole message fits into a single L2_PDU) or BOM slot. This means that an SMDS switch need only examine the first slot to make a switching decision.

The addressing plan for SMDS is based on the ITU-T Recommendation E.164, which includes the North American Numbering Plan (NANP) used for telephone service. As the SMDS E.164 address is globally unique, SMDS provides the capability for ubiquitous connectivity. The IEEE 802.6 standard also allows the option for 48-bit IEEE Media Access Control (MAC) addresses to be employed in the DA and SA fields.

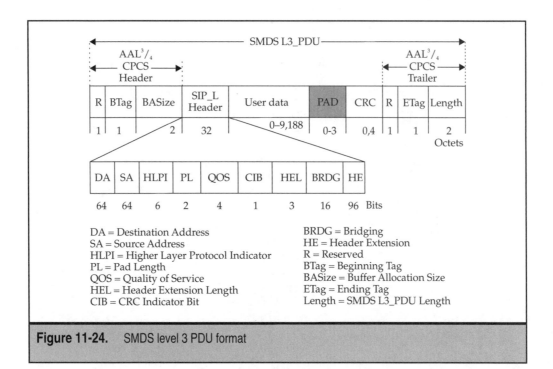

Figure 11-24. SMDS level 3 PDU format

Figure 11-25 illustrates the 48-octet SMDS level 2 PDU format encapsulated in a 53-octet DQDB slot. The other four octets of SMDS level 2 overhead in the DQDB payload are used for the SMDS segment type (ST), message identifier (MID), payload length, and a CRC on the 44-octet payload. The SMDS level 2 overhead and function are identical to the ATM AAL3/4 SAR. The ST field identifies either a SSM, BOM, COM, or EOM slot. The MID field associates the BOM with any subsequent COM and EOM segments that made up an SMDS L3_PDU. The MID value is the same for each cell that makes up a packet, and all cell sequence integrity is done through the MID. When an SMDS switch receives an SSM or BOM segment, the destination address determines the outgoing link on which the slots are transmitted. This is especially important in 802.6 implementations, because the protocol interleaves cells during transport and the MID offers the method of resequencing these cells at the egress port.

ATM implementation MID using ATM Adaption Layer (AAL) 3/4 and AAL 5 are different. With AAL 3/4, cells associated with different packets can be interleaved within the same 802.6 bus or ATM virtual channel connection (VCC). When AAL 5 on an SMDS VCC is used, the 48-byte cell loses the MID and must keep the cell order concurrent on the ATM VCC. Even though this limitation must be observed, cells on an AAL 5 SMDS VCC can be mixed with other cells from other VCCs within the same virtual path (VP). Delay between cell arrivals will have much less impact with AAL 5 service.

The DQDB access control field (ACF) and header are used to provide a distributed queue for multiple stations on a bus, provide self-healing of the physical network, pro-

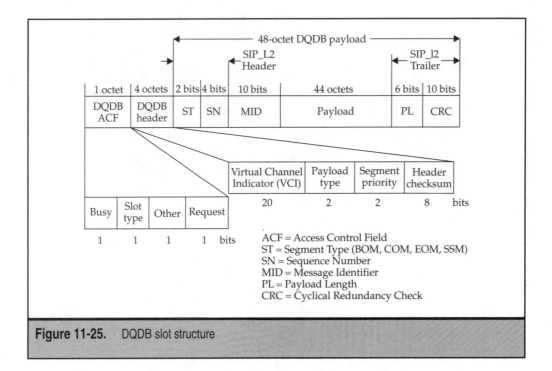

Figure 11-25.   DQDB slot structure

vide isochronous support, and control management functions. Note that the DQDB ACF and header taken together are exactly 5 bytes, exactly the same size as the ATM cell header. This choice was made intentionally to make the design of a device that converted between DQDB slots and ATM cells simpler (plus to have a cell optimized for both voice and data traffic transport).

SUBSCRIBER INTERFACE AND ACCESS PROTOCOLS

There are five major methods for users to access an SMDS network. Examples of these methods are presented in Figure 11-26.

▼ SMDS subscriber network interface (SNI)

■ SIP or access DQDB

■ Data exchange interface (DXI)

■ SIP relay access

▲ ATM UNI access

Each of these access methods is explained in this section, along with evolution of the CPE environment. First, we need to review the heart of the SMDS protocol—the level 3 PDU (L3_PDU).

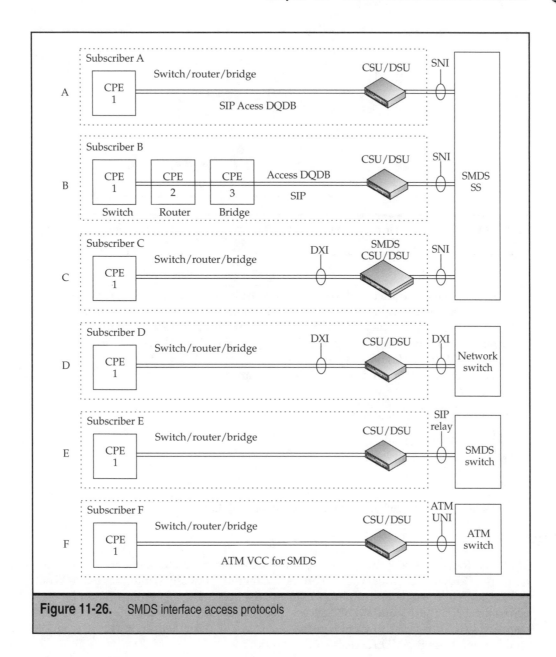

Figure 11-26. SMDS interface access protocols

SMDS L3_PDU

The first level of user data encapsulation when using SMDS is within the L3_PDU. The L3_PDU carries the real protocol value of SMDS. The most common version of the L3_PDU, shown in Figure 11-27, is detailed in RFC 1209, *The Transmission of IP Datagrams over the*

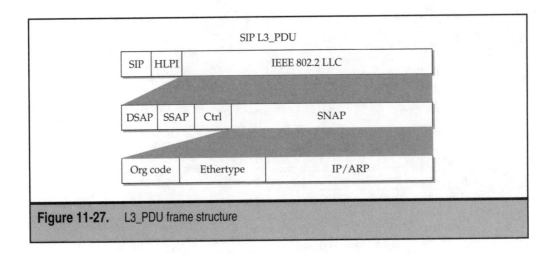

Figure 11-27.   L3_PDU frame structure

SMDS Service. Here we see the SNAP fields encapsulated within the LLC frame, which in turn is encapsulated within the SIP L3_PDU. The High-Layer Protocol Identifier (HLPI) field value is *1.* All other fields compose the standard IEEE 802.2 LLC frame and have a fixed value depending on whether you are sending IP or ARP packets. The Org Code, Ethertype, and IP/ARP fields compose the SNAP.

An L3_PDU can be moved across the WAN in any of four ways, all of which are transparent to the user:

▼   DXI frame

■   FR frame

■   802.6 cell (L2_PDU)

▲   ATM cell

Let's now explore each, along with the SIP and SNI.

SNI

The SNI is the subscriber physical and administrative interface and boundary to the SMDS network or service provider. The SNI offers one method for CPE to interface a SMDS network. The SIP in single and multiple CPE access *(access DQDB)* protocols can be used across this SNI. These standard SNI access methods use the access DQDB protocol and a standard CSU/DSU, as shown in Figures 11-26A and B. Now let's look at the two more common methods of SMDS access—SIP and DXI.

SIP

The SIP was the original access protocol that operates across the SNI. SIP provides for many CPE devices to communicate over the SNI using the DQDB protocol. SIP operation is primarily the exchange of L3_PDUs between CPE and SMDS network switching nodes.

This operation is called an access DQDB, which is distinguished as CPE-to-MAN switching system access, as opposed to switching-system-to-switching-system (SS-to-SS) access. The SMDS access DQDB is based on the open bus topology. One (single-CPE access) or multiple CPE (multi-CPE access) devices may be attached to one access DQDB via DS1, DS3, E1, or E3 circuits. These CPE devices may be a variety of devices, such as bridges, routers, gateways, or switches. If all CPE devices attached to a given access DQDB require autonomy, no other alien CPE may be attached to the same access DQDB; thus, if there are multiple customers at a site, each customer must be provided a separate access DQDB into the SMDS network. Figure 11-26A shows an example of SIP access across an SMDS SNI for a single CPE (single-CPE access). Figure 11-26B shows multi-CPE access. Figure 11-28 illustrates an end-to-end network using DXI over an SNI.

DXI

DXI, a variation of SIP, was first developed by the SMDS Interest Group as a cost-effective access method that required only the upgrade of the CSU/DSU equipment and software on the CPE device (typically a router) rather than a hardware upgrade to the CPE device. This allowed for easy integration and upgrade capability to SMDS for the existing router base; thus, the router equipment is not required to do the "slicing and dicing" of the SMDS L3_PDU into L2_PDUs, and the task is relegated to select SMDS CSU/DSU vendors, as shown in Figure 11-26C. Here, the router places the user data into an L3_PDU, and uses a logical level protocol—DXI—to move the L3_PDU to the SMDS CSU/DSU. When the SMDS CSU/DSU receives the L3_PDU, it strips the DXI header, takes the original user data, and then chops it into L2_PDU segments and encapsulates it into the SMDS L2_PDU frame for transmission to the SMDS network.

The DXI Local Management Interface (LMI) Protocol is used for signaling across the DXI. A high-speed serial interface (HSSI) can also provide transport for DS3 DXI access. DXI standards are defined in the *Generic Requirements for Low Speed Access*, TA-TSV-1239 and *Frame Relay Access to SMDS*, TA-TSV-1240.

The DXI is an enhanced version of the standard HDLC protocol and frame, as shown in Figure 11-29. As shown, the SMDS CSU/DSU performs the L3_PDU-to-L2_PDU segmentation and reassembly. MCI Communications later improved the specification by eliminating the need for a special CSU/DSU for speeds of 56 Kbps to 1.544 Mbps, and this

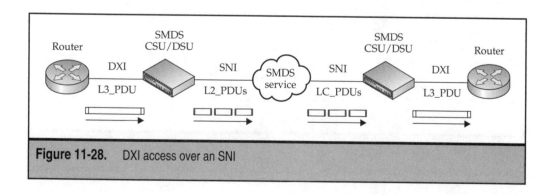

Figure 11-28.   DXI access over an SNI

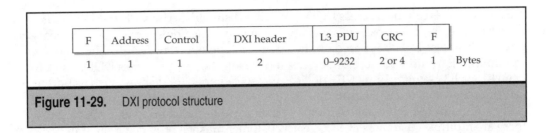

F	Address	Control	DXI header	L3_PDU	CRC	F	
1	1	1	2	0–9232	2 or 4	1	Bytes

Figure 11-29.   DXI protocol structure

specification was later ratified in 1993 with the Bellcore Technical Advisory 1239—Generic Requirements for Low Speed SMDS Access. This standard spawned a new SMDS DXI service that allowed for DXI access straight from the CPE, through the CSU/DSU, and into the SMDS network switch, as shown in Figure 11-26D. The SMDS network switch performs the functionality of the SMDS CSU/DSU in example C. This service provided lower SMDS speeds for greater ubiquity and cost-effective service. Many service providers then provided this direct L3_PDU DXI interface to their SMDS service, so a special DXI CSU/DSU was not required. Vendors also provide an access server technology to convert the customer DXI into a SIP, as shown in Figure 11-30.

FR Access

What alternatives exist for FR users that want to communicate with SMDS users? SIP Relay is the method of using an FR protocol and access circuit as access to an SMDS service. Again, an HDLC deviation is used similar to the DXI access protocol, but with the FR information as the L3_PDU and the frame header address (data-link connection identifier, DLCI) as the SIP relay interface PVC (SRI PVC). Figure 11-26E shows the FR SIP PVC access, where the CSU/DSU simply relays the L3_PDU to the SMDS switch. Note that this method passes L3_PDUs into the FR frame and extracts them out of a FR frame at the destination end. The protocol format for SRI PVCs is shown in Figure 11-31, and the network

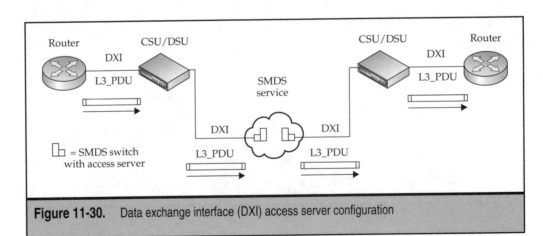

Figure 11-30.   Data exchange interface (DXI) access server configuration

F	DLCI = SRI PVC ID	L3_PDU	CRC	F	
1	2	0–9232	2	1	Bytes

Figure 11-31.   FR SRI PVC protocol structure

access connectivity is shown in Figure 11-26E. This implementation is defined by the Frame Relay Forum (FRF) implementers agreement as link access procedures frame (LAPF) mode, the format of which is shown in Figure 11-32. This allows the use of a single interface port for both FR and SMDS access to a public network.

Figure 11-33 illustrates an FR user in Georgia who has established PVCs over an FR network to FR users in Texas and New York. Now the Georgia user wants to communicate with a user in California. But the user in California is already using SMDS service with the same service provider that is providing FR to the other three users. The provider will offer the user in Georgia an SRI PVC through the FR network. The job of the internetworking unit within the carrier's network is to receive the L3_PDU frame, and if it is connected to a DXI switch, convert the L3_PDU back into a DXI frame. If it is connected to a SIP SNI, it slices the L3_PDU into 802.6 L2_PDU cells. In our example, the interworking unit (IWU) translates the SRI PVC into a SIP and forwards through an SS onto an SMDS SNI to the SMDS user in California. Access classes (defined later in SIR Access Classes subsection) and CIRs are not defined on the SRI PVC, so for engineering purposes, ensure that the SRI PVC and SIP has similar bandwidth requirements. The Annex D specification is used for signaling. SIP relay and signaling operations are further defined in Bellcore Technical Advisory 1240.

SMDS to ATM Access

Figure 11-26F illustrates ATM VCC connectivity for access to SMDS service through an ATM UNI access protocol. The standards for SIP access can be found in Bellcore Technical Reference 772. It is interesting to note that there is also a SIP variant for ATM access that allows use of one or more VCCs to be allocated as SMDS SIPs.

F	Header	L3_PDU	CRC	F	
1	2	<4096	2 or 4	1	Bytes

Figure 11-32.   LAP-F FR SRI PVC protocol structure

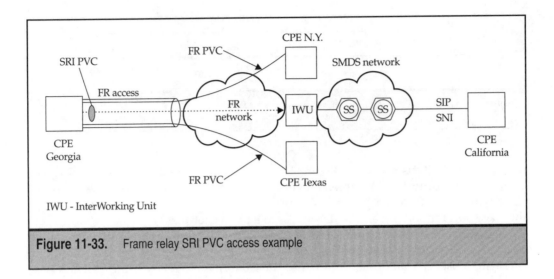

Figure 11-33.   Frame relay SRI PVC access example

ADDRESSING AND TARIFF CONTROL

The addressing scheme used by the SMDS network is formatted using the same structure as the North American Numbering Plan (NANP), which uses the ITU-T Recommendation E.164 numbering plan containing up to 15-digit addresses. This scheme was chosen to speed the integration of SMDS into the telephone network addressing infrastructure for integration of voice and data operations. As a result, the source and destination addresses have 15 digits reserved to accommodate *any* E.164 address. The NANP (world zone) has 10-digit numbering schemes, plus it adds a 1 (for world zone 1) for a total of 11 digits. Within these 11 digits, SMDS uses the first seven digits (including the world zone 1) to define one switching system from which individual and group addresses can be defined. The last four digits of this number are used to find a specific access line on the switching system.

CPE interface methods to an SMDS network device via multiple access protocols across the SNI include SIP, DXI, SIP relay, ISDN, and ATM. The SMDS service provider will assign each SNI one or more unique addresses. The subscriber will have full control over the use of each individual address, and may assign multiple SMDS addresses per CPE. SMDS can assign a group address to multiple devices so that they can multicast their data to other members of their group address. The standard specifies that up to 16 subscribers are possible per SNI, however, no user in the network will have the same address.

There are many addressing functions available, such as unicasting and multicasting. Source address validation and address screening are performed on all SNIs, and access classes are offered as a means of controlling traffic patterns and congestion.

NOTE: Many of these addressing functions are now being built into public and private IP network services.

Unicasting and Multicasting (Group Addressing)

SMDS offers either a point-to-point datagram delivery service called *unicasting*, or a point-to-multipoint service defined as a group multicast address. Group-addressed data unit transport provides the CPE capability to transmit to a maximum of 128 individual recipient addresses, similar to a broadcast but different in that specific destinations are specified versus all destinations in a broadcast. The source address can send a group address to a group-address agent. The group-address agent copies the packet and sends a copy on to each destination, with an appended BOM cell in front of the original L3_PDU. The new BOM cell carries the individual address of the member of the group the copy is intended for. Each SS can support up to 1024 of these group addresses, and each address on the network could be assigned up to 32 group addresses. One addressing example is to assign all the SMDS nodes (members of the same group address) the same IP network and subnet address. Then, each of these nodes would ARP each other as if they were on the same physical LAN with common higher-layer protocols.

Source Address Validation and Address Screening

SMDS service operates using E.164 source and destination addresses. The SMDS source address is screened by the network to ensure that it is valid for the source SMDS access line. SMDS customers can screen incoming data and accept only data from specific source SMDS addresses or block data from specific SMDS addresses. SMDS users can also limit the destination SMDS addresses that can be reached from their SMDS access lines. SMDS customers can have ubiquitous connectivity, or they can use these screening tools to achieve tightly controlled, closed user groups. Source address validation is an incredibly valuable feature to provide added security.

When a data unit is transmitted via the SNI to the SS, the source address is verified to ensure that it was assigned to the SNI from which it originated. This will be performed for each data unit sent. If the source address is not assigned to the SNI that originated the call, the L3_PDU is not delivered. The SMDS network also has the capability of authorization and address screening for both source and destination if closed user group network service is required. It is the network designer's job to ensure that VPNs are built within the public data network, in effect provisioning a private virtual network, and that the subscriber receives every feature required by the private SMDS network. Care must be taken when establishing address screening and group addressing to eliminate conflicts in both.

The standard ranges and limitations of each subscription parameter are shown in Table 11-1. Service providers often deviate from these Bellcore standards in their SMDS services.

Subscription Parameters	Ranges and Limitations
SNI addresses	16 maximum per SNI
Group addresses	128 maximum addresses per group, 32 group memberships per address
Address screens	Four maximum per SNI

Table 11-1.   SMDS Range and Limitations

SIR Access Classes as Traffic and Congestion Control

SMDS controls congestion and traffic through the use of an open-loop flow-control mechanism called sustained information rate (SIR) regulated through the assignment of access classes; thus, the SIRs are designed to control congestion conditions. SMDS SIR is based on the aggregate of all data originating on the SMDS access line regardless of its destination. SIRs are defined by access class.

SIR Access Classes

SIR access classes are assigned to SNIs based on many factors, but primarily to control congestion conditions and ensure an efficient access traffic engineering design by placing limits on the bursts of data. Access classes are a method of providing bandwidth priorities for times when there is network congestion at the SNI. Network congestion occurs when there is an attempt by the network to transfer one or more SMDS data units without an interval of time between the units. This means that more data is attempting transfer than can be supported by the SIP across the access path. The access class places a limit per user on the rate of sustained information transfer available. When the user creates a burst of traffic across the shared SMDS access link, the access class determines the duration of time that the user controls the link. In actual practice on an SNI, the SMDS CSU/DSU chooses the access class and then clocks and meters the traffic from the router to average the traffic to meet the SIR rate. When using an entire DS3 access, the user will be able to burst to the entire DS3, then back off to the average SIR, then burst, then back-off, and so forth; thus, the user achieves the average access speed and throughput of the SIR—but beware of the effect this might have on total, or variation of, throughput.

The only time the access class is not equal to the access bandwidth is with DS3 access classes. For DS3 access lines, five access classes are defined in Table 11-2. This table shows the class number assigned to the user, the maximum rate of transfer that the user can use over extended intervals (SIR), and the LAN traffic each was designed to support. Data arriving at a rate higher than the SIR is discarded at the originating SMDS switch. Access classes are regulated by a credit manager scheme. The table also shows the maximum

Access Classes	SIR (Mbps)	LAN Mapping	Burst Size in kbytes
1	4	4Mbps Token Ring	10.4
2	10	10Mbps Ethernet	13.0
3	16	16Mbps Token Ring	17.6
4	25	16–34Mbps Subrate	33.7
5	34	No enforcement	Unlimited

Table 11-2. SMDS Access Classes for DS3 Access

burst size in kbytes per access class. These values can help designers determine the average delay they can expect to see over the SMDS access.

Note that access classes 1 through 3 line up with standard legacy LAN speeds so that traffic from a single LAN cannot experience loss due to the SIR credit manager operation. It is apparent that T1 access does not warrant an access class, as the maximum amount of bandwidth achievable using SIP over a T1 SNI trunk is about 1.17Mbps (due to overhead). The 34Mbps for access class 5 is the maximum throughput achievable on a 45Mbps access line after Physical Layer Convergence Protocol (PLCP), and L2_PDU or ATM cell overhead are taken into account, and can be used for 100Mbps Ethernet extensions. SIR uses a credit manager, or "leaky bucket," type of rate enforcement method. Basically, no more than M of N cells may contain nonidle slots or cells. For class 5 $M = N$, while for the lower numbered classes, the relationship is SIR $= M \times 34/N$ Mbps. The value of M controls the number of consecutive slots or cells that can be sent at the DS3 rate.

SMDS has a L3_PDU loss objective of 10^{-4}, which is several orders of magnitude greater than that caused by transmission errors. This is consistent with the character of the SMDS service, emulating that of a LAN but providing MAN or WAN coverage.

DESIGN CONSIDERATIONS

When looking at using SMDS, it is important to understand the scope of your network. If your network is going to be worldwide, you need to verify that you have Interworking Units that will allow you to use other interfaces when SMDS access is not available. Compare your other options, such as FR, ATM, with newer services such as Optical/Gigabit Ethernet in the MAN, to meet your requirements.

Since SMDS isn't used much in the market, make sure you understand your costs of CPE equipment so that you don't pay more than required. Bottom line, make sure that you want to deploy an SMDS network, because the future isn't bright and support for legacy hardware and software will not last forever.

REVIEW

This chapter allowed us to review how we got to where we are today with respect to packet switched networking. We learned how packet switched networking started with X.25 packet switching as the parent for the modern day packet switch progeny. We discussed how its three levels of physical, link, and packet map to the OSIRM of physical, data link, and network. The discussion of network error correction and retransmission provided the foundation to understand why FR, SMDS, and ATM don't require these functions anymore and teach the basics of understanding a packet network.

Covering SMDS provided some history and also completeness, and we find many of the IP services public service providers are striving to offer today were pioneered in SMDS. As SMDS was one of the best-documented services that we have ever come across (in our dark pasts, we read all of the original SMDS Bellcore specifications), it provides a detailed view of a complete and well-designed service offering that spanned and was supported by all major carriers in the late twentieth century. Understanding the reasons for its failure can provide insight into the success or failure of future technologies.

PART V

Requirements, Planning, and Choosing Technology

CHAPTER 12

Requirements Definition

Requirements analysis is the first and most important step in network design, but before you can determine the network requirements, you need to understand the business requirements and challenges. Networks are designed to facilitate the business. In fact, in most instances, the network serves as an extension of the business. There must be a direct correlation between the goals of the business and those of the network and staff who support it. The network is built for the end users, and as such it must meet their needs. No single aspect of the design is more important than fully understanding the user's needs, for they ultimately dictate the technology, protocols, services, hardware, software, and resources devoted to both access and backbone design.

The two major views of requirements are those of the user and those of the designer. The designer can either be within the enterprise or a service provider. In our discussion of WAN design, these viewpoints can also be clarified as the enterprise (from the premises into the network) and the service provider (from the network out to the premises). The user looks at the network from the outside (premises) in, and the designer or service provider looks at it from the inside (backbone network) out. This creates two myopic views that must merge to provide a comprehensive complementary analysis beyond simple network ingress-and-egress design. Many questions must be asked before beginning the design. Both parties must "get to know each other" to begin the "marriage" of user and designer. This working relationship is essential to the success of the network's design and use. Changes and inaccuracies in user requirements can have devastating effects on both the access and backbone network design. While user requirements change, the designer needs to set a time limit when the addition of any new requirements is frozen and the current ones analyzed, thus the initial design is a snapshot in time, and requires constant tuning and optimization. This chapter examines how to look at the requirements from both the user's and the network design engineer or manager's perspective, beginning with an exploration of the many aspects of user requirements that set the stage for the traffic-analysis and capacity-planning phases.

BACKGROUND

It is important to understand that customer satisfaction is driven primarily by how the designer works with the user. Even the best designs and implementations will have problems, but conflict can be kept at a minimum if clear expectations are set appropriately and the designer builds a good working relationship with the user from day one. This chapter is designed to aid in this working process by defining expectations and detailing a number of areas that the designer needs to understand before beginning the network design.

To provide some background on documenting and managing expectations, some history of the development of requests for comments (RFCs) is appropriate. In 1969, while at UCLA, Steve Crocker established RFC series of notes. These memos were intended to be an informal fast way to share ideas with other network researchers. At first, the RFCs were printed and distributed via postal delivery; later, they were distributed via FTP and then the Internet. The effect of the RFC was to create a positive feedback loop, with ideas or proposals presented in one RFC triggering another RFC with additional ideas, and so on.

When some agreement was reached, a specification was then prepared based on the consensus. E-mail has been a significant factor in all areas of the Internet, and that is certainly true in the development of standards and consensus.

The point of discussing the creation of RFCs is that the communication process between the designer and end user is critical to get feedback during the process and buy-in on the final design. Good design engineers and managers do not design in a vacuum.

BUSINESS CHALLENGES AND REQUIREMENTS

Before a network design can begin, the network designer must understand the business and technical challenges and requirements facing the "CxO" (CEO, CFO, CIO, CTO, et al). This section reviews the business requirements and drivers, and the next section covers the technical requirements.

Table 12-1 summarizes typical key business requirements and typical company strategies to accomplish them. Corporate management objectives typically involve

▼ Growing the business

■ Maintaining strong financial control while improving shareholder value

■ Remaining competitive in an increasingly competitive environment

▲ Integrating operations with customers, suppliers, and partners

One often-overlooked concept is that of using network and technology to achieve these business requests. Many executives look at the network and technology only as a necessary expense. They make decisions based on budget constraints that exist within their current

Business Requirements	Strategies to Accomplish
Business growth and expansion	-Mergers and acquisitions -Industry consolidation or fragmentation -Globalization
Financial control	-Expense Control—lower capital and operating expenses (CapEx and OpEx) -18-month return on investment (ROI) -Reduce costs by deploying evolutionary versus revolutionary technologies and services

Table 12-1. Key Business Requirements and Strategies

Business Requirements	Strategies to Accomplish
Remain competitive	-Keeping up with technological change -Evaluating and deploying e-business and e-commerce initiatives -Automating and integrating customer and supplier interactions -Deploying new web- and Internet-based platforms -Enhancing web sites to include personalization and interaction, support financial and customer service transactions, and advanced functionality and services to make highly personalized and intelligent
Business coverage through infrastructure, network reach	-Support, connect to corporate users ("on net") -Support, connect to customers and suppliers ("off net") -Provide access for mobile and remote workers -Support any-to-any communications patterns and technologies -Provide capacity on demand
Adapt to changing environments	-People changes—human resources (find, hire, train, retain) -Adapt to changes in deregulation -Convergence of business and home—SOHO, remote access
Maintain security	-Implement security policy -Implement firewalls, IDs, etc.
Provide premier customer support	-7×24×365 customer network service and coverage -Speed and instant gratification -Personalization and customization -Customer and supplier communications

Table 12-1. Key Business Requirements and Strategies *(continued)*

business and operations model. Technology and network expenses are better viewed in the cost/opportunity business model. While there is a variety of network and technology options that indeed cost money, they can create a tremendous return on investment for the business. Each technology and network option should be evaluated based on its cost and impact on the business, otherwise known as return on investment (ROI).

TECHNICAL CHALLENGES AND REQUIREMENTS

Next, the network designer must understand the business and technical challenges and requirements facing the CIO, CTO, and network managers. Table 12-2 provides some sample technical requirements. Note that many of these parallel the business requirements.

Businesses often struggle with how to bridge the technology assimilation gap. Said differently, technology advances become available faster than businesses can assimilate

Technical Requirements	Comments, Examples
Scalability	Can you network grow to support company mergers and growth?
Flexibility	Can the network add other differently designed systems?
Accessibility	-Are there geographic limitations on access? -What are the different access methods?
Reliability and availability	In today's business environment, the network should rarely be down.
Performance	Throughput?
Security	How protected is your network? Make sure that security violations have minimal impact on the businesses.
Applications	-Packetized voice alternatives -e-enablement of network applications -Application growth while supporting legacy systems HTTP, XML, Java
Legacy network and systems	-Transparent access to legacy systems -Conversion—legacy to client-server
Architecture	-Selection of LAN, WAN-distributed, client-server, and Internet-based networking -Voice, video, and data integration over a shared architecture

Table 12-2. Business Requirements and Strategies

Technical Requirements	Comments, Examples
Storage	Do you have offsite data storage and restoration plans?
Maintaining service levels	-Will the users experience same level of service they have today? -Is the network monitored to verify the service level in the future?

Table 12-2.   Business Requirements and Strategies *(continued)*

them into the business. This creates a gap that grows as fast as the business grows. In a fairly static business, this gap might be smaller and thus the opportunity of using new technologies to accelerate the business might be less, but in a rapidly growing company, this gap and thus opportunity could be huge. Businesses either rely on internal resources to bridge this gap, or turn to outsourcing (which will be explored later).

EXAMPLES OF BUSINESS AND TECHNICAL REQUIREMENTS BY INDUSTRY

Here are a few examples of requirements by industry:

- ▼ **Financial services**   Agents require instant access to client financial information
- ■ **Medicine**   Hospitals access and share patient records and X-rays in minutes during emergencies
- ■ **Publishing**   Large text and graphic files are sent across the Web, stored, and printed
- ■ **Travel**   Timeliness of data important in distributed database computing and reservation system; many users during 8:00 A.M.–5:00 P.M. traffic pattern
- ■ **Engineering**   Share large CAD/CAM/CAE graphics, text, and video around campus
- ■ **Web hosting**   Internet-based software and information distribution company
- ■ **Architecture**   Large graphic files, multimedia conference room, and desktop videoconferencing
- ■ **Law**   Instant access to web-based legal, discovery, and client data
- ▲ **Database archival startup**   Large, high-use file backups at 1:00–4:00 A.M.

When determining business and technical requirements, review the following list and make sure to cover every aspect of the business:

▼   Marketing

■   Product and service development

■   Engineering

■   Sales

■   Operations

■   Customer service and support

■   Human resources and training

■   Distribution

▲   Supply-chain and inventory management

The goal of the network designer is to determine how the network can deliver meaningful results to the business. When you communicate with business management, make sure that meaningful results are communicated in specific, measurable results. Table 12-3 pro-

Meaningful Results	Specifics
Shortens time-to-market of goods and services by days or weeks	Allows company to launch new product in 5 months vs. 6 months
Enables faster development and implementation of new applications by days, weeks, or months	Reduces integration of new applications from 4 weeks to 1 week, reducing project costs by $10,000
Reduces cost of doing business	-Reduces equipment and access costs 50 percent -Eliminates redundant networks to lower total network costs by 50 percent
Improves cash flow and handling	-Shortens cycle time of A/R by two days -Streamlines automated payroll systems for 2 percent more accuracy -Cuts inventory reporting time by 75 percent or two weeks' labor cost -Processes and sends invoices 10 times faster, improving cash flow by two days and saving $5 million annually -Saves employee time -Cuts 1 day from A/P processing time -Cutting a 5-minute search to 15 seconds increases speed 20 times and employee productivity 10 times

Table 12-3.   Examples of Networks Driving Meaningful Results

Meaningful Results	Specifics
Enables rapid scalability of the business	-Able to add new applications, devices, or sites in days vs. months -Able to integrate new partner and customer extranets in days or hours vs. months
Enables ubiquitous access	-Enables extranet support for workforce dispersion and SOHOs to improve productivity by 10 percent -Achieving total workforce mobility increases employee productivity 20 percent -Internet-extranet-intranet communications adds revenue opportunities -International expansion captures larger market share
Improves communications	Company-wide communications now possible: -Enables electronic mail (bane or boon?) -Enables online sales support tools to increase sales -Enables instant messaging to shorten sales cycle by an average of two days -Enables extranet communications with customers and partners -E-enabled network adds 20 percent more revenue in first year -Online customer documentation reduces customer service labor costs 30 percent
Secure communications protects the businesses' assets	Decreases the probability of financial loss and regulatory embarrassment or prosecution

Table 12-3   Examples of Networks Driving Meaningful Results *(continued)*

vides examples of results that companies can achieve and specific objectives. As a designer, you will be more likely to get funding if your network improvements will provide measurable improvements and cost savings or revenue increases that executives can understand.

In summary, the WAN now carries more mission-critical traffic, will extend to clients, partners, and suppliers across the intranet, extranet, and Internet, and in essence become the lifeblood of the business. The old model of using a network for best-effort, nonmission-critical transport that offered no service-level guarantees has yielded to a new network that enable the business, requiring *and* providing:

▼ High performance and reliability

■ High security

■ High speed

■ Rapid scalability

■ Ubiquitous access

▲ Ability to integrate with customers, partners, and suppliers

USER REQUIREMENTS

Before being able to begin the design process, there are two initial steps that need to be accomplished by the designer: performing and documenting an inventory of the current network, and uncovering and documenting the customer's expectations of the new network. In this section, we substitute "customer" for "end user."

Cisco recommends 12 items to be inventoried in the customer's current network. These are listed in Table 12-4. The customer should provide most of this information, but

Inventory Step	Description
Existing applications	Document current applications running across the network.
Existing network protocols	Document current protocols running across the network.
Network topology and addressing	Create a high-level topology map of the current network, including all major segments, routers, bridges, switches, servers, and other network devices.
Potential bottlenecks in current network	Monitoring bandwidth use and traffic patterns: Using a protocol analyzer can determine on-net and off-net traffic patterns. These bottlenecks might be real or perceived, but both hold clues to design requirements.

Table 12-4.   Twelve Items to Inventory on Current Network

Inventory Step	Description
Business constraints	Understand nontechnical and political factors as they relate to current network and determine if these factors might affect future design.
Exiting network availability	Understand current amount of downtime and mean time between failure (MTBF). If possible, calculate cost associated with downtime.
Existing network performance	Measure network performance between various hosts and servers. Understand how application performance is driven by latency versus bandwidth. Some measurements will need to be repeated on the new design to document improvements.
Existing network reliability	Understand current network error conditions such as number of CRC errors, collisions, runts/giants. Reliability can be measured at all layers of the OSIRM; for example, reliability of the access circuits, FR network, IP routers, and TCP/IP file servers.
Existing network use	Understand network use by links, segments, and protocols. Collecting this information will probably require a protocol analyzer.
Status of existing routers	Document revision levels, memory use, CPU use, and buffer drops. Determine if there is a processing limitation under load.
Existing network management system	Document all network management tools being used and which platform they run on.
Overall health of existing network	Measure the perceived existing health of the network, based on specific criteria such as the following Cisco recommendations: -Ethernet segments should not exceed 40 percent use. -Token Ring segments should not exceed 70 percent use. -WAN links should not exceed 70 percent use. -Broadcast/multicast should not be more than 20 percent of overall traffic. -On Ethernet, should be no more than 1 CRC error per one million bytes of data. -Routers CPU use should not exceed 75 percent.

Table 12-4. Twelve Items to Inventory on Current Network *(continued)*

in reality customers rarely have this level of information documented. The designer often must collect this information himself or herself. Using a protocol analyzer can confirm protocols and applications and reduce surprises later.

Once the current network is inventoried and documented, understanding the customer's expectations is in order. Below are five categories to assist in gathering information from the customer.

▼ Business constraints include items such as timelines, staffing, training, budgets, and project approvals. Understand downtime requirements and set expectations for network implementation. How critical is the network as measured by the cost of downtime?

■ Security requirements are critical to most businesses. Who can access the network? Each resource? What can be accessed and when? Determine the appropriate security level for the resources and network you are trying to protect. Chapter 18 covers securing your network.

■ Manageability requirements can vary across the board from a simple PING program documenting that each device in the network is alive and operational to full-blown network-management systems with intelligent correlation engines that can relate alarms to events and recommend appropriate actions. Chapter 19 covers operations and network management. Determine whether 7×24×365 reactive or proactive management is required.

■ Define the current and future application requirements, which in turn will refer back to network protocols and performance requirements.

▲ Performance requirements cover bandwidth requirements and QoS (lost packets, jitter, and latency). Applications along with users drive performance requirements, but the final driver is budget justification. For example, in the early 1990s, many customers wanted OC-3 (155 Mbps) connectivity but very few were willing to pay the price.

As a continual theme, user expectations must be properly managed to ensure satisfaction not only after the new network becomes operational, but also through continued service of the network. The best way to ensure this is by jointly establishing these requirements with the user, documenting them, and then designing the network to meet and exceed these initial levels of customer satisfaction. Clearly understand what is expected on both sides and then set expectation levels accordingly. If this is a new network, make sure users know that initial service is in its test stages. Establish graduated levels of new technology introduction: technology trial, then alpha test, then beta test, and finally full production. These levels of network or service introduction are defined as

▼ **Technology trial** A test environment in which both the user and network designer are learning from each other. Network downtime and reconfiguration are expected often. This phase is primarily for both parties to learn about the new technologies. The network services are limited in scope and functionality.

The target group should be limited to experienced users or people not heavily affected by downtime. This phase is certainly not to be tested on mission-critical users or applications.

- ■ **Alpha test**   A prerelease version of the network service in which the customer is still learning from the network provider, but the provider now has the network design completed and the hardware is fully operational. Downtime is minimal, and very few users are on the network. This is a small-scale version of the "real thing," often an internal trial run, and expected to be "buggy." Again, users should not be severely affected by downtime.

- ■ **Beta test**   Final test phase before offering commercial or public user availability. Most, if not all, of the bugs should be out of the system, and users should experience little or no downtime. The beta test phase is close to the actual network offering, but since it is new, everyone expects some minor instability. Most new network technologies will be tested in parallel with older legacy systems through at least the beta test phase.

- ▲ **Production**   The network officially goes live! All bugs have been eliminated (in theory) and the network is running with full functionality. There is no downtime (unless scheduled in advance).

The final version of the production network should be transparent to the average user. Each user should feel that he or she has full connectivity when required, and with the required amount of bandwidth, to every destination he or she communicates with, per their original requirements. After a short time, the network will become viewed as a utility, something that always works—not a luxury, but a necessity. Above all, remember that the user is the customer and the network designer or service provider is the provider. The primary responsibility of the network manager or designer is to provide network capabilities and performance as close as possible to the user's expectations. Keep a professional, friendly attitude toward users, treat them as partners, and they will treat you in the same way. From the network provider perspective, *user perception is reality*.

The problem with many of the new technologies is that they require application design and use to understand the mid- to high-layer protocols more than ever before. The protocol used across the WAN can be just as much a limiting factor as the WAN bandwidth. It is the job of network engineers and managers to make this environment as transparent as possible to the user while still providing the feature functionality in a user-friendly manner to the desktop applications. The network should look like the transparent cloud in Figure 12-1, where users A, B, C, and D can communicate with whomever and whatever they require.

The rest of this chapter discusses user requirements from the designer's viewpoint. Obviously, the network designer has to understand much more than the input and information provided by the user, as user information is often incomplete and sometimes inaccurate. While reading the following sections, you might want to compile a working list of each user's requirements. Refer to earlier chapters for clarification on technologies, hardware, and services to meet these requirements. You should also understand both user and network-designer constraints. You will rarely receive all the user requirements, and even if you do, they will change throughout the development of the design and life of the network.

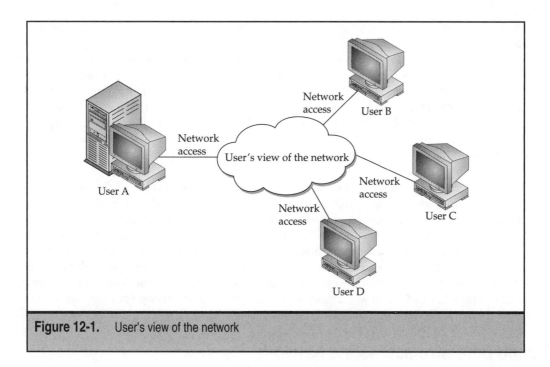

Figure 12-1.   User's view of the network

We cannot stress enough that the first phase of network design is to understand the top business requirements that CxOs must meet and the business and technical requirements that derive from them, and then design the network to meet these requirements.

TRAFFIC SIZING

Traffic comes in many shapes and sizes, conforms to many protocols and formats, travels in many types of patterns, and requires special methods of processing and handling. The next few sections cover these aspects and more. The format of this and later sections, and the approach of this chapter, is provided in a questioning tone. You should ask the questions identified here for each application planned for the network, using the answers to draw an aggregate picture of traffic patterns that will in turn be used in the access and backbone design phases.

Message or Data Size Basics

The two common formats for data traffic are the units of measure and the packaging of these units. Units of measure, in progression, include bit, byte, octet, message, and block. These units can be packaged into files, packets, frames, or cells or left as plain units for transfer across a physical medium using transmission packaging (for example, DS1). Another name for a data package is a protocol data unit (PDU), which is how ATM standards define the term.

Data rate is measured by the number of units or packages transmitted per unit of time. Some examples include packets/frames/cells per second, bytes per second, messages per hour, and number of transactions per second (using a fixed or variable unit of measure for each transaction). These values translate into channel transmission rates, and the transmission rate determines the amount of time it takes to transmit a unit of data. Table 12-5 shows examples of data size and transmission times based on network bandwidth available (these times assume no overhead and unlimited window size, so times are typically longer).

Another way to think about traffic is using the concept of "flows." A flow is a stream of data going from one point to another, for example, a file transfer from an HQ site to a remote site, or a web-browsing session from a TCP/IP computer in a home to a web server site within the Internet. Each flow has an asymmetrical transmission rate in both directions. For example, a remote workstation retrieving files from a central server could have an average 4 kbps request flow and an average 50 kbps response flow (the files being sent back to the requestor requiring much more bandwidth than the requests). In a large network, these flows are aggregated together to form throughput rates, which in turn drive the "feeds and speeds" of the network design.

Tuning Data Size across the Network

From the local and wide area network perspective, the data units are typically packets, frames, or cells, which are a combination of data and protocol overhead. From our discussion of the OSIRM, we know that the higher-layer data (for example, files) are segmented and encapsulated into these packets, frames, and cells for transport, switching, and routing. Many LAN and WAN technologies set limits of minimum and maximum packet

Data Sent	Data Size	Transmission Speed	Time to Send Data
Basic text file	60KB	56 Kbps	8.57 seconds
		DS1	0.0313 second
PowerPoint presentation	2MB	56 Kbps	285.71 seconds
		DS1	10.42 seconds
CAD/CAM graphics file	10MB	56 Kbps	23.8 minutes
		DS1	52.08 seconds
Database backup	250MB	56 Kbps	9.92 hours
		DS1	21.70 minutes

Table 12-5.   Data Transmission Comparison

size, such as a maximum Ethernet packet size of 1518 bytes or a maximum frame relay frame size of 8096 bytes (maximum frame relay size varies based on service provider). Table 12-6 provides a summary of maximum transfer unit (MTU) by media (MTU is the amount of data that can be transferred versus maximum packet size which includes the protocol overhead). The tradeoff here is typically packet size versus throughput, and the biggest influencing factor is typically packet loss or discard.

Many protocols, such as Transmission Control Protocol (TCP) provide windowing for acknowledgments of data sent and received. Protocols such as TCP manage a "flow" of IP packets (that in turn contain the user data) from one point to another. TCP windowing algorithm adjusts based on network conditions to try to achieve a large window size for a clean network that doesn't require retransmission. Segmentation of data across the network can happen when there are many varying technologies. TCP negotiates the maximum segment size (MSS) at the start of a connection but it is still possible for network segmentation to exist when a network has different LAN/WAN technologies. Based on the protocol used by the application, network segmentation could cause a problem but protocols such as TCP make the effects of segmentation transparent to the application.

TRAFFIC CHARACTERISTICS

How do applications perform based on different network designs and conditions? Which network variables—such as delay, loss, jitter, and throughput—are important to which applications? Which network variables should a designer be aware of? Are all applications created equal?

All applications are not created equal, and each application's performance might depend on one or more network variables. The most common network variables are shown in Table 12-7 with definitions for easy reference. How tolerant is your application to delay?

Media Type	MTU (Bytes)
16 Mbps Token Ring	17914
4 Mbps Token Ring	4464
FDDI	4352
Ethernet	1500
IEEE 802.3/802.2	1492
X.25	576
PPPoE	</=1492

Table 12-6. Default Maximum Transfer Unit (MTU) by Media

Characteristic	Definition
Delay	Measures the time for a packet to travel between two network devices. PING measures round-trip delay between two network devices. Delay in networks might not be symmetrical so the delay from A to B might be different than the delay from B to A. This is especially true in packet-based networks, but rarely in circuit-based networks.
Jitter/delay variation	Measures the difference in one-way delay over time for different packets sent between two network points.
Lost packet percentage	Measures the number of packets deleted or dropped in the network due to an error or congestion over the total number of packets transmitted.
Burstiness	Measures how infrequent a source sends traffic. Burstiness is defined as the ratio of peak to average rate of traffic based on a specific sampling period for the data.
Throughput	Measures how much data is required to be transmitted in a specified time frame. Measurements such as bits per second and packets per second are used.

Table 12-7.   Traffic Characteristics Defined

Can you wait an extra second or minute for your e-mail to be sent to the destination (high delay tolerance)? Can you wait 10 seconds (which might seem like an eternity) for your videoconference picture to catch up with the voice (low delay tolerance)? How does your voice conversation sound if your end-to-end delay increases or decreases by 200 milliseconds throughout the conversation (low jitter tolerance)? How does your videoconference or voice conversation react if you are losing 20 percent of your transmitted packets? Twenty percent loss of your voice traffic might not seem significant, but it definitely would be if you are using 16:1 compression and your compressed silence was part of that 20 percent!

Table 12-8 lists various applications and provides feedback by application on the defined characteristics. E-mail is defined as very bursty, as the traffic is infrequent and generated only when a user clicks the send button after writing a message, so the average bandwidth required by a user might be 2 kbps but the peak is 1 Mbps. E-mail is delay-, jitter-, and lost-packet tolerant because e-mail is not a real-time application while throughput varies based on size of e-mail attachments. Voice has medium burstiness due to how often

Application	Burstiness	Delay Tolerance	Jitter Tolerance	Lost-Packet Tolerance	Throughput (Mbps)
E-mail text (no attachments)	High	High	High	High	0.004–0.020
Voice	Medium/ low	Low	Low	Low	0.008–0.064
File transfer	Often high	High	High	High	0.01–600
CAD/CAM	High	Medium	High	High	1–100
Transaction processing	High	Low	Low	Low	0.064–1.544
Imaging	High	Medium	Medium	Low	0.256–25
Business real-time video	Low	Low	Low	Low	0.256–16
LAN-LAN	High	High	Medium	Medium	4-100
Server access	Avg.	High	Medium	Medium	4-100

Table 12-8.   Application Characteristic Attributes

someone is on the phone, but has low burstiness when a call is active . Voice applications typically require less than 200 milliseconds one-way delay for toll quality, and require low jitter and lost-packet percentage. This is especially true for packetized voice. Throughput required per voice channel can vary from 8 Kbps to 64 Kbps, not including overhead, and some compression schemes offer down to 4 Kbps voice.

Implementing networks that can support different qualities or classes of service is important to meet the design requirements of users who have multiple applications that require different network characteristics. Many CPE devices support priority queue schemes to allow specified traffic to cut in line or get to the front based on their QoS requirement. Real-time voice and video traffic, which are delay- and jitter-sensitive, can be queued in priority, allowing traffic to get in front of lower priority, big file transfer packets. In addition, network packet services are now offered by service providers that provide QoS features at the physical circuit, logical circuit, and even per-flow basis, with appropriate pricing and billing schemes. Users can either control or set this QoS within their CPE equipment, or the network can set the QoS, or both. Note that if a user sets their own QoS within their originating CPE, matching and compatible QoS features are required in the network service to prioritize traffic at the egress point of the network cloud to the remote CPE device. QoS, once set at the network ingress, must be carried through by the service provider all the way to network egress.

Sessions and Usage Patterns

What is the relationship between network devices? What are the characteristics of the user's sessions between two devices and thus across the network? Network traffic can be limited due to bandwidth or competing resources, and understanding the limiting factors will assist in solving the correct problem. Said differently, applications can be bandwidth- or processor/application-limited. If your host computer or application is the bottleneck (processor/application-limited), the doubling of network bandwidth will not resolve the processor application bottleneck, but if bandwidth is limited, then additional bandwidth might indeed solve the problem. Some characteristics of traffic patterns include

▼ Number of sessions or virtual circuits

■ Number of call setups

■ Number of times a session is initiated

■ Number of calls

■ Polling intervals

■ Reporting intervals

■ Maximum output rate

▲ Maximum rate receivable

What are the time patterns of user sessions? Time patterns occur in

▼ Peak work/traffic hours (Figure 12-2A)

■ Specific hours of bulk data transfer (Figure 12-2B)

▲ Random times, but predictable averages (Figure 12-2C)

Again, think of each communication, like a phone call in the voice world or a file transfer in the data world, as a flow. Then, aggregate these flows to calculate a 24-hour snapshot of user traffic use. Figure 12-2 has three examples of these snapshots, using an aggregation of flows across the network showing total bandwidth use. A shows a typical workday traffic use for a business, where most of the bandwidth use is 9:00–11:00 A.M., and 1:00–4:30 P.M.—standard business hours. We note that during the lunch break, fewer users are on the network, as is also true in the off hours of 5:30 P.M.–9:00 A.M. B shows a typical file backup that occurs every night from 1:00–3:00 A.M. C shows a pattern of general usage 7×24, such as with an ISP backbone network. Note that these snapshots can be calculated per network, node, access circuit, or even virtual circuit.

Also note that these time intervals can typically be anywhere from milliseconds to hours. What are the traffic patterns during the peak usage times? Here are a few calculations used to size physical (for example, port speed) and logical bandwidth (for example, PVC CIR rate) and are all measured in bps increments:

▼ Peak burst of traffic (not same as peak traffic condition)

■ Average peak condition

■ Maximum peak condition

- Sustained peak condition
- Constant data flows for x duration
- ▲ Minimum bandwidth required (e.g., 64 Kbps for voice)

One way to get a handle on existing traffic flows is to evaluate the average, average peak, and maximum peak of traffic on the network at time slots throughout the day, say at 15-minute intervals. This sampling technique, when graphed on an x-y axis, will resemble those in Figure 12-2.

NOTE: There will often be multiple flows or sessions that need to be aggregated into a single graph for physical and logical port and circuit sizing.

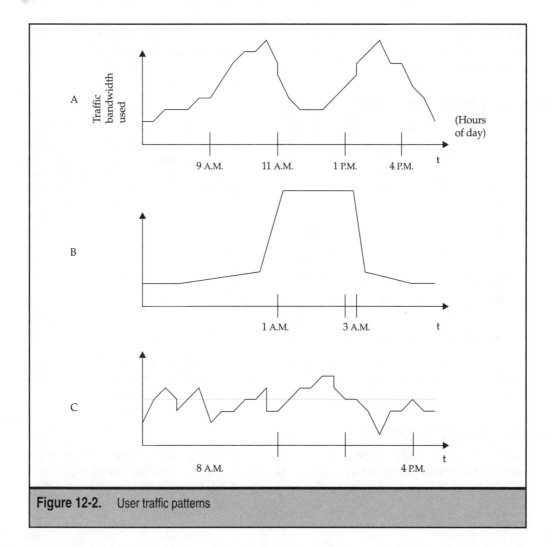

Figure 12-2. User traffic patterns

PROTOCOLS

The full suite of user protocols must be defined for both existing and planned applications. This includes all protocols serving all seven layers of the OSI reference model, which includes everything from lower-level physical media requirements to upper-level presentation software and operating systems. Multiple protocols per layer are often present, especially at the higher layers.

Next, define what protocols are to be used on both the application side and the network side. What functions are specific to applications that warrant special consideration? Also, define how users will internetwork these protocols. The bridging, routing, or switching required will depend heavily upon the protocols. For example, some protocols such as NetBEUI and DEC LAT are not network-layer-addressable protocols and must be bridged, while others such as FTP can be routed through the use of TCP/IP at the network level. Will the user require protocol encapsulation, conversion, translation, or just bridging and switching? Are higher-level directory services required (for example, X.400, X.500)? Also, know if there are any special or proprietary implementations of these protocols and how they operate.

Common Application Requirements

As there are thousands of applications available to businesses from desktop word processing to enterprise resource planning (ERP), you need to understand the capabilities that applications require from the network. Enterprise software market is defined as software used by companies to automate their business operations. Business applications focus on providing solutions to business-related issues. Five primary areas of application solutions are

- ▼ Supply-chain management (SCM)
- ■ Enterprise resource planning (ERP)
- ■ Customer relationship management (CRM)
- ■ Business-to-business (B2B) and business-to-consumer (B2C) e-business software
- ▲ Desktop productivity software (e.g., Microsoft Office Suite)

Table 12-9 lists some departmental functions that could use the network. You must understand application requirements on the network, such as what application architecture is used, as covered in the next section.

Application Architecture

Applications generally follow a specific application architecture, which establishes the standard user and programmer interface. When developers use an application architecture, they set the standard method of protocols for programming, data transfer and stor-

Departments	Functions
Sales and Marketing	-Product information -Customer information -War stories -Leads -Competitive information -Online training -Presentations -Customer database access -Newsgroups—feedback, what works, issues
Product Development	-Product specs -Schedules -Team assignments -Customer issues -Competitive information -Project information -Software libraries -Engineering information -Design drawings
Customer Sales/Services	-Sales support centers -Product information -Product support database -Problem status -Customer concerns -News flashes -Online training
Human Resources	-Benefits updates -Employee and group information -Policies and procedures -Job postings -Phone directories -Employee information databases -Maps -Medical referrals -Lookup of personal information -Training and registration

Table 12-9. Application Examples by Department

Departments	Functions
General Applications	-Access to data warehouse
	-Newswire clippings
	-Conference-room reservations
	-Libraries
	-Subscription services
	-Historical information
	-Technology centers
	-Competitive analysis
	-Strategies
	-Literature ordering
	-Surveillance
	-Application front-end
	-Whiteboarding

Table 12-9. Application Examples by Department *(continued)*

age, and data-access methods for consistency across the network. Some examples of application architectures include

▼ TCP/IP Internet architecture

■ IBM Systems Application Architecture (SAA)

■ DEC Network Applications Support (NAS)

▲ Novell's NetWare

The trend towards consolidation within a single protocol architecture, such as TCP/IP, continues, so your design might be simplified. Many networks today support only TCP/IP architectures, as Novell and other vendors have implemented TCP/IP stacks into their solutions.

Addressing and Naming Schemes

What are the user addressing and naming schemes currently being used? Are they flat addressing conventions or are they hierarchical in nature? Are they permanent? If not, can changes, modifications, and new adaptations be made easily? Can they fit in with a global addressing scheme?

With the increase in TCP/IP implementations, understanding the current addressing plan will be critical. Are the addresses private or public? Is there a corporate addressing plan or did every site just choose an address?

Overhauling a network addressing plan can be painful but might be necessary; however, you can use dynamic address servers such as DHCP servers and services such as IP-enabled frame relay to avoid the requirements to change addresses.

TIME AND DELAY CONSIDERATIONS

One of the most important aspects of data communications networking is time and delay considerations and how applications and protocols manage delay or are affected by delay. *Response time* is defined as the round-trip delay from source to destination, or the time it takes a user to send a request until he or she receives a reply. Response time can be broken into various components, including host processing time and network time. Figure 12-3 shows a picture of a basic network and breaks out the various delay components:

▼ **Media access delay**   The time it takes to access the media or LAN. The time will be very small under normal conditions but under load and congestion, the delay could be a factor.

■ **Serialization delay**   The time it takes to output a packet onto a serial link. Serialization delay is a major factor on low-speed links.

▲ **Network delay**   The time it takes for a packet/frame/cell to travel across the service provider's network. Network delay components can include propagation delay, equipment switching/routing delays, and software/hardware processing delays.

Serialization delay can become a dominant delay element when large packets are transferred across low-speed links. The components that affect serialization delay are packet size, link speed, and the end-to-end distance of the low-speed link. Table 12-10 shows the serialization delay for various FR frame sizes and link speeds. Serialization delay is computed as the frame size in bits divided by the link bandwidth in bits per second. The third component might not be directly controllable via the designer because the distance of the low-speed local loop depends on the distance from the customer site to the service provider's network switch. If the distance is long, your serialization delay will be close to a multiple of two of the serialization delay for that link. If the distance is short, the multiple will be close to 1. The less time you are on an access road to an interstate, the shorter your total trip time. As discussed in Chapter 8, network switches can implement cut-through techniques to keep the multiple closer to 1 for long local loops.

In high-speed packet networks, network delay is mainly driven by propagation delay (traveling at the speed of light, it takes 8 milliseconds to travel 1000 miles). Network delay other than propagation delay involves switch, processing, and routing delays and will vary based on a service provider's offering or service (a private line offers far less delay than an IP packet network) and the service provider network architecture (some FR architectures have inherently lower network delay than others).

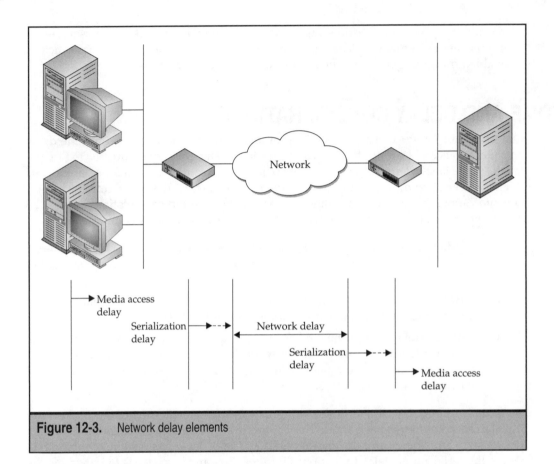

Figure 12-3. Network delay elements

Line Speed	1 Byte	64 Bytes	256 Bytes	1500 Bytes
64 kbps	125 us	8 ms	32 ms	187 ms
256 kbps	31 us	2 ms	8 ms	47 ms
512 kbps	15.5 us	1 ms	4 ms	23.4 ms
1536 kbps	5 us	320 us	1.28 ms	7.8 ms

* ms = milliseconds and us = microseconds

Table 12-10. Serialization Delay for Various Frame Sizes and Speeds

As delay is a major component relating to application throughput, how the application is written and the protocols that the application use will also greatly affect throughput. The TCP/IP implementation of windowing, which allows multiple packets to be transmitted before waiting for an acknowledgment, can reduce the impact of delay. In addition to windowing, packet size will drive application throughput as will host processing time. As the designer, make sure that you understand the application characteristics and make sure that your network will offer equal or better delay than your objective.

Blocking versus Storage versus Queuing

Invariably, every network will eventually encounter some network congestion. It is important to understand how the user applications and protocols will respond to congestion conditions. Congestion conditions are generally handled by the network in three ways: by employing blocking, storage, or queuing. Each of these can have major effects on the user traffic. When a technology uses blocking, the user traffic flow is blocked until sufficient bandwidth is available to continue the transmission. Some technologies just "drop the information out onto the floor" during congestion conditions, assuming that the user has employed some form of higher-level protocol at the CPE transport through application level to stop the flow of information until congestion clears. Others notify the user and simply block the transmission flow until the congestion clears or the user slows down transmission of data. The determination to use or not use blocking is very important; many delay-sensitive applications cannot handle blocking or data dropping and, more importantly, the retransmission of data after the original transmission data has been blocked or dropped. SNA applications are one example, as is real-time traffic such as voice and video.

Storage and queuing are similar and often used together. Queuing is the method of allowing data to be stored in buffers in the order it was received (FIFO) until there is sufficient bandwidth to transmit it to its destination; it is sent out in the same order it was received. The primary example of queuing discussed already is the packet switch, which queues packets until transmission bandwidth is available. Storage is used in store-and-forward networks, and typically signifies the use of memory buffers in a FIFO arrangement. Both queuing and storage increase delay through the network.

Blocking, storage, and queuing vary by technology and by implementation within each technology. Please refer to hardware and software vendor's implementation specifics.

CONNECTIVITY

Now that we have a handle on the types and characteristics of traffic required by the user for transport, we now take the next step to define user connectivity requirements. In many cases, user connectivity will be defined by existing or available connectivity methods. For example, some remote locations might have only dial, xDSL, or cable access. First, we look at the differences between user-to-network and network-to-network connectivity. Geographic connectivity requirements play an important factor in traffic patterns, as the current infrastructure and design of cabling and local connectivity. Finally, remote access requirements are introduced.

User-to-Network and Network-to-Network Connectivity

What is the minimum speed (data-access and data-transfer rate) required for connectivity? What types of devices will be connected and what data rates can they transmit? What is the distance involved between user equipment and data-communications equipment? What vendors and models are now used? What are the vendor's software and hardware vendor specifics? What mode of addressing is required for the access and backbone portions? What are the protocols (physical, data-link, and so on) required for basic connectivity?

Once the user-to-network interface (the connectivity specified between the user and the service provider) has been defined, any network-to-network interface requirements for internetworking new and existing networks to the data-transport network must also be defined. To what extent is ubiquitous connectivity required? Any-to-any connectivity can take on many forms and can occur at any of the seven protocol layers. Will the connectivity community be homogeneous or heterogeneous? Will private, public, or a hybrid network access and transport be required? What form of technology will be used for network interfaces and internetworking? Examples include

- ▼ Multipoint or point-to-point
- ■ Multiplexing or concentration
- ■ Switched (circuit, packet, frame, or cell)
- ■ Bridged or routed
- ▲ Hybrid

Geographical Requirements

Where do the applications reside? Is the planned network local, national, or global in nature? Are remote locations at major cities or "bandwidth-challenged" locations? Are there specific geographical location restrictions based on topology, transport media availability or quality, user communities, existing facilities, or any other limitations? Are the users fixed or mobile?

Structure: Central versus Distributed

What type of data processing structure is required? The technologies described in this book apply to both distributed and centralized processing. Is the design hierarchical in nature? Hierarchical LAN/MAN designs are the first step in building WANs because of the importance of the segmentation of data user groups. The proliferation of LAN switching has made hierarchical LAN design hierarchical and in some enterprises virtual in nature.

Figure 12-4 shows an example of a hierarchical LAN/MAN configuration. Here, Ethernet LANs are built in a three-tier hierarchy. Tier 1 is the local floor LAN segment

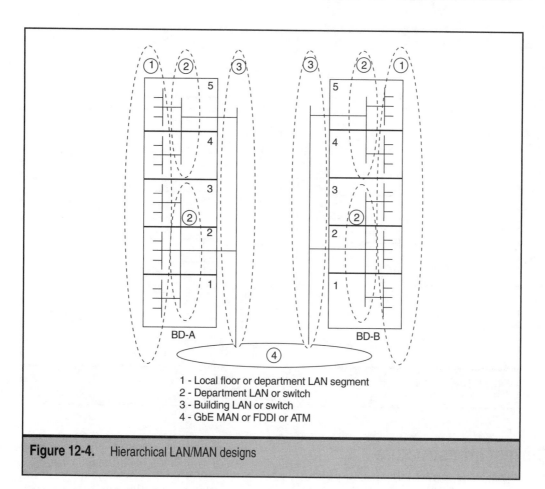

Figure 12-4.   Hierarchical LAN/MAN designs

(100 Mbps Ethernet), tier 2 is the departmental LAN segment or switch, and tier 3 is the building LAN segment (1000 Mbps switched or routed). The fourth tier is the Gbps Ethernet, FDDI, or ATM MAN connecting users in both buildings. Department 1 comprises floors 1, 2, and 3 of building A, department 2 comprises floors 4 and 5 of building A, and so on, and has a 100 Mbps shared Ethernet. This allows segmentation of user traffic and prevents "flooding" the Gbps Ethernet MAN with information transfers it never needs to process. Most enterprises combine these junction points between LAN segments with switches or routers, depending on the number of users and what they are sharing. Figure 12-5 shows an example of how to design a LAN/MAN *without* this hierarchical design. Here we see an FDDI or 100/1000 Ethernet or ATM building LAN ring that could be a collapsed backbone within a single device, such as an intelligent hub, router, or switch.

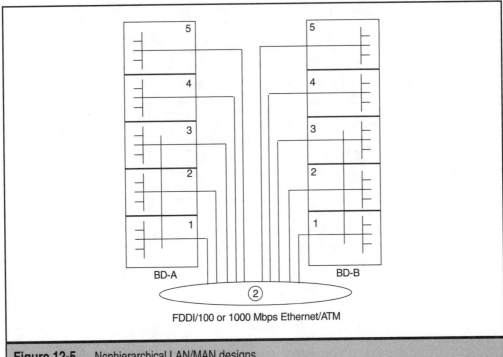

Figure 12-5.   Nonhierarchical LAN/MAN designs

Current Infrastructure

What is the current infrastructure being used? Are user communities heterogeneous or homogeneous? What impact will implementing a new platform or architecture have on existing facilities? The designer must understand the existing voice, data, and other media structures to effectively use all existing resources in the new network. Migration from an existing architecture to new platforms is often an arduous and difficult process, and this is why designers should select evolutionary technologies and services over revolutionary ones whenever possible. The designer must consider the use of temporary gateways as the first step at internetworking the current infrastructure with a new architecture.

Remote Access

Do remote users operate in a fixed or mobile environment? If users are in a fixed environment, what type of access facilities are available—dedicated or switched? If users are mobile, what geographic or virtual connectivity areas do they typically travel through? What access facilities are available in these areas, and how do they communicate today?

Remote access facilities could be

▼   Point-to-point dedicated circuits (private line, FR, ATM)

■   Dial access (asynchronous, ISDN)

■   Wireless access

■   Dedicated access services to a public switched service (xDSL or cable to IP)

▲   Combination of these access services (IP-VPN)

AVAILABILITY, RELIABILITY, AND MAINTAINABILITY

A user is concerned with three major measures of network quality: availability, reliability, and maintainability. While availability and reliability calculations are defined thoroughly in Chapter 13, a user must also look at availability as related to available network-wide capacity. A user always wants to have enough capacity to transmit his or her message (regardless of the message size) in a reasonable amount of time. The network allocates capacity across the network, rather than to a specific user. Maintainability is defined as the measure of effort a user or network provider must put into the network to maintain its operating efficiency. Maintainability can include

▼   Defining how the designer will expand the network as requirements increase

■   Expandability and flexibility of the hardware platform

■   Ease of software upgrades

▲   Built-in tools for network monitoring, management, troubleshooting, trending, and reporting

Does the protocol require fault tolerance, and what is the level of error tolerability? How much sharing of resources and capacity is tolerable? Does the user protocol require guaranteed delivery? These are some of the questions that are asked of the user regarding the reliability of existing systems.

AMOUNT OF USER CONTROL

To what degree does the user need control of network resources? Many public network service providers are struggling with this question. Today, many users want more and more control over setting their service parameters than in the past. In practice, many users want the comfort level of "seeing" the network while allowing the vendor to actually administrate the network under the "control" of the customer. Customers require the capability of intelligent network management and tools that they can use to monitor the health of and reconfigure network resources. The designer must draw the line as to which resources users can access and which they cannot. One option is to allow users to see the network status of resources but in a manner that will not permit the resources to be directly modified. Too much information can be dangerous, so carefully evaluate what the user really will need to see of the network. The best solution is to provide a true level of transparency while providing optimal user control of network resources even if the vendor administrates it.

Control can take on either a centralized or distributed nature. In private networks, control rests within the corporation. Public networks are typically managed and controlled by the service provider, but visibility can be provided through managed services portals. Many management services provide the user a browser interface to the Network Management System. Centralized control is often the case for networks managed by local or regional network-management centers. Distributed control is often the case where a corporation has distributed operations of their networks. Managed services offered by most service providers can allow users to view their network in a distributed manner while the service provider proactively manages and controls the network from a centralized management center.

EXPANDABILITY, SCALABILITY, AND EVOLUTION

The network must be able to react to change. Therefore, it must be designed with the capability to expand, evolve, and be scaled either up or down. Network contracts should allow at least 20 percent room for network increase or decrease. The network plan should define an evolutionary cycle, not a revolutionary change. It should provide the capability to change configuration rapidly to meet changes in a dynamic user environment. This change could involve hardware and software configurations, addition or deletion of services, constant technology updates and upgrades, and protocol flexibility. Strict change procedures should accompany any change, so that the network manager understands the scope of the change, no matter how trivial it might seem. Expansions and migrations should be planned in advance, based on user projections for expanding current applications or adding new ones. Dates should be achievable yet provided in the broadest form available (for example, 2H2005).

One method of ensuring that the network can handle future growth is to overbuild the network with capacity (hardware, software, processing power, memory, and bandwidth), but this can become expensive, and can prove to be misguided if the excess allocations are in the wrong location, the technology changes, or the network requirements were overestimated in the first place. Effective network capacity planning is the answer to this problem, along with education of the users on how to forecast their needs as far in advance as possible. Another option is to use a public data service as the network of choice, thus placing the burden of escaping network technological obsolescence in the backbone network onto the public service provider.

SERVICE ASPECTS

Service aspects such as network management, billing, security, user support, and disaster recovery are important topics with a broad range of standard and proprietary solutions.

Network designers must understand the capabilities offered by each technology and protocol and make their decisions based on sound business criteria along with principles defined in this book.

Network Management

Most users require fast end-to-end fault identification and isolation during network failure conditions. This can be accomplished through a proactive network monitoring and management system that provides configuration capabilities and dynamic capacity allocation through a user-friendly network management interface. Much more is said on network management in Chapter 19, but the primary idea is to have a proactive approach to network management.

Billing

For public data networks, billing is based on either public pricing or tariffs. Does the user require special billing arrangements? Are costs allocated by individual, department, or company-wide? Does the customer agree with these methods? Is itemized billing required, and to what extent does each user analyze network costs?

For strictly internal company networks, determine how the network and traffic transport costs are charged back to the user departments or customers. If it is strictly an internal enterprise network, can a charge-back scheme be implemented? What method of expense allocation accounting is preferred? Can bills for different services be consolidated?

Redundancy and Disaster Recovery

What level of redundancy and disaster recovery is required? The highest level of redundancy and disaster recovery is one fully redundant system element for every live system (1:1). A more conservative approach is one redundant system for N systems (1:N) or (N+1) systems. Is the user prepared to incur the higher cost of such redundancy, or will fewer systems suffice? Is outsourcing of disaster recovery to a public data service provider an option? Remember, disaster recovery plans should be periodically tested at least twice per year to ensure they indeed work and provide true backup.

Security

What level of security is required? What levels of passwords and access are required? What resources require what levels of access, and how are they accessed? Does the user require end-to-end security? How sensitive is the information being passed? Can someone actually compromise your operations though any part of the network access? This question becomes extremely important as enterprises open their internal network applications to partners, customers, and the public Internet. Do you have the appropriate firewalls, packet and circuit filters, application filters, and intrusion detection? What is your security policy? Can you track down and catch an intruder once you have identified an intrusion? As security is a major concern, more detail is covered in Chapter 18. Often, security comes down to how much the enterprise can afford relative to what they are trying to protect.

User Support

User support should be tailored to the user's needs. Users with highly complex routing protocols, proprietary protocol implementations, and executive level users will require many more resources than a standard, single protocol user, mostly because of the complexity of the problems that can occur. The more complex the protocols and the more mixed the protocol environment, the greater will be the complexity and level of support required. User expectations should be managed from the day the network is first announced through the day the user gains actual access to the network. The levels of user support should be agreed on before the design is complete.

It is sometimes difficult to understand what the user defines as "excellent service" or "quality service." These values vary based on the users past experience with similar networks. One gauge of user support requirements is to monitor existing systems support and the level of dedication and time required. Ask what services the users currently operate, or what access will be required with the new network. It is important to establish lines of communications with users so that they can alert the network designer of future requirements as they occur. Start the long-term planning process in the initial design.

BUDGET CONSTRAINTS

Though users try to spend as little money as possible on the network, they still want access to every resource possible. Either way, the designer must design the network within a given budget, accommodating the largest number of users and applications within the available budget. This becomes a balance between cost, capabilities, and connectivity. How far can you push the economics and still provide functionality and connectivity?

A network becomes cost-justified if it improves operating efficiency, helps users meet corporate objectives, provides a potential revenue increase, and/or avoids larger expenditures. Many networks have an ROI of less than one year. Additional criteria include improving customer service and creating new services for the user. Ultimately, the question must be asked, Can the network expenses be related back to the user, and will the network meet the desired business and technical criteria?

There is also the concern of who controls the network budget, the network managers or the users. Most often, it is the network manager. This is heavily influenced by how much control the user has over network expenditures. The rule is, the more critical the application and the closer it gets to the revenue stream, the more control the user has over what is purchased. When users have budgetary control, more care is exercised about what is placed on the network. When the network manager has control and the user is a customer, the user tries to place everything possible over the network. This is the point where departmental charge-back schemes might be implemented. The manager can also allocate a communications budget to each department based on the requirements discussed in this chapter. Either way, network costs must be controlled. Customers and users might have an existing hardware base, so the cost of additional equipment, or savings thereof, might not be the major consideration. What happens when the internal budget cannot meet the requirements? Outsourcing might then become a viable option.

POLITICS

Politics can cause a perfectly good network plan to go awry. Politics is part of the every-day business world, and it is also part of the requirements process. The user requirements should be scanned for hidden political agendas and decision criteria based upon political rather than technical or economical factors. This is not to say that we should have the equivalent of the McCarthy purges of the 1950s, looking for "communist" bits in every data stream. The network designer should be aware, however, and be prepared to dig a little deeper into the requirement should it appear that executive politics, vendor or application favoritism, turf wars, or any other politically based bias is negatively influ-encing the network-design process.

REVIEW

There are two viewpoints to requirements: that of the user and that of the designer or ser-vice provider. Obviously, the designer and service provider viewpoint is much more ex-tensive, and has warranted a more detailed discussion. We began with a discussion of the business challenges and requirements. We then moved on to the technical requirements, delving into the detailed technical user requirements gathering phase. Many characteris-tics of traffic affect the network design. The characteristics of protocols and the impor-tance of their addressing schemes play a major role. Understanding the transmission time and delay requirements for all traffic types is critical. Methods of connectivity were also discussed, and the calculations to help the designer meet availability, reliability, and maintainability of users were outlined. Two issues that plague every network designer were discussed: budget constraints and politics. The network designer, therefore, must compile all of the user requirements in the manner presented above and feed them into the traffic engineering and capacity planning phase.

CHAPTER 13

Traffic Engineering and Capacity Planning

Capacity planning used to be fairly straightforward for voice networks and private-line data networks. Traffic growth and volume figures were calculated, and the appropriate number of dedicated access circuits and trunks were added or subtracted with each design iteration, or incrementally added as required. If capacity exceeded projections, more bandwidth was ordered. With the advent of distributed computing and communications environments, the number of capacity contingencies has grown at an exponential rate. Advanced protocols, dynamic traffic patterns and characteristics, LAN to LAN and peer-to-peer internetworking has changed capacity planning into more of a heuristic guesswork approach than one based on concrete calculations. The traffic matrix is no longer a two-dimensional spreadsheet, but a multidimensional matrix including variables such as protocol types, multiple protocols, multiple traffic-flow patterns, multiple technologies, circuit options, many-to-many communication patterns, and more. These new technologies and traffic types and patterns have caused capacity planners to throw away the old traffic design books and simply over-engineer the network. This is especially true with packet-based networks, the Internet being the best example. Capacity planning and traffic engineering tools have come a long way in the past decade, but packet networks have also become more complex and distributed. New tools continue to emerge on the market that take these changes into account.

This chapter mixes some new views on traffic analysis with some older traditional methodology, leading you into the next generation of traffic engineering, analysis, and capacity planning. In this edition, we continue to present our tried-and-true methods for creating a traffic matrix, including enhanced calculations applied to traffic patterns for both old and new technologies, other methods of modeling traffic sources and switch performance, and some useful approximations for estimating performance that will help you accurately predict the required network capacity. We have left out the analysis of current vendor tools for two reasons: the material would go out of date too quickly, and the requirement to keep the book less than three feet thick. Also note that the beginning of this chapter is more theoretical and mathematical, while later on the chapter is more practical and implementation-oriented.

BACKGROUND: THROUGHPUT CALCULATIONS

Every user-access circuit is regulated by throughput. Throughput is the actual amount of user protocol data (as measured in bps) that is transmitted over the access circuit and received by the network node. Throughput can also be measured end to end across the entire network, and is always regulated by the weakest (speed) link. Access-circuit speeds are represented as a total capacity number, for example, a DS1 private line circuit can transmit up to 1.544 Mbps. The actual throughput that the user receives might be much less than that, depending on the protocols (that is, TCP/IP compared to frame relay [FR]) and equipment used. Each protocol contributes, in the most basic sense, a particular amount of overhead. Essentially, the throughput is the total transmission speed minus the protocol overhead. Overhead takes many forms, from pure header and trailer data wrapped around the user data (packet encapsulation and reformation) to time spent waiting for acknowledgments when data is not even being transmitted. When engineering a network, be concerned with the total throughput you will receive, not the total circuit capacity.

The common units of measurement for throughput are bits, bytes, packets, frames, and cells per second. These rates can be applied not only to transmission, but also to processing, filtering, and forwarding capability of network equipment. The amount of overhead affects the total throughput provided to the application sending data over an access line. The technology used and the number of encapsulations incurred before user-data transmission actually occurs also contribute to overhead.

Packets, Frames, and Cells per Second

If one were to ignore the intricacies of each higher-layer protocol, the maximum achievable throughput could be calculated. The terms *packets*, *frames*, and *cells per second* are used throughout the calculation, but to simplify the discussion, we typically default to *packets*. Let's first take an example using X.25 or IP packet switching or routing. The maximum achievable packets-per-second (PPS) rate on a physical circuit can be calculated as follows:

$$\text{PPS} = (P_K \text{ bits per second})\left(\frac{1 \text{ byte}}{8 \text{ bits}}\right)\left(\frac{1 \text{ packet}}{x \text{ bytes}}\right)$$

For example, a DS0 circuit ($P_K = 56{,}000$) has a maximum PPS transmission when using a 128-Byte ($x = 128$) packet size like this:

$$(56{,}000)\left(\frac{1}{8}\right)\left(\frac{1}{128}\right) = 55 \text{ PPS}$$

Assuming this is FR and that 128-byte frames are being used, this number would be 55 frames per second. The same calculations are carried forward for frames and cells per second, adjusting for the speed of the medium and the overhead involved (for example, packets might have 3 percent overhead per packet, whereas a frame might have 5 percent overhead per frame, both further reducing the effective throughput).

Effects of Overhead

The PPS calculated in the last example is actually somewhat misleading. It does not account for the overhead incurred in the switching and protocol handshaking operations. For example, take a 512-kbps FR fractional T1 access line. The frame size of 1024 bytes with overhead of 13 bytes (using extended addressing) per frame is used. The total frame size would be $1024 + 13 = 1037$ bytes. The actual frames per second throughput would be

(512 Kbps)(1/8)(1/1037) = 61.72 frames per second

Consider the same example using a frame size of 56 bytes. The same amount of overhead is 13 bytes, for a total frame size of $56 + 13 = 69$ bytes. The actual frames per second throughput would be

(512 Kbps)(1/8)(1/69) = 928 frames per second

At first blush, it appears that throughput has been improved, but, actually, it has degraded drastically. The overhead in the first example was only 1.25 percent, whereas in the second example it jumped to 18.84 percent. The calculations are as follows:

Overhead (example 1) = 13/1037 = 1.25 percent
Overhead (example 2) = 13/69 = 18.84 percent

This illustrates that the larger frame sizes are more efficient and provide higher line throughput than the smaller ones, but only up to a certain point. A low CIR PVC used with large frame sizes together with many DE frame discards could prove to be disastrous, as one error in a 1024-byte frame is more detrimental than one in a 56-byte frame. Think of how one flat tire on a bus full of people delays many more people than a flat tire on a car with four people, but the bus can be a much more efficient mode of transportation than 20 cars. These are the trade-offs of packet size to potential throughput.

In packet switching, the larger the packet size, the higher the probability of error, causing data to require retransmission. For any given bit error rate (BER), the probability of error increases with packet (or frame) size. If the BER is high enough, and packet/frame size is large enough, you are almost guaranteed to make an error for every packet/frame. This is why 128 bytes was chosen as the best compromise for packet switching. For noisy and error-prone lines, throughput can be increased by decreasing packet size to 64 bytes. The added overhead is offset by reduced retransmissions. The same problem applies to FR, where choice of frame size is a function of both the protocol being transported and the probability of frame discard.

Figure 13-1 illustrates the theoretical range for packet/frame size versus delay incurred. Cell-relay technologies such as SMDS and ATM have a fixed overhead per cell, effectively reducing throughput by approximately 9 percent (5-octet overhead out of the 53 total for ATM cells). This throughput reduction is made up for with large access-circuit speeds (typically DS3 and higher). It also shows the inefficiency of lower-speed cell services.

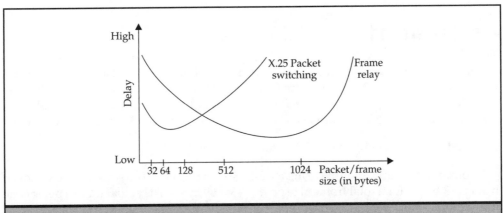

Figure 13-1.   Theoretical delay curves for packet/frame transmissions

TRAFFIC ENGINEERING BASICS: TRAFFIC CHARACTERISTICS AND SOURCE MODELS

Now that we have viewed performance from a throughput and overhead perspective, let's turn our attention to methods of approximating and estimating performance based on the traffic sources. These analytical methods focus on the modeling of real traffic patterns through source models.

Source Model Traffic Parameter Characteristics

There are two basic philosophies for characterizing source traffic parameters: deterministic and random. Deterministic parameters are based upon a specific traffic contract, with conformance verifiable on a unit-by-unit basis, for example, frames for FR and cell-by-cell for ATM. The agreement as to the traffic throughput that achieves a given performance is unambiguously stated.

The probabilistic (also called stochastic) model is typically measurable only over a very long-term average. Since the method and interval for computing the average can differ, conformance testing defines the details of the measurement method. Specification of the statistical model is also required.

Both statistical methods are useful approximations to the deterministic traffic contract behavior. These methods are very useful in analysis if a simple statistical model is chosen. Most of the following examples are based on an ATM cell as the base unit of measure, as it is easier to learn these models based on a fixed unit of measure.

General Source Model Parameters

This section defines some general source-model parameters used throughout the remainder of this chapter. There are some general terms used that need to be defined.

Burstiness is a commonly used measure of how infrequently (or frequently) a source sends traffic. A source that infrequently sends traffic is said to be very bursty, while a source that always sends at the same rate is said to be nonbursty. The formula that defines burstiness in terms of the peak traffic unit (that is, packet, frame, cell) rate and the average unit rate is defined as this:

$$\text{Burstiness} = \frac{\text{Peak Rate}}{\text{Average Rate}}$$

A good example of nonbursty traffic is a one-hour 384-Kbps videoconference. A bursty traffic source would be a standard TCP/IP user sending e-mail over an Ethernet LAN.

The *source activity probability* is a measure of how frequently the source sends, defined by the probability that a source is bursting:

$$\text{Source Activity Probability} = \frac{1}{\text{Burstiness}}$$

Utilization is a commonly used measure of the fraction of a transmission link's capacity that is used by a source, theoretically measured over an infinite period of time; however, in practice, it is measured over a long time interval. The definition of utilization is given in terms of the peak (packet, frame, or cell) rate and transmission link (access-circuit) rate, as follows:

$$\text{Utilization} = \frac{\text{Peak Rate}}{\text{Link Rate}}$$

and is calculated after all (protocol and switching) overhead is accounted for.

Poisson Arrivals and Markov Processes

Random arrival processes are described in general, and the Poisson (or Markov) process in particular, with reference to Figure 13-2. Poisson arrivals occur such that for each increment of time (T), no matter how large or small, the probability of arrivals is independent of any previous history. These events might be individual cells, a burst of cells, cell or packet service completion, or other, arbitrary events in models.

There is a probability that the interarrival time between events t, as shown in Figure 13-2, has a certain value called the *interarrival time probability density*. The following formula gives the resulting probability that the interarrival time t is equal to some value x when the average arrival rate is λ events per second:

$$\Pr(t = x) = \lambda\, e^{-\lambda x}$$

This is called a *memoryless process*, because the probability that the interarrival time will be x seconds is independent of the *memory* of how much time has already expired. This fact greatly simplifies the analysis of random processes since no past history, or

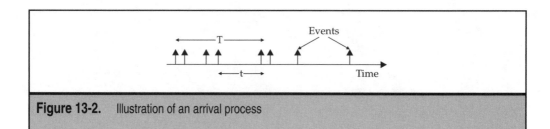

Figure 13-2. Illustration of an arrival process

memory, must be kept. These types of processes are commonly known as *Markov processes*, named after the Russian mathematician of the 19th century.

The famous Poisson distribution gives the probability that n independent arrivals occur in T seconds:

$$PR(n,T) = \frac{(\lambda T)^n}{n!} \, e^{-\lambda T}$$

These two thoughts are combined in a commonly used model called the Markov Modulated Poisson Process (MMPP). There are two basic types: the *discrete* (which corresponds to frame or cells) and the *continuous* (which corresponds better to higher-layer PDUs, which generate bursts of frames, packets, or cells). Figures 13-3 and 13-4 give equivalent examples for the discrete and continuous models.

The labels on the arrows of Figure 13-3 show the probability that the source transitions between active and inactive bursting states, or else remains in the same state for each cell time. In other words, during each cell time the source makes a state transition, either to the other state, or back to itself, with the probability for either action indicated by the arrows in the diagram.

The burstiness, or peak-to-average ratio, of the *discrete* source model is given by the following formula:

$$b = \frac{\alpha + \beta}{\beta}$$

where α is the average number of bursts arriving per second, and β is the average rate of burst completion. Often we think in terms of β^{-1}, which has units of the average number of seconds per burst. We define D as the cell quantization time having units of seconds per cell. Therefore, αD defines the probability that a burst begins in a particular cell time, and βD defines the probability that a burst ends in a particular cell time. The average burst duration d (in units of packets, frames, or cells) is then computed from the standard geometric series as follows:

$$d = \frac{1}{(\beta)(D)}$$

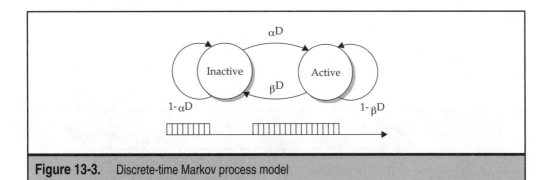

Figure 13-3.   Discrete-time Markov process model

The second, *continuous* time case is illustrated in Figure 13-4. The time elapsed from the beginning of the burst to the end of the burst is modeled instead of modeling the individual cells (frames, or packets). Some accuracy is lost in that the quantization inherent in segmentation and reassembly is not considered; however, we use in this book the simplicity in modeling it provides. The diagram is called a *state transition rate diagram* since the variables associated with the arrows refer to the rate exponent in the negative exponential distribution introduced earlier in the "Title" section. Both the discrete and continuous Markov models yield equivalent results except for the (unit) quantization factor D.

The corresponding burstiness b for the continuous process is

$$b = \frac{\alpha + \beta}{\beta}$$

and the average burst duration in seconds is given by the following formula:

$$d = \frac{1}{\beta}$$

Note how these formulas are identical to the discrete case except for the absence of the discrete cell time D in the denominator of the equation for the average burst duration of the continuous model.

Another distribution that is sometimes used to model extremely bursty traffic is that of the *hyperexponential*, which is effectively the weighted sum of a number of negative exponential arrivals. This turns out to be a more pessimistic model than Poisson traffic because bursts and burst arrivals are more closely grouped together.

Real LAN traffic measurements often indicate that these traditional traffic models are overly optimistic and represent ideal conditions. These results show that the LAN traffic measured at Bellcore is *self-similar*, which means that the traffic has similar properties regardless of the time scale on which it is observed. This is in sharp contrast to the Poisson and Markovian models, where the traffic tends to become smoother and more predictable as longer and longer time averages are considered. Tools are readily available as software that can be run on a laptop to measure these traffic flows.

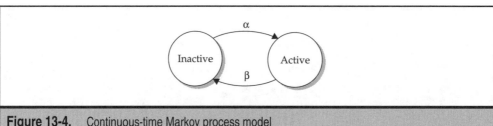

Figure 13-4. Continuous-time Markov process model

TRADITIONAL TRAFFIC ENGINEERING

In this section, we look at traditional traffic modeling, starting with the basis of voice traffic modeling, the traditional Erlang analysis. These fundamentals will help us lay the foundation for exploring basic packet, frame, and cell traffic modeling.

Statistical Behavior of User Traffic

Traffic patterns can be calculated in many ways. User information arrives at the network node based on statistical arrival rates. Typically, not all users need to communicate with all other users at the exact same time, therefore, statistical approximations can be used to model these traffic patterns. These approximations can either be based on mathematical calculations that first generalize the messages or packets and their arrival rates and second calculate the required bandwidth to support the total traffic, or they can be performed through packet-level modeling where each type of packet transmission is calculated and bandwidth is sized from the aggregate. This chapter presents aspects of both methods. For voice networks, the primary parameters to be concerned about are the call arrival rate, usually in calls per hour, (λ) and the average hold time or duration of message per call (τ). With these numbers, demand on the access node can be predicted in units called *erlangs*. Erlangs can be used in voice network modeling as well as circuit-switched data network designs, and have been used successfully for many years. They are much easier to understand than discrete packet transmissions and modeling and are, therefore, our first building block to traffic modeling.

Voice Traffic Modeling (Erlang Analysis)

The standard for statistically calculating an estimate of user demand based on random call arrival and holding was modeled by A. K. Erlang in the 1920s. This unit of measure, called the erlang, is calculated as

$$E = \lambda\tau = 1 \text{ erlang}$$

where λ = the call arrival rate in calls/hour, and τ = average holding time in hours.

This measurement was developed for analog voice communications, where calls would arrive at a voice switch or circuit switch (see Figure 13-5) at λ and whose total transmission time would be τ hours. In this example, there are five users at switch A. If each user calls every 12 seconds and talks for six seconds before hanging up, the total utilization of the transmission line is 0.5 erlang: $(1/12)(6) = 0.5$. It is obviously possible to offer 1 erlang for every user, but the laws of statistics show that much lower numbers of circuits can be maintained, since every user will not try to place a call at the same time. The actual utilization on an access line is normally much less than 1 erlang. One erlang is also equal to 36 call century seconds (CCSs). A camera took a picture of the call peg counters on the electromechanical switches every 100 seconds, thus the term call century seconds. Bell Labs was the first to standardize CCSs.

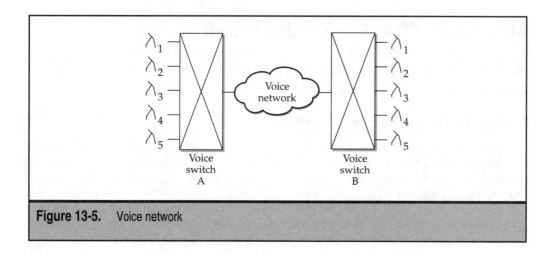

Figure 13-5. Voice network

The number and duration of calls vary, and therefore so must the erlang calculation. The formula for calculating erlangs with multiple call duration is

$$\sum_{n=1}^{k} \tau_n = \text{average erlangs}$$

where k is the total number of calls completed in an hour and τ_n is the length of the call in hours.

Thus, if 100 150-second calls, 200 100-second calls, and 300 50-second calls took place over a one-hour period, the number of erlangs would be 13.89. This number then drives the engineering of voice trunk and switch bandwidth. Since all blocked calls are "cleared," blocking should be calculated from the erlang calculations shown previously. The formula to calculate the probability of blocking is

$$B = \frac{E^N / N!}{\sum_{k=0}^{k=N} E^k / k!}$$

where $B = B(N, E)$ = percent of blocking as a function of the number of lines available and the number of affected Erlangs and

$$N! = N(N-1)(N-2)...(3)(2)(1)$$

For example, 20 calls per hour at three minutes per call would equal 1 erlang (or 36 CCS). The number of trunks required for 2 percent blocking would be four. As the call arrival rate increases, the probability that a new call will be blocked or dropped increases. There are erlang B (lost calls cleared) tables in most voice and packet-switch design books that graphically demonstrate blocking versus erlangs for various volumes of traffic.

QUEUED DATA AND PACKET-SWITCHED TRAFFIC MODELING

While erlangs work well predicting voice network and circuit-switched traffic rates, they do not work well with packet-switched and routed networks. In packet networks, some level of queuing is employed so that packets are queued in buffers and transmitted when congestion ceases, rather than being immediately blocked. Also, packet networks provide a mix of protocol and traffic types, whereas voice and circuit-switched networks provide point-to-point, transparent, homogeneous transport of information. Therefore, packet switching and routing demands a different analysis of traffic handling. Knowledge of the way packet/frame/cell modes of traffic are measured combined with a knowledge of the user traffic allow you to calculate the patterns provided to the access network so that a model of the access node can be simulated. We will now see how the statistical characteristics of the traffic directly affect the access design. We start with the notation used in queuing systems, and move through the common models for traffic modeling. Then we discuss some of the complex calculations for approximating traffic, overflow, and performance issues and analysis, and modeling of statistical multiplexer gain and LAN/MAN systems.

Queuing System Models Notation

There are three major queuing formulas for dealing with voice, TDM, and packet (queuing) models. Each of these formulas follows the same format.

The notation shown in Figure 13-6 gives this usual categorization of queuing systems. This is industry-standard technical notation that is used throughout the book.

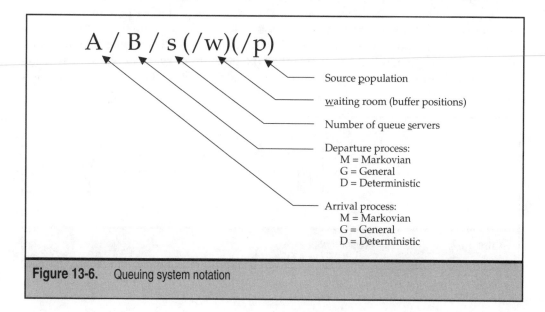

$$A \ / \ B \ / \ s \ (/w)(/p)$$

Source population

waiting room (buffer positions)

Number of queue servers

Departure process:
M = Markovian
G = General
D = Deterministic

Arrival process:
M = Markovian
G = General
D = Deterministic

Figure 13-6.   Queuing system notation

The three major modeling formulas include

> Erlang-B: $M/G/s/s$

which is used for voice-blocked calls cleared and TDM modeling,

> Erlang-C: $M/G/s/k$

which is used when the waiting room or queue (k) is greater than the number of servers (s) for voice with blocked calls held, or for operator services, and

> Packet: $M/G/1$

which is used for one server and infinite waiting and population, and commonly used to model packet, frame, and cell networks.

The third formula is of primary concern: packet modeling with $M/M/1$, where M designates a Markovian process (or Poisson arrival distribution—previously G designated the Gaussian arrival distribution). Thus, formulas are based on a single server with Poisson arrivals or equivalently negative exponential service times, and first-in-first-out (FIFO) service. Figure 13-7 shows this relationship between arrival rates λ service times, and a single server μ. Buffers and buffer overflow are discussed next.

Markovian Queuing Systems Models

Two particular examples of queuing systems are presented: $M/D/1$ and $M/M/1$. From this notation, each of these queuing systems has Markovian arrivals (negative exponential or memoryless burst arrivals) at a rate of λ bursts per second. The $M/M/1$ system has random-length bursts with a negative exponential distribution (Markov), while the $M/D/1$ system has constant-length bursts. The parameter μ^1 defines how many seconds (on average) are required for the transmission link to send each burst. For the $M/M/1$ system, this is an exponentially distributed random number of this average length, while in the $M/D/1$ system, this is the constant or fixed length of every burst. Both systems also have a single server (that is, physical transmission link) and an infinite population

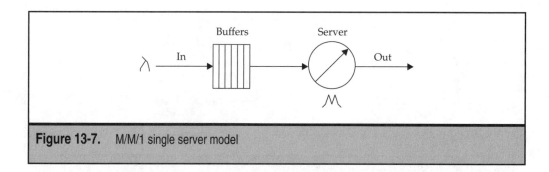

Figure 13-7. M/M/1 single server model

(number of potential bursts) and infinite waiting room (buffer space). The units of the buffer in the $M/D/1$ model are units (packets, frames, cells), while in the $M/M/1$ case the units of the buffer are bursts of units. Figure 13-8 illustrates these physical queuing systems and their specific relationship to a cell-based technology (such as ATM).

This is a good example of the trade-offs encountered in modeling. The $M/D/1$ system accurately represents the fact that the buffers in the switch are in units of cells; however, the bursts are all of fixed length. The $M/M/1$ system does not model the switch buffers accurately since it is in units of bursts and not cells; however, the modeling of random burst lengths is more appropriate to many traffic sources, such as with FR. The $M/M/1$ model is also very simple to analyze, and therefore it is used extensively to illustrate specific tendencies in FR and ATM systems. In general, if the traffic is more deterministic than the $M/M/1$ model (for example, more like the $M/D/1$ model), then the $M/M/1$ model will be pessimistic (there will actually be less queuing and less delay in the modeled network). If the traffic is burstier than the $M/M/1$ model, then the $M/M/1$ results will be optimistic (there will actually be more queuing and more delay in the modeled network).

Utilization and Capacity Calculations

In many of the following results, the system delay and loss performance is presented in terms of the offered load or utilization ρ, given by the following formula:

$$\rho = \frac{\lambda}{\mu}$$

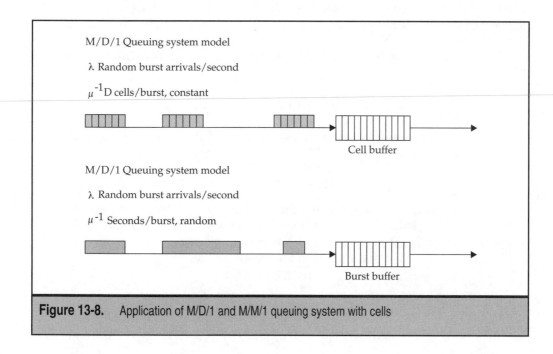

Figure 13-8.   Application of M/D/1 and M/M/1 queuing system with cells

Recalling that λ is the average number of arriving bursts (packets, frames, or cells) per second, and that μ^{-1} is the average number of seconds per burst, you can see that the offered load ρ is unitless. Thus, the offered load has the interpretation of the average fraction utilization of the resource capacity that is in use.

For a burst of B bytes at a line rate of R bits per second, the service rate μ is computed as follows:

$$\mu = \frac{8B}{R}\left(\frac{bursts}{seconds}\right)$$

The utilization calculated determines the average amount of time required to serve each message (τ):

$$\tau = \frac{B}{R}$$

The probability that there are n bursts waiting in the $M/M/1$ queue is given by the following formula:

$$\text{Prob [n burst in M/M/1 queuing delay]} = \rho^n (1-\rho)$$

When dealing with $M/M/1$ queues, as in packet switching, there is an average of N users in the queue:

$$N = \left(\frac{\rho}{(1-\rho)}\right)$$

where ρ is the probability that the queue is not empty and $(1-\rho)$ is the probability that the queue is empty. Figure 13-9 shows how the increase in utilization (ρ) causes an increase in the average queue size (N).

The average queuing delay (that is, waiting time), or w, in the $M/M/1$ system is given by the following formula:

$$w = \text{Avg [M/M/1 queuing delay]} = \frac{\rho/\mu}{1-\rho}$$

then the average delay ($d$avg) equates to the sum of the waiting time and the service time during stable queue conditions:

$$d\text{avg} = w + \tau = \tau/(1-\rho).$$

$M/D/1$ queuing predicts better performance than $M/M/1$. Indeed, the average delay of $M/D/1$ queuing is exactly one-half of the $M/M/1$ delay. The probability for the number of cells in the $M/D/1$ queue is much more complicated, which is one reason the $M/M/1$ model is used in many of the following examples.

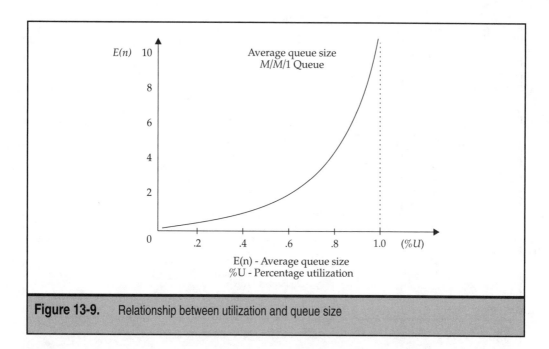

Figure 13-9. Relationship between utilization and queue size

Markovian Queuing Packet-Switching System Example

Take the following example for a packet-switched network. If a packet switch has five users, each transmitting ten messages per second at 1024 bits per message, with the packet switch operating over a DS0 (56 Kbps) trunk, the following applies:

$\lambda B = (5)(10)(1024) = 51{,}200$ bps
$p = 51{,}200$ bps$/56{,}000$ bps $= 91.4$ percent utilization
$\tau = 1024/56{,}000 = 0.0183$ seconds
$N = (0.914)/(1 - 0.914) = 10.63$ users in queue
$w = (10.63)(.0183) = 0.195$ seconds average wait time
$davg = 0.0183 + 0.195 = 0.213$ seconds average delay

Note that the queuing delay is an order of magnitude much greater than the transmission delay. Now, one portion of overall network delay is known, that which is within the packet-switch queue. Based on the queuing theory shown, the utilization of a trunk is directly influenced by the delay in queuing.

Figure 13-10 shows that as system utilization (*p*) increases, so does the delay through the system (*d*avg). This shows that the greater the utilization, the longer the delay. The cause and effects are simple; if delay in queuing becomes a problem, either move some users to additional trunks or increase the bandwidth of the trunk.

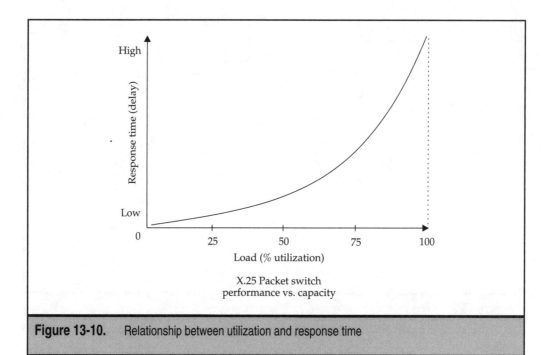

Figure 13-10. Relationship between utilization and response time

Bernoulli Processes and Gaussian Approximation

A Bernoulli process is essentially the result of N independent coin flips (or Bernoulli trials) of an "unfair coin." An unfair coin is one where the probabilities of heads and tails are unequal, with p being the probability that heads occurs as the result of a coin flip and $(1 - p)$ being the probability that tails occurs. The probability that k heads occur (and hence $[N - k]$ tails) as a result of N repeated Bernoulli trials ("coin flips") is called the *binomial distribution*, as given by

$$\text{PR}[k \text{ "heads" in } N \text{ "flips"}] = \binom{N}{k} \rho^k (1 - \rho)^{N-k}$$

where

$$\binom{N}{k} \equiv \frac{N!}{(N - k)!k!}$$

The Gaussian, or Normal, distribution is a continuous approximation to the binomial distribution when Np is a large number. Figure 13-11 compares the binomial and Gaussian distributions, for example, where $N = 100$ and $p = 0.1$. The distributions have basically the same shape, and for large values of Np, in the $Np(1 - p)$ region about Np, the Gaussian distribution is a reasonable approximation to the binomial distribution.

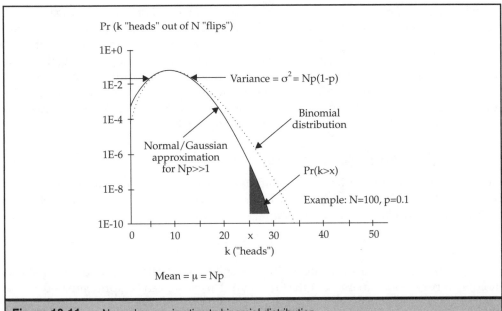

Figure 13-11. Normal approximation to binomial distribution

This is helpful in analyzing relative performance in that the probability area under the tail of the Gaussian, or normal, distribution is widely tabulated and implemented in many spreadsheets and mathematical programming systems. We approximate the tail of the binomial distribution by the cumulative distribution of the normal density, $Q(\alpha)$. We will use the following approximation several times to estimate loss probability or statistical multiplex gain:

$$\Pr[k > x] \approx Q\left(\frac{x-\mu}{\sigma}\right) = Q(\alpha) \approx \frac{1}{2}e^{-\alpha^2/2}$$

where

$$Q(\alpha) \equiv \frac{1}{\sqrt{2\pi}}\int e^{-x^2/2}\,dx$$

Traffic Engineering Complexities

Realistic source and switch/route traffic models are not currently amenable to direct analysis, with the results presented in this book providing only approximations under certain circumstances. Such approximate methods might have large inaccuracies, which can be ascertained only by performing detailed simulations or actual tests. Simulations are time consuming and, in the case of modeling complex high-speed technologies such as ATM and IP, cannot effectively model low cell-loss or packet-loss rates since an inordinate number of cells or packets must be simulated. For example, to simulate a cell-loss rate of one in a billion, at least 100 billion to 1 trillion cells must be simulated. Even with today's computers, this is a lot of computations to obtain a single point on a loss curve. Where possible, methods for extrapolating loss rates and estimating the occurrence of unlikely events should be used instead. Also, constantly changing source, switch, and network characteristics create a moving target for such traffic engineering models. For greater detail on traffic engineering specifically with ATM, see McDysan and Spohn's *ATM: Theory and Application* (McGraw-Hill, 1998).

Buffer Overflow and Performance

While it is important to understand the limits of the queue and delay imposed, it is also important to calculate when a buffer will overload and data will be lost. The probability that there are k packets in the $M/M/1$ queue is approximated by

$$Pk = \rho^k(1 - \rho)$$

With this value, we can calculate the probability of overflowing a buffer capable of holding B packets of variable length ($\Pr[u \geq B]$). This value can be approximated as

$$\Pr[u \geq B] = \sum_{k=B}^{\infty} P_k = r^B$$

Cell Buffer Overflow Analysis

This section analyzes several simple models of switch delay and loss performance as impacted by various aspects of a switch buffer architecture. For simplicity, Poisson arrivals and negative exponential service times are assumed. Output queuing delay performance then behaves like a classical $M/M/1$ system. Input queuing incurs a problem known as head-of-line (HOL) blocking. HOL blocking occurs when the cell at the head of the input queue cannot enter the switch matrix because the cell at the head of another queue is traversing the matrix.

For uniformly distributed traffic with random message lengths, the maximum supportable offered load for input queuing is limited to 50 percent, while fixed message lengths increase the supportable offered load to only about 58 percent. On the other hand, output queuing is not limited by utilization as in input queuing. Figure 13-12 illustrates this result by plotting average delay versus throughput for input and output queuing. For a more detailed analysis of input versus output queuing, which shows that these simple types of models are valid for switches with a large number of ports, see McDysan and Spohn's *ATM: Theory and Application*.

The consequence of this result is that almost all TDMs and cell switches have some form of output buffering. If input buffering is used on a cell switch that you are considering, check to make sure that some means to address HOL blocking is implemented. Examples of methods to address HOL blocking are: a switch fabric that operates much

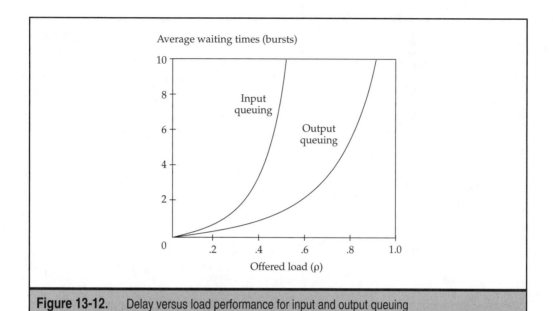

Figure 13-12.   Delay versus load performance for input and output queuing

faster than the cumulative input port rates, schemes where an HOL-blocked cell can be bypassed by other cells, or the use of priority queuing on the input. Some services and equipment offer the capability for priority ingress queueing, and this capability is extremely important for CoS IP WAN implementations.

The next example gives a simple, useful approximation for the output buffer overflow probability. For simplicity, an $M/M/1$ queuing system, which has an infinite buffer, is assumed, instead of a $M/M/1/B$ system, which would have a finite buffer. The overflow probability for a buffer of size B cells is approximately the probability that there are B/P bursts in the infinite queue system. Comparison with simulation results and exact analysis has shown that this is a reasonable approximation. When the average higher-layer *protocol data unit* (PDU) burst size is P cells, the approximate buffer overflow probability is given by the formula:

$$\text{Prob[Overflow]} \approx \rho^{B/P+1}$$

Figure 13-13 plots the approximate buffer overflow probability versus buffer size for various levels of throughput ρ assuming a PDU size of $P = 1$ cells. The performance for other burst sizes can be read from this chart by multiplying the x axis by the PDU burst size P.

Note that for a specific overflow probability objective and a fixed buffer size the load must be limited to a maximum value. We illustrate this concept by solving the above

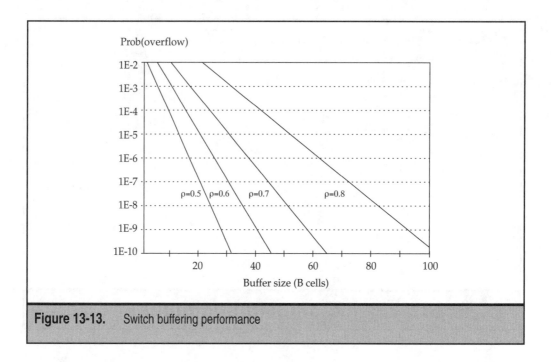

Figure 13-13. Switch buffering performance

equation for the overflow probability in terms of the required buffer size B to achieve an objective *cell loss ratio* (CLR). The result is the following:

$$B \approx P\frac{\log(CLR)}{\log(\rho)}$$

Buffer overflow probability in packet, frame and cell networks increases as the higher layer PDU sizes increase. When the PDU size approaches the buffer size, the loss rate is almost 100 percent. Figure 13-14 illustrates the impact of higher-layer PDU size (P) on buffer overflow performance for various output buffer sizes (B frames or cells).

The shared output buffer scheme has a marked improvement on buffer overflow performance because of sharing a single, larger buffer among many ports. Since it is unlikely that all ports are congested at the same time, the loss will be substantially less than an equivalent number of individual output buffer positions dedicated to each port.

Since the exact analysis of shared buffer performance is somewhat complicated, a simple approximation is presented based on the normal distribution. In the shared-buffer architecture, N switch ports share the common buffer, each with approximately the $M/M/1$ probability distribution requirement on buffer space. The sum of the individual port determines the shared-buffer probability distribution. The normal distribution ap-

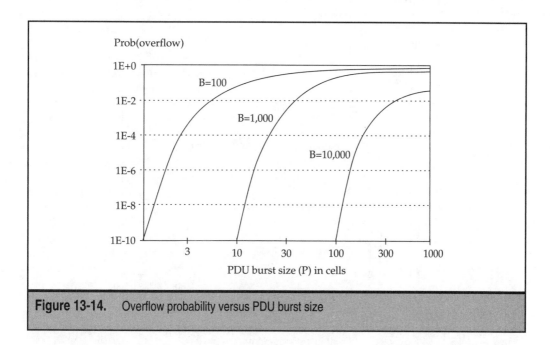

Figure 13-14.   Overflow probability versus PDU burst size

proximates a sum of such random variables for larger values of N. The mean and variance of the normal approximation are then given by the following:

$$\text{Mean} = \frac{N\rho}{(1-\rho)^2} \qquad \text{Variance} = \frac{2N\rho}{(1-\rho)^2}$$

Figure 13-15 shows a plot of the overflow probability versus the equivalent buffer size per port for shared buffers on switches of increasing port size (N), along with the dedicated output buffer performance for the large N from Figure 13-15 for comparison purposes. The offered load is $\rho = 0.8$, or 80 percent load. The total buffer capacity on a shared buffer switch is N times the buffer capacity on the x axis. Note that as N increases, the capacity required per port approaches a constant value. This illustrates the theoretical efficiency of shared buffering. Of course, a practical implementation has limits in terms of the shared buffer access speed.

Statistical Multiplexing Gain

The statistical multiplexing gain G is defined as the following ratio:

$$G = \frac{\text{Number of Sources Supported}}{\text{Required Number of Channels}}$$

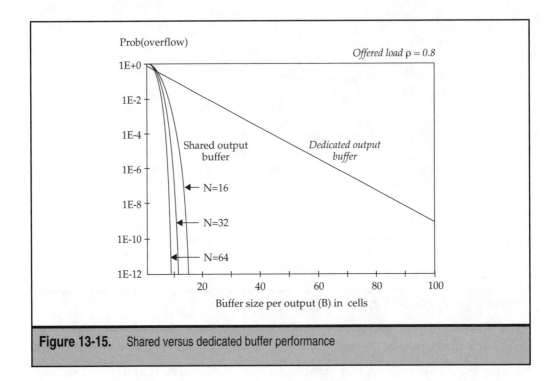

Figure 13-15.   Shared versus dedicated buffer performance

The statistical multiplex gain G can be computed from the binomial distribution, or estimated from the Normal distribution with the following parameters:

$$\text{Mean} = \frac{N}{B} \qquad \text{Variance} = \frac{N}{b}\left(1 - \frac{1}{b}\right)$$

where N is the number of sources, b is the burstiness (peak/average rate).

The required number of channels, C (in units of the number of peak rate sources), to achieve an objective CLR of $Q(\alpha)$ is given by

$$C \approx N/b + a\sqrt{N(b-1)}/b$$

The parameter η defines the peak source-rate-to-link-rate ratio, which means that the link capacity is $1/\eta$. Therefore, the statistical multiplex gain reduces to $G = N/C = N\eta$. Setting C in the previous equation equal to this link capacity $1/\eta$ and solving for N using the quadratic formula yields the result:

$$G \approx \frac{N(\sqrt{\alpha^2(b-1) + 4b/\eta} - \alpha\sqrt{b-1})^2}{4}$$

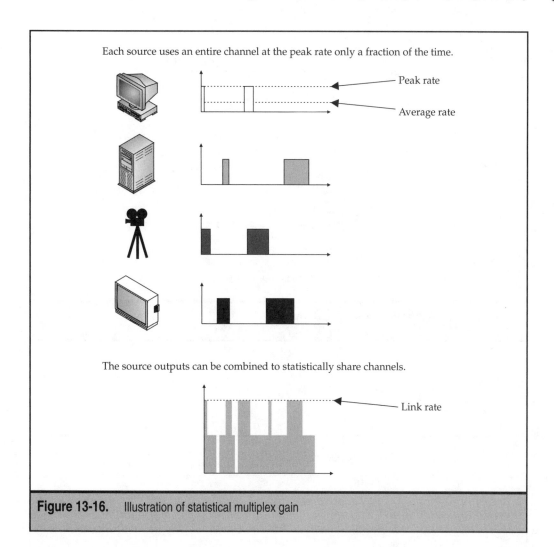

Each source uses an entire channel at the peak rate only a fraction of the time.

Peak rate

Average rate

The source outputs can be combined to statistically share channels.

Link rate

Figure 13-16. Illustration of statistical multiplex gain

Figure 13-17 plots the achievable statistical multiplex gain G versus the peak-to-link rate ratio η with burstiness b as a parameter for a CLR of 10^{-6}. This figure illustrates the classical wisdom of statistical multiplexing: the rate of any individual source should be low with respect to the link rate η, and the burstiness of the sources b must be high to achieve a high statistical multiplex gain G.

NOTE Traffic designers of large service provider backbone networks struggle with providing enough bandwidth to provide good and fair throughput to all sources, while selecting a high statistical multiplexing gain to achieve lower network infrastructure costs. Too high a gain could lead to customer dissatisfaction; too low a gain could lead to lower service margins.

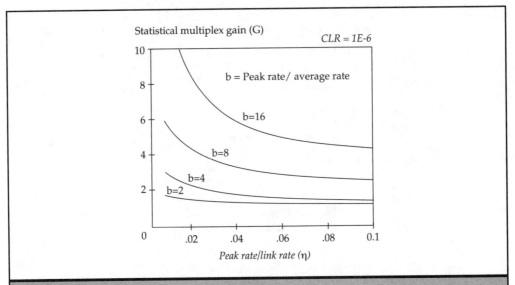

Figure 13-17. Achievable statistical multiplex gain

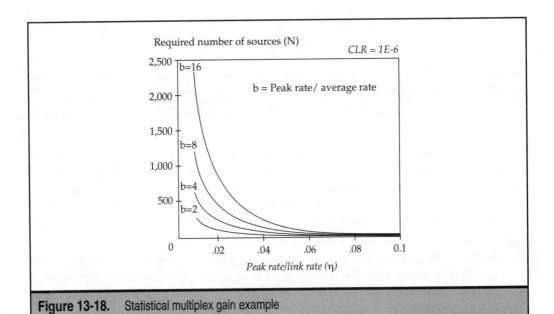

Figure 13-18. Statistical multiplex gain example

LAN Traffic Modeling

LAN traffic modeling is a difficult process and is subject to further study. Many LAN traffic characteristics, such as performance and throughput based on number of users, have been thoroughly studied and are provided by LAN equipment vendors. Figure 13-19 shows a comparison of Token Ring 4 Mbps LANs to Ethernet 10 Mbps LANs. Notice that the Token Ring throughput increases when the number of users increases because less time is spent token passing, whereas on the Ethernet (CSMA/CD) LAN the throughput decreases as the number of users increases due to the increased likelihood (and number) of collisions. FDDI response curves resemble that of the Token Ring, yet are more efficient, and Fast Ethernet response curves resemble 10Mbps Ethernet. More detailed calculations can be obtained using LAN traffic analyzers.

LAN switching and routing designs are concerned primarily with frames and packets forwarded per second and frames and packets filtered per second. Any design should also take into account packet and frame forwarding and filtering buffers, as well as the depth of LAN address table memory. Proprietary vendor overhead, as well as routing algorithm traffic (especially the distance-vector routing protocol) and routing protocol selected, can generate substantial traffic that reduces the bandwidth available to user traffic.

DQDB Traffic Modeling

The SMDS DQDB bus operates as a LAN, but handles calls similarly to the Erlang method, where messages contending for the bus have to wait until they can reserve a

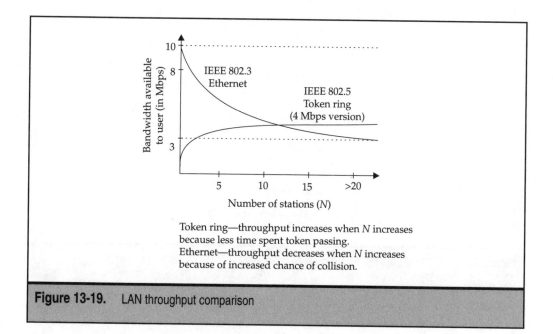

Figure 13-19. LAN throughput comparison

space on the bus. Call arrival rates are modeled differently. Even though the SMDS DQDB standard is almost obsolete, we still present this method as a transition into true packet modeling. Note that the last edition explained the SMDS DQDB bus in detail, but was omitted in this edition, as SMDS is rarely available today.

The traffic characteristics of a LAN (bursty traffic) attached to a MAN are shown in Figure 13-20. The variables of concern are

▼ **B**   Bandwidth consumed during burst (peak rate) in bps

■ **ts**   Average time slot used for transmission in seconds

■ **n**   Number of time slots between starts of bursts

■ **tb**   Time of each burst (average) in seconds $(\mu^{-1}) = 8(Db)/B$

▲ **Db**   Burst duration (bytes)

Note that a burst might contain one or more packets. For more than one packet per burst, use $(tb)(x) \Rightarrow tb$, where x equals the number of packets per burst.

Previous calculations can be taken one step further to model an IEEE 802.6 DQDB MAN where the traffic characteristics of the individual LANs attached are known. The required capacity of a DQDB MAN to handle all user traffic is calculated with the sum of

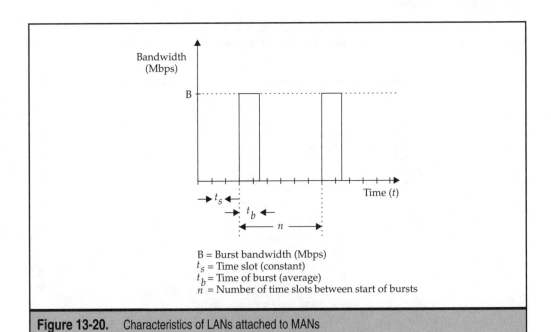

B = Burst bandwidth (Mbps)
t_s = Time slot (constant)
t_b = Time of burst (average)
n = Number of time slots between start of bursts

Figure 13-20.   Characteristics of LANs attached to MANs

the λ's (packets per second) of the local, remote traffic from and to the MAN, and the pass-through traffic. The formula is

$$\sum I_1 + \sum I_{rf} + \sum I_{rt} = \lambda^1$$

where $\sum I_1$ = local traffic

$\sum I_{rf}$ = traffic from remote MAN

$\sum I_{rt}$ = traffic to remote MAN

such that $\lambda^1 = 1/(n)(t_s)$

where all λ's are the sum of the users in that category and λ' represents the minimum required capacity of the local MAN. The capacity of the MAN would obviously be higher than the capacity required.

Since MANs often provide high-bandwidth connectivity to a small number of users, the traffic approximations just discussed become valid (where aggregations tend to have Poisson distributions). Huge bursts on the MAN can dwarf the normal large packet transmissions normally seen on the LAN.

Now let's look at a LAN/MAN traffic model that allows for the approximation of the number of LANs, based on traffic characteristics, that can be attached to a MAN.

The probability that a LAN time slot will be busy (ρb) is calculated as

ρb= Average number of slots consumed by burst/n = (tb/ts)/n = $8(Db)/[(B)(n)(ts)] = \lambda'/\mu$

Suppose a DS3 DQDB network has the following characteristics:

B = Class of Service (4, 10, 16, 25, and 34 Mbps) = 16 Mbps
ts = 53 octet time slot of 125 μs
$n = 5$
$Db = 1024$

The probability that a slot will be busy = $[(8)(1024)]/[(16 \text{ Mbps})(5)(125 \text{ μs})/13] = 0.8192 = 81.92$ percent.

And the probability that a LAN will transmit onto a particular MAN slot, in theory, is

$$\rho m = (\rho b)(\rho \text{inter-LAN})$$

where ρinter-LAN represents the fraction of inter-LAN bursts.

If there are N LANs connected to the MAN, the probability that k out of N LANs will be transmitting bursts onto the MAN at any given time is represented by the binomial distribution:

$$\binom{N}{k} \rho_m{}^k (1 - \rho_m)^{N-k} = P_N(k)$$

Assume that the MAN is y times faster than each LAN (for example, $y = 4$ for a DS3 SMDS MAN connecting to multiple 10 Mbps Ethernet LANs). If the number of LANs currently sending bursts exceeds y, then some or all of the LAN bursts will have to be queued or discarded. Approximating the DQDB MAN as an $M/M/1$ queue with average utilization (or throughput) of

$$\rho_{MAN} = (N)(\rho_m)/y$$

then the average $M/M/1$ delay is proportional to $1/(1 - \rho_{MAN})$.

We can optimize the ratio of throughput to delay, usually called the queuing power (P), as follows:

$$P = throughput/delay = \mu(1 - \mu)$$
$$P = [(N)(\rho_m)/y] - [(N)(\rho_m)/y]^2$$

The queuing power versus network utilization is plotted in Figure 13-21.

If $\partial P/\partial N$ is set to 0 ($\partial P/\partial N = 0$), the optimum number of LANs that can be connected to the MAN ($Nopt$) can be solved for

$$N_{opt} = \frac{y}{2\rho_m}$$

DESIGNING FOR PEAKS

When calculating the arrival rate of calls (λ), a figure was used called "busy hour." Any network must be designed to handle the busiest traffic periods, or data will be blocked or lost. Take, for example, the U.S. long-distance carriers (historically called interexchange carriers or IXCs), which need to design their voice networks based on the nation's busy

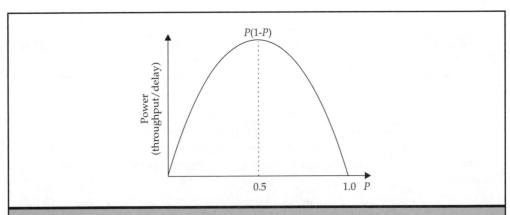

Figure 13-21.   Queuing power versus network utilization

hour. How long would you keep your long-distance carrier if there was a good chance that your calls would be blocked from 9:00 to 10:00 A.M. each day during the average five-day work week (one of the busiest hours for phone calls)? These carriers specifically design their networks to handle periods of peak usage (such as Mother's Day, the busiest calling day of the year), understanding the potential for blocking and loss during those time periods. Data networks must be designed with a similar thought process, but with potentially smaller increments in busy minutes!

Standard Busy-Hour Calculations

When λ is calculated and applied to the formulas for traffic load, it is assumed that the designer will use a call arrival rate measured or estimated during the peak busy period. This period is called the busy hour, and an hourly measurement is fine for most voice networks.

Data Equivalent of Busy Hour

Data networks have their own equivalent of busy hour. Take, for example, the New York Stock Exchange (NYSE), which each day after 5:00 P.M. New York time transmits huge amounts of information about the day's transactions across the world; the data center that performs switch/billing/file updates at 2:00 A.M. each morning; or the distribution company that synchronizes worldwide databases at the top of each hour, or offers real-time shipping information to anyone in the world, and, worse yet, due to a major event, has 30 percent of its customers requesting a shipment status at the same time! These are the times when the highest throughput is required for these networks. Thus, a network is designed to accommodate the peaks of its particular "busy hour" traffic requirements. It's too bad our highway systems cannot be designed to accommodate busy hour where every car could continue to travel up to the speed limit at any time of the day or night, and during any day of the year. But a highway design of this type would be cost-(if not space) prohibitive. Often, a cost tradeoff is used to balance the need of a larger network that might accommodate all traffic during busy hour with little to no delay compared to a less robust network that buffers or delays transmissions during busy hour.

The other major component of data is its burstiness. The bandwidth allocated to a phone call is usually the same: 56 or 64 Kbps for a standard voice channel, and down to 8 Kbps or less for compressed toll-quality voice. In data, however, an average user might transmit anything from a 2-kbit text file to a multimegabit graphics file. To complicate matters, multiple users might be simultaneously accessing a LAN or MAN, which in turn uses the WAN, and peak traffic patterns could vary drastically across the entire enterprise network with virtually no notice. Because of these characteristics, data traffic can be analyzed on a "busy hour" basis, but is more accurately represented with multiple snapshots down to a "busy minute" basis.

Now let's take a look at some methods of calculating data busy hour, keeping in mind that if applications warrant, these bandwidth requirements and thus calculations could require busy minutes or even seconds.

busy hour PPS = (busy hour packets sent + busy hour packets received) (3600 seconds/hour)

busy hour (BH) bps = (busy hour PPS × packet size) × 8 bits
link utilization = BH bps/speed of link

For example, to calculate the PPS required during busy hour:

BH PPS = (5 PPS + 5 PPS)(3600) = 36,000 PPS

To calculate the bps capacity required during busy hour:

BH bps = (5 PPS)(128 bytes)(8 bits) = 5120 bps

To calculate the maximum link utilization during busy hour:

link utilization = 5120 bps/9600 bps = 53.33 percent utilization

These statistics will tell if you need to add more processing power or bandwidth to accommodate busy hour traffic volumes.

Chapter 16 will show how busy hour statistics fit into the access node design.

DELAY OR LATENCY

When a network begins to slow down because of buffering, retransmissions, and/or any other time-affecting factor, its users begin to experience *delay* and might experience *loss* of traffic. Delay measured across a LAN, MAN, or WAN is also called "latency." Delay and loss will most likely cause response time and throughput to degrade, potentially cause application time-outs and retransmissions to occur, and might even cause users to lose data. The potential impacts of delay and loss can affect an application's design when performance is a major consideration, which is true in most networks and for most applications. Loss will impact the usable throughput for most network- and transport-layer protocols. This is true for almost all applications that are either bandwidth-limited (throughput is limited by the bandwidth available, and could be increased if more bandwidth were available) or latency-limited (throughput is limited by the network or receiving station delay, and could be increased if this delay were decreased). The accumulation of delay variation in multiple hop networks is important to delay-variation-sensitive applications, such as video, audio, and real-time interactive traffic. Variations in delay are also called "jitter." Appreciable variations in delay, on the order of 50 milliseconds or more, will be observed by most data users, particularly for applications that used a command-response mode of communications.

Causes of Delay

While actual transmission-path delay does contribute an element of delay to the network, the primary contributors to delay include

- ▼ Propagation path length
- ■ Line speed
- ■ Number of hops between routing or switching nodes
- ■ Hardware and software interface buffers
- ■ Load on every component across the path
- ■ Hardware/processor elements traversed (each adds delay)
- ■ Window sizes
- ■ Bit-setting selections (for example, D-bit)
- ■ Memory and buffers
- ■ Pad functions
- ■ Address or route database or table lookup and verification
- ■ Security
- ■ Changes in traffic load
- ▲ Filtering, forwarding, and processing packets, frames, and cells

Most network design tools routinely model delay, but they also need to account for the components of delay listed here. There are many ways by which to decrease delay, including decreasing network load, increasing circuit and switch capacity, more efficient routing, and adjusting device- and protocol-specific tuning parameters.

Circuit-, Message-, Packet-, and Cell-Switching Delay Basics

In circuit switching, the delay incurred by a user is based upon the message size and the time it takes to transmit it over the available bandwidth. For example, if a 2Mbit graphics file is being transmitted over a 128Kbps FR trunk, the total delay in transmission (assuming zero network and protocol delay elements) would be 2Mbit/128Kbps = 15.625 seconds.

Message switching delay closely resembles that found in FR networks. This is where the total delay is calculated the same as in circuit switching, but multiplied by the number of nodes the frame must traverse, minus 1. For example, assume that a user is transmitting the same 2Mbit file through the 128Kbps port on the user device. The frames are being passed through a four-node FR network (not counting the origination and destination nodes), with the middle two nodes passing the information at T1 speeds. The total delay would be [(2)(2Mbit/128Kbps)] + [(2)(2Mbit/1.544Mbps)] = 33.84 seconds. This calculation assumes that the user has the entire bandwidth of each link (and might vary for different implementations of FR).

Packet-switching delay is based on many of the packet-switching calculations examined above. The total message delay is calculated as

$$[\left(\frac{p}{c}\right)(n = 1)] + \left(\frac{r}{c}\right)$$

where p = packet size of first packet

n = number of nodes

c = capacity available in the transmission medium

r = remaining number of bits to be delivered in message

For example, if the 2Mbit graphics file is transmitted over the four-node network connected by 56 Kbps trunks, using packet sizes of 1024 bits, total delay in transmitting the entire graphics file would be $[(1024/56,000)(4 + 1)] + (1,998,976/56,000) = 35.79$ seconds.

Cell-switching delay best resembles packet-switching delay. There is some queuing (as in packet switching) but with a *fixed* number of cells. Data exceeding the available throughput is discarded, with no retransmissions. In most cases, the *entire* frame/cell needs to be completely read and processed before it can be transmitted out.

Impact of Delay on Applications

Two situations occur when a source sends a burst of data at a certain transmission rate across a network with a certain delay, or latency: these situations are called bandwidth limited and latency limited. A *bandwidth-limited application* occurs when the receiver begins receiving data before the transmitter has completed transmission of the burst. A *latency-limited application* occurs when the transmitter finishes sending the burst of data before the receiver begins receiving any data.

Figure 13-22 illustrates the consequence of sending a burst of length b equal to 100,000 bits (100Kb) at a peak rate of R Mbps across the domestic United States with a propagation delay τ of 30 milliseconds. It takes 30 milliseconds for the bit stream to propagate from the originating station to the receiving station across approximately 4000 miles of fiber since the speed of light in fiber is less than that in free space, and fiber is usually not routed along the most direct path. When the peak rate between originator and destination is 1 Mbps, and after 30 milliseconds, only about one-third of the burst is in the transmission media, and the remainder is still buffered in the transmitting terminal. This is called a bandwidth-limited application because the lack of bandwidth to hold the transmission is limiting the transmitter from releasing the entire message immediately.

Now let's look at the case where the transmitter has sent the *entire* transmission before the receiver has received any data. When the peak rate is increased to 10 Mbps, the situation changes significantly: The entire burst is sent by the workstation before it can even reach the destination. Indeed, only about one-third of the bits propagating through the fiber transmission system are occupied by the burst! If the sending terminal must receive a response before the next burst is sent, then we see that a significant reduction in throughput will result. This type of situation is called *latency limited*, because the latency of the response from the receiver (or the network) limits additional transmission of information.

Now let's apply the basic $M/M/1$ queuing theory from earlier as an additional element of end-to-end delay that increases nonlinearly with increasing load, and thus is of key concern to an application. The average $M/M/1$ queuing-plus-transmission delay in the network is $b/R/(1-\rho)$, where ρ is the average trunk utilization in the network. The point where the time to transfer the burst (that is, the transmission-plus-queuing time)

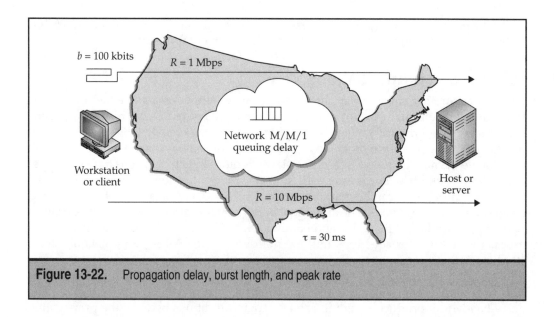

Figure 13-22.   Propagation delay, burst length, and peak rate

exactly equals the propagation delay is called the latency/bandwidth crossover point, as illustrated in Figure 13-23.

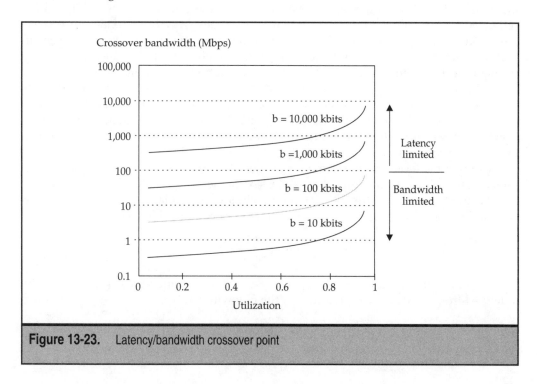

Figure 13-23.   Latency/bandwidth crossover point

In the previous example, for a file size of $b = 100$Kb the crossover point is 3.33 Mbps for zero utilization, and increases to 10 Mbps for 66 percent utilization.

Impact of Loss on Applications

Loss can be another enemy of applications. For many applications, the loss of a single frame or cell results in the loss of an entire packet (or an entire PDU). This is because the higher-layer network protocol (such as an IP packet) or ATM SAR sublayer in the AAL will fail in attempts at reassembly. Loss (or even excessive delay) can result in a time-out or negative acknowledgment in a higher-layer protocol, such as at the transport layer (TCP). If the round-trip time is long with respect to the application window size, then the achievable throughput can be markedly reduced. This is a basic aspect of all flow- and congestion-control methods. The amount of buffering required in the network is proportional to the product of the delay and bandwidth. In Figure 13-22, the delay-bandwidth product is 300 bits for a 1-Mbps link (30 milliseconds × 1 Mbps) and 3000 bits for a 10-Mbps link.

This situation is analogous to what occurred in early data communications over satellites, where the data rates were low, but the propagation delay was very high. The delay-bandwidth product is high in satellite communications because the propagation delay is high, while in terrestrial B-ISDN and ATM communications, the delay-bandwidth product becomes large because the transmission speeds are high.

Higher-layer protocols recover from detected errors, or time-outs, by one of two basic methods: either all information that was sent after the detected error or time-out is retransmitted, or only the information that was actually in error or timed out is selectively retransmitted. Resending all the information means that if N packets were sent after the detected error or time-out, then N packets are retransmitted, reducing the usable throughput. This scheme is often called a *Go-Back-N* retransmission strategy. The second method is where the packet that has a detected error, or causes a time-out, is explicitly identified by the higher-layer protocol; then only that packet need be retransmitted. This scheme is often called a *selective-reject* retransmission strategy. The usable throughput is increased because only the erred or timed-out information is retransmitted, however, this type of protocol is more complex to implement.

A simple model of the performance of these two retransmission strategies is presented here to illustrate the impact of cell loss on higher-layer protocols.

The number of cells in the retransmission window W is determined by the transmission rate R, the packet size p (in bytes), and the propagation delay τ as follows:

$$W = \left\lceil \frac{2\tau R}{8p} \right\rceil$$

The probability that an individual packet is lost due to a random cell loss, probability π derived from the CLR, is approximately the following:

$$\pi \approx \left\lceil \frac{p}{48} \right\rceil CLR$$

In the Go-Back-N strategy, if a single packet is in error of a window of W packets, then the entire window of W packets must be retransmitted. For the Go-Back-N retransmission strategy, the usable throughput η(Go-Back-N) is approximately the inverse of the average number of times the entire window must be sent, which is approximately

$$\eta(\text{Go} - \text{Back} - \text{N}) \approx \frac{1-n}{1+nW}$$

In the selective reject strategy, if a single packet is in error, then only that packet is retransmitted. For the selective reject retransmission strategy, the usable throughput η(Selective-Reject) is approximately the inverse of the average number of times any individual packet must be sent, which is

$$\eta(\text{Selective} - \text{Reject}) \approx (1 - n)$$

This formula is valid for the case in which only one packet needs to be transmitted within the round-trip delay window. It also applies to a more sophisticated protocol that can retransmit multiple packets, such as ATM's Service Specific Connection-Oriented Protocol (SSCOP).

Figure 13-24 plots the usable throughput (or "goodput") for Go-Back-N and selective-reject retransmission strategies for a DS3 cell rate R of 40 Mbps, a packet size p of 200

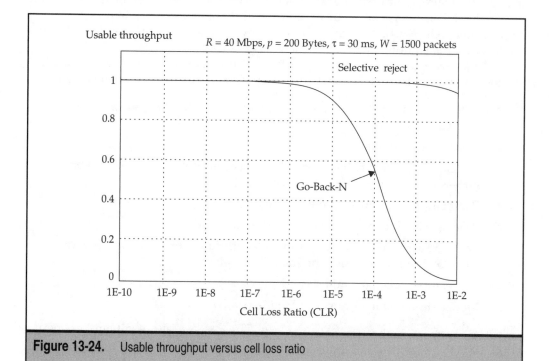

Figure 13-24. Usable throughput versus cell loss ratio

bytes, and a propagation delay of 30 milliseconds. The resultant window size W is 1500 packets. The retransmission protocols have nearly 100 percent usable throughput up to a CLR of 10^{-6}. As the CLR increases, the usable throughput of the Go-Back-N protocol decreases markedly because the probability that an individual window (of 7500 cells) will be received error free decreases markedly. As the CLR increases toward 10^{-2}, the probability of an individual packet having a lost cell starts to become significant, and even the selective-reject protocol's usable throughput begins to degrade.

These examples illustrate the importance of selecting a QoS class with loss performance that meets the application requirements. For example, TCP uses a Go-Back-N type of protocol and hence works best with low loss rates.

Data Services Delay

Sometimes delay components are not readily visible. For example, a PAD or a FRAD receiving asynchronous transmissions might packetize or frame this traffic at 128 bytes at a time, or it might wait until it receives 4 Kbytes and then split the message into packets and transfer (store-and-forward). Thus, greater delay is incurred when an entire message must be read into a node before being transferred. This example is very important when designing FR networks. In most FR networks, when an FR device receives a frame, it must read the entire frame into memory, calculate the CRC to verify the frame, and then transmit the entire frame on to the next node or to the user. The larger the frame size, the greater the serialization delay incurred, and the more buffer space required. Some combination frame/cell switches eliminate this delay by segmenting the frames into cells and immediately transmitting them across the WAN.

Let us take a remote user accessing a packet switched network via dial access and calculate total network delay. The total network delay is composed of many elements, such as

▼ Call setup delay (20 milliseconds—Call RQ, Call CN, ENQ, Auth, Resp, Ack, Clear RQ, and Clear CF)

■ Node delay (variable)

■ Buffer filling time for characters (32 milliseconds per 4 async on 1200-bps line—so 8 milliseconds for each access line)

■ Packet formation time (50 milliseconds)

■ Processor instruction execution (11–33 milliseconds)

■ Each hop across network (for example, if utilization on a 56 Kbps line was 10 percent, the delay would be 28 milliseconds)

■ Modem-to-modem (80 milliseconds) initiate

▲ Modem-to-modem terminate (10 milliseconds)

for a total network round-trip delay on a three-hop network of $(2)[(20)+(8)+(28)] + (3)[(50)+(11)] + 80 + 10 = 385$ milliseconds, best case. It is important to note that the modems in this example contributed to much of the delay, while CSU/DSUs in an FR or LAN/MAN environment would contribute very little delay.

Delay would be handled differently in an FR network, where the result depends on how the user applications higher-level protocols deal with delay. Most services, such as FR, will state a guaranteed delay and jitter *service level agreement* (SLA) and objective.

With larger frame sizes, the service that is providing the transport might segment or lose the frame. Also, delay might be incurred in storing portions of frames in buffers until they can be received and retransmitted in their entirety. In most FR switches, the entire frame is received and verified (via a CRC) before being retransmitted. There is also the danger of large frames being segmented by other protocols, such as IP and even ATM. This causes additional overhead in proportion to the frame size. The effects of protocol conversions, encapsulations, and translations on delay must all be accounted for by the network designer.

AVAILABILITY AND RELIABILITY

Two quality measures of hardware and software must be known by the network designer: availability and reliability. These values are found through vendor-provided calculations such as mean time between failures (*MTBF*) and mean time to repair (*MTTR*) or restore. Note that mean time to *respond* is sometimes calculated by service providers, and should not be confused with *MTTR*. Read the service contract. *MTBF* is calculated based on stress tests, the results of which are projected into the future, as well as through theoretical model projections, possibly using compilations based on the individual parts that make up the system. Other methods of measuring availability and reliability performance will also be explored.

Availability

Availability is the amount of time the system is working when compared to the measured lifetime of the system. Availability is calculated by

$$A_1 = \text{Availability} = \frac{MTBF_1}{MTBF_1 + MTTR_1} = \frac{\text{time system is working}}{\text{time system exists between failures}}$$

For highly reliable systems, this number should be at least 0.999, or 99.9 percent. This is commonly referred to as "three nines." Networks that provide public service offerings often have availability figures of 99.95 percent or higher. Each additional nine increases the order of magnitude by 10, thus an increase from 99.99 percent to 99.999 percent is a drastic increase in availability. But what does it cost for an extra 9? It might be more than one is willing to pay, as the cost increase in hardware, software, and services to provide 99.99 percent might also be tenfold.

Another way to look at availability is through its complement or reciprocal: *unavailability*.

$$U = \text{Unavailability} = 1 - \frac{MTBF}{MTBF + MTTR} = \frac{MTTR}{MTBF + MTTR}$$

Unavailability is a calculation of the time the system will be unavailable or, in other words, its probability of failure. The system is unavailable *MTTR* hours out of every *MTBF* + *MTTR* hours.

Another way to look at the number of failures during a given period is by the formula:

$$\text{Average number of failures in } t = t/(MTBF + MTTR) \cong t/MTBF$$

where *t* is the number of hours of operation. *MTTR* is included in the formula because each failure must be repaired. When *MTBF* is much greater than *MTTR* (*MTBF* >> *MTTR*), *MTTR* can be omitted from the equation. Thus, if the *MTBF* was 1000 hours (a very poor MTBF) and the number of failures must be determined within a year (8760 hours), there would be the likelihood of 8.76 failures that year, or 0.024 failures per day (almost one failure each month). If there are 100 nodes in your network, 0.024 failures per day means that there are 2.4 failures per day throughout the entire network. Now it can be seen why an MTBF of 1000 hours is quite poor. Consider a good MTBF of 40,000 hours, which would calculate to one failure every 4.57 years. Now this 100-node network has less than two failures per month.

For multiple network elements with different MTBFs, as in a hybrid network, availability (*Ai*) and unavailability (*Ui*) would be calculated for each element and then one of the following formulas would be used, depending on whether the elements were in serial or parallel.

For a serial network, as seen in Figure 13-25, the availability with two devices would be calculated as

$$A_s = (A_1)(A_2) = \left(\frac{MTBF_1}{MTBF_1 + MTTR_1}\right)\left(\frac{MTBF_2}{MTBF_2 + MTTR_2}\right)$$

Thus, the greater the number of nodes, the greater the chance of network failure. The unavailability would then be calculated as

$$Us = (U1)(A1) + (A1)(U2) + (U1)(U2)$$

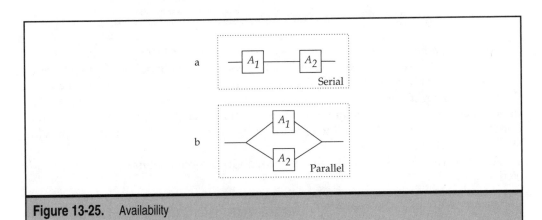

Figure 13-25.   Availability

For a parallel network, as seen in Figure 13-25, the unavailability with two devices would be calculated as

$$Up = (U1)(U2) = (1 - A1)(1 - A2) = 1 - A1 - A2 + A1A2$$

The availability would then be calculated as

$$Ap = (1 - Up) = A1 + A2 - A1A2$$

Thus, the greater the number of nodes placed in parallel, the less chance of network failure. Meshing also has the potential to increase *network* or *system* reliability.

Reliability

Reliability is the distribution of time between failures. Reliability is often specified by the MTBF for Markovian failures. A high-reliability MTBF figure means that the system contains many reliable components that together constitute a reliable system. Reliability is specified as the probability that the system does not fail prior to t hours.

$$\text{Reliability} = e^{-t/\text{MTBF}}$$

Take a sample MTBF of 10,000 hours and a time interval t of 1 year (8760 hours). The reliability would be 41.64 percent. If we were to increase the MTBF to 20,000 hours, the reliability jumps to 64.53 percent. For multiple network elements with different MTBFs, as in a serial hybrid network (such as a bus environment), the total failures calculation would be

$$R(\text{total}) = e^{-t[(\frac{1}{\text{MTBF}_1}) + (\frac{1}{\text{MTBF}_2}) + (\frac{1}{\text{MTBF}_3})]}$$

As an example, if we had MTBF figures of 20,000, 25,000, and 30,000 hours, respectively, measured over one year, the network would yield a 34 percent reliability! Thus, reliability can also be cumulative, but is always as weak as the weakest network element and always decreases as network devices are added. It can be seen that reliability is a tradeoff with redundancy when adding additional network resources.

Three additional performance measurements to MTTF are

▼   **Mean time to isolate (MTTI)**   The time it takes to identify the cause of the problem or outage.

■   **Mean time to repair (MTTR)**   After finding a problem, how long does it take to repair the problem or outage? This figure is usually stated in minutes or worse case hours. Note that DSL service has emerged to take on frame relay as a preferred corporate access service, but the MTTR on most DSL access loops is one to two days (and could take weeks) versus typically two to four hours for an FR access circuit. You do get what you pay for.

▲ **Mean time between service outages (MTBSO)**   Historically, how long has it been since the system has been down for a service outage? This figure is usually stated as greater than 2000 hours. More than 2000 hours translates to 2.5 hours downtime per year (250 weekdays × 8 hours per day).

Also, with 1:N live spares, the overall $MTBF$ can be much higher, by a factor of 10 to greater than 100. Sparing of 1:1 would be much better, but most likely cost-prohibitive.

Additional Performance Measurements and SLAs

In service or maintenance contracts, negotiated penalties apply if performance objectives provided by the vendor (SLAs) are not met. For enterprise networks that purchase managed services from the service provider, these SLAs are reported by the service provider to the enterprise customer. On standard network services, such as FR, ATM, or IP transport and access services (nonmanaged services), it is incumbent on the enterprise customer to measure, report, and track their achievement of the SLAs. This can become a false hope for an enterprise user who is promised strict SLAs but is left to prove the service provider's conformance to those SLAs. Ultimately, an SLA becomes a refund plan, with the service provider refunding some or all of the enterprise's monthly network fees. SLAs rarely contain clauses for remuneration that match the business impact of low- performing networks. Also note that each network performance parameter must be tested before placing users or applications on it. Not only must the level of error tolerability be determined, but also how much sharing of resources and capacity is tolerable. Some common performance objectives for packet-, frame-, and cell-switched services, with a sample of each, include

▼ **On-time provisioning**   1+ days late

■ **Mean time to restore**   4 hours

■ **Transfer delay**   Less than 140 milliseconds round-trip cross-country

■ **Data delivery ratio**   99.99 percent of packets/frames/cells delivered to destination address

■ **Network availability**   99.99 percent network availability

▲ **Error-free seconds**   99.99 error-free seconds

Plan for Failures

Is there extra capacity to allow for failures in the network backbone nodes, access nodes, links, network hardware, and network software? Make sure that the system is designed to survive failures. Select hardware and software with high availability and reliability figures. Implement designs that minimize weak points by adding additional redundant subsystems and implementing network meshing within available cost constraints. Increasing reliability and availability is bounded only by availability of budget and diversity alternatives. It might also be prudent to force a failure early in the life of the network (or before it goes "live") to determine if fault-tolerant system backups are working properly. Always periodically test your backup hardware, software, and systems.

REACTION TO EXTREME SITUATIONS

Another important consideration in network design is the desired behavior of the network under extreme situations. Next, we will consider the extreme situations of significant failure, traffic overload, and unexpected peak traffic patterns. For example, what will happen during a significant failure, such as one or more critical circuit or equipment failures, headquarters site, or failure of the entire network. The general guideline is that any element of the network should not become isolated by a single circuit, node, or if possible site failure. If you can survive with some loss of connectivity, costs can be significantly reduced in a private network; however, public networks are usually designed to survive single circuit and node failures. The exception and most vulnerable point is usually the user's access to the public network, in both single-point-of-failure CPE or access circuits (such as the local loop, which typically has the greatest failure rate often attributed to "back-hoe fade"). This can be solved with equipment diversity, circuit diversity, or dial or dedicated backup facilities (including wireless alternatives). You might have different performance objectives under failure situations than under normal circumstances. Also, you might desire that some traffic be preempted during a failure scenario so that support for mission-critical traffic is maintained. A failure without redundant facilities can effectively reduce either a bandwidth or switching resource, and hence can be a cause of congestion or outage.

Traffic overloads and unexpected traffic parameters can also cause congestion. For example, offered traffic in excess of the service contract (such as exceeding the CIR rate in FR) might create congestion. Some network services such as ATM mark this excessive traffic (under normal circumstances) for selective cell discard, and those cells in excess of the contract will be discarded first. But if the network is overbooked with contracted traffic parameters, the selective cell, frame, or packet discard might not be enough. As pointed out earlier, congestion can drive a switch or multiple points in a network into overload, reducing overall throughput significantly if congestion collapse occurs. If you expect this situation to occur, then a mechanism to detect congestion, correlate it with its cause, and provide some feedback to isolate various traffic sources and achieve the required measure of fairness is desirable. If you are uncertain as to how long such overloads will persist, then some slow-reacting feedback controls might actually reduce throughput because the reaction might occur after congestion has already abated (such as we saw with higher-layer protocols such as TCP, and why FECN/BECN did not scale in large FR networks).

To support time-varying traffic patterns, there are two fundamentally different approaches: one based upon the telecommunications concept of reserving bandwidth and the other based on the communications concept of fairly shared resources. A network service that offers bandwidth on demand, such as a switched virtual channel (SVC) or equivalent capability such as that found in IP-enabled FR and ATM services, allows an application to request the network to reserve bandwidth for its exclusive use, very similar to circuit switching. It might even reserve specific CoS or QoS parameters. These new implementations of SVC-like services though MPLS-based services such as IP-enabled FR, will allow the bandwidth to be dynamically established and CoS/QoS negotiated on demand.

Another possibility is dynamic flow control, where feedback from the network regarding congestion is used to throttle back sources in a fair manner, which also isolates applications that are "good citizens" from those that aren't following the flow-control rules. The choice of approach will depend on the characteristics of your applications, and on which approach is adopted and available by the vendor and service provider.

NETWORK PERFORMANCE MODELING

Most users are concerned with modeling the performance of a network. There are two basic modeling approaches: simulation and analysis. A simulation is usually much more accurate, but can become a formidable computational task when trying to simulate the performance of a large network. Analysis can be less computationally intensive, but is often inaccurate. Which is the best approach? The answer is similar to nodal modeling: It depends on how much information you have and how accurate an answer you require.

Simulation models are very useful in investigating the detailed operation of a system, which can lead to key insights into equipment, network, or application design. Detailed simulations generally take too long to execute to be used as an effective network design tool, and in many cases, the user does not know all the application traffic characteristics to simulate.

A good way to bootstrap the analytical method is to simulate the network technology or switch performance under the expected mix of traffic inputs. Often an analytical approximation to the empirical simulation results can be developed as input to an analytical tool. An assumption often made in network modeling is that the nodes operate independently, and that the traffic mixes and splits independently and randomly. If better information is not available, then this is a reasonable assumption, and simulation might be the only recourse. Analytical models become very complex without the assumption that nodes are independent of each other.

The inputs and outputs of a network model are similar for any packet/frame/cell-switched network design problem. The inputs are the topology, traffic, and routing. The network topology must be defined, usually as a graph with nodes and links. The characteristics of each node and link relevant to the simulation or analytical model must be described. Next, the pattern of traffic offered between the nodes must be defined. For point-to-point traffic this is commonly done via a traffic matrix. The routing, or set of links that traffic follows from source to destination, must be defined. Most applications work point to point and can be modeled in this fashion (for example, TCP/IP sessions between two IP addresses).

The principal outputs are measures of performance and cost. The principal performance measures of a model are loss and delay statistics. A model will often produce an economic cost to allow the network designer to select an effective price-performance tradeoff.

Now let's take a look at the first step in traffic modeling: the traffic matrix.

CREATING THE TRAFFIC MATRIX

Now that the user requirements have been defined and we have categorized the traffic modeling and engineering, we can compile and sort these requirements into meaningful data to develop a network design. In the most simple terms, we can create a traffic matrix of who needs to talk with whom, and what traffic patterns need to go where. We can then analyze the traffic matrix and start the capacity-planning cycle. At an even higher level, these traffic patterns are typically driven by the business traffic. Look at the way any company does business, and certain traffic patterns emerge: a centralized HQ communicating with remote offices (hub-and-spoke) or many distributed sales offices communicating in peer-to-peer arrangements (distributed or meshed topology). The application traffic patterns will generally follow these business topologies.

Asymmetric versus Symmetric Distribution

Is the distribution of traffic by direction asymmetric or symmetric? *Asymmetrical* traffic lacks directional symmetry through an imbalance of flows, speeds, or a variety of other characteristics. It originates from large sites to small, or vice versa, and does not follow a normal distribution. Access devices vary in quantity, design, engineering, and loading. On the other hand, symmetric traffic often originates from communities of similar interest, such as specific geographic regions, and is uniformly spread across these sites within each region, and the bidirectional quantity is similar.

In *symmetrical* networks, many of the access devices are similar in quantity, design, engineering, and loading. Hierarchical networks, such as those using the SNA protocols, are often symmetrical in nature. Distributed networks often resemble asymmetrical rather than symmetrical traffic distributions. LAN traffic and WAN traffic made up of LAN traffic feeds tend to be asymmetrical and very hard to diagnose. In this instance, average and peak traffic patterns should be used in the traffic matrix. Figure 13-26 illustrates symmetrical and asymmetrical traffic distributions.

Creating the Traffic Matrix

The traffic matrix is an essential part of the access node design, and illustrates traffic flows not otherwise readily apparent. Traffic interfaces to the network through an access node or access point. Access nodes could take the form of a concentrator (for example, PAD or FRAD), DXC, access multiplexer, hub, bridge, switch, router, or any other device concentrating user inputs but not operating as a switching backbone. The traffic matrix helps define details about the access node requirements, such as location, size, operation, protocol support, performance characteristics, and device type.

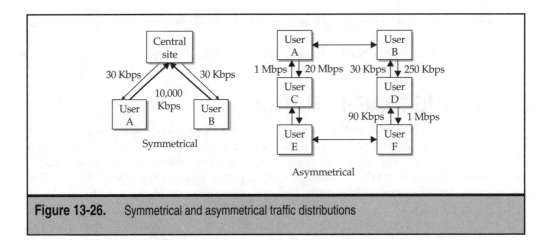

Figure 13-26. Symmetrical and asymmetrical traffic distributions

The traffic matrix is, in effect, a spreadsheet or table mapping traffic flows from origin to destination. The FROM nodes are listed vertically down the left side of the matrix, and the TO nodes are listed horizontally across the top. Figure 13-27 shows a sample traffic matrix with simple data units (for example, bytes, calls, packets) per second for each site.

		To location				
i \ j	A	B	C	D	E	F
A	20	0	2	1	20	12
B	2	3	3	*	6	5
C	2	0	12	2	8	3
D	8	*	1	10	22!	5
E	12	4	0	31!	6	3
F	22	8	2	1	2	2

(From location)

Traffic flow units (for example, packets, frames, bytes, calls per second)

Figure 13-27. Traffic matrix with all routes

Each box represents a traffic flow from the FROM node i to the TO node j (this is sometimes referred to as the ij matrix). All traffic that remains local to a node will be found in the A-A box, B-B box, and so forth. Notice that node A has 20 intranodal traffic units per second, while node B has only three. Notice also that node B sends two traffic units per second to node A.

It is good practice to start with a local geographic area as node A and work out from there, so that letters that are lexically close represent nodes in a geographic region. Keeping to this scheme as much as possible simplifies the process. Traffic flows, or profiles, will be represented by any of the previously discussed formats, including packets, frames, bytes, calls, or even protocols, priorities, or other dependencies. Traffic measurements used should have a similar message (packet) length and should be measured in "mean busy hour" throughput (in bps) or in the peak-to-mean ratio. Traffic patterns are often provided in units per second (that is, packets, frames, cells) during average, peak, and maximum traffic patterns throughout a 24-hour period, and are designed for busy-hour traffic as previously discussed. Traffic measurements should be measured from either the network or the application point of view. Thus, a matrix can be built that shows specific application traffic flows (such as FTP or Telnet file transfer protocol traffic) or generic packet flows, such as Ethernet packets from a LAN interface. Rarely does an enterprise network know their traffic patterns to these levels, so gross approximations are often made. Also mark invalid and preferred routes. Figure 13-28 shows the same matrix,

	To location					
i $\diagdown$ j	A	B	C	D	E	F
A	20	0	2	1	20	12
B	2	3	3	*	6	5
C	2	0	12	2	8	3
D	8	*	1	10	22!	5
E	12	4	0	31!	6	3
F	22	8	2	1	2	2

From location

Traffic flow units (for example, packets, frames, bytes, calls per second)

Figure 13-28. Traffic matrix with invalid and preferred routes

with the additional detail of invalid routes indicated with an asterisk, while preferred routes are indicated with an exclamation point.

Interpreting the Matrix

In its simplest use, the matrix shows the connectivity required between each site. Let M be the binary matrix, with a 1 indicating connectivity and a 0 indicating no connectivity. The following are then true:

▼ M = connectivity for one node (that is, direct connectivity)

■ $M \times M$ = connectivity for a 2-hop path

■ $M \times M \times M$ = connectivity for a 3-hop path

▲ $M + M^2 + M^3$ = all paths up to path length of 3 hops

Note that this method can include "cycles" or loops (paths that traverse the same node more than once), which should be eliminated. For example, each level of connectivity between nodes might require a private line, PVC if FR, VC or VP if ATM, an IP routing protocol route, or tandem node.

All traffic identified as remaining local to a given node would be placed into the same access node. Circles are then drawn around boxes that represent a small geographic area that could be served by a single concentrator. This is done by grouping nodal traffic distributions in a local geographical area together to form larger access nodes. This reduces the number of access devices required.

Figure 13-28 shows the same matrix from the last example. Node A has 20 units of traffic (this could be 20 PPS, 20 frames per second, or 20 Kbps average traffic during busy hour), which remains local and node B has only three units of traffic. Also note that node A sends no traffic to node B, and node B sends only two units of traffic to node A. Since in this example node A and node B are in the same geographic region, the traffic from both nodes is combined at node A, where a single access node is placed. The small amount of traffic originating at node B is "backhauled" to node A. Some amount of backhaul access is required in many public data services, where there are limited access points into the switched network, or where lower-cost regional hub-and-spoke subnetworks are required. This also assumes that no other large amounts of traffic are generated or sent to node B from other nodes.

This process continues until the number of access nodes required to begin the design is established. Ideally, one would like to place a separate concentrator node at each site, but often economics do not justify this, so the network design usually settles for smaller nodes at less concentrated regions and larger ones in more dense regions, or backhaul from less to more concentrated regions.

Network designs for multimedia and multiprotocol networks are much more complicated. These complex designs often require many traffic matrices combined into a multidimensional matrix (for example, a z-axis forming a three-dimensional matrix to accommodate interdependencies such as priority of information, budget trade-offs, or protocols), or in large networks, design tools to perform these calculations. Ideally, this analysis would be performed by a design tool. Design tools are briefly covered next.

CAPACITY PLANNING AND NETWORK VISION

Capacity planning was once done on a five- to ten-year cycle. It is now a one- to three-year cycle, and many times even shorter. In fact, packet networks often demand a capacity review on a monthly basis. There are two elements to the plan, a *short-term* objective and task-oriented plan usually revised each year, and the *long-term* three- to five-year plan, which should also take into account the strategic vision of corporate communications for the next five to ten years. As the cost of computing hardware decreases, the entropy of capacity requirements increases. This makes capacity planning for communications networks a challenging task. Short- and long-range capacity planning can provide the corporation with a competitive advantage, assuming that the plans fit in with the long-range strategic business plan. Each design must provide the flexibility to change technology as business needs change without major network restructuring. Both plans must take into account the business needs, customer needs, and the technologies available.

One method is to migrate multiple network platforms to a consolidated network platform that conforms to industry standards. Decide early on whether to maintain the existing architecture and build upon it, or plan to build a new integrated network architecture in the future. Better yet, look for migratory (evolutionary) versus forklift upgrades (revolutionary) strategies. One of the best architectures is built in a hierarchical nature that caters to flexible peer-to-peer communications and can be replaced in layers over time. Plan for port expansion, CPU capacity, hardware storage requirements, memory storage requirements, growth in user application traffic, and many other critical growth areas discussed in this chapter. Many design tools have the capability to model future network changes and assist in both the short-term and long-range capacity planning process.

DESIGN TOOLS

This section provides the reader with insight into the selection of network design tools. Design tools provide an accurate method of modeling and designing networks. In this chapter, the criteria necessary to choose a design tool will be explained. This section will serve to describe types of network tools and state which features belong to each tool, describe typical network design tasks, state standard requirements for a design tool, and analyze and describe the features available on current commercial design tools. You can then use this chapter to select a design tool that meets your specific requirements.

Commercially available network design tools for packet, frame, and cell networks have been around since the late 1980s. The capabilities of these tools include analyzing existing networks, providing meshed and hierarchical network designs, modeling design change and failure scenarios, and modeling capacity planning scenarios. While these tools exist, few are actually used by most network designers and managers. This is in part due to the lack of tool flexibility and the inherent constraints of limited options, and also in part by the sheer difficulty of modeling distributed hybrid networks. The complexity of these tools greatly increases from circuit to packet switched networks. Some available tools are also well suited for modeling a specific vendor's networks, or specific protocols, but quickly break down in large routed and switched networks.

Design tools analyze two types of data networks: circuit-switched and packet/frame/cell-switched networks. When choosing a design tool, certain criteria should be present in the tool. At a minimum, it should support the basic user requirements defined in Chapter 12. Before a tool can be successful, the data fed into it must be accurate. Hence the importance of the detailed requirements analysis of Chapters 15 and 16, so that good input will produce good outputs.

Design tools use either mathematical modeling or packet-level simulation. Mathematical modeling uses statistics to predict user traffic flows and model their characteristics. Packet-level simulation is the most common method, however, where the tool inputs are a snapshot of the network at a *single point in time*. Since the traffic on packet networks is often bursty in nature, *multiple* snapshots are required. This type of modeling works well for small networks where the user traffic characteristics are well known, but processing times and the sheer computing power required to perform a large, dynamic network design often makes this process very time-consuming, resource insensitive, and difficult. Some design tools use neither of the above approaches. Instead, they model each user input as a single demand, based on their file-transfer protocol characteristics or "flows." The author has found that the best network-design tools focus on heuristic routing algorithms based on user-definable parameters and queuing theory, rather than any one form of mathematical simulation of theory.

Terminology

There are two primary terms used throughout this section: transport and demand.

▼   *Transport* is a term used to define the bandwidth that is used to create user channels. Transport carries user data from point A to point B. Transport comprises the bandwidth (private lines, FR, ATM, and so on) between switching devices (digital cross connects, switches, multiplexers, and so on). Transport is also referred to as *backbone.*

▲   *Demand* is the portion of the transport bandwidth that contains the user data. In private line networks, the demand traffic is the unit of circuit used such as 56 Kbps, 64 Kbps, fractional-T1, and T1 or packet/frame/cell flow into the network. No distinction is made between the amount of bandwidth required for a particular user, and the amount of bandwidth that is added due to overhead or routing inefficiencies. A session, file transfer, client-server application, or switched circuit are all types of demand. Demand is also referred to as the *circuits* that are carried by the backbone.

CATEGORIES OF TOOLS

There is a general differentiation among design, configuration-management, and event-management tools. The term *design tool* is used to describe a wide range of applications that are concerned with topics such as selection of the proper software and hardware, optimization of network topology, and failure analysis. The term *configuration-management tool* is used to describe a wide range of applications that address topics such as storing software and hardware configurations, designing racks and cabling, and equipment placement. The term *event-management tool* is used to describe a wide range of applications that are used for real-time network event monitoring, correlation, and notification.

Design Tools

The attributes of and the services provided by a design tool include

- ▼ **Cost model**   Calculates the cost of the transport, hardware, and software portions of the network
- ■ **What-if analysis**   Recommends design changes based on failure or network configuration changes
- ■ **Failure analysis**   Describes completely the effects on demand traffic of a failure of some portion of the transport network or devices (nodes) within the network
- ■ **Visualize**   Shows network elements and connections on screen and on paper
- ■ **Simulate**   Models the operation of the network devices with respect to physical, data link, network, layers and so forth, parameters
- ■ **Characterize**   Calculates key performance indicators (KPIs) that describe design, efficiency, utilization, and so on
- ■ **Optimize**   Changes the network design to achieve higher utilization or performance and models cost trade-offs
- ■ **Design**   Produces transport from demand and demand from profiles
- ▲ **Report**   Produces utilization, link, equipment, site reports

Configuration-Management Tools

The attributes of, and the services provided by, a configuration-management tool include

- ▼ Keeps detailed records of the setting of network elements, including ports, cards, and devices. Settings include all software- and hardware-defined attributes of equipment. Other details such as serial numbers, revision levels, software options, and setup parameters can be stored by a configuration-management tool.

  ▲   Keeps detailed records of the layout of racks of equipment. This information will most likely be graphical in nature. The connections made by cables and routing information will also be stored.

Event-Management Tools

The attributes of and the services provided by an alarm- and event-management tool include

  ▼   Storage of events, some of which will represent faults in the network (alarms)

  ■   Correlation of events, which reduces multiple events related to a particular failure to a single event relaying the proximate cause of the multiple events

  ■   Presentation of events

  ▲   Reporting and trending results

CLASSES OF DESIGN TOOLS

Design tools can be broken down into three categories. Physical-design tools are those tools that take into consideration attributes of equipment only to the physical level. Circuit switching is essentially the only type of network covered by physical-design tools. By contrast, logical-design tools are those tools that take into consideration attributes of equipment beyond the physical level. Networks of this type frequently employ the concept of virtual circuits or datagram delivery. Logical-design tools cover packet-, frame-, and cell-switched networks. Statistical-design tools are those tools that take into consideration applications and the statistical nature of the traffic that they generate. These tools consider delay and throughput requirements of the applications. Their models are inherently statistical in nature, and cover all the previously mentioned connections.

Physical-Design Tool

A physical-design tool has the capability to design networks that incorporate only physical entities. Transport facilities are always considered as physical when they are primary. Primary refers to a configuration where there is not a lower level of network providing the transport. Figure 13-29 shows a model for a physical design.

Demand circuits are considered physical entities when they consist only of portions of transport circuits that are created at a physical level. For example, a physical time-division multiplexer divides a transport circuit into multiple demand circuits.

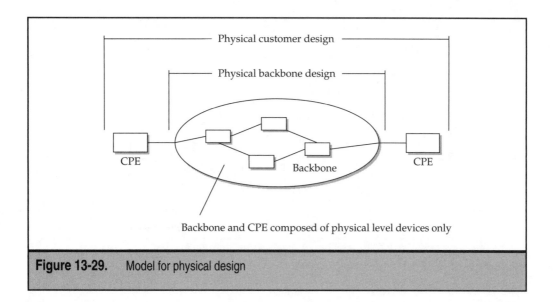

Figure 13-29.   Model for physical design

Logical-Design Tool

A logical-design tool has the capability to design networks that incorporate logical entities such as permanent virtual circuits and switched virtual circuits. One example would be a FR switch that has multiple PVCs. Also included are networks that provide connectionless services such as IP. This type of tool converts a virtual circuit demand or packet flow into an optimized physical-transport network. Figure 13-30 shows a model for a logical design.

Statistical-Design Tools

For work with multiprotocol environments, the ultimate demands placed on the data network will be specified in terms of end-user quantifiable entities. Sample entities are SNA sessions, client-server sessions, and connections to network servers. For each of these requirements, there is a native protocol associated with the application that provides the service. For each native protocol, there are special requirements for data throughput, priority, and latency. A model is needed to convert the user requirements in terms of sessions into logical circuit demand. Figure 13-31 shows a model for a statistical design.

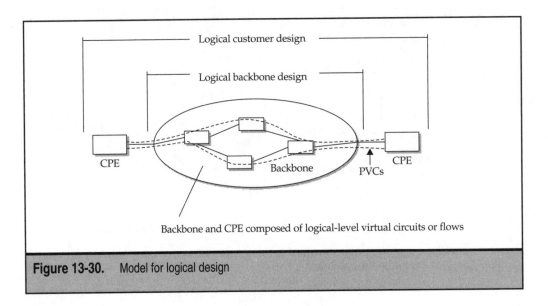

Figure 13-30. Model for logical design

Integration of the Physical, Logical, and Statistical

To perform network design from the level of user demand to the level of physical transport, the three levels of design tool must be integrated, as shown in Figure 13-32. Ultimately, the three levels should exist in one tool.

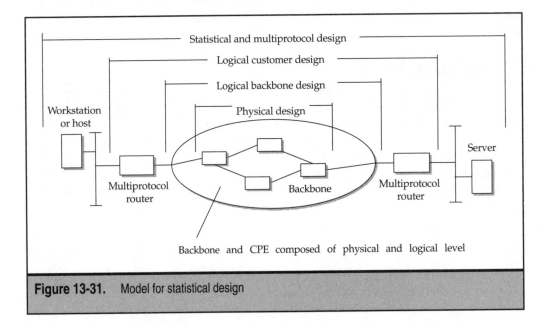

Figure 13-31. Model for statistical design

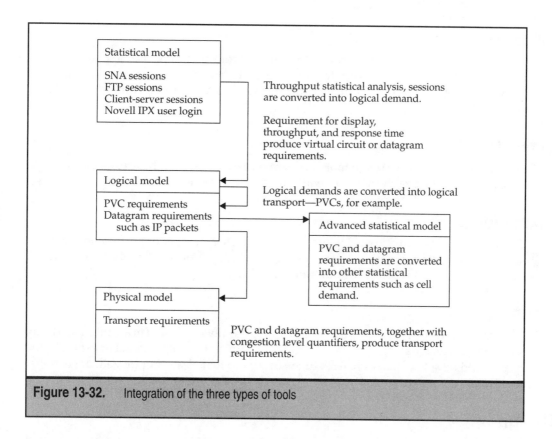

Figure 13-32.   Integration of the three types of tools

COMPONENTS OF DESIGN PROJECTS

Design projects typically require a design tool to perform one or more of the following activities:

▼ **Visualize**   Show network elements and connections, on screen and on paper

■ **Simulate**   Model the operation of the network devices with respect to physical, data link, network, and sometimes higher-layer parameters

■ **Characterize**   Calculate performance metrics that describe design, efficiency, utilization, and so on

■ **Optimize**   Change the network design to increase performance metrics, use directives, strategies

■ **Design**   Produce transport from demand, and demand from profiles

■ **Test**   Evaluate survivability, loading

■ **Report**   Produce utilization, link, equipment, site reports

▲ **Analyze**   Investigate performance parameters

Visualize

A design tool should have a versatile user interface that allows the user to place and connect network components. In addition, the tool should allow physical and logical network topology maps to be manipulated, saved to standard graphics formats (like JPG), and printed.

Simulate

A function at the core of design tools, and sometimes invisible to the user, is the ability to simulate the actions of the network equipment placed in the model.

Characterize

To quantify changes made during the design process, a number of performance metrics should be calculated by the design tool. These indicators could include utilization, efficiency, cost, survivability, throughput, and delay.

Optimize

Services should be provided by the design tool to modify the design in an automated way such that certain parameters of the design are maximized or minimized. For example, the tool should be able to make changes to the design so that cost is minimized, or such that survivability is maximized.

Design

Design is the most important collection of services provided by a design tool. The tool should be able to take as input a set of parameters and produce as output a description of a network design that can be manipulated by the operator, or by automated services of the design tool. Listed as follows are examples of the input and output for various types of network technologies.

- ▼ **Time-division multiplexing (TDM)**   Demand (switch locations, transport) based on minimum cost or maximum survivability, and so on
- ■ **LAN to physical**   Demand (switch or router locations, transport) based on delay, priority, and so on
- ■ **LAN to virtual**   Demand based on delay, priority, and so on
- ■ **FR access**   Demand (switch location, access [PVC])
- ▲ **FR backbone**   Demand (switch or router locations, transport)

Test

Services should be available to test the design once created. Tests should include failure and stress analyses. During failure analysis, the output should describe any user traffic that is not carried by the network during the tested outage. Stress analysis should describe the degradation of service in terms of reduced throughput and increased delay due to increased offered load on the network.

Report

A versatile set of reports should be available to describe the components of the network that has been designed. In addition, performance metrics should be reported along with details of utilization, throughput, and efficiency of each component or circuit of the network.

Performance Analysis

This area is particularly applicable to tools that address statistical networks. Ideally, a design tool should perform the design in stages. In the early stages, the placement of nodes and links, along with the determination of the size of links, are calculated based on aggregate parameters such as maximum packet-processing speed. At a later stage of the design, the simulation should switch to a more detailed level, and advanced statistical models should be employed to analyze packet throughput and delay and queue depth.

TYPES OF DESIGN PROJECTS

Design projects include

- ▼ Digital cross-connect backbone
- ■ Private line or dedicated circuit backbone
- ■ Data services switched backbone such as FR and ATM
- ■ Single-protocol switched design
- ▲ Multiprotocol routed or switched design such as IP or MPLS

Each of these is typically approached from both an access and backbone perspective.

REQUIREMENTS

Next, list all the design tool interface requirements specific to your network. These might include

- ▼ Interface to the existing database of record (for example, relational database)

- Data flows between the design tool and your configuration and event management systems
- Capture all cost elements (transport, demand, equipment, management, installation)
- Conform to rules or limitations for optimization
- Plan for future expansion
- Support protocol specifics (for example, CIR for FR)
- ▲ Support circuit and session prioritization

User Inputs

Network-design tool user-input parameters vary widely, based on the type of network to be modeled. Some of the more important parameters include

- ▼ Packet/frame/cell size (average or peak)
- Number of packets/frames/cells per second (mean and in each direction)
- Minimum/maximum bandwidth per user access
- Time between packets (burstiness)
- File size per transmission
- Links/trunks required (length, speed, priority, and so on)
- Cost and priority factors
- Overhead statistics per protocol
- Network device (node) specifics
- ▲ Protocol specifics

This information is typically input to the tool through an application profile input file. This file also includes application specifics such as name, description, traffic type, and co-ordinates origin(s) and destination(s), and so on.

Tool Support

While the features and functions of design tools vary widely, listed here are some of the more important items to be supported:

- ▼ Multiple protocols (HDLC, FR, ATM, IP, MPLS)
- Multiple architectures (OSI, TCP/IP, SNA)
- Layered view of each protocol and architecture
- Multimedia traffic (voice, data, video—time-sensitive/insensitive)
- End-to-end view upon selection
- Support for both hierarchical (LAN/MAN) and meshed network designs

- User-friendly interface—graphical user interface (GUI) and applications program interface (API), CAD/CAM capabilities, multilevel graphics, international application

- Location inputs in vertical and horizontal (V&H) of serving CO, latitude and longitude, NPA/NXX, LATA, and CRT screen coordinates

- Conversions for the location finders above

- Display utilization

- Powerful high-level user language accessible by user (user able to make coding changes to tool)

- Online editing of links, nodes, and other properties

- Flexible data structures (circuits/packets/frames/cells)

- Flexible input parameters (distance, cost, quality, bandwidth)

- Flexible parameters for defining link and node placement

- Capability to upgrade/add new technologies, protocols, and parameters

- Modular design (run each step of design separately)

- General-purpose design criteria

- Capability to input national and international tariff and network specifics

- Dialup capability

- Varied node and link types

- Survivability analysis

- Unlimited number of nodes

- Configuration and clocking design

- Industry-standard platform

- Current software revision

- Multiple homing of links to multiple or same node

- Variable equipment costs

- Fast, efficient algorithms

- Data export including laser printing and plotting

- Multiple save file formats: text and graphics

- Sensitivity analysis

- Tariff manager

- Multivendor, multicarrier device libraries

- Short-run and processing times

- Add-in for growth

- Thorough debugger, editor, journalizing
- Performance analysis simulator
- Enhanced query capability
- Traffic generator
- Least-cost topology design
- Assess network delay and throughput
- Applications profiler
- Variable decision matrix
- ▲ Price-performance modeling

Reporting Capability

Design tools need to report their findings to the user so the user can understand what the tool has modeled, what can now be modeled, and how the modeling can be translated to a design. Some of the more important reporting characteristics include

- ▼ End-to-end response time
- Topology options
- Throughout, delay, cost (per link and node)
- Effect of link or node failure
- Individual link and node views
- Bandwidth usage per user/port/protocol
- "What changed?" analyses (for topology, node/link demand, link load, node throughput, routing differences, and packet throughput)
- Topology changes
- Link and node upgrades
- Protocol type changes (routing, switching)
- Maximum hop count
- Delay and throughput analysis
- Traffic type and pattern changes
- Link and node characteristics changes (PPS processing)
- Busy hour/minute/second changes
- Black box support for unrecognized devices
- Constraints in link and node demand
- ▲ Hybrid topologies

User Functionality

User functionality defines the level of control the user can exert over both the design and the design tool. The functions the tool provides to the user should include

▼ Complete design
■ Incremental design
■ Multinetwork design
■ Subnetwork design
■ Built-in redundancy
■ Specific rules of routing
■ Layered (protocol or architecture) design
■ User-specified specific parameter design
■ Manual additions
■ Time interval design
■ Specialized routing
■ Forced homing
■ Connectivity constraints
■ Import traffic statistics recorded by data analyzers
■ Macro functions
■ Zoom-in and zoom-out capability
▲ Printing capability

The tool should also have the capability to import current configuration files in native down to simple ASCII format, ranging from database downloads of existing equipment to entire network maps of available routes and the tariff information for each. All parameters should be displayed and be configurable in both domestic and international measurements, distances, tariffs, maps, and so on.

Private Line Customer Network Design Requirements

The input to the tool would be a list of demands, and the output would be the optimal placement of nodes and access lines.

Features of the tool include

▼ Ability to gather data on current demand, import into the tool
■ Utilization report
■ Price components of the design

- Minimum cost design
- Performance analysis
- Maps of proposed design
- ▲ Easy modification of design

FR and ATM Customer Network Design Requirements

For FR networks, the input to this tool would be a list of demands, possibly the same as the input to the multiprotocol customer network design. The output of the tool would be a list of node locations, access line speeds, and PVC speeds. The node locations would be chosen to reduce access costs, and would be a subset of the available public and private FR switch locations. The tool should account for MPLS-based FR implementations such as IP-enabled FR services, which use a single enterprise PVC per port. ATM support should include TP, VP, and VC engineering with all QoS classes, with output similar to FR.

Packet Switched and Routed Customer Network Design Requirements

For packet switched and routed networks, the input to this tool would be a list of packet flows or site-site maps. The output of the tool would be a list of node locations, routing tables, access and trunk circuit speeds, and general or specific routing configurations. The node locations would be chosen to provide optimal routing while reducing access and transport costs as required.

Multiprotocol Customer Network Design Requirements

The network design tool should have the ability to design networks carrying the following user protocols:

- ▼ SNA
- IPX
- IP
- DECNET
- ▲ ISO

It is presumed that the design tool will contain a model for each protocol, and that the tool will be able to simulate demand based on user requirements for each protocol.

Input to the tool would include user demand in terms of traffic profiles. A traffic profile specifies the amount of traffic generated by a user, and characterizes the burstiness of the traffic. Parameters such as throughput and delay requirements are also specified.

Profiles would be predefined for common applications such as a file server, print server, or client workstation.

The traffic profiles would be converted by the tool into either physical or virtual demands. The physical demands could then be directed as input to the physical design module. The virtual demands could likewise be directed to the virtual design module described previously as the FR access-design module.

Customization Requirements

The tool should be flexible and allow the network designer to create links to other systems.

The tool should include

- ▼ API for extensibility and customization (with hooks for object messaging)
- ■ Full support for customized network objects
- ■ Rule customization and extension (to support new types of connectivity not yet dreamed of by the developers)
- ■ Extension of existing objects to add attributes needed for integration into existing systems
- ■ Ability to call other applications (with context) in response to user or object/rule events
- ▲ Ability to be called and provided with a context (such as a database zoom into a specific object initiating the circuit diagram with specific object selected)

Other Requirements

The chosen design tool should automate as many of the following as possible.

- ▼ Integration of network equipment cost with network bandwidth cost
- ■ Pending order activity (new, disconnect, and change)
- ■ "Auto price" bandwidth
- ■ All nonrecurring charges on installs and rearrangements
- ■ Circuits not on least-cost-routing paths
- ■ Trends on bandwidth activity to support projected bandwidth requirements
- ■ Network utilization reports
- ■ Graphical representations of network bandwidth
- ▲ Maintain an inventory of all network equipment

COMMERCIAL TOOLS

Finally, choose a tool. The last edition of this book rated the top-six vendor tools in the industry. Because this information goes out of date so quickly, only the key criteria to rate each vendor are listed here.

▼ Scalability versus cost

■ Market share and reputation

■ Extent of integration with software and hardware of devices being modeled

■ Hardware requirements

■ Software/operating system requirements

■ Features: analyze, design, plan, optimize, simulator, and so on

■ Interface: graphical or text

▲ Extent of tool automation

HOW OFTEN SHOULD I OPTIMIZE?

Remember that the design-tool process does not stop with the initial design. It is a cyclical process to be completed every few months by the network-engineering organization, and optimized in even shorter timeframes. Design tools can drastically improve the efficiency of an existing network, provide significant cost savings through reducing access and thus reducing costs, and recover underutilized hardware from the network. Network-design tools can optimize efficiency from the servers and workstations, through the LAN, and across the WAN. These tools can also help perform the fine tuning discussed in Chapter 20.

REVIEW

Going beyond the voice world and standard circuit-switched traffic modeling, the queued data and packet-switched traffic modeling of data services and technologies such as packet switching, FR, ATM, and IP were introduced. We started the chapter with some basic throughput calculations.

We next moved to the key aspect of traffic engineering philosophy: *source modeling*. Various source models affect the accuracy and complexity of the traffic-engineering calculations. In general, the more accurate the model, the more complicated the calculation. There are models that average, but deterministic models that use actual data structures and equipment propagation delays are far more complex, but have a vastly better level of accuracy. This book opts for simplicity in modeling and introduces only a few of the popular, simple source models.

After traditional erlang traffic engineering was introduced, we next turned to the key aspects of modeling switch performance, including a comparison of buffering methods and statistical multiplexing. Your network design has been sized to accommodate standard and peak traffic conditions, and to determine what theoretical level of delay and loss will be tolerable. Guidelines were provided to aid in the choice of link speed, burst duration, and loss ratio. Methods for calculation of delay, loss, and error rate in a multiple switched-node network were described, along with some suggestions and alternatives for managing delay variation (jitter). The tradeoffs and critical factors boil down to cost versus performance.

Part of the network design should consider what would happen under extremes, such as failures, overload, and unexpected peak traffic patterns, and each subject was explored in detail. The availability, reliability, and other performance measurements required of vendor products with which to build the network have been identified. Calculating the traffic matrix, or possibly even multiple traffic matrices, allows you to determine network access resource requirements and size access nodes.

We then identified capacity needs, including how much capacity, what the utilization will be, how performance will be affected by these decisions, and how to improve performance. A network vision and organized plan was set forth to accommodate future growth in capacity. Next, the best technology must be chosen to suit network access requirements, and a choice of the vendor(s) to supply this technology established, and only then can the access network design be completed. Finally, this chapter has provided you with the capability to choose a network design tool that meets the requirements of user-input parameters, user functionality, feature and function support, and reporting capability.

CHAPTER 14

Technology Comparisons

Now that we understand our traffic requirements, we can move to the next step in the design process—choosing the access and backbone technology or hybrid of technologies or the public network service that will offer this choice of technologies. Previous chapters have covered a working knowledge of circuit-, packet-, and cell-switching technologies, the standards that define them, and the services that can be offered. This knowledge will be coupled with the user's requirements and the level of capacity required from the network. The most popular technologies vying for command of the WAN include private lines, the Internet Protocol (IP), frame relay (FR), and ATM. We do not include Ethernet as it fits more as a LAN and Metro technology. Neither do we cover SONET or DWDM as they fall into the category of private lines. We do not include cable, xDSL, or wireless as they are more common access technologies compared with transport technologies and services. X.25 and SMDS appear in some of the comparisons as they are still used internationally but have extremely limited support in North America.

This chapter draws comparisons between these technologies and services, their protocols and interfaces, and the details of each switching, routing, and transport technique. Comparisons are based on objective measures, suitability to application needs, network attributes, and services provided to end users. Some comparison to traditional LAN technologies such as FDDI and 100 Mbps Ethernet are also provided. A good understanding of these technologies and services and their pros and cons of use are essential for the network design engineer to make wise design decisions. Thus, the access and backbone portion of the network design can be accomplished using the best mix of technologies to meet user requirements and to ensure designing to meet the current and future capacity requirements.

CIRCUIT-, MESSAGE-, PACKET-, AND CELL-SWITCHING METHODS

This section summarizes all of the circuit-, message-, packet-, and cell-switched data communications methods that have been developed throughout modern data history. Motivations for the choice between circuit switching versus packet-switching technologies in terms of some simple application examples are also provided.

Taxonomy of Data Communication Methods

There are basically three switching methods that can be used to communicate data: circuit switching, message switching, and packet switching. All other categories of data communications can be placed into this taxonomy, as illustrated in Figure 14-1. The packet-switching branch is further broken down into packet/frame/cell switching. The large number of techniques under the packet-switching branch is indicative of the industry focus on this method.

Message switching started the era of modern data communications in 1847, with the invention of the telegraph by Morse and the system of message relays. Message switching evolved into paper-tape teletype relay systems and the modern telex messaging sys-

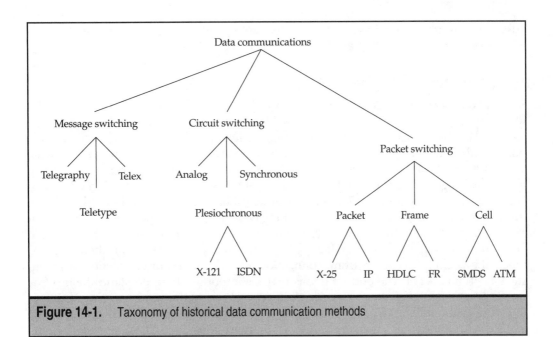

Figure 14-1. Taxonomy of historical data communication methods

tem used for financial transfers and access to remote locations. But although digital data communications began with the telegraph, which initially employed human operators to perform the message-switching function, it is not a prevalent data communications technology today. The telegraph was eventually replaced by the teletype, which yielded to Telex systems, without which you could not wire money or reach remote locations. True message switching today has evolved to become a higher-layer protocol, and in many cases, an application that operates over packet switching and routing in modern data-communication networks. One example is the ISO X.400 messaging system. The Simple Mail Transfer Protocol (SMTP) of the Internet also provides a higher-layer protocol for messaging.

Circuit switching in data communications started more than 60 years ago through modems designed for use on analog transmission systems. This evolved into plesiochronous digital transmission systems over the past 40 to 50 years. The main technologies derived from these efforts include digital private lines, X.21 fast circuit switching, and ISDN BRI and PRI circuit switching.

Packet switching was developed in the past 40 years to overcome the expense and poor performance of transmission systems. Three major classes of packet switching have evolved over time. The first packet-switching systems of X.25 and IP were designed to operate over very poor transmission networks. A simpler protocol such as HDLC could be used for local connections when the quality of the links was better. HDLC, in turn, has evolved into the wide area through the FR standard. The desire to achieve even higher performance and flexibility lead to the development of SMDS, which was further enhanced by the development of ATM. IP took a parallel course, albeit with less dramatic advances. Improvements in transmission technology, electronics, and protocol design are key enablers in each new generation of data communications technology.

Dedicated or Switched Networks?

Should you choose a dedicated network connection or a switched service? Figure 14-2A illustrates the trade-offs between a dedicated facility between two points and a switched facility. This figure shows that there is a point when a dedicated facility between two points will be more economical than a switched facility for a certain amount of daily usage. For example, if the usage duration is high, such as two minutes per transfer, but the total daily usage is only about 2000 seconds, or about 30 minutes, then a switched service is probably more economical. This crossover could be different if the individual usage duration is so small that the required switching capability is too expensive. Services such as ISDN are offered with both a flat-rate charge and a flat-rate-plus-usage charge. If the point-to-point usage indicates switching is economically desirable, then there are two types of switching to choose from: connectionless, such as IP, or connection-oriented, such as FR and ATM. The bottom line is that it's important to understand the tariff or public pricing structure of each service. As a general rule of thumb, the average transaction duration should be an order of magnitude greater than the circuit (either physical or logical) setup time when choosing a CONS, otherwise consider a CLNS, as shown in the setup time regions of Figure 14-2B.

Figure 14-3 illustrates this example of usage duration by showing the time required to transfer an object of a certain size for a range of representative PDH circuit transfer rates.

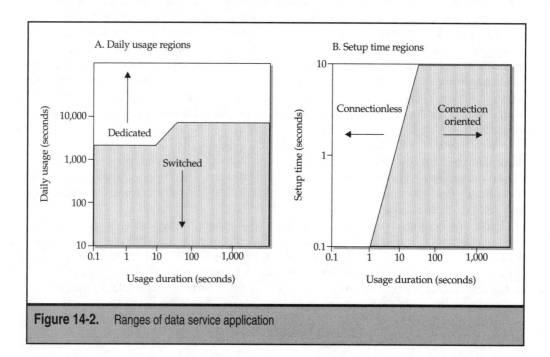

Figure 14-2. Ranges of data service application

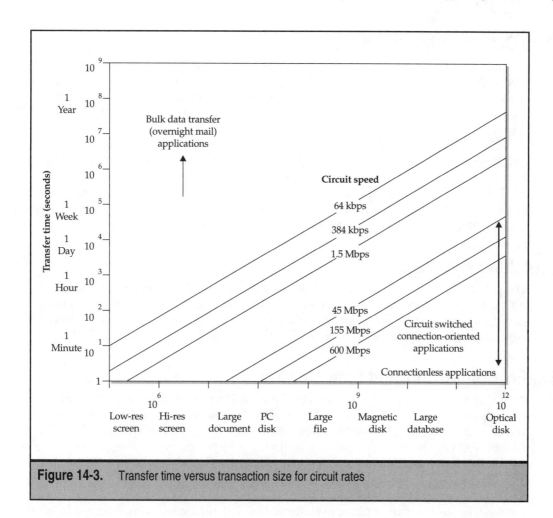

Figure 14-3.   Transfer time versus transaction size for circuit rates

There obviously exists a linear relationship. The range of transfer times is divided into three regions based on applicability of technology: connectionless, connection-oriented, and bulk data transfer (for example, overnight mail). Note that there is a gap in the transfer time between 1.5 Mbps and 45 Mbps in the PDH and SDH transmission granularity. This is one area where the flexibility of packet or cell transfer over fixed-rate circuits is prevalent.

PACKET-SWITCHING SERVICE ASPECTS

This section compares the service aspects of packet-switching technologies. These include the philosophy of data delivery, congestion control, flow control, protocol functions, and how the service relates to the OSI Reference Model (OSIRM).

Data Delivery Philosophy

A fundamental aspect of a packet-switching service is whether the packets are guaranteed to be delivered or not. An assured data service guarantees delivery of the packets, while an unassured data service does not. The assured mode is tolerant of errors. The unassured mode is also called a datagram service, a term that originated in the older X.25 standards.

X.25 and TCP assure that packets are delivered reliably on a link-by-link basis. FR and SMDS operate in unassured mode. ATM can offer either mode of service, depending on the service class selected.

The packet-switching service might guarantee that data arrives in the same sequence as it was transmitted, or might reorder the packets on delivery. If a packet service has sequence integrity, the order of transmitted packets is preserved end-to-end.

Switching Approach

The packet-switched network can operate as either a connection-oriented network service (CONS) or a connectionless network service (CLNS), as defined in Chapter 3. Connection-oriented packet-, frame-, and cell-switching services can establish their connection as either permanent virtual connections (PVCs) or switched virtual connections (SVCs).

Traffic, Congestion, and Flow Control

A packet service can reserve bandwidth for a connection-oriented service, or enforce other limits on access to the service. This bandwidth reservation can take the form of an end-to-end committed information rate (CIR) as with FR, or peak cell rate (PCR) and sustainable cell rate (SCR) traffic-control functions per virtual channel connection (VCC) as with ATM. For connectionless services, bandwidth reservation is only an attempt. SMDS uses access classes and limits bandwidth at the ingress. IP uses class of service (CoS) mechanisms on a hop-by-hop basis.

A packet service can implement flow control. The flow-control method can be window-based as with X.25, congestion-based as with FR (FECN/BECN) and ATM (forward congestion notification), or rate- and credit-based as with ATM. Alternatively, a packet service such as IP can have no flow control whatsoever. A packet service can detect and react to congestion on either a link-by-link basis or an end-to-end basis. The reaction to congestion can be receiver-controlled, transmitter-controlled, both, or neither.

Comparison of Protocol Functions

Table 14-1 shows a comparison of public data service protocol functions. The terms used in the table were summarized in the preceding sections.

Function	X.25	IP	FR	SMDS	ATM	MPLS
Switching type	Packet	Packet	Frame	Cell	Cell	Packet/ Frame/Cell
Mode	CONS	CLNS	CONS	CLNS	CONS w/CLNS	CONS for CLNS
CONS elements	PVC, SVC	N/A	PVC, SVC	N/A	PVC, SVC	Flow
Assured mode	Yes	No	No	No	via SSCOP	Yes
Sequence integrity	Yes	No	Yes	Yes	Yes	Yes
Retransmission	Yes	No	No	No	via SSCOP	No
Traffic control	None	None	CIR, EIR	Access Class	PCR, SCR	FR or ATM
Flow control	Yes	No	No	No	No	No
Congestion control	Transmit	No (but possible)	Transmit, Receiver	No	Receiver	No

Table 14-1.   Comparison of Protocol Functions

OSI Functional Mapping

Figure 14-4 depicts an approximate mapping of data communications protocols, services, and their common interfaces to the OSIRM. These protocols were covered in previous chapters.

GENERIC PACKET-SWITCHING NETWORK CHARACTERISTICS

This section covers aspects of addressing, switching, routing, and network design. A tabular presentation summarizes the comparison of the networking aspects of data communication services.

Network-Addressing Philosophies

Addressing can be geographically oriented, as with the E.164 Address plan. The North American Numbering Plan (NANP) is a subset (that is, country code, area code, NPA, NXXX) of E.164. Addressing may also be network-oriented as with the Internet IPv4 or IPv6 plans (198.5.3.2). Addressing may also be hardware-oriented as with a MAC address. The most common addressing schemes employed today include E.164, IPv4 and IPv6, X.121, NSAP, and IEEE MAC, as covered in Chapter 10.

OSIRM	Protocol	Service	Interface
Application	Operating system file management X.400 / X.500	Distributed file sharing, multimedia, messaging	User, software
Presentation	NCP, NetBIOS, NETBeui, FTP, NFS FTAM	Multimedia	Software
Session	SPX, NetBIOS, NETBeui, FTP, SMTP	LU6.2	Software
Transport	TCP, XNS, SPX	TCP/IP	Software
Network	IP, IPX, XNS, IEEE, 802.1, X.25 (packet), ISDN, ARP	ISDN, X.25, IP, SMDS, ATM AAL	Software
LLC	IEEE 802.2 LLC, HDLC, SDLC, X.25 (link), PPP, FR, SIP_L2	X.25, PPP, ATM, FR	Software
MAC	IEEE 802.X, SMDS SIP, FDDI	ATM, FDDI, High-speed-Ckt switching	Ethernet, Token Ring, FDDI X3.139
Physical	DS0, FT1, DS1, DS3	DS0, FT1, DS1, DS3, HSCS	Copper/coax/fiber media systems and interfaces

Figure 14-4. Mapping of services and protocols to the OSIRM

The standard IPv4 (most common) IP address is 32 bits and is assigned on a network basis. The E.164 addressing plan is 15 binary coded decimal (BCD) digits and is currently assigned on a geographic basis. The 48-bit IEEE MAC addresses are assigned on a vendor-chip basis. X.25 uses a logical channel number (LCN). Switched X.25 connections use a 14-digit X.121 address, which is allocated to networks based on the first four digits, with the network provider specifying use of the remaining digits.

FR frames are assigned a data-link connection identifier (DLCI). FR SVCs can use the E.164 numbering plan, or be created using MPLS. ATM cells are assigned a virtual path identifier (VPI) and virtual channel identifier (VCI) that can have meaning on an end-to-end basis through translation at intermediate nodes. Switched virtual ATM connections can use either E.164 or NSAP addresses. The ISO NSAP addressing plan is assigned on a network-administrator basis.

Routing Approaches

The routing of packets in data communications services can range from static to dynamic. The routing can be unspecified for the service, or standardized. Examples of standard routing protocols are the Open Shortest Path First (OSPF) and Routing Information Protocol (RIP). The primary protocol when routing to the Internet is Border Gateway Protocol (BGP). Each of these routing protocols was covered in Chapter 10.

Network Access and Topology

A packet service can provide user access via a shared medium or a dedicated medium. The access medium can be dedicated to a single type of service, or shared between multiple service types. The service can provide either point-to-point, multicast (that is, multipoint-to-multipoint or broadcast), or point-to-multipoint connectivity, as defined in Chapter 3.

Protocol-Specific Functions

A key characteristic of packet services is the existence of standard methods to carry other protocols, defined as protocol interworking. For example, an Internet Engineering Task Force (IETF) request for comment (RFC) standard is defined for how IP can be carried over each data communication service protocol.

Summary of Networking Aspects

Table 14-2 compares the networking aspects of public data communication services. The preceding sections defined the terms, concepts, and acronyms listed in this table.

PRIVATE VERSUS PUBLIC NETWORKING

Is a dedicated private network or a shared public network better for your suite of protocols and applications? Or would a combination of private and public networks serve the enterprise better? This section providers objective criteria for assistance in making this sometimes difficult decision.

One key element to be considered is the overall cost, which can include planning, design, implementation, support, service, maintenance, management, and ongoing optimization and technology upgrades. Building and running your own private network can require the dedication of significant resources, whereas these same capabilities can be found in public network service offerings at a fraction of the cost.

The current network will likely consist of legacy hardware (mainframes, controllers), and routed/switched equipment riding over LANs interconnected by bridges, routers, switches, and hubs supporting workstations and servers. Many existing network contains some form of legacy SNA protocols. Their interconnections can use private lines, or an existing private or public data service. Identify if there are some applications, or concentrations of traffic, at certain locations that require connectivity with other locations.

Aspect	X.25	IP	FR	SMDS	ATM
Addressing Plan Layer 3	X.121	IPv4/IPv6	—	E.164	E.164, NSAP
Addressing Plan Layer 2	LCN	—	DLCI	MID	VPI/VCI
Maximum packet length	< 1024 octets	< 65,535 octets	< 8192 octets	< 9188 octets	< 65,535 octets[1]
IP encapsulation	RFC 877	Native	RFC 1490	RFC 1209	RFC 1483
Routing standard	None	RIP, OSPF, E-IGRP, BGP, MPLS	None	ISSI	P-NNI
Access medium	Dedicated	Dedicated or shared	Dedicated	Shared or dedicated[2]	Dedicated
Access sharing	No	Yes	Yes	Yes	Yes
Point-to-point	Yes	Yes	Yes	Yes	Yes
Multicast	No	Yes	Yes[4]	Yes	No
Point-to-multipoint	No	No[3]	No	No	Yes

1 Depends on AAL

2 Multiple users share same access bus.

3 Multicast can be achieved by point-to-multipoint operations.

4 Can be achieved with MPLS and multipoint services

Table 14-2.   Comparison of Networking Aspects

Construct a traffic matrix of what throughput is required between major locations. You can then build a trial network design for a private network to achieve the QoS availability and performance that your applications require. In a private network, it is important to estimate the capital and ongoing expenses accurately. It is a common mistake to overlook or underestimate the planning, ongoing labor support, management, security, and upgrade costs of a private network.

If you have the site locations and estimated traffic between sites, a carrier will often be able to respond with fixed-cost and recurring-cost proposals. These proposals often offer both fixed- and usage-pricing options. Thus, the cost of a public network service can be a fixed recurring amount, versus a private network that is a huge initial capital expense. The performance of the public service will be guaranteed by the service provider through service level agreements (SLAs), while in a private network the performance is almost exclusively controlled by the design and optimization performed by the network designer. In a public network, switches and trunks can be shared across several customers, reducing cost and achieving economies of scale which are difficult to achieve in private networks. Carriers often implement a shared-trunk speed higher than any access-line speed (for example, OC-192), and consequently can achieve lower delay and loss than in a private network due to the economy of scale inherent in the large numbers required for statistical multiplexing gain. This decreases costs for the individual user yet provides performance that is suitable for most applications.

If your application has unique performance requirements that are not met by any of the carrier's quality of service (QoS) offerings, then you might be forced to build a private network. This solution will probably be more expensive yet meet the QoS requirements. Be very sure that your current and future application requirements will justify this decision.

Assuming comparable performance, the decision then becomes a matter of choosing which costs less yet meets your current and future requirements, and assessing risk. This will require a return on investment (ROI) study for each solution. Of course, the least costly (and least risky) design might be a hybrid private and public network. In the very general sense, large volumes of high-utilization point-to-point traffic might be better handled via a private network or circuit switching, while diverse, time-varying connectivity might be supported better in public packet-based networks. For example, some enterprises will run their own dark fiber and build a private, high bandwidth network within their campus or metro area, and then purchase public network services for WAN connectivity.

If a public network service is chosen, then a key question is whether fixed- or usage-based billing should be selected. Not all carriers offer these billing options, so if your application can be more economically supported by a choice of billing options, then this should be an important factor in your selection process. A fixed-rate option would charge a fixed monthly price for a certain traffic contract, which specifies a target throughput and QoS. Examples would be FR, in which the minimum CIR predictable frame delivery rate is guaranteed, or ATM, in which the QoS is expressed in terms of cell loss and delay. Internet access services can be fixed- or usage-price based. Some examples of Internet access services are fixed bandwidth (T1), tiered bandwidth (3 Mbps, 6 Mbps, 12 Mbps, and so on), and burstable (usage fee based on average bandwidth usage over period of one month). Usage billing is usually subject to a minimum and maximum charging amount, usually 100 percent or more of the equivalent fixed rate, so users that do not understand their traffic patterns cannot hurt themselves.

Most users who are unfamiliar with their traffic patterns will chose a fixed-rate option with a guaranteed QoS level (such as a DS1 port and 56 Kbps CIR rate for FR). Only after users become intimately familiar with their traffic patterns and volumes will they consider migrating to usage rates with maximum price caps to protect them from times of unpredictable excess traffic or growth. Accurate traffic forecasts are rare, and due to the accelerating bandwidth principle forecasting future traffic is difficult. Check to see what the minimum charge is for usage-based billing, and if there is a cap on the usage-based option in relation to the fixed-rate option. If the minimum is low and the cap is reasonable, then usage-based billing might be your best choice. Knowledge of your network traffic volumes and patterns is valuable here. If the public service provides traffic-measurement capabilities, you can use them to obtain more accurate traffic data and make a better-informed decision in the future. Most service providers offer managed services that provide detailed traffic reports that can help you size feeds and speeds.

PUBLIC NETWORK SERVICE SELECTION

Now that you have decided to use a public network service, how does one choose the correct service offering (or combination thereof)? Design methodologies and selection criteria have been defined throughout each technology chapter. Some additional rules of thumb are provided in this section, but are by no means exclusive. Each technology transports, switches, or routes data differently. The primary transport technologies reviewed in this section include X.25 packet switching, IP, FR, SMDS, ATM, and SONET. Note that IP traffic can be transported over any of these technologies, as can non-real-time, near-real-time, and real-time traffic. Private line transport mode is provided as a baseline.

When do you require a specific technology? Here are a few guidelines.

When Do You Need a Private Line?

A private line, or dedicated circuit between two points, might be required when

▼ Point-to-point connectivity is required between only two locations.

■ Average link utilization (traffic volume) between two points is very high (more than 30 percent average utilization during the busy hour of the busy day), such as with LAN extension.

■ Building a star (hub-and-spoke) network configuration to a single hub site.

■ Integrated access of voice, video, and data is required over a single circuit from an existing CPE device such as a PBX, channel bank, or multiplexer.

■ Traffic characteristic is constant-bit rate (CBR), as with video conferencing.

▲ A consistent QoS is required that can be provided only by a dedicated circuit (for example, less than 30 milliseconds delay).

The quality of private-line circuits has drastically improved in recent years with the advent of all fiber-optic (SONET- and DWDM-based) transmission facilities and high-quality PL service architectures such as AT&T's FASTAR.

When Do You Need X.25 Service?

X.25 public service might be required when

▼ Traffic is bursty and delay-insensitive in nature.

■ Reliable data transport is required at speeds from 150 bps to 56,000 bps.

■ Facilities with poor-quality communications are prevalent.

■ Error checking and flow control are required to be built into the protocol.

▲ International connectivity to countries and cities without fiber-optics is required.

When Do You Need FR Service?

FR might be required when

▼ Consolidation of multiple protocols (that is, IP, IPX, and SNA) over a single network access circuit and technology is needed.

■ A large amount of LAN-to-LAN traffic must be transported.

■ Traffic is variable bit rate (VBR), very bursty, and non-delay-sensitive.

■ Multiple locations (usually more than three) require interconnectivity (physical and/or logical meshing).

■ Multiple traffic prioritization down to the protocol or session level is required.

■ In-band management capability such as SNMP is required.

■ Flexibility for rapid network reconfiguration (at PVC level) is needed.

▲ Cost-effective alternatives over international PL are required.

When Do You Need ATM Service?

ATM might be required when

▼ High-speed interconnectivity is required (DS1–DS3).

■ Native LAN interconnect speeds of 100 Mbps (and higher) are required.

■ Multiple QoS levels are required within a single physical circuit or path.

■ Multiple-service interconnection (that is, FR to ATM, LAN to PSTN) is required.

▲ Integrated access or transport of multiple services, such as PL, FR, SMDS, voice, video, and legacy service, is required.

When Do You Need an IP Service?

There are three general types of IP services: remote IP network access (dial, xDSL, cable, private IP services, and public IP services such as the Internet), access to the public Internet (remote and dedicated), and dedicated site-to-site IP connectivity (IP VPN or over a public service like PL, FR, or ATM). These forms of IP services might be required when

▼ Traffic is bursty and delay-insensitive.

■ Remote access such as dial, xDSL, or cable modem is required, but higher-speed dedicated services (PL, FR, ATM) are not available.

■ Facilities with poor-quality communications are prevalent.

■ High and intermittent quantities of data retransmission are acceptable.

■ International connectivity to countries and cities without fiber-optics is required.

▲ CoS vs. QoS is required.

When Do You Need a Public Data Service?

What criteria drive the decision to consider a public data service?

▼ Total cost of ownership: lower cost to buy network services versus build private network

■ Access to redundant/diverse facilities (no common facilities) in access and backbone

■ Want to achieve the benefits of a public SONET/DWDM redundant, self-healing architecture

■ Guarantees of availability, reliability, and performance as defined and guaranteed through SLAs with refund of predefined damages if not met

■ Fixed, recurring price

■ Multiprotocol and multiservice transport and interoperability

▲ Gateway services (Internet, PSTN)

Transport Transmission Characteristics

Figure 14-5 illustrates a comparison of circuit-switched, X.25 packet-switched, FR, cell-switched (ATM), SONET, IP (typically PPP), and private-line transmissions. Notice in

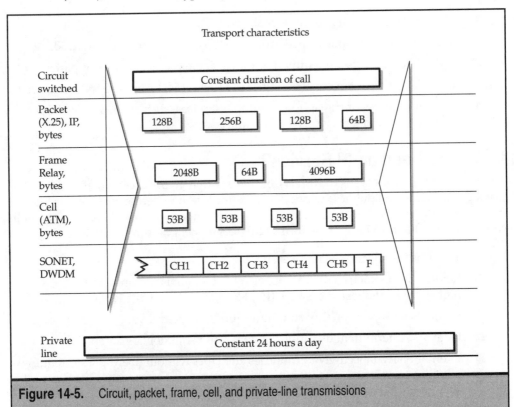

Figure 14-5. Circuit, packet, frame, cell, and private-line transmissions

circuit switching that variable bandwidth is not available to the user, whereas in packet/ frame/cell switching, bursty data can be allocated the appropriate bandwidth-on-demand by the CoS/CIR/ATM service class. Packet, frame, and cell technologies also allow for the capability to dynamically route around failures at the packet/frame/cell virtual circuit or protocol flow (TCP/IP session) level, rather than at the circuit level, and virtual circuit or protocol flow reconnect time is in milliseconds rather than seconds. Usually, in circuit switching, the entire call has to be reestablished in the event of a failure or disconnect. Thus, packet/frame/cell services can survive node and circuit failures with minimal session interruption.

Which technology is better suited to smaller or larger networks? As the number of meshed or semimeshed circuits increase, which technology is better suited? Figure 14-6 illustrates one method of viewing technology selection based on network size. There are obviously many similar charts that can be drawn to compare technologies based on network characteristics. The bottom line is that the greater the number of circuits and meshing required, the more economic packet/frame/cell solutions become. Note that IP can be transported over all of these technologies.

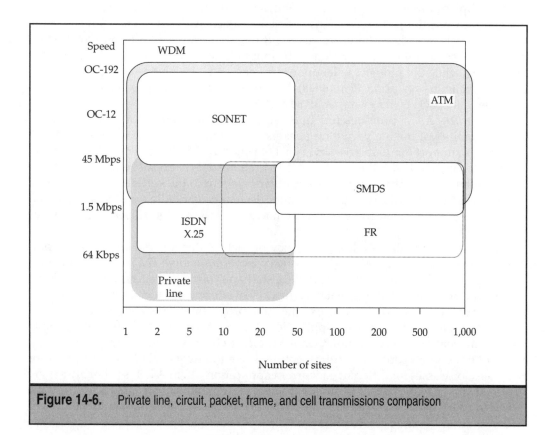

Figure 14-6.   Private line, circuit, packet, frame, and cell transmissions comparison

BUSINESS ASPECTS OF PACKET-, FRAME-, AND CELL-SWITCHING SERVICES

This section compares several business aspects of data communication services. These include the trade-off between efficiency and features, impacts on user hardware and software, a quantification of the savings due to integration, an assessment of the market demand, and pricing comparisons of various data communications services.

Efficiency versus Features

One thing that you might want to consider is the trade-off of efficiency versus features. Both might affect your higher-layer protocols and thus your applications, as well as the cost of operating/managing your network. Increasing the number or quality of features often comes at the expense of decreased efficiency and increased support costs. In this section, the efficiency and features of three major data protocols used in private or public networking are compared: FR, ATM (using AAL5), and IP. Protocol efficiency is compared in this section, and is shown in Figure 14-7.

FR supports variable-length packets, with an overhead of 5 to 7 bytes per packet (excluding zero insertion). This is the most efficient protocol with respect to overhead of the three protocols considered here. However, FR might not support multiple QoS classes, especially if some frames are very long. The longest standardized frame size required is 1600 bytes, while the protocol will support frames up to 8192 bytes long (but the CRC check is accurate only up to 4000 bytes). Its efficiency approaches 100 percent for very long user data packets (for example, IP packets).

ATM using AAL5 provides functions very similar to FR, and provides the additional flexibility of mixing very long packets with other delay-sensitive traffic. AAL5 also allows support for up to a 64-kbyte packet length which FR does not. The 8 bytes in the trailer combined with the 5 bytes of ATM cell header overhead reduce the achievable efficiency by 17 percent. Because the variable-length packet must be segmented into fixed-length cells, the resultant efficiency decreases markedly when this segmentation results in one or a few bytes of packet data in the last cell. Its efficiency approaches 90 percent for very large packets.

Figure 14-7 plots the resulting efficiency of each protocol versus user packet size. Note how very short packets are handled very inefficiently by ATM Adaptation Layers (AALs) 3, 4, and 5. In one further example, a study performed on current Internet traffic produced calculations showing that the efficiency of offering this traffic over ATM would be approximately 60 percent because of the large proportion of very short packets!

Which protocol is best for your application? It depends. If you need a feature that only the less-efficient protocols support, then the choice is clear; you can't use a more efficient protocol if it doesn't support a critical feature. If your network will require support for multiple QoS classes for different concurrent applications, then ATM is probably a good choice. If you need to connect to other networks via a public service, access users on the public Internet, IP or FR are probably good choices, either as a stand-alone service or carried over an ATM-based service. If raw efficiency is key, and support for multimedia applications is not required, then FR is a good solid choice.

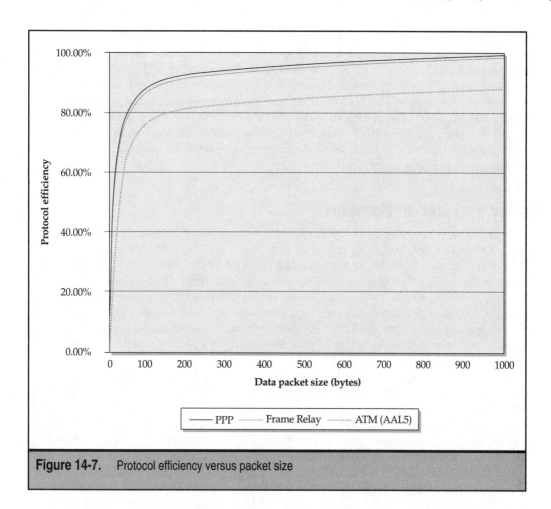

Figure 14-7. Protocol efficiency versus packet size

CPE Hardware and Software Impacts

What are the hardware and software cost and change impacts of adding a new protocol to, or changing the existing protocol of, your WAN or LAN? IP already works on most existing hardware platforms, and therefore could require minimal upgrade, whereas upgrading from FR to ATM might require all new CPE. Software support for all three of these protocols is widely available, but might require new software loads be applied to all CPE. Hardware changes might include new interface cards, switches, hubs, routers, and potentially new CSU/DSUs. Software changes might include operating systems, device drivers, and entirely new applications, or could have an impact on existing applications.

Integration Savings

Services such as FR and ATM offer economies of integration. For example, an enterprise can purchase a public FR service and access the public Internet over the same FR access circuit. Access (through a gateway) to the PSTN is also available from a FR access circuit. ATM supports integrated access and transport of voice, data, and video, and also allows Internet and PSTN access and termination from an originating ATM port. The need for multimedia and mixed services over a single integrated access line or shared switch port is a key advantage of ATM. Technologies that integrate multiple forms of traffic (voice, data, and video) and can prioritize between them can achieve and sustain higher bandwidth utilization patterns than single traffic pattern technologies. This integration capability enables cost savings that must be measured against the additional cost of new hardware and network complexity.

Ubiquity and Market Demand

X.25 and IP services have been around for many years. They are widely available in Europe, Latin America, and Asia, and IP is extensively available in North America (most X.25 services have been decommissioned in North America, but remain active in other parts of the world). Part of the reason for this is the relatively expensive cost of a private line and the lack of fiber-optic transmission facilities in most areas of the world. Furthermore, X.25 is slow and has high processing overhead and long delays. On the other hand, it has accuracy and guaranteed delivery, both of which are critical for low-quality transmission environments, and native IP provides a ubiquity of access better that any other public network service short of the PSTN.

IP network services continue to experience phenomenal growth, which indicates the pent-up demand for ubiquitous data communications access and cost-effective transport. Plus many IP services now offer the capability to purchase multiple CoS or reserve bandwidth. Most global IP service is provided over the public Internet, a good bit over private carrier IP infrastructres, and some is transported over transport-protocol service such as FR, ATM, and MPLS where access is paid through an Internet service provider (ISP) in either a flat rate or usage-pricing configuration.

FR services continue to see strong growth. Most users are large corporations who use it for site-to-site corporate virtual private network connectivity. New MPLS deployments and consequently services such as IP-enabled FR and ATM have made virtual meshing of IP network communications routing over FR/ATM networks even more economical and flexible. And FR continues to be an excellent alternative to private lines.

The SMDS market has largely dissipated, especially in the United States, but some services are supported in Europe. Most SMDS users have converted to IP VPNs or ATM services.

ATM PVC and SVC services are being used by many corporate customers in a manner similar to FR to construct virtual private networks. In many cases, ATM is used at the HQ or central site due to port speed requirements (FT1 or DS3) with FR at remote sites. Most providers offer ATM DS1 at the same cost as FR DS1 to make it attractive for the user to economically justify an upgrade from FR to ATM. Plus IP operates seamlessly over ATM.

General Pricing Structures

Services such as FR, SMDS, IP, and ATM can either be classified as enhanced services, and thus would not be offered under a structured tariff, or else would be offered under a tariff. Most are now nontariff public pricing. The pricing and billing policies of these enhanced data services are based on many factors, including

▼ Local Access Physical Circuit based on speed and distance to local serving PoP

■ Physical Port access speed based on bandwidth available

■ Total virtual connection bandwidth per port or per virtual channel/circuit based on defined traffic parameters

■ CIR for FR

■ Access class for SMDS

■ PCR and SCR (or their PVC CIR equivalents) for ATM

■ CoS for IP

■ Other QoS class

▲ Fixed, Tiered, or Usage rates

Usage-based billing rates can be measured in packets, frames, cells, or just total bytes delivered over a time period and rounded off to some accuracy. For example, the charge can be based on millions of cells delivered per month.

Fixed charges include a port charge, access charges (for the circuit from the customer premises to the service provider switch), installation charges, and other fees. A fixed-rate billing option might also include a charge based on the virtual connection bandwidth, priority, and QoS class. There are also many credits, bulk discounts, time-of-day discounts, and nonrecurring charges that for large accounts are typically waived.

The excessive cost of dedicated access services often limit users to low-speed dial or shared circuits (xDSL or cable modems) for LAN-to-LAN traffic, creating a WAN bottleneck. If these circuits are analyzed, it is often seen that they are flooded during the busy hour but are not used much during off-peak, nonbusiness hours. These applications are ideal candidates for virtual networking. For many users, the initial deployment of any virtual data service should be limited, allowing the users to learn their traffic patterns.

Users should look for price caps on a usage-based service so that it can be no greater than a certain percentage above the comparable flat-rate fee or leased line service. Pricing should not penalize users who are just trying out the service and who are not familiar with their traffic patterns. There will still be access charges, but a virtual data network using fewer dedicated access circuits in the local loop will decrease bottom-line access costs.

Intra-LATA, inter-LATA, and interstate data services (FR, IP, ATM) are offered as either public pricing or under a tariff. Public pricing varies, so make sure you get a true "apples-to-apples" pricing comparison for your network. Some "public" pricing is published openly, some is bundled, and some is still "double secret." Tariffs are public and available to anyone. Regulatory structures constantly change.

Private Line Pricing Example

Private line pricing characteristics usually include all of the following:

▼ Fixed monthly recurring charge

■ Mileage sensitivity

■ Linear rate structure

■ Rate increases over longer distances (especially international)

▲ Significant rate increases with shorter terms (that is, month-to-month or one-year terms)

Common private line rates include DS0, FT1, T1, FT3, DS3, and OC-n. The number of circuits to achieve a break-even point for purchasing a single DS1 instead of multiple DS0s is now around three to eight (and as low as three to four in some metropolitan areas). The number of circuits to achieve a break-even point for purchasing a single DS3 instead of multiple DS1s is now around 5 to 10 (again, less in metropolitan areas). Fractional DS1 and DS3 offerings provide further economic alternatives.

FR Pricing Example

FR pricing is typically broken down into LEC and IXC components. Pricing characteristics usually include

▼ Flat rate monthly charge per FR port based on bandwidth selected

■ Flat rate monthly charge per local loop (sometimes bundled with FR port)

■ Flat rate charge per month per PVC typically based on CIR rate

■ No mileage component (usually)

▲ Possibly a higher cost per MPLS (IP-FR) PVC, also called an enterprise PVC

Typically, the greater the PVC meshing of the network configuration, the more cost-effective the overall design compared with a private line meshed network. Some carriers also offer usage-based pricing at a few cents per megabyte of data received, but beware that the data received includes overhead plus the file being sent (the amount depends on the protocols being used) and customers rarely buy usage pricing.

With mileage-based private line and non-mileage-based FR rates, private lines and FR have a crossover point, as shown in Figure 14-8, where the FR service becomes more cost-effective at greater distances. Here we see that in an apples-to-apples comparison, FR-loaded costs of a CIR equal to the private line speed are cheaper between two cities at distances greater than 500 miles. The greater the meshing, the greater the cost savings because the port and access charges are already established for FR, but required for each new point-to-point connection with private lines. Note that the speeds of this crossover point will vary widely by service provider, and this chart is presented a methodology versus an accurate cost comparison.

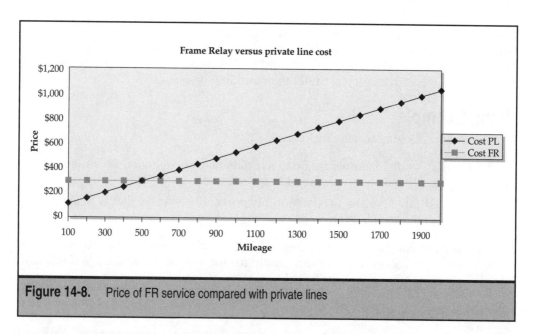

Figure 14-8.   Price of FR service compared with private lines

Also note that some local FR pricing has the port and local access bundled into a single price, and often charges a specific price per PVC regardless of the CIR rate, as long as the aggregate CIRs do not exceed the port speed.

"Zero CIR" service is one option where the provider transports all FR frames with the DE bit marked for discard. Thus, there is no CIR guaranteed, and all data could potentially be discarded. This service could be more cost-effective for remote locations that have low-speed requirements, intermittent access, and delay-tolerant applications. But beware, the actual throughput might be 0 Kbps. Remember that CIR does not always "guarantee" delivery of a CIR (non-DE) frame; it just means that CIR frames may be dropped only after all DE frames are discarded.

Sometimes regional FR providers will tie together multiple FR platforms with a network-to-network interface (NNI). This might be the only way a regional provider can offer inter-LATA FR transport. While this option can provide for less expensive rates, beware of performance issues when using a shared NNI: these networks can be hard to troubleshoot (multiple switch platforms and multiple vendors), offer inconsistent SLAs, and in general create finger-pointing between vendors. Make sure all these issues are explored before selecting a network that relies on NNIs.

Balance the volume, term, and discounts you can obtain against the price. Shorter term (for example, one year) contracts can be obtained but at a premium over two- or three-year contracts. Ask yourself how long it will take to get the network implemented. If the answer is three to four months and you sign a one-year contract, or if it is prudent to begin contract renewal negotiations at least three months before your current term expires, you could find yourself renegotiating your contract just a few months after your network is installed! Longer term contracts can carry deeper discounts; just make sure they include technology upgrade, obsolescence, and economic downturn clauses.

Lease CPE when it makes sense, which might make upgrades easier. Technical obsolescence moves at a fast rate, and it might be worth the lease money to make your service provider shoulder much of the upgrade burden. This is one of the primary reasons you are purchasing a network service rather than building it yourself.

IP Pricing Example

IP pricing characteristics usually include

▼ **For dial**   A flat monthly fee up to a certain amount of hours, OR a monthly usage fee based on minutes used in given month

▲ **For Dedicated Access**   A flat monthly port connection fee that typically includes the local loop

IP pricing can vary widely; for example, IP VPN pricing can be fixed- or usage-based, while IP Internet access can be a flat monthly fee for a T1. xDSL and cable-modem IP Internet access range all across the board.

ATM Pricing Example

ATM pricing characteristics are broken down into the type of service required. VBR service is offered with a defined SCR (minimum peak BW) and PCR (maximum peak BW), but with only the SCR guaranteed. For example, some service providers equate the PCR with a CIR rate for VBR (similar to FR CIR). With ABR (Available Bit Rate) service you pay for a minimum throughput level. With unspecified bit-rate (UBR) service, there is no such specification. VBR can come in both connection-oriented (CO) and connectionless (CL) modes. A maximum burst duration and CDV rate is assigned for each VC. CBR service might be charged as a defined bandwidth similar to a traditional, dedicated private line. The primary elements of ATM service fees include a flat monthly fee per ATM access port (usually with the local loop bundled into the port price) (depending on speed) and a fee per PVC based on speed. There could also be usage- and mileage-sensitive cost components, and potentially enterprise PVC costs if using MPLS IP-ATM service. All services aforementioned might include additional nonrecurring and bundling charges, many of which can be partially or fully waived for very large networks.

Summary of Business Aspects

Table 14-3 provides a comparison of business aspects of the currently available public data services.

HIGH-SPEED LAN PROTOCOLS COMPARISON

Moving closer to the user, we inevitably come to the discussion of high-speed LAN technologies. The key contenders in 100 Mbps and higher-speed LAN technologies include FDDI, 100 Mbps Ethernet, ATM, and Gigabit Ethernet (GbE). Table 14-4 shows a comparison of these technologies.

Aspect	X.25	IP	FR	SMDS	ATM
Efficiency (1 best, 4 worst)	2nd	3rd	1st	4th	1st, 2nd, 3rd, and 4th
Multiple service support	Possible	Possible	Possible	Some	Best
CPE hardware use	Existing	Existing	Existing	Existing	New
CPE software use	Existing	Existing	New	New	New
Access ubiquity	Limited	Best	High	None	Medium
Market demand and geographic coverage	Low	High	High	Low	Moderate
Evolution potential	Low	Some	Some	None	High
Service	Low	Varies	Low	Varies	Medium
Technological obsolescence factor	High	Low	Low	High	Low

Table 14-3. Comparison of Business Aspects

Attribute	FDDI	100BASE-T (100 Mbps Ethernet)	ATM	Gigabit Ethernet (GbE)
Standard	ANSI X3T12	IEEE 802.3u	ATM Forum, ITU, IETF	IEEE 802.3ae
Throughput	100-Mbps simplex	100-Mbps Simplex	1-Mbps to 1.2-Gbps duplex	1-Gbps simplex
Packet or frame type	FDDI frame	Ethernet frame	Cell	Ethernet frame
Evolution potential	Fair	Excellent	Good	Excellent
Reserved bandwidth	No	No	Yes	No
Isochronous support	No	No	Yes	No
Multiple traffic classes	No	No	Yes	No
Cost to implement	High	Low	Medium	High
Uses existing wiring	Yes (CDDI)	Yes*	Yes*	Yes*
Scalable in speed	No	No	Yes	No
Scalable to MAN	No	Yes	Yes	Yes*
Scalable to WAN	No (MAN)	No	Yes	No

*Distance, category of wiring, and number of wire pairs required must be considered.

Table 14-4. Comparison of FDDI, 100 Mbps Ethernet, ATM, and GbE

APPLICATION PERFORMANCE NEEDS

This section compares the various services introduced in this book to meet the performance needs of applications with their key distinctive characteristics. First, the relative throughput of each service type and its underlying technology is summarized. Then the trade-offs between burstiness, throughput, response time, and delay are examined. This section analyzes the attributes of user application needs for throughput, burstiness, and delay tolerance over a wide range of public data services.

Throughput

Figure 14-9 shows the history of maximum available throughput for commercially available data services. The time frame is the historical or projected year in which the maximum data rate was widely offered and became cost-effective. From this perspective, there is some differentiation in maximum throughput with ever-increasing maximum bandwidths on the horizon. However, throughput is not the only dimension of performance that must be considered.

Burstiness

Figure 14-10 plots the characteristic of burstiness, defined in Chapter 12 as the ratio of peak to average rate, on the vertical axis versus the supportable peak rate of the service,

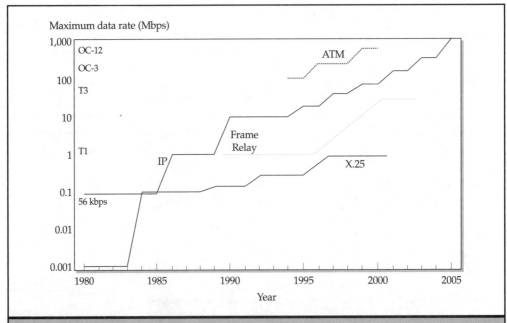

Figure 14-9.   Comparison of maximum data-rate by service

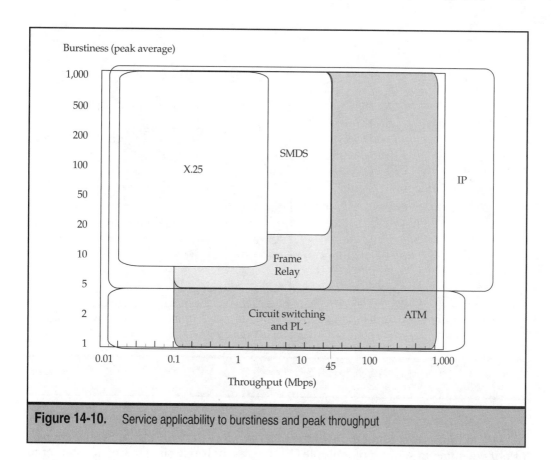

Figure 14-10.   Service applicability to burstiness and peak throughput

or throughput, on the horizontal axis. The term *circuits* encompasses both circuit switching and private lines, the choice being based on the economics summarized earlier in this chapter. The enclosed region for a particular service indicates that it is applicable to that region of burstiness and the throughput characteristic. A number of the services overlap in their range of applicability. As described in the previous section, note that the time frame in which peak rate throughput has been available progresses from left to right.

Response Time and Delay Tolerance

Figure 14-11 depicts the applicability of services in another dimension, namely the range of nodal delay on the vertical axis versus peak throughput on the horizontal axis. The chart shows that circuit switches have essentially constant nodal delay. Any form of packet switching will introduce some variations in delay, and, typically, the lower the speed of the packet/frame/cell-switching circuits, the more the variation in delay, as shown by the general trend of the services to support better (that is, lower) nodal delays as the peak throughput increases. Note that FR can support specific values of delay through the use of prioritization. ATM can support delay close to that of dedicated cir-

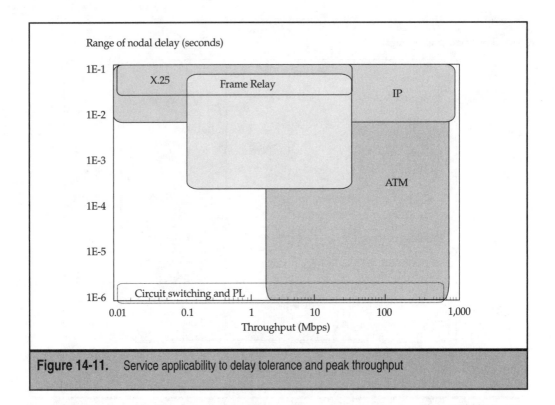

Figure 14-11. Service applicability to delay tolerance and peak throughput

cuits up to ranges exceeding those of the other services through the implementation of priority queuing in support of multiple QoS classes. IP is relegated to CoS to attempt to meet response time and delay tolerance requirements, but still predominantly remains a best-effort service.

Figure 14-12 depicts the applicability of services in the dimension of range of nodal delay on the vertical axis and burstiness on the horizontal axis. As can be observed from the previous charts, dedicated circuits are best suited to applications that are not bursty and have a strict delay tolerance, such as video, audio, and telemetry data. X.25 and IP services depict the classic wisdom of packet switching targeted to bursty applications that can accept significant variations in delay. Again, some prioritization and use of CoS can make IP more conducive to transport delay tolerant applications. FR and SMDS support a broader range of application burstiness, while FR has the potential to support better delay tolerance through prioritization. ATM supports the broadest range of burstiness and delay tolerance through the implementation of multiple QoS classes.

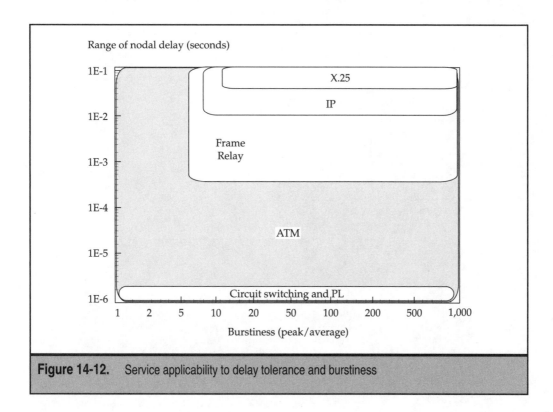

Figure 14-12. Service applicability to delay tolerance and burstiness

REVIEW

This chapter compared technologies and data services from several points of view. Data communications was first categorized based on the method—message, circuit, or packet/frame/cell switching. We identified that most modern methods are based on some form of packet switching, hence packet/frame/cell-switching service aspects and network characteristics were covered in detail. A detailed comparison of the X.25, IP, FR, SMDS, and ATM data services was next presented. It was shown that each technology has its specific area of advantages and disadvantages, with some overlap. The comparison covered functional, technical (switching, architecture, and addressing), and business aspects of these services. Existing and emerging LAN standards were also compared. The chapter concluded with an analysis of application performance requirements and the applicability of each of these technologies to meet those requirements.

PART VI

Choosing the
Service Provider

CHAPTER 15

Choosing Service Providers

Choosing a service provider is similar to searching for a marriage partner. Proposals for a relationship are extended through solicitations—requests for information (RFIs) and, later, proposals (RFPs)—providing a list of requirements by which to build a long-lasting relationship. The service provider (the user's future partner) responds to the RFI/RFP with a list of what it can provide, when it can provide it, and at what expense or expectations. The capabilities of each provider are examined carefully, and ultimately one is chosen (in some cultures, more than one) to build a network. A contract is written and the future (network) is committed to the service provider as the service provider commits its services to the user. Both find out how they must live with each other. Partnerships are expected to last for the life of the network, although the capability of "divorcing" the network from the service provider might become necessary if service becomes poor or the service provider's priorities change. The key is to never stop communicating. Vendors or service providers must be chosen sometime after the requirements have been defined, the technologies and services selected, and the high-level design process begun. Vendor selection should be done with care. The success of the network can affect the network manager's job, the users who rely on the network, and the business itself. All these rely directly or indirectly on vendor performance.

In this chapter, the RFP process is summarized. Conformance to standards, the business parameters of the company, and the industry as a whole are critical. The RFP is the one chance to "get it all in writing." If a requirement or conformance is not included in the RFP, and subsequently is not in the contract, the vendor does not have to provide it. The watchword is be thorough in the selection and contract process.

This chapter presents a method of choosing vendors based on weighted business and technical needs. Critical issues include what trade-offs to expect, how to derive various levels of support from the vendor, how to ensure industry standardization in the hardware and software purchased, and how to ensure vendors deliver on promises. The vendor-user relationship must benefit the strategic and technical direction of both parties to be a lasting relationship. In this chapter, the end user, network designer, network manager, partners, suppliers, and so on, are all "users" when considering vendor relationships. Vendor responsiveness to user needs is critical. Vendor selection can affect the future business success of the company. This was especially true at the turn of the century when many telecommunications companies suddenly (some with days' notice) went out of business and caused customer outages.

The network is designed, the purchase orders are written, hardware and services are ordered, and the network sites are awaiting the equipment's arrival. Vendor XYZ promised that the hardware would arrive in six weeks. It has now been more than three months, and still no equipment. The recent trade magazine shows that vendor XYZ is having financial problems. A call is placed to the sales representative at vendor XYZ. He or she tells you, "No problem, the stuff is on the way; it's only rumors." A week later the hardware arrives and the bill is paid. The next month, XYZ goes out of business. When finally the equipment you bought is up and running, it does not work properly. When it is interfaced to another vendor's equipment, it does not work because the interfaces are proprietary. The network is eventually scrapped; the network designer loses his or her job. The same story could happen with network connectivity services (such as FR or IP connectivity services). This story, of course, is exaggerated to emphasize the point that a thorough vendor analysis must be completed prior to choosing a vendor. This chapter helps separate promises from reality. Don't be an XYZ fatality!

RFI PROCESS

An RFI is designed to obtain enough information from potential suppliers to enable the user to eliminate suppliers who cannot meet the minimum requirements. Thus, the user arrives at a short list from which a final candidate can be chosen. The RFI simply offers prospective suppliers a version of the desired end result and allows them the opportunity to provide their solution. This is the "feeling out" stage, and many vendors can be provided an opportunity to respond. There are usually parameters placed on the selection of vendor and technology, and guidelines are offered.

The user typically provides

- ▼ Rules of engagement during the RFI process
- ■ Business and network performance objectives
- ■ Existing applications and technologies to replace or integrate
- ■ Traffic volumes and characteristics (as explained in this chapter)
- ■ Future plans and requirements
- ■ Evaluation criteria
- ▲ All information in electronic and hardcopy format

The user typically requests from the supplier respondents:

- ▼ A specific response for each request or line item
- ■ Specific vendor capabilities to meet each requirement by date
- ■ Service and product delivery dates
- ■ Complete supporting documentation
- ▲ General pricing

The user then uses the RFI responses to select a short list of vendors who will receive the RFP.

RFP PROCESS

The evaluation of the RFI responses has narrowed the field of potential vendors. It is now time to begin the RFP process. Generally, the rule is that RFIs go to 10 to 15 vendors, and RFPs to three to five. RFPs are used

- ▼ To clarify buyer needs
- ■ As a "soft" legal agreement of vendor provisions and capabilities

- ■ To weed out competition
- ■ To finalize the network design and direction
- ■ To solve pricing discrepancies
- ▲ To give a true apples-to-apples comparison of the short-list vendors

RFPs are a means of requesting multiple vendors to formally commit detailed solutions, propose the appropriate technology and service, and quote services to satisfy designated requirements. Before issuing the RFP, the buyer must

- ▼ Understand the technology alternatives
- ■ Properly define what is required from the vendor
- ■ Clearly define the technology, business, and financial issues with priorities
- ▲ Clearly define support requirements

Make sure that user requirements are clearly articulated and define what you will and will not accept. All correspondence should be thoroughly documented. All answers to questions should be posted to all respondents as frequently asked questions (FAQs). This might seem harsh for two businesses that are trying to establish a lasting relationship, but it is necessary to build a professional relationship and to avoid finger-pointing later.

RFP Structure

RFPs vary, based on the systems being bid, from simple requests for a specific piece of hardware or software or service offering to an entire network solution complete with vendor support and possibly even an outsourcing agreement. A general RFP format includes

- ▼ Synopsis or business objectives
- ■ General contractual terms and conditions (explanations, interpretations, rules of engagement)
- ■ Scope of work
- ■ Timeline schedule with milestones and deliverables
- ■ Qualifications of bidder
- ■ Current systems, technologies, architectures, protocols, services, and applications
- ■ Hardware and software technical specifications or proposed configurations with accepted substitutions
- ■ Environmental requirements
- ■ Vendor-required engineering and installation
- ■ Implementation plan
- ■ Performance objectives
- ■ Service level agreements (SLAs)

- Warranty or availability requirements
- Summary of financial bid
- Payment options
- Statement of Work with specific responsibilities
- Proposal assumptions
- Training requirements
- Vendor credibility and reference requirements
- ▲ Legal or contractual considerations

Sample Networks

In the case of sending out an RFP for a complete network design, even though you have included the network application and transport requirements in the RFP, each vendor might come back with a different network solution. For example, equipment vendor solutions, choice of WAN service, and "feeds and speeds" all might vary widely. One of the best ways to ensure that all vendors provide similar responses is to provide a sample network design, or at least a minimum and maximum configuration. This design could take the form of a spreadsheet of equipment and circuit details, a topological map, or a written document. For example, if you are building a statewide FR network and want to connect ten cities, four of which are large cities and six, smaller (remote) cities, you might want to provide a design that requires specific port and PVC speeds per site. In this manner, the responses can be compared more closely to apples to apples in cost and configuration. Otherwise, you might get back five designs from five vendors, each with different port and PVC speeds, all at different prices, which would be difficult to compare.

Solicitation

Solicit the RFP to the vendors short-listed by the RFI process. Number all questions for response. Offer equal and fair guidance to all vendors. Set a maximum return date for all responses and stick to it. If vendors want your business, they will respond in time. Make sure you have given ample time for a comprehensive response. Keep in mind holidays. A time to respond that is too short will yield shoddy responses that can be vague or noncompliant. Set up a question-and-answer session with each respondent to clarify and amplify any areas that are not quite clear. A good rule of thumb is to allow two times the length of time it took to create the RFP for vendor questions, and at least two more weeks for a good response. Don't hurry the process; it takes a long time for the vendor to gather all the information requested.

Analyzing and Evaluating RFP Responses

Each respondent to the RFP should respond paragraph by paragraph. Responses will be varied, but this seems to be the best format. Beware of terms such as "substantial compliance," "intend to comply," and "will be contained in future releases." Look for terms such as "full compliance" with an explanation of how they comply and to what extent. Vendors should clearly specify what they do *not* support. Replies should contain

▼   Price of product

■   Maintenance requirements

■   Training and learning curve

■   Ongoing expenses

■   Tax financing

■   Contract termination fees

■   Warranties

■   Documentation

■   Purchase or lease decisions

▲   All nonrecurring and recurring costs

In the next section, each factor is examined for a determination of which vendor to choose.

CHOOSING VENDORS

There are many reasons for choosing one vendor over another. The vendor is not chosen only for meeting all the requirements of the RFI or RFP. Factors such as politics; business, financial, and operational needs; future position or potential partnership with the vendor; balance of trade; goals of both businesses; and a variety of others might outweigh the technical abilities of the vendor to meet the requirements. This is particularly true for large corporations or users seeking large national or international vendors for multiple services.

The relationship established with the choice of a vendor must be both practical for the business needs and affordable to the user and vendor. The most successful contracts represent a win-win solution for both parties. While the term "win-win" is often overused, the concept of both parties believing they are benefiting by doing business with the other is a very important concept. Contract relationships are sometimes termed as "sleeping with the vendor." Look into the vendor's past for not only the product or service you are purchasing, but financial history, payment history, billing accuracy, shipping and receiving procedures and policies, past and present customer base, and industry experience. Ask for references and, more importantly, *check* references. Some evaluation criteria for hardware and service providers include

▼   Vendor history

■   Product/service versatility and ability to provide a total solution

■   Processor and packet/frame/cell-processing speeds and capabilities

- Interface and protocol support
- Local or remote support ability
- Standard versus proprietary protocol support and operation
- Performance characteristics
- Features and functions
- Network management
- Security
- ▲ Price to performance, or cost-effectiveness

Remember, price is often not the most important evaluation factor, because the labor and resources committed to making the network operate often exceed hardware costs. Do not allow the focus to become myopic on cost—technical decisions based strictly on cost constraints might place the design in jeopardy. Do not condone foolhardy or frivolous spending, but bargaining away technology and performance for low cost is foolhardy. There is often a point on all technology in which cost outweighs benefit. It is your job to find the balance point.

Requirements Matrix and Weighting Methods

The next step is to build a requirements matrix, and assign a weight to each requirement based on its importance. More important criteria are given a greater weight, less important, a lower weight. Some requirements such as "total cost of solution" are often weighted more heavily than others, such as security. With the advent of Internet access and transport and the inherent security risks, security has lately taken a much higher priority.

Table 15-1 shows a sample weighting of ten typical requirements for an RFP, specifying a three-node router network. Each was provided a weight from 1 to 99 percent, with a total weight of all requirements of 100 percent. Each requirement was then assigned a rating from 1 to 10, with 10 being the highest score and 1 the lowest. In Table 15-1, the vendor scored a total of 700 points out of a possible 1000.

The weighting could be adjusted to provide an equal weighting for all requirements, or more requirements could be added. Either way, the vendor with the highest number of total points is probably the best choice for you. Another method of requirements analysis is the cost-benefit analysis, in which the costs of each requirement are weighed against the benefits realized by the requirement. This is similar to the weighting method shown previously.

Some companies perform an exposure analysis, which measures the potential expenses if the contract is a partial or total failure. This includes both the capital expenditures and the operational and personnel costs involved in the project from conception through implementation. Maximum exposure is usually measured from one to two years, with the vendor stretching out delivery and then finally not delivering or, worse yet, going bankrupt after spending the user's prepaid money.

Requirement	Weight	Score	Total Points
Total cost of solution	10	7	70
Pricing and billing options	5	8	40
Features and functions (protocols and interfaces)	10	10	100
Vendor and product reputation and philosophy	5	4	20
Architecture flexibility and technology migration path	5	6	30
System capacity and performance	15	8	120
Availability, reliability, and disaster recovery	15	4	60
Network management	25	8	200
CPE hardware support	5	8	40
Customer and field service and support aspects	5	4	20
Total	100	-	700

Table 15-1.   Requirements Matrix Weighting

Which Trade-Offs Are Critical?

The weighting method is an excellent way to determine which vendor to choose. But how can it be determined which trade-offs are critical and warrant higher weighting factors? This section presents a broad range of criteria to consider when choosing a data communications public service. This list is by no means comprehensive, but does represent the most commonly proposed options. These options can be converted to vendor questions for the RFI and RFP process. You should make your own detailed list, prioritize it, and use it to select the service or product that best meets your needs. There might be a large equipment base already existing in the corporation that will need integration and interoperability. If this is the case, integration must be factored into the requirements analysis. Following are some of the areas to consider:

▼ Pricing and Billing Options
  - Order intervals
  - Fixed or usage billing
  - Minimums and maximums on usage billing
  - Delivery options for bills (hardcopy, fax, e-mail, disk/tape)
  - Frequency of billing
  - Capability to bundle all services (equipment, management, transport/circuit costs) in one bill

- Hardware/Service Features and Functions (Protocols and Interfaces)
  - Processor capability (PPS/FPS/CPS)
  - Packet/frame/cell filtering/forwarding capability per protocol and in total
  - Bus and data-transfer speeds
  - Switching/routing protocols supported
  - Physical interfaces required/supported
  - Access classes and speeds (DS0 through STS-Nc)
  - Multiple-service access supported
  - Expansion capability
  - Local- and remote-load software for operation
  - Classes of service (CoSs) and quality of service (QoS) offered and fully supported to standards
  - Prioritization handling
  - Traffic parameters supported (that is, CIR, SIR, PCR, SCR, MBS)
  - Multiple, fully redundant, load-sharing options
  - Portability of service
  - Security features supported
  - In-band or out-of-band network management
- Vendor and Product Reputation and Philosophy
  - Industry leader or follower
  - References and recommendations—be sure to check them!
  - Large range of internetworking products or single solution source
  - Commonality of common logic across entire product line
  - Service-level guarantee with refunds
- Product Architecture Flexibility and Technology Migration Path
  - Ability to migrate to future technologies (with minimal impact to CPE)
  - Future product line migration path (no disjointed software or hardware upgrades/revisions/fixes and proven architecture)
  - Standards-based for future investment protection
  - Plug-and-play CPE-to-network compatibility
  - Type of network architecture/equipment used

- Architecture/System Capacity and Performance
  - Fault tolerant robust network (1:N or 1:1 switch and component redundancy and availability)
  - PPS/FPS/CPS transmission over lightly loaded and heavily loaded ports, cards, and nodes
  - Minimal back-haul to closest switch (number of switches)
  - Ease of expansion
  - Amount of end-to-end network delay (latency) at normal- and peak-traffic conditions
  - Minimal data loss rate
  - Consistent and high throughput
  - Type of equipment used by network
  - Network architecture with high MTBF and low MTTR
  - Minimal switching delay and buffer delay per switch
- Availability, Reliability, and Disaster Recovery
  - Fault tolerance (no single physical or electronic point of failure)
  - Multiple processors per interface card (look at processor MIPS, bus speed, PPS/FPS/CPS processing, memory, and so on) or live backup processors
  - Symmetric multiprocessing
  - Easy device configuration and customization (local and remote)
  - Minimum/maximum network availability
  - Redundancy in all components and systems
  - Parallel back-plane/bus for reliability
  - Independent load-sharing over data paths
  - Redundant power supplies, common logic boards, local media
  - Hot-swap functionality
  - Dynamic reconfiguration while on line
  - No single point of failure (1:N system redundancy)
  - Automatic isolation of failed components, cards, and buses
  - Disaster recovery options
  - Number of switches, location, and back-haul required
  - Network-loadable firmware upgrades

- Network Management
  - SNMP-compliant at a minimum
  - Network management system compatibility and portability with current systems
  - Customer network management (CNM) features
  - Reporting capabilities
  - NMS costs and reporting costs
  - Monitoring and real-time configuration capabilities
  - Change management procedures
  - Performance management and engineering provided
  - Enhanced user interface, for example, web browser
- Premises Hardware Support
  - Flexible leasing/rental/purchase plans
  - Software and firmware revision testing and implementation
  - Meets all relevant industry standards
  - Upgrade-capable equipment (software, hardware, new technologies)
  - Free initial training provided
  - Ongoing support
- Total Cost Involved
  - Total cost of the network for the configuration provided
  - Price performance ratio—processing power and cost per unit (that is, packets/frames/cells per second and cost per packet/frame/cell per second)
  - Modularity expansion or upgrade costs
  - Price per port or trunk (DS1, DS3, OC-N)
  - Lowest total cost of ownership (TCO)
- ▲ Service Aspects: Operations and Support
  - Defined and measurable quality of service levels
  - 7×24×365 live customer support and troubleshooting expertise
  - Same level of service regardless of customer size
  - Large support staff with demonstrable talent
  - Ease of software and hardware installation
  - Online Documentation
  - Customer intimacy and communications

Public Service Network Offerings versus Private Networks

Users must at some point decide whether to access a public network or to build their own private network. If the decision is made to use a public network service, the user must decide between global (traditional large IXCs), national (traditional IXCs), local (traditional RBOCs), or metro service providers. This decision will be based primarily on intra-LATA, inter-LATA, interstate, or international access as well as connectivity requirements, availability, and cost of similar services.

Public network service offerings have the following advantages over private networks:

▼ Lower capital investment required

■ Higher network availability with large shared optical backbone

■ Extensive points of presence (PoPs) and switches for less backhaul and higher network availability

■ Broad choice of interface speeds

■ Integrated access capabilities—support multiple service access over a single access circuit

■ Sophisticated network management support and performance management capabilities

■ Portfolio of services (X.25, FR, IP, ATM, IP-FR/ATM) that minimize technological obsolescence

■ Smooth migration between services—minimal CPE changes required

■ Usage-based and flat-rate billing structure flexibility

■ Carrier-provided CPE offerings

■ Outsourced solution packages available

■ Highly skilled service- and equipment-support structures

■ Inherent reliability, redundancy, and survivability of a virtual private shared backbone

■ Access to public resources, for example, the Internet

▲ Ability to support simultaneous internetwork, intercompany, and intranet connectivity and communications

Another very important deciding factor is the architecture that the service provider employs for the access and backbone network. Whereas the tariff or public pricing structure is key in the initial selection, the service provider's architecture is the long-term insurance that costs will remain stable, that service quality will be delivered per the SLAs, and that new features and technologies will be offered in a timely manner. International connectivity requirements often make public networking the only cost-effective option. Earlier chapters described additional benefits of public networks compared with private networks, such as value-added services, economy of scale, network redundancy, and network management.

Adherence to Industry Standards

In today's age of data communications standardization and open systems, it becomes increasingly important to choose vendors who adhere to de facto standards and justify this commitment to standards by continuing to develop products around them. Beware of vendors that are banking on a single-standard product (especially a proprietary-standard product), even though they might promise eventual standards compliance. These rules also apply to regulatory, protocol, and manufacturing compliance on both a national and international scale. Compliance to the standards previously listed leads to interoperability from the client-server level through the network access and into the network. A complete guide to standards support is found in Chapter 3.

Vendor Promises and Support

Vendors will make many promises when courting a contract. Just make sure that all verbal commitments are fully explained in writing and included in the contract. If it is not in writing, it does not have to be honored. To verify information, research the vendor. Ask around. Talk to other customers of the vendor, and even to their competitors (and weigh their responses accordingly). Ask the vendor for a few good references and then ask for one or two that had problems with their service. From them you might get a clearer picture of the vendor. Documentation of all vendor correspondence should be compiled and stored for future reference.

One of the most hotly contested issues among vendors and buyers is support. When the vendor is first courting the user, look for vendors who both educate and consult your staff on the technologies and issues involved, and sell a *solution* rather than just a product. Look for the following support from the vendor:

▼   Well-defined onsite or remote maintenance and customer services

■   Support 24 hours a day, 7 days a week, 365 days a year (7×24×365) by trained staff who understand your network—test this support before you buy!

■   How much assistance will be provided with the installation, test, and turn-up? After the sale with billing support and reconciliation?

■   Percentage and size of staff assigned to support—does the vendor have a specific project manager assigned to its success?

■   Ongoing training by the vendor for your staff (including features and functions, options, and fixing unforseen problems)

▲   Automated tools available from vendor

Vendor Expertise

What expertise does the vendor hold in sales, marketing, product, design, security, networking, and systems-level support? Have its account references been checked? Also check the manufacturer's position in the industry. A vendor might have to delay a product delivery because it has been short of power supplies from its overseas power-supply vendor (which has gone out of business), or might be trying to get that next round of funding to complete the fiber route it just sold you! Make sure the vendor's supply sources are easily accessible and that it has alternate sources for its parts or infrastructure.

Vendor Delivery Dates and Reality

Again, check the vendor's references for its delivery track record. Does it often miss or postpone deliveries or installations? Does it build products at order levels or does it build at 80 percent of orders? If the latter, the vendor might look good to the financial industry but shipments might be delayed. What have been some of its other customers' experiences with late deliveries or installations? How does the vendor ship and track these shipments? In the United States, it is common to have two-week to two-month delivery cycles from the date the order is placed to the date the equipment ships from the vendor, and circuit installations sometimes exceed several months. Does the vendor have the required network capacity for when you order the service, or will it be built after your order is placed? In Europe and Asia, the average delivery time is much longer, typically two to four months. This average is getting shorter, however, as many international vendors are now competing in U.S. markets, where project timelines and delivery dates are more competitive and much shorter.

Product Announcements and Product Futures

Be aware of all product announcements and the future product direction of each vendor. Product announcements should be received free of charge through data sheets, advertisements, and electronic mail bulletins. If information is sensitive in nature and not yet public, a user-vendor mutual nondisclosure form can be used, which states that neither party will divulge information about the other without express written consent or until after a specific date. This contract is legally binding and strictly enforced. Nondisclosure agreements can be either selective or blanket agreements.

Also ask for the future product direction of the company. Discern its dedication to R&D activities, and what percentage of its profit goes toward research and new product development. Make sure that the vendor's spending direction for new products is the same as your product requirements direction.

The Proprietary Vendor and Futures

While using the same vendor over time can provide backward compatibility, it can also lock the user into an obsolete product. The vendor could get off track from technological change, and take the user with it. Avoid proprietary vendor implementations, with the exception being cutting-edge prestandards products. While proprietary implementations provide specialized solutions for the short term, they cause atrophy in the long term. Lastly, look at the overall future potential of the vendor. This includes market position, product futures, financial condition, strategic partnerships, existing and potential competition, and a myriad of other company "health" factors, which paint the true picture of whether the vendor is in for the short haul or the long haul. Many people disparage vendors that hold a predominant market share, but remember that they got there for a reason (a good product, strategy, large market, management team, and so on). A dominant player can also make some mistakes and recover, while a niche player might not. Brand name should be weighted heavily in the requirements matrix.

THE VENDOR-DESIGNER RELATIONSHIP

A user-vendor relationship can be a rewarding experience. As mentioned before, this is similar to a marriage, where both parties benefit under good conditions. Both must clearly understand each other's business needs, and maintain good communications channels to head off any misunderstandings. If you do not like or trust your salesperson, then a "divorce" might be eminent.

There are some rules to follow to achieve these goals. Don't let the vendor experiment with your network. This is especially true when you are trying to stabilize your network, and the vendor is experimenting with untried solutions such as new software revisions. All upgrades should be planned to eliminate these surprises, and strict change management procedures should be followed.

Maintain good interpersonal relationships. Make sure that what is expected of the vendor and the user is clearly understood. Speak honestly and cooperatively with the vendor, and work together to achieve your goals. Understand the levels of peer-to-peer relationships and the roles and responsibilities of the account team. Frequent presales and post sales support calls, as well as user visits to vendor facilities and labs are desirable. The vendor should make available a business and technical contact, such as a knowledgeable sale support person and network engineer, and provide some level of continuous on-site support for large accounts; but remember, true 7×24×365 maintenance support is left to maintenance contracts.

Make sure you are purchasing the products and services you want and need, not what the vendor wants you to purchase. When signing vendor development contracts, make sure you do not get locked in for long periods of time. These days, three years might be too long. Balance a good price for a long-term commitment with what you might pay in early cancellation penalties. Have the vendor produce good documentation before project/product hand-off.

Look for vendors who are choosy about their business partners, and how the vendor relates the chosen customers to its long-term strategy. Does the vendor deal only with interexchange carriers, or does it also deal with local access providers? Do they focus on specific vertical markets, or sell to virtually anyone? The primary customer base of a vendor can tell much about how the vendor is positioning itself for the future.

The relationship between vendor and user will usually last a long time; therefore, the vendor will have a profound impact on the user's business. The two are tied together. If the primary vendor for a communications network suddenly goes out of business, it could mean substantial budgetary impacts on the user's business to either replace the existing product base or migrate to a new one.

STRATEGIC USER-VENDOR AGREEMENTS

Strategic agreements between users and vendors take many forms, depending on the level of commitment of each party. Flexibility is the most important aspect of the agreements listed below. Both user and vendor will learn through the process, and both will be required to adapt to each other's needs. Large users typically have enough buying clout to affect the R&D direction of the vendor. These agreements can offer many advantages, such as guaranteeing a revenue stream for both parties, providing the lowest prices, skipping the repetitive, resource-intensive, and expensive RFP process, and building on the strengths of both user and vendor. Often, the vendors achieve greater control, for without them there is no product. The following are some common terms of agreement defined:

▼ **Affiliate**   No legal contract, but work together for business purposes

■ **Alliance**   Nonexclusive contractual agreement; separate funding, but might lead to a joint product or service venture

■ **Joint venture**   Central or pooled funds; often exclusive contract language or separate incorporation

▲ **Strategic partnership**   Work together to solve complex problems; might involve any level of those relationships listed earlier

SERVICE LEVELS

It is important to define the service expectations of the vendor. This includes the vendor's perspective—how service is defined, how that service is provided, and measurements for both. What are the categories of service provided, and what are its priorities? What priority is the user to the vendor—what size account—and how does the user compare to other users of that vendor? It is a fact of life that the customers that represent the largest amount of revenue typically are provided the greatest amount of vendor resources. What are the vendor's response and repair times, parts and sparing plan, software and hardware support hours? Are spares centrally located or dispersed to areas of dense customer-service areas? Are backup and fault tolerance inherent within the network service? These elements are critical to maintaining a highly available network.

Vendors provide many service levels to users. Four general levels of service can be provided, and the user must decide which best suits the business strategy and is most cost-effective. The four levels of service are nonparticipant, value-added, full-service, and joint-development.

▼ **Nonparticipant vendors** deliver their products to their customers and do not provide continued service after receipt of delivery. These are typically off-the-shelf products not requiring vendor installation or maintenance. They are also often low-cost items with sales based on price, availability, and speed of delivery. An example is Black Box, a company that specializes in delivery of well-known low-end and midrange data communications products.

- **Value-added vendors** include some level of service and support with their products and services. These vendors are judged by factors other than price and availability, such as quality, feature function, and support staffs, and make it a part of their business to communicate with each customer. These vendors offer some long-term commitment to their products and services, as well as to the customers who purchase them. While value-added vendors provide customer support, they typically draw the line when it becomes a financial burden to do so; customer service is an added value for their product, not part of their revenue-generating business.

- **Full-service vendors** are differentiated by their dedication to, and relationship with, each customer. These vendors typically have large corporate accounts and support users who require a dedicated account team and are willing to pay for it. Often, this service is provided only to the vendor's largest customers. Full-service vendors interface much more with the end user, and might be involved with the actual implementation of the product or services purchased. Full-service vendors provide customer service and account teams and relate this service directly to revenue. These vendors often prefer long-term relationships with the user based on joint service offerings and future business potential. Service in this case is often measured and conforms to strict guidelines. Outsourcing and out-tasking fit into this category.

- ▲ **Joint-development vendor** not only work with users, but also develop products in and around users. Vendors that can partner with large businesses can gain a strategic advantage in the marketplace. Small vendors can claim interoperability with major users and cut a niche into the market at the expense of time spent on development work with the user.

Sometimes a vendor will not be able to provide all the service or product that is required. A good design will incorporate alternate sources and strategies for network support that will not leave you out in the cold. It is the network manager's job to find and implement these alternatives.

NETWORK AND SYSTEMS MANAGEMENT CAPABILITIES

Network and systems management should be one of the most important decisions in the vendor-analysis process. Networks can be managed via a single network management platform with distributed analysis and data and alarm collection from all equipment and elements compiled and correlated at a central location. Network management can span the WAN, LAN, down to the desktops and servers, and all three can be performed by one network management *system.* Thus, integrated network management needs to be incorporated into the RFP process. Some users might already have an existing hardware base that will be integrated with the new—mixing protocols, operating systems, billing, alarms, and operating platforms, making integrated network management all the more important. This creates a need for a network management platform that can do many things—provide proactive and reactive global fault detection, analysis, and correction; measure network performance; and help with proactive performance engineering, security control and accounting measures, alarm and event correlation, and local and remote configuration capability. Each of these capabilities should be available for every manageable device on the network.

There are two network-management protocols that provide the integrated capability needed in today's computing networks: all versions of TCP/IP's Simple Network Management Protocol (SNMP) and OSI's Common Management Information Protocol/Common Management Information System (CMIP/CMIS). Both management protocol schemes enable integrated network management for network elements on a communications network and can be managed through hardware and software platforms such as HP OpenView.

Much of the burden still lies with the user, who must both interpret the information provided by the network manager and develop interfaces for the translation of this data into a workable form. Just monitoring SNMP feeds on an HP OpenView platform will not suffice. Some important network-management requirements that should be incorporated include

▼ Integration of all OSIRM layer of alarms

■ Intelligent interpretation of alarm and management data

■ Flexible alarm presentation and log structure

■ Real-time geographical network status

■ Real-time point-and-click graphics

■ Statistical collection

■ Remote and local downloads, nodal configuration, board diagnostics, and inventory management capabilities

■ Local hard drive/floppy storage

■ Multiple security levels other than system logon

■ Data scope functions

■ Accounting and billing collection (ASCII or binary)

▲ Integration of nonproprietary implementations

Of course a more cost-effective option might be to outsource the management of your network.

FUTURE BUSINESS OF YOUR COMPANY

It cannot be stressed enough that the future success or failure of a business (not to mention the designer's job) can ride on the success or failure of the vendors chosen for the data and computer communications networks. For this reason, a user will rarely give the entire business to a single vendor. Occasionally, a business relationship, partnership, or joint strategic direction will dictate a single vendor solution, however, a multivendor environment is a healthy and safe one. It creates a competitive environment so that the prime vendor works harder for the business and a secondary supplier is available in case the primary supplier falters. If all vendors meet the criteria presented in this chapter, especially standards compliance, there should be minimal difficulty in network integration and interoperability.

INTERNATIONAL NETWORKS

Much of the structure of international telecommunications has changed in a manner similar to U.S. telecommunications reform over the past 30-plus years. Policy changes and regulatory liberalization have swept the globe. Global telecommunications corporations have found opportunities in countries where new competitive markets were created by the privatization and liberalization of the traditional PTT monopoly. These countries are moving through a life cycle of monopoly to privatization and liberalization to partial or open competition and deregulation. This evolution into privatization changes the legal status of a PTT or PTO from public or government to private ownership. Sometimes these changes take place in niche markets, such as cellular or digital radio, and sometimes they encompass the entire communications infrastructure of the country. When operating in these new markets, the service provider must understand the politics, laws, economic and labor restrictions, social policies, and limitations to each technology. The past decade has seen rapid expansion by global carriers into many countries not available in the past, and typical high-speed data coverage for a large carrier encompasses 50-plus countries. But the bottleneck in most instances remains in the local access circuit.

The next section highlights both the business and technology aspects of international network design. The focus is on the changing role of many national communications systems and regulations and how these changes affect the way we design global networks. The advantages and drawbacks of public and virtual private global network services are covered.

INTERNATIONAL DATA NETWORK TYPES

This section discusses many network configurations and services provided by international carriers and dominant public providers. We will now define these terms and their relationship to providers.

▼ **Public data networks (PDN)** provide a common-access network to allow many users to share a common network facility as well as the services it offers (PDN also could refer to a private data network, where a set of common users share private facilities and services). PDNs support voice, data, or both, and provide access for users who cannot cost-justify building a private data network of their own. Many countries have moved from allowing a single PDN provider (historically the PTT) monopoly to a competitive environment with multiple national and foreign providers.

■ **Packet-switched networks (PSN)** are shared-data networks where customers are charged based on flat circuit rates to access the PSN or usage-based on how much data (measured in packets, frames, or cells) they send across the network. Frame relay, SMDS, ATM, and IP (private, public, and Internet access/VPN) services fall into this category.

■ **International value-added networks (IVAN)** are privately owned service providers who offer public services not available through the local service (or local PDN). Typical services include basic file or voice transfer, and enhanced services include electronic data interchange (EDI), electronic mail (e-mail), and protocol interpretation and conversion. A user interfaces to an IVAN through direct connect or dial access. Dial access can be plain old telephone service (POTS) or ISDN. IVANs provide a good alternative to private lines. If the country's communications are PTT owned, IVANs will interface to monopoly providers through the local PDN gateway.

■ **International virtual private network (IVPN)** is an international public network service where facilities and services are offered to customers in a manner where it appears they are operating their own private data network.

▲ **International record carriers (IRC)**—Prior to 1980, IRCs were the only international telex and packet-switch providers that worked with the PTTs through gateways to each country's PDN.

Figure 15-1 shows the evolution of these various service providers.

THE CHANGING ROLE OF THE PTT

The dominant provider for many countries worldwide remains the post, telegraph, and telephone (PTT) entity. Many PTTs are government owned or franchised. They are regulated as public utilities and considered a natural or privatized monopoly. PTTs are also called public telecommunication organizations (PTOs). While PTT/PTOs enjoy a monopoly, they remain under many restrictions, such as the need to cross-subsidize service (think of the old RBOC model in the United States). Cross-subsidization still occurs in many countries where the population is dispersed and the classes of service and types of users vary.

Some PTTs have been partially released to competitive environments such as cellular and paging, while their core telecommunications transport services remain monopolistic. In some countries, the PTT or PTO operates in a closed market where the government favors the PTT over potential competition. In this case, they are referred to as the national favorite or hero. Their labor force is often unionized. Let's now look at these changes in detail.

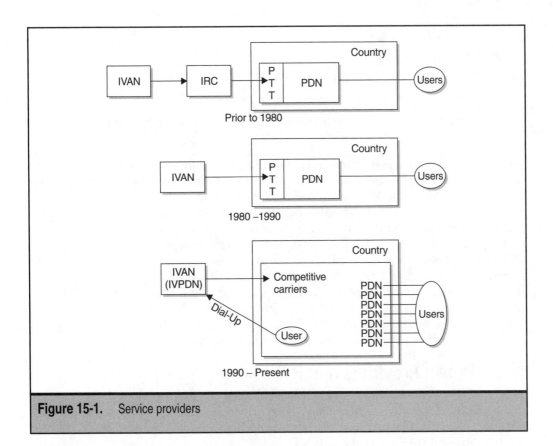

Figure 15-1.   Service providers

Worldwide Divestiture and the User

Until recently, the PTTs of many countries worldwide held control of the voice and data communications services within their country. Government owned and influenced, the PTTs operated in a monopolistic environment, primarily for government profit (or loss in some cases).

As in the U.S., carrier monopolies collapsed and free competition occurred in the same manner as deregulation occurred in the U.S.—driven by the regulatory climate and the end user. The same exorbitant costs for communications that drove users in the U.S. to rebel against the monopolies have taken place all over the world. Many of the companies that built business empires out of divestiture in the U.S. have profited (and lost) from European and Pacific Rim divestiture.

As previously mentioned, this move away from PTT monopolies and toward divestiture has been driven by the customers. These customers demanded

▼ Regulatory change for fair competition

■ Separation of regulatory from operating company

■ Cost-effective value-added services

- Cost-based tariffs
- Guaranteed service levels
- Further liberalization and competition
- Strategic alliances with major global carriers
- ▲ Privately owned companies that are competitive, customer driven, and responsive to the market

The PTTs have changed their role. Historically, their primary interest was to generate government revenues. Customer service suffered, and the cost of that service was high. Now with privatization, PTTs have reversed their historical priorities and focused on customer satisfaction and the introduction of new services. This means offering better quality services at lower prices. To date, international providers have had to deal with each PTT, or local competition, one-on-one to form partnerships. This remains true as the PTTs still represent the driving factor in the global markets, and basic services remain largely regulated. As privatization spreads through PTT-owned countries, PTTs are selling government assets to the private industry sector in an effort to obtain the substantial investments required to fully restructure. The PTTs have also tried to gather funds by selling portions or the entire PTT holdings, by offering public stock, and through employee buyout options. These trends continue with privatization.

Dominant Public Providers and PTTs

Table 15-2 shows the dominant public voice and data service providers, or PTTs if prior to privatization, worldwide. Many have been privatized in the last two decades. This is not a complete list. Most African, Eastern European, Central American, and Caribbean countries are still running on the old PTT model.

Country	Dominant Carrier(s) or PTT
Australia	Telstra
Austria	Radio-Austria A.G. (RADAUS)—PTT—Telecom Austria
Argentina	Privatized with Consortiums
Belgium	Regie des Telegraphes et Telephones (RTT)—PTT
Brazil	Telecomunicacoes Brasileira, S.A.—PTT
Canada	Teleglobe Canada
Chile	CTC and ENTEL=Ayuda
China	AsiaSat Franchise

Table 15-2.   Dominant Global Data Providers

Country	Dominant Carrier(s) or PTT
Colombia	Ministry of Communications—PTT
Denmark	Kopenhagen Telecom AS (KTAS)—Privatized PTT
Finland	Telecom Finland Int'l—PTT
France	France Telecom
Germany	Deutsche Bundepost
Greece	Hellenic Telecommunications Organization—PTT
Hong Kong	Hong Kong Telecom International Ltd. (HKTI)
Hungary	Privatized PTT
India	Videsh Sanchar Nigam, Ltd.
Indonesia	PT Indonesian Satellite Corp.
Italy	SIP, Italcable, Telespazio
Japan	International Digital Communications (IDC)
Korea	Korean Telecommunications Authority (KTA)—PTT
Mexico	Telmex (France Telecom and SBC)
Netherlands	Administration des Postes et Netherlands—Restructured PTT
New Zealand	Telecom New Zealand
Norway	Teledirecktoratet—PTT
Peru	Ministerio de Transportes y Comunicacion—PTT
Philippines	Privatized PTT
Portugal	Companhia Portuguesa de Radio Marconi—PTT
Puerto Rico	Privatization of PTT
Saudi Arabia	Cable & Wireless Riyadh, Ltd.
Singapore	PTT Singtel
South Africa	Department of Posts & Telecommunications—PTT
Spain	Telefonica of Spain
Sweden	Televerket Sverige—PTT
Switzerland	Swiss Telecom—PTT Swisscom
United Kingdom	British Telecom
Venezuela	CANTV

Table 15-2. Dominant Global Data Providers *(continued)*

TRANSMISSION NETWORKS

Many factors are hindering the modernization of worldwide networks. The primary cause is the lack of quality in existing transmission networks and the expense of upgrading to quality digital or fiber facilities. Location also influences the cost and availability of quality transmission facilities. With today's technology, optical transmission facilities are required to move data around the globe, and many digital and satellite facilities no longer provide sufficient quality or bandwidth. Government stagnation and bureaucracy are also factors. In some fast-growing economies, technology acceleration has caused a country to consider upgrading very old facilities to very new facilities, in effect skipping a few generations of technology cycles in the upgrade.

Expensive, Poor Facilities in Developing Areas

The problem plaguing many developing countries is the lack of quality access and transmission facilities. Eastern Europe, Africa, South and Central America, and some Far East and third-world countries still have a poor infrastructure with little or no existing digital or optical communications facilities. In fact, the wait time for residential phone connectivity in some countries is still ten years (contributing to the worldwide cell-phone explosion), and modern data services such as xDSL and cable are almost nonexistent. Optical transport facilities are the predominant intercontinental and intracontinental transport media, replacing digital, satellite, and even older microwave facilities. International fiber-optic transport was introduced in 1988 with TAT-8, and new optical builds have far overtaken older digital and satellite, but it is still virtually impossible for fiber to reach many underdeveloped, geographically, or environmentally challenged areas. It is these areas that are still served by satellite and microwave systems.

Importance of Location

The pervasive nature of data communications in all countries is based on location of facilities in areas of large population and in high-growth markets. These are the locations where global network connectivity supports global business. Many European and Asian cities form hubs or focal points for inter- and intra-country traffic. These locations serve as the primary origination and termination points for international fiber and satellite drops. Some examples include London, Paris, Frankfurt, Zurich, Munich, Dusseldorf, Brussels, Amsterdam, Tokyo, Hong Kong, and Moscow. They are also prime locations for international network-management centers. Typically, in-country quantity and quality of service degrades drastically as the distance from these hubs increases.

Cost of International Dedicated versus VPN Services

Intercountry bandwidth is considerably more expensive than intra-country. Dedicated circuits can cost thousands of dollars per month, compared to shared packet/frame/cell VPN services.

The IVPN market exists for both voice and data, often in a merged environment such as with VoP. The IVPN data market can be segmented into six major technologies and services, including

▼ Dedicated connectivity (PL, xDSL, cable)

■ X.25 and SMDS packet/cell switching

■ FR and ATM public services

■ Public IP services (Internet, private IP-VPNs)

■ Satellite services such as VSAT

▲ Switched services (dialup, ISDN, switched 56/DS1/DS3)

These technologies and services will be offered by either the locally predominant carrier, local or metro service provider, or foreign service provider. The first two have been discussed; foreign service providers are next.

Foreign Service Providers

An alternative to the locally dominant carrier is a foreign service provider. These companies provide IVPN service when the local PDN cannot adequately service the user's needs. Most common carriers such as AT&T offer complete end-to-end communications between the United States, Europe, and Asia (the last edition had a longer list of international carriers, but due to the provider shake-up still occurring, there were few of the traditional carriers left standing). The two types of services offered are basic transport and enhanced or value-added services. The IVPNs provide international virtual private data network services (IVPDNs) to the foreign country. This connects local data networks to an international data network, as well as offering voice and data services. Often, these services will predominate over the local or domestic virtual network services.

One of the largest international networks is obviously the Internet, but this Internet is fueled by the interconnection of many independent service providers.

International Outsourcing and Joint Partnerships

Many of the leading service providers and predominant carriers of the late 1990s tried to form joint partnerships but most failed in their attempts. The goal was to provide a complete end-to-end international outsourcing package to multinational corporations. Today, many of the carriers are building their networks alone, as the era of telecommunications acquisitions and joint partnerships has slowed significantly.

INTERNATIONAL DESIGN

When designing an international network, all of the steps discussed in this book apply and should be followed in the same sequence and order. Designing an international network is similar to designing a national network, with the priority weighted more toward reducing the cost of facilities and transport and less toward creating a "balanced" design. Such conveniences as diversity and redundancy are often sacrificed in international designs, or are provided with lower cost and typically lower bandwidth alternatives. All architectures discussed might be present, although the OSIRM, TCP/IP, and SNA architectures predominate throughout the world. OSI as a common worldwide standard has still not been realized. The major international standards institute is the International Telecommunications Union (ITU).

Look for business overlaps when planning traffic patterns. One example is the early morning overlap of business hours between the United States and Europe. This yields high voice-traffic volumes. Similar patterns can be found with bank transactions, stock market information transfers, and other industrial and financial traffic. Also, look for ways to save money on the network design by using port oversubscription on packet services where global traffic patterns do not overlap but rather are complementary.

REVIEW

This chapter is designed to assist you in choosing a vendor or service provider capable of providing the features, functions, and services required by the network design. This decision is based on the criteria defined in previous chapters and reviewed here. After the RFI is analyzed and the choice of vendors is narrowed down to a "short list," the RFP is issued. RFP responses are then analyzed based on a host of weighted criteria including cost-effectiveness, performance, features and functions, manageability, and perception of the vendor's ability to provide the required services. A look at real-world user-vendor issues revealed the importance of items such as delivery dates, product announcements and features, and the vendor-designer and vendor-user relationships required for successful vendor implementations and ongoing relationships. Finally, existing vendor network-management capabilities were reviewed along with how the vendor becomes an integral part of the future network. The next phase of the design comprises the access and backbone network designs. The choice of vendors can and often does follow the access and backbone designs.

This chapter also reviewed the state of the telecom industry on a global scale. We see a continued move toward privatization and change in PTT posture from that of a government-owned monopoly to that of a private enterprise in a deregulated environment. With this change have come opportunities for international network and service providers to compete in areas previously monopolized by the PTTs. Many opportunities have been identified for these providers, as well as new ground rules that they must follow to compete in the international arena. International network designs resemble national designs with a shift in priorities toward cost and quality of facilities. These factors also influence the base technologies that can be used.

PART VII

Network Design
and Management

CHAPTER 16

Access Network Design

This chapter is the first of two chapters focused on network design (access and backbone). Before defining access design, let's review the four primary layers of network design based on standard industry-accepted terminology.

▼ *Applications* are the programs and protocols that run on the workstations, servers, and terminal equipment that communicate across the data network. Applications can operate across all the OSIRM layers. Applications include operating systems.

■ *Premises architecture, or local enterprise architecture,* is the hardware and software that makes up the desktop, servers, and local area networking within a premises—equipment commonly referred to as customer premises equipment (CPE). This layer can operate across all the OSIRM layers. Note that for this discussion on access network design we are merging LANs into access, since the LAN and its WAN-connecting device are often part of enterprise access.

■ *Access,* in this chapter, is defined as the environment and elements providing the interface between a premises or enterprise network and the service provider's WAN environment. In a strictly local environment (and based on Cisco's definition of access), access includes the devices that interface multiple LANs or workstations to one another, thus blurring the distinction between access and premises. This chapter, therefore, begins with a review of LANs as the first step to access design, and spends less time on LAN design and optimization, leaving that to you for further study. This chapter focuses primarily on access as the infrastructure that ties the premises to the backbone network. In many cases, the backbone is a service-provider transport or networking service, such as a frame relay (FR) or IP service, and the access technology can be Ethernet, private line, switched service (SW56, SWT1), packet service (FR, ATM, IP), xDSL or cable, or some form of wireless access technology.

▲ *Backbone* is the environment and elements providing transport, switching, and routing between access elements and backbone devices. The backbone can be a service provider's network cloud, such as FR, ATM, or IP services, or just a private line between two sites.

Access network design has changed considerably over the last decade. The trend has been toward IP and Ethernet as the dominant LAN protocols, while the price point of Ethernet switches, Fast Ethernet (100 Mbps), and Gigabit Ethernet has blurred the distinction between local and metropolitan access and allowed very high-speed access and metropolitan networks to emerge. Access technologies such as xDSL and cable have just about overtaken traditional 56 Kbps dial as the preferred small office/home office (SOHO) access medium, and the corporate environment has continued to move toward FR, ATM, and various forms of native IP and Ethernet access types, occasionally relying on lower-cost xDSL, cable, and dial alternatives. Most corporate access still requires traditional physical access circuits, but the rules of engineering and capacity management have changed radically. In addition, the requirements to support mobile and remote connectivity and security of that connectivity, along with the convergence of voice, video, and data on the network, have provided additional challenges. These trends are discussed in more detail later in the chapter.

NETWORK DESIGN LAYERS

The four general layers of network design—application, premises, access, and backbone—are shown in Figure 16-1 and explained in detail in this section. The access and backbone layers roughly relate to Cisco's three-layer hierarchical model of core, distribution, and access.

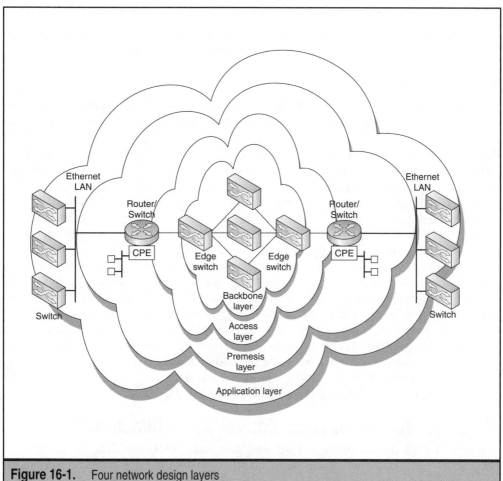

Figure 16-1. Four network design layers

Cisco's model defines responsibilities at each layer that are logical and not physical, and looks at network design from an equipment-centric view. For example, logical and not physical means that one physical device such as a router may reside in all layers. Here is a summary of Cisco's model:

▼ **Core** This is the core or backbone of the network. The core needs to be reliable and fast. No filtering or packet manipulation is done so as not to affect speed. This layer typically has fault tolerance as a design goal.

■ **Distribution** As the core layer is about speed, the distribution layer is about control. The distribution layer implements network policies for security, routing control, and filtering.

▲ **Access** Access controls user and workgroup access to the network. Collision domain segmentation accomplished with Ethernet switches falls in this layer.

You can see that an equipment-centric model misses the key aspects of network infrastructure. Each of the layers in our four-layer model is defined next.

Application Layer

As the access and backbone layers focus on transport and communication, the application layer defines what is transported and how. The application layer defines the various protocols (such as TCP/IP, NetBEUI, AppleTalk, and IPX) and the services (such as DNS, DHCP, FTP, and NFS) that the lower-layer protocols need to support and transport. When discussing network design, the application layer covers all the OSIRM layers, not just the application layer. The FTP protocol, for example, spans OSIRM Layers 5 through 7. The OSIRM also includes operating systems, such as Windows, UNIX, and Linux.

As discussed in Chapter 12, collecting information about the application layer is critical to how the access and backbone layers are designed and what capabilities are required. Before designing a highway system, you would need to know the user traffic patterns, who drives which type of vehicle where and how often. In the same way, you need to understand application flows to design the network infrastructure to support them. One example would be LAN-based telephony, in which the application layer transports voice across the data network to make telephone calls between stations and to the PSTN. The application layer requires low delay, minimum jitter, and preferably no lost packets. In addition, the bandwidth requirement per voice calls on the LAN might be 80 Kbps in each direction (64 Kbps for noncompressed and overhead). There is also typically a call-routing or switching plan that is somewhat predictable. This information must be understood to effectively design the access and backbone layers.

Premises Architecture or Local Enterprise Architecture Layer

This layer defines the hardware and software that make up the desktop, servers, and local area networking within a premises—equivalent to the intrastate highway system for the applications within an enterprise. Equipment is commonly referred to as CPE. This layer can operate across all the OSIRM layers. Note that for our discussion on access network design we are merging LANs into access. For example, enterprise users might use

100 Mbps Ethernet as their access media to a router that then attaches to the WAN (Internet). Typical premises devices include hubs, Layer 2 and 3 switches, routers, bridges, PBXs, and any device that provides communication between hosts within a premises or to the access layer.

Access Layer

This layer defines the premises layer access or interface to the backbone layer or WAN, and communication between the premises layer (typically LAN) and the backbone (WAN). An enterprise's application layer (for example, a user running TCP/IP and HTTP web browser doing an FTP file transfer) might interface through the premises layer (Ethernet LAN switched environment), through the access layer (xDSL), and into the backbone (in this case, the public Internet) to terminate their application session *within* the backbone layer (versus just transporting across the backbone layer to a remote site premises).

A typical access device could be a router, L2 switch (FR, ATM, Ethernet), integrated access device (IAD), V.90 modem, XDSL modem, cable modem, PBX, wireless modem, or any device that provides communication between the premises and the backbone. Protocols supported in this layer typically relate to the network, data-link, and physical layers of the OSIRM, but with the advent of seven-layer switches, sophisticated firewalls, and intrusion-detection devices, can relate to all layers. The separation between the access layer and backbone layers is typically at the router or switch that is shared by the two layers. The access layer relates to the access and distribution layers of the Cisco model and is responsible for control and segmentation. Control involves security and prioritization of traffic, while segmentation involves managing collision and broadcast domains. The access layer is typically made up of LAN technologies such as Ethernet, Token Ring, FR, ATM, xDSL, cable, and wireless, and hardware such as DXCs, multiplexers, hubs, Layer 2 and 3 switches, and routers.

Backbone Layer

This layer defines the backbone transport, switching, and routing between access layer elements. It is generally transparent to the access portion of the network, except in cases such as IP-FR and IP-ATM, or more advanced backbone intelligent services that communicate with the access, premises, or application layers. To the user, the backbone can be a carrier-provided switched service. In this case, the backbone is the "network cloud" to which the access devices send and receive traffic. This cloud could be an independent medium such the public Internet, an intelligent switched backbone service as in AT&T's INCS ATM service, or just a "big transport pipe" from point A to point B. One example of a backbone layer service is FR, in which the user-access device (a router) interfaces with a backbone node (frame switch). Backbone layer services include private line (SONET, Packet Over SONET, DWDM, and more), FR, ATM, and IP (transport and Internet access). Note that the backbone layer can provide an access layer with a standard platform interface, protocol (or multiple protocols), architecture, technology, quality of service (QoS), and potentially many other standard services. Backbone topologies and capacity design are covered in Chapter 17.

ACCESS LAYER DESIGN

Designing a network involves understanding the technology options and trade-offs. As discussed in Chapter 12, gathering the information you need to perform a design and determining that information's completeness and accuracy requires some investigative reporter traits.

Access layer design involves selecting or modifying the LAN, MAN, dial, or dedicated access topology. Before beginning the process of traffic analysis, capacity planning, and network infrastructure design, you first need to assess information you've collected in five key areas:

▼ **Physical connectivity** Is there an existing network? If so, what are the physical and logical configurations and why? If not, what design makes the most sense given the current and future requirements? Sometimes the access network is designed based on what is available versus what is desired (such as opting for V.90, xDSL, or cable modem access for a SOHO).

■ **Protocols** Do you have a mixed Layer 2 or 3 networking protocol environment or a 100 percent Ethernet/IP environment? If the latter, you are lucky. If the former, you have to consider protocol consolidation and redesign, or build the access to accommodate the legacy protocols. Networks that have been around for a long time are typically multiprotocol and require some consolidation for optimal design.

■ **Switching versus routing** Do you have LAN switches, routers, or both? When and where does it make sense to switch versus route?

■ **QoS** Which of your applications need to support QoS, and what level of QoS do they need? Will CoS do? Does your network need to or plan to support Voice, Video, Data, and Internet access in a separate or integrated fashion? If integrated, how are you going to guarantee voice and video requirements on delay, jitter, and lost packets?

▲ **Fixed versus mobile versus SOHO** How many users are fixed on corporate LANs versus require mobile access? How many sites are SOHO and not on the corporate LAN yet require corporate LAN access?

There are many more questions than these, but these should give you a start on designing your access layer connectivity requirements.

Physical Connectivity

Perhaps the widest variance of any connectivity requirements are at the physical media level. Copper, fiber, and air (wireless and satellite) are the three most common media for physical connectivity. The access layer design needs to accommodate user-side premises interfaces such as Ethernet, Token Ring, FDDI, and ATM LANs connecting hosts (workstations, servers, and printers). Typically, equipment is shared between the premises and access layer, and in some cases, such as Internet access, with the backbone layer—all of which have unique physical interfaces to copper, fiber, and air.

The interface from the access layer into the backbone layer is typically on a router or switch using serial or telephony interfaces such as T1, DS3, or OC-3, again over copper, fiber, or air. This interface might be just point-to-point links between locations or connectivity such as FR, ATM, or IP into a service provider's service. Each interface may have multiple logical ports on the single physical port (details in Chapter 17).The existing wiring configurations at each access site dictate many connectivity options. The typical options of building wiring are unshielded twisted pair (UTP), shielded twisted pair (STP), thin and thick coax (all copper media), and glass (single mode or multimode) or plastic (multimode) fiber-optic media. UTP is probably seen most often, and it is important to understand what type of UTP you have. Table 16-1 shows the various UTP categories. The category of UTP drives premises bandwidth options, and can force an infrastructure upgrade (rewiring) to achieve higher bandwidth rates.

Category	Maximum Bandwidth	Application	Specifications	Comments
6	250 MHz	1000 Base T		
5e	100 MHz	Same as CAT 5 plus 1000 Base T	TIA/EIA 568-A-5	Developed specifically for channel support of Gigabit Ethernet. Has enhanced performance requirements over CAT 5 for near-end crosstalk, attenuation, return loss, and impedance.
5	100 MHz	1000 Base T 100 Mbps TPDDI (ANSI X 319.5) 155 Mbps ATM	TIA/EIA 568-A (CAT 5) NEMA (Extended Frequency) ANSI/ICEA	Characterized by tightly twisted pairs to reduce crosstalk loss. Plenum versions are expensive due to demanding transmission requirements combined with challenging flame and smoke resistance. Some manufacturers are offering a CMX rated CAT 5 for residences.

Table 16-1.   UTP Categories

Category	Maximum Bandwidth	Application	Specifications	Comments
4	20 MHz	10 Mbps Ethernet 16 Mbps Token Ring	TIA/EIA 568-A (CAT 4) NEMA (Extended Distance) ANSI ICEA S-90-661)	Almost nonexistent. So similar to CAT 5 that it is not economical. CAT 5 provides five times the bandwidth for about the same cost.
3	16 MHz	10 Mbps Ethernet	TIA/EIA 568-A (CAT 3) NEMA (Extended Distance) ANSI/ICEA S-90-661	Widely used for voice, especially digital voice, installations in commercial sites.
2	4 MHz	IBM Type 3 1.544 Mbps T1 1 Base 5 4 Mbps Token Ring	IBM Type 3 ANSI/ICEA S-90-661 ANSI/ICEA S-80-576	Requirements based on the IBM cabling systems. Referred to as low-speed data cable.
1	1 MHz	RS232 RS422 ISDN Basic Rate	ANSI/ICEA S-80-576 ANSI/ICEA S-90-661	Conductorized station wire fits this category. Suitable for low data-rate-device communication over short distances.

Table 16-1. UTP Categories *(continued)*

While most physical-wiring people discuss maximum bandwidth in MHz, most designers want to know the maximum bandwidth in Mbps. MHz expresses a frequency of a pure sinusoidal signal, so a maximum bandwidth of 100 MHz indicates that a cabling system in general can transmit sinusoidal signals with a frequency of up to 100 MHz with an acceptable level of performance. The relationship between Mbps and MHz depends on the signal encoding used for the binary data. The Manchester encoding technique used by Ethernet and Token Ring is a one-to-one relationship (10 MHz equals 10 Mbps) while MLT-3 encoding used by Fast Ethernet can produce 100 Mbps with 80 MHz of bandwidth.

Coaxial (coax) cable was the second generation of wiring to proliferate, but in some cases (for example, Wang, Unisys, and legacy SNA networks), it was the predecessor of twisted pair. Coax cable is used extensively for Ethernet. Many buildings have existing coax cable wiring to each floor. Previous to fiber deployment, coax cable was used for interbuilding wiring. Coax can handle much higher bandwidths than twisted-pair wiring, up to 500 MHz.

Fiber-optic cable provides the highest bandwidth options available, into the terabits-per-second data-transfer rates. Data is transmitted through light-wave pulses converted from electrical signals. Advantages to fiber are the obvious high-bandwidth capability, high security, the lack of copper-media-affecting disturbances, and the logistical advantages of smaller, lighter cable. For new installations, the cost of running fiber to the desktop is not much more than copper alternatives.

For computer and LAN communications, each LAN architecture provides multiple interfaces. Most personal computers contain network interface cards (NICs) that have RJ-45 outputs. A twisted-pair cable runs from the NIC to an RJ-45 wall jack. This wall jack is wired through the building to the telephone closet, where it is terminated on a 66 punch-down block (a row of wire prongs extended from the main distribution frame for "punching down" the wires, while stripping back the insulation of the wire to provide contact with the prong). This punch-down block interfaces the user to the destination device, which could be an Ethernet switch or hub or another type of concentrator. Most wiring closet designs also include some form of patch panel before the concentrator for testing and ease of reconfiguration. Figure 16-2 shows one example of user connectivity to the network-access device. The PC interfaces to the wall jack in the office via a LAN NIC with an RJ-45 interface plug. This wall jack is wired to the patch panel in the local wiring closet (the point at which everyone else on the LAN is also wired). The patch panel is wired to a 66 block, where patching capability is provided. The four wires are run down to a LAN switch or hub, where all four-wire circuits terminate onto the LAN media. The LAN switch or hub is then connected to either another LAN switch or hub or to a distribution or WAN device such as a router. Wireless connectivity was covered in Chapter 6.

Protocols

What protocol support is required? Protocol support can range from providing transparent transport for a homogeneous protocol environment such as IP, to translating and converting multiple protocols from multiple architectures, to protocol interworking or tunneling. First, each protocol that operates over each interface must be defined by identifying its syntax, semantics, timing, and proprietary implementations and idiosyncrasies. Next, determine which portion of each protocol is used. When possible, identify and use protocols that do not depend on physical media or hardware.

Identify the characteristics of the file-transfer protocols for impacts, specifically, their packet sizes in each direction (such as NFS, which from the file server's perspective trans-

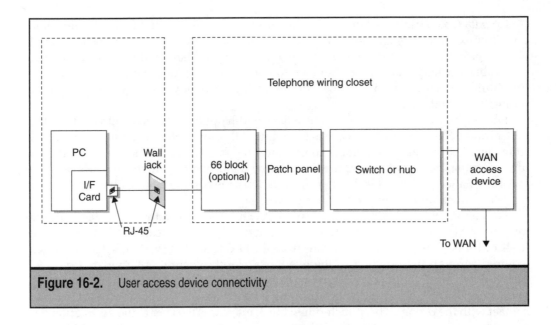

Figure 16-2.   User access device connectivity

mits large packet sizes and receives small ones back, or IPX, for which the window and packet size can vary drastically). Determine each protocol's mean data unit size and ratio of transmit-to-receive data units, then determine which protocols can be bridged, routed, or switched, and which cannot. Isolate the media-access protocols, and determine if they will be passed transparently to the network, encapsulated (tunneled), translated, or converted by the network. Also, many protocols depend on other protocols, which limits their handling and operation. Analyze which protocols will be affected by error detection, correction, notification, flow control, or buffering. Analyze the effects of the end-to-end latency on each protocol.

There will most likely be many dissimilar protocols in the application layer, and most will not communicate directly with any other, or, if they do, they will do so via some form of protocol conversion or gateway. When mapping these protocols, you need to understood their interdependencies and conflicts clearly. Look at the protocol requirements from the perspective of the access layer. What protocol requirements are expected from the access portion of the network (bandwidth, delay, broadcast, multicast)?

This brings up the question of the amount of control that the access network needs to exert over the application, or more importantly, the amount of access-device-to-application interaction required. These interactions will be different depending on the protocol(s) being used. You must clarify all these interdependencies before progressing with the access design. These details become important for an accurate and functional network design.

As IP became the dominant networking protocol, many vendors, such as Novell, joined the bandwagon by supporting IP versions of their systems. Novell's NetWare 5 allows the user to use IP or IPX. When designing and thinking about operational support costs, if the number of protocols can be reduced, it will pay dividends in reduced design complexity and operational support once implemented. Whenever possible, consolidate protocols and total traffic before they are transmitted to the backbone layer.

Switching versus Routing

LAN switches have become very popular in IP networks. In the 1990s, LAN switches were typically Layer 2 (data-link protocols such as Ethernet) devices providing high-speed, low-latency, and in some cases intelligent bridging. Now, LAN switches exist that can switch at Layers 2 and 3, and are Layer 4-plus aware, meaning they can make Layer 2 and 3 switching and routing decisions based on Layer 4-plus protocol information and prioritization. Routers are typically Layer 3 devices that provide routing functionality for Layer 3 protocols such as IP and IPX.

Switching in the LAN provides many advantages: reducing collision domains, increasing bandwidth to hosts, providing full duplex communications, and the flexibility to support different speed interfaces (10/100 Mbps Ethernet switches are very common) in the same device. The downside of implementing switches is the possibility of a forklift upgrade to the building's wiring, as discussed earlier. Note that switches send only unicast frames (frames with specific destinations versus broadcasts that go to everyone) to the port the user is attached to once the switch has learned the topology. So, if you usually pull a network analyzer off a LAN segment so you can view all the local traffic, you will be disappointed with the results.

To review, implementing a switch over a hub sets up different collision domains. This increases network performance by reducing collisions that require retransmission and by reducing traffic on each segment to broadcast frames and frames either originated or terminated to stations on your segment. In addition, switches allow for full-duplex interfaces when servers or workstations are directly attached to the switch, thus providing twice the total bandwidth. (On a 100 Mbps full-duplex connection to a server, you can both send and receive 100 Mbps.)

Routers divide the network into various broadcast domains. Broadcasts are used for protocols such as DHCP and name services, so make sure when implementing routers that services required by users can either reach local servers or be passed through your router.

Taking these concepts forward into the access layer, we most often find some version of routing as the primary interface between access and backbone layers. For example, almost every major enterprise implements a router as their WAN access device when using private line, FR, ATM, and IP WAN services. V.90, xDSL, and cable all use modems as their access protocol, but the wise SOHO user will implement a router and firewall between their xDSL and cable modem, and many already have these capabilities in an integrated access device. This does not have to be the same router that is used as their premises aggregation device.

QoS

Being able to prioritize traffic in both the LAN and WAN is becoming more important every year as voice and video traffic migrate to the data network and mission critical ERP, CRM, and other business applications vie for bandwidth beside low priority web browsing. Historically, bandwidth has been cheap in the LAN. A 100 Mbps Ethernet NIC and a switch port can cost as little as $100 per user, while 1.544 Mbps WAN DS1 can cost hundreds or thousands of dollars *per month*. Keeping this imbalance in mind, it is important to design and implement a network that will easily support major bandwidth growth in both the LAN and the WAN and also is able to prioritize traffic as required. Due to the high cost of bandwidth in the WAN, congestion is more of an issue and often mixed traffic requires prioritization techniques.

When the user interfaces to the WAN through an access network device, certain features, functions, and services are required over and above the normal interface and protocol support. These features and functions are specific to the combination of interface and protocol selected, such as FECN, BECN, and DE bit usage with FR, and IP-precedence bits in IP. The basic protocol might support these functions, but how do the application and access devices use them to implement flow control? How does the service provider implement and guarantee these schemes across the backbone WAN? And how do they affect the applications (such as discarding traffic in an open loop FR transport environment)?

Some access devices, such as routers, switches, and intelligent multiplexers, allow prioritization of user traffic. This prioritization is often performed in conjunction with large variable-size buffers so that traffic with a lower priority can be queued. The most common term used is "priority queuing." Priority can be assigned by protocol, packet/frame/cell message size, physical or virtual port, or logical unit (LU) device. When used correctly and in conjunction with passing SNA and non-SNA traffic over the same access circuit (as in Figure 16-3), priority queuing can prevent SNA time-outs by larger file transfer traffic such as with TCP/IP. This is close to assuring a QoS over a service such as FR. In this example, we see three types of traffic, with SNA-based accounting traffic taking the highest priority, TCP/IP file transfers second, and NetBIOS traffic the lowest. The SNA traffic will receive the bandwidth required to transmit its traffic before the other two protocol streams (or be allowed to use a majority of available bandwidth), and the TCP/IP file transfers will have priority over NetBIOS traffic. Priority queuing implementations vary, but be aware that if the high-priority traffic (in our example, the SNA traffic) requires most of the bandwidth most of the time, the lower-priority traffic (especially the NetBIOS traffic) might achieve marginal to no throughout for long periods of time while sitting in the queue waiting to be transmitted. Care must be observed when using this approach, as incorrect allocation of high-priority buffers or high-use patterns of higher-priority traffic can cause lower-priority traffic to be drowned out. This could further cause a cascade or avalanche effect if the lower-priority protocols are sensitive and have short retransmission sequences, causing effective throughput, or "goodput," to be drastically degraded.

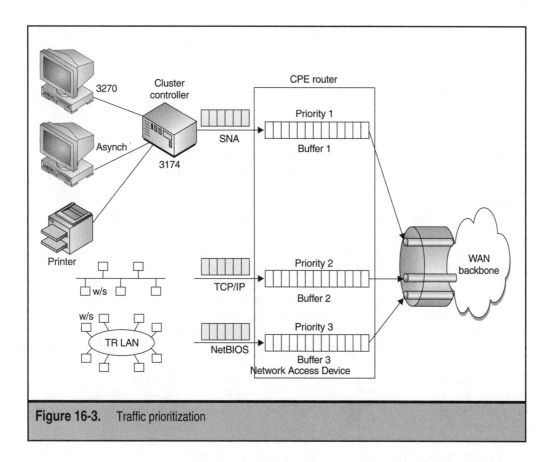

Figure 16-3. Traffic prioritization

Prioritization can also be carried through on the WAN side of the access device. Specific PVCs within a single FR access circuit can be provided different priorities, along with the traffic being transmitted over that PVC. The same goes for ATM VP/VCs. Prioritization can also be performed at the packet level for IP services.

Ethernet switches can support various class of service (CoS) settings. The three main CoS techniques are

▼ IEEE 802.1p/Q standard functioning at Layer 2 of the OSIRM

■ IP-precedence type of service in IP version 4, or Differentiated Services Code Point (DSCP) function at Layer 3 of the OSIRM (note that the service provider must propagate these CoS settings through every router).

▲ Vendor-specific solutions that can tag based on port or MAC address, functioning at Layer 1 and 2 of the OSIRM, respectively.

Remember that QoS, to be effective, must be end to end. QoS is only as good as its weakest link!

ACCESS NETWORK CAPACITY

Chapter 13 covered calculating the loading on each access device based on known inputs. If the user applications and inputs are well known, the access network capacity is either already known or easily determined, but bursty LAN traffic patterns and the peer-to-peer, many-to-many communication patterns of client-server applications create extremely unpredictable traffic patterns. Many designers, therefore, are not fortunate enough to have current and future capacity requirements of users and bandwidth.

When there is an information vacuum, you need to make some approximations and make sure that the design can be easily modified. Users can plan for future modifications by using T1 facilities from service providers and keeping just a few channels active for remote sites, or for example, using FR with CIR values that can be upgraded or lowered in days (versus weeks for dedicated circuits). In the LAN, an enterprise can use Layer 2 and 3 switches, which reduce collisions and allow software definition of VLANs (software-defined LAN segments), where networks can be reconfigured logically versus physically. Modular LAN switches can allow easy expansion by adding higher-bandwidth NICs for congestion points or switches that support QoS features that can prioritize different types of traffic.

Advances in switching and routing are changing the LAN landscape as they provide cost-effective, high-bandwidth port switching and support VLANs, full-duplex ports, gigabit interfaces, 10/100 Mbps auto discovery, and network management capabilities.

NETWORK TOPOLOGY AND HARDWARE

The network topology for the access layer includes LAN, remote access, and dedicated access methods. Drivers for selecting the topology and hardware are the existing network, access technology and service availability, and equipment and budget constraints. When reviewing options, keep in mind the following:

▼   Scalability and flexibility

■   Reliability and availability

■   Performance

▲   Security

Will your design adjust to changes in the company? What if application usage exceeds your bandwidth projections? Can the LAN segments be upgraded, and what is the cost to upgrade? If the company has rapid growth, how will you rapidly and cost-effectively expand the network?

Can you design a fault-tolerant network? Can you design a fault-tolerant network within budget? If the network has a hardware failure, how long can you be down and what is the cost of downtime? Do all applications have the same performance requirements?

On the LAN, implementing Ethernet switching closer to the end user is a viable solution today due to the cost. This type of distributed switch design can reduce collision domains in Ethernet networks by reducing the number of stations per segment and thus increasing the bandwidth throughput potential per segment. When evaluating cost-to-performance trade-offs, review the following:

▼ Implementing 100 Mbps Ethernet segments versus 10 Mbps. Upgrade cost is minimal.

■ Implementing a pure switched environment versus a hub-based solution. Upgrade cost is low, and removing collision domain increases speed dramatically.

▲ Adding routing and firewall capability at the switch level can increase security—but at a high cost. The same principle applies to manageability.

What information should be accessed by whom? Should payroll information have just network passwords, or should it be located on separate LAN segments? Using VLAN technology allows segmentation logically versus physically, as companies don't always locate each department in the same geographic area.

There are two major topologies of providing connectivity in the LAN: *ubiquitous* and *hierarchical* access. We will now explore both.

Ubiquitous Access

The ubiquitous access approach allows all users to transmit and receive data from all areas of the network across a shared device or medium. This is also sometimes called the "matrix" or "flat" approach. One example of ubiquitous access is shown in Figure 16-4, in which a single intelligent Layer 2 or 3 switch or router provides WAN access for the entire building's LAN connectivity between LANs in 12 departments (A through L). Any user on any LAN can pass data through the hub or routing device, as well as access any other device in the network. This style of access is good for organizations that are spread out and nonstructured (nonhierarchical) in nature. The ubiquitous access style provides a one-dimensional flat network and is often used with smaller networks. This type of network becomes difficult to manage as it grows in size, especially when multiple interfaces, technologies, architecture,

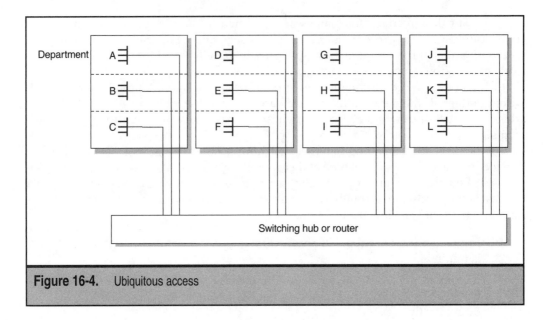

Department

Figure 16-4. Ubiquitous access

protocols, and vendors are involved. Problems with performance degradation are not easily diagnosed and the network can become more difficult to manage. It also offers a very large single point of failure that can take *every* user down at one time. This design becomes less practical daily as the cost of switches and routers has now fallen below $1000.

Hierarchical Access

Hierarchical designs provide a user access hierarchy in which traffic destined for its own local, metropolitan, and wide area remains in that geographical area rather than accessing the common switching or routing point to the backbone, as in the ubiquitous access approach. Figure 16-5 illustrates a building with a four-tier hierarchy. Each user is connected to a floor LAN, each floor LAN is connected to a building LAN, the four building LANs are connected to one campus MAN, and the campus MAN is connected to the WAN. In this example, connectivity between segments, or subnetworks, is accomplished via bridges, routers, or LAN switches. The hierarchical design is often used in larger networks warranting the segmentation of user traffic. In this design, users typically do not require access to every server in the network, instead going through their local server for most applications, thus servers are generally more specialized. This is also a good architecture for implementing VLANs.

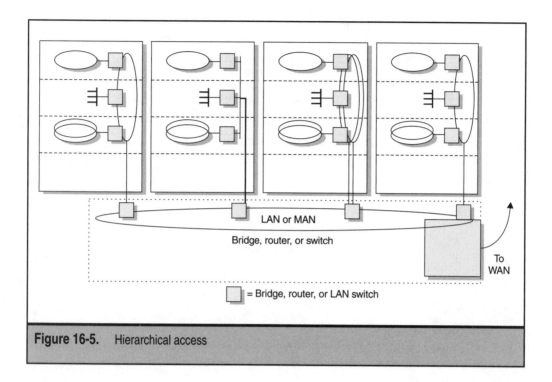

Figure 16-5.   Hierarchical access

A deviation of the hierarchical design would be to use LAN switches instead of bridges or routers on each floor, and the building LAN or MAN would be internal to an L2/L3 switch/router. This is shown in Figure 16-6. LAN switching provides concentration of traffic from points within each floor and between floors. LAN and WAN switching and routing are performed in the L2/L3 switch/router.

The segmentation of hierarchical networks starts at the work-group subnet. This unit provides interconnection of resources (workstations) between LANs typically through a LAN switch. The next higher level is the departmental subnet, where switches connect a larger local area. This unit provides LAN-to-LAN internetworking and connection to WAN routing and switching. The next higher level is MAN and WAN networking. Departmental subnets should be arranged to provide flows of connectivity, which form the enterprise backbone. The enterprise backbone could be the network, as portrayed in Figure 16-6, or many such networks connected over the WAN. Typically, the enterprise network is the latter, with many local designs connected via router or switches to a carrier providing a public network service (for example, IP, FR, or ATM).

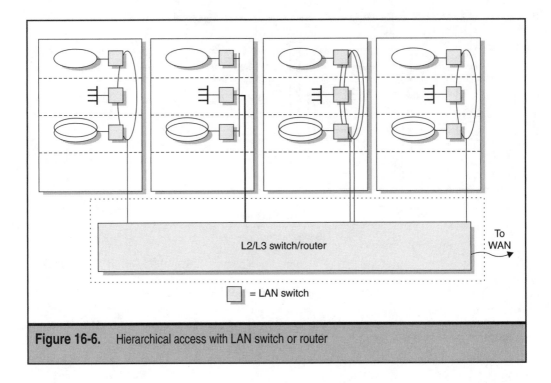

Figure 16-6. Hierarchical access with LAN switch or router

The hierarchical access topology allows the capability of connecting low-speed LANs to high-speed LANs, MANs, and WANs. It allows the designer to understand performance bottlenecks and thus manage or architect the network to alleviate these bottlenecks. The rule that the transport is only as fast as its "slowest link" still applies, and with a hierarchical style, the bottlenecks can be eliminated by ensuring that each level of the hierarchy is at least as fast as the previous one. Hierarchical-style networks help protect users from broadcast storms, and make it easier for administrators to regulate and secure traffic flows between segments.

Hierarchical versus Ubiquitous Access

The hierarchical approach to local access design provides many advantages over the ubiquitous access style, including

▼ Cost-efficient use of network media

■ Performance enhanced due to limited segment size

- ■ Protection from broadcast storms
- ■ Hierarchical address schemes can be used to provide route summarization
- ■ Access control filters in routers to police segments
- ■ Ease of security administration
- ▲ Isolation and diagnosis of problems are easier and faster

Obviously, the ubiquitous access method causes more internetwork traffic because much of the traffic could be limited to the area of transmission and reception of data. In large WAN designs, this could be disastrous for WAN throughput and performance. Sometimes it is difficult to quantify the trade-off of up-front capital equipment costs compared with the ongoing (recurring) costs of operating and using an inefficient network. The major drawback of the hierarchical style is the additional cost of network equipment (switches or routers) and servers to localize the traffic. Also, ubiquitous access is sometimes required when many remote LANs need to communicate due to application requirements but features of switches networked together might not accommodate.

Regardless of which topology is used, the resources (for example, servers) of each LAN should be designed in line with hierarchical or ubiquitous access layers. In the hierarchical style, more servers are needed to ensure local access of server-based information and segmenting of that access. Putting servers and clients in the same location keeps backbone WAN traffic reasonably low. In ubiquitous access, all servers can talk to all other servers so all resources can be shared across the entire LAN. VLANs offer one method of alleviating these geographic restrictions. The network or subnetwork addressing should also correspond to the topology chosen. In hierarchical networks using routers, parts of the network can be isolated or protected to provide fault isolation and keep data contained to specific areas to prevent broadcast storms. Remember, LAN switches and bridges limit collision domains, while routers limit broadcast domains. Cost and network control (turf) issues also become factors in choice of style, and hybrids of both are the norm.

Collapsed Backbone

Figure 16-7 shows a legacy LAN that implemented a 100 Mbps shared Ethernet LAN segment for a company's server farms and provided user connectivity through a combination of 10/100 hubs and switches. As the traffic and number of users grew, the LAN segment became congested, and the backbone needed to be collapsed. Note the collision and broadcast domains.

The first step in alleviating the situation is to replace the 100 Mbps shared LAN segment with a LAN switch, as shown in Figure 16-8. When selecting the LAN switch, your

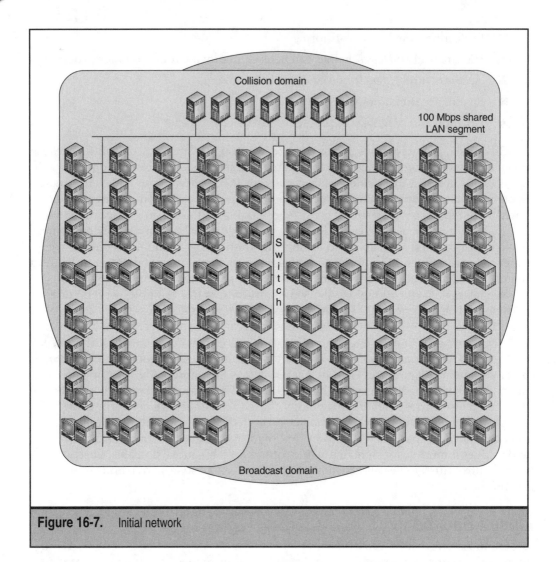

Figure 16-7. Initial network

options are full-duplex connections to the directly attached servers or higher-speed LAN connections to the server such as 1 or 10 Gbps. (Remember, before purchasing 1 or 10 Gbps interfaces, first check if your server drive supports that amount of bandwidth, then check the severe distance limitations on these technologies—literally tens of feet!)

The second step might be retiring some of the 10/100 Mbps hubs for switches or migrating the hubs closer to the user to save money. The current trend is to connect

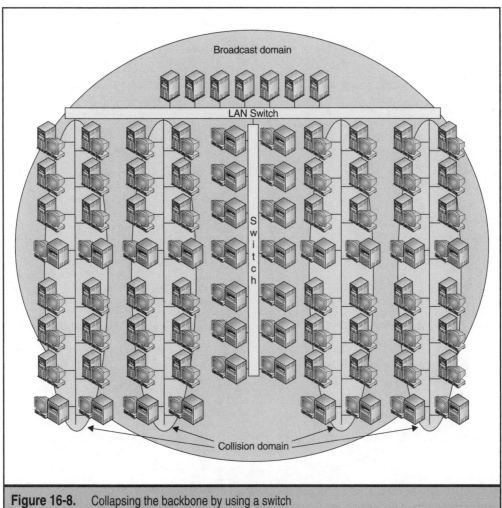

Figure 16-8. Collapsing the backbone by using a switch

workstations directly to the switch, where each host receives the full bandwidth of the LAN segment (for example, 10 Mbps).

The third step is to collapse the broadcast domain by using a router, or a switch with router functionality, as shown in Figure 16-9. An ATM switch might be the solution for large installation or customer requiring high-speed dedicated-bandwidth LAN-to-WAN connectivity.

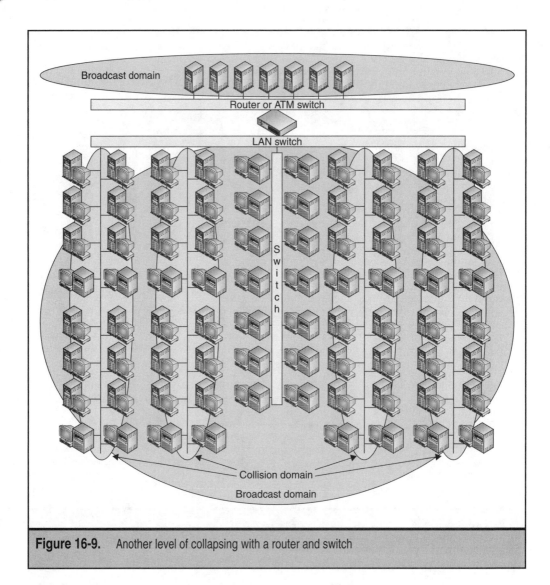

Figure 16-9. Another level of collapsing with a router and switch

COMPLETING THE ACCESS NETWORK DESIGN

The steps for completing the access-network design include verifying the application intelligence, confirming the design and choice of the access device(s), choosing the number and type of access devices, and verifying the total access topology. Most of these steps might have already been fixed from design practices explained in previous chapters, but are presented here as a wrap-up to ensure that every step in completing the network access design phase portion of the network is summarized.

Application and Protocol Intelligence Verification

When the access network design was performed, it was assumed that there was some level of intelligence in the user devices and applications. The greater this level of intelligence, the less network intelligence that is required from the access and backbone network, and the more the access and backbone networks can concentrate on passing data. If not done in the initial requirements phase, some time should be spent reanalyzing the user application intelligence to confirm the expectations of both the user and the network from the application and protocols standpoint. Remember, FR is a Layer 2 transmission protocol only. It drops errored or congested frames and does not retransmit them, and relies on a higher-layer protocol such as TCP for retransmission of lost packets and subsequent frames. Confirm that the required intelligence is in the access device selected, and that this device will be able to communicate that intelligence to the backbone network, or confirm where that intelligence lies before the applications get to the access network.

Access-Device Level

The next level of verification is of the access device itself. The access device should be the feeder portion of the network design, where user applications, devices, and protocols of a defined geographic area are fed into a single or multiple device(s). This access device(s) will then communicate with other access devices or directly with the backbone. The typical access node will aggregate and transmit voice, data, and video traffic from many different interfaces, protocols, architectures, and technologies to the backbone via a single protocol and technology. Access devices, therefore, should reduce the number of access ports, protocols, conversions, and data formats fed to the backbone. With technologies such as FR, access to the WAN is in terms of multiple logical channels rather than single physical channels per port. ATM is one technology that can offer true integrated access of all forms of communication—specifically voice, data, and video.

Number and Type of Access Nodes

The number of access nodes is determined by the traffic matrix, the optimized grouping of traffic, and the placement options for access nodes. The network design should always allow for a multiple node-failure scenario, as well as alternate routes for a minimum of a single failure. No single site failure should take the entire network down.

By now, the reader should be able to choose the type of access node required. Here are a few extra tips on the selection of access hardware. Most router and switch vendors make almost all common protocols available for their devices either at no cost or at a very low cost. Consider using a LAN hub over a router for segmentation and cost savings.

TELECOMMUTING

Telecommuting refers to the ability of company employees to work outside of a company office. With the advent of broadband access to the home, SOHO workers can connect to the company resources at high speeds through virtual private network (VPN) connections. VPN is an extension of a company's LAN and allows the remote user or telecommuter to access the same information as if they were at the office. VPN access can be accomplished from any Internet connection by creating a secure tunnel into the corporate network or as previously accomplished thru dialup to a company modem bank or remote access server (RAS). As dial-up solutions have existed for years, affordable broadband Internet connections have become available in the 21st century and should be an enabler to additional telecommuting. As a success story for telecommuting, Cisco Systems has more than 70 percent of its employees telecommuting at least part-time since the turn of the century.

Using a VPN versus company-specific dialup for telecommuting provides the ability to use access methods from dialup when on the road, to xDSL, ISDN, and cable at the house. In addition to high-speed access, a corporate VPN can be accessed via a national Internet services with local numbers versus dialing 800 numbers while traveling on business.

Understanding your solution for remote user access for telecommuting and traveling employees is critical to productivity. Securing this access is equally important and is covered in Chapter 18.

TELEPHONY-ENABLED LAN

The vision of a single network device, access, and transport or switched service to support voice, video, and data communications has become a reality. The telephony-enabled LAN and voice over data (VoIP, VoFR, VoATM) WAN services have enabled this reality. Many vendors have IP-based phone systems on the market and total voice and data network integration has reached down to the applications. The key trade-off for voice over the LAN and data WAN include trading bandwidth, hardware, and software to achieve and guarantee QoS. This is an opportunity cost, and with the cost of corporate voice dropping to lower than three cents per minute, and data service costs increasing, the business case to put voice traffic over the data network gets worse every day. Applications will be key enablers for voice-over packet wide-scale deployment.

If the business case makes sense, however, there are many technologies and innovations that enable rapid voice and data integration. Inline power is an option for some of the IP phones. Ethernet switches or separate panels can provide this power. Understanding your company's future direction might save money and the forklift later. An issue that is still being worked in the VoIP industry is firewall proxy devices to allow the VoIP traffic to pass through firewalls without larger number of ports open. See Chapter 18 for more detail.

REVIEW

This chapter focused on designing two of the four network layers: premises and access. In the LAN, the demarcation blurs between the two, so both were grouped into the access layer. All four layers of network design—application, premises, access, and backbone—were defined and compared to Cisco's three-layer hierarchical model. We then stepped through the key areas of access layer design—physical connectivity methods, access protocols, switching versus routing at the access, QoS requirements, designing access network capacity, network topology and hardware, design differences between hierarchical and ubiquitous access topologies, benefits of collapsed backbones—and concluded with some additional network access design concerns. Chapter 17 covers the next step: backbone design.

CHAPTER 17

Backbone Network Design

A s a review of Chapter 16, the four layers of network design are as follows:

▼ **Applications** are defined as the programs/protocols that run on workstations, servers, or terminal equipment that communicates across the data network. Applications can operate across all the OSIRM layers. Applications include operating systems.

■ **Premises or local enterprise architecture** is defined as the hardware and software that makes up the desktop, servers, and local area networking within a premises. Equipment is commonly referred to as customer premises equipment (CPE). This layer can operate across all the OSIRM layers. Note that for this discussion on access network design, we are merging LANs into access.

■ **Access** in this chapter is defined as the environment and elements providing the interface between a premises or enterprise network and a service provider wide area network (WAN) environment. In a strictly local environment, access (based on Cisco's definition of "access") defines the devices that interface multiple LANs or workstations to one another, and thus this definition blurs access with premises. So in the beginning of this chapter, we review LANs as the first step to access design. We do not spend excessive time on LAN design and optimization, leaving that to you for further study. For the purposes of this chapter, we stick to the former definition for access: the infrastructure that ties the premises to the backbone network. In many cases, the backbone is a service provider transport or networking service, such as a frame relay (FR) or IP service, and the access technology can be Ethernet, private line, packet service (FR, ATM, IP), or some form of wireless technology.

▲ **Backbone** is defined as the environment and elements providing transport, switching, and/or routing between access elements and backbone devices. The backbone can be a service provider's network cloud such as FR, ATM, or IP services, or just a private line between two sites. The backbone layer is related to connecting various sites or networks together. The backbone layer could refer to a MAN or campus network but typically is a WAN. In designing a WAN, network costs along with performance and reliability tradeoffs can drive the topology and technology chosen. Availability of public network services can also be a limiter.

BACKGROUND: HISTORY OF WIDE AREA NETWORKS (WANS)

The history of the individual WAN technologies is covered in Chapters 5, 8, 9, and 11. This chapter will allow an opportunity to look at WAN network history from a high-level design point-of-view.

▼   Modern-day WAN communications technologies were created in the 1970s with the first public networks using X.25. Companies began using data networks for communications, but the voice network continued to be the primary communications method.

■   In the 1980s, public X.25 networks continued to serve as the predominate public network service, but a number of companies began building and operating private networks for their companies' voice and data communications needs. Many of the private networks used circuit multiplexing technology, such as that found in Network Equipment Technologies' Integrated Digital Network Exchange (IDNX) equipment. Private multiplexer networks allowed companies to manage and partition the expensive private-line bandwidth to support both voice and data.

▲   In the 1990s, major telecommunication providers began providing virtual private network (VPN) voice solutions that allowed companies to have private number schemes and cost savings when communicating intracompany. This was the first true VPN—providing only voice transport! VPN solutions soon appeared in the form of public data services with the deployment of FR and later ATM services. The late 1990s also brought the Internet to the corporate and consumer markets as both a transport medium and a public intercommunications network forum. This move of consumers and corporations to Internet communications and e-enablement of their businesses revolutionized communications. This revolution was so profound, many businesses flocked to the Internet and its associated services and business models. The dot-com bust of 2000 showed an over-dependence on the Internet as a business medium, and now corporations are finding alternate ways of using the Internet as cost-effective transport, hence the interest in IP VPNs while still relying on PL, FR, and ATM services for core business networking.

Some of the trends in the first decade of the new millennium include

▼   Customers building VPN networks across the Internet using tunneling encryption such as IPSec versus using VPNs such as FR and ATM

■   The move from traditional FR and ATM networks to MPLS-based services.

■   Network security has become a critical element of network design due to the dependence on the Internet for extranet and e-commerce applications

▲   The move of legacy voice to Voice over Packet

BACKBONE REQUIREMENTS

Backbone networks can consist of virtual public network services such as IP, FR, ATM, VPNs, private networks such as fiber-optic connections; dedicated yet expensive private lines (T1, DS3, OC-3); and the public Internet (the ultimate public network). Today, most companies have Internet access, and many companies are using VPN technologies such as IPSec to create encrypted tunnels between locations and home offices in their IP VPN designs. Still, the predominant WAN public service technologies are private line, FR, ATM, and IP (private and public).

Some of the efficiencies/tradeoffs in selecting the appropriate technology or service for your backbone designs are

▼ Traffic consolidation and convergence—will/can voice/video/data share the same network/transport/access?

■ Reliability—redundancy and rerouting capabilities

■ Economies of scale

■ Sharing of equipment and facilities by multiple locations

■ Dynamic bandwidth resource allocation

■ Flexible topologies (CPE, access, and backbone) and styles of design

■ Distributed or centralized network management

▲ Bandwidth and CPE Flexibility

As in any design, the selection of topology, technology, and service are driven by cost, performance, availability, and reliability objectives, bandwidth and throughput requirements, the QoS objectives that need to be met, and ultimately, the application and business requirements.

Figure 17-1 shows a private line WAN with fully meshed trunk topology between six access/concentrator nodes. As the number of dedicated point-to-point circuits (or trunks) grows between access nodes, it becomes necessary to design a backbone layer hierarchy that can save circuit costs and improve design scalability. Thus, a three-node backbone has been added with groupings of the access nodes by region. The backbone "cloud" could be a public service such as PL, FR, ATM, and IP, or a private network built between regional corporate facilities. By adding the backbone layer, the network costs are reduced as the number of local loops/private lines is reduced and the number of ports on the access devices is reduced, yielding a much more scalable and cost-effective design.

NOTE: As Figure 17-1 shows, the number of private lines to support a fully meshed design even on a six-node network is 15. The formula is n(n − 1)/2 where *n* is the number of sites. As each private line has two local loops, the total number of local loops is double the number of private lines, or 30 in our example. If the customer uses FR, the number of local loops is *n*, or six in the example. Also, the number of router ports in the private line example per site is (n − 1), and in the FR example, it is one per site. This shows the scalability of FR over private lines.

Protocols

Many of the user applications and protocols will be transparent to the backbone, but the design of the backbone might still have an effect on them. For example, the L4/L3 protocol TCP/IP is transparent to the transport (L2) protocol FR, but a poorly performing FR WAN service can have a devastating impact on a host-to-host TCP/IP file transfer. Delay, packet loss, jitter (delay variation), and a decrease in throughput across the backbone

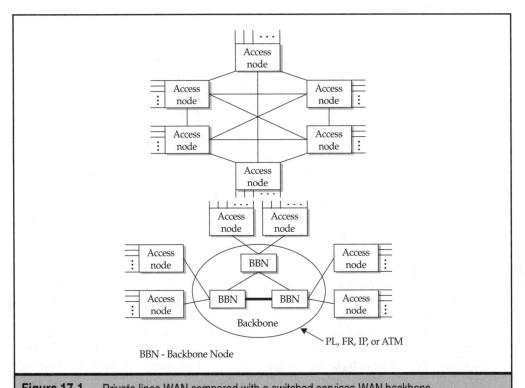

Figure 17-1.   Private lines WAN compared with a switched services WAN backbone

might ripple back all the way down to the desktop applications. The backbone design must be flexible enough to accommodate multiple protocols and operating systems, whether switching them transparently or actually becoming involved in the intelligent internetwork operations of the protocol. From the previous study of network protocols, it is known that routable protocols such as IP are often the preferred protocols for WAN internetworking, while protocols such as LAT, IBM SRT, and NetBIOS (NetBEUI) can only be bridged and therefore are inefficient across a WAN. In fact, most methods of passing bridged protocols involve IP encapsulation or translation bridging. Determine whether the user applications use protocols that support windowing, which allows the sender to send more than a single packet while waiting on an acknowledgment. Then, analyze the impact of the WAN protocol on these windowing protocols and fine-tune the performance as appropriate.

IP remains the most common backbone network and internetwork protocol, and can be deployed in many ways. This statistic counts public and private IP backbones, as well as the public Internet. IP addressing schemes provide unique identifiers to access network components (called "hosts" in IP terminology) such as router and switch ports,

Protocol Windowing

Windowing is utilized to reduce latency and increase efficiencies in connection-oriented services. Without a window, we would send only one packet and then wait for the reply. With windowing, we have the ability to send ahead x amount of packets and then receive a singular reply. The sliding window expands upon this even further by varying the amount of send-ahead packets based upon previous replies. The goal of windowing is to transmit the greatest amount of packets with the smallest amount of replies, and to dynamically react to changes in path quality by decreasing the window size in times of errored transmission and increase the window size during error-free periods.

Protocol windowing allows more than a single packet to be sent while waiting on an acknowledgment. A TCP window size is based on the number of bytes that can be sent, but in this example, the window size will relate to the number of packets requiring transport.

So, each packet is a car. Each car will take a planned trip from New York to Washington, D.C., which takes five hours each direction. If we have a window size of one, or say one driver and a car, we can move a car full of stuff at a rate of one car per ten hours, assuming that our drivers don't sleep.

If we have a window size of ten (ten cars/drivers), the rate is ten cars per ten hours. These calculations assume no packet retransmission is required (no cars break down or get lost in transit). One car with a single driver could return to Washington, D.C., to acknowledge that all cars arrived intact and on time, thus reducing bandwidth on the road from Washington, D.C., to New York.

If you relate to 1000-byte packets and a round-trip of one second, a window size of one has a rate of 1000 bytes per second and a window size of 10 has a rate of 10k bytes per second. This is one method to measure maximum transmission rate of a protocol. We covered earlier how applications can be bandwidth-constrained (not enough bandwidth to achieve maximum window-size transmission) or application-constrained (window size is at its maximum yet there is still plenty of bandwidth available were the window size able to grow larger).

servers, and desktop computers. IP routing protocols such as OSPF allow network devices to keep track of who's on first, and to constantly and dynamically reconfigure the internetwork routing optimal configuration. In FR and ATM networks, the backbone uses virtual circuits while the access devices such as routers use IP to determine the virtual circuit to route on.

Many routing protocols such as RIP add extra overhead to the WAN through their constant exchange of routing table information. Routing protocols such as OSPF take up drastically less overhead (about 1 percent of RIP), but with this reduction of overhead and dynamic routing capability comes complexity. It is very important to minimize and localize the routing tables in each router. Also, the backbone design should always attempt to use standard protocols to avoid potential pitfalls in equipment and circuit compatibilities.

Technology

The business requirements determine the network architecture, technology, and service. Table 17-1 shows a comparison of the most common WAN services. The comparison looks at private lines, FR, ATM, and IP (private and public IP networks).

▼ **Speeds** FR service providers currently support DS3 (45 Mbps) interfaces and may support OC-3 (155 Mbps) in the future. ATM, IP, and private lines maximum speeds relate more to your budget than the technology, and range from low-speed DS0 at 56kbps up to OC-n Gbps speeds.

■ **Protocol efficiency** Private lines are the most efficient as they have the lowest overhead and you can control configuration of the CPE. FR is next highest with typically a 2-byte header and 4-byte CRC, typical overhead is less than 4 percent. IP requires a data link protocol such as PPP or FR and a 20-byte IP Version 4 header, so overhead can exceed 5 percent. The smaller the packet, the greater the overhead. ATM has 5 bytes of headers in every 53-byte cell plus the AAL, so it starts with 16 percent overhead.

WAN Services Comparison	FR	ATM	IP Service	Private Lines
Speeds	56 kbps to 45 Mbps	1.5 Mbps to OC-3	56k dial to OC-n	56 kbps to OC-n
Protocol efficiency (1–4, best to worst)	2	4	3	1
QoS controls (1–4, best to worst)	3	2	4	1
Ubiquitous access (U.S.)	Yes	Most areas	Yes	Yes
Ubiquitous access (global)	Many major cities	Some major cities	Most countries	Most countries
Price components	Port, local loop, and VC charges	Port, local loop, and VC charges	Port and local loop charges	Local loops and distance-sensitive charge
Security (1–4, best to worst)	2	2	4	1
Price	Medium	Medium	Medium to low	High

Table 17-1   WAN Services Comparison

■ **QoS controls**   Private lines offer the best control over QoS due to control of the end equipment segmentation and prioritization of bandwidth. QoS becomes important when implementing time- and bandwidth-sensitive traffic such as voice or video. ATM is next-best efficient with the support of five classes of service and very granular virtual circuit design (VPs and VCs). ATM has the ability to provide five services from high-priority constant bit rate (CBR) services to low-priority unspecified bit rate (UBR) services ("pump and pray" service similar to zero CIR in FR). FR has CIR (throughput QoS) controls for bandwidth along with some service-provider proprietary priority queuing, but typically a design can't prioritize traffic flow between the network service provider and the CPE. IP services are ranked last because the IP protocol has class of service (CoS) notification bits versus true CoS, but most service providers haven't supported true end-to-end CoS services due to technology/performance and complex billing issues. Multiprotocol label switching (MPLS)–based services are being deployed to solve this QoS versus CoS problem, but only time will tell of its success or failure. MPLS is covered in Chapter 20.

■ **Ubiquitous access**   All these technologies have become mature technologies and services internationally. In the global world, IP service and private lines are accessible in the developed countries while FR networks exist in the larger countries and ATM in the very large countries/cities. Dial access to the Internet (IP) is ubiquitous.

■ **Pricing**   Private lines are priced as distance-sensitive, which means there is a charge per mile, while the other services discussed (IP, FR, ATM) are not distance-sensitive. The difference between FR/ATM and IP is that FR/ATM has a charge per logical connection and IP does not. The tradeoff is the QoS of FR/ATM logical connection versus the most common best-effort transport of IP. Stated differently, IP allows any-to-any connectivity but FR/ATM requires you to pay for the level of connectivity. These logical circuit charges increase dramatically as networks grow in size. One way FR/ATM has become more price-scalable is through the deployment of IP-enabled FR/ATM services based on MPLS that only require a single logical circuit per physical access port. Private lines might be the cheapest and best solution when there is limited distance.

▲ **Security**   Chapter 18 provides further insight into this subject, but we find that security is a key factor in the network design and service selection. Private lines are the most secure because the connection is physical between the two locations. FR/ATM is a logical connection between two locations across a service provider's network, and thus essentially as secure as a private line. IP services between locations can be across the Internet unencrypted, encrypted in a tunnel, or transferred across a private IP network, offering varying degrees of security. Using an encrypted tunnel across a private IP Network would be similar to a FR/ATM logical connection, assuming the network has no public connectivity.

BACKBONE NETWORK CAPACITY

Chapter 13 helped you calculate the loading on each access device based on known inputs. If the user applications and inputs are well known, the access-node configurations are either already known or can easily be determined, and you can proceed directly to the topology section. If not, please read on.

When interfacing an access design to a large private or public data network, however, the user applications and transport specifics such as bandwidth use are usually not well defined. In fact, most network designers are faced with few facts on user application and traffic requirements. This is especially true when designing a network from scratch, and the user inputs are estimations or, worse yet, speculations. In this case, some broad approximations of user traffic can be placed into a model to make a mathematical guess or educated assumption at the number of access and backbone ports required, their speeds, and use. This assumes that *all* user application and protocol characteristics are either the same or similar, and that a single technology and set of protocols is used for internetworking these users, which in practice is rarely the case. These requirements must take into account service-specific aspects, such as the ACK/NACK overhead in SNA, TCP window sizes, IPX burst capability, and CIR in FR, which provide logical constraints that might be and probably will be exceeded by the user at any time.

Link Use

Now we look at calculating required backbone design capacity using only raw bandwidth numbers. These calculations are protocol- and technology-independent, and require modification for statistical multiplexing, queuing, or any other buffering or efficiency increases or decreases. These calculations are most applicable to calculating bandwidth and equipment requirements to access the backbone network such as FR, ATM, or IP. Obviously, since we have limited initial information, network tuning will be required.

A company will transmit a given number of bytes of information per day over the network M through a given number of access-node ports n. A model for the access network can be built with n user input ports and T backbone access trunks. A limit must be set on the size (in ports) of the access devices, as well as the access and trunk speeds available. Once this access model is done, modifications can be made to these variables by adding factors that model queuing delays, statistical multiplexing, and internodal traffic.

Figure 17-2 shows an example where M = number of Mbytes/day/network = 950,000 and the number of access ports in the network n = 1000. For simplicity, we designated that all access ports speeds s = 1.544 Mbps (DS1). If we divided all transmitted traffic equally among all access ports, the average one-way utilization for each port (or link) would be calculated as 5.7 percent. The formula for average utilization per port is shown below. Naturally, some ports (such as the headquarters site in a star network) would have higher utilization than others, such as higher port-access speeds for headquarters and centralized processing sites and lower speeds for remote-access sites.

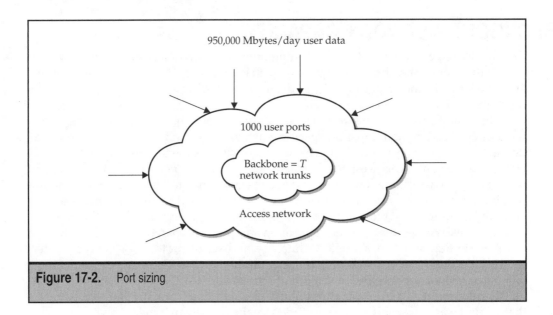

Figure 17-2.   Port sizing

This utilization needs to be adjusted for protocol overhead but is acceptable for an estimate. These calculations should not take the place of protocol- and device-specific design modeling.

$$\frac{M}{n} \times \frac{1\,\text{day}}{24\,\text{hours}} \times \frac{1\,\text{hour}}{3600\,\text{seconds}} \times \frac{8\,\text{bits}}{1\,\text{byte}} \times \frac{1}{\text{port speed}} = \text{avg \% Utilization per port}$$

$$\frac{950,000}{1000} \times \frac{1\,\text{day}}{24\,\text{hours}} \times \frac{1\,\text{hour}}{3600\,\text{seconds}} \times \frac{8\,\text{bits}}{1\,\text{byte}} \times \frac{1}{1.544\text{Mbps}} = 5.7\% \text{ Utilization}$$

Now add a busy-hour calculation where 20 percent of the total traffic occurs during the busy hour. The new calculation would include a factor of five hours per day to attain the 20 percent busy-hour peak (if 20 percent of total traffic is transferred during the busy hour, five hours represents all busy hours and 100 percent of the traffic).

$$\frac{950,000}{1000} \times \frac{1}{5} \times \frac{1}{3600} \times \frac{8}{1} \times \frac{1}{1.544} = 27.35\% \text{ Utilization}$$

Notice that port utilization has increased from 5.7 to 27.35 percent during the busy-hour period (again assuming a flat traffic distribution; this utilization would be even greater in a star or hub-and-spoke network with a headquarters site). Remember: as the busy hours increased the utilization from 5.7 to 27.35 percent, the busy second is probably near or equal to 100 percent due to the "bursty" nature of data traffic. Data networks have buffers, which can keep packets from dropping during these spikes of traffic load. In addition to the buffers, queuing schemes can help your QoS-sensitive traffic make it through ahead of traffic that isn't QoS-sensitive.

Backbone Capacity

This section covers computing the backbone capacity. Backbone capacity relates to the total amount of bandwidth required to transport the input traffic to a remote destination (backbone ingress port to backbone egress port). Figure 17-3 shows a sample backbone node where the access ports go to remote sites and output trunks connect to other backbone nodes. To find the backbone node input-to-output utilization, a comparison is made concerning the number of ports, the speed of each port, and the port utilization to the output trunk utilization.

The following formula can be used to either compute number of trunks or trunk utilization based on number of access ports, their speeds, and their utilizations:

$$(T)(S)(\%UT) = \sum (p_i)(s)(\%Up_i)$$

where the

number of trunks required = T
number of ports of type i = p_i
speed of trunks = S
speed of port = s
percent utilization of trunks = %UT
percent utilization of ports of type i = $\%Up_i$

▼ **Example 1**   There are three remote sites single-homed into a backbone node. Each remote site is connected via a T1 and each T1 has an average utilization of 27 percent. Your design objective is to have trunk ports designed for an average utilization of 50 percent. How many T1 trunk ports are required?

$(T)(1.536)(.5) = (3)(1.536)(.27)$, then T= 1.62, or 2 T1 trunks

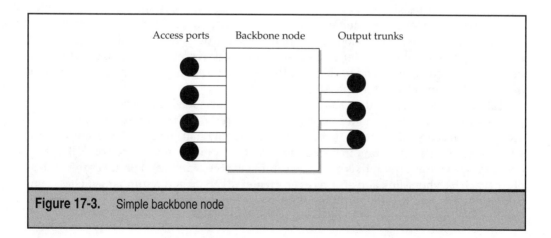

Figure 17-3.   Simple backbone node

NOTE: The average utilization is 27 percent, but the peak might be 100 percent in the busy second.

▲ **Example 2** There are 27 remote sites. The ports speeds/utilizations for the remote sites are as follows: 5 T1s at 37 percent utilization, 10 FT1s (256 Kbps) at 57 percent utilization, and 12 DS0 (64 Kbps) at 75 percent utilization. Your design objective is to have trunk ports designed for an average utilization of 50 percent. How many T1 trunk ports are required?

$$(T)(1536 \text{ Kbps})(.5) = (5)(1536 \text{ Kbps})(.37) + (10)(256 \text{ Kbps})(.57) + (12)(64 \text{ Kbps})(.75)$$

$$T = 6.35 \text{ or } 7 \text{ T1 trunks}$$

NOTE: You can bond multiple T1s together using inverse multiplexing algorithms in routers or an external hardware device. You also could use routing techniques to share the traffic across the T1s, but these schemes can be complicated and may not allow the design to scale affectively.

The numbers computed by this formula will vary based on statistical multiplexing efficiencies, time variances in utilization and busy-time periods, protocol overhead, and usage patterns, to name a few. It is important to note that you should not only design to the bandwidth required during normal transmission, but also design to the peak bandwidth during the busy hour/minute/second. The intelligent queue capabilities of devices today allow the utilization to be higher on average by allowing delay-sensitive traffic to go to the front of the line and quickly to its destination. If your backbone design doesn't have intelligent queuing options and you design it to run QoS-sensitive traffic such as voice/video, you will need to design the overall backbone to lower average utilizations.

The previous discussion assumed that all traffic was destined to cross the backbone node, but in real networks some percent of the traffic is regionalized and thus goes "in and out" the same backbone node. Figure 17-4 shows an example of typical traffic patterns for a 12-node network with single-trunk access nodes. Notice that each access node is trunked to a single backbone node. Fifty percent of the user traffic remains local (to and back out of the same *access* node), 50 percent of the traffic remains regionalized within the same state or province (to and back out of the same *backbone* node), leaving 25 percent of the traffic that must transit the backbone.

Taking this one step further, assume that each access node is dual-trunked: one trunk to two separate backbone nodes, as shown in Figure 17-5. The same amount of traffic accesses each access and backbone node; however, only half the previous amount actually transits each access trunk to backbone node (12.5 percent per access trunk if evenly load balanced—traffic pattern is based on routing in access device). This takes the utilization of each backbone link and affords even greater diversity and redundancy. These considerations are used together with topology styles defined later in this chapter to choose the number and location of the backbone nodes and trunks.

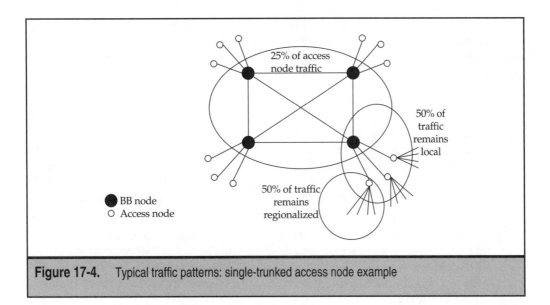

Figure 17-4.   Typical traffic patterns: single-trunked access node example

Given the backbone-access traffic patterns, backbone capacity can be calculated in two ways:

▼   Determine capacity per node based on a chosen number of nodes. Number of nodes may be determined geographically or at central facilities.

▲   Determine number of nodes based on capacity restrains of node equipment.

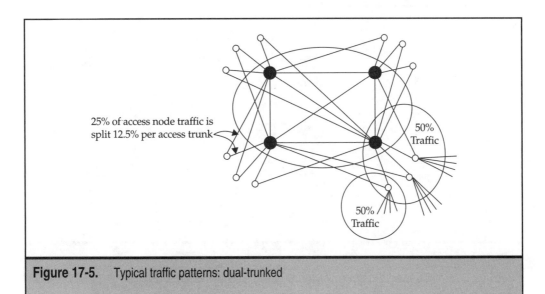

Figure 17-5.   Typical traffic patterns: dual-trunked

Take the case where users are single-trunked to a network backbone. Once a topology configuration is decided on, and if the number of nodes in the backbone *N* and capacity of each node *c* is known, the total capacity of the backbone *T* based on the type of traffic it will carry can be determined. There are four major types of traffic patterns:

▼ *Most or all traffic that enters a node leaves the same node and does not transit any other backbone node.* There are times when a majority of, or *all,* traffic that enters a node will leave the same node, as shown in Figure 17-6. In the case where most of the traffic that enters leaves the same backbone node, the backbone trunking from this node to other backbone nodes is minimal; many good network designs operate by this concept, where the backbone nodal trunks are primarily used for backup and redundancy. The formula for calculating the total backbone capacity in this arrangement is: $T = (N)(c)$.

■ *Traffic originating on a backbone node is transmitted symmetrically to every other backbone node.* This is the case for a broadcast network. The backbone nodes' trunks are primarily used for switching and the links between them are heavily used. The formula for calculating the total backbone capacity in this arrangement is: $T = (N+1)(c)/2$.

■ *All traffic patterns are asymmetrical and are divided into user classes such as terminal-to-host and LAN-to-LAN (IP) communications.* The backbone nodes' trunks are again primarily used for switching or routing and the link usage varies. The formula for calculating the total backbone capacity in this arrangement is $T = (N^2)(c)/(2N-1)$.

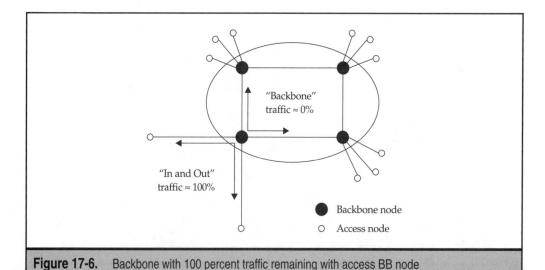

Figure 17-6. Backbone with 100 percent traffic remaining with access BB node

▲   Users never talk to nodes on the same backbone (this is a multiple backbone
    scenario with backbone nodes connected via WAN links). The applications for
    these are varied, but again this relates to a public-network service. One
    example might be peering, where all traffic on a peering arrangement is
    destined for a remote network. The formula for calculating total backbone
    capacity in this arrangement is: $T = (N)(c)/2$.

Say we select a Cisco 7206 with a NPE-400 process as our backbone node, which can process 400k packets per second (pps). The network configuration can be found in Figure 17-7.

▼   **Example 1**   If all the traffic stays local to the backbone node, what is the backbone
    capacity?

    $T = (400 \text{ kpps})(4) = 1600 \text{ kpps}$

■   **Example 2**   What if Figure 17-7 is changed from dual-homed to single-homed
    and the backbone is fully meshed? If all traffic crosses the backbone to another
    backbone node, what is the backbone capacity?

    $T = (400 \text{ kpps})(4)/2 = 800 \text{ kpps}$

▲   **Example 3**   If traffic is distributed asymmetrically between the sites, what is
    the backbone capacity?

    $T = (4^2)(400 \text{ kpps})/((2)(4)—1) = 914.28 \text{ kpps}$

As the traffic patterns become more distributed, the network capacity decreases. This
is because there are more options for traffic to use the limited bandwidth resources.

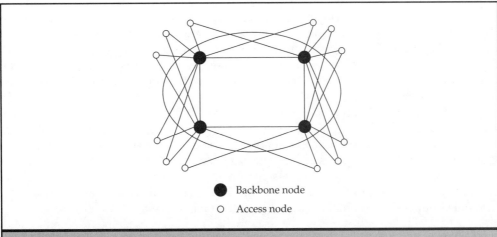

○   Backbone node
○   Access node

Figure 17-7.   Dual-homed backbone network

This is a design challenge, particularly with the next-generation packet networks covered in this book. Many novice network designers are finding that the only way to add extra capacity to this type of network is to over-engineer from the beginning. Unfortunately, many networks were built over-engineered this way in the late 1990s, and now companies are going back and trying to recover the cost out of incorrectly designed networks. Remember that these calculations are approximations only, and should be confirmed through a good design and modeling tool.

Route Determination

As reliability and availability are typically key user requirements, data networks need the intelligence to route around failures, thus increasing reliability and availability. FR, ATM, and IP networks provide an improvement to the customer over private lines because these packet networks can automatically route around network node and link failures.

In addition to network reliability, the designer can implement intelligence on the access device such as a routing protocol (OSPF, E-IGRP, BGP) for IP traffic to select the best route and if that is down, select alternate routes. Route selection is typically based on a variety of variables (hop count, cost, bandwidth, priority, quality of line). In addition to dedicated facilities, critical data can be protected using dial-backup solutions from ISDN to dialup modem. Selecting the right routing protocol and an address scheme to work with the routing protocol can improve network reliability and overhead.

Future Capacity

User requirements typically are always changing based on new application, growth, or seasonal trends of the business. So when designing, it is important think about how to add capacity. Load factors should be low early in the life of the network, and the network should have the capability to quickly add capacity when and where required. Again, this means increased processing power, memory, and extra access and trunk bandwidth capacity at each backbone site. When turning up a new service, make sure that this extra capacity is available. For example, in FR, measure all the CIRs of each user input to the switch, calculate the total burst that might reach the backbone, and determine if the backbone can handle that burst or drop traffic. Then plan on providing more than what is required based on the growth rates.

IP traffic planning is a bit more difficult, and you might need to take a rough ratio of port speed to backbone transport circuit speed. If you follow the design practice of building a backbone with a lower factor of technology obsolescence and larger transport circuits than the access actually requires, the design will prove effective. Remember, compare the cost of upgrading equipment and access proactively now versus the capital and expense cost of later going back to a site and changing out the equipment or access circuits.

Some implementation hints to keep in mind when designing:

▼   Local loops from carriers take weeks and sometimes months to get installed.

- Increasing bandwidth on an existing T1 from, say, one channel (64 Kbps) to four channels (256 Kbps) can typically be done in less than two weeks, a lot faster than ordering a new DS1 access circuit, which can take 30–40 business days on average.

- Increasing PVC CIR bandwidth can be done in days.

- The cost of a DS3 is about 8–10 T1s (varies by location and distance).

- Using standard protocols allows vendor swapping, which might be important if your company merges with another company.

▲ Monitor the network thresholds on a regular basis to see trends or problems before they happen.

BACKBONE TOPOLOGIES

Backbone topologies come in two styles: those planned and those that just grow. All private and public data networks seem to fit these stereotypes. Private networks, especially LANs that grow into MANs and then into WANs, tend to take on very asymmetrical shapes, with definable communities of interest. On the other hand, public networks respond to user needs and applications and are often designed largely on the procedures outlined in this book. It is easier to plan a backbone design and then build the network than to try and modify an existing mesh of WAN connectivity. Either way, the backbone network topology should be a function of the user application traffic patterns, the access-network topology, traffic volume, and range and profile of connectivity (local to global). Do not cement yourself into a single technology, service, or protocol suite. Now we will examine some of the more popular backbone topologies and the designs that go with them.

Star

The *star* design, also called *hub-and-spoke*, is similar to the star topology, where there is a central node serving as the hub node and all other nodes are connected via point-to-point circuits to the central node. All communications pass through the central node. A minimum of $N-1$ links are required to support N node(s) including the hub. This star style is often used in an environment such as a LAN/ATM switch or networks using a public service such as FR or ATM. The central node is often a multiport, scalable device that can handle large amounts of concentration, bridging, switching, or routing. While this configuration provides a maximum of two hops, it is unreliable and susceptible to an entire network failure when the hub node fails. Despite star-network inefficiencies, however, this type of management has certain advantages.

It should be noted that the *majority* of FR networks are star topology with the HQ site being the central node. In an FR star topology, each site has a physical loop into the FR cloud and then a logical virtual circuit to each site (except in MPLS IP-FR services, which require only one virtual circuit per site regardless of the number of interconnected sites). In FR networks, there are also dual star configurations to support redundancy (a virtual circuit to both HQ site and a backup). Figure 17-8 illustrates a star-style backbone configuration.

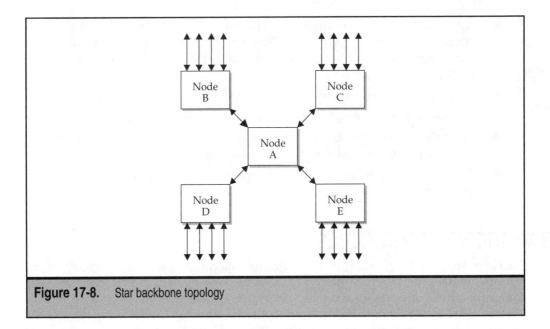

Figure 17-8.   Star backbone topology

Loop

The loop backbone design is similar to the loop or ring topology. Each network node is connected to two other network nodes. A minimum of *N* links are required for *N* nodes. This style is often used for distributed networks where nodes primarily talk to local nodes or point-to-point communications are required over short distances (or cannot operate over extended distances such as MAN links). There is no maximum to the number of hops across this network, but it is reliable up to the point of two link failures, which would then separate the network into two pieces. Capacity planning is difficult with loop topologies, and upgrades are difficult if the traffic patterns are not symmetric and consistent across different access nodes. Figure 17-9 illustrates the loop-style topology.

Meshed and Fully Meshed

While the meshed network is discussed in Chapter 5, the degree to which a mesh is built depends on the hardware and software expense of the ports, incremental cost of the links, network resource availability, and the amount of reliability and redundancy required. The number of links required for a fully meshed design is $N(N - 1)/2$. The number of links required drastically increases with the number of network nodes (thus pointing to the advantages of virtual private network services such as FR). Obviously, a fully meshed network is highly desirable, but often cost-prohibitive and rarely required. Again, design

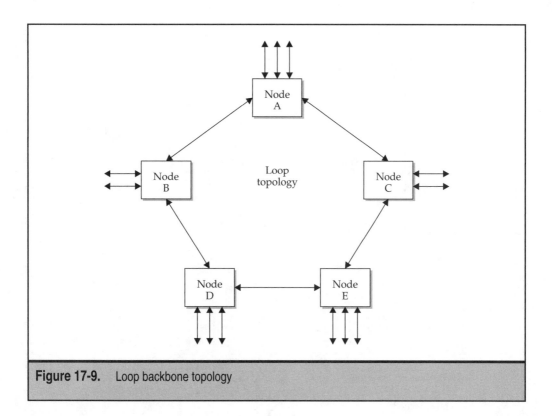

Figure 17-9. Loop backbone topology

tools have the capability of modeling various scenarios of meshing. Figure 17-10 shows both a partially meshed and fully meshed backbone.

Daisy-Chained

Consider, as an example of daisy-chained nodes, the packet network depicted in Figure 17-11A. All network-access devices are dual-homed to two high-capacity backbone switches. While this provides for high availability, it wastes bandwidth if the applications are regional or their processing is distributed. Figure 17-11B shows an alternative, where each access device also acts as a switch through a daisy chain.

In this example, the number of links required has been decreased from 54 to 32. This has lowered the equipment costs of the larger centralized switches, while retaining the connectivity requirements. The distance between nodes is also shortened. Unfortunately, these gains are not without potential costs. If a single link to the backbone is lost, an access node could be five hops from the nearest backbone node. Also, each link might be required

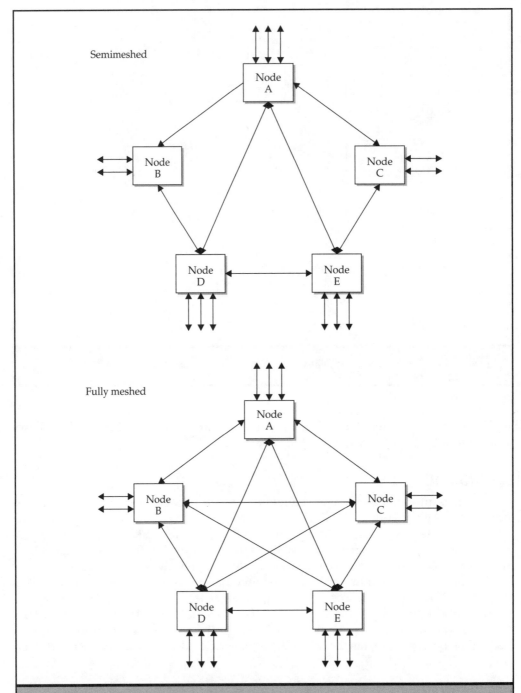

Figure 17-10.   Semimeshed and fully meshed backbone topologies

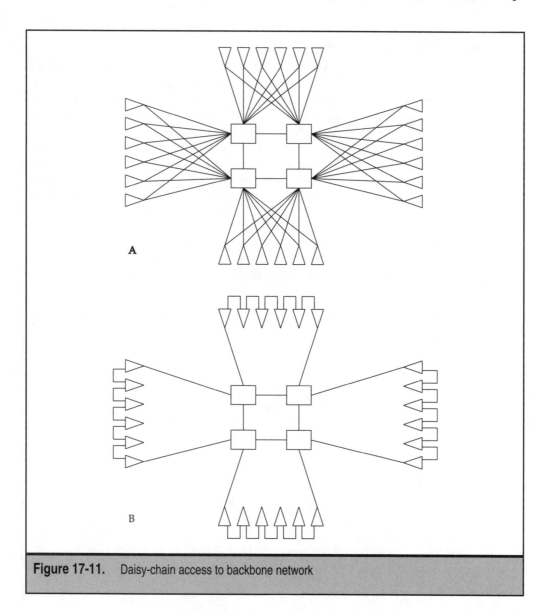

Figure 17-11. Daisy-chain access to backbone network

to carry all the capacity required to get all traffic from the isolated access nodes to the closest backbone node in the case of a single trunk failure. Careful cost and traffic analyses should be performed before using this design, as it almost always adds complexity and decreases reliability, with little cost reduction. It is interesting to note that much of the hodge-podge connectivity of the public Internet uses this topology—but not by design!

Backbones within Backbones

In the last section, it was assumed that the location of network backbone nodes was dictated by the requirements of the access nodes. In many cases, however, the backbone nodes and their topology are separate from the access-node topology. In fact, many network providers often build multiple backbones within backbones in a hierarchical nature. This approach has both advantages and disadvantages, as we will soon see.

Figure 17-12 shows an example of a network where ten access nodes receive user CPE traffic, and the design is based on DS1 and DS3 circuits. Each Local Access and Transport Area (LATA) is served by two access nodes. These network access nodes are configured in a loop-access topology, where each access node is connected to two other access nodes. These access nodes are then, in turn, connected to two different backbone nodes. Up to this point, all circuits are of DS1 speed. The backbone nodes are also configured in a loop backbone topology and provide a majority of the inter-LATA high-bandwidth transport. The backbone provides high-capacity DS3 circuits between backbone nodes. This network topology allows each user a maximum of three hops to get to any destination, or two if the

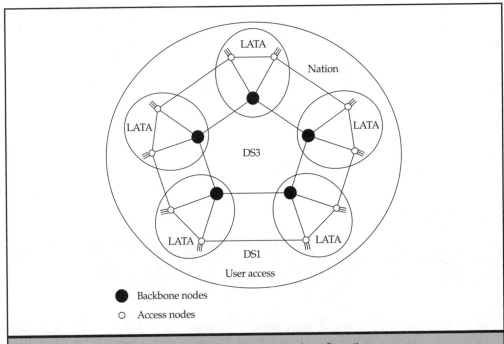

Figure 17-12. Single-access and single-backbone network configuration

destination is in the same or adjacent LATA. This topology could be used for either hier-archical TCP/IP networks or flat FR network designs.

Figure 17-13 shows the same network, this time with an additional high-speed (level 2) backbone (that is, SONET) within the existing (level 1) backbone. Assume that the distance between access (level 0) nodes is increased, and the LATAs are now countries. The original backbone now has a network node at each country and spans a continent. The addition of a higher-level backbone will be built with three nodes in a fully meshed configuration. Each level 1 backbone node will then connect to two level 2 backbone nodes. The new level 2 backbone can provide high-speed switching at gigabit or terabit levels.

From this analysis, it is plain that networks are built using hierarchical structures offering not only redundancy and availability, but also a reduced hop count (and the processing delay that goes along with it) and an increased speed of traffic that transits long distances across the network.

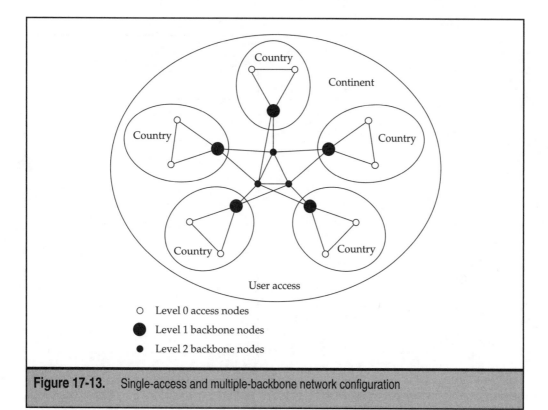

Figure 17-13.   Single-access and multiple-backbone network configuration

BACKBONE TOPOLOGY STRATEGIES

User requirements drive backbone topologies, which this section examines further, along with hybrid networks that mix different WAN technologies.

Requirements Drive the Topology

Always review all technologies and routing algorithms available, and do not confine yourself to a single transport technology, service, or protocol during the design process.

One method for designing the topology of a network is to add the links that are absolutely required first, and proceed to add more links until all possible links are added where capacity is required for data flow. You then eliminate links and combine traffic over other existing links based on many factors such as shortest path, link cost, and quality of facilities. This method can also be performed by a design tool.

This method is called *shortest path*. Figure 17-14A shows six links that have been added in order of the *largest* flow required to the *smallest* flow required (links 1 through 6,

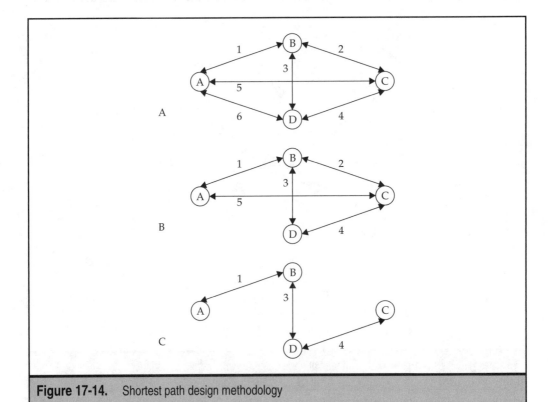

Figure 17-14.   Shortest path design methodology

respectively). Figure 17-14B shows the selection of links 1, 2, 3, 4, and 5 to remain, and 6 to be deleted, because it was too expensive not to route the traffic through node B (over links 1 and 3) rather than directly from node A to node D and vice versa. Figure 17-14C shows the final iteration where link 2 was eliminated due to only analog transmission facilities being available (traffic from B to C was rerouted from B to D to C and vice versa) and link 5 was eliminated due to its excessive distance (and traffic rerouted from A to B to D to C and vice versa). While this is a simplistic view of a network-topology design, it does provide some insight into the method of selection for topologies and aggregation of backbone links.

Never lose sight of the original user requirements during the backbone design. Understanding the effects that your backbone design will have on user applications is critical in optimizing the backbone design. This is a two-way process. Note that high-bandwidth access and backbone transport might not be required if the application can stand a bit of delay during times of congestion, but if the opposite is true, and a backbone is designed with too few links, the extra network transport delay incurred across the backbone might have an adverse effect on the application. When signing up for a carrier-offered service, you need to fully understand the carrier's access and backbone design and its potential effects on user applications. For example, if a carrier is quoting a 50-millisecond total delay across its public data network, how does this affect your file-transfer sessions? Is the delay variable? Will this delay, when added to your access and egress delay to the carrier's service, affect your applications? These questions and many more from previous chapters must be asked of the carriers.

Hybrid Topologies

Hybrid designs mix both private lines and public networks such as FR, ATM, or IP. Switched services are often used as backup to leased facilities such as ISDN or for locations where private lines are too expensive. When designing private networks, the design should allow integration with a public network-switched services. Public and private network hybrids allow control of critical resources to be retained while taking advantage of public services functionality and pricing. When designing a hybrid backbone network, attempt to keep all speeds fairly constant, and beware of bottleneck bandwidth points. Beware of multiple encapsulation schemes in hybrid networks, and understand that similar network devices must often be used at both network ingress and egress points.

TUNING THE NETWORK

Network tuning should be performed at the same time you are designing the backbone-network design, as well as at specific intervals throughout the lifetime of the network. This section addresses five specific areas that are critical to your network and application performance: packet size, segmentation on a per-link basis, application window sizes, bandwidth limitations of both physical port, and logical limits and queuing.

Optimizing Packet/Frame/Cell Size

In packet-, frame-, and cell-switched networks, there is a tradeoff between large and small packet/frame/cell sizes (we shall refer to "packets" from this point on). When small packets are used (and each packet has a small amount of data), the amount of overhead increases. This causes a disproportionate amount of overhead generated versus data passed, and the data throughput of the line degrades. Remember the definition of throughput: how much *data* a user can pass across a given circuit or device (less the "overhead"). Small packets have the advantage of better response time.

Packet size tuning is a balancing act, where additional factors influence the size. A user application like FTP typically prefers the largest packet size possible. In voice over packet, as the packet size grows, the end-to-end delay of the voice is increased, and since more voice samples are in a larger packet, each packet lost causes detectable sound degradation.

As a summary, large packet sizes are critical to performance of web traffic, e-mail traffic, and FTP traffic, where throughput is the critical driver; smaller packets are typically better for jitter sensitive, and delay applications like multimedia. There isn't a correct answer other than continually tuning for optimal performance.

Segmentation

Segmentation is the process where a packet size that originates at the source is broken into multiple packets at some point in the network. Table 17-2 shows different LAN media and the default MTU; an example of segmentation would be a client attached to a 16 Mbps Token Ring segment sending a 4000-byte packet to a client on an Ethernet segment. For the packet to be received at the Ethernet station, it has to receive the 4000-byte packet segmented in at least three packets.

Media Type	MTU
16 Mbps Token Ring	17914 bytes
4 Mbps Token Ring	4464 bytes
FDDI	4352 bytes
Ethernet	1500 bytes
IEEE 802.3/802.2	1492 bytes
X.25	576 bytes
PPPoE	<=1492 bytes

Table 17-2. Default Maximum Transfer Unit (MTU) by Media

Another term used for segmentation is link fragmentation. Table 17-3 shows the serialization delay added to the end-to-end delay based on line speed and packet size. The voice over packet objective is typically to have a one-way delay of less than 200 milliseconds for quality voice; Table 17-3 illustrates that if a voice packet gets behind a 1500-byte FTP packet on a 56 Kbps line, you are in trouble. Segmentation works with queuing schemes to allow multimedia traffic to meet QoS objectives.

When adding a MTU restriction to a link, it should be understood that the MTU restriction may cause some problems, such as some web pages not being accessible and applications/protocols that cannot segment may no longer work. Some router vendors have implemented a TCP maximum segment size (MSS) manipulation to help address some of the web issues, but beware.

Window Sizes

Window sizes can be tuned at each level of the X.25 packet-switched network, or at the network layer (that is, TCP) portion of the protocol stack (usually in the user or access device). These windows provide transmission-flow control. The window size determines how many packets can be outstanding in the network before an acknowledgment is received from the last unacknowledged packet sent. In packet switching, high-error lines should use a window size of two and low-error full-duplex lines should use a window size of seven. TCP, on the other hand, will adjust its window size automatically based on the current network throughput. If there are more errors in the network, it will *decrease*

	1 Byte	64 Bytes	128 Bytes	256 Bytes	512 Bytes	1024 Bytes	1500 Bytes
56 Kbps	143 us	9 ms	18 ms	36 ms	72 ms	144 ms	214 ms
64 Kbps	125 us	8 ms	16 ms	32 ms	64 ms	126 ms	187 ms
128 Kbps	62.5 us	4 ms	8 ms	16 ms	32 ms	64 ms	93 ms
256 Kbps	31 us	2 ms	4 ms	8 ms	16 ms	32 ms	46 ms
512 Kbps	15.5 us	1 ms	2 ms	4 ms	8 ms	16 ms	32 ms
768 Kbps	10 us	640 us	1.28 ms	2.56 ms	5.12 ms	10.24 ms	15 ms
1536 Kbps	5 us	320 us	640 us	1.28 ms	2.56 ms	5.12 ms	7.5 ms

Table 17-3.   Serialization Delay for Various Frame Sizes on Low-Speed Links

window size; if there are fewer errors, it will *increase* window size. Increased window size provides increased throughput. It should now be apparent how excessive lost packets/ frames/cells in the data services transport can have a devastating effect on window sizes.

Bandwidth

Bandwidth limitations caused by the physical port speed, logical constraints of logical circuits (such as of CIR for FR), and limits on bursting over port speed can all cause performance problems of increased, end-to-end delay due to network buffering or dropped packets from buffer overruns. As network tuning goes, it is important to monitor the CIR usage and port speed usage at each site as due diligence against signs a bottleneck is starting. As discussed earlier, it is important to remember the ordering/installation interval required to resolve congestion problems.

Queuing

Queuing schemes is an area that continues to be enhanced in networks due to the requirements of users to have special handling for multimedia traffic and other special needs traffic.

In the most basic queue of first in, first out (FIFO), there is still tuning of the depth of the buffer. If the traffic is really bursty (a big blast of traffic and then nothing followed by a big blast—defined as peak/average traffic), increasing the depth of the FIFO buffer will reduce drops and increase performance. But if you have a mix of traffic types, increasing buffer depth will increase end-to-end delay so modeling and trial and error may be required.

Priority queue schemes vary by vendors. The main purpose of priority queuing is to allow delay- and loss-sensitive traffic to cut to the front of the line. Many priority schemes allow multiple levels of queues and schemes to prevent queue starvation (when a queue isn't serviced). Understanding which applications require special handling and a method to notify network devices is critical to designing to application performance. Methods of notifying network devices could be TCP/UDP port, IP source or destination address, or IP Precedence bits, to name a few.

TYING NETWORKS TOGETHER

As the growth of networks continues, the requirement for connecting different network services continues to rise. Connecting networks together is fairly simple in that a physical connection is made between two different pieces of equipment, but reliability, routing, network management, billing, and trouble isolation is really where the fun begins. When tying networks together, it is important to understand the possible bottleneck between the two networks and size the interface to prevent congestion.

As the Internet is a collection of many networks, connecting networks together in the Internet environment has 20-plus years of history using interior and exterior routing protocols. The Internet community is currently using Border Gateway Protocol Version 4 (BGP-4) as the exterior routing protocol for communicating routes between different networks. Since reliability is a key in connecting different networks, BGP-4 provides routing information that allows routing devices to select the best path and also the ability to reroute around failures. The Internet's billing model simplifies the network-to-network interfaces (NNI) in that carriers typically split the cost for private peering.

As for FR, the NNI interface typically is implemented between two pieces of equipment next to each other because automatic rerouting due to an NNI failure isn't standardized. There are some NNI proprietary vendor solutions but each carrier has to be utilizing the same vendors equipment. FR NNIs are found in global carrier interconnections down to local carriers or national carriers as in the U.S. model.

As for ATM, time was invested in the standard bodies to provide fully functional interfaces as well as addressing other problems from billing, and network management thru operations. The ATM standards specify two interfaces:

▼ BISDN intercarrier interface (B-ICI) is an interface between two different public network service providers.

▲ Private network-to-network interface (PNNI) is protocol that distributes topology information between networks much like BGP-4. PNNI can also stand for private network node interface, as the same protocol can be used between switches in the same network.

REVIEW

In this chapter, we completed the backbone network design. This network design supports enough capacity to meet existing user access requirements, as well as future network growth. The backbone style and topology was chosen based on many factors, such as user requirements, the access and backbone technologies, and future networking concerns. The importance of strong network design principles, confirmed through network performance and trend analysis modeling, was reviewed. The chapter attempted to present multiple topological examples of designs.

As no design is perfect due to original assumptions/information or just unforeseen changes, tuning the network is critical to having a network that will continue to meet the user's requirements. To complete our coverage of data network design, we will discuss how to secure your network and also how to maintain/monitor your network once it is operational.

CHAPTER 18

Securing Your Network

The importance of network security has risen to the critical level for many companies, especially with the growth of the Internet and its many uses for businesses. As companies rely more on the Internet and their computer infrastructures, the opportunities for damage from a hacker (cracker is a better description) and the amount of damage that can be inflicted increase exponentially.

This chapter has been added to explain techniques and processes that are required to secure your network. As a caveat, this chapter in no way provides all the knowledge required to secure a network. No network can be 100 percent secure. This chapter provides only an elementary discussion on network security as it relates to network design, and refers you to more thorough sources for further study. It gives you a high-level overview of firewalls and VPN design, and a discussion of implementing a network security policy.

BACKGROUND

The modern history of network security starts at the development of the first computer. In the 1960s at MIT, the term "hacker" was borrowed from a term used to describe members of a model train group at the school who "hacked" the electric trains, tracks, and switches to make them faster and different. A few members transferred their enthusiasm and curiosity to the new mainframe computer being studied and developed.

The 1970s ushered in the decade of the "phreaks," who were phone hackers. One phreak, known as Cap'n Crunch, learned that a toy whistle given away inside Cap'n Crunch cereal generated a 2600 hertz signal, which was the same tone that accessed the AT&T long distance network. The phreaks created a "blue box" that, along with the whistle, could make free calls. Two college students, Steve Wozniak and Steve Jobs, launched a home business making and selling these blue boxes before going on to found Apple Computer.

Bulletin board systems (BBSs) began appearing in the 1980s. Designed as an information-sharing medium between computer users, BBSs were a precursor to newsgroups and e-mail. BBSs with names such as Sherwood Forest and Catch-22 became the home of phreaks and hackers to talk and share information—including computer passwords and credit card numbers. As the phone networks got smarter by implementing Signaling System 7 (SS7), phreaks began focusing on computer networks. In 1988, Robert T. Morris, Jr., a graduate student at Cornell University, launched a self-replicating worm/virus on the government's ARPANET. The worm affected about 6000 computers, and provided a glimpse of what was to come.

In 1990, the U.S. Secret Service conducted a nationwide crackdown on computer hackers, which resulted in numerous arrests, criminal charges, and seized equipment. The crackdown, however, did not stop the hackers. The 1990s are filled with stories of hacking from the Justice Department's home page modifications, to AOHell, a freeware application that allowed unskilled hackers to wreak havoc on America Online's network for days. As BBSs were replaced with web pages, accessing and sharing information only got easier.

In 1999, in the wake of Microsoft's Windows 98 release, the focus on security became a mainstream activity as software vendors mass-produced antivirus software for home users as well as businesses. In 2000, distributed denial-of-service (DDOS) attacks against web sites such as eBay, Yahoo, Amazon, and others provided a new method of disruption. DDOS attacks have moved to Domain Name System (DNS) servers and to routers via SNMP. The need for security remains the forefront as the number of different attacks and viruses affects our reliance on computers and information. Network security has become a huge market, and continues to be one of the most critical issues a network manager or engineer has to face.

Overview

Before understanding security threats and safeguards, we need to understand the need for security. The question most network managers ask is "Do I need security?" Figure 18-1 shows that of 532 companies responding to the Computer Security Institute's 2001 study, more than 60 percent had unauthorized computer use in the last 12 months. Figure 18-2 shows the amount of financial loss by type of attack.

Most people think security violations come from outside their network, that is, from the Internet and professional hackers. The truth is that (based on the Computer Security Institute's 2002 study) company employees initiate approximately 79 percent of security breaches. These employees are not just disgruntled individuals out for revenge, but their

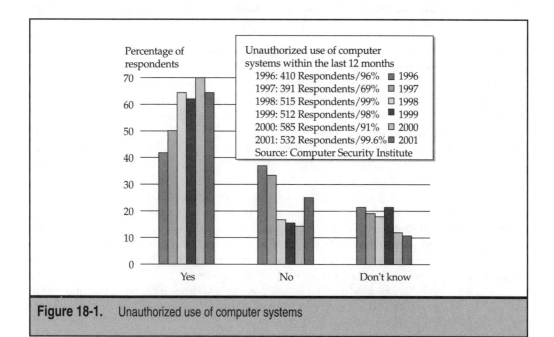

Figure 18-1.   Unauthorized use of computer systems

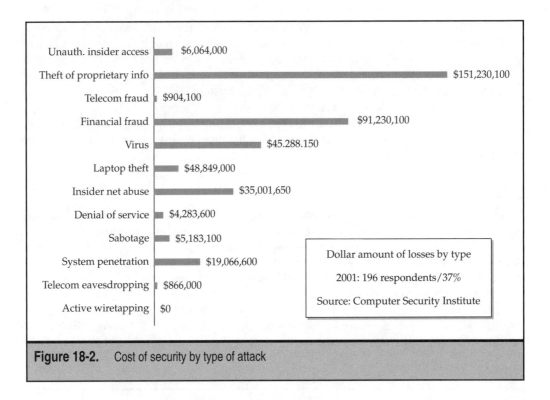

Figure 18-2. Cost of security by type of attack

behavior can range from plain curious to illegal and abusive. Figure 18-3 shows companies' views on who are likely sources of attacks.

Network security is all about identifying the real risks to your network and making proper security decisions. Security is like an insurance policy for the business. The cost of deploying security features should be less than the cost of a potential security incident.

The term "hacker" is used throughout this chapter and the industry. Actually, there are two distinct groups, known as "hackers" and "crackers." A hacker is an independent-minded law-abiding computer enthusiast who pursues the freewheeling intellectual exploration of computer systems. A hacker understands the internal workings of a computer system and is totally engrossed in computer programming and technology. Hackers are usually nonthreatening, nondamaging types of people.

A cracker has the same interests as a hacker, but illegally accesses computer systems for fun, profit, and personal gain. Crackers don't always harm a computer system once they gain access, but sometimes just snoop around undetected. In this book, the term "hacker" is used for both groups to simplify the discussion.

A third group is "script kiddies," who download prewritten tools from the Internet to run attacks on networked systems. Script kiddies normally have very few skills but cause a large percentage of damage done on the Internet.

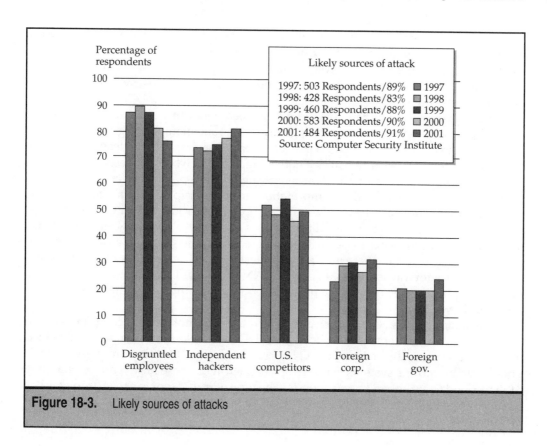

Figure 18-3.   Likely sources of attacks

SECURITY THREATS

Security threats can be classified into three groups:

▼   **Unauthorized access or "break-ins"**   A system or network data is accessed by unauthorized personnel or system. An example of this is a hacker using a compromised server on a distribution site for pirated software (warez) or MP3s.

■   **Privacy violation or "impersonation"**   Data is viewed either in transit over your network or by other means, which allows someone to present an authorized user's credentials. An example of this is breaking into an SMTP server and installing a sniffer. Receipts for items purchased with a credit card are automatically e-mailed back to the hacker. It is not uncommon for credit card information to be contained in the e-mail. Once this is obtained, items such as access to services can be purchased on the Internet.

▲   **Unavailable service or DDOS**   An attack that floods a network's access so that user data or the system cannot be accessed. An example of this is the DDOS attack that put UK-based ISP Cloud Nine out of business.

Unauthorized access occurs when unauthorized entry is gained to an asset such as a computer, and the unauthorized individual has the possibility of tampering with the asset. Access can be gained by a privacy violation or by exploiting a weakness in the security of a machine or software or hardware product. Once access to a system is achieved, data alteration or destruction can happen.

Viruses, worms, and Trojan horses are some techniques that cause data alteration or corruption in addition to hackers accessing the machine and manipulating or deleting data.

Privacy violations can happen via packet snooping or simply a user leaving access information unsecured (such as a sticky note listing all passwords posted on a monitor). Packet snooping or eavesdropping is accomplished using a packet sniffer on the LAN or anywhere on the network where information is not encrypted. Sniffer technology is available as software that can be run on any laptop, so if a hacker puts a PC on a LAN segment, they might be able to view all the packets on the LAN. As LAN technology has moved from hubs to switches, security has increased in the switched environment because only broadcast packets and packets destined for computers off an Ethernet switch port are forwarded from a specific LAN segment. To protect against privacy violations, physical security of the network is an important step, along with encryption and firewalls.

Unavailable service occurs when authorized users cannot access a computer system due to an attacker's attempt to disrupt access. DDOS attacks have been well publicized in the last few years. In such an attack, hackers send (flood) traffic or requests to computer systems and the systems get so overwhelmed with these false requests that they can't respond to authorized user requests. The type of traffic sent to cause problems has included ping ICMP, HTTP, DNS, and SNMP. Some common DDOS attacks are shown in Table 18-1.

Name of DDOS Attack	Vulnerability Exploited
TCP SYN attack	Memory is allocated for TCP connections such that not enough memory is left for other functions.
Ping of Death	Fragmentation implementation of IP whereby large packets are reassembled and can cause machines to crash
Land.c attack	TCP connection establishment
Teardrop.c attack	Fragmentation implementation of IP whereby reassembly problems can cause machines to crash
SMURF attack	Flooding networks with broadcast traffic such that the network is congested

Table 18-1.   Common DDOS Attacks

SECURITY SAFEGUARDS

As using Internet access and computer systems to manage businesses continues to rise, security vendors continue to come out with new products to assist in safeguarding networks. Designing and enforcing a security policy at your company is the first course of action, and is covered in the "Security Policy" section. Understanding the safeguard tools available will assist you in implementing a security policy.

Secure Network Equipment

The first safeguards date back to the earliest buildings, where locks were used to protect possessions. Your network equipment needs to be secured behind a locked door and access limited to authorized personnel. As noted earlier in this section, employees cause the majority of the problems that are not always intentional, so prevent the opportunity. The following provides a facility access checklist to assist in understanding your vulnerabilities:

▼ Who has keys to which doors?

■ Is your building's leasing company bonded?

■ What's above those ceiling tiles? Could someone crawl over the wall?

■ Do network cables or power lines run through exposed and vulnerable areas of the building?

■ Would a motion-detecting alarm be valuable?

■ Do you enforce policies about controlling visitors?

■ Who has physical and logical access to your computers?

■ Do your employees bring family members to work on weekends or after hours?

■ Who has access to your administrator passwords, and how often are they changed?

■ Do you change locks and passwords immediately when an employee leaves the firm?

■ Is your cleaning crew bonded?

■ Do you let vendors and other employees know immediately when someone departs the firm?

■ Is your building management company bonded?

▲ Do you have a policy detailing what gets shredded before it is put in the trash?

Password Procedures

Passwords are required to access almost any resource in a network environment, but poorly selected passwords can be determined easily. Software is available on the Internet to break poorly selected passwords, so implementing policies on passwords is an important step in security. Table 18-2 provides a list of Do's and Don'ts on creating passwords.

Antivirus Software

Computer viruses such as the "ILOVEYOU" virus that affected the world in May 2000 have helped educate us on the destruction that viruses can cause.

A virus is a hacker program than normally has malicious intent. It can infect legitimate programs or attack the operating system directly. Polymorphic viruses can modify their own code to try to defeat signature-based antiviral software. A virus can be just an annoyance—such as those that modify the display or replicate e-mail to your entire distribution list—or a real problem, such as those that reformat the hard drive or modify data. More and more viruses are being transmitted through defects in e-mail programs. Many take advantage of the scripting languages built into systems such as the Microsoft Outlook and Microsoft Office suite.

A Trojan horse is a hacker program that searches out other programs and infects them by embedding a copy of itself in them so that they become "Trojan horses." The term

Don't	Do
Use your login name in any form.	Use a password of mixed-case alphabetics.
Use your first, middle, or last name in any form or use your spouse's or child's name.	Use a password with nonalphabetic characters (digits or punctuation).
Use other information easily obtained about you, including license plate numbers, telephone numbers, social security numbers, the make of your automobile, the name of your street, etc.	Use a password that is easy to remember, so you don't have to write it down.
Use a password of all digits.	Run a password cracker regularly to weed out users with easily guessed passwords and make them change them.
Use a word contained in any dictionary, spelling list, or other word list.	
Use a password shorter than six characters.	

Table 18-2. Good Password Procedures

refers to a program that appears legitimate but is designed to have destructive effects. When these programs are executed, the embedded virus is executed too, thus propagating the infection. This process is normally invisible to the user. A virus might allow the program to run normally and remain silent for a while before it starts doing things, from writing "cute" messages on the terminal to irreversible damage such as deleting files. A virus cannot infect other computers without assistance, such as people trading programs with friends, while a worm is a hacker program that replicates itself and can spread via e-mail without assistance.

As virus or worms can cause major problems on your network and computers. It is critical to implement network or individual computer antivirus software and keep it up to date. The National Computer Security Association estimates that if just 30 percent of computer owners regularly used up-to-date antivirus software, the virus problem would virtually disappear. Table 18-3 provides a list of precautionary steps to prevent problems, but antivirus software is a minimum requirement.

Implement a Firewall

The term "firewall" is a general term because a firewall is simply some type of mechanism (hardware, software, or both) for protecting your network from the outside world. Another use of a firewall is to separate critical data, such as HR or product design data, from internal network users. The first rule of a firewall is that it is only as good as it is configured. In other words, just because you have a firewall doesn't mean your network is

Prevention Steps	Description
Screen your e-mail.	Never download or run an attached file from an e-mail from an unknown address.
Don't automatically open attachments.	Never set your e-mail program to open attached files automatically. Turn off the option to launch or execute any programs after receiving an e-mail.
Don't download programs from web sites.	If you need to download, do so in a separate isolated drive and scan it with your antivirus software.
Update your antivirus, e-mail software, and OS regularly.	Security patches and updated antivirus definitions are coming out frequently. Getting the latest updates might save you from getting infected.

Table 18-3. Precautionary Steps to Prevent Viruses and Worms

secure. In fact, firewalls need constant updates and attention, and were not meant to be static devices. Designing firewalls is covered later in the "Firewall Design" section.

As firewall is used as a general term, it is important to understand the different functions of a firewall so that you can choose a firewall to meet your requirements. The functions of a firewall are broken into the following areas:

▼ **Packet filtering**　Specify packet conditions to allow or disallow entry into the network. Packet filters can be based on protocols, protocol ports, or IP addresses. Packet filtering capabilities are available on most routers today.

■ **Application proxies**　A program or server that is empowered to act on behalf of one or more other computer(s) on the network.

▲ **Stateful inspection or dynamic packet filtering**　Filtering has intelligence to be based on prior packets and can view the packet payload versus just the packet header.

Packet filtering is the highest performance firewall mechanism, but it can be hard to configure because the configuration depends on a low-level understanding of protocols and ports. Packet filtering can be specified on output packets (packets being sent by the device), input packets (packets being received by the device), or in both directions. For example, spoofed packets that appear to have originated from an acceptable source can defeat simple packet filtering.

Application proxies are also called proxy servers or application gateways. An application proxy acts as a relay agent or mediator between two systems attempting to communicate. Figure 18-4 shows a proxy server configuration. The process might be something like this:

1. A user connects to the application gateway via software that tells the proxy what system the user wants to connect to, and for what reason (such as a web request).

2. The gateway checks the user's source IP address and accepts or rejects based on access criteria.

3. The proxy might authenticate the user.

4. The proxy service creates a connection between the gateway and the host.

5. The proxy service passes data between the two connections.

6. The proxy server logs the connection information.

7. Steps 5 and 6 are repeated until all the information is transferred.

Application proxies conceal the identity of the host so the user never knows the identity or IP address of the server where the application resides. Application proxies have to be set up for each required service such as HTTP or FTP, which can make configuration complex, but if configured correctly, application proxies can provide a high level of security.

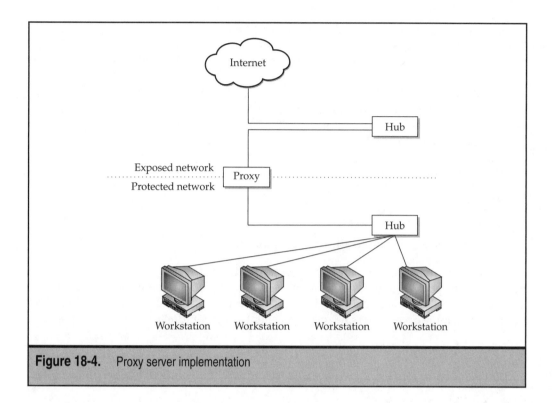

Figure 18-4.   Proxy server implementation

A variant of an application proxy is a circuit-level gateway. A circuit-level gateway doesn't function at the application layer but typically at the transport layer (TCP, UDP) or network layer (IP). Network address translation (NAT) or port address translation (PAT) performs the function of translating an internal IP address to an external IP address. The difference between PAT and NAT is that a NAT has a single external IP address for every internal IP address while a PAT has fewer external IP address for the number of internal IP addresses and thus uses ports to track connections. In addition to NAT and PAT, an IETF protocol called SOCKS is a well-known circuit-level gateway. To function, SOCKS version 5 requires modifications either to the application or client TCP/IP stacks.

Implement a Virtual Private Network (VPN)

A VPN is implemented to secure remote access or communication between facilities over the Internet. A VPN is a private connection between two or more network elements over a shared (typically public network) infrastructure. The "virtual" in VPN defines a logical definition between the networks, not a separate physical network. The "private" in VPN defines separate addressing and routing. A VPN is used to describe service provider services of frame relay and ATM and also for encrypted tunnels between networks over an IP infrastructure, which could also be the public Internet. The discussion in this chapter focuses on the IP-VPN definition of a secured tunnel across the Internet for remote user access or remote site-to-site connectivity.

IP-VPN connectivity is achieved through a combination of tunnels and encryption (although L2TP doesn't always use encryption). Encryption is the process of using a secret code to alter data to make it unintelligible to unauthorized parties. Encryption uses cryptography, which is the technology that helps ensure that private communication remains private.

There are three types of VPNs:

▼ Secure remote access

■ Intranet access (site-to-site)

▲ Extranet access (site-to-site or site-to-Internet)

Secure remote access, which provides connectivity for the "road warriors" or remote users in your organization, is shown in Figure 18-5. These users dial (56 Kbps, V.90) into an ISP account or connect through a broadband connection such as DSL or cable. Secure remote access users have a VPN client either vendor-provided or embedded

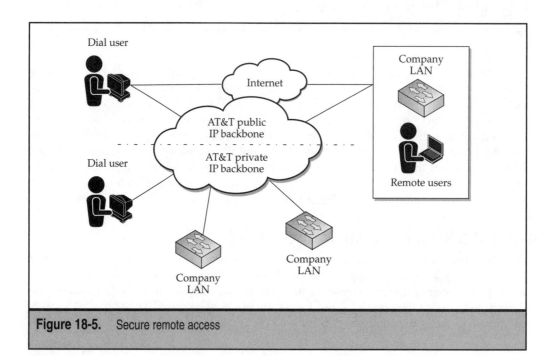

Figure 18-5.   Secure remote access

in the operating system (OS) on their machine. A VPN client typically performs the following functions:

▼   Negotiates tunnel parameters and establishes the tunnel

■   Authenticates users and establishes user access rights

■   Manages security keys for encryption and decryption

■   Authenticates, encrypts, and decrypts the data

▲   Keeps message digests to ensure the integrity of the data

Intranet access is shown in Figure 18-6. Intranet access is used to connect remote offices. As remote access requires one client per computer, Intranet access is typically configured from the firewall or a separate server that provides the VPN functions of authenticating, encryption, and encapsulation.

Extranet access is shown in Figure 18-7. Extranet access is used to allow access to parts of your network for suppliers and business partners. It is important to make sure that your firewall design and extranet access design are integrated and designed optimally to limit a supplier's or business partner's access.

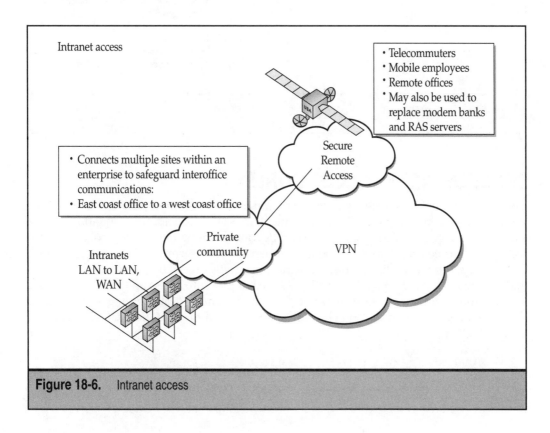

Figure 18-6.   Intranet access

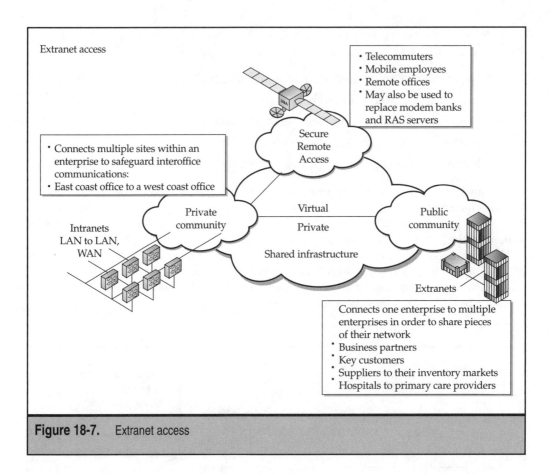

Figure 18-7. Extranet access

DESIGN FOR NETWORK SECURITY

The first step in network security design is to implement a security policy that matches the needs and vulnerability protection requirements of your business. Implementing a security policy involves risk analysis and baselining, documenting the security policy, and selecting a dedicated team to implement and manage your security. Once risk analysis is accomplished and a baseline security design completed, you can begin tactical discussions and implementation of firewalls and VPN as needed to secure access and reduce your risk.

Designing for network security is not a one-time event of implementing a firewall and you're done, but a continual process. At Spohn Consulting, the NetAUDIT process is used, which is

▼ Analyze

■ Understand

- Design
- Implement
- ▲ Train

To achieve network security, the NetAUDIT is not a one-time process but a continual or cyclical process of analyzing and understanding security threats.

Security Policy

The goal in developing an official network security policy is to define the organization's expectations of proper computer and network use and to define procedures to prevent and respond to security incidents. RFC 1244, "Site Security Handbook," provides additional detail on the process and procedures that need to be covered in your security policy. The corporate security policy documents the corporate security stance.

The first rule of network security is stated:

"That which is not expressly permitted is prohibited. Simply, a security policy should start by denying all access to all network resources, and then expressly add back access on a specific basis. Implemented in this way, your network security policy will not allow any inadvertent actions or procedures."

Part of the process of setting up a security policy is to define a process of reacting to a security violation. Who is responsible for what, and how much authority does the security team have when reacting to security violations?

To assist in implementing a security policy, monitoring current issues, and reacting to violations, an organization named CERT Coordination Center (CERT/CC) exists for reporting major Internet security problems. Staff members of CERT/CC provide technical assistance, coordinate responses to security compromises, identify trends in intruder activity, work with other security experts to identify solutions to security problems, and disseminate information to the Internet community.

Preparation

Prior to being able to implement a security policy, you must

- ▼ Conduct a risk analysis.
- Establish a security team structure.
- Define roles and responsibilities.
- Create a security policy statement.
- ▲ Define procedures.

Risk Analysis   A risk analysis involves determining what you need to protect, what you need to protect it from, and how to protect it. All risks need to be examined and the risks need to be ranked by level of severity. Here are three risk levels that can be used for risk analysis:

▼ **Low risk**   Systems or data that, if compromised, would not disrupt the business or cause financial, legal, or regulatory ramifications. The targeted system or data can be easily restored and does not permit further access to other systems.

■ **Medium risk**   Systems or data that, if compromised, would cause a moderate disruption in the business, minor financial, legal, or regulatory ramifications, or permit further access to other systems

▲ **High risk**   System or data that, if compromised, would cause an extreme disruption in the business, or major financial, legal, or regulatory ramifications

Once the risks are assigned a level of severity, identify the types of users of that system or device. Five common types of users are

▼ **Administrators**   Internal users responsible for network resources

■ **Privileged**   Internal users with a need for greater access

■ **Users**   Internal users with general access

■ **Partners**   External users with a need to access or share some resources

▲ **Others**   External users or customers

Table 18-4 provides an example of a risk analysis matrix created using the methods of describing the level of severity and the type of user access. The risk analysis matrix provides a quick reference to review security measures and make sure the selected security strategy is accomplishing its goal.

System	Description	Risk Level	Types of Users
ATM switches	Core network device	High	Administrators for device configurations (support staff only); all others for use as transport
Network routers	Distribution network device	High	Administrators for device configurations (support staff only); all others for use as transport

Table 18-4.   Risk Analysis Matrix

System	Description	Risk Level	Types of Users
Closet switches	Access network device	Medium	Administrators for device configurations (support staff only); all others for use as transport
ISDN or dialup servers	Access network device	Medium	Administrators for device configurations (support staff only); partners and privileged users for special access
Firewall	Access network device	High	Administrators for device configurations (support staff only); all others for use as transport
DNS and DHCP servers	Network application	Medium or High	Administrators for configuration; general and privileged users for use
External e-mail server	Network application	Low	Administrators for configuration; all others for mail transport between the Internet and the internal mail server
Internal e-mail	Network application	Medium	Administrators for configuration; all other internal users for use
Database	Network application	Medium or High	Administrators for configuration; privileged users for data updates; general users for data access; all others for partial data access
External web server	Network application	Medium or Low	Administrators for configuration; all others for accessing information; you might want to implement a proxy

Table 18-4.   Risk Analysis Matrix *(continued)*

The United States Department of Defense has defined seven levels of computer OS security in a document known as the Trusted Computer Standards Evaluation Criteria, otherwise known as the Orange Book. Table 18-5 shows the Orange Book security levels. There are various certified secure OS in commercial operating systems such as UNIX and Windows. Implementing the highest security level OS is probably not practical in most business environments, but on critical servers, understanding the OS and reviewing the logs on a regular basis might be justified.

NOTE: On secure operating systems, the features and capabilities require significant amounts of CPU processing power and disk space.

Establish a Security Team Structure   The success or failure of a security policy greatly depends on management buy-in and appropriate resources and training. Create a cross-

Security Level (Lowest to Highest)	Description (Each Level Builds on the Previous)
D1	States that the system is untrusted.
C1	System has file and directory read and write controls and authentication through user login.
C2	System also includes an auditing function to record all security-related events and provides stronger protection on key system files, such as password file.
B1	System supports multilevel security, such as secret and top secret, and mandatory access control, which states that a user cannot change permissions on files or directories.
B2	System requires that every object and file be labeled according to its security level and that these labels change dynamically depending on what is being used.
B3	System extends security levels down into the system hardware; for example, to ensure there is no unauthorized access, terminals can connect only through trusted cable paths and specialized system hardware.
A1	The design must be mathematically verified. To prevent tampering, all hardware and software must have been protected during shipment.

Table 18-5.   Orange Book Security Levels

functional security team, led by a security manager, with participants from each of your company's operational areas. The security operations and management staff should be organizationally as separate from the network staff as possible. Note that additional training might be required for the team members so that they are aware of the technical aspects of security design and implementation.

The security team's objectives:

▼ Establish and review security policies.

■ Review at least yearly both the risk analysis and security policy.

■ Be prepared for a problem. Practice how the team would react to violations.

▲ Respond to problems. Work as a team to troubleshoot and fix violations.

Create a Security Policy Statement   Creating a security policy statement is required to advise users' roles and responsibilities. Your policy statement might want to cover the following:

▼ What guidelines you have regarding resource consumption

■ What constitutes abuse in terms of system use

■ Which users are permitted to share which accounts

■ How often users should change their passwords and password restrictions

■ Whether you provide backups or expect users to create their own

■ Process for disclosure of information which might be proprietary

■ Statement on e-mail privacy: Does the company consider e-mail private to each employee or do they consider it the property of the organization?

■ Statement on web access: What restrictions are on users?

■ Statement on instant messaging

▲ Statement on e-mail use

RFC 1244, now replaced by RFC 2196, suggests five criteria for evaluating any policy:

1. Does the policy comply with the law and with duties to third parties?

2. Does the policy unnecessarily compromise the interest of the employee, the employer, or third parties?

3. Is the policy workable as a practical matter and likely to be enforced?

4. Does the policy deal appropriately with all different forms of communications and record keeping with the offices?

5. Has the policy been announced in advanced and agreed to by all concerned?

Now that security risks have been tabulated and the security team assembled, the process of designing systems to protect your network needs to be reviewed.

Firewall Design

Designing a firewall requires an understanding and identification of boundaries between security domains in your networks. A network security domain is a contiguous region of a network that operates under a single, uniform security policy. The places where these domains intersect create a potential for policy conflict, and firewalls can help resolve this conflict. The most common boundary is between an organization's internal network and the Internet or extranet. When designing a firewall, the first decision is selecting architecture. The two classes of firewall architecture are single-layer, as shown in Figure 18-8, and multiple-layer, as shown in Figure 18-9.

In single-layer architecture, one network device connects the public and private networks and performs access controls. The single-layer architecture is simple and very cost-effective. The firewall security policy completely resides in a single device. Since there is only one layer of security, any configuration errors or flaws in the firewall might allow firewall penetration. Remember, the first rule on any firewall is to drop any traffic directed at a firewall interface. This prevents mapping of the firewall.

In multiple-layer architecture, firewall functions are distributed between different devices, typically connected in a series, with a demilitarized zone (DMZ) network between them. A DMZ is your frontline when protecting valuables from direct exposure to an untrusted environment. It is sometimes referred to as a "perimeter network." The advantages of a multiple-layer design is that you have more than one layer to protect the intranet, and errors in a single firewall device won't open the whole network to attack. Although more expensive, using two different firewall devices is recommended to reduce risk of common implementation flaws or configuration errors. The disadvantages are cost and complexity.

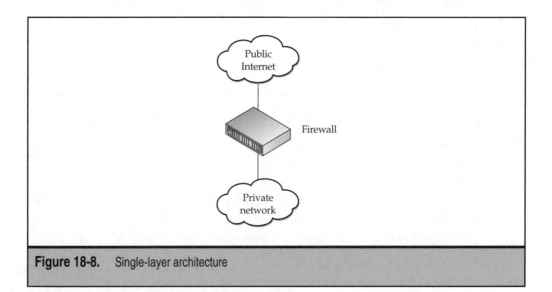

Figure 18-8. Single-layer architecture

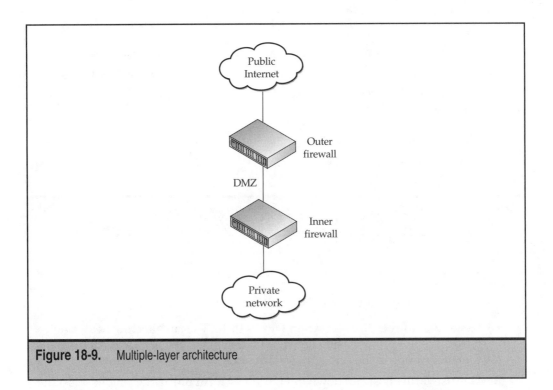

Figure 18-9.   Multiple-layer architecture

The next decision is to select firewall functions. Firewall functions include packet filtering, application proxies, and stateful inspection filtering. Many firewalls support all
three functions, and it is recommended to support multiple functions in your design.
Table 18-6 provides trade-off analysis of the three functions as defined by CERT
guidelines.

Function	Packet Filtering (PF)	Application Proxies (AP)	Stateful Inspection (SI) and Packet Filtering
Protocol/Service[a]	A	S	A
Security Requirements[b]	L	H	M

Table 18-6.   CERT Guidelines on Choosing Firewall Functions

Function	Packet Filtering (PF)	Application Proxies (AP)	Stateful Inspection (SI) and Packet Filtering
Performance/Scale Requirements[c]	H	L	M

a. A: any; S: only specific protocols or services

b. L, M, H: low, medium, high

c. L, M, H: low, medium, high

Table 18-6. CERT Guidelines on Choosing Firewall Functions *(continued)*

Firewall Topology

There are four common topologies of firewalls:

▼ Basic border firewall, as shown in Figure 18-10. This architecture has a single firewall connecting a trusted network and an untrusted network. All firewall functions reside in the single firewall device.

■ Untrustworthy host, as shown in Figure 18-11. An untrustworthy host is added to the network between the firewall and the untrusted network. The firewall is configured to require incoming and outgoing traffic to go through the

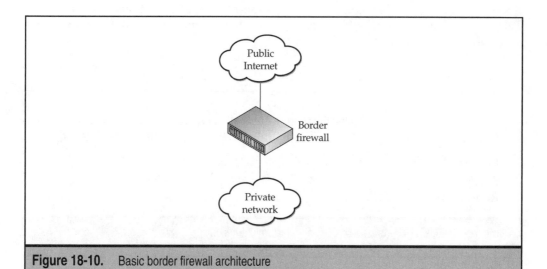

Figure 18-10. Basic border firewall architecture

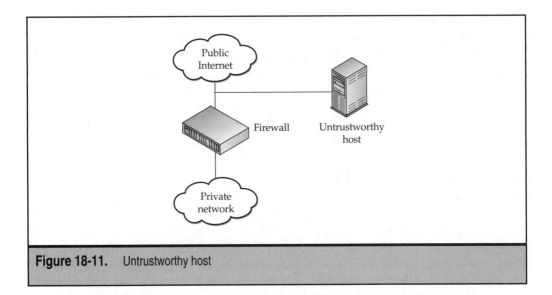

Figure 18-11. Untrustworthy host

untrustworthy host. The untrustworthy host is minimally configured and managed to be as secure as possible.

■ DMZ network, as shown in Figure 18-12. The untrustworthy host is brought "inside" the firewall but placed on a network by itself. The firewall has connectivity to three separate physical networks. The DMZ network increases

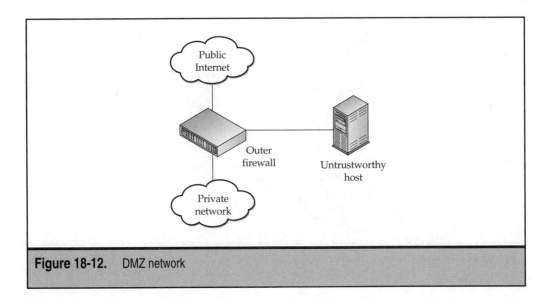

Figure 18-12. DMZ network

the security, reliability, and availability of the untrustworthy host. Additional untrustworthy hosts such as web servers and FTP servers can be placed on the DMZ network (often a 100 Mbps Ethernet LAN segment).

▲ Dual firewall with DMZ, as shown in Figure 18-13. The trusted network is further isolated from the untrusted network by a second firewall. Traffic from the trusted network to the untrusted network must transverse two firewalls. Using two different firewall products for the firewall is recommended to increase security by eliminating a possible firewall hole in one of the products.

Virtual Private Network (VPN) Design

Remote access and site-to-site VPN growth will continue at least over the next few years due to the cost and ubiquitous access of the Internet. With broadband access availability continuing to increase and more people interested in working from home, remote access VPN connectivity is a critical component of any network design. A VPN is an overlay network over a public network. The overlay is accomplished by creating a tunnel between two networks or machines so that traffic can be passed and also so that the data can be encrypted. This section covers cryptography fundamentals, VPN topologies, and different tunneling protocols.

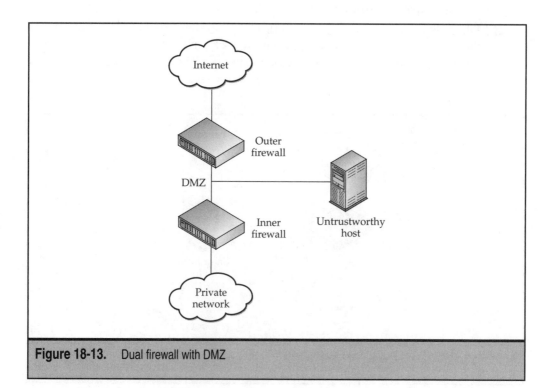

Figure 18-13.   Dual firewall with DMZ

Cryptography Fundamentals

Cryptography is defined as the process or skill of communicating in or deciphering secret writings. There are two kinds of cryptosystems:

▼ **Symmetric** Use the same secret key to encrypt and decrypt a message.

▲ **Asymmetric** Use public key to encrypt a message and a private key to decrypt it. Asymmetric cryptosystems are also called public key cryptosystems.

Encryption, key management, and authentication are the three fundamentals of cryptography. Encryption is the process of taking a code or key and encrypting a message. The key is analogous to a combination to a lock. The more numbers a given combination has, the more work that must be done to guess the combination. Selecting the appropriate key strength is critical to achieve your objective. Table 18-7 compares key strength and different threats based on 2000 technology to a brute-force attack. You might find the results surprising. A key size of 80 bits would take several years, even with an investment of hundreds of millions of dollars, so it is advised to select key lengths in excess of 128 bits. The trade-offs of implementing a larger key size are cost for the key solution and CPU usage.

Table 18-8 provides a list of current encryption algorithms as well as the new AES standard published in November 2001. When dealing with encryption algorithms, U.S. import/export laws might affect your use of these algorithms outside the U.S.

Threat	Budget	Technology	Time to Break 40 Bits	Time to Break 56 Bits
Hacker	Tiny	Scavenged time	1 week	Unfeasible unless distributed processing is used
Small business	$10,000	FPGA	12 min.	556 days
Corporation	$300,000	FPGA or ASIC	24 sec.	19 days
Big corporation	$10 million	FPGA or ASIC	7 sec.	13 hours
Government	$300 million	ASIC	.0002 sec	12 sec.

FPGA: field programmable gate array

ASIC: application-specific integrated circuit

Source: *Defending Your Digital Assets* by Nichols, Ryan, and Ryan

Table 18-7. Key Strength versus Attack Technology

Name of Algorithm	Block Size (bits)	Key Size (bits)
DES (Data Encryption Standard, IBM)	64	56
Skipjack (NSA, clipper chip, was classified)	64	80
3DES (Triple DES)	64	168
IDEA (Lai/Massey, ETH Zurich)	64	128
CAST (Canada)	64	128
Blowfish (Bruce Schneier)	64	128…448
RC2 (Ron Rivest, RSA)	64	40…1024
RC5 (Ron Rivest, RSA)	64…256	64…256
AES (Advanced Encryption Standard)	128	128, 192, 256

Table 18-8. Popular Data Encryptions

Key management is the process of how key information is transferred between the users. In secret-key cryptography, the secret key must be kept secret and entered into the end equipment to allow an encrypted tunnel to function. In public-key cryptography, each receiver publishes its public key. The key publishing has to be authenticated. Public-key encryption schemes use more CPU cycles than secret-key schemes.

Public key infrastructure (PKI) is defined by the Internet X.509 Public Key Infrastructure PKIX Roadmap document. The purpose of PKI is to provide trusted and efficient key and certificate management. PKI consists of five types of components:

▼ Certification authorities (CAs) that issue and revoke certificates. The best known CA is VeriSign

■ Organizational registration authorities (ORAs) that vouch for binding between public keys, certificate holder identities, and other attributes

■ Certificate holders that are issued certificates and that can sign digital documents

■ Clients that validate digital signatures and their certification paths from a public key of CA

▲ Repositories that store and make available certificates and certificate revocation lists (CRLs)

Authentication is the process of verifying the source is who they say they are. Authentication techniques guard against packet insertion, deletion, delay, and replay. The simplest form of authentication is your username and password used to connect to your VPN, but most VPNs use message authentication codes (MAC). MAC uses a hash function (SHA and MD5 are most common) that provides a digital signature or a fingerprint of the messages. Using the digital signature or fingerprint allows the receiver to authenticate the sender. As part of the authentication process, there are a number of protocols used for processing the authentication from Radius, TACACS, and Kerberos.

VPN Topologies

The three primary VPN topology options are

- ▼ **Mesh**   All VPN servers are interconnected. May be partial or full meshed.
- ■ **Star**   There is a central site VPN server and all remotes connect to the central site (also called "home-run").
- ▲ **Ring**   Each VPN server is connected to two neighbors.

In designing a VPN, a number of decisions are dictated by need, such as what type or types of VPN do you require: secure remote access, intranet, or extranet? Are you going to use a corporate backbone, which has some security, or an ISP backbone? Do remote sites require connectivity only to the HQ site or some or all remotes? Do you need to support remote users or remote sites or both?

In addition to answering topology questions, VPN server function can be purchased as a stand-alone or integrated into your firewall. A stand-alone VPN server is a higher security option because access to the VPN server can be managed by the firewall as well as the VPN server security. An integrated option might be less expensive and easier to implement without having to understand and support another product.

Figure 18-14 provides a high-level view a Global VPN that includes all three access types.

Tunnel Protocols

The four most common tunneling protocols are

- ▼ **Point-to-Point Tunneling Protocol (PPTP)**   PPTP is a protocol that allows PPP to be tunneled through an IP network. PPTP does not specify any changes to the PPP protocol, but rather is a vehicle for carrying PPP.
- ■ **Layer-2 Tunneling Protocol (L2TP)**   L2TP is a combination of Cisco Systems' Layer-2 Forwarding (L2F) and PPTP. L2TP supports any routed protocol and any WAN backbone technology. A key to L2TP is its use of PPTP, which is available in most Windows clients.
- ■ **Multi-Protocol Label Switching (MPLS)**   MPLS is a protocol for transporting various protocols over a Layer 2 network such as frame relay and ATM.
- ▲ **Internet Protocol Security (IPSec)**   IPSec is a suite of protocols that provide security features for IP VPNs. IPSec supports two encryption modes: Transport

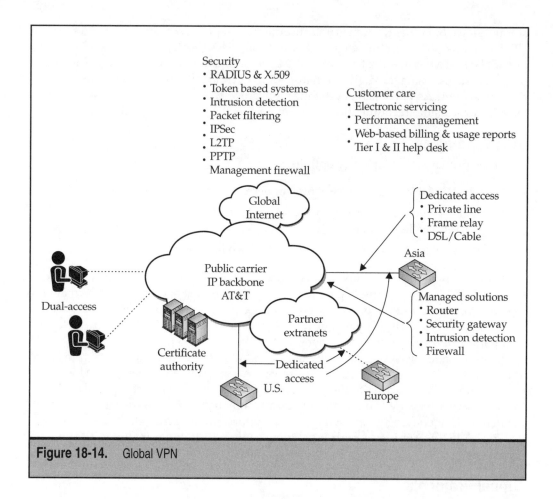

Figure 18-14. Global VPN

and Tunnel. Transport mode encrypts only the payload of each packet, leaving the header untouched. The more secure Tunnel mode encrypts both the header and the payload. On the receiving side, an IPSec-compliant device decrypts each packet.

Another protocol that requires discussion is Generic Routing Encapsulation (GRE) protocol. GRE is used with PPTP, L2F, and L2TP if IP packet authentication and confidentiality is required on top of the multiprotocol data tunnel. GRE is also used in IPSec environments when there is a requirement to encrypt and certain IP routing protocols such as OSPF and E-IGRP.

The selection of a tunnel protocol is driven by your network protocols. PPTP and L2TP are Layer 2 protocols that allow different protocols other than IP, such as Novell and Appletalk, to be transported in a tunnel across an IP network.

Intrusion Detection Systems

A critical and often missed component of network security are intrusion detection systems (IDS) and how they operate in both CPE- and network-based VPNs. Customer premise-based IDS can be both network-based and host-based.

Network-based IDS, as shown in Figure 18-15, are systems that reside on a network segment and monitor the inbound and outbound traffic on that segment using a network interface card (NIC) in promiscuous mode. In most cases, network-based IDS are handicapped if the enterprise operates in a switched environment. In a switched infrastructure, the IDS must use port spanning to monitor multiple segments (or use the IDS blade in the Cisco 6500-series catalyst switch). The network-based IDS examines each packet for evidence of hostile or suspicious activity. The examination is based on either knowledge (port signatures and string signatures) or anomalies (header signatures). If the IDS determines an attack is in progress, either it sends an alert or an action such as modifying the firewall rule set is performed to deny access from the offending address. Network-based IDSs may be connected to a common point, aggregation port, or a blade that is installed into a higher-end switch and monitors traffic at that point.

Host-based IDS, as shown in Figure 18-16, is software that resides on a device (typically a server) and keeps track of the unauthorized intrusion attempts and suspicious processes of that server, using log files or other auditing tools that reside on the server.

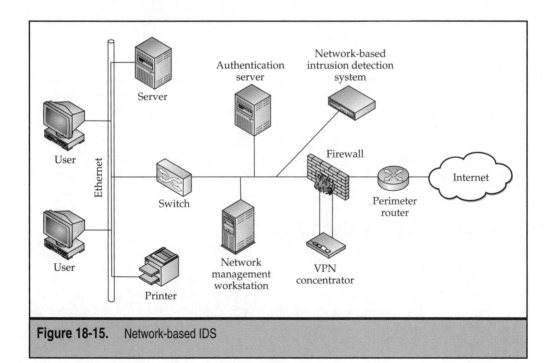

Figure 18-15.   Network-based IDS

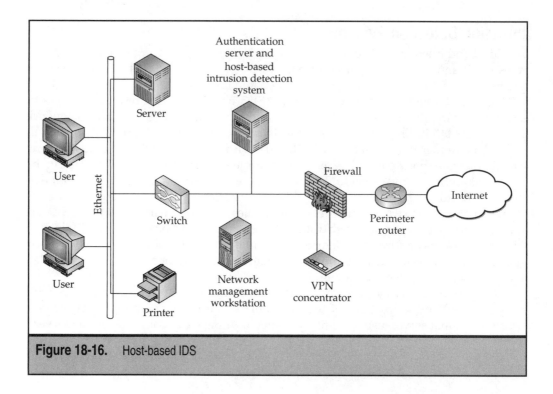

Figure 18-16.   Host-based IDS

The best method of security is to use a combination of the two types of IDS. Network-based IDSs can be susceptible to flooding, while a host-based IDS will not detect attacks on other devices. Signatures must be updated on a regular basis for the systems to detect newer attacks. An IDS on the internal network will also help in detecting internal threats to systems.

IDSs provide little value unless their activities are monitored and specified individuals react to their alerts. Based on the size of the network, the company might require 24×7×365 monitoring but, at a minimum, network alerts must be sent to someone who will act on them.

Performance and Design Considerations

In designing security for your network, there are a number of tradeoffs that need to be considered, including

▼ **Availability**   Understand the reliability of your vendors, and if Internet access is critical to your business, redundant internet "pipes" and firewalls might be required.

- ■ **Performance** Separating firewall functions and selecting hardware-based vendors with better throughput or multiple firewalls might be required.
- ▲ **Security** Dual firewall systems provide higher security but have a higher price point (benefits versus cost).
  - ■ If compromised, how will you recover?
  - ■ How will you monitor security? Regular checking of logs and automated notification of problems is a requirement.

In VPN designs, the key items to consider include

- ▼ If less than an 80-bit secret key is selected, you might be vulnerable.
- ■ Will you use a stand-alone VPN server or integrate it into the firewall?
- ▲ Select Authentication method that meets the level of security required. (Simple UserName/Password or MAC.)

REVIEW

This chapter provided an overview of issues that must be addressed to secure your network, focusing on five areas required to secure your network:

- ▼ History of security and network requirements
- ■ Security threats and safeguards
- ■ Strategic security design including the security policy
- ■ Firewall and VPN design
- ▲ Intrusion detection systems

The chapter also covered implementing a network security policy to specify the do's and don'ts along with the implementation of a security team to help educate, enforce, and react to security issues.

As a final note, remember that the majority of security threats originate within the network. Make sure that policies are in place to limit and monitor access to your network and servers. Also, implement policies to change passwords and access when there are changes in staff.

CHAPTER 19

Documentation and Network Management

Documentation is an often overlooked and neglected step in the design process, yet it is the most important for future cost control and effective network management. This chapter first covers documentation, then moves on to the critical and also often overlooked topic of network management. Our discussion of network management spans the technical details of Simple Network Management Protocol (SNMP) and Remote Monitoring (RMON). An analysis of network management is presented, covering the history of network management standards and detailing the three versions of SNMP and two versions of RMON protocol. Proper documentation requires both an engineering plan, which steps a user or manager through the how's and why's of the enterprise network design, and an operations and maintenance (O&M) manual, which explains how to run the network and defines the required support structure for both implementing and maintaining the network. The responsibilities of each department must be identified, and documenting each area helps ensure a successful design implementation. Outsourcing and out-tasking options are explored as a method of lowering cost while improving network reliability and performance.

Finally, some soul searching must be done to decide when to exercise some constraint. At this point, we must stop designing and start implementing the network.

BACKGROUND

Network management standards have a history involving three standards organizations: Internet Engineering Task Force (IETF); International Organization for Standardization (ISO), which developed the OSI standards; and the International Telecommunications Union (ITU-T). Marshall Rose and Jeffrey Case are two individuals who were driving forces in the development of SNMP and are still active today in standards development.

Modern network management history began in the early 1980s when the ISO started to work on a network management standard and architecture. Around 1987, the Internet was growing rapidly and required a network management architecture and protocol to help manage the network. A group in the IETF determined that the ISO effort wasn't going to be able to provide a standard in the required time, so they developed an interim solution termed SNMP which was based roughly on the ISO work and Simple Gateway Monitoring Protocol (SGMP). This SNMP effort was intended to be only a stopgap measure until the ISO completed their effort. SNMP borrowed the ideas of manager/agent, ASN.1 encoding, and MIBs from the ISO development. As if two efforts were not enough, the ITU-T started development on the Telecommunications Management Network (TMN) framework and published its recommendation in 1988.

Frustration grew at the pace and direction of the ISO effort, and new ideas entered the process in the late 1980s and changed the direction of the development effort. In addition, the TMN effort discovered that there was a large body of work already existing in the ISO, so the two groups were able to come together and the TMN group published a revised publication in 1990, which used much of the ISO effort.

The ISO defined five generic functional areas for network management:

▼ Fault
■ Configuration
■ Accounting
■ Performance
▲ Security

The ISO original vision was that there would be five protocols, with one protocol for each functional area, but the ISO was able to develop the Common Management Information Protocol (CMIP) and Common Management Information Service (CMIS) to support all five functional areas.

So the battle was on between SNMP, which was an interim solution to support fault- and performance-management areas, but which lacked security, and the CMIP/CMIS standard, which covered work by both the TMN ITU-T and the ISO. As Internet growth exploded in the early 1990s, SNMP deployments in devices became ubiquitous and the management protocol of choice. The result was that when the CMIP/CMIS standard finally became ratified, many did not want to spend the money to upgrade devices. Plus both the vendor and user community had become comfortable with the more simplistic yet less expensive and more ubiquitous SNMP. So SNMP was here to stay (again, cheap and easy!). The TMN standard has been adopted in public voice networks, but public and private data networks use SNMP almost exclusively.

The initial SNMP standard known as SNMPv1 did not support appropriate security, so the IETF working group began work on SNMPv2 to fix the problem. SNMPv2 was commercialized but never became widely accepted, so a new group in the IETF published and approved the SNMPv3 set of standards. Only time will tell if SNMPv3 is fully accepted or not.

Following the SNMP framework, RMON standards were developed in the early 1990s to provide a method for collecting detailed information about remote networks such as LANs.

Before getting into designing a network management solution, we will cover an understanding of the players and required documentation.

ORGANIZATIONAL RESPONSIBILITIES

To achieve success in a network design and implementation, many groups within the company must participate to gain consensus on design and drive toward implementation. Active participation from all groups ensures a smooth implementation and continued operation of the network. These group responsibilities are only guidelines, as many of these groups fall under a single engineering or operations organization. The following list shows the major groups involved in a network:

▼ **Planning** Provides future architecture direction based on business direction, plans on how future services will integrate and on which technology platforms they will ride, and design concepts for engineering.

■ **Network engineering** Performs engineering of network from the user requirements through the desktop, server, LAN, access and backbone WAN design. This includes the initial design and continued engineering support after the network is operational. Capacity is forecasted and operations metrics are established.

■ **Systems engineering** Provides the same service as engineering, but for the software, control systems, and network management of the network, with more of a software and services orientation to ensure interoperability. The prime difference could be having the information systems (IS) group responsible for the software and applications infrastructure, and the information technology or internal telecommunications (IT) group responsible for the hardware and network infrastructure.

■ **Order entry/order provisioning (OE/OP)** Orders the required access and backbone circuits and services, tracks circuit orders to completion, notifies the user of potential jeopardy, and provisions the required circuits and services.

■ **Network administration** Provides all node, circuit, address, and other administrative responsibilities for the network, including configuration management, database management, security administration, and performance reporting.

■ **Billing** Handles the generation of billing to the customer or paying the bills as a customer for the network transport, access, hardware, software, and any other cost aspect of the network. Also performs billing reconciliation.

■ **Operations** Reviews the network design; installs the network devices (hardware and software); performs the operations, maintenance, performance monitoring, preventive engineering, and network management of the network once it is installed, including support structure for trouble reporting and trouble management to vendors and customers based on performance metrics.

■ **Testing** Tests and troubleshoots all applications on the network-access devices as well as over the backbone, provides component to system end-to-end network testing, and certifies vendor hardware and software releases. Includes prototyping.

■ **Training** Ensures all support personnel are trained on all network systems, and trains users on the network applications and services.

■ **Program and project management** Manages the project resources from design conception through implementation (entire life cycle) and maintains overall responsibility for the project and the budget. Most importantly, program management gets the buy-in and cooperation early on from all support groups listed previously in the project and manages their interdependencies. Figure 19-1 shows average project cycles, from technology that rapidly becomes obsolete (curves A and B) to newer technologies (curve C).

▲   **Security**   The security audit and management function should be separate from the network design and implementation teams.

DOCUMENTATION

Documentation is one of the most important steps in the network design process. Documentation helps people understand a design created sometime in the past, allows them to remember the assumptions made during the design, and allows them to keep a record of updates and modifications to that design. It should be an ongoing process, and never an afterthought. Both designer and user suffer from poor documentation. It must be developed as a joint consensus during the network design project.

The four primary documents required to support a network design are the business case document, the user specifications and acceptance document, the engineering plan,

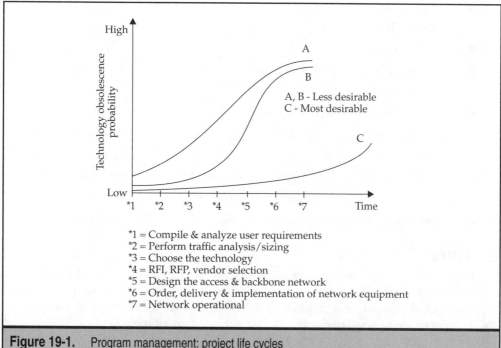

Figure 19-1.   Program management: project life cycles

and the O&M manual. The first two documents must be completed before the design begins. The business case document will map the business mission, vision, goals, objectives, and specific requirements to that of the three-to-five-year IT/IS mission, vision, goals, objectives, and specific requirements. The business case will then go on to define the cost justification for the current and future network design. The user specifications and acceptance document will define the requirements of the cars, buses, emergency vehicles, and other traffic that will transit the network; the network will be the highway system designed to support this traffic. The engineering plan is developed throughout the design and distributed when the design is completed. The O&M manual will be distributed after network design completion, but it requires specific inputs from the engineering plan.

Engineering Plan

The engineering plan explains the history behind your present connectivity, the reasons for the network design, what the network will support and why it needs support, and the entire design from application to backbone connectivity. Of course, it should include everything discussed in this book about design. Capacity planning could also be included in the plan, or it could be a separate document.

Specific information in the engineering plan includes

▼ Requirements matrix
■ Design assumptions and constraints
■ Node configuration
■ Circuit diagrams
■ Physical and logical configurations
■ Site-specific information
■ Bridge/router/hub/switch/gateway/ID addressing
■ Segment/port name/ID address plan and design
■ Serial and model numbers
■ LAN/MAN/WAN addressing (for example, Ethernet, E.164, and TCP/IP)
■ Current software and firmware version level
▲ Technology and service details—PL, FR, ATM, IP, MPLS, and so on

O&M Manual

The O&M manual presents all information required to install and maintain the network. Many sections of O&M are taken directly from the engineering plan, and many sections represent standard operating procedures for installing and maintaining network equipment. Some of the topics represented in the O&M document include

▼ System/network description
■ Physical/topological description

- Logical/functional description
- Design of network (reference design document)
- Budgetary impacts
- System/network administration
- OE/OP procedures
- Network management procedures
- Installation and testing
- Billing procedures
- Support structure and escalation procedures
- Hardware/software maintenance and sparing
- Test equipment requirements
- Training
- Vendor-specific documentation
- ▲ Glossary, acronyms, and references

At the site-specific level, the details provided include

- ▼ Installation power and grounds
- Implementation and cut-over
- Naming and addressing conventions
- Device-specific wiring
- Device-specific testing
- Floor plan construction
- Layout of SAN/CAN/LAN/MAN/WAN
- Topology
- Device locations
- Shared resources locations
- Network management/administration locations
- ▲ Maintenance schedules

OAM&P

Operations, administration, maintenance, and provisioning (OAM&P) functions form the cornerstones of managing a network. First, we will look at the OAM&P functional model for insight into the key areas of operations. Next, each area is defined, followed by a study of centralized versus distributed management.

OAM&P Functional Model

One of the best examples of a network management functional model is the OAM&P model, as shown in Figure 19-2.

▼ **Operations** involve the day-to-day, and often minute-to-minute, care and feeding of the data network in order to ensure that it is fulfilling its designed purpose. It also involves comparing measured performance against objectives and taking corrective action and/or invoking maintenance. These objectives are often mapped to service provider service-level agreements (SLAs).

■ **Administration** involves the set of activities involved with designing the network, processing orders, assigning addresses, tracking usage, change management, and accounting.

■ **Maintenance** involves the inevitable circumstances that arise when everything does not work as planned or when it is necessary to diagnose what went wrong and repair it. It also includes preventive measures.

▲ **Provisioning** involves installing equipment and facilities, setting parameters, and verifying that the service is operational. It also includes deinstallation.

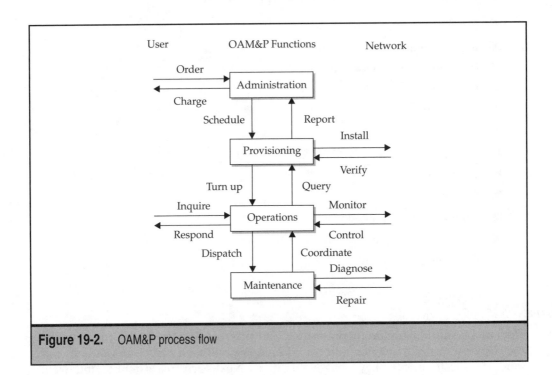

Figure 19-2. OAM&P process flow

Centralized versus Distributed Network Management

When designing your network, it is important to consider how the network management system (NMS) affects operational philosophy. A key decision is whether to adopt a centralized or distributed NMS architecture for managing network elements (NEs), as depicted in Figure 19-3.

Some will opt for a centralized approach with the expertise concentrated at one or, at most, a few locations with remote site support for only the basic physical actions, such as installing the equipment, making physical connections to interfaces, and replacing cards. In this approach, the software updates, configurations, and troubleshooting can be done by experts at the central site. The centralized approach requires that the requisite network management functions defined in the previous section be well developed, highly available, and effective.

Others might have only a few sites, and hence they might want to have expertise at every site. This approach might be required if the NMS is not sophisticated or the equipment has a number of actions that can be done only at the site. Some lower-level, well-

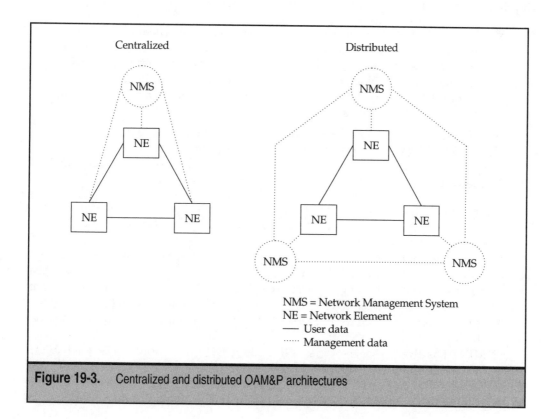

Figure 19-3.   Centralized and distributed OAM&P architectures

defined automated functions are best performed in a distributed manner. Most RMON and LAN management is performed in a distributed manner.

SNMP

SNMP is based on three concepts: managers, agents, and the management information base (MIB). Simple network management covers the following key elements:

▼ **Which information is interesting** The objective is to get standardization of the form and meaning of information stored across many different vendors' products.

■ **What to name it** You need the name of an item to ask for it.

▲ **How to get it or change it** SNMP is a protocol defined to get and change an item.

SNMP uses the Internet-Standard Management Model to examine device data and update configuration and status information. This model defines two types of entities:

▼ **Agent** The agent is software located on each device, which receives incoming messages from the manager. The messages from the manager either request read or write operations on the device's data. The agent software receives the messages and sends response messages back to the manager. A TRAP (notification message) can be sent from the agent without a request to notify the manager of a serious or significant event.

▲ **Manager** The manager is software located on a management station that collects information from the agent and can display TRAP information. The purpose of the management station is to provide status on the health of the network and notification of problems or significant events.

Figure 19-4 shows the interworking of the manager and agent. It should be noted that a typical network might have a single manager and many agents, as every PC, router, switch, and so on has an agent.

Located on each device is a MIB, which can be considered a database of information. A MIB is defined as a logical database made up of the configuration, status, and statistical information stored at each device. There are standard MIBs, such as MIB I, defined in RFC 1156, and MIB II, defined in RFC 1213, which provide information for TCP/IP networks. Also, many vendors have implemented vendor-specific extensions into their devices' MIB structures.

SNMPv1 has five messages types: GET REQUEST (or simply GET), GET NEXT REQUEST (or simply GET NEXT), SET REQUEST (or simply SET), RESPONSE, and TRAP (which is like an alarm). The SET, GET, and GET NEXT messages are all replied to by the RESPONSE message. A GET is issued from an SNMP management station to an

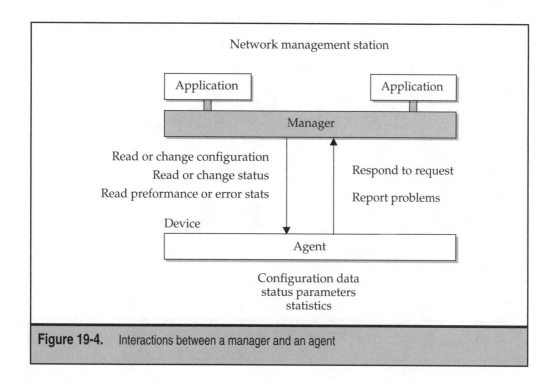

Figure 19-4.   Interactions between a manager and an agent

SNMP agent within an SNMP-managed device. The TRAP message is very important since it is the notification of an unexpected event, such as a failure or a system restart.

Figure 19-5 shows the messages types communicated between the manager and agent when using SNMPv1 and shows the MIB or database that is located on each device. The messages are transported between the agent and manager using UDP, which is connectionless and unreliable. Why choose an unreliable protocol and not TCP? UDP was chosen over TCP because UDP is well suited for small request and response messages. TCP requires three messages to set up a connection and four messages to disconnect a connection; it requires more memory and CPU to support a TCP stack. The SNMP manager sends GET, GET NEXT, and SET messages to the agent using UDP port 161 and the agent sends TRAP messages to the managers using UDP port 162.

MIB Structure

Understanding the basic structure of a MIB will be helpful in getting information out of a MIB. SNMP uses a subset of Abstract Syntax Notation 1 (ASN.1) to define a MIB as a data structure that can be referenced in SNMP messages. The syntax of these messages is specified in the Structure of Management Information (SMI) RFC 1155. SNMP network managers access each MIB through a function called a *proxy agent*. The MIB defines objects in terms of primitives such as strings, integers, and bit maps, and allows a simple form of

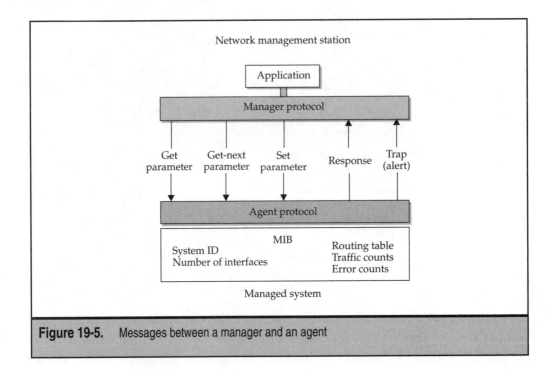

Figure 19-5.   Messages between a manager and an agent

indexing. Each object has a name, syntax, and an encoding. The MIB variables have a textual object identifier (OID), which is commonly used to refer to the objects. The MIB objects are defined in a tree structure that allows organizational ownership of subtrees to be defined. A dotted decimal notation identifies the branches of the tree. For example, the prefix of the subtree registered to the ATM Forum is 1.3.6.1.4.1.353. Each of the other branches is identified by the decimal number assigned to the OID as defined in the ATM Forum UNI specification version 3.0.

Each MIB object has the following components:

▼   A unique name, OID. An OID is a string of numbers derived from a global naming tree, used to identify an object

■   Attributes such as data type, description including details required to build, and status information

▲   Valid operations that can be performed on the object (read, write, set)

The formal template used to define MIB is shown in Figure 19-6 and specified in RFC 1213.

Figure 19-7 shows the global naming tree for ISO/ITU, which is the basis for generating the unique object identifier.

Figure 19-8 shows the MIB-II tree structure. It should be noted that MIB-II originally had 11 groups, but Common Management Information Services and Protocol over

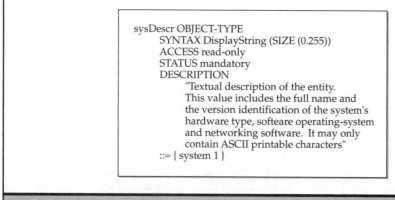

```
sysDescr OBJECT-TYPE
        SYNTAX DisplayString (SIZE (0.255))
        ACCESS read-only
        STATUS mandatory
        DESCRIPTION
                "Textual description of the entity.
                This value includes the full name and
                the version identification of the system's
                hardware type, softeare operating-system
                and networking software.  It may only
                contain ASCII printable characters"
        ::= { system 1 }
```

Figure 19-6.   Formal template

TCP/ IP (CMOT) is not used anymore because the project was abandoned based on the success of SNMP. As you follow down the tree, iso_org_dod_internet_mgmt_ mib-2_interfaces_ifTable_ifEntry_ifOperStatus might describe 1.3.6.1.2.1.2.2.1.8, and 1.3.6.1.2.1.2.2.1.8.2 might represent interface 2.

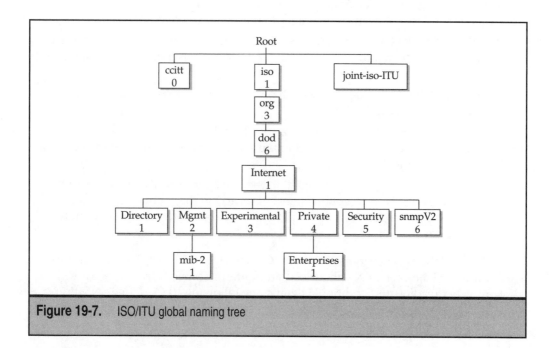

Figure 19-7.   ISO/ITU global naming tree

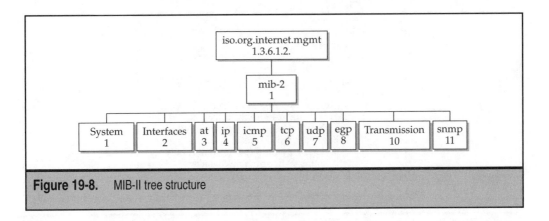

Figure 19-8. MIB-II tree structure

SNMPv1

Even with the development of SNMPv2 and SNMPv3, many vendors still support only SNMPv1. So it is safe to predict that SNMPv1 will continue to dominate the market for many years. The driving force in moving to SNMPv3 is primarily security, because SNMPv1 is vulnerable to DOS attacks and also passes clear text passwords. This one benefit alone might accelerate the move to SNMPv3.

There are five commands in SNMPv1:

▼ **GET REQUEST**   Fetches a value from a specific object by name. This command is sent from the manager to the agent to collect specific information.

■ **GET NEXT REQUEST**   Fetches a value without knowing the objects exact name. This command is used to walk a tree of objects and is sent from the manager.

■ **GET RESPONSE**   Reply to a fetch operation. The agent responds to the manager's request.

■ **SET REQUEST**   Store a value in a specific object. This command is sent from a manager to configure an object in the end device. Set commands are used in configuring the device remotely.

▲ **TRAP**   Message sent by the agent to the manager to notify the manager of a specific event. Trap reception is not confirmed so the agent does not know if the manager has received the trap. Agents can be configured to send more than a single trap.

SNMPv1 defines seven types of traps: Coldstart, Warmstart, Linkdown, Linkup, Authentication Failure, EGPNeighborloss, and Enterprisespecifictrap.

For further reading and additional details, the following RFCs define SNMP:

▼ **RFC 1155** "Structure and Identification of Management Information for TCP/IP-based Internets," which describes how management information has been structured in a global tree, lays down some restrictions to keep the protocol simple, and introduces the rules for assigning names to objects.

■ **RFC 1212** "Concise MIB Definitions," which improves on the definition techniques defined in RFC 1155

■ **RFC 1213** "Management Information Base for Network Management of TCP/IP-based Internets: MIB-II," which specifies the second addition of a MIB to manage a TCP/IP network

▲ **RFC 1157** "A Simple Network Management Protocol (SNMP)," which defines the message formats and interaction of messages between the manager and agent

SNMPv2

The main problems with SNMPv1 include authentication of the message source, protecting these messages from disclosure, and placing access controls on the MIB database. SNMPv2 tried to solve these problems, but made significant changes to the messages format that increased the complexity and size of implementations. SNMPv2 acceptance in the market has been limited, or stated differently, SNMPv2 remains alive partly because the original objectives of SNMPv1 weren't completely met.

SNMPv2 security framework recommends use of the Digest Authentication Protocol. This protocol is based on the message digest to authenticate message source and prevent message tampering. In addition to the authentication protocol to verify the source, encryption is supported to keep the messages private.

SNMPv2 added two commands to the initial five commands of SNMPv1, both focused on improving management system scalability:

▼ **INFORM REQUEST** This command enables a manager to send some information to another manager, which allows managers to share trap information. As networks continue to grow, this command allows a network management hierarchy of manager stations.

▲ **GET BULK REQUEST** This command allows the manager to retrieve as much data as is possible in a response message from the agent. The command can retrieve stand-alone scalar variables and/or columns from a table. This request alleviates the limitation from SNMPv1, whereas if an agent received a request that was more than could be returned due to agent limitations or network packet size, the agent would return an error message of "too big" without data.

More details on SNMPv2 can be found in RFC 1901, 1902, 1903, 1904, 1905, 1906, 1907, and 1908.

SNMPv3

SNMPv3 builds upon SNMPv1 and the work done in the SNMPv2 standards and corrects the security deficiencies of both SNMPv1 and SNMPv2. SNMPv3 standards, as shown in Table 19-1, were proposed standards in 1998 and approved as full standards in April of 2002.

SNMPv3 provides three important services, as shown in Figure 19-9, which are authentication, privacy, and access control. SNMPv3 introduces the concept of a principal. RFC 2271 defines

A principal is the "who" on whose behalf services are provided or processing takes place. A principal can be, among other things, an individual acting in a particular role; a set of individuals, with each acting in a particular role; an application or a set of applications and combinations thereof.

A principal operates a management station and issues SNMP commands to agents. The identity of the principal and target agent together determine the security features that will be invoked, including authentication, privacy, and access control, as shown in Figure 19-9. Security policies can now be designed to specific principals, and agents and specify the information exchanged. This provides the capability of assigning different levels of authorization or views to different users.

The SNMP entity, as shown in Figure 19-10, is an implementation of SNMPv3, and each such entity consists of a single SNMP engine and one or more associated applications. An

RFC Number	Title
2271	An Architecture for Describing SNMP Management Frameworks
2272	Message Processing and Dispatching for the Simple Network Management Protocol (SNMP)
2273	SNMPv3 Applications
2274	User-Based Security Model for SNMPv3
2275	View-Based Access Control Model (VACM) from SNMP

Table 19-1. SNMPv3 RFCs

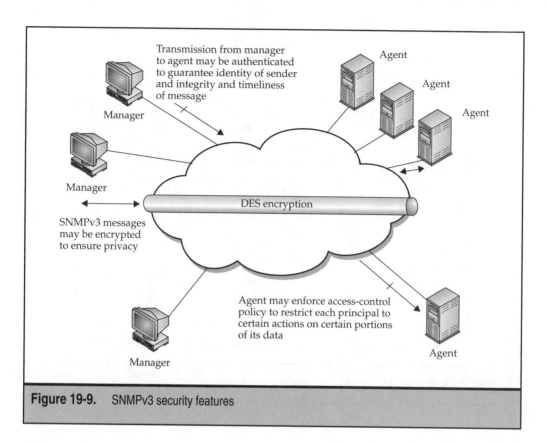

Transmission from manager
to agent may be authenticated
to guarantee identity of sender
and integrity and timeliness
of message

Manager

Agent

Agent

Agent

Manager

DES encryption

SNMPv3 messages
may be encrypted
to ensure privacy

Agent may enforce access-control
policy to restrict each principal to
certain actions on certain portions
of its data

Agent

Manager

Figure 19-9.   SNMPv3 security features

SNMP engine implements functions for sending and receiving messages, authenticating and encrypting/decrypting messages, and controlling access to managed objects. These functions are provided as services to one or more applications that are configured with the SNMP engine to form an SNMP entity. The modular architecture of SNMPv3 provides the following advantages:

▼   The modules that are implemented determine the role of an SNMP entity. An SNMP entity can be an agent based on certain modules and a manager based on other modules.

▲   The specification lends itself to defining different versions of each module. This provides architecture for enhanced capabilities versus a new version and allows different versions such as SNMPv1 and SNMPv3 to coexist.

Table 19-2 provides a brief description of each module shown in Figure 19-10.

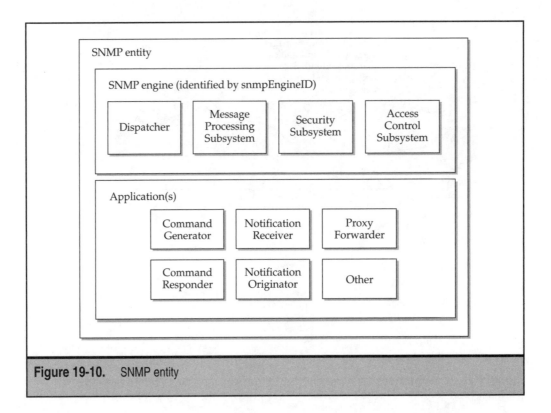

Figure 19-10.   SNMP entity

SNMPv3 Component	Description
Dispatcher	Allows for concurrent support of multiple versions of SNMP messages in the SNMP engine. It is responsible for (1) accepting protocol data units (PDUs) from applications for transmission over the network and delivering incoming PDUs to applications; (2) passing outgoing PDUs to the message processing subsystem to prepare as messages, and passing incoming messages to the message processing subsystem to extract the incoming PDUs; and (3) sending and receiving SNMP messages over the network.

Table 19-2.   SNMPv3 Components of an SNMP Entity

SNMPv3 Component	Description
Message processing subsystem	Responsible for preparing messages for sending and for extracting data from received messages.
Security subsystem	Provides security services such as the authentication and privacy of messages. This subsystem potentially contains multiple security models. The security subsystem should protect against the four principal threats: modification of information, masquerade, message stream modification, and disclosure.
Access control subsystem	Provides a set of authorization services that an application can use for checking access rights. Access control can be invoked for retrieval or modification request operations and for notification-generation operations.
Command generator	Initiates SNMP GET, GET NEXT, GET BULK, or SET REQUEST PDUs and processes the response to a request that it has generated.
Command responder	Receives SNMP GET, GET NEXT, GET BULK, or SET REQUEST PDUs destined for the local system as indicated by the fact that the contextEngineID in the received request is equal to that of the local engine through which the request was received. The command responder application performs the appropriate protocol operation, using access control, and generates a response message to be sent to the originator of the request.
Notification originator	Monitors a system for particular events or conditions, and generates Trap or inform messages based on these events or conditions. A notification orginator must have a mechanism for determining where to send messages, and which SNMP version and security parameters to use when sending messages.
Notification receiver	Listens for notification messages, and generates response messages when a message containing an Inform PDU is received.
Proxy forwarder	Forwards SNMP messages. Implementation of a proxy forwarder application is optional.

Table 19-2.   SNMPv3 Components of an SNMP Entity *(continued)*

Deciding on implementing SNMPv3 will be determined by device support of SNMPv3 and the support of your manager software along with the upgrade cost. HP Openview, the industry-leading SNMP manager, can interact with SNMPv3 as of Network Node Manager (NMM) version 5.01 and 6.X, but requires a third-party Security pack to support SNMPv3 security features. The security vulnerabilities of SNMPv1 will probably force many enterprises to upgrade to v3. Since IETF approved SNMPv3 as a full standard in April of 2002, the IETF also moved SNMPv1 and SNMPv2 to historical status, which means that there will be no additional development on those standards.

RMON

RMON is a method of collecting and analyzing information from remote NEs. RMON provides the information required to determine where to place the boundaries between collision and broadcast domains, functions provided by LAN switches and routers, respectively. An RMON agent attached to a local network element captures information and statistics on protocols and traffic activity and communicates the information back, sometimes formatted, to a central RMON management console for processing. RMON probes (dedicated RMON agents) and other RMON agents provide this data when polled. They send TRAPs only to alert the console of a condition but do not send significant data via these TRAPs.

RMON is especially critical when managing a switched LAN environment, because LAN segments, which previously served many users, are now micro segmented (splitting large single-segment LANs into multiple LAN segments, each with fewer hosts per segment). This micro segmentation creates more segments to manage, closer to the user. RMON extends the visibility into these micro segmented LANs, providing traffic analysis at the packet level along with trending capability for performance engineering. When extended to the VLAN environment, physical and logical topology design can be optimized. Remote LAN troubleshooting can be performed proactively, with the engineer using RMON reports to look for things that are abnormal based on threshold criteria.

RMON probes can provide a great deal of information on the performance of your LAN and WAN, capturing protocol traffic patterns that enable trending of protocol performance. This information is especially critical when migrating from a routed environment to a switched one. The engineer can then optimize the switched or LAN topology. Most importantly, RMON allows the network manager to provide bounding between the collision (MAC) and broadcast (IP/ARP) domains.

RMON can be justified if the application performance on a specific portion of the network is mission critical. RMON can catch utilization patterns that are exceeding thresholds and alert the engineer to take action. All of this monitoring can be done remotely, and thus eliminates the need for on-site LAN managers to watch LAN performance, while providing proactive management alerts of potential network outages. Figure 19-11 illustrates a network where remote SNMP devices are monitored through an SNMP management platform. An RMON probe is also placed on the Ethernet LAN.

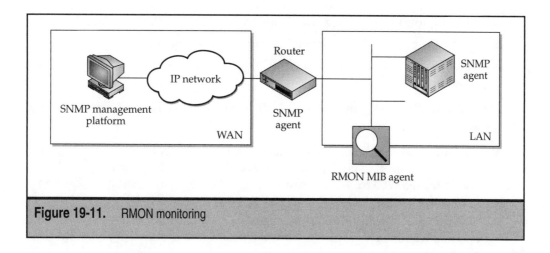

Figure 19-11. RMON monitoring

RMON standards began with RFC 1098, which defined SNMP in 1989, and was later standardized in 1994 as RFC 2222. The first RMON specification—RFC 1271—was developed in 1994. RFC 1757 was next specified defining the RMON 10 groups, and is the standard used today. RMON2 specifies enhancements to the original RMON RFC. RMON groups operate at the MAC layer, while the newer RMON2 groups operate at the network layer and above.

RFC 1757 defines 10 RMON groups, where each group collects information on variables and sends it back to the central management station for analysis. These groups include

▼ **Statistics**   Maintains error and utilization statistics for the specific LAN segment or subnetwork being monitored by the RMON agent. Some examples include CRC/alignment, fragments, multicast, broadcast, and bandwidth utilization.

■ **History**   Obtains statistical samples, such as packet count, error count, and utilization and stores them for later retrieval. This also includes a history of conspicuous statistics.

■ **Alarm**   Administration control of sampling interval and threshold for any variable monitored by the RMON agent. Some examples include absolute or relative values and rising or falling thresholds.

■ **Host**   Host traffic measurements such as packets or bytes sent and received, errors, multicast, and broadcasts.

■ **Host TopN**   Reporting on top *N* hosts statistics.

■ **Traffic Matrix**   Stores the errors and statistics (packets, bytes, and errors) between source and destination nodes on a network.

■ **Filter**   Provides a filter engine for packet recognition.

- ■ **Packet Capture**   Buffering criteria for packets that match filter criteria.
- ■ **Event**   Time- and date-stamped logging and printing of events.
- ▲ **Token Ring**   Configuration and statistical information on source routing and stations on a ring.

RMON2 provides new groups that operate at the network layer and higher. These groups include

- ▼ **Network and Application Layer Host**   Statistics for each network address and each application-layer protocol on the segment or ring, such as packets and bytes received for Layer 3 traffic (not just Layer 2) and port number of an application, respectively.
- ■ **Network and Application Layer Matrix**   Traffic statistics at the network and application-layer protocols between source and destination nodes on a network.
- ■ **Protocol Directory**   User-selectable protocols that are monitored and counted.
- ■ **Protocol Distribution**   Table of statistics for each protocol in directory.
- ■ **User Definable History**   Sampling of any MIB object monitored by the RMON agent.
- ■ **Address Mapping**   Listing of MAC to network-layer address bindings such as with ARP.
- ▲ **Configuration Group**   Listing of RMON agent configurations and capabilities.

DESIGNING A NETWORK MANAGEMENT SOLUTION

Now that we have an understanding of SNMP, RMON, and group responsibilities, we can take the next step of beginning the design of a network management solution. TMN and ISO standards were touched on early in this chapter in the background section, but reviewing ISO's five functional areas, as shown in Table 19-4, and TMN's management/responsibility layers, as shown in Table 19-3, is warranted. These areas provide the view of what network management encompasses. Figure 19-12 shows a visual representation of the relationship between TMN and ISO groupings.

Understanding your network, level of expertise of operational personnel, and your budget are a few areas that will drive your design of a network management system.

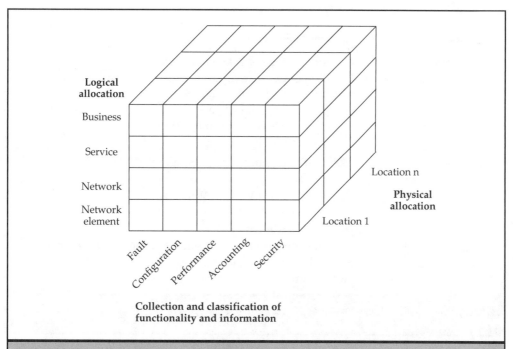

Figure 19-12.   Visual relationship of the TMN logical layers and ISO's functional areas

Layers	Examples of Functions
Element management	-Detection of equipment errors -Measuring power consumption, resources such as CPU and temperature of equipment -Logging statistical data -Updating firmware

Table 19-3.   TMN's Management/Responsibility Layers

Layers	Examples of Functions
Network management	-Creation of the complete network view -Creation of dedicated paths through the network for QoS -Modification of routing tables -Monitoring of link utilization -Optimizing network performance -Detection of faults
Service management	-QoS Management (delay, loss, jitter) Accounting -Addition and removal of users -Address management -Maintenance of group addresses
Business management	-Responsible for the management of the whole enterprise -Strategies and implementation of policies -Goal setting

Table 19-3. TMN's Management/Responsibility Layers *(continued)*

Functional Areas	Description
Fault management	Provides facilities that allow network managers to discover faults in network and determine their cause and take remedial action.
Configuration management	Monitors network configuration information so that the effects of specific hardware and software can be managed and tracked. It provides the ability to initialize, reconfigure, operate and shut down managed devices.
Accounting management	Measures network utilization of individual users or groups to provide billing information, regulate users or group, and keep network performance at an acceptable level.

Table 19-4. ISO's Key Functional Areas

Functional Areas	Description
Performance management	Measures various aspects of network performance including the gathering and analysis of statistical data about the system so that it can be maintained at an acceptable level. Includes utilization and error reports by device.
Security management	Controls access to network resources so that information cannot be obtained without authorization. Includes limiting access to network resources and providing notification of security breaches and attempts.

Table 19-4.   ISO's Key Functional Areas *(continued)*

Network management design for an enterprise network will be much different than for a service provider network that will support public service offerings. In a service provider design, understanding order entry and billing, as previously discussed in the OAM&P section, will be critical for all of the systems to communicate effectively. For an internal corporate enterprise network, the key NMS objectives include monitoring and measuring reliability, performance, security, and costs. The level of expertise of the operational personnel and budget will determine whether complete graphical and intelligent rule systems are worth the effort and money, and to what extent middleware correlation and interpretation tools can be developed or purchased. This is an area that is typically overpromised and under delivered, so beware.

As in the model of SNMP, keep it simple. Drive your network vendors to support SNMP and eliminate, if possible, vendor specific element managers. Remember, many vendors' products have element managers for configuration. As SNMP is an in-band network management protocol in that it rides the same network as it is managing, set up a backdoor or dedicated dial-backup solution so that you can troubleshoot the network versus dispatching or calling remote personnel after hours.

The typical network management architecture consists of the following NEs:

▼ **Network management (NM) stations**   NM stations run the NM application which gathers managed device information and typically polls the devices via an IP address to make sure that they are alive. The NM station should be able to gather large amounts of information and provide trending reports to see real or potential problems. The NM station should have the ability for proactive pager, e-mail, and other messaging alarm or event notification methods based on certain events to allow troubleshooting of problems in the off-hours and also not require operational personnel to be continually monitoring the system.

■ **Managed devices** A managed device such as a router, switch, printer, or PC is any device that contains a NM agent that the NM station can receive information and status from.

■ **Management agents** Software running on a managed device that provides information such as statistics and trap notification of problems about the managed device.

■ **NM protocols** In data networks, the protocol will typically be SNMP but you might come across some of the other NM protocols, such as CMIP.

▲ **Management information** This is the information that is collected from a management agent about the managed device. This is an area that requires some expertise and time to collect useful information from the device versus everything or nothing. If you are running an IP network, you can poll MIB-II information, however, to see performance requires using vendor-specific MIBs and loading these MIBs into your network management system. Don't just pull the whole MIB; rather, try to understand what information you want to track because you don't want to be moving more network management traffic than actual data.

When selecting a network management system, here are a few areas to understand:

▼ **Protocols** Make sure that SNMP is supported and understand the road map to SNMPv3.

■ **Openness** Understand how easy it is to add vendor-specific element managers for configuration into the system and vendor-specific MIBs. Also, connectivity from a NM system into a database might allow easy data analysis and enhanced reporting capability.

■ **Scalability** How many devices can be pulled in a 15/5/1 minute interval? If you have a large number of devices, how will you be notified? Many systems become overloaded or unusable as the network grows larger.

■ **Security** Is the information to the agents secure? Is your NM station secure and does it support various levels of access? Note the SNMP vulnerability discovered in 2002.

▲ **Remote access** Remote notification of problems and either a Web access or some remote method of connecting into the system from your home.

The final area to discuss is the use of network/RMON probes to track application problems. As a network manager, you require information on who is using the network and what they are using it for. Many switch vendors currently have RMON probes built into switches, which can be used to provide traffic patterns and application trouble-shooting.

Network Management Response Categories

There are several key areas of network management services, including the following. These response categories correspond to current lines of demarcation within networks and represent best practices of network management.

▼ O&M management

■ Monitoring and fault management

■ Administration (OE/OP) management

■ Configuration management

■ Network planning

■ Performance management and engineering

■ Information management and reporting

■ Restoration management

▲ Security management

O&M Management

O&M management involves the day-to-day, and often minute-to-minute, care and feeding of the network in order to ensure that it is fulfilling its designed purpose. This includes installation, implementation, project management, and coordination. Maintenance involves the inevitable circumstances that arise when everything does not work as planned, or when it is necessary to diagnose what went wrong and repair it. It also includes preventive measures.

Monitoring and Fault Management

Monitoring and Fault Management is used to detect, isolate, and repair problems. This category encompasses such activities as tracing faults, carrying out diagnostics, maintaining error logs, and analyzing error information to recommend changes. Trouble-ticket management functions are provided in the case of line problems, and historical analysis of past problems tracked by trouble tickets (chronic problems) and their resolution.

Administration (OE/OP) Management

Administration (OE/OP) management encompasses the set of activities involved with designing the network, order entry, processing orders, assigning addresses, tracking resource usage, change management, and accounting. This service allows for general administrative chores, notification procedures, file indexing and transfer, system configuration, security access, and administrative messaging via e-mail. Provisioning Management involves installing equipment and facilities, setting parameters, and verifying that the service is operational. It also includes de-installation. Inventory and Provisioning Management provide information concerning services inventory, order entry, order status, provisioning details, and delivery dates.

Configuration Management

Configuration Management is used to identify and control managed objects in the network. This category includes such activities as creating and maintaining an inventory of network hardware and software and maintaining a topology map of the relationships between those inventory items. Network Configuration Management provides the ability to monitor and reroute on a dynamic basis to meet changing user and network needs. It allows on-demand allocation of bandwidth, preprogrammed configuration scenarios based on changing traffic patterns, and connectivity requirements. This category also includes Software and Firmware Control.

Network Planning

Network Planning is used primarily to plan for major additions/deletions of sites and/or equipment. This category includes such activities as scheduling major projects that change the overall configuration and topology of the network, and supporting MAC (move/add/change) activities that change the network configuration and/or topology. It includes planning and implementation of Software Distribution to distribute new releases to remote sites for network and user applications.

Performance Management and Engineering

Performance Management and Engineering is used to evaluate the performance of the network in carrying traffic according to preset parameters. This category includes such activities as establishing a system to measure traffic flows, measuring traffic to identify under- and over-utilized network components, and analyses of collected data to support planning for changes in the network configuration and/or traffic patterns through optimizing network traffic and equipment. This category also provides information and reporting on present performance, via real-time transmissions, and correlates it to historical trends in network performance. Then take action! This is the proactive portion of network management—fixing problems before they can cause a network outage. It includes Traffic Management, which provides information on present and past traffic patterns, allowing trunk and circuit analysis, trending, and optimization; cost-performance data analysis; and so forth. It also defines vendor- and equipment-specific SLAs.

Information Management and Reporting

Information Management and Reporting provides the user with a means to update and maintain the basic physical and logical information contained in the user's databases that define the network. This might include physical and logical addresses, contact databases, circuit layout information, and escalation lists. It includes traditional *Operations Management* functions of tracking information concerning the present operation of the system, including network alarms for all protocol layers and escalation procedures. It also ties into restoration management in disaster situations. Reporting defines reporting methods, procedures, and deliverables.

Restoration Management

Restoration Management relates to, but is different from, configuration management. The Restoration Management function tracks disaster recovery plans and other contingencies that have been preprogrammed to be executed—manually or automatically—when a circuit outage or some other disaster occurs.

Security Management

Security Management is used to establish and maintain security levels, procedures, and clearance. Some key areas of security management include Forced password changes, Automatic screen saver passwords, Firewall monitoring, Token management, War dialing, Port scans, Intrusion detection systems, and Virtual Private Networks.

TRENDS IN NETWORK MANAGEMENT

What are some of the trends now occurring in network management? The dependence on networks to carry mission critical information drives the importance of proactive, around-the-clock, 7×24×365 management. Multivendor and multitransport media-management, improvements in display management, and artificial intelligence (AI) and neural networks are all covered.

7×24×365 Around-the-Clock Operations

Just as the local supermarket is now open 7 days a week, 24 hours a day, and 365 days a year, networks too require the same level of management monitoring, management, and availability. Extended hours and around-the-clock operation of world stock exchanges and economic markets from Tokyo to New York to London show this trend. Data critical for global decision making is being passed over networks at all hours of the day and night. Multinational (also called transnational) businesses are run and managed from across the globe. Older human-based systems of network management must be increasingly automated to meet these challenges.

Key features of NM systems include

▼ Interactive graphical user interfaces (GUIs)

■ Windows, menus, icons, color graphics, and so on

■ Rapid mouse-clicking on icons to display or change status

■ Enhanced human-factors engineering (ergonomics)

■ "Exception" report to prioritized alerts, alarms, status

■ Alarm and event correlation

▲ Object-oriented coding and database support

The sheer volume of network status, alerts, and alarms flowing over a network demands that network managers and operators have all the help they can get to keep control. The information provided to the operator must be summarized, correlated, condensed, and made quickly digestible. It should be graphically oriented so the network operator can make operations decisions by observing symbols, color changes, and various condition states on color-CRT screens rather than being forced to decipher, with constant reference to paper documentation, the cryptic messages of network status, alarms, and alerts rapidly scrolling past in a text format on a CRT. Prioritization of alarms is a critical factor, and alarm and event logs should be similarly organized.

Information, too, should be displayed in hierarchical fashion, with the ability to "telescope" from the macro view down to the micro view—for example, looking at the overall network of 100 nodes represented by icons, and then further isolating a problem by rapid mouse-clicking down to the individual icon trunk card level of, let us say, a router in Denver, with the icon showing the router port or IP address as a status light in color on the workstation's windows. Action can then be taken based on status. Icon clicking with the mouse can take the network operator from the macro view to the micro view in 3 to 6 seconds—from the overall network down to the card or individual virtual circuit level of a specific location, device, circuit, and address.

There is an exception to this rule—as systems scale and require an operator to manage hundreds or thousands of devices, a graphical interface, no matter how tiered, cannot provide the sorting and rapid display of critical information, and at that point managers turn back to text-oriented systems and can sort and display critical information based on priority that requires immediate attention.

Multivendor, Multitransport Network Issues

Multiple vendor network product and service implementations can cause inter-operability problems. Proprietary designs evolve even within the implementation of standards-based design. Often, there are dissimilar transport infrastructure, hardware, software, programming, command structures, and displays. As multiple network-management platforms have developed, multiple display terminals have also developed. Interoperability is a key issue for users with multivendor networks. More than 90 percent of major commercial users have equipment from at least two different vendors and 50 percent from at least four different vendors. These are data networks, composed of modems/CSUs/DSUs, multiplexers, packet/frame/cell switches, routers, and other communications devices with mixed protocols and architectures. What happens with the addition of voice and legacy protocols (for example, SNA) into the area of network management? There is no simple answer to this question. The answer lies in knowing that the hybrid networking environment consists of voice/data, public/private NEs, CPE/POP-based switching systems, and varying degrees of user/vendor control.

To address this multivendor environment, the leading vendors have developed "umbrella" platforms or architectures to deal with the multivendor problem. This approach is called "managing the managers" or "manager of managers (MoM)." An integrated network management system (INMS) is developed which monitors existing disparate network management systems through some common interface. However, the problem is not just multiple vendors but also multiple products *within* the same vendor.

Mother of Management systems—or MoM—rolls all capabilities into a single system. The pros to this approach are the integration of all systems into a single platform giving broad coverage of most systems, but the primary con is that each element of a MoM system is typically not as deep or full-featured as the single element approach purchased separately.

Most enterprise network management systems use reactive management techniques instead of proactive ones. Existing network management systems tend to flood the network operator with alarms and status information. And the operator tries to react as quickly as possible. As networks grow more complex, however, the operator is flooded with still more information. Rapid decisions must be made on *more* information, in *less* time, and with *escalating penalties* for mistakes.

Automation of human factors must step in to help. Network management systems must be built to adapt to the human mind's ability to process information. People are not good at parallel processing or handling multiple streams of information simultaneously. People are mono, serial processors one thing at a time, although they can be interrupt-driven. Network management systems must take information coming in from the network in parallel fashion, correlate and sort it according to predefined priorities, and adapt it to the human mind's ability to serially process events and actions.

Network management systems now interface to the parallel incoming information sources streaming in from the network. By neural networks and rule-based expert systems, network management systems can reconfigure incoming parallel information streams for serial presentation to the human network operator thus automating the analysis of information.

Some basic requirements for adapting new technologies to network management include

▼ Improve display management

■ Implement rule-based and neural AI systems

■ Employ object-oriented coding and databases

■ Handle growing networks with more NEs

■ Correlate and summarize network data for decision making

■ Move rapidly from macro to micro views of NEs

■ Automate the control process

■ Improve data presentation and alarm annunciation

■ Accommodate emerging technologies and standards

▲ Replace reactive network management with proactive network management

Improvements in Display Management

Improved graphic-display management software allows the network operator to now scan detailed network diagrams and determine the general health and status of a several-hundred-node network in seconds. This is a major improvement over the chore of reading text-related messages for each network element.

User interfaces have become more mouse-, menu-, and windows-oriented, allowing the operator to interact with the actual equipment represented by the icons to program or take in and out of service through vendor-proprietary element managers. Using toolkits and window managers, users can draw complex network diagrams to allow an operator to view the status of hundreds of network nodes and elements simultaneously. Yet with the click of a mouse-button, the operator can, within a few seconds, focus on a particular icon and observe its alarm lights for the state of the actual element or object represented by the icon.

The network operator's attention can be enhanced by the animation of icons to represent "living" systems, turning red, green, blue, or yellow, as well as blinking, showing happy or sad faces, or using speech processing to literally cry out for "Help!" in a strident manner like some video games. Work space on the screen can be maximized by the ability to resize and open or close windows on the network-management workstation. Closed windows, however, continue in real time to monitor the status of the NEs for later recall and display if required. When a window is reopened later, the current, cumulative network status is displayed in nearly real time. This timeliness and availability of information makes network decision making easier and faster. This allows quick resolution of problems with less downtime. This equates to reduced costs and increased revenues.

Artificial Intelligence (AI)/Neural Networks

Since voluminous amounts of network management information must be processed, and network information arrives at the control point in parallel streams as status/alarms originating from perhaps thousands of NEs—such as a modem, multiplexer, router, switch, or CSU/DSU—the parallel streams must be analyzed and patterns and statuses recognized. The "real" alarms, or the "trigger" alarms must be isolated by exception methods from "sympathy" alarms set off by the original "trigger" alarm. Otherwise, thousands of alarms would have to be dealt with.

To move from reactive to proactive network management, rule-based expert systems and neural networks will allow for the detection of deteriorating conditions on the network before a full-fledged outage or breakdown. This allows for proactive effecting of changes before the faults actually occur. Artificial intelligence monitors hundreds of points for traffic flow rates, user transaction response times, and equipment health and status. These data streams are correlated to recognize trends that can predict problems by extrapolation.

The knowledge of experienced network operators can be captured by AI methods by storing various corrective procedures. It also stores "memory" for things *not* to be done. These procedures can be stored and referenced later as holiday or after-hours outages occur so that, in a sense, network operations experience is available in almost real time. Rule bases are produced over time (the experiences of expert human network operators) and these rule bases predict ranges of decisions of things "to do" or "not to do" in certain situations in the network.

To release this overload, a neural network is used. A neural network computer processor gathers and correlates high volumes of measurement data for input to the rule-based expert systems. Unlike traditional computers, which must be programmed to produce certain outputs based on specific input data, neural networks are "trained" to recognize patterns by running sample data. Neural networks can also process many inputs simultaneously, that is, perform "parallel processing" while conventional computers are limited to serial-like processing, performing one operation at a time. Neural nets can correlate multiple measurement data streams against preprogrammed measurement trend-data ranges that could cause network faults and either alarm or take action to fix them. This is proactive network management! Neural network output could also be used by the rule-based expert systems to select corrective courses of action. Thus, "self-healing" networks are possible not only by physical design but by software design.

OUTSOURCING AND OUT-TASKING TRENDS CONTINUE

The trend toward outsourcing continues, with Forrester projecting that 90 percent of all corporations will have some form of carrier-managed VPN by 2003. The salaries of technical experts continue to rise, and having an IT department with the knowledge base necessary can be expensive, so carriers and service providers provide various outsourcing or out-tasking options from complete implementation and management to specific tasks such as after-hours monitoring. Network components from firewalls, routers, and CSU/DSUs down to LAN and individual workstations and servers can be covered. More details on outsourcing are covered later in this book.

WHEN TO STOP DESIGNING AND START IMPLEMENTING

The design process is an iterative one, but the designer must know when to stop designing and start implementing. There is new technology emerging on the market every day. Don't give in to the temptation to stop the design process based on a new product some vendor says will be out "next quarter." The design will never be perfect, and modifications can always be made after the network is up and running. If the network is designed based on the guidelines provided in this book, it will be easier to integrate new technology into the network when required.

REVIEW

Standardization of network management is usually considered later in the technology life cycle because only after you have built the network, determined what can go wrong, and discovered what is needed to make it work can you finalize how to operate, administer, maintain, and provision it. This chapter introduced a model of OAM&P functions and how they interact to meet the overall needs of network users. Good planning can provide these OAM&P functions in a much more productive manner soon after the introduction of technology; however, there is no substitute for experience.

The importance of documenting both the network design (engineering plan) and the method by which it will be implemented (O&M document) was covered. It takes teamwork among many departments to design and implement a network. The importance and the capabilities of network management were noted: the responsibility to provide thorough network management to the user and to make the best use of standards-based protocols when implementing network management. SNMP and RMON were covered and a discussion on designing a network management solution. Network management best practices of O&M management, monitoring and fault management, administration (OE/OP) management, configuration management, network planning, performance management and engineering, information management and reporting, restoration management, and security management were reviewed. Finally, the design was reviewed again before beginning the implementation phase.

PART VIII

Emerging Technologies

CHAPTER 20

What's New on the Horizon

This chapter introduces new technologies that have seen significant advancement since the last edition of this book. The 1990s were a decade of worldwide fiber-optic infrastructure deployment, and many of these advancements were designed to take advantage of that infrastructure. In some cases, two or more legacy technologies were merged to produce a new technology or service offering. Multiprotocol Label Switching (MPLS) merges FR/ATM-switched services and IP-routed services to provide a single service that offers the best of both worlds, along with the equivalent of a network-based VPN. MPLS services are now being deployed in many service-provider backbones. Interestingly enough, except for some prioritization and QoS standards, few advancements have occurred to legacy IP. Voice over packet technologies and services have proliferated, but their success has been somewhat dampened by the severe drop in legacy voice-switched service prices. Enhancements to xDSL technology, such as VDSL, are covered, along with new advances in wireless broadband. We start our discussion with packet over SONET, optical switching and routing, and metro Ethernet.

PACKET OVER SONET

Packet over SONET (PoS), also referred to as IP/PPP over SONET, is a data transport technology that offers high-bandwidth capacity with efficient link utilization. PoS was developed as an alternative to ATM network backbones to improve link utilization and reduce network costs. RFC 2615 (PPP over SONET) defines a protocol for transporting IP packets inside PPP over SONET. The overhead of PoS averages about 3 percent, which is significantly lower than the 15 percent average for ATM.

Figure 20-1 shows the OSI model view of PoS. SONET/SDH was covered in Chapter 5. Since PoS is built on top of SONET, the OAM&P and restoration capabilities become inherent in the protocol.

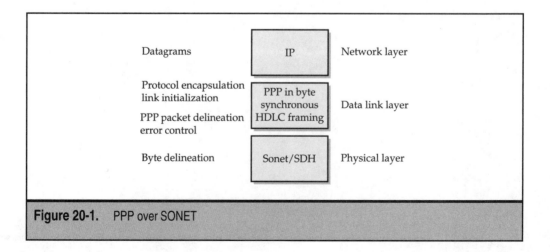

Figure 20-1. PPP over SONET

PoS Frame

PoS uses PPP in High-level Data Link Control (HDLC)-like framing, which is defined in RFC 1662. As shown next, PPP functions as the Layer 2 Data Link Protocol.

Flag 8	Address 8	Control 8	PPP packet	FCS 16/32	Flag 8

The fields for this frame format are defined here:

▼ **Flag** Each frame begins and ends with a flag sequence, which is binary sequence 01111110 (Hex 0x7e). All implementations continuously check for this flag, which is used for frame synchronization. Only one flag sequence is required between two frames. Two consecutive flag sequences constitute an empty frame.

■ **Address** The address field is a single octet, which contains the binary sequence of 11111111 (Hex 0xff), the all-stations address. Individual station addresses are not assigned. The all-stations address must always be recognized and received.

■ **Control** The control field is a single octet, which contains the binary sequence 00000011 (Hex 0x03), which is the unnumbered information (UI) command with the poll/final (P/F) bit set to 0.

▲ **FCS** The Frame Check Sequence field defaults to 16 bits (two octets). The FCS is transmitted least significant octet first, which contains the coefficient of the highest term. A 32-bit FCS is also defined and can be negotiated. The FCS field is calculated over all bits of the address, control, and PPP packet.

PPP was designed for use on point-to-point links, and is suitable for SONET links, which are provisioned as point-to-point circuits. PoS specifies STS-3c as the basic data rate, which has 149.760 Mbps usable data bandwidth. Figure 20-2 shows the framing process

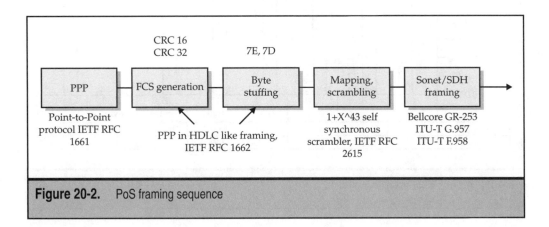

Figure 20-2. PoS framing sequence

of PoS. PoS standards recommend payload scrambling, which provides some level of security. PoS circuits are typically configured for looped/network timing, but can run off an internal clock source when dark fiber is used.

Figure 20-3 shows the PoS percentage efficiency for various packet sizes. The PoS bit efficiency is approximately 96 percent for a 300-byte packet, compared with 80 percent with ATM for a similar packet size.

PoS Applications

PoS has been most successful in high-speed point-to-point IP transport in the WAN. PoS interfaces are connected to carrier SONET rings via add/drop multiplexers (ADM). Figure 20-4 shows a picture of a Cisco gigabit switch router (GSR) connected to a SONET ADM, then to a SONET backbone, with the same termination equipment on the distant end. In this example, the PoS interface is synchronized with the carrier's time source. In WAN configurations, the PoS interface can be connected directly to a DWDM transponder or directly to dark fiber, thus providing efficiency and cost savings over connecting to a SONET network.

In addition to WAN configurations, the low cost of a PoS interface can allow connection to access routers, as show in Figure 20-5. An enterprise can also move the access routers into the customer premises and use PoS versus Gigabit Ethernet in the metro.

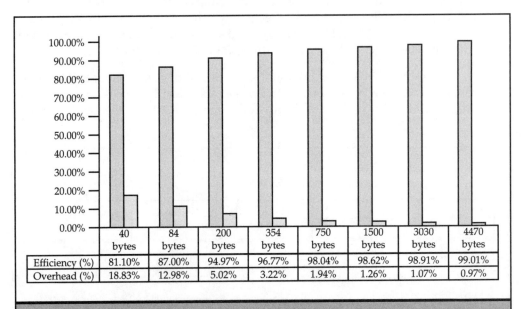

	40 bytes	84 bytes	200 bytes	354 bytes	750 bytes	1500 bytes	3030 bytes	4470 bytes
Efficiency (%)	81.10%	87.00%	94.97%	96.77%	98.04%	98.62%	98.91%	99.01%
Overhead (%)	18.83%	12.98%	5.02%	3.22%	1.94%	1.26%	1.07%	0.97%

Figure 20-3. PoS efficiency chart

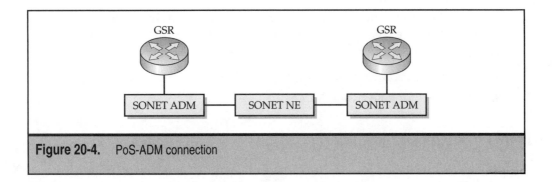

Figure 20-4.   PoS-ADM connection

PoS Advantages Summarized

PoS was developed to provide a cost-effective, low-utilization, high-capacity technology for connecting backbone routers together. PoS has many of the advantages of SONET:

▼   Fast restoration (50 milliseconds)

■   OAM&P—performance monitoring and fault detection via SONET/SDH framing

■   High-capacity interfaces ranging from OC-3 (155 Mbps) to OC-192 (10 Gbps)

▲   Utilization of the existing SONET networks

Adding to the advantages of SONET, PoS also provides

▼   More efficient link utilization than ATM

■   Reduced complexity as compared with ATM

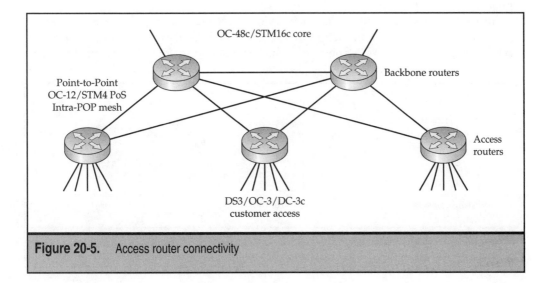

Figure 20-5.   Access router connectivity

■ Reliability and performance—PoS solutions have been shipping since 1997, with more than 20,000 total interfaces deployed

■ Standards-based multi-vendor approach

■ Can be implemented in the core, edge, and metro

▲ Optimized for both IP and MPLS

OPTICAL SWITCHING/ROUTING

A new class of backbone switches and routers is emerging, aimed at providing a migration path from legacy switching, routing infrastructures, and DWDM-transport infrastructures into a single, converged, all-optical architecture. The plan is to eliminate legacy DWDM "dumb optical pipes" running on unintelligent DWDM multiplexers by replacing most of the optical core with intelligent optical switches and routers. Optical, also called wavelength, switching and routing works in conjunction with legacy DWDM transport systems, creating an intelligent optical layer between the DWDM sublayer and the IP (L3 or routed) and/or FR/ATM/PPP (L2 or switched) layers. Optical switching and routing places additional switching (L2) and routing (L3) intelligence into legacy DWDM technology either at the network edge or core. This technology is being driven by the real-world requirements of achieving better optical network scalability, operational (provisioning and support) efficiencies, faster restoration (on the order of 50 milliseconds) at all levels, and higher reliability across backbone networks.

DWDM multiplexers feed the optical router, as shown in Figure 20-6, which then breaks down the optical feed into its multiple wavelengths, then switches or routes each wavelength to another optical switch/router or combines the wavelength back into an egress DWDM feed. Thus, each wavelength can be switched between one or multiple fiber-optic cables. Remember that a single, physical, optical link can carry several logical signals transmitted on different wavelengths.

Since optical switch/routers do this function at the wavelength level, they can establish meshing efficiencies at a much more granular level. This provides huge efficiencies over legacy, meshed, DWDM networks that function only point to point. In legacy

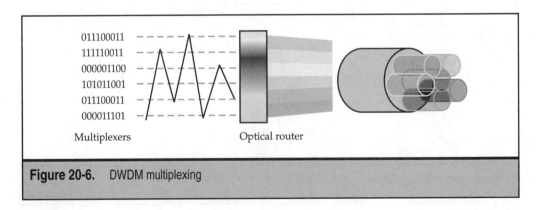

Figure 20-6. DWDM multiplexing

DWDM, when a point-to-point circuit fails, so do all the calls on that path. In fact, all wavelengths are down until the DWDM multiplexer can establish an alternative path and re-establish all wavelengths. Optical switched/routed networks therefore offer greater bandwidth efficiency and higher reliability over the point-to-point DWDM alternative, as they contain the intelligence to switch or route around failures. Additionally, each optical router/switch can share capacity information to enable intelligent routing and rerouting decisions.

Another benefit of optical routing is that elements do not depend on legacy operational support systems (OSSs) to provision and restore the network. Each optical routing element is network-aware, so it can route services through the network based only on source and destination routing. In the traditional approach, each system is provisioned at the circuit or packet level throughout the network. A legacy approach might require 10 to 20 times more steps to provision a single service than an optical approach. In addition, routing itself is traditionally performed using a centralized, manual method, adding significant cost and time to the process through an error-prone procedure. An all-optic network could greatly reduce provisioning staff and thus lower the operating expense (OpEx).

There is a huge savings potential in automated bandwidth management of optical routers over legacy transparent optical patch panels and digital cross-connect (STS-1 or 51.84 Mbps switching) systems. Added to the fact that optical routing provides true routing functionality beyond what a transparent optical patch panel can provide.

If this deployment is done correctly, it allows carriers to leverage their core network technologies alongside IP and ATM technologies to support the massive growth of data services across an all-optical, intelligent backbone. In fact, it helps them collapse multiple backbones into a single optical architecture. Traditional carrier backbones have *at least* four layers:

▼   IP-routed backbones

■   FR and ATM service platforms and/or ATM backbones used for
    traffic engineering

■   A SONET/SDH physical layer transport network

▲   DWDM for point-to-point fiber capacity

This approach has functional overlap among its layers, cumbersome and lengthy provisioning, and manual bandwidth reconfigurations; contains outdated functionality; requires wasted bandwidth as reserved in SONET/SDH rings; and is too slow and expensive to scale. This makes it ineffective as the architecture for optical data networks. The bottom line is that scalability and functionality is limited by the least common-denominator of all layers, and any one layer can limit the scalability of the entire network. In fact, there are many inefficiencies, and potential problems, in overlap of restoration schemes. Figure 20-7 shows the current legacy switched, routed, and transport-carrier environment.

Alternatively, carriers can turn to a converged optical platform using optical switches and routers. Many legacy IP, FR, and ATM switches and routers today use optical interfaces,

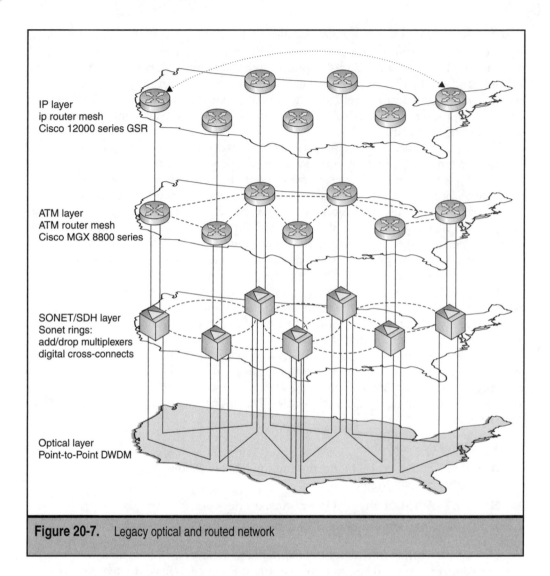

Figure 20-7. Legacy optical and routed network

but here we are discussing taking the next step to wholesale replacement of the legacy hardware with all-optical switches and routers, as shown in Figure 20-8.

So we find that huge efficiencies can be had in the core of carrier networks and local fiber-access rings. The age-old nemesis of carriers—OpEx—can be greatly reduced, but this utopian dream is not without challenges. This reduction must be analyzed against the one-time capital expense (CapEx) of this new network deployment. Routing protocols and algorithms are complex; there is only a limited number of wavelengths for switching and routing; and compatibility problems exist between different vendor switches and routers. Today, all optical switches and routers do so only at the wavelength (L1) layer. The holy grail of optical routing is the true optical router, or the device that can

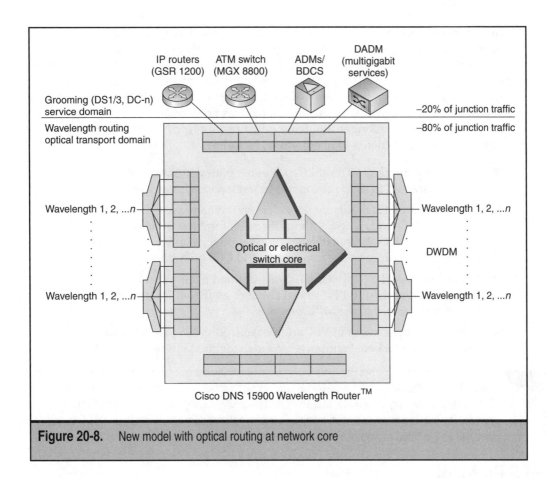

Figure 20-8.   New model with optical routing at network core

switch photonic data at the packet level (L3). These devices did not exist at time of publication, but prototypes were in development. If these issues are solved, wavelength routing might become the dominant carrier backbone switching and routing engine, along with providing similar benefits in the metro network.

MPLS

MPLS is a promising technology that provides the traffic management and QoS support found in legacy ATM networks, speeds up the IP packet-forwarding process, and retains the flexibility and dynamic routing of IP networking. The roots of MPLS go back to efforts to combine IP and ATM in the mid-1990s. Some of the numerous prior technologies include Cisco's tag switching, IBM's aggregate route-based IP switching (ARIS), and Toshiba's cell-switched router. The goal was to improve throughput and delay performance of IP equipment—in other words, increase Layer 3 switching speed to that of Layer 2.

In response to these various proprietary solutions, the IETF set up the MPLS working group in 1997, which produced the first proposed standards in 2001. Label-based switching allows routers to make forwarding decisions based on the contents of a simple label, rather than by performing a complex route lookup based on the destination IP address. By 2001, Layer 3 switches or ASIC-based routers were on the market that performed at the speeds of Layer 2 switches, so the initial goal was now moot.

As the speed was no longer the driving justification for MPLS, MPLS technology brought other needed benefits to IP networks, including

▼ **Traffic engineering**   The ability to set the path that traffic takes through the network and to set performance characteristics for a class of traffic

■ **VPNs**   Using MPLS, service providers can dynamically create IP tunnels throughout their network, without the need for encryption or end-user applications. But whereas IP VPN tunnels attempt only end-to-end CoS, MPLS tunnels can provide true end-to-end QoS guarantees.

■ **Layer 2 transport**   New standards are defined to allow service providers to transport Ethernet, FR, PPP, and ATM over an IP/MPLS core, and use these protocols as access to the MPLS service.

▲ **QoS**   With the growth in VoP and packetized video products, having a backbone network that supports QoS management is a requirement.

TIP: I find the best way to describe MPLS is as taking "fast but dumb switching" and combining it with "slow but smart routing" to achieve "fast and smart switching/routing." MPLS gives you the best of both worlds. The most common implementation is in carrier network services, in which an MPLS-based service has all the smart routing of IP, yet achieves this with the speed of FR and ATM.

MPLS Protocol

The MPLS Protocol adds a 32-bit (4-octet) header on top of the IP packet and inside the Data Link Protocol. Figure 20-9 shows the MPLS label, which has the following elements:

▼ **Label value**   A 20-bit label carries the actual value of the MPLS label that is locally significant.

■ **CoS**   A 3-bit field that can affect queuing and discard algorithms applied to the packet. This is also called a "shim" header.

■ **S**   A 1-bit field that is set to 1 for the oldest entry in the label stack, and 0 for all other entries. See the "Label Stacking" section later in this chapter for more detail.

▲ **Time to live (TTL)**   The 8 bits used to encode a hop count or TTL value.

Figure 20-10 shows how the MPLS label is added after the data-link layer but before any network layer headers. If more than one label is present, the top or initial label appears closest to the network layer header, and the bottom or last label appears closest to

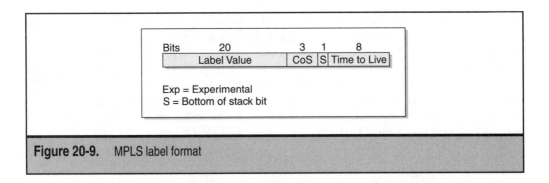

Figure 20-9. MPLS label format

the data-link header. The network layer packet immediately follows the label, which has the S bit set to 1. If MPLS is used over a connection-oriented network service, the topmost label is placed into either the VPI/VCI field in the ATM cell header or DLCI field in the FR header. Using the connection-oriented data-link layer address allows MPLS switching to be done through standard FR and ATM switches, but the entire MPLS label is still placed between the data-link and network layers. Note that in most cases, the TTL field is not visible to FR and ATM switches and not decremented, as is discussed in the "Time-to-Live Processing" section that follows.

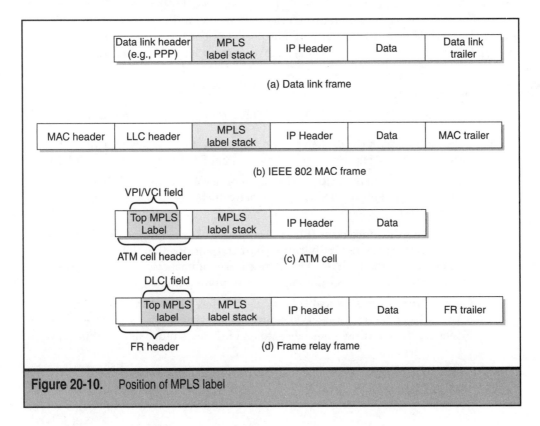

Figure 20-10. Position of MPLS label

Now let's take a high-level view of the MPLS protocol operation. First, a packet comes into an ingress network device called a label switch router (LSR). The LSR performs a lookup based on the destination address, and determines the preferred route to the destination. The LSR adds an MPLS header on top of the IP packet and sets the label value to represent the determined path, adds the data-link header for the specific interface (FR, Ethernet, ATM, whichever), and sends the packet out the specific interface.

The next LSR removes the data-link header, looks at the label, and determines the next step. It will take one of two actions:

▼ **End of the line**   Removes the MPLS header and processes the packet as a normal router would

▲ **Forward on**   Performs a label lookup, changes the label, adds the data-link protocol, and forwards to the next LSR

Time-to-Live Processing

A key IP header field is the TTL field in IPv4 and Hop Limit field in IPv6. The field is decremented at each router, and if the count falls to zero, the packet is dropped to avoid looping or having a packet remain too long within the network due to faulty routing. As MPLS is based on the idea of not looking at the IP header except at the end LSR devices, the TTL field is included in the MPLS label. At the ingress LSR, the TTL field is set to the TTL value of the IP packet and returned to the IP header at the egress router. If the TTL field expires while in the MPLS network, the packet can be discarded or passed to the appropriate network layer for processing, such as with an ICMP error message.

Detailed Operations

Before discussing the detailed operations of MPLS, it is important to define its main terms:

▼ **Label switch path (LSP)**   A specific, logical traffic path through an MPLS network. An LSP is provisioned using a Label Distribution Protocol (LDP).

■ **Label switch routers (LSRs)**   The nodes or devices that are capable of switching and routing packets on the basis of a label, which has been, or will be, appended to each packet

■ **Forward equivalence class (FEC)**   Defines a distinct flow across the network. Each FEC is associated with traffic characterizations that define the QoS requirement of the path. An FEC defines a set of packets that will be forwarded in the same manner (over the same path with the same forwarding treatment).

▲ **Label Distribution Protocol (LDP)**   Establishes a path through an MPLS network and reserves necessary resources to meet predefined service requirements for the path. LDP distributes labels to its LDP peers much as a routing protocol such as OSPF would. Currently, there are two different proposed LDP standards: CR-LDP, which proposes to extend LDP originally designed for hop-by-hop label distribution to support QoS signaling and explicit routing; and RSVP-TE, which is a specification to extend RSVP to support label distribution.

Now that we have defined the primary terms, let's describe how they are used. The essence of MPLS functionality is that traffic is grouped into FECs. The traffic in an FEC transmits an MPLS domain along an LSP. Individual packets in an FEC are uniquely identified as being part of a given FEC by means of a label that is significant only to the local port. At each LSR, each labeled packet is forwarded on the basis of its label value, with the LSR replacing the incoming label value with an outgoing label value.

To accomplish this functionality, the following steps must be taken:

1. The traffic must be assigned to a particular FEC.

2. A routing protocol is used to determine the topology and current conditions in the domain so a particular LSP can be assigned to an FEC. Current IP routing protocols require extensions to achieve all the MPLS benefits. Explicit routing, in which the ingress LSR specifies the complete path through the network, is required so the MPLS network has the ability of traffic engineering and policy routing. Some of the metrics that require support in enhanced version of OSPF are maximum link data rate, current capacity reservation, packet loss ratio, and link propagation delay.

3. An individual LSP must become aware of the LSP for a given FEC, assign an incoming label to the LSP, and communicate that label to any other LSR that might send it packets for this FEC. The communication of the labels is accomplished through the use of an LDP protocol.

Label Stacking

Label stacking is a powerful feature of MPLS. A labeled packet can carry many labels, which are organized as a last in, first out stack. Label stacking allows MPLS networks to create tunnels through the MPLS network. Label stacking can allow customers or other service providers to have separate MPLS networks and use another service provider for connectivity between different LSRs of their network.

Label stacking also allows a VPN to be set up between sites. The innermost label can be set up to have no meaning in the carrier network.

Enhancements to MPLS

MPLS deployments continue to grow, and the industry is working on what is to come next. Generalized MPLS (GMPLS) extends the capability of MPLS to encompass time division (for example, SONET and ADMs), wavelength (optical lambdas) and spatial switching (for example, incoming port or fiber to outgoing port or fiber). GMPLS extended

MPLS to control configuring paths in non-packet-based devices such as optical switches, TDM MUXs and SONET/ADMs. Some of the features of GMPLS are

▼ **Link bundling** The grouping of multiple, independent physical links into a single, logical link

■ **Link hierarchy** The issuing of a suite of labels to support the various requirements of physical and logical devices across a given path

■ **Unnumbered links** The ability to configure paths without requiring an IP address on every physical or logical interface

▲ **Constraint-based routing** The ability to automatically provision additional bandwidth or change forwarding behavior based on network conditions such as congestion or demands for additional bandwidth

Traffic Engineering with MPLS

If we combine this discussion of MPLS with the previous on optical switching and routing, we find an interesting story emerging for a converged network. One option is to split traffic engineering between the IP layer at the packet granularity level and the optical layer at the wavelength granularity level. Thus, the network designer has only two levels of traffic engineering, versus five in IP, FR, ATM, DWDM, or SONET. We will see over time that TDM- and ATM-based traffic engineering will give way to MPLS and wavelength-level traffic engineering in the core.

GMPLS, LMP, and WaRP

GMPLS is an optical networking standard being developed by the IETF, and it might become a key integration standard to bridge legacy IP and MPLS with the optical switching and routing standards and across multivendor implementations. The Link Management Protocol (LMP) is then used to manage and monitor interconnections between nodes in the GMPLS network. GMPLS extends the functions of existing MPLS routing and signaling protocols, developed for delivery of advanced IP services, to include optical networking functions, such as dynamic provisioning of optical bandwidth. The GMPLS protocols also provide a bridge between traditional devices, such as routers, ATM switches, SONET multiplexers, and optical switches, by creating common control plane software across the entire network.

Cisco uses a distributed protocol called Wavelength Routing Protocol (WaRP). In Cisco's words:

"WaRP views the network as a fluid bandwidth pool and provides for point-and-click auto-provisioning of end-to-end wavelength paths in seconds. Depending on the class of service required by the service layer, the Wavelength Router can present bandwidth with varying guarantees of availability, latency, and restoration times. As a result, bandwidth can be provided for services ranging from highly mission-critical applications to intranet or Internet access and bulk transport. WaRP views the network as a single pool of wavelengths, so any wavelength added to the network becomes immediately available for service and can be provisioned as part of an arbitrary end-to-end path across the network."

CIENA's version of this protocol is called the Optical Signaling and Routing Protocol (OSRP) standard, and other similar vendors exist.

METRO ETHERNET

Ethernet has proven that it is the dominant LAN technology. Will it now prove that it is the dominant metro technology? Most service providers now offer high-speed Ethernet point-to-point connectivity and Internet access in the metro area. In the past, SONET was the solution to provide point-to-point connectivity, but now metro Ethernet looks to become a dominant solution. Metro Ethernet connections range in speed from 50 Mbps up to multigigabit. As 95 percent of Internet communications begin and end as Ethernet frames, the idea behind WAN Ethernet solutions is to use Ethernet instead of SONET as the primary transmission technology for public multiservice networks.

Customers like the idea of Ethernet connectivity because it is simple and familiar, and interfaces are much cheaper than their SONET peer. As Ethernet's price in the LAN drove its dominance, it seems to be going the same direction in the metro.

There are various architectures used to provide metro Ethernet services:

▼ Transparent LAN services (TLS) that use RFC 1483 and bridge over ATM networks to a second site. A PVC is configured for each pair of sites in the MAN. The scalability and cost is driven by the SONET/ATM equipment costs. An addition PVC can be set up to access the Internet.

▲ Architecture based on long-haul Ethernet and Ethernet Layer 2/3 switches. Figure 20-11 shows metro Ethernet network based on Layer 2/3 switches. The Ethernet frame from the customer would be encapsulated with a unique IEEE 802.1Q virtual LAN (VLAN) header and bridged over the MAN. Internet access would be offered through a network-based router. Meshing and redundant links with fast-spanning tree failovers are used in the event of link failures. To improve reliability and capacity, DWDM and coarse wavelength division multiplexing (CWDM) rings can be added between the core switches and the Layer 2/3 switches. CWDM provide four or eight wavelengths over each fiber strand, compared with up to 32 or 64 wavelengths in the case of DWDM.

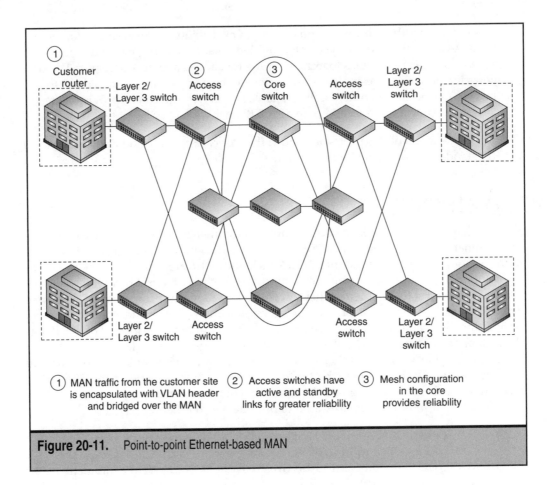

Figure 20-11. Point-to-point Ethernet-based MAN

VDSL

Very-high-speed digital subscriber line (VDSL) service is both symmetric and asymmetric, and provides up to 52 Mbps of bandwidth on a single twisted-pair copper loop. Table 20-1 shows the rates and loop restrictions for the family of xDSL services.

VDSL, like other xDSL technologies, uses the higher-frequency spectrum available over standard copper that operates above the frequencies used for POTS and ISDN services. This technology enables telcos to use existing legacy copper infrastructure for the delivery of broadband services over the same physical plant. The VDSL spectrum is specified to range from 200 kHz to 30 Mhz. Figure 20-12 illustrates an example of spectral allocation for asymmetric VDSL running at 26 Mbps downstream and 3 Mbps upstream.

Asymmetric VDSL was designed to support asymmetric broadband services such as broadcast TV, video-on-demand service, and Internet access. Symmetric VDSL supports symmetric requirements such as video conferencing and business Internet access. High-bandwidth applications such as HDTV and video-on-demand (which requires 18 Mbps) require VDSL because other xDSL technologies do not offer as much bandwidth.

DSL Type	Symmetric/Asymmetric	Loop Range (kft)	Downstream (Mbps)	Upstream (Mbps)
IDSL	Symmetric	18	0.128	0.128
SDSL	Symmetric	10	1.544	1.544
HDSL (2 pairs)	Symmetric	12	1.544	1.544
ADSL G.lite	Asymmetric	18	1.5	0.256
ADSL	Asymmetric	12	6	0.640
VDSL	Asymmetric	3	26	3
	Asymmetric	1	52	6
	Symmetric	3	13	13
	Symmetric	1	26	26

Table 20-1.   xDSL Types

WIRELESS BROADBAND NETWORKS

Wireless networking covers many different technologies that solve different business problems. Wireless networking covers the following different areas:

▼ **Office networking**   Use wireless technology to remove the requirement for cabling of computers and peripherals. This covers wireless computer peripherals such as mice and wireless LANs. Wireless technologies include IEEE802.11 and Bluetooth.

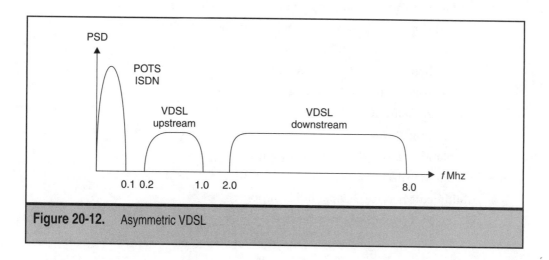

Figure 20-12.   Asymmetric VDSL

- ■ **Last-mile solutions** Use wireless technology to bypass the local exchange carrier and for disaster backup. Technologies include IEEE 802.11, 802.16 wireless local loop (WLL), Wireless Access Protocol (WAP), and some proprietary solutions.

- ▲ **Service providers** Use wireless technology to offer cellular phones, messaging products, and mobile Internet access. Terms include 2G, 2.5G, 3G, and future 4G solutions, plus technologies such as GPRS and W-CDMA (also known as Universal Mobile Telecommunication System [UMTS]). Note that service providers also offer a full suite of wireless local access services, typically at DS1 and DS3 speeds.

As wireless networking is such a broad subject, and our focus is on service-provider solutions, we will not cover office networking and last-mile solutions in any further detail.

Service Providers

The dream of pulling out your laptop anywhere and connecting to the Internet at broadband speed continues to drive service providers to upgrade their cellular and wireless infrastructure. Throughout the late '90s, carriers spent large sums on government auctions to get the spectrum to offer what is known as third-generation (3G) technologies. The realization of 3G technologies enabling high-speed Internet access could dramatically transform wireless broadband phone application and drive use. However, delays in 3G technology and economic drivers have also opened the door to 2.5G technologies that provide an interim solution for less money. As 3G technologies slipped, dreams of fourth-generation technologies, which will support 100 Mbps or higher connectivity rates and were projected for 2006, are now projected for 2010.

3G Wireless

The ITU's International Mobile Telecommunications 2000 initiative (IMT-2000) 3G mobile system services began being deployed in 2001. A system overview follows.

- ▼ Circuit and Packet Data Support at High Bit Rates
  - ■ 144 Kbps or higher in high-mobility (vehicular) traffic
  - ■ 384 Kbps for pedestrian traffic
  - ■ 2 Mbps or higher for indoor traffic
  - ■ Interoperability and roaming
- ■ Common Billing/User Profiles
  - ■ Sharing of usage/rate information between service providers
  - ■ Standardized call-detail recording
  - ■ Standardized user profiles
- ▲ Multimedia Services/Capabilities Support
  - ■ Fixed- and variable-rate bit traffic

- Bandwidth on demand
- Asymmetric data rates in the forward and reverse links
- Multimedia mail store and forward
- Broadband access up to 2 Mbps

To support the 3G system capabilities, wideband code division multiple access (W-CDMA), an ITU standard derived from CDMA, is officially known as IMT-2000 direct spread. W-CDMA uses a 5-MHz wide carrier versus a 200-kHz wide carrier for narrowband CDMA. Figure 20-13 shows a graphical view of W-CMDA technology and 3G services available.

Figure 20-14 shows how actual packet speed achieved varies greatly on the location and the rate that the terminal device is moving. UMTS or W-CDMA technology functions

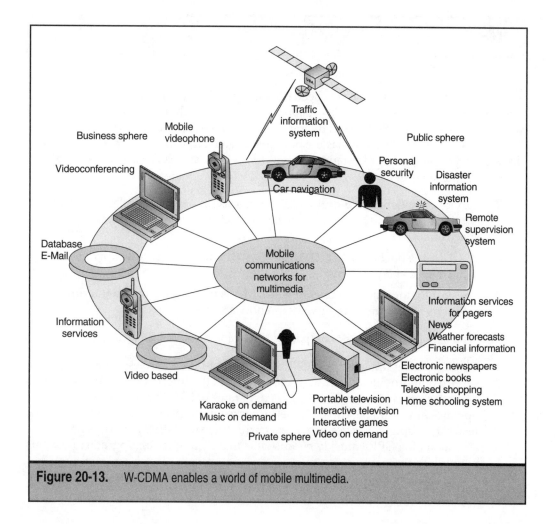

Figure 20-13.   W-CDMA enables a world of mobile multimedia.

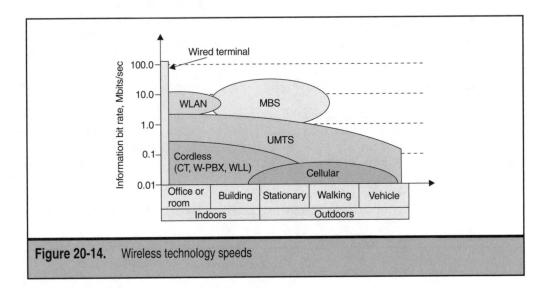

Figure 20-14. Wireless technology speeds

across the spectrum, but the packet speed (throughput achieved) decreases when driving in your car. MBS stands for Mobile Broadband System, which represents the high-speed wireless LAN products that are on the market supporting rates of 100 Mbps.

W-CDMA is a standard that has the potential to gain large market-share over the next decade, so you need to understand what all these 2.5G and 3G discussions are about. Here are some key points:

▼ Service providers that didn't win the auctions for new 3G wireless spectrum want to offer high-speed data services on their existing networks and spectrums.

■ W-CDMA is not based on CDMA IS-95, so the technology has experienced some delays and problems.

▲ The cost to upgrade networks to W-CDMA is very expensive, so interim solutions to provide data services are now a strategy.

Here is a list of the interim or competing technologies of W-CDMA:

▼ General packet radio service (GPRS) is a packet-based wireless communication service that provides continuous connection to the Internet for mobile-phone and computer users. GPRS promises data rates of 56–114 Kbps but in reality operates at around 33 Kbps. The service is asymmetrical, with downlink speeds faster than uplink. Service providers currently using GPRS networks have been able to deploy GPRS quickly because it is mainly a software upgrade of various network components.

■ Enhanced data GSM environment (EDGE) is a radio-based high-speed mobile data standard. EDGE, formerly called GSM384, allows data transmission speeds up to 384 Kbps when all eight time slots are used. EDGE was initially developed for mobile network operators who failed to win UMTS spectrum because EDGE gives incumbent GSM operators the opportunity to offer high-speed data services on the operators' existing spectrum.

▲ CDMA2000 1X also known as 1XRTT is a backward-compatible upgrade to CDMA IS-95. 1XRTT is delivering data rates between 80 to 100 Kbps. The service is symmetrical, which means uplink and downlink speeds are the same. 1XRTT is a cost-effective solution to add higher data speeds to an existing CDMA-based network.

As voice communications have become a commodity, adding more data services such as Internet access, e-mail, and messaging to their networks has become critical to wireless providers. The options and time frames for these services will continue to play out over the next couple of years. Many industry pundits hang their hat on 4G to solve all the problems of wireless, but isn't that what they said about 3G?

VOICE OVER PACKET

Transporting packetized voice has become commonplace in private and public networks. This has been especially true when a majority of the voice traffic remains "on net" for international transport of voice calls. Voice over Packet (VoP) is a grouping of

▼ **Voice over Internet Protocol (VoIP)**   The leading VoP technology. VoIP allows voice communication between any VoIP-enabled device that has an IP address that is reachable from another VoIP-enabled device. There are also Internet access services that allow users to originate a call on VoIP, then gateway the call to the Public Switched Telephone Network (PSTN) for termination on a legacy phone.

■ **Voice over frame relay (VoFR)**   Allows voice communication between VoFR-enabled devices that have assigned DLCI addresses. VoFR is limited to routers or devices that terminate into an FR network.

■ **VoDSL**   Allowed service providers to offer voice service access over DSL. Voice is placed on an ATM PVC and transported to a gateway device that connected into a Class 5 switch. VoDSL was designed to resolve the last-mile problem and provide an integrated service bundle from competitive local exchange carriers (CLECs).

■ **VoATM**   Allows voice communication using AAL2 for packetized voice.

▲ **PacketCable**   A set of specifications to provide voice and multimedia communication across cable networks. PacketCable was developed by CableLabs, which is a R&D consortium of the cable industry.

While there are many VoP technologies, the fundamentals of sending voice across a data network are the same.

Fundamentals

Understanding some basics about telephony is important to be able to implement a VoP network. As VoP phone quality is improving and VoP equipment is getting cheaper, the majority of your VoP network integration will be into existing Private Branch Exchange (PBX) or the PSTN.

Figure 20-15 shows a flowchart representation of voice processing across a data network.

1. When a person talks into a phone, their speech is represented by an analog signal.

2. At the PBX, PSTN, or in a VoP device, the analog signal is converted into a digital signal by performing an analog to digital (A/D) conversion. A standard A/D conversion in voice networks is to sample a signal 8000 times per second and represent each sample with an 8-bit code. The digital signal from this conversion is represented in a 64-Kbps stream of information in either μ-law encoding (North America and Japan) or A-law encoding.

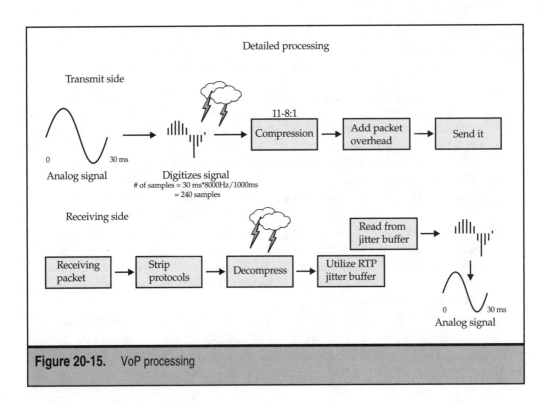

Figure 20-15. VoP processing

3. The digital signal can be compressed to reduce the required network bandwidth but this compression can cause voice quality degradation. Various standard compressions are shown next. The mean opinion score (MOS) is a rating of the voice quality, and frame size is the amount of data that must be at a minimum contained per packet.

Compression methods

Compression method	Bit rate (kbps)	Framing size	MOS
G.711 PCM	64	0.125 ms	4.1
G.726 ADPCM	32	0.125 ms	3.85
G.728 LD-CELP	16	0.625 ms	3.61
G.729 CS-ACELP	8	10	3.92
G.729a CS-ACELP	8	10	3.7
G.723.1 MP-MLQ	6.3	30	3.9
G.723.1 ACLEP	5.3	30	3.65

4. Now that a sample of voice is captured and possibly compressed, a protocol such as Real-time Transport Protocol (RTP) for VoIP is added to the packet. RTP, as shown next, is an unreliable protocol that provides information to allow the packets to be reformed into a stream of voice at the other end of the conversation. For VoIP, an additional UDP and IP header is added to the packet before it is sent into the network. An unreliable protocol is used because adding delay to retransmit to a real-time conversation is unacceptable.

Real-Time Transport Protocol (RTP)

0					16	32 bits
V=2	P	X	CC	M	PT	Sequence Number
Timestamp						
Synchronization Source (SSRC) Identifier						
Optional: Contributing Source (CSRC) Identifiers						

- Protocol is unreliable. Why not utilize reliable?
- Information to re-create and synchronize stream with timing properties.
- Identifies Payload—aka Compression algorithm.

Source: From RFC 1889 - http:\\www.normos.org/rfc/rfc1889.txt

At the receiving end of the network, the process is reversed to re-create the original analog signal. A technique known as a *jitter buffer* is used to compensate the stream of packets to allow for a continuous signal at the egress. A jitter buffer delays sending the signal to the egress interface if there is a high probability that network events will cause packets to be late. One problem with VoP networks is echo, which occurs when you hear your own voice after you speak. VoP networks implement Echo cancellers to resolve this problem, but the quality of the implementation varies by product. Another problem is DTMF digits not passing through the network, which causes callers not to be able to use IVR (Interactive Voice Response) systems. When an analog signal is compressed, the DTMF digits are distorted, and interactive voice response (IVR) units can detect the tones. VoP equipment typically detects the tones at the ingress side of the network and sends the tones to the egress side in a signaling message, then the egress equipment regenerates the signal.

Two more important terms in VoP networks are silence suppression and comfort noise. An advantage of VoP networks is that if you are not speaking, packets do not have to be transmitted to the egress side to represent silence. The method of detecting silence is known as voice activity detection (VAD). Comfort noise is how silence is represented at the egress device. Many tests have shown that people prefer a little noise on the line because a completely silent connection makes them think the connection is broken.

Signaling Control Protocols

Signaling control protocols are used for setting up and taking down calls and implementing various phone features such as conferencing and call waiting. There are three competing protocols/architectures in the VoP space for signaling control protocols:

▼ H.323, which was originally developed for videoconference, has been adapted for the VoP space. A graphical representation of the ITU standard and the various components is shown next. H.323 is currently on version 3, which has resolved some of the problems associated with earlier versions.

ITU-H.323 — Packet-based multimedia
communications systems

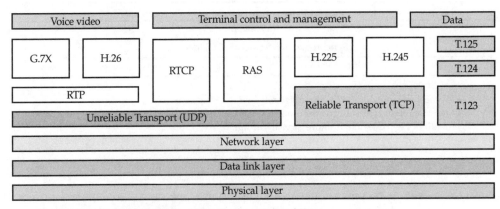

- First published in 1996 supporting Video Conferencing and Voice.
- Complex system -# of protocols working together.
- ASN.1 encoding of the messages.
- Updated since 1996.
  - Speeding up call setup.
  - Added Signaling Features such as Call Transfer, Forward.

■ Session Initiation Protocol (SIP) is an application-layer control protocol for creating, modifying, and terminating sessions with one or more participants. SIP was driven by the IETF versus the ITU and is based on HTTP principles versus telephone principles.

▲ Megaco Protocol and Media Gateway Control Protocol (MGCP) are two different control protocols but have similar architectures. Both specify communication between control elements and telephony devices. As SIP and H.323 are distributed solutions, Megaco and MGCP use central signaling devices known as *call agents* and allow the end device to be dumb. A debate over which is the best protocol has raged the last couple of years, but it looks as if both are going to have their uses. Devices known as *soft switches* are being created that speak more than one of the control protocols and will allow VoP equipment to replace Class 5 telephony switches in the future.

VoP Design Basics

When designing VoP networks, there are a couple of trade-offs:

▼ **Bandwidth versus quality** Select the appropriate level of compression that meets your quality. Very few people can tell the call is compressed when using G.729 and G.723.1.

▲ **Bandwidth versus latency** Figure 20-16 shows perceived quality when one-way delay goes up. Bandwidth required can be reduced by sending more information per packet, but delay is increased due to waiting for more samples to arrive.

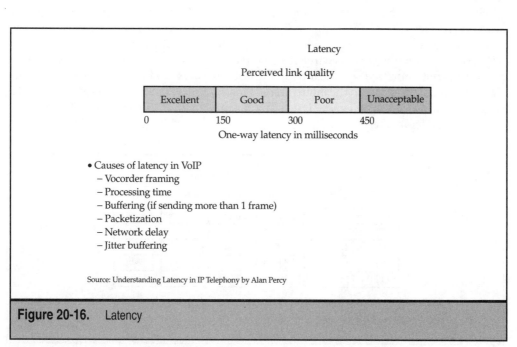

Figure 20-16. Latency

Figure 20-17 provides bandwidth utilization based on G.729 and the number of frames used in a ten-minute speech. cRTP is a standard for compressed RTP but can be used only over point-to-point links between facilities.

We now detail some design rules for VoP networks:

▼ Reduce bottlenecks when possible.

■ Reducing bandwidth requirements reduces the probability of congestion.

■ Use cRTP.

■ Choose lower bandwidth vocoder/compression rates and choose more frames per packet.

■ Use VAD/silence suppression if possible.

■ Use fragmentation on low-speed links.

■ Beware that fragmentation can cause trouble with https and some web pages.

■ Use queuing schemes to prioritize voice and multimedia traffic.

▲ Restrict or limit traffic to reduce congestion.

REVIEW

In this chapter, we introduced many of the newer technologies that have seen some level of significant deployment since the last edition of this book. We started with packet over SONET as a cost-effective alternative for long-haul and metro IP networking. We next moved on to the use of optical switching and routing to collapse the five legacy networks into a single, all-optical converged network. We briefly covered metro Ethernet and VDSL as new broadband access technology options. MPLS offers a merging of traditional switched services (FR/ATM) with traditional routed services (IP) to provide a single service that offers the best of both worlds, along with the equivalent of a network-based VPN. We explored the various wireless broadband alternatives and saw that the wireless market has not improved significantly in the last few years, and remains a splintered and limited alternative except in the metro arena. Finally, VoP was covered in some detail; despite the rapid decrease of legacy switched-voice pricing, it is still a viable technology for international deployment.

Overhead summary

Table summarizes bandwidth by frame using G.729-8Kbps

Protocol	1 frame	2 frame	3 frame	6 frame
PPP(VoIP)	44.8 Kbps	26.4 Kbps	20.3 Kbps	14.1 Kbps
ATM/AAL5(VoIP)	84.8 Kbps	42.4 Kbps	42.4 Kbps	21.2 Kbps
VoFR	12.8 Kbps	10.4 Kbps	9.6 Kbps	8.8 Kbps
PPP(VoIP) cRTP	14.4 Kbps	11.2 Kbps	10.1 Kbps	9.1 Kbps

Figure 20-17. Overhead summary

PART IX

Appendixes

APPENDIX A

Acronyms and Abbreviations

C omments in parentheses are a clarification or refer to the standard or protocol from which the term is derived. Many acronyms are used by multiple standards; only the most prevalent are mentioned.

AAL   ATM Adaptation Layer

AAL1   ATM Adaptation Layer 1

AAL2   ATM Adaptation Layer 2

AAL3/4   ATM Adaptation Layer 3/4

AAL5   ATM Adaptation Layer 5

AARP   AppleTalk Address Resolution Protocol

ABM   Asynchronous Balance Mode (HDLC)

ABR   Area Border Router

ABR   Available Bit Rate (ATM)

AC   Access Control (IEEE)

ACF   Access Control Field (DQDB)

ACK   Acknowledgment

ACR   Allowed Cell Rate

ADCCP   Advanced Data Communications Control Procedure

ADM   Add/Drop Multiplexer

ADSP   AppleTalk Data Stream Protocol

ADSU   ATM Data Service Unit

ADSL   Asymmetric Digital Subscriber Line

AEP   AppleTalk Echo Protocol

AFI   Authority and Format Identifier

AFNOR   Association Francaise de Normalisation (France)

AFP   AppleTalk Filing Protocol

AIEE   American Institute of Electrical Engineers

AIP   ATM Interface Processor

AIS   Alarm Indication Signal (SONET)

ALPS   Automatic Line Protection Service

AM   Amplitude Modulation

AMI   Alternate Mark Inversion

ANS   American National Standards

ANSI   American National Standards Institute

API   Application Programming Interface

APPC   Advanced Peer-to-Peer Communications (IBM)

APPN   Advanced Peer-to-Peer Networking (IBM)

APS   Automatic Protection Switching

ARIS   Aggregate Route-based IP Switching (IBM)

ARM   Asynchronous Response Mode (HDLC)

ARP   Address Resolution Protocol

ARPANET   Advanced Research Projects Agency NETwork

ASBR   Autonomous System Boundary Router

ASCII   American Standard Code for Information Interchange

ASICs   Application-Specific Integrated Circuits

ASP   AppleTalk Session Protocol

AST   Automatic Spanning Tree

Async   Asynchronous

ATDM   Asynchronous Time-Division Multiplexing

ATG   Address Translation Gateway

ATIS   Alliance for Telecommunications Industry Solutions

ATM   Automated Teller Machine

ATM   Asynchronous Transfer Mode

ATMM   ATM Management

ATP   AppleTalk Transaction Protocol

AU   Access Unit (DQDB)

AUI   Attachment Unit Interface (Ethernet 802.3)

B2B   Business-to-Business

B2C   Business-to-Consumer

B8ZS   Bipolar with 8 Zero Substitution

BBS   Bulletin Board System

BCC   Block Check Characters

BCD   Binary Coded Decimal

BCN   Backbone Concentrator Node (Nortel)

BDXC   Broadband Digital Cross-Connect

BECN   Backward Explicit Congestion Notification (FR)

BER   Bit Error Ratio or Rate

BERT   Bit Error Rate Testing

BGP   Border Gateway Protocol (IP)

BGP4   Border Gateway Protocol: Version 4 (IP)

BIP   Bit Interleaved Parity (8)

BIPS   Billion Instructions Per Second

B-ISDN   Broadband Integrated Services Digital Network

BLSR   Bi-directional Line-Switched Ring (SONET)

B-NT   Broadband Network Terminator

BO   Bit Oriented (SONET)

BOC   Bell Operating Company

BOM   Beginning of Message (DQDB)

BONDING   Bandwidth-ON-Demand Interoperability Group

BPDU   Bridge Protocol Data Unit

bps   bits per second (B=bytes; b=bits)

BRI   Basic Rate Interface (ISDN)

BSC   Binary Synchronous Communications protocol (IBM)

BSI   British Standards Institution

B-TA   Broadband Terminal Adapter (ATM)

B-TE   Broadband Terminal Equipment (ATM)

CA   Certification Authority

CAD/CAM   Computer Aided Design/Computer Aided Manufacturing

CAC   Connection Admission Control (ATM)

CAN   Customer Access Node (SMDS)

CAP   Competitive Access Provider

CapEx   Capital Expense

CBDS   Connectionless Broadband Data Service

CBEMA   Computer and Business Equipment Manufacturers Association

CBR   Constant Bit Rate (ATM)

CC   Communications Controller (IBM)

CCI   Carrier-to-Carrier Interface

CCITT   Consultative Committee International Telegraph & Telephone

CCS   Call Century Second

CD   CountDown counter (DQDB)

CD   Carrier Detect

CDDI   Copper Distributed Data Interface

CDP   Cisco Discovery Protocol

CD-ROM   Compact Disk-Read Only Memory

CDV   Cell Delay Variation (ATM)

CDVT   Cell Delay Variation Tolerance (ATM)

CE   Connection Endpoint

CEN   Comite Europeen de Normalisation

CEPT   Conference on European Post & Telegraph

CER   Cell Error Rate (ATM)

CES   Circuit Emulation Service (ATM)

CHAP   Challenged Handshake Authentication Protocol (PPP)

CIDR   Classless Interdomain Routing (IP)

CIM   Common Information Model

CIP   Channel Interface Processor (Cisco)

CIR   Committed Information Rate (FR)

CL   Connectionless (SONET)

CLLM   Consolidated Link Layer Management (FR)

CLNP   Connectionless Layer Network Protocol

CLNS   ConnectionLess Network Service (OSI)

CLP   Cell Loss Priority (ATM)

CLR   Cell Loss Ratio (ATM)

CLSF   ConnectionLess Server Function (ITU-T)

CMIP   Common Management Interface Protocol (ISO)

CMIS   Common Management Information Service (ISO)

CMISE   CMIS Element (ISO)

CMT   Connection Management (FDDI)

CNMS   Customer Network Management System

CO   Central Office

COAM   Customer Owned and Maintained

COCF   Connection-Oriented Convergence Function (DQDB)

COM   Continuation of Message (DQDB)

CONS   Connection-Oriented Network Service (ITU-T)

CPCS   Common Part Convergence Sublayer (ATM)

CPE   Customer Premises Equipment

CPU   Central Processing Unit

C/R   Command/Response Indicator or Bit (FR)

CRC   Cyclic Redundancy Check or Test (FR)

CRL   Certificate Revocation List

CRM   Customer Relationship Management

CS   Convergence Sublayer (DQDB)

CSA   Canadian Standards Association

CSMA/CD   Carrier-Sense Multiple Access with Collision Detection (Ethernet)

CSU   Channel Service Unit

CTD   Cell transfer Delay (ATM)

CV   Coding Violations (SONET)

CWDM   Course Wavelength Division Multiplexing

DA   Destination Address field

DAL   Dedicated Access Line

DARPA   Defense Advanced Research Program Agency

DAS   Dual-Attach Station connection (FDDI)

DCC   Data Country Code (ATM)

DCE   Data Communications Equipment

DCS   Digital Cross-connect System

DDCMP   Digital Data Communications Message Protocol (DEC)

DDD   Direct Distance Dialing

DDN   Defense Data Network

DDP   Datagram Delivery Protocol

DDR   Dial-on-Demand Routing

DDS   Digital Data Service

DE   Discard Eligibility (FR)

DEC   Digital Equipment Corporation

DG   Datagram

DH   DMPDU Header (DQDB)

DHCP   Dynamic Host Configuration Protocol (IP)

DIN   Deutsches Institut fur Normung (Germany)

DIS   Draft International Standards

DLC   Data Link Control

DLC   Digital-Loop Carrier

DLCI   Data Link Connection Identifier (FR)

DLL   Data Link Layer

DLL   Dynamic Link Library

DLS   Data Link Switching (IBM)

DLUR   Dependent LU Requester

DM   Line Depredated Minutes (SONET)

DMPDU   Derived MAC PDU (DQDB)

DMZ   DeMilitarized Zone (IP)

DNA   Digital Network Architecture (DEC)

DNS   Domain Name System (IP)

DoD   Department of Defense

DPG   Dedicated Packet Group (FDDI)

DQDB   Distributed Queue Dual Bus (IEEE)

DS   Dansk Standardiseringsrad (Danish)

DS   Digital Stream

DS0   Digital Signal Level 0

DS1   Digital Signal Level 1

DS3   Digital Signal Level 3

DSAP   Destination Service Access Point (LLC)

DSF   Dispersion-Shifted Fiber

DSG   Default Slot Generator (DQDB)

DSR   Data Set Ready

DSU   Data Service Unit

DT   DMPDU Trailer (DQDB)

DTE   Data Terminal Equipment

DTMF   Dual Tone MultiFrequency

DTR   Data Terminal Ready

DUV   Data Under Voice

DVMPR   Distance Vector Multicast Routing Protocol

DWDM   Dense Wavelength Division Multiplexing

DXC   Digital Cross-Connect

DXI   Data Exchange Interface (SMDS, ATM)

E1   European Transmission Level 1

E3   European Transmission Level 3

EA   Extended Address

EBCDIC   Extended Binary-Coded Decimal Interchange Code (IBM)

ECMA   European Computer Manufacturers Association

ECN   Explicit Congestion Notification (FR)

ECSA   Exchange Carriers Standards Association

ECU   Establishment Controller Unit (IBM)

ED   End Delimiter (IEEE 802)

EDGE   Enhanced Data GSM Environment

EFCI   Explicit Forward Congestion Indication (ATM)

EFT   Electronic Funds Transfer

EGP   Exterior Gateway Protocol (IP)

EGRP   Exterior Gateway Routing Protocol (IP)

EIA   Electronics Industries Association

EIGRP   Enhanced Interior Gateway Routing Protocol (Cisco™) (IP)

EIR   Excess Information Rate (FR)

ELAN   Emulated LAN

ELAP   Ethertalk Link Access Protocol

EMA   Enterprise Management Architecture (DEC)

EOM   End Of Message

EOT   End Of Transmission

ERP   Enterprise Resource Planning

ES   End System (OSI)

ES   Errored Seconds (SONET)

ESCON   Enterprise Systems Connection Architecture™ (IBM)

ESF   Extended SuperFrame

ES-IS   End System-to-Intermediate System protocol (OSI)

ETB   End of Transmission Block

ETSI   European Telecommunications Standards Institute

ETX   End of Text

F   Flag

FC   Frame Control field (FDDI)

FCAPS   Fault, Configuration, Accounting, Performance, Security

FCC   Federal Communications Commission

FC-PH   Fibre Channel Physical and Signaling Interface

FCS   Frame Check Sequence (FR)

FCS   Fiber Channel Standard

FDDI   Fiber Distributed Data Interface (ANSI)

FDDI-II   Fiber Distributed Data Interface Version II

FDL   Facility Data Link

FDM   Frequency Division Multiplexing

FEBE   Far End Block Error

FEC   Forward Error Correction

FEC   Forward Equivalence Class (MPLS)

FECN   Forward Explicit Congestion Notification (FR)

FEP   Front End Processor (IBM)

FERF   Far End Reporting Failure

FICON   Fiber Connection

FIFO   First In First Out

FM   Frequency Modulation

FMBS   Frame Mode Bearer Service

FOIRL   Fiber-Optic InterRepeater Link (Ethernet 802.3)

FPM   Fast Packet Multiplexing

fps   frames per second

FPS   Fast Packet Switching

FR   Frame Relay

FRAD   Frame Relay Assembler/Disassembler, or Access Device

FRF   Frame Relay Forum

FS   Frame Status field (FDDI)

FT1   Fractional T1

FTAM   File Transfer and Access Management

FTP   File Transfer Protocol (IP)

FTTC   Fiber To The Curb

FTTH   Fiber To The Home

FUNI   Frame UNI (FR)

GAN   Global Area Network

Gbit   Gigabits (billions of bits)

Gbps   Gigabits per second (10^9 bps)

GFC   Generic Flow Control (ATM)

GFID   General Format Identifier

GFI   General Format Identifier (X.25)

GGP   Gateway-Gateway Protocol (DoD)

GigE   Gigabit Ethernet (also labeled GbE)

GM   General Motors

GMPLS   Generalized MPLS

GNS   Get Nearest Server (IPX)

GOS   Grade of Service

GOSIP   Government Open System Interconnection Protocol

GPRS   General Packet Radio Service

GRE   Generic Routing Encapsulation (Cisco)

GSM   Global System for Mobil Communications

GSR   Gigabit Switch Router (Cisco)

GUI   Graphical User Interface

HCS   Header Check Sequence (DQDB)

HDTV   High Definition TeleVision

HDLC   High-Level Data Link Control (ISO)

HEC   Header Error Control

HILI   Higher Layers and Management Interface standards

HIP   HSSI Interface Processor

HOB   Head of Bus (DQDB) A or B

HOL   Head of Line (DQDB)

HPPI   High Performance Parallel Interface

HPR   High Performance Routing

HSCI   High-Speed Communication Interface

HSRP   Hot Standby Router Protocol (Cisco)

HSSI   High-Speed Serial Interface

HTTP   HyperText Transfer Protocol (IP)

Hz   Hertz or cycles per second

IAB Internet Activities Board

IANA Internet Assigned Numbers Authority

ICD International Code Designator (ATM)

ICF Isochronous Convergence Function (DQDB)

ICIP Inter-Carrier Interface Protocol (SMDS)

ICMP Internet Control Message Protocol (IP)

IDNX Integrated Digital Network Exchange

IDP Internetwork Datagram Protocol (IP)

IDRP InterDomain Routing Protocol (IP)

IDS Intrusion Detection System

IEC InterExchange Carrier

IEC International Electrotechnical Commission

IEEE Institute of Electrical and Electronics Engineers

IETF Internet Engineering Task Force

IGMP Internet Group Management Protocol (IP)

IGP Interior Gateway Protocol (IP)

IGRP Interior Gateway Routing Protocol (Cisco™) (IP)

ILMI Interim Local Management Interface (FR)

IMPDU Initial MAC Protocol Data Unit (DQDB)

IMSSI Inter-MAN Switching System Interface (DQDB)

I-MAC Isochronous Media Access Control (FDDI)

INMS Integrated Network Management System

intraLATA intraLocal Access Transport Area

IP Internet Protocol (DoD)

IPCP Internet Protocol Control Protocol (DoD)

IPSec   Internet Protocol Security (IP)

IPX   Internetwork Packet Exchange protocol (Novell)

IRE   Institute of Radio Engineers

IRTF   Internet Research Task Force

IS   Intermediate System (OSI)

ISA   Industry Standard Architecture

ISDN   Integrated Services Digital Network

ISDU   Isochronous Service Data Unit (DQDB)

IS-IS   Intermediate System-to-Intermediate System (OSI)

ISL   Inter-Switch Link (Cisco)

ISN   Initial Sequence Number (DoD)

ISO   International Organization for Standardization

ISO/IEC   ISO/International Electrotechnical Commission

ISOC   Internet Society

ISP   Internet Service Provider (IP)

ISSI   Inter-Switching System Interface (SMDS)

ISU   Isochronous Service User (SMDS)

ITU   International Telecommunications Union

ITU-T   ITU—Telecommunications Standardization Sector

IVR   Interactive Voice Response

IXC   IntereXchange Carrier

JISC   Japanese Industrial Standards Committee

JTC 1   Joint Technical Committee 1

kbit   kilobit (thousands of bits)

Kbps   kilobits per second (10^3 bps)

km   kilometers (10^3 meters)

L2F   Layer-2 Forwarding

L2TP   Layer-2 Tunneling Protocol

LAN   Local Area Network

LANE   LAN Emulation (ATM)

LAP-B   Link Access Procedure—Balanced (X.25)

LAP-D   Link Access Procedure—D Channel (ISDN/FR)

LAP-F   Link Access Procedure—Frame Mode (FR)

LAT   Local Area Transport protocol (DEC)

LATA   Local Access Transport Area

LB   Letter Ballot

LCGN   Logical Channel Group Number

LCN   Logical Channel Number

LCP   Link Control Protocol

LDM   Limited-Distance Modem

LDP   Label Distribution Protocol (MPLS)

LEC   Local Exchange Carrier

LEC   LAN Emulation Client (ATM)

LECS   LAN Emulation Configuration Server (ATM)

LES   LAN Emulation Server (ATM)

LLAP   LocalTalk Link Access Protocol

LLC   Logical Link Control (IEEE 802.X)

LMD   Limited-Distance Modems

LME   Layer Management Entity (DQDB)

LMI   Local Management Interface (FR)

LMP   Link Management Protocol

LMT   Layer ManagemenT

LNNI   LAN Emulation Network-to-Network Interface (ATM)

LQM   Link Quality Management

LSA   Link-State Advertisement

LSB   Least Significant Bit

LSP   Label Switched Path (MPLS)

LSR   Label Switched Router (MPLS)

LT   Line Termination

LTE   Line Terminating Equipment (SONET)

LU   Logical Unit (SNA)

m   meter

MAC   Media Access Control (IEEE 802.X)

MAN   Metropolitan Area Network (DQDB, FDDI)

MAP   Manufacturing Automation Protocol (GM)

MAU   Multistation Access Unit (IBM)

MA&E   Market Awareness and Education Committee (ATM)

Mbit   Megabits (millions of bits)

Mbps   Megabits per second (10^6 bps)

MBS   Maximum burst Size (ATM)

MBS   Mobile Broadband System

MCDV   Maximum Cell Delay Variation (ATM)

MCF   MAC Convergence Function (DQDB)

MCLR   Maximum Cell Loss Ratio (ATM)

MCP   MAC Convergence Protocol (DQDB)

MCR   Maximum Cell Rate (ATM)

MCTD   Maximum Cell Transfer Delay (ATM)

MGCP   Megaco and Media Gateway Control Protocol (ITU-H323)

MHz   Megahertz

MIB   Management Information Base (SNMP)

MIC   Media Interface Connector (FDDI)

MID   Message IDentifier (DQDB), Multiplexing IDentifier (ATM)

MIPS   Millions of Instructions Per Second

MIS   Management Information Systems

MLP   Multilink PPP

MMF   Multimode Fiber

MMP   Multichannel Multilink PPP

MoM   Mother of Management system

MOP   Maintenance and Operation Protocol (DEC)

MOSPF   Multicast Open Shortest Path First (IP)

MPEG   Moving Picture Experts Group

MPLS   MultiProtocol Label Switching

MRCMBS   MultiRate Circuit Mode Bearer Service

MRU   Multiport Repeater Unit

ms   millisecond (one-thousandth of a second, 10^{-3} seconds)

MSAP   MAC Service Access Point (SMDS)

MSB   Most Significant Bit

MSDU   MAC Service Data Unit (SMDS)

MSS   MAN Switching System (SMDS)

MTBSO   Mean Time Between Service Outages

MTBF   Mean Time Between Failures

MTU   Maximum Transmission Unit

MTU   Multiport Transceiver Unit

MUX   Multiplexer

NANP   North American Numbering Plan

NAT   Network Address Translation (IP)

NAFTA   North American Free Trade Agreement

NBP   Name Binding Protocol

NBMA   NonBroadcast MultiAccess

NCP   Network Control Protocol or Point (SNA)

NDSF   NonDispersion-Shifted Fiber

NE   Network Element

NEMA   National Electrical Manufacturers Association

NetBEUI   NetBIOS Extended User Interface

NetBIOS   Network Basic Input/Output System protocol

NFS   Network File System

NHRP   Next Hop Resolution Protocol

NHS   Next Hop Server

NIC   Network Interface Card

NIU   Network Interface Unit

NLSP   NetWare Link Services Protocol (Novell)

nm   nanometer (10^{-9} meter)

NMP   Network Management Process (SMDS)

NMS   Network Management System or Station

NNI   Network-Node Interface (SONET)

NNI   Network-to-Network Interface (FR)

NNI   Nederlands Normalisatie Instutuut

NOS   Network Operating System

NP   Network Performance

NPA   Numbering Plan Area

NRM   Normalized Response Mode (ISO)

nrt-VBR   non-real-time Variable Bit Rate (ATM)

NRZ   Non-return to zero

NRZI   Non-return to zero invert ones

ns   nanosecond (10^{-9} second)

NSAP   Network Service Access Point

NSAI   National Standards Authority of Ireland

NSF   National Science Foundation

NTx   Network Termination x (where X = 1, 2, ...)

NTSC   North American Television Standard Coding

NVRAM   Non-Volatile RAM

NYSE   New York Stock Exchange

NZ-DSF   Non-Zero-Dispersion-Shifted Fiber

OADM   Optical Add Drop Multiplexer

OAM&P   Operation, Administration, Maintenance, and Provisioning

OC-N   Optical Carrier Level N (SONET)

ODA   Office Document Architecture

OEO   Optical-Electrical-Optical

OE/OP   Order Entry/Order Provisioning

OH   Overhead

OID   Object Identifier (SNMP)

OOF   Out of Frame

ONA   Open Network Architecture

OpEx   Operational Expense

ORA   Organizational Registration Authority

OS   Operating System

OSI   Open Systems Interconnection

OSI CLNS   Connectionless Network System (OSI)

OSIRM   OSI Reference Model

OSNR   Optical Signal-to-Noise Ratio

OSPF   Open Shortest Path First (IP)

OSRP   Optical Signaling and Routing Protocol (CIENA)

OSS   Operations and Support System

OTC   Operating Telephone Company

OUI   Organizationally Unique Identifier

OXC   Optical Cross-Connect

PA   PreArbitrated segment or slot (DQDB)

PABX   Private Automatic Branch Exchange

PAD   Packet Assembler/Disassembler (X.25)

PAF   PreArbitrated Function (DQDB)

PAP   Password Authentication Protocol (PPP)

PAT   Port Address Translation

PBX   Private Branch Exchange

PC   Personal Computer

PCR   Peak Cell Rate (ATM)

PDA   Personal Digital Assistant

PDC   Packet Data Channel (FDDI)

PDH   Plesiochronous Digital Hierarchy

PDN   Public Data Network

PDS   Packet Driver Specification for public domain

PDU   Protocol Data Unit (IEEE)

PGP   Pretty Good Privacy

Ph-SAP   Physical layer SAP (DQDB)

PHY   PHYsical layer standard (FDDI)

PID   Protocol IDentification

Ping   Packet Internet Groper (IP)

PIR   Protocol Independent Routing

PKI   Public Key Infrastructure

PL   PAD Length (DQDB)

PLP   Packet Layer Protocol (X.25 Level 3 – X.25 Protocol)

PLCP   Physical Layer Convergence Protocol (DQDB)

PM   Performance Monitoring

PM   Physical Medium (B-ISDN/ATM)

PMD   Physical Medium Dependent (FDDI)

PNNI   Private Network-Network Interface (ATM)

POH   Path Overhead (SONET)

POI   Path Overhead Identifier (DQDB)

PON   Passive Optical Network

PoP   Point of Presence

POS   Point-Of-Sale

POTS   Plain Old Telephone Service

PPP   Point-to-Point Protocol

Pps   Packets per second

PPTP   Point-to-Point Tunneling Protocol

PRI   Primary Rate Interface (ISDN)

PSE   Packet Switch Exchange (X.25)

PSPDN   Packet-Switched Public Data Network

PT   Payload Type

PTE   Path-Terminating Equipment (PTE)

PTT   Postal, Telegraph & Telephone Ministry/Administration

PU   Physical Unit (SNA)

PVC   Permanent Virtual Circuit or Channel (FR, X.25)

QA   Queued Arbitrated (DQDB) segment, slot, access function

QAF   Queued Arbitrated Function (DQDB)

QoS   Quality of Service

QPSX   Queued Packet and Synchronous Exchange

RARP   Reverse Address Resolution Protocol

RBOC   Regional Bell Operating Company

RCP   Remote Console Protocol (DEC)

RDI   Remote Defect Indication (ATM)

REJ   Reject frame

RFC   Request For Comments

RFI   Request For Information

RFP   Request For Proposal

RFQ   Request For Quote

RHC   Regional Holding Company

RISC   Reduced Instruction Set Computer

RIF   Routing Information Field (Token Ring)

RIP   Routing Information Protocol (IP)

RISC   Reduced Instruction Set Computer

RJE   Remote Job Entry

RMT   Ring Management (FDDI)

RMON   Remote Monitoring

RNR   Receive Not Ready

ROC   Return On Communications

ROI   Return On Investment

RPC   Remote Procedure Call

RQ   Request Counter (DQDB)

RR   Receive Ready frame

rt-VBR   real-time Variable Bit Rate (ATM)

RTMP   Routing and Management Protocol (Apple)

RTP   Real-time Transport Protocol

RTS   Request To Send

s   second

SA   Source Address field

SADM   SONET Add/Drop Multiplexer

SAID   Security Association IDentification

SAN   Storage Area Network

SAP   Service Access Point (ISO)

SAPI   Service Access Point Identifier (ISO)

SAR   Segmentation and Re-assembly (ATM)

SAS   Single-Attach Station connection (FDDI)

SASO   Saudi Arabian Standards Organization

SCM   Supply Chain Management

SCR   Sustainable Cell Rate (ATM)

SD   Start Delimiter

SDH   Synchronous Digital Hierarchy (ITU-T)

SDLC   Synchronous Data Link Control protocol (IBM)

SDM   Space Division Multiplexing

SDSAF   Switched Digital Services Application Forum

SDSL   Symmetric Digital Subscriber Line

SDU   Service Data Unit (DQDB)

SDXC   SONET Digital Cross-Connect

SEF   Severely Errored Framing (SONET)

SES   Severely Errored Seconds (SONET)

SF   SuperFrame

SFS   Suomen Standardisoimisliito (Finland)

SGMP   Simple Gateway Monitoring Protocol

SIG   SMDS Interest Group (SMDS)

SIP   SMDS Interface Protocol (SMDS)

SIP   Session Initiation Protocol (ITU-H323)

SIR   Sustained Information Rate (SMDS)

SIS   Standardiseringskommissionen i Sverige (Sweden)

SLA   Service Level Agreement

SLIP   Serial Line Internet Protocol (IP)

SMDS   Switched Multimegabit Data Service

SMF   Single-Mode Fiber

SMT   System Management protocol (FDDI)

SMTP   Simple Mail Transfer Protocol

SN   Sequence Number

SNA   System Network Architecture (IBM)

SNAP   SubNetwork Access Protocol (SMDS)

SNI   Subscriber Network Interface (SMDS)

SNMP   Simple Network Management Protocol (DoD)

SOGA   SNA Open Gateway Architecture

SOH   Section Overhead

SOHO   Small Office, Home Office

SONET   Synchronous Optical Network (ANSI)

SPE   Synchronous Payload Envelope (SONET)

SPF   Shortest Path First algorithm

SPID   Service Profile Identifier (ISDN)

SPM   FDDI-to-SONET Physical Layer Mapping standard

SPM   Statistical Packet Multiplexing

SPX   Sequenced Packet Exchange (Novell)

SRB   Source-Route Bridging (IBM)

SRDM   SubRate Data Multiplexing

SREJ   Select Reject frame

SRP   Source Routing Protocol (IBM)

SRT   Source Routing Transparent protocol

SS   Switching System (SMDS)

SSAP   Source Service Access Point (LLC)

SSB   Single Side Band

SSCOP   Service-Specific Connection Oriented Protocol (ATM)

SSCS   Service-Specific Convergence Sublayer (ATM)

STDM   Statistical Time Division Multiplexing

STE   Section Terminating Equipment (SONET)

STM   Synchronous Transfer Mode or Station Management (SDH)

STM-n   Synchronous Transport Module Level *n* (SDH)

STP   Shielded Twisted Pair

STP   Spanning Tree Protocol (IEEE 802.1d)

STS-n   Synchronous Transport Signal Level *n* (SONET)

STS-Nc   Concatenated Synchronous Transport Signal Level *N*

STUN   Serial Tunnel (HDLC to SDLC)

SVC   Switched Virtual Circuit or Signaling Virtual Channel (FR, ATM)

SYN   Synchronous Idle

t   time

TA   Terminal Adapter

TAG   Technical Advisory Group

TC   Transmission Convergence sublayer of PHY layer (ATM)

TCP   Transmission Control Protocol (DoD)

TCP/IP   Transmission Control Protocol/Internet Protocol (DoD)

TDM   Time Division Multiplexing

TDMA   Time Division Multiple Access

TDS   Time Division Switch

TE   Terminal Equipment

TEI   Terminal Endpoint Identifier (FR)

TFTP   Trivial File Transfer Protocol

TIA   Telecommunications Industries Association

TLAP   Token Talk Link Access Protocol

TLS   Transparent LAN Service (ATM)

TMN   Telecommunications Management Network

TOP   Technical and Office Protocol (Boeing)

TOS   Type Of Service

TP   Transport Protocol (CCITT)

TP4   Transport Protocol Class 4 (ISO)

TR   Technical Report

TTL   Time To Live (IP)

TUD   Trunk Up-Down (ATM)

UBR   Unspecified Bit Rate (ATM)

UDP   User Datagram Protocol (DoD)

UMTS   Universal Mobile Telecommunication System

UNI   User-to-Network Interface

UNMA   Unified Network Management Architecture (AT&T)

UPC   Usage Parameter Control

UPSR   Unidirectional Path-Switched Ring

UTP   Unshielded Twisted Pair

VAD   Voice Activity Detection

VAX   Virtual Address eXtension (DEC)

VBR   Variable Bit Rate (ATM)

VBR-rt   Variable Bit Rate-real-time (ATM)

VBR-nrt   Variable Bit Rate-non-real-time (ATM)

VC   Virtual Channel or Virtual Call (ATM)

VCC   Virtual Channel Connection (ATM)

VCI   Virtual Channel or Circuit Identifier (DQDB)

VC-n   Virtual Container-n (SDH)

VDSL   Very High Data Rate Digital Subscriber Line

VLAN   Virtual LAN

VLSI   Very Large Scale Integration

VLSM   Variable Length Subnet Mask (IP)

VoATM   Voice over ATM

VoDSL   Voice over DSL

VoIP   Voice over IP

VoFR   Voice over Frame Relay

VoP   Voice over Packet

VP   Virtual Path (ATM)

VPC   Virtual Path Connection (ATM)

VPDN   Virtual Private Data Network

VPI   Virtual Path Identifier (ATM)

VPN   Virtual Private Network

VT   Virtual Tributary (SONET)

VTAM   Virtual Telecommunications Access Method (SNA)

VTP   VLAN Trunk Protocol

VTx   VT of size x (currently $x = 1.5, 2, 3, 6$)

VTx-Nc   Concatenated Virtual Tributary (SONET)

WAN   Wide Area Network

WAP   Wireless Access Protocol

WaRP   Wavelength Routing Protocol (Cisco)

W-CDMA   Wideband Code Division Multiple Access

WDM   Wavelength Division Multiplexing

WDXC   Wideband Digital Cross-Connect

WLL   Wireless Local Loop

WWW   World Wide Web

XNS   Xerox Network Systems protocol (XEROX)

xDSL   x-Type Digital Subscriber Line

ZIP   Zone Information Protocol

µs   microsecond (10^{-6} second)

APPENDIX B

Standards Sources

Alpha Graphics

10215 N. 35th Avenue, Suites A&B
Phoenix, AZ 85051
(602) 863-0999 (IEEE P802 draft standards)

American National Standards Institute—ANSI—Sales Department

New York City Office
25 West 43rd Street, 4th Fl.
New York, NY 10036
(212) 642-4900 / Fax (212) 398-0023

ATM Forum

Presidio of San Francisco
P.O. Box 29920 (mail)
572B Ruger Street (surface)
San Francisco, CA 94129-0920
(415) 561-6275 / Fax (415) 561-6120

British Standards Institution (BSI)

389 Chiswick High Road
London W4 4AL UK
(44) 20-8996-9000 / Fax (44) 20-8996-7001

Canadian Standards Association

178 Rexdale Boulevard
Rexdale
ON M9W 1R3 Canada
(416) 747-4044 / 1 (800) 463-6727 / Fax (416) 747-2510

Comite Europeen de Normalisation

36 rue de Stassart
B1050 BRUXELLES Belgique
(322) 550-08-19 / Fax (322) 550-08-11

Deutsches Institut für Normung (DIN)

Burggrafenstrasse 6
10787 Berlin, Germany
(49) 30-2601-0 / Fax (49) 30-2601-1231

Electronics Industries Alliance (EIA)

Electronic Industries Alliance
2500 Wilson Blvd.
Arlington, VA 22201
(703) 907-7500

European Computer Manufacturers Association (ECMA)

ECMA 114 Rue du Rhône
CH-1204, Geneva, Switzerland
(41) 22-735-36-34 / Telex (41) 3237-ECMA-CH /
Fax (41) 22-786-52-31

European Conference of Postal and Telecommunications Administrations—CEPT

Radiocommunications Agency Wyndham House,
189 Marsh Wall, London E14 9SX UK
(44) 207-211-0660 / Fax (44) 207-211-0047

Exchange Carriers Standards Association (ECSA)

5430 Grosvenor Lane
Bethesda, MD 20814-2122
(301) 564-4505 (ANSI T1 secretariat)

Information Handling Services

15 Inverness Way East
Englewood, CO 80112
(800) 854-7179 / Fax (303) 397-2599

Information Technology Industry Council

1250 Eye Street NW, Suite 200
Washington, DC 20005
(202) 737-8888 / Fax (202) 638-4922

Institute of Electrical and Electronics Engineers (IEEE)— Computer Society

445 Hoes Lane
Piscataway, NJ 08854-1331
(732) 981-0060 / Fax (732) 981-1721

International Organization for Standardization

1 Rue de Varembe, Case Postale 56
CH-1211 Geneva 20, Switzerland
(41) 22-749-01-11 / Fax (41) 22-733-34-30

International Telecommunications Union—General Secretariat—Sales Service

Place de Nation, CH 1211
Geneva 20, Switzerland
(41) 22-730-5111 (ITU Switchboard) / Fax (41) 22-733-7256

Internet Access to Request for Comments (RFCs)

Internet: logon "anonymous"; password "guest"

Japanese Industrial Standards Committee (JISC)

Standards Department, Agency of Industrial Science & Technology
Ministry of International Trade and Industry
1-3-1, Kasumigaseki, Chiyoda-ku, Tokyo 100 Japan
(81) 3-501-9295-6 / Fax (81) 3-680-1418

National Institute of Standards and Technology

100 Bureau Drive, Stop 3460
Gaithersburg, MD 20899-3460
(301) 975-NIST (6478) / TTY (301) 975-8295

National Standards Authority of Ireland

Glasnevin
Dublin 9, Ireland
(353) 1-8073800 / Fax (353) 1-8073838

Nederlands Normalisatie-Instituut

Vlinderweg 6
2623 AX Delft, Netherlands
(015) 2-690-390 / (015) 2-690-190

Omnicom, Inc.

12700 Shelbyville Road - Barkley Building, Suite 100
Louisville, KY 40243
(502) 244-4215 / Fax (502) 244-4216

SRI International

333 Ravenswood Avenue
Menlo Park, CA 94025
(650) 859-2000 / Fax (650) 326-5512
(Requests for Comments [RFC] documents)

Suomen Standardisoimisliitto

P.O. Box 205, SF-00121
Helsinki 12, Finland
(358) 0-645-601 / Telex:122303-STAND-SF

U.S. Department of Commerce—National Technical Information Service—NEC Research Institute

5285 Port Royal Road
Springfield, VA 22161
(703) 487-4650
(ITU recommendations, U.S. Government and
Military standards)

APPENDIX C

IP Mask
Reference Table

This reference contains a guideline for choosing an IP subnetwork mask. The following table is arranged so that the user can select the number of networks and hosts available per mask. Note that the number of actual networks per mask is two less than what is possible because all 1's and all 0's are reserved. The actual network numbers available per mask are provided in the rightmost column.

Mask	B7	B6	B5	B4	B3	B2	B1	B0	Possible Networks (Available Networks)	Hosts	Net numbers
128	1	0	0	0	0	0	0	0	2 (0)	128	0, 128
192	1	1	0	0	0	0	0	0	4 (2)	64	0, 64, 128, 192
224	1	1	1	0	0	0	0	0	8 (6)	32	0, 32, 64, 96, etc., to 224
240	1	1	1	1	0	0	0	0	16 (14)	16	0, 16, 32, etc., to 240
248	1	1	1	1	1	0	0	0	32 (30)	8	0, 8, 16, 24, etc., to 248
252	1	1	1	1	1	1	0	0	64 (62)	4	0, 4, 8, 12, etc., to 252
254	1	1	1	1	1	1	1	0	128 (126)	2	0, 2, 4, 6, 8, etc., to 254
	128	64	32	16	8	4	2	1			

Note: All 1's and 0's are technically reserved for network (0) or broadcast (1) (typical configuration), so masks like 128, 64, etc., are invalid.

B = bit position, Hosts = number of hosts

APPENDIX D

IP Network: Addressing Reference

T his table can be used to find the network subnet mask that provides a specific number of hosts and networks for classes A, B, and C IP addresses.

128 Subnet Mask Example (256-128=128)

Network	Net#	Binary	Address Class A	Address Class B	Address Class C
.000	res	0XXX.XXXX	XXX.000.XXX.XXX	XXX.XXX.000.XXX	XXX.XXX.XXX.000
.128	res	1XXX.XXXX	XXX.128.XXX.XXX	XXX.XXX.128.XXX	XXX.XXX.XXX.128

192 Subnet Mask Example (256-192=64)

Network	Net#	Binary	Address Class A	Address Class B	Address Class C
.000	res	00XX.XXXX	XXX.000.XXX.XXX	XXX.XXX.000.XXX	XXX.XXX.XXX.000
.064	1	01XX.XXXX	XXX.064.XXX.XXX	XXX.XXX.064.XXX	XXX.XXX.XXX.064
.128	2	10XX.XXXX	XXX.128.XXX.XXX	XXX.XXX.128.XXX	XXX.XXX.XXX.128
.192	res	11XX.XXXX	XXX.192.XXX.XXX	XXX.XXX.192.XXX	XXX.XXX.XXX.192

224 Subnet Mask Example (256-224=32)

Network	Net#	Binary	Address Class A	Address Class B	Address Class C
.000	res	000X.XXXX	XXX.000.XXX.XXX	XXX.XXX.000.XXX	XXX.XXX.XXX.000
.032	1	001X.XXXX	XXX.032.XXX.XXX	XXX.XXX.032.XXX	XXX.XXX.XXX.032
.064	2	010X.XXXX	XXX.064.XXX.XXX	XXX.XXX.064.XXX	XXX.XXX.XXX.064
.096	3	011X.XXXX	XXX.096.XXX.XXX	XXX.XXX.096.XXX	XXX.XXX.XXX.096
.128	4	100X.XXXX	XXX.128.XXX.XXX	XXX.XXX.128.XXX	XXX.XXX.XXX.128
.160	5	101X.XXXX	XXX.160.XXX.XXX	XXX.XXX.160.XXX	XXX.XXX.XXX.160
.192	6	110X.XXXX	XXX.192.XXX.XXX	XXX.XXX.192.XXX	XXX.XXX.XXX.192
.224	res	111X.XXXX	XXX.224.XXX.XXX	XXX.XXX.224.XXX	XXX.XXX.XXX.224

240 Subnet Mask Example (256-240=16)

Network	Net#	Binary	Address Class A	Address Class B	Address Class C
.000	res	0000.XXXX	XXX.000.XXX.XXX	XXX.XXX.000.XXX	XXX.XXX.XXX.000
.016	1	0001.XXXX	XXX.016.XXX.XXX	XXX.XXX.016.XXX	XXX.XXX.XXX.016
.032	2	0010.XXXX	XXX.032.XXX.XXX	XXX.XXX.032.XXX	XXX.XXX.XXX.032
.048	3	0011.XXXX	XXX.048.XXX.XXX	XXX.XXX.048.XXX	XXX.XXX.XXX.048
.064	4	0100.XXXX	XXX.064.XXX.XXX	XXX.XXX.064.XXX	XXX.XXX.XXX.064
.080	5	0101.XXXX	XXX.080.XXX.XXX	XXX.XXX.080.XXX	XXX.XXX.XXX.080
.096	6	0110.XXXX	XXX.096.XXX.XXX	XXX.XXX.096.XXX	XXX.XXX.XXX.096
.112	7	0111.XXXX	XXX.112.XXX.XXX	XXX.XXX.112.XXX	XXX.XXX.XXX.112
.128	8	1000.XXXX	XXX.128.XXX.XXX	XXX.XXX.128.XXX	XXX.XXX.XXX.128
.144	9	1001.XXXX	XXX.144.XXX.XXX	XXX.XXX.144.XXX	XXX.XXX.XXX.144

.160	10	1010.XXXX	XXX.160.XXX.XXX	XXX.XXX.160.XXX	XXX.XXX.XXX.160
.176	11	1011.XXXX	XXX.176.XXX.XXX	XXX.XXX.176.XXX	XXX.XXX.XXX.176
.192	12	1100.XXXX	XXX.192.XXX.XXX	XXX.XXX.192.XXX	XXX.XXX.XXX.192
.208	13	1101.XXXX	XXX.208.XXX.XXX	XXX.XXX.208.XXX	XXX.XXX.XXX.208
.224	14	1110.XXXX	XXX.224.XXX.XXX	XXX.XXX.224.XXX	XXX.XXX.XXX.224
.240	res	1111.XXXX	XXX.240.XXX.XXX	XXX.XXX.240.XXX	XXX.XXX.XXX.240

248 Subnet Mask Example (256-248=8)

Network	Net#	Binary			
0	res	0000.0XXX	XXX.000.XXX.XXX	XXX.XXX.000.XXX	XXX.XXX.XXX.000
8	1	0000.1XXX	XXX.008.XXX.XXX	XXX.XXX.008.XXX	XXX.XXX.XXX.008
16	2	0001.0XXX	XXX.016.XXX.XXX	XXX.XXX.016.XXX	XXX.XXX.XXX.016
24	3	0010.0XXX	XXX.024.XXX.XXX	XXX.XXX.024.XXX	XXX.XXX.XXX.024
32	4	0010.1XXX	XXX.032.XXX.XXX	XXX.XXX.032.XXX	XXX.XXX.XXX.032
40	5	0011.0XXX	XXX.040.XXX.XXX	XXX.XXX.040.XXX	XXX.XXX.XXX.040
48	6	0011.1XXX	XXX.048.XXX.XXX	XXX.XXX.048.XXX	XXX.XXX.XXX.048

And so forth in increments of 8 until

.232	29	1110.1XXX	XXX.232.XXX.XXX	XXX.XXX.232.XXX	XXX.XXX.XXX.232
.240	30	1111.0XXX	XXX.240.XXX.XXX	XXX.XXX.240.XXX	XXX.XXX.XXX.240
.248	res	1111.1XXX	XXX.248.XXX.XXX	XXX.XXX.248.XXX	XXX.XXX.XXX.248

252 Subnet Mask Example (256-252=4)

Network	Net#	Binary	Address Class A	Address Class B	Address Class C
.000	res	0000.00XX	XXX.000.XXX.XXX	XXX.XXX.000.XXX	XXX.XXX.XXX.000
.004	1	0000.01XX	XXX.004.XXX.XXX	XXX.XXX.004.XXX	XXX.XXX.XXX.004
.008	2	0000.10XX	XXX.008.XXX.XXX	XXX.XXX.008.XXX	XXX.XXX.XXX.008

And so forth in increments of 4 until

.248	62	1111.10XX	XXX.248.XXX.XXX	XXX.XXX.248.XXX	XXX.XXX.XXX.248
.252	res	1111.11XX	XXX.252.XXX.XXX	XXX.XXX.252.XXX	XXX.XXX.XXX.252

254 Subnet Mask Example (256-254=2)

Network	Net#	Binary	Address Class A	Address Class B	Address Class C
.000	res	0000.000X	XXX.000.XXX.XXX	XXX.XXX.000.XXX	XXX.XXX.XXX.000
.002	1	0000.001X	XXX.002.XXX.XXX	XXX.XXX.002.XXX	XXX.XXX.XXX.002
.004	2	0000.010X	XXX.004.XXX.XXX	XXX.XXX.004.XXX	XXX.XXX.XXX.004
.006	3	0000.011X	XXX.006.XXX.XXX	XXX.XXX.006.XXX	XXX.XXX.XXX.006

And so forth in increments of 2 until

.252	126	1111.110X	XXX.252.XXX.XXX	XXX.XXX.252.XXX	XXX.XXX.XXX.252
.254	res	1111.111X	XXX.254.XXX.XXX	XXX.XXX.254.XXX	XXX.XXX.XXX.254

APPENDIX E

Glossary

10BASE2	IEEE 802.3 standard specifying Ethernet over thin coax cable.
10BASE5	IEEE 802.3 standard specifying Ethernet over thick coax cable.
10BASET	IEEE 802.3 standard specifying Ethernet over UTP.
10BASEF	IEEE 802.3 standard specifying Ethernet over fiber.
100BASEFX	100 Mbps standard specifying Ethernet over fiber.
100BASET4	100 Mbps standard specifying Ethernet over category 3, 4, or 5 cabling. Compatible with 802.3 MAC sublayer format.
100BASETX	100 Mbps standard specifying Ethernet over category 5 and Type 1 cabling. Compatible with 802.3 MAC sublayer format.
100VG-AnyLAN	IEEE standard specifying 100 Mbps Ethernet and Token Ring over 4-pair UTP.
Access unit	In DQDB, the functional unit within a node that performs the DQDB layer functions and controls access to both buses.
Address	An identifier of a source or destination in a network. Examples of addresses are IP, E.164, and X.121.
Address Resolution Protocol (ARP)	Protocol used to resolve a destination host MAC address from its known IP address.
Address Translation	A method of converting a user-protocol address into the standard address format of the network protocol, and vice versa.
Agent	Software residing in a managed network device that reports MIB variables through SNMP.
American National Standards Institute (ANSI)	A private, nongovernmental, nonprofit national organization that serves as the primary coordinator of standards within the U.S.
Analog	Voice or data signals that are continuously variable and possess an infinite number of values (compared to digital, which has discrete variables).
Application Layer (OSI)	Layer 7 of the OSIRM. Provides the management of communications between user applications. Examples include e-mail and file transfer.
Asynchronous Transfer Mode (ATM)	A high-speed, connection-oriented multiplexing and switching method specified in international standards utilizing fixed-length cells to support multiple types of traffic. It is asynchronous in the sense that cells carrying user data need not be periodic.

Asynchronous Transmission	The transmission of data through start and stop sequences without the use of a common clock.
ATM Adaptation Layer (AAL)	A set of internationally standardized protocols and formats that define support for circuit emulation, packet video and audio, and connection-oriented and connectionless data services.
Available Bit Rate (ABR)	A traffic class of ATM.
B-channel	An ISDN bearer service channel that can carry either voice or data at a speed of 64 Kbps.
Backward Explicit Congestion Notification (BECN)	Convention in frame relay (FR) for a network device to notify the user (source) device that network congestion has occurred.
bandwidth	The amount of transport resource available to pass information (passband), measured in hertz for analog and bits per second for digital carriers.
Bandwidth Balancing	A DQDB scheme where a node that is queued for access will occasionally *not* seize an empty QA slot. This helps to ensure effective sharing of QA slots.
Basic Mode	An FDDI mode of ring operation that supports packet-switching services only where MAC PDUs are transmitted directly by the PHY protocol.
Basic Rate Interface (BRI)	An ISDN access interface type composed of two B-channels each at 64 Kbps and one D-channel at 16 Kbps (2B+D).
B-channel	An ISDN bearer service channel that can carry either voice or data at a speed of 64 Kbps.
Bell Operating Company (BOC)	One of the 22 local telephone companies formed after the divestiture of AT&T (for example, Illinois Bell, Ohio Bell).
Bisync (BSC) or Binary Synchronous Communications Protocol	An IBM proprietary bit-oriented protocol.
Bridge	A LAN/WAN device operating at Layers 1 (physical) and 2 (data link) of the OSIRM.
Broadband	A general term for bandwidth that exceeds Mbps.
Broadband ISDN (B-ISDN)	A set of services, capabilities, and interfaces supporting an integrated network and user interface at speeds greater than that of ISDN. The ITU-T initially decided to develop B-ISDN using ATM in 1988.

Broadcast A transmission to all addresses on the network or subnetwork.

Broadcast Address A predefined network address that indicates all possible receivers on a network.

Brouter A device that combines some elements of both bridging and routing.

Busy Slot A DQDB slot that is "in use" and not available for access by the QA access functions.

Cell A fixed-length 53-octet packet, or Protocol Data Unit (PDU) used in ATM. The ATM cell has a 5-octet header and a 48-octet payload.

Cell Header A 5-octet header that defines control information used in processing, multiplexing, and switching ATM cells.

Central Office (CO) Telephone company switching office providing local user access to the local switched telephone network and its services; often the first interface to inter-exchange carriers.

Central Office Vendors A reference to vendors who provide switching equipment conforming to central office standards, such as Lucent, Siemens, and Alcatel.

Circuit Switching A connection-oriented technique based on either time- or space-division multiplexing and switching providing minimal delay. Bandwidth is dedicated to the connection.

Client-Server Architecture The distribution of network control across many computing elements within the network. Thus, some elements act as servers, controlling the transfer, and some as clients that transmit and receive the information. Servers can do all three functions, and are often the workhorse computing elements (multi-GHz machines), while the clients are typically workstations and terminals.

Colocated Devices near one another at the same site.

Committed Information Rate (CIR) A term defined for frame relay service that defines the minimum rate at which a user can send frames and be guaranteed delivery by the network. Transmissions exceeding the CIR may be subject to lower-priority treatment or discard.

Concatenated Virtual Tributary (VTx-Nc) A combination of VTs where the VT envelope capacities from N VTx's have been combined to carry a VTx-Nc that must be transported as a single entity (as opposed to being transported as separate signals).

Concentrator A device providing a single network access for multiple user devices. In FDDI, a device that has additional ports beyond what is required for its own attachment to the ring.

Congestion The condition where network resources (bandwidth) are exceeded by an accumulation of demand.

Consolidated Link Layer Management (CLLM) In frame relay, an ANSI-defined method of sending link layer management messages over the last DLCI (1023). These messages are used to identify the exact cause of congestion and modify transmissions based on each DLCI.

Convergence Function A DQDB protocol layer that interfaces service-specific interfaces to higher-layer protocol functions.

Countdown Counter (CD) A queued, arbitrated access method for determining how many empty slots must pass before a node has access to the DQDB bus.

Customer Premises Equipment (CPE) Equipment that resides and is operated at a customer site.

Cycle The Protocol Data Unit (PDU) used in FDDI-II.

Cyclic Redundancy Check (CRC) An algorithm that detects bit errors caused in data transmission.

D4 AT&T-defined framing and synchronization format for T1 transmission facilities.

Data Communications (or Circuit Termination) Equipment (DCE) Data communications equipment defined by the standards as a modem or network communications interface device.

Datagram A packet mode of transmitting data where there is no guaranteed sequential delivery (connectionless service).

Data Link Connection Identifier (DLCI) A FR address designator for each virtual circuit termination point.

Data Link Layer (OSI) Layer 2 of the OSIRM. Provides for the error-free communications between adjacent network devices over a physical interface. Examples include the LLC and MAC layers that manage LAN and MAN operation.

Data Terminal Equipment (DTE) Data-processing equipment defined by the standards as interfacing to the communications network (DCE).

D-channel The ISDN out-of-band (16 Kbps or 64 Kbps, depending on BRI or PRI, respectively) signaling channel that carries the ISDN user signals or can be used to carry packet-mode data.

Default Slot Generator Function In DQDB, the function defining the identity for each bus in the dual bus network. In the looped bus topology, this function also provides the head of bus function for both buses.

Delay-Insensitive *See time-insensitive.*

Delay-Sensitive *See time-sensitive.*

Derived MAC Protocol Data Unit (MAC-PDU or DMPDU) In DQDB, single 44-octet portion of the original IMPDU, composed of 4 overhead octets and a 44-octet segmentation unit.

Digital Signals that have discrete values, such as binary bit streams of 0's and 1's.

Digital Cross-Connect System (DXC) Breaks down a T1 into individual DS0s for testing and reconfiguration (DS3s into DS1s).

Digital Signal 0 (DS0) One 56 Kbps framed channel out of the 24 contained in a DS1 channel.

Digital Signal 1 (DS1) The North American standard 1.544 Mbps digital channel.

Digital Signal 3 (DS3) The North American standard 44.736 Mbps digital channel.

Discard Eligibility (DE) Bit Used in frame relay, this bit signals (when set to 1) that the particular frame is eligible for discard during congestion conditions.

Distributed Processing Sharing of applications, data, and the tasks operating among several small or midrange processing devices, as opposed to a single mainframe in centralized processing.

Distributed Queue The operation of the DQDB Queued Arbitration MAC scheme, where all nodes keep track of the number of stations queued for access in their request counter; when a station queues itself for access, it keeps track of its position in the queue using its countdown counter and it counts the number of stations behind it in the queue in the request counter.

Distributed Queue Dual Bus (DQDB) The IEEE 802.6 MAN architecture standard for providing both circuit-switched (isochronous) and packet-switched services.

DQDB Layer The lower portion of the DQDB link layer that provides the connectionless MAC data service, connection-oriented data service, and an isochronous service with the help of physical layer services.

Dual-Attachment Station (DAS)
A workstation that attaches to both primary and secondary FDDI MAN rings that enables the capability for network self-healing.

Dual Bus
Bus A and bus B, dual DQDB bus structure. The dual bus supports both the open dual bus and the looped dual bus.

E1
The European T1 CEPT standard digital channel operating at 2.048 Mbps.

E1 Carrier
Part of the European and Asian (excluding Japan) digital TDM hierarchy: a single multiplexed 2.048 Mbps channel.

E.164
A CCITT Recommendation for defining addresses in a public data international network, varying in size up to 15 digits.

Enterprise Network
A network that spans an entire organization.

Entity
In the OSIRM, a service of management element between peers and within a sublayer or layer.

Ethernet
A LAN that uses CSAM/CD media access method and operates at 10, 100, or 1000 Mbps.

Explicit Congestion Notification (ECN)
In FR, the use of either FECN and BECN or CLLM messages to notify the source and destination of network congestion (as opposed to implicit congestion notification).

Fast Packet
The generic term used for advanced packet technologies such as FR and ATM.

Fiber Distributed Data Interface (FDDI)
Fiber-optic LAN operating at 100 Mbps.

FDDI-II
FDDI standard with the additional capability to carry isochronous traffic (voice/video).

FDDI Follow-On (FDDI-FO)
Future ANSI standards for extending the speed of FDDI up to 600 Mbps.

Fiber Optics
Plastic or glass fibers that transmit high data rates using optical signals.

Filtering
The selection of frames not to remain at the local LAN but to be forwarded to another network by a network device (for example, router).

Flag
Character that signals a beginning or end of a frame.

Forward Explicit Congestion Notification (FECN)
Convention in frame relay for a network device to notify the user (destination) device that network congestion is occurring.

Fractional T1 (FT1) The transmission of a fraction of a T1 channel, usually based on 64 Kbps increments but not less than 64 Kbps total.

Frame An OSI data link layer unit of transmission whose length is defined by flags at the beginning and end.

Frame Check Sequence (FCS) A field in an X.25, SDLC, or HDLC frame that contains the result of a CRC error-checking algorithm.

Frame Relay An ANSI and CCITT LAN/WAN networking standard for switching frames in a packet mode similar to X.25, but at higher speeds and with less nodal processing (assuming digital transmission).

Frame Relay Assembler/Disassembler (FRAD) A device that acts as a concentrator and protocol translator from nonframe relay protocols (for example, SDLC, SNA) to a standard frame relay transmission.

Frequency Division Multiplexing (FDM) The method of aggregating multiple simultaneous transmissions (circuits) over a single high-speed channel by using individual frequency passbands for each circuit (for example, RF Broadband LANs).

Full-Duplex The simultaneous bidirectional transmission of information over a common medium.

Gateway A network device that interconnects dissimilar types of network elements through all seven layers of the OSIRM.

Global Addressing A frame relay addressing convention where a single, unique DLCI value is given to each user device on the network.

Half-Duplex The bidirectional transmission of information over a common medium, but where information may only travel in one direction at any one time.

Head of Bus (HOB_A and HOB_B) In DQDB, the node responsible for generating empty slots and management information octets.

Host An end-communicating station in a network; also an IP address.

Implicit Congestion Notification A congestion indication that is performed by upper-layer protocols (for example, TCP) rather than network or data link layer protocol conventions.

Individual Address The address of a specific network station or node. In IP, the format is XXXX.XXXX.XXXX.XXXX—for example, 192.8.13.1.

Initial MAC Protocol Data Unit (IMPDU) In DQDB, the PDU formed by the DQDB layer providing a connectionless MAC service to the LLC.

Integrated Services Digital Network (ISDN)	CCITT I-series Recommendation defining the digital network standard for integrated voice and data-network access and services and user-network messages.
Integrated Switching	The method of performing multiple switching techniques with one device or within a single hardware architecture, including consolidated configuration and network management.
IntereXchange Carrier (IXC)	The provider of long distance (inter-LATA) service in the U.S.; also the provider of worldwide switched voice and data services.
Interface	In OSI, the boundary between two adjacent protocol layers (for example, network to transport).
Interim Local Management Interface (ILMI)	An SNMP-based management protocol for an ATM UNI defined by the ATM Forum.
Internetwork	A master network made up of multiple smaller networks, or the concept of bridging, routing, switching, or gateway between homogeneous network devices, protocols, and standards.
Interoperability	The ability of multiple, dissimilar vendor devices and protocols to operate and communicate using a standard set of rules and protocols.
Intra-LATA	LEC-defined geographic areas (Local Access Transport Area). LEC must pass cells to IXC to go inter-LATA.
Isochronous	The circuit-switched transmission service offered in DQDB and FDDI-II. This allows a consistent timed access of network bandwidth for time-sensitive transmission of voice and video traffic.
Layer Management	Network management functions that provide information about the operations of a given OSI protocol layer.
Layer Management Entity (LME)	In DQDB, the entity within the protocol layer responsible for performing local management of the layer.
Layer Management Interface (LMI)	In DQDB, the interface between the LME and network management systems.
Line-Terminating Equipment (LTE)	A device that either originates or terminates an OC-*N* signal and that may originate, access, modify, and terminate the transport overhead.

Link Access Protocol on the D-channel (LAPD)	CCITT Recommendations Q.920 (I.440) and Q.921 (I.441) defining standards for the data link layer operation of ISDN D and FR.
Local Area Network (LAN)	A MAC-level data and computer communications network confined to short geographic distances.
Local Bridge	A high-throughput, colocated LAN-to-LAN interconnectivity device.
Local Exchange Carrier (LEC)	In the U.S., traditionally a local phone service provider that now can compete in inter-LATA service.
Local Management Interface (LMI)	A set of user device-to-network communications standards used in ATM DXI and FR.
Logical Link Control (LLC)	The upper half of the OSIRM data link layer, Layer 2, as defined by the IEEE 802.2 standard. This layer provides a common LAN platform for all IEEE 802.X protocols.
Logical Ring	The circular closed set of point-to-point links among network stations on a Token Ring and FDDI network.
Looped Dual Bus	A DQDB bus configuration where the head of bus functions for both A and B buses are contained within the same node.
MAN Switching System (SS)	A single metropolitan area network composed of many MAN switches, usually linked by a common DQDB bus.
Media	The plural form of medium, or multiple mediums (twisted-pair wire, coax cable, fiber, and so on).
Medium	The single common access platform such as a copper wire, fiber, or free space.
Medium Access Control (MAC)	IEEE 802 protocol defining media-specific access control.
Message Identifier (MID)	In DQDB, a value used to identify all DMPDUs that together make up the same IMPDU.
Metropolitan Area Network (MAN)	A MAC-level data and computer communications network that operates over metropolitan or campus areas, and recently has been expanded to nationwide and even worldwide connectivity of high-speed data networks.
Multicast	A connection type with the capability to broadcast to multiple destinations on the network. Also called a selective broadcast.
Multimode Fiber (MMF)	50- to 100-μm core diameter optical fiber with many propagation paths for light, typically used for lower speed or shorter distances (compared to single-mode optical fiber).

Multiplexing	The technique of combining multiple single channels onto a single aggregate channel for sharing facilities and bandwidth.
Network	A system of autonomous devices, links, and subsystems that provide a platform for communications.
Network Layer (OSI)	Layer 3 of the OSIRM. Provides the end-to-end routing and switching of data units (packets), as well as managing congestion control.
Network Management	The process of managing the operation and status of network resources (for example, devices, protocols).
Node	A device that interfaces with the transmission medium through the physical layer (and often the data link layer) of the OSIRM.
Octet	An 8-bit transmission unit of measure. Also called a Byte.
Open Systems Interconnection Reference Model (OSIRM)	A seven-layer model defining the international protocol standards for data communications in a multiple architecture and vendor environment. Both the OSI and CCITT define standards based on the OSIRM.
Optical Carrier level N (OC-N)	The optical carrier level signal in SONET that results from an STS-N signal conversion. In SONET, the basic transmission speed unit is 58.34 Mbps.
Packet Assembler/ Disassembler (PAD)	A concentration and network-access device that provides protocol conversion into X.25 packet format.
Packet Switch Public Data Network (PSPDN)	A public data network utilizing packet-switching technology (X.25, SMDS, IP, and ATM).
Packet Switching	A method of switching that segments the data into fixed or variable units of maximum size called packets. These packets then pass the user information (addressing, sequencing, error control, and user-controlled options) in a store-and-forward manner across the network.
Packet Type	Identifies the type of packet and its use, such as for user data, call establishment and termination, and routing information.
Path Overhead (POH)	Overhead transported with the SONET payload and used for payload transport functions.

Payload Pointer — Indicates the starting point of a SONET synchronous payload envelope.

Permanent Virtual Circuit (PVC) — A logical dedicated circuit between two user ports in a point-to-point configuration.

Physical Layer (OSI) — Layer 1 of the OSIRM. Provides the electrical and mechanical interface and signaling of bits over the communications medium.

Physical Layer Convergence Protocol (PLCP) — The IEEE 802.6 standard defining the physical layer that adapts the actual capabilities of the underlying physical network to provide the services required by the DQDB or ATM layer.

Physical Layer Medium Dependent (PMD) — In FDDI, the medium-specific layer corresponding to the lower sublayer of the OSIRM physical layer.

Physical Layer Protocol (PHY) — In FDDI, the medium-independent layer corresponding to the upper sublayer of the OSIRM physical layer.

Plastic Optical Fiber (POF) — A low-cost, low-distance plastic alternative to glass fiber.

Presentation Layer (OSI) — Layer 6 of the OSIRM. Identifies the syntax of the user data being transmitted and provides user service functions such as encryption, file-transfer protocols, and terminal emulation.

Primary Rate Interface (PRI) — An ISDN T1 access interface type comprising 23 B-channels each at 64 Kbps and one D-channel at 64 Kbps (23B+D). The European version will operate at 2.048 Mbps (30B+D).

Primary Ring — The main ring for PDU transmission in FDDI, and the only attachment for SAS FDDI stations.

Private Network — A network providing interorganizational connectivity only.

Private [Automatic] Branch Exchange (PBX/PABX) — An [automatic] customer-site telephone switch, with some capability to integrate data.

Protocol — The rules and guidelines by which information is exchanged and understood between two devices.

Protocol Data Unit (PDU) — The unit of information transferred between communicating peer layer processes.

Public Data Network (PDN) — A network designed to provide data transmission value-added services to the public.

Queued Arbitrated Access	In DQDB, packet-data users contend for access to the bus by queuing their requests; since all of the nodes know the length of the queue and their position in the queue, the access scheme is referred to as distributed queue.
Regional Bell Operating [or Holding] Company (RBOC or RBHC)	One of seven U.S. regional holding companies formed after the divestiture of AT&T (for example, Ameritech, Southwestern Bell). The RBOCs also manage the 22 BOCs.
Remote Bridge	A high-throughput bridge that provides remote LAN-WAN connectivity.
Ring	A closed-loop, common bus network topology.
Router	A LAN/WAN device operating at Layers 1 (physical), 2 (data link), and 3 (network) of the OSIRM. Distinguished from a bridge by its capability to switch and route data based upon network protocols such as IP.
Secondary Ring	In FDDI, the ring that carries data in the opposite direction as the primary ring; primarily used for backup to the primary ring.
Section	A transmission facility between a SONET Network Element and regenerator.
Segment	In DQDB, the payload (user data) portion of the slot.
Segmentation Unit	The 44-octet unit of data transfer in DQDB.
Self-Healing	The ability for a LAN/MAN to reroute traffic around a failed link or network element to provide uninterrupted service.
Service	The relationship between protocol entities in the OSIRM, where the service provider (lower-layer protocol) and the service user (higher-layer protocol) communicate through a *data service*.
Service Access Point (SAP)	The access point at a network node or station where the service users access the services offered by the service providers.
Service Data Unit (SDU)	Unit of information transferred across the OSI interface between service provider and service user.
Session Layer (OSI)	Layer 5 of the OSIRM. Provides the establishment and control of user dialogues between adjacent network devices.

Shielded Twisted Pair (STP)	A twisted-pair wire with jacket shielding, used for long distances and less subject to electrical noise and interference than UTP.
Simplex	One-way transmission of information on a medium.
Single-Attachment Sations (SAS)	In FDDI, stations that are attached only to a single ring (primary ring).
Single-Mode Fiber (SMF)	8- to 10-μm core diameter optical fiber with a single propagation path for light; typically used for higher speeds or longer distances (as compared to multimode optical fiber).
slot	The basic unit of transmission on a DQDB bus.
SMDS Interface Protocol (SIP)	The three layers of protocol (similar to the first three layers of the OSIRM) that define the SMDS SNI user information frame structuring, addressing, error control, and overall transport.
SNA	IBM's communications networking architecture.
Source Routing	A routing scheme where the routing of packets is determined by the source address and route to the destination in the packet header.
Station	An addressable logical or physical network entity, capable of transmitting, receiving, or repeating information.
Station Management (SMT)	FDDI station management entity.
Subnetwork	The smaller units of LANs (called LAN segments) that can be more easily managed than the entire LAN.
Subscriber-Network Interface (SNI)	A DQDB user access point into the network or MAN switch.
Switched Multimegabit Data Service (SMDS)	A MAN service offered over the IEEE DQDB bus.
Switched Virtual Circuit (SVC)	Virtual circuits similar to PVCs, but established on a call-by-call basis.
Synchronous Digital Hierarchy (SDH)	The CCITT original version of a synchronous digital hierarchy, based on optical fiber, called SONET in ANSI parlance.
Synchronous Optical Network (SONET)	A U.S. high-speed, fiber-optic transport standard for a fiber-optic digital hierarchy (speeds range from 51.84 Mbps to 2.4 Gbps).

Synchronous Transmission	The transmission of frames that are managed through a common clock between transmitter and receiver.
Synchronous Transfer Mode (STM)	The T1 carrier method of assigning time slots as channels within a T1 or E1 circuit.
Synchronous Transport Module level N (STM-N)	The SDH line rate of N STM-1 signals.
Synchronous Transport Signal level N (STS-N)	SONET transmission signal created with byte interleaving of N STS-1 (51.84 Mbps) signals.
Synchronous Transport Signal level Nc (STS-Nc)	Concatenated SONET synchronous payload envelope.
T1	A four-wire repeater system; commonly used to refer to a DS1 signal.
T1 Carrier	The TDM digital T1 hierarchy used in North America and Japan, with 24 voice channels constituting a single 1.544 Mbps T1 trunk.
T3	Commonly used to refer to a DS3 signal.
Telecommunications	The transmission of voice, video, data, and images through the use of both computers and a communications medium.
Time-Division Multiplexing (TDM)	The method of aggregating multiple simultaneous transmissions (circuits) over a single high-speed channel by using individual time slots (periods) for each circuit.
Time-Insensitive	Traffic types whose data is not affected by small delays during transmission. This is also referred to as delay-insensitive.
Time-Sensitive	Traffic types whose data is affected by small delays during transmission and cannot tolerate this delay (for example, voice, video, real-time data).
Token	A marker that can be held by a station on a Token Ring or bus indicating the station's right to transmit.
Token Ring	A LAN that uses a token-passing access method for bus access and traffic transport between network elements, where bus speeds operate at either 4 or 16 Mbps.
Transmission Control Protocol/Internet Protocol (TCP/IP)	The combination of a network and transport protocol developed by ARPANET for internetworking IP-based networks.

Transport Layer (OSI)	Layer 4 of the OSIRM. Provides for error-free, end-to-end communications between two "host" users across a network.
Transport Overhead	In SONET, the line and section overhead elements combined.
Twisted Pair	The basic transmission medium consisting of 22 to 26 American Wire Gauge (AWG) insulated copper wire. TP can be either shielded (STP) or unshielded (UTP).
Unshielded Twisted Pair (UTP)	A twisted-pair wire without the jacket shielding, used for short distances but subject to electrical noise and interference.
User Channel	Portion of the SONET channel allocated to the user for maintenance functions.
User-to-Network Interface (UNI)	The point where the user accesses the network.
User-to-User Protocols	Protocols that operate between users and are typically transparent to the network, such as file transfer protocols (for example, FTP).
Virtual Channel Identifier (VCI)	In DQDB, a field within the segment header that determines whether a node is to read, write, or copy the segment payload. In ATM, a field within the cell header that is used to switch virtual channels.
Virtual Circuit	A virtual connection established through the network from origination to destination, where packets, frames, or cells are routed over the same path for the duration of the call. These connections seem like dedicated paths to the users, but are actually network resources shared by all users. Bandwidth on a virtual circuit is not allocated until it is used.
Virtual Path Identifier (VPI)	In ATM, a field within the cell header that is used to switch virtual paths, defined as groups of virtual channels.
Virtual Tributary (VT)	An element that transports and switches sub-STS-1 payloads or VTx (VT1.5, VT2, VT3, or VT6).
Wide Area Network (WAN)	A network that operates over a large region and commonly uses carrier facilities and services.
Window	The concept of establishing an optimum number of frames or packets that can be outstanding (unacknowledged) before more are transmitted. Window protocols include X.25, LAP, TCP/IP, and SDLC.
X.25	CCITT recommendation of the interface between packet-switched DTE and DCE equipment.

Index

G

J

 L

M

N

O

P

Q

R

S

U

X

INTERNATIONAL CONTACT INFORMATION

AUSTRALIA
McGraw-Hill Book Company Australia Pty. Ltd.
TEL +61-2-9415-9899
FAX +61-2-9415-5687
http://www.mcgraw-hill.com.au
books-it_sydney@mcgraw-hill.com

CANADA
McGraw-Hill Ryerson Ltd.
TEL +905-430-5000
FAX +905-430-5020
http://www.mcgrawhill.ca

GREECE, MIDDLE EAST,
NORTHERN AFRICA
McGraw-Hill Hellas
TEL +30-1-656-0990-3-4
FAX +30-1-654-5525

MEXICO (Also serving Latin America)
McGraw-Hill Interamericana Editores S.A. de C.V.
TEL +525-117-1583
FAX +525-117-1589
http://www.mcgraw-hill.com.mx
fernando_castellanos@mcgraw-hill.com

SINGAPORE (Serving Asia)
McGraw-Hill Book Company
TEL +65-863-1580
FAX +65-862-3354
http://www.mcgraw-hill.com.sg
mghasia@mcgraw-hill.com

SOUTH AFRICA
McGraw-Hill South Africa
TEL +27-11-622-7512
FAX +27-11-622-9045
robyn_swanepoel@mcgraw-hill.com

UNITED KINGDOM & EUROPE
(Excluding Southern Europe)
McGraw-Hill Education Europe
TEL +44-1-628-502500
FAX +44-1-628-770224
http://www.mcgraw-hill.co.uk
computing_neurope@mcgraw-hill.com

ALL OTHER INQUIRIES Contact:
Osborne/McGraw-Hill
TEL +1-510-549-6600
FAX +1-510-883-7600
http://www.osborne.com
omg_international@mcgraw-hill.com